D0405581

JEWISH
WISDOM

By Rabbi Joseph Telushkin

NONFICTION
Nine Questions People Ask About Judaism (with Dennis Prager)
Why the Jews? The Reason for Antisemitism (with Dennis Prager)
*Jewish Literacy: The Most Important Things to Know About the Jewish Religion,
Its People, and Its History*
Jewish Humor: What the Best Jewish Jokes Say About the Jews

FICTION
The Unorthodox Murder of Rabbi Wahl
The Final Analysis of Dr. Stark
An Eye for an Eye

JEWISH WISDOM

Ethical, Spiritual, and
Historical Lessons from the Great Works
and Thinkers

RABBI JOSEPH TELUSHKIN

WILLIAM MORROW AND COMPANY, INC.
New York

Copyright © 1994 by Joseph Telushkin

Permissions, constituting a continuation of the copyright page, can be found on page 635.

All rights reserved. No part of this book may be reproduced or utilized in any form or by any means, electronic or mechanical, including photocopying, recording, or by any information storage or retrieval system, without permission in writing from the Publisher. Inquiries should be addressed to Permissions Department, William Morrow and Company, Inc., 1350 Avenue of the Americas, New York, N.Y. 10019.

It is the policy of William Morrow and Company, Inc., and its imprints and affiliates, recognizing the importance of preserving what has been written, to print the books we publish on acid-free paper, and we exert our best efforts to that end.

Library of Congress Cataloging-in-Publication Data

Telushkin, Joseph, 1948–
    Jewish wisdom : ethical, spiritual, and historical lessons from the great works and thinkers / Joseph Telushkin.
        p. cm.
    Includes bibliographical references and index.
    ISBN 0-688-12958-7
    1. Judaism—Essence, genius, nature. 2. Ethics, Jewish.
    3. Judaism—Quotations, Maxims, etc. 4. Jews—Quotations.
    I. Title.
    BM565.T45   1994
    296.3—dc20   94-9186
                                                            CIP

Printed in the United States of America

20 19 18 17 16 15 14 13 12

BOOK DESIGN BY MICHAEL MENDELSOHN/MM DESIGN 2000, INC.

FOR DVORAH

With whom I look forward to growing old,
while remaining young

ACKNOWLEDGMENTS

A number of friends were very generous in expending the time to read and critique large sections of this book. In addition to providing concrete stylistic and editorial advice, a few reminded me of important passages I had forgotten to include, while others challenged the significance of some that I did. I am deeply grateful to all of them, and apologize to anyone whose name I have inadvertently omitted: Rabbi Irwin Kula, Rabbi David Woznica, Beverly Markus Woznica, J. J. Goldberg, Rabbi David Wolpe, Professor David Shatz, Dennis Prager, Dr. David Elcott, and my wife, Dvorah Menashe Telushkin.

Rabbi Michael Berger, a Jewish scholar of wide-ranging knowledge and deep insights, has checked my translations of rabbinic texts. He has challenged some points of view expressed in my running commentary, and his input and critiques have enriched the manuscript.

My good friend David Szonyi, a man of broad Jewish and general knowledge, has read this manuscript several times, and made thousands of stylistic and editorial changes. This is the third book on which he has worked with me, and I am profoundly grateful for his insights and improvements. He is a blessing to any writer.

At William Morrow and Company, I have been singularly fortunate in working with Adrian Zackheim. Adrian has encouraged this book from the very first time I described it to him, and his continuing enthusiasm and support have inspired me to keep trying to raise *Jewish Wisdom* to an ever higher level. Ann Bramson and Gail Kinn stepped in at a point when I was sure the book was finished, and challenged and goaded me to go even further. I am indebted to them.

As always, it is a pleasure to express my appreciation to, and love for, Richard Pine, my agent since the earliest days of my writing career. Richard and his father, Arthur, have a roster of many distinguished writers, yet it is Richard's singular gift to make each feel as if he or she is his most important client. Richard's impulse to do this is due not only to his being a master diplomat, which he is, but also to his being a particularly decent and kind human being. In a highly competitive, often brutal world, it is reassuring to know that such people exist and succeed.

Over the past year and a half, I have commuted monthly to Los Angeles, where I serve as rabbi of the Synagogue for the Performing Arts, a congregation consisting, in the main, of Jews associated with the entertainment industry. The experience has been a wonderful, and growing, one for me. Nothing makes the Jewish texts cited in this book come so alive as teaching and talking about them to people who are open to applying these biblical, talmudic, and modern Jewish insights to their daily lives. I thank the members of my congregation for letting me into their lives, and acknowledge six particular individuals with whom I have worked most closely, and who have become dear friends: Judy Fox, Barry Rubin, Susie Ross, Ted Tobias, Ron Temkin, and Beverly Santana.

Since the publication of my last book, *Jewish Humor,* dedicated to my three daughters, Rebecca, Naomi, and Shira, my wife, Dvorah, and I have been blessed with a fourth child, Benjamin. Some day, God willing, he will read this Preface and learn that this book was largely conceived between midnight and two A.M., during walks up and down the ground-floor hallway of our large apartment building as I pushed him, awake and crying, in his stroller. Benjamin is sleeping a lot better now, and has brought immense joy into our lives.

CONTENTS

Introduction   *xix*

I. Between People: How to Be a Good Person in a Complicated World

1. Does Judaism Have an Essence?   3

2. When to Give, What to Give, How to Give:
   Why *Tzedaka* Is Not Charity   11

3. Helping the Helpless: What Are Our Obligations to
   Society's Most Vulnerable Members?   26

4. *Mensch*—Nine Challenges a Good Person Must
   Meet   33

5. Honesty, Dishonesty, and the "Gray Areas" in
   Between   46

6. "You Must Pay Him His Wages on the Same
   Day": Between Employers and Employees   54

7. Truth, Lies, and Permissible Lies   58

8. "Sticks and Stones" and Words: The Ethics of
   Speech   65

9. Arguing Ethically   70

Contents

10. The Obligation to Criticize, How to Do So, and
     When to Remain Silent   76

11. When Life Is at Stake   80

12. "It Is As If He Saved the Entire World":
     The Infinite Value of Each Human Life   88

13. "All Jews Are Responsible One for Another":
     Communal Responsibilities   91

14. Models of Leadership   99

15. "Listen to Her Voice": Conflicting Biblical and
     Talmudic Views of the Character of Women   104

16. "It Is Not Good for Man to Be Alone":
     Jewish Perspectives on Marriage   118

17. "For Love Is As Strong as Death": Romantic Love   128

18. Sex: The Commanded, the Permitted, the
     Forbidden   131

19. "Be Fruitful and Multiply": The Duty to Have
     Children   143

20. Between Parents and Children   147

21. If the Fetus Is Not a Life, What Is It?:
     Judaism and Abortion   161

22. "Even the Altar Sheds Tears": Divorce   168

23. "Love Your Neighbor"   174

24. "Either Friends or Death": Friendship   178

25. "When I Was Young, I Admired Clever People.
     Now That I Am Old . . . ": Kindness and
     Compassion   182

26. "What Does a Good Guest Say?": Good Manners   187

27. "If You See Your Enemy's Donkey": A Jewish
     Alternative to Jesus' Command: "Love Your
     Enemies"   191

28. The Terrible Toll of Hatred   196

29. Good Advice on Fifteen Subjects   199

II. *Personal Issues: Judaism and the Quest for Meaning*

30. Human Nature—A Somber Look   207

31. The Human Condition: Four Parables and a Bushel of Quotes   216

32. On Suffering   222

33. "One Does More, and One Does Less": Humility   225

34. "Did You See My Alps?": Against Asceticism   230

35. "What Have I in Common with Jews?": Alienation   239

36. "A Person Is *Always* Liable for His Actions": Free Will and Human Responsibility   243

37. Old Age: Anguish and Opportunities   248

38. "The Anniversary of a Death, *That* a Jew Remembers": Death and Mourning   255

39. "A Sentinel Who Has Deserted His Post": Suicide   271

40. The Afterlife   276

41. "Who Is Rich?"   279

III. *Between People and God: What God Wants from Us*

42. God   283

43. Is God Necessary for Morality?   290

44. Idolatry and Its Attractions   294

45. Chosen People: A Beautiful, but Often Misunderstood, Concept   298

46. Jews and God After the Holocaust   303

47. How Does One Sanctify God's Name? How Does One Desecrate It?   316

Contents

48. Martyrs: Those Who Died *al Kiddush ha-Shem* (to Sanctify God's Name)   320

49. *Mitzvah* (Commandment) and Some of the Distinguishing Characteristics of Judaism   329

50. Studying Torah   336

51. "How Can We Tell When a Sin We Have Committed Has Been Pardoned?": On Repentance and Sin   345

52. Prayer   356

53. Rabbis   371

54. "Your People Shall Be My People": Converts   374

55. "You Shall Rejoice in Your Festival": A Few Scattered Thoughts on Jewish Holidays   382

IV. Between People and the World: Jewish Values Confront Modern Values

56. "People Would Swallow Each Other Alive": Against Anarchy   393

57. "Let the Law Cut Through the Mountain": Jewish Principles of Justice   398

58. Murder and the Death Penalty: The Conflicting Views of the Bible and Talmud   407

59. "Must the Sword Devour Forever?": Jewish Reflections on War   417

60. Against Utopianism   425

61. "Poverty Would Outweigh Them All": The Curse of Poverty   427

62. "A Physician Who Heals for Nothing Is Worth Nothing": Medicine and Doctors   433

63. "For There Will Be No One to Repair It After You": Toward a Jewish Ecology   438

Contents

64. "His Mercy Is upon All His Works": Jewish Ethics
Toward Animals   444

V. *Modern Jewish Experience: Major Themes*

65. Antisemitism   457

66. Antisemitism and the American-Jewish Experience   480

67. Philosemitism   496

68. Assimilation and Intermarriage   503

69. A Miscellany: On Sports, Jewish Denominations,
and Communism   508

VI. *The Holocaust*

70. The Holocaust: A Prologue   515

71. What the Nazis Said   517

72. The Experience of the "Final Solution": Six Stories
out of Six Million   522

73. Before and During the Holocaust: Reactions in
the West   528

74. "Like Lambs to the Slaughter": Why Did More
Jews Not Fight Back?   532

75. "Then They Came for Me, and There Was No One
Left": Heroic Words and Tragic Quotes   536

76. "Let Them Go to Hell": Jewish Rage at the Nazis   542

77. "Let Not the Murderers of Our Nation Also Be Its
Heirs": The Debate over German Reparations   545

78. "As Your Sword Has Made Women Childless . . .":
The Eichmann Trial   550

79. "That Place Is Not Your Place:" Ronald Reagan
and the Bitburg Controversy   552

80. On Holocaust Deniers   554

81. The Holocaust and Its Meaning for Christians   557

82. "One, Plus One, Plus One": Six Final Quotes on the Holocaust   561

VII. *Zionism and Israel*

83. The Land of Israel in the Bible, the Talmud, and Jewish Law   567

84. Theodor Herzl: Zionism's Founder   572

85. Chaim Weizmann and the Balfour Declaration   579

86. Vladimir Jabotinsky   584

87. David Ben-Gurion   588

88. Golda Meir   593

89. Menachem Begin   596

90. "It Is Good to Die for Our Country": Other Zionist Leaders and Other Quotes About Israel   601

91. Anti-Zionism and Antisemitism   607

VIII. *On Being a Jew: Modern Reflections*   613

Bibliography   619

Index   638

JEWISH
WISDOM

INTRODUCTION

Since my teenage years, I have generally marked up the books I have read, putting large checks or other signs around passages that moved or infuriated me, or taught me something new, or just caused me to consider a perspective to which I had previously been oblivious. For many years, I also have written at the front of a book the page number of passages that I wish to recall, along with a very brief summary of their contents. These marked passages, drawn from some thirty-five hundred Jewish books in my home library, constitute a large percentage of the texts cited in *Jewish Wisdom*.

For me, the writing of *Jewish Wisdom* has been a singularly satisfying event. I have always been drawn to books of quotations (over the years I've assembled more than two hundred), and long have dreamed of putting together a compilation of Judaism's most insightful and inspiring statements. What attracts me to a good quotation is its ability to "cut to the core" of the most complicated issue and present one with a fresh and essential truth.

Two thousand years ago, when a non-Jew asked Hillel, the leading rabbi of his age, to define Judaism's essence, the sage could have responded with a long oration on Jewish thought and law, and an insistence that it would be blasphemous to reduce so profound a system to a brief essence. Indeed, his contemporary, Shammai, furiously drove away the questioner with a builder's rod. Hillel, however, responded to the man's challenge: "What is hateful to you, do not do to your neighbor: this is the whole Torah. The rest is commentary; now go and study"—a model statement that has defined Judaism's essence ever since.

As Hillel knew, the right words at the right time can inspire people for generations. Theodor Herzl, the nineteenth-century founder of Zionism, declared at the end of his novel *Altneuland,* "But if you will it, it is no fantasy." With those words, he fashioned a goad that helped move Jewish life in radically new ways for generations. As I explain later, Herzl's words in Hebrew, *Im tirzu, ein zoh aggadah,* quickly became a slogan that galvanized early Zionist pioneers to settle previously uncultivated swampland, and to persevere in turning it into fertile fields. They also motivated Zionist activists to work for Hebrew's reestablishment as a modern, spoken language (although no other "dead language" ever had been resurrected), and inspired Jewish activists to lobby non-Jewish leaders to recognize their right to reestablish a homeland, and then a state, in Palestine. Five simple Hebrew words! Yet Herzl's insistence that people can transform a fantasy into reality itself shaped reality.

In *Jewish Wisdom,* I have endeavored to choose the words that have really mattered, or that should really matter, the phrases and texts that have shaped Judaism's and the Jewish people's responses to the key issues in their lives and their history. This book is intended as a companion to *Jewish Literacy,* in which I strove to transmit a brief summary and overview of the most important concepts, events, and people in Judaism and Jewish history.

What distinguishes *Jewish Wisdom* from almost all other collections of Jewish quotations is the running commentary following many of the quotations. In it, I have tried to show how the words cited affected Judaism, the Jewish mind, and Jewish history, and how they continue to challenge Jews today. On a few occasions, quotations are repeated because I found them to be relevant in more than one section of the book.

The words cited in *Jewish Wisdom* are, in large measure, the words that have helped make me the kind of human being I am. I can only hope that many of these words, drawn from more than three thousand years of Jewish thought and history, will similarly inspire and energize you.

ON THE BIBLE, THE TALMUD, AND OTHER RABBINIC WRITINGS: THE PRIMARY SOURCES OF THIS BOOK

The Bible and the Talmud are the most important sources cited in *Jewish Wisdom*. Beginning with the five books of the Torah, the Hebrew Bible contains the Jewish people's earliest writings. The first, Genesis, describes God's creation of the world and the story of humankind's earliest generations, and goes on to relate the story of Judaism's founding patriarchs and matriarchs. The Torah's other four books speak of the ancient Hebrews' enslavement in and exodus from Egypt, and their forty years of wandering in the desert.

Interspersed with the narrative, the Torah sets down many of the laws that have governed Jewish life ever since. It is here that Jews are first commanded to worship only one God, to honor parents, to observe the Sabbath, to "Love your neighbor as yourself," to "pursue" justice, and much more.

The Bible's remaining books are divided into two categories, the Prophets and the Writings. Generally, these books contain few legal instructions, and much historical narrative and moral exhortations. In Isaiah, for example, we find the classic messianic vision of a utopian world in which "Nation shall not lift up sword against nation, neither shall they learn war anymore" (2:4), words emblazoned, more than twenty-five hundred years later, on the "Isaiah Wall" across the street from the United Nations building in New York.

The writings of the eighth-century B.C.E. prophet, Micah, beautifully summarize what matters most to God: ". . . to do justice, and to love goodness, and to walk modestly with your God" (6:8).

The Writings contain a mixture of historical, philosophical, and theological reflections. The most influential book, Psalms, is the source of many of the prayers in the Jewish *siddur* (prayer book). Job, the story of a righteous man who suffers, perhaps speaks most to our contemporary sensibility; it also helped establish the Jewish tradition of challenging and questioning God about this world's injustices.

That so many biblical texts are cited throughout *Jewish Wisdom* reflects how pervasively the Bible has shaped, challenged, and inspired the Jewish mind throughout history.

The literary style of the Talmud, which was written and edited during the early centuries of the Common Era, is markedly different (granted, however, that biblical books employ various styles—e.g., the two Books of Samuel are straightforward narrative, while Psalms consists of poetry). Much of the Talmud consists of lengthy, often unresolved, disputes concerning Jewish law. Other parts are not concerned with legal matters at all, consisting instead of ethical guidance, anecdotes about the Rabbis' lives (throughout this book, I use the capital "R" when referring to the Rabbis of the talmudic era), folklore, and even medical advice.

The British-Jewish scholar Hyam Maccoby notes, "The total impression [generated by the Talmud] is of a corporate literary effort, in which a large number of experts, belonging to successive generations, is engaged in a common enterprise: the clarification of Scripture and the application of it to everyday life" (*Early Rabbinic Writings,* page 1). Just as one wanting to know what the constitutional guarantee of free speech has meant in American life will read relevant Supreme Court opinions and rulings, so one who wishes to know how Jews have understood "Love your neighbor" or "Honor your father and mother" will examine the appropriate talmudic and rabbinic discussions of these texts.

There are two editions of the Talmud, one set down in final form by the Rabbis in Palestine about the year 400, a second by the Rabbis in Babylon about a century later. They came to be called respectively the Yerushalmi (after Jerusalem) and the Bavli (Hebrew for Babylonia). The Babylonian is the more extensive and came to be considered authoritative (i.e, if you hear that someone is studying the Talmud, he or she is almost certainly studying the Babylonian). However, in recent years, particularly since Israel's creation in 1948, scholars and students are paying greater attention to the Yerushalmi (in English, the Palestinian Talmud) than was done previously.

All talmudic quotes cited in this book are identified as being from the Palestinian or Babylonian Talmud (over 90 percent come from the latter). Page citations from the Babylonian Talmud will enable any reader to quickly locate the quotes, since all editions of it adhere to the same pagination. Thus, if a quote is identified as appearing in the tractate *Ketubot* 5a, you can find it in that volume on side one of page 5.

Of the other major works that comprise the talmudic literature, all are represented in this book, some quite extensively. Most important is the Mishna, which Rabbi Judah the Prince edited into its current form around the year 200 of the Common Era. The Mishna classifies Jewish law into sixty-three discrete, short books. For example, one book, *Shabbat,* summarizes the Sabbath laws in twenty-four chapters; three books, *Bava Kamma, Bava Mezia,* and *Bava Bathra,* summarize Jewish business law and ethics. *Kiddushin* explains the procedures involved in becoming married, and *Gittin,* in getting divorced. The best-known, the pithy *Pirkei Avot* (*Ethics of the Fathers*), which is represented by over twenty quotes in this book, relates the favorite maxims of different Rabbis over a period of many generations.

Many rabbinic statements made during the mishnaic period, which were not incorporated into that work, are found in other significant, but less authoritative, works of rabbinic literature. The most important of these is the *Tosefta.* This might be described as an enormous appendix to the Mishna, although it is four times as long. A number of statements from the *Tosefta* are cited in *Jewish Wisdom.*

Other important compilations of early rabbinic teachings include the *Mekhilta,* which consists of rabbinic insights into the Book of Exodus, the *Sifra,* a rabbinic commentary on the Book of Leviticus, and *Sifre,* the school of Rabbi Ishmael's commentary on Numbers, as well as the school of Rabbi Akiva's commentary on Deuteronomy.

Midrash Rabbah, a collection of commentaries, parables, and rabbinic reflections on all five books of the Torah, is a particularly significant, and later, rabbinic work cited extensively in *Jewish Wisdom.*

Almost all of these works are available in English translations, and can be found at the beginning of the bibliography.

Jewish Wisdom also cites the medieval "codes," particularly the *Mishneh Torah,* Maimonides's twelfth-century, all-encompassing, fourteen-volume summary and codification of Jewish law. Probably the most influential Jewish book issued since the Talmud, this work strongly influenced Rabbi Joseph Karo's great sixteenth-century code of Jewish law, the *Shulkhan Arukh,* a knowledge of which is required for those seeking rabbinical ordination.

Yet another important source of Jewish legal writings is the responsa literature, which consists of wide-ranging questions on Jewish law addressed to rabbis in every generation, and their answers. For example, my chapter on animals quotes the eighteenth-century Rabbi Yehezkel Landau's response to a Jew who wished to know whether it was permissible, according to Jewish law, for him to go hunting for sport.

By and large, the other texts cited in *Jewish Wisdom,* drawn from philosophical and historical writings and incidents, are self-explanatory. When this is not the case, I have generally supplied an explanation immediately following the quotation.

PART I

BETWEEN PEOPLE

*How to Be a Good Person in
a Complicated World*

1

DOES JUDAISM
HAVE AN ESSENCE?

GOD'S FIRST QUESTIONS

In the hour when an individual is brought before the heavenly court for judgment, the person is asked:
    Did you conduct your [business] affairs honestly?
    Did you set aside regular time for Torah study?
    Did you work at having children?
    Did you look forward to the world's redemption?
             —Babylonian Talmud, *Shabbat* 31a

Note that the first question asked in heaven is not "Did you believe in God?" or "Did you observe all the rituals?" but "Were you honest in business?" Unfortunately, despite many texts that insist on the primacy of ethics, most Jews associate being religious solely with observing rituals. Throughout the Jewish community, when one asks, "Is so-and-so a religious Jew?" the response invariably is based on the person's observance of ritual laws: "He (or she) keeps kosher, and observes the Sabbath; he is religious" or "She does not keep kosher or observe the Sabbath; she is not religious."

From such responses, one could easily conclude that Judaism regards ethical behavior as an "extracurricular activity," something desirable but not essential.

The above passage unequivocally asserts that ethics is at Judaism's core; God's first concern is with a person's decency.

The second question concerns Torah study, for Judaism teaches that through studying Torah, a person learns how to be fully moral (see Chapter 50), and how to be a part of the Jewish people.

Third comes having children (those who are childless can adopt). Rabbi Irving Greenberg notes that raising a family fulfills the "covenantal obligation to pass on the dream and work of perfecting the world for another generation."

Fourth is hoping for and working toward this very perfection. The first three questions address "micro issues," matters that would be sufficient were Judaism exclusively addressed to the individual. But Jews also are part of a people and a broader world, and Judaism imposes upon the Jewish people the obligation to help bring about *tikkun olam*, the repair (or perfection) of the world. In a frequently quoted passage in the *Ethics of the Fathers* (2:21), Rabbi Tarfon teaches: "It is not your obligation to complete the task [of perfecting the world], but neither are you free to desist [from doing all you can]."

One final thought about this talmudic passage: When a Jewish baby is born, the prayer offered expresses the hope that the child will be able to respond affirmatively to the first three questions:

> May the parents rear this child [son or daughter] to adulthood imbued with love of Torah and the performance of good deeds, and may they escort him [or her] to the wedding canopy.

This prayer is recited in the synagogue (or at another naming ceremony) for a girl, and at the boy's circumcision. My friend Rabbi Irwin Kula notes that the fourth question is alluded to through the *kisei eliyahu*, the chair of Elijah, that is set up at every circumcision. In Jewish tradition, Elijah is the prophet who will usher in the world's redemption.

OTHER BIBLICAL AND RABBINIC VIEWS OF WHAT MATTERS MOST TO GOD

Both the Bible's prophets and the greatest figures of talmudic Judaism have also expressed the view that ethical behavior is God's central demand of human beings:

> He has told you, O man, what is good, and what the Lord requires of you:
>   Only to do justice,
>   to love goodness,
>   and to walk modestly with your God.
>   —Micah 6:8 (eighth century B.C.E.)

> Thus said the Lord: Let not the wise man glory in his wisdom; Let not the strong man glory in his strength; Let not the rich man glory in his riches. But only in this should one glory: In his earnest devotion to Me. For I the Lord act with kindness, justice and equity in the world; For in these I delight.
>   —Jeremiah 9:22–23 (sixth century B.C.E.)

Jeremiah, like Micah, enumerates three types of behavior that give God pleasure: in his case, kindness, justice, and equity.

> It happened that a certain heathen came before Shammai [he and Hillel were the two leading rabbis of their age] and said to him, "Convert me to Judaism on condition that you teach me the whole Torah while I stand on one foot." Shammai chased him away with the builder's rod in his hand. When he came before Hillel, Hillel converted him and said, "What is hateful to you, do not do to your neighbor: this is the whole Torah. The rest is commentary; now go and study."
>   —Babylonian Talmud, *Shabbat* 31a (shortly before
>   the beginning of the Common Era)

5

That Hillel, one of the greatest figures of talmudic Judaism, was willing to convert a non-Jew on the basis of his accepting this ethical principle surely proves that ethical behavior constitutes Judaism's essence (in the same way that Protestant fundamentalists would insist on a would-be convert's acceptance of what they see as Christianity's essence, that Jesus Christ was the son of God who died to atone for mankind's sins). As Hillel remarks of this ethical principle, "this is the *whole* Torah." Significantly, Hillel instructs the man to start learning Torah, for only by studying this "commentary" will he be able to carry out Judaism's teachings.

A century after Hillel, Rabbi Akiva, the greatest scholar and teacher of his age, reiterated the primacy of ethics in Judaism:

> "Love your neighbor as yourself" (Leviticus 19:18)—this is the major principle of the Torah.
> —Palestinian Talmud, *Nedarim* 9:4 (second century C.E.)

While Micah, Jeremiah, Hillel, and Akiva were all concerned with finding the specific "way" that matters most to God, Rabbi Yochanan ben Zakkai was concerned with isolating the personality trait most apt to guarantee that its practitioners lead a good life:

> Said he [Rabbi Yochanan ben Zakkai] to them [his five preeminent students]: "Go out and see which is the best way a person should follow."
> Rabbi Eliezer said, "[One should have] a good, kindly eye."
> Rabbi Joshua said, "[One should be] a good friend."
> Rabbi Yossi said, "[One should be] a good neighbor."
> Rabbi Simeon said, "One who foresees the future consequences of his acts."
> Rabbi Elazar said, "[One should have] a good heart."
> Said he [Rabbi Yochanan ben Zakkai to them]: "I prefer Elazar's words to yours, for in his words yours are included."
> —*Ethics of the Fathers* 2:9 (first century C.E.)

An ancient rabbinic tradition teaches that there are 613 laws in the Torah (the Torah itself never states a number). A famous talmudic passage attempts to decipher which are the most essential:

> Rabbi Simlai taught: 613 commandments were revealed to Moses; 365 negative commandments . . . and 248 positive commandments. . . . When David [to whom authorship of the Psalms is attributed], came, he summed up the 613 commandments in eleven [ethical] principles: "Lord, who may sojourn in Your tent, who may dwell on Your holy mountain?
>   (1) He who lives without blame
>   (2) who does righteous acts
>   (3) who speaks the truth in his heart
>   (4) whose tongue speaks no deceit
>   (5) who has not done harm to his fellow
>   (6) or borne reproach for [his acts toward] his neighbor
>   (7) for whom a contemptible person is abhorrent
>   (8) who honors those who fear the Lord
>   (9) who stands by his oath even when it is to his disadvantage
>   (10) who has never lent money for interest
>   (11) or accepted a bribe against the innocent."
>
> —Psalms 15:1–5

What does principle number three, "who speaks the truth in his heart," mean? It refers to a person who follows the truth even when it is known only to him/her, and yet is disadvantageous in practical terms. The commentaries on the Talmud cite the case of Rabbi Safra: One day, while the Rabbi was reciting the *Sh'ma* ("Hear, O Israel"), a man entered his office and made an offer for an item the Rabbi was selling. Not wishing to interrupt his prayers, Rabbi Safra said nothing. The would-be buyer interpreted the silence as rejection, and raised his offer several times. When Rabbi Safra finished praying, he explained why he had been silent and accepted the original bid, explaining that when he first heard it, he knew that he would be willing to sell the item at that price.

> When Isaiah came [the talmudic passage continues] he summed up the 613 commandments in six [ethical] principles:
> (1) He who walks in righteousness
> (2) who speaks honestly
> (3) who spurns profit from fraudulent dealings
> (4) who waves away a bribe instead of taking it
> (5) who closes his ears and doesn't listen to malicious words
> (6) who shuts his eyes against looking at evil.
>
> —Isaiah 33:15–16

The Talmud next cites Micah, in the passage quoted earlier, who summed up the 613 commandments in three principles.

Then it returns to a different verse in Isaiah, which summarizes the 613 commandments in two principles:
> (1) Do justice
> (2) carry out acts of righteousness (or charity)
>
> —Isaiah 56:1

There then follows a short dispute whether or not Amos summarized the laws in one principle: "Seek Me and you will live" (5:4), and finally,

> When Habakkuk came, he summed up the 613 commandments in one principle, for he said, "The righteous shall live according to his faith" (2:4).
> —Babylonian Talmud, *Makkot* 23b–24a

Many people who profess to be religious do not in their daily lives live according to the faith they profess. Habakkuk, therefore, offers a simple test for determining the sincerity of a person's religiosity: Does he or she carry out the actions commanded by God?

> The Jewish nation is distinguished by three characteristics; they are merciful, they are modest [alternatively, bashful], and they perform acts of loving-kindness.
>
> —Babylonian Talmud, *Yevamot* 79a

While large numbers of Jews certainly do not possess these traits (I know more than a few who are distinguished neither by modesty nor by bashfulness), the Rabbis were suggesting what values and behavior each Jew should aspire to; once again, all the traits enumerated are ethical.

ADDITIONAL STATEMENTS OF JUDAISM'S ESSENCE

> The world endures because of three activities: Torah study, worship of God, and deeds of loving-kindness.
>
> —*Ethics of the Fathers* 1:2; for the meaning of "deeds of loving-kindness," see page 24.

> The following are the activities for which a person is rewarded in this world, and again in the World-to-Come: honoring one's father and mother, deeds of loving-kindness, and making peace between a person and his neighbor. The study of Torah, however, is as important as all of them together.
>
> —Mishna *Peah* 1:1

> If a man learns two paragraphs of the law in the morning and two in the evening and is engaged in his work all day, it is considered as though he had fulfilled the Torah in its entirety.
>
> —*Tanhuma Beshallakh* #20

Because Torah study teaches one how to live, the most important characteristic to cultivate in its study is consistency. As long as you set aside time for daily Torah study, even a short period sufficient to learn only two paragraphs, it will influence you.

These statements on the significance of Torah study notwithstanding, other Rabbis regarded the dispensing of charity as the pre-eminent commandment (see page 14).

> Whoever repudiates idolatry is called a Jew.
> —Babylonian Talmud, *Megillah* 13a; on idolatry,
> see pages 294–297.

The Torah's central message is the belief in one universal and moral God. Idolatry, with its insistence on a multitude of gods and its denial of a universal morality, negates Judaism's essence.

Finally, a post-talmudic statement; the conclusion reached by Moses Maimonides, the preeminent Jewish philosopher and rabbinic scholar of the Middle Ages:

> The purpose of the laws of the Torah . . . is to bring mercy, loving-kindness and peace upon the world.
> —Moses Maimonides, *Mishneh Torah,* "Laws of
> the Sabbath," 2:3 (twelfth century)

For more on Judaism's essence, see Chapter 23: "Love Your Neighbor."

2

WHEN TO GIVE, WHAT TO GIVE, HOW TO GIVE

Why Tzedaka *Is Not Charity*

> If, however, there is a needy person among you . . . do not harden your heart and shut your hand against your needy kinsman. Rather you must open your hand and lend him sufficient for whatever he needs.
>
> —Deuteronomy 15:7–8

> There are eight degrees of charity, each one higher than the next. The highest degree, exceeded by none, is that of the person who assists a poor Jew by providing him with a gift or a loan, or by entering into a partnership with him, or helping him find work; in a word, by putting him where he can dispense with other people's aid.
>
> —Moses Maimonides, *Mishneh Torah,* "Laws Concerning Gifts to the Poor," 10:7

According to Jewish law, the highest form of charity is to ensure that a person not need it, at least not for more than a short period. Maimonides apparently intuited what is today widely accepted, that ongoing reliance on charity demoralizes the recipient. For this reason, his emphasis is on making loans to the poor and finding work for them.

11

When your brother Israelite is reduced to poverty and cannot support himself in the community [literally, and his hand falls], you shall uphold him as you would a resident stranger. . . . You shall not charge him interest on a loan. . . .

—Leviticus 25:35–37

[Concerning the words "and his hand falls," a rabbinic commentary teaches that one must not allow him to fall into utter poverty]: This injunction may be explained with an analogy to a heavy load on a donkey: as long as the donkey is still standing up, one person may take hold of him and lead him [and keep him standing upright]. But once he has fallen, five men cannot raise him up again.

—*Sifra Leviticus* on 25:35–38

As for the injunction "You shall not charge him interest on a loan . . ." biblical law actually forbids taking interest on *all* loans. However, as ancient Jewish life expanded from an exclusively agricultural economy to one that combined farming and small businesses, the Rabbis enacted a "legal fiction" that allowed a lender to earn interest by sharing in a business's profits. (I call this a "legal fiction," and not a normal investment, because the lender "earns" his set percentage whether or not the business is profitable.)

However, this provision applies only to business loans; to this day, Jews are forbidden to collect any interest on a loan extended to a person to purchase necessities. Throughout history, Jewish communities have established "Free-Loan Societies" (known in Hebrew as *Gemakh*) to extend interest-free loans to the poor, and to those trying to avoid going on welfare.

Because not everyone's needs can be satisfied with a loan or job offer, Jewish tradition offers two distinct messages about charity: To those on the brink of poverty, it insists that every feasible alternative be tried before turning to welfare; to those possessing ample means, it insists on generosity.

12

THE JEWISH MESSAGE TO THE POOR

Skin an animal carcass in the street and earn a wage, and don't say, "[Support me], I am a great sage and this work is degrading to me!"

—Babylonian Talmud, *Bava Bathra* 110a

Make your Sabbath [meals plain] as [those of] a weekday, and don't ask others for help.

—Babylonian Talmud, *Shabbat* 118a

Some rabbinic writings created a difficult dialectic for the poor: on the one hand commanding them to accept charity when there was no alternative; on the other, praising those who defer that day for as long as possible:

Whoever cannot survive without taking charity, such as an old, sick, or greatly suffering individual, but who stubbornly refuses to accept aid, is guilty of murdering himself ... yet one who needs charity but postpones taking it and lives in deprivation so as to not trouble the community, shall live to provide for others.

—Rabbi Joseph Karo (1488–1575), *Shulkhan Arukh*
(*The Code of Jewish Law*), *Yoreh Deah* 255:2

In nineteenth-century Vilna, a wealthy man lost all he had. He was so greatly ashamed of being poor that he informed no one of his situation, and eventually died of malnutrition. Rabbi Israel Salanter (1810–1883) consoled the ashamed townspeople: "That man did not die of starvation, but of excessive pride. Had he been willing to ask others for help and admit to his situation, he would not have died of hunger."

—Based on Shmuel Himelstein, *Words of Wisdom,*
Words of Wit, page 169

13

To prevent recipients of charity from seeing themselves as nothing more than mendicants, the Rabbis legislated a remarkable law:

> Even a poor man who himself survives on charity should give charity.
>
> —Babylonian Talmud, *Gittin* 7b

THE IMPERATIVE TO RESPOND: JUDAISM'S MESSAGE TO EVERYONE EXCEPT THE POOR

Jewish law hardly intended for prosperous citizens to cite the teachings directed to the poor as an excuse for not giving charity, or worse, for using them to humiliate beggars (e.g., "Why don't you go skin an animal in the marketplace?"):

> [If a rich man says to a poor man], "Why don't you go out and work at a job? Look at those thighs! Look at those legs! Look at that belly! Look at that brawn!," the Holy One will then say to the rich man, "Is it not enough for you that you gave him nothing of yours? Must you also begrudge what I gave him?"
>
> —*Leviticus Rabbah* 34:7

When Jewish texts address people with money, their message, therefore, is totally different from their teachings to the poor:

> Charity is equal in importance to all the other commandments combined.
>
> —Babylonian Talmud, *Bava Bathra* 9a

> One who gives charity in secret is greater than Moses.
>
> —Babylonian Talmud, *Bava Bathra* 9b

This sort of greatness, however, British-Jewish writer Chaim Bermant has quipped, "is one to which few Jews aspire."

According to Maimonides, anonymous giving (wherein the donor and the recipient do not know each other, i.e., a third party or charitable organization is involved) ranks as the second-highest form of charity. My grandfather, Rabbi Nissen Telushkin, of blessed memory, once was raising money for a rabbinic scholar who had become impoverished. In his appeal to other rabbis, he concealed all information that might betray the recipient's identity. One man, Rabbi Eliezer Silver of Cincinnati, sent a signed check to my grandfather with the amount left blank. "Since you are the one person totally familiar with the circumstances and identity of the recipient," he wrote, "only you know the proper sum to fill in."

People often wonder what Maimonides designates as the lowest of the eight levels of charity: "One who gives morosely" (*Mishneh Torah*, "Laws Concerning Gifts to the Poor," 10:14). Of course, it is still preferable to give reluctantly than not to give at all. Ideally, one should aspire to give joyfully. As a United Jewish Appeal campaign slogan of several years ago encouraged, "Give until it doesn't hurt!"

> A Hasidic rebbe, known as the Leover, taught, "If a person comes to you for assistance, and you tell him, 'God will help you,' you are acting disloyally to God. For you should understand that God has sent you to aid the needy person, not to refer him back to the Almighty."
> —Based on Lionel Blue with Jonathan Magonet,
> *The Blue Guide to the Here and Hereafter,* page 168

> Rabbi Shmelke of Nikolsberg (d. 1778) said: "When a poor man asks you for aid, do not use his faults as an excuse for not helping him. For then God will look for your offenses, and He is sure to find many."

Arthur Kurzweil argues that this quote "is somewhat helpful when dealing with the question of the alcoholic who asks for money. . . . My denying him money 'because he'd only use it for booze' is not helping anyone" ("The Treatment of Beggars According to Jewish Tradition," page 110).

On the issue of beggars, I confess to not knowing what is ethically correct. Most charitable organizations and social workers who have commented on this issue argue that giving to beggars is ultimately bad both for them and for the agencies which, ultimately, are the only places that can consistently help these people.

Overwhelmed by the sheer number of beggars (a pedestrian in New York City, where I live, may be solicited two dozen or more times a day), I find that my behavior is inconsistent: I give to some and walk past others, with no clear rationale determining when or to whom I give. I only know that when someone says, "I haven't eaten. I'm hungry," I find it hard to walk away.

> If a person closes his eyes to avoid giving [any] charity, it is as if he committed idolatry.
> —Babylonian Talmud, *Ketubot* 68a

This seemingly farfetched connection between stinginess and idolatry is explained by a contemporary Talmud scholar, Rabbi Adin Steinsalz: "A person who knows that his money comes from God will give from his money to the poor. One who doesn't give to the poor, however, apparently believes that his own strength [and wisdom] are solely responsible for all he has. This is a form of idolatry, insofar as he posits himself as the exclusive source of everything" (Commentary on *Ketubot,* page 302; Hebrew edition of Steinsalz Talmud).

A major modern rabbinic figure, Rabbi Israel Meir Ha-Kohen Kagan (1838–1933), known as the Haffetz Hayyim, connects this talmudic dictum to the biblical verse: " 'You shall not make for yourselves gods of silver and gods of gold' (Exodus 20:20), i.e., do not make gold and silver into a god" (*Ahavat Chesed,* Chapter 10).

From the Rabbis' perspective, one of the damning features of the aesthetically advanced but idolatrous Roman society was its cruel indifference to the poor. Of one sage it is reported:

> When Rabbi Joshua ben Levi went to Rome, he saw marble pillars covered with sheets, so they wouldn't crack from the heat, nor freeze from the cold. He also saw a

16

poor person with only a reed mat under him, and a reed mat over him.

—*Pesikta de-Rav Kahana* 9:1

We support the non-Jewish poor along with the poor of Israel.

—Babylonian Talmud, *Gittin* 61a

STEADY GIVING

It is good to give charity before praying.
—*Shulkhan Arukh, Orakh Chayim* 92:10

In most traditional synagogues today, a small *pushke* (charity box) is passed around during the weekday morning service (on Sabbath and most holidays it is forbidden to handle money), and people are expected to contribute, even if just a small amount.

A person who gives a thousand gold pieces to a worthy person is not as generous as one who gives a thousand gold pieces on a thousand different occasions, each to a worthy cause.

—Anonymous; sixteenth century *Orhot Zaddikim*
(*The Ways of the Righteous*)

The author assumes, correctly I believe, that the very act of giving habitually, rather than sporadically and impulsively, accustoms one to become more generous. That is why it has long been a custom, still observed by many Jews, to have children put money into charity boxes every Friday afternoon just before the Sabbath.

The merit of fasting is the charity [dispensed].
—Babylonian Talmud, *Berakhot* 6b

In his commentary on the Talmud, a medieval scholar, the Maharsha, explains that before a fast, it was customary for people to

17

dispense as charity the amount of money they would save by not eating (see also Babylonian Talmud, *Sanhedrin* 35a). Unfortunately, this beautiful custom is unknown among most modern Jews; it should be revived.

HOW MUCH CHARITY SHOULD A PERSON GIVE?

Ideally, one should donate a minimum of 10 percent of his or her net income, although Jewish law places an upper limit as well:

> One who wishes to donate [generously] should not give more than a fifth of his income, lest he himself come to be in need of charity.
>
> —Babylonian Talmud, *Ketubot* 50a

The talmudic law might well have been a response to early Christianity's idealization of poverty, as epitomized by the oaths of penury undertaken in monastic orders. In contrast, the Rabbis viewed poverty as a curse: "There is nothing in the world harder to bear than poverty, for one who is crushed by poverty is like one to whom all the troubles of the world cling. . . . Our Rabbis said: If all the sufferings and pain in the world were gathered [on one side of a scale], and poverty was on the other side, poverty would outweigh them all" (*Exodus Rabbah* 31:14; see pages 427–432 on the curse of poverty).

Thus, Jewish law never saw anything wrong in the accumulation of wealth, provided it was done honestly, and as long as the person of means gave appropriate amounts of charity.

The psychological wisdom in specifying minimum and maximum donations of charity is twofold: It encourages people to give more than they would otherwise (I have noticed that people who give 2 or 3 percent of their income to charity usually think of themselves as generous), and it enables sensitive people who have donated the requisite amount to enjoy their possessions without guilt.

BUT AREN'T MANY BEGGARS FAKERS?

We all know people, perhaps including ourselves, who don't give to beggars because they claim that most are charlatans. How do Jewish sources deal with this argument?

Rabbi Hanina knew a poor man to whom he regularly sent four *zuzim* [a substantial sum] before every Sabbath. One day, he sent that amount through his wife, who came back and told him [that the man was in] no need of it. "What did you see?" [Rabbi Hanina asked her. She replied,] "I heard him being asked, 'On what will you dine, the silver colored table cloths or the gold ones?'"

"It is because of such cases [Rabbi Hanina responded] that Rabbi Elazar ben Pedat said: 'We should be grateful to the rogues among the poor; were it not for them, we [who don't respond to every beggar's appeal] would be sinning every day.'"

—Babylonian Talmud, *Ketubot* 68a

This approach is reinforced by a Hasidic sage:

Rabbi Chaim of Sanz (d. 1786) said: "The merit of charity is so great that I am happy to give to 100 beggars even if only one might actually be needy. Some people, however, act as if they are exempt from giving charity to 100 beggars in the event that one might be a fraud."

Chaim of Sanz's hyperbolic statement notwithstanding, the Rabbis despised welfare cheats, both because of their thievery and because they alienated some people from giving charity. Because it was impossible to eliminate charlatans by fiat, they implored heaven to convert their lies into truths:

Our Rabbis taught: If a man pretends to have a blind eye, a swollen belly, or a shrunken leg, he will not leave this world before actually coming into such a condition. One who accepts charity and is not in need of it, his end will be that he will not leave this world before he comes to such a condition.

—Babylonian Talmud, *Ketubot* 68a

The Babylonian Talmud also teaches (*Bava Bathra* 9a) that while one need not give a beggar a large sum, one should try to give at least a little. Maimonides rules that if one gives nothing at all, one should at least extend a pleasant greeting. This seems an important guideline, given that so many of us turn coldly from the beggars who overwhelm our large cities.

> When a [poor] man says, "Provide me with clothes," he should be investigated [lest he be found to be a cheat]; when he says, "Feed me," he should not be investigated [but fed immediately, lest he starve to death during the investigation].
>
> —Babylonian Talmud, *Bava Bathra* 9a

> A beggar once came to the city of Kovno and collected a large sum of money from the residents. The people of the town soon found out that he was an imposter; he really was a wealthy man. The city council wanted to make an ordinance prohibiting beggars from coming to Kovno to collect money. When Rabbi Yitzchak Elchanan Specter (1817–1896), the rabbi of Kovno, heard about the proposed ordinance, he came before the council and requested permission to speak. . . . "Who deceived you," he asked, "a needy person or a wealthy person? It was a wealthy person feigning poverty. If you want to make an ordinance, it should be to ban wealthy persons, not needy beggars, from collecting alms."
>
> —Irving Bunim, *Ethics from Sinai*, Vol. 3, page 121

ISN'T IT GOD'S WILL THAT THE POOR BE POOR?

The talmudic rabbis often were presented with the now infrequently cited argument that the sufferings of the poor must be the will of God. In fact, this was the argument advanced by a distinguished Roman official to one of the Talmud's greatest sages:

> Rabbi Meir used to say: "A critic [of Judaism] may bring against you the argument, 'If your God loves the poor, why does He not support them?' Say to him, 'So that through them we may be saved from punishment after we

die.' This question was actually put by Turnusrufus [the Roman governor of Judea] to Rabbi Akiva: 'If your God loves the poor, why does He not support them?' He replied, 'So that through them we may be saved from punishment after we die.'

"On the contrary," said [Turnusrufus], "it is this which will condemn you to punishment after you die. I will prove it to you through a parable. Suppose an earthly king was angry with his servant and put him in prison and ordered that he should be given no food or drink, and a man went and gave him food and drink. If the king heard, would he not be angry with him?" . . .

Rabbi Akiva answered him: "I will answer you through a parable. Suppose an earthly king was angry with his son, and put him in prison and ordered that no food or drink should be given to him, and someone went and gave him food and drink. If the king heard of it, would he not send him a present?"

—Babylonian Talmud, *Bava Bathra* 10a

Although Rabbi Akiva seems to accept Turnusrufus's argument that poverty is a punishment from God (a point of view hardly uniformly accepted in rabbinic writings), he continues to insist that poor people are children of God, and entitled to be treated accordingly. Most important, he suggests that God delights in our helping the poor. In addition, being children of God entitles poor people not only to food, drink, and money, but to be spared humiliation as well.

GUARDING THE DIGNITY OF THE POOR

A poor person's self-respect is safeguarded in several ways:

1. by reminding everyone that a certain amount of poverty is inevitable:

For there will never cease to be needy people in your land, which is why I command you: open your hand to the poor and needy.

—Deuteronomy 15:7–8

2. by teaching that rich people have a personal *need* to fulfill God's commandments through giving charity:

> Said Rabbi Joshua ben Hananiah: The poor man does more for the rich man [by accepting charity] than the rich man does for the poor man [by giving it].
> —*Leviticus Rabbah* 34:11

Rabbi Joshua's teaching helped create the image of the *shnorrer* (beggar) in Jewish folklore. In numerous jokes (several of which Sigmund Freud cites in his *Jokes and Their Relationship to the Unconscious*), the *shnorrer* is proud and assertive rather than ashamed and submissive. He feels "entitled" to the donor's money, for he is doing the donor a big favor by giving him or her the opportunity to carry out a *mitzvah* (commandment). A revealing tale:

A *shnorrer* is accustomed to receiving a set donation from a certain man every week. One day, when he comes for the money, the man tells him that he can't give him anything: "I've had terrible expenses recently. My wife became very sick, and I had to send her to a health resort in Carlsbad. It's very cold there, so I had to buy her new clothes, and a fur coat."

"What!" the beggar yells. "With my money?"

3. by impressing upon fortunate people that their current economic status may dramatically change:

> Rabbi Hiyya advised his wife, "When a poor man comes to the door, be quick to give him food so that the same may be done to your children." She exclaimed, "You are cursing our children [with the suggestion that they may become beggars]." But Rabbi Hiyya replied, "There is a wheel which revolves in this world."
> —Babylonian Talmud, *Shabbat* 151b

A man should meditate on the fact that life is like a revolving wheel, and in the end he, or his children or his grandchildren, may be reduced to taking charity. He

22

should not think, therefore, "How can I diminish my wealth by giving it to the poor?" Instead he should realize that his property is not his own, but only deposited with him as a trust to do with as the Depositor [God] wishes.

—*Abridged Code of Jewish Law,* by Rabbi Solomon Ganzfried
(1804–1886), 34:1

Reuben, an honest man, asked Shimon to lend him some money. Without hesitation, Shimon made the loan but said, "I really give this to you as a gift."

Reuben was so shamed and embarrassed that he would never ask Shimon for a loan again. Clearly, in this case, it would have been better not to have given Reuben a gift of that kind.

—Judah the Pious, *Sefer Hasidim* (the thirteenth-century
Book of the Pious), paragraph 1691

Although undoubtedly well intentioned, Shimon's behavior humiliated the recipient by making him feel that he no longer was an equal, but part of a lower social class, a beggar. This episode reminds me of a critique a rabbi once made of a big philanthropist, "He likes giving charity too much to be a really good person"; i.e., he derives too much satisfaction from others being dependent on his giving.

SUBTLETY IN GIVING

Rabbi Aharon Kotler, a prominent twentieth-century Orthodox sage, knew that his behavior was subjected to careful scrutiny. Once, when he entered a synagogue and again when he left, he was observed giving money to the same beggar. Questioned as to why he gave to the man twice, Kotler replied that he feared someone might see him passing the beggar, and conclude that the man was unworthy of being helped.

IF ALL ELSE FAILS: PRAGMATIC REASONS FOR GIVING CHARITY

Charity saves from death.

—Proverbs 10:2

Most Jewish sources understand this as meaning that charity saves the donor from an early death: Quite possibly, the verse should be interpreted literally, that it saves the recipient.

> If a person says, "I am giving this coin to charity so that my child will live," or "so that I will make it into the next world," he is regarded as completely righteous [his self-centered motives notwithstanding].
>
> —Babylonian Talmud, *Pesachim* 8a–b

SOMETHING GREATER THAN CHARITY: *GEMILUT CHESED*, ACTS OF LOVING-KINDNESS

> Our Rabbis taught: *Gemilut Chesed* (loving-kindness) is greater than charity in three ways.
>
> Charity is done with one's money, while loving-kindness may be done with one's money or with one's person [e.g., spending time with a sick person].
>
> Charity is given only to the poor, while loving-kindness may be given both to the poor and to the rich [e.g., consoling one who is in mourning or depressed].
>
> Charity is given only to the living, while loving-kindness may be shown to both the living and the dead [e.g., by arranging a proper burial for a person who died indigent].
>
> —Babylonian Talmud, *Sukkot* 49b

The Rabbis considered God to be the original exemplar of acts of loving-kindness; the Torah itself commands people to walk in His ways (Deuteronomy 13:5). Thus, because God clothed the naked—"And the Lord God made garments of skin for Adam and his wife, and clothed them" (Genesis 3:21)—you too should clothe the naked.

Because God visited the sick—"The Lord appeared to [Abraham] by the terebinths of Mamre" (Genesis 18:1; this was immediately following Abraham's circumcision at the age of ninety-nine)—you too should visit the sick.

Because God buried the dead—"He buried [Moses] in the valley of Moab" (Deuteronomy 34:6)—you too should bury the dead. Because God comforted mourners—"And it came to pass after the death of Abraham that God blessed his son Isaac" (Genesis 25:11)— you too should comfort mourners (based on the Babylonian Talmud, *Sotah* 14a).

The Rabbis saw burial of the dead as the act of *gemilut chesed* par excellence because it necessarily is done without any hope that the "recipient" will repay the good deed. (In Hebrew it is called *chesed shel emet,* a true act of loving-kindness.) Indeed, the Haffetz Hayyim defined *gemilut chesed* as "any good deed that one does for another without getting something in return" (*Ahavat Chesed*).

A FINAL THOUGHT

A person should be more concerned with spiritual than with material matters, but another person's material welfare is his own spiritual concern.
—Rabbi Israel Salanter (1810–1883), founder of the Mussar movement, a movement that put particular emphasis on ethical self-improvement

The Russian religious existentialist Nikolai Berdyaev (1874–1948) expressed the same thought more poetically: "The question of bread for myself is a material question, but the question of bread for my neighbor is a spiritual question."

3

HELPING THE HELPLESS

What Are Our Obligations to Society's Most Vulnerable Members?

THE POOR, THE WEAK, AND THE VULNERABLE

> You shall not wrong a stranger or oppress him, for you
> were strangers in the land of Egypt. You shall not ill-treat
> any widow or orphan.
>
> —Exodus 22:20–21

The Torah appreciates how common it is for people to take advantage of society's weakest, most marginal members, and fears that an appeal to sympathy alone would be insufficient to motivate people to act sensitively. It thus adds a "kicker" to the second of these commandments, warning those who mistreat widows and orphans that "your own wives shall become widows and your children fatherless" (Exodus 22:23).

Concerning strangers, the Torah claims that they are the sole category of people whom God is identified as loving. "And God loves the stranger" (Deuteronomy 10:18).

German-Jewish philosopher Hermann Cohen (1842–1918) believed that the biblical commandments protecting the stranger represented the beginning of true religion: "The stranger was to be protected, although he was not a member of one's family, clan, religion, community, or people; simply because he was a human being. In the stranger, therefore, man discovered the idea of humanity" (cited in Richard Schwartz, *Judaism and Global Survival*, page 13).

> A person must be especially heedful of his behavior toward widows and orphans because their souls are deeply depressed and their spirits low. Even if they are wealthy, even if they are the widow and orphans of a king, we are warned concerning them, "You shall not ill-treat any widow or orphan." How are we to conduct ourselves toward them?
>
> One must always speak to them tenderly.
>
> One must show them unwavering courtesy; not hurt them physically with hard toil, or wound their feelings with harsh speech.
>
> One must take greater care of their property and money than of one's own. Whoever irritates them, provokes them to anger, pains them, tyrannizes over them, or causes them loss of money, is guilty of a transgression.
>
> —Moses Maimonides, *Mishneh Torah*, "Laws of
> Character Development and Ethical Conduct," 6:10

As Maimonides makes clear, neediness is not always synonymous with poverty; it can refer also to those who are emotionally and/or psychologically destitute. Thus, even the widow and orphans of a king may be vulnerable and in need of emotional support.

> Let all who are *hungry* come in and eat, let all who are *needy* come in and make Passover.
>
> —Traditional prayer recited near the beginning of the
> Passover Seder

Shmuel Yosef Agnon, the Israeli Nobel Laureate, wrote a story, "The Passover Celebrants," whose whole point is to highlight the difference between "hungry" and "needy."

In a small Eastern European town lived a *shammas* (a synagogue sexton), who was so poor that, when Passover arrived, he lacked money to purchase food for the Seder. He walked around the town hungry and alone. In the same village lived a wealthy woman, whose husband recently had died. This was the first Passover Seder that she was observing without him; out of habit, she set a beautiful Seder table, but she was in distress, for she too was alone.

But then the widow meets the destitute *shammas*, and they celebrate the Seder together. By the evening's end, they forge a powerful connection, and there is reason to hope that soon he will no longer be "hungry," and she will no longer be "needy."

THE PHYSICALLY, AND OTHERWISE, DISADVANTAGED

> You shall not place a stumbling block in front of a blind man: You shall fear God.
>
> —Leviticus 19:14

In addition to mandating not playing cruel tricks on the physically blind, the Rabbis broadly interpreted this verse as forbidding taking advantage of anyone who is "blind" in the matter at hand. Anyone who takes advantage of another's ignorance and gives him or her inappropriate advice is considered to have violated this biblical law. A rabbinic commentary on Leviticus teaches:

> If a man seeks your advice, do not give him counsel that is wrong for him. Do not say to him, "Leave early in the morning," so that thugs might mug him.
>
> Do not say to him, "Leave at noon," so that he might faint from heat.
>
> Do not say to him, "Sell your field and buy a donkey," so that you may circumvent him, and take the field away from him.
>
> —*Sifra Leviticus* on 19:14

As the final example makes clear, when someone seeks your advice, you must disclose whether you have a personal interest in the matter at hand.

VISITING AND HELPING THE SICK

It happened that one of Rabbi Akiva's students became sick, but none of the sages went to visit him. Rabbi Akiva, however, went to visit him. Because he swept and cleaned the floor for him, the student recovered. The student said to him, "Rabbi, you have given me life!" Rabbi Akiva came out and taught, "Those who do not visit a sick person might just as well have spilled his blood."

—Babylonian Talmud, *Nedarim* 40a

"Where [our sages asked] shall we look for the Messiah? Shall the Messiah come to us on clouds of glory, robed in majesty, and crowned with light?" The [Babylonian] Talmud (*Sanhedrin* 98a) reports that Rabbi Joshua ben Levi put this question to no less an authority than the prophet Elijah himself.

"Where," Rabbi Joshua asked, "shall I find the Messiah?"

"At the gate of the city," Elijah replied.

"How shall I recognize him?"

"He sits among the lepers."

"Among the lepers?" cried Rabbi Joshua. "What is he doing there?"

"He changes their bandages," Elijah answered. "He changes them one by one."

That may not seem like much for a Messiah to be doing. But, apparently, in the eyes of God, it is a mighty thing indeed.

—Rabbi Robert Kirschner, sermon on AIDS, quoted in Albert
Vorspan and David Saperstein, *Tough Choices:
Jewish Perspectives on Social Justice*, pages 236–237

This was the conclusion of Rabbi Kirschner's 1985 Yom Kippur sermon, urging his San Francisco congregants to reach out to those with AIDS. It was not by accident that Kirschner quotes Rabbi Joshua's teaching about the Messiah sitting among the lepers, since the response of many people in the ancient world to lepers parallels the response of many contemporary people to AIDS sufferers. As Kirschner explains: "In the days of our sages, to be a leper was not only to be afflicted with a disease but to be despised for it. It was not only to die a terrible death, but to be accused of deserving it." Thus, in announcing that the Messiah chose to live among lepers, Rabbi Joshua was breaking not only with a popular prejudice against lepers, but even with many of his rabbinic colleagues who believed that lepers should be pushed away with both hands. A midrashic text reports that Rabbi Yochanan used to say, "It is forbidden to get closer than four cubits [about six feet] to a leper." Rabbi Ammi and Rabbi Assai would not even go near to a place where lepers were known to live; and of Resh Lakish it was taught, "When he saw a leper in the city, he would throw stones at him shouting, 'Stop contaminating us and go back where you came from' " (*Leviticus Rabbah* 16:3).

POLITICAL ASYLUM

> You shall not return a runaway slave to his master. . . . Let him stay with you anywhere he chooses in any one of your settlements, whatever suits him best; you shall not wrong him.
>
> —Deuteronomy 23:16–17

In the 1857 Dred Scott case, in what was probably the most immoral and unfortunate Supreme Court ruling ever handed down, the justices ruled that a black slave who had been brought by his master to a free state could be forcibly returned to slavery in the South. In contrast to this three-thousand-year-old biblical ruling that all people, slaves included, are endowed with certain inalienable rights, Chief Justice Roger Taney wrote that blacks "had no rights which the white man was bound to respect."

The Supreme Court's violation of this biblical law wrought havoc; historians today regard the Dred Scott decision, and the revulsion it inspired, as a major cause of the Civil War. Supreme Court Justice Felix Frankfurter observed that later justices never mentioned this decision, any more "than a family in which a son had been hanged mentioned ropes and scaffolds" (cited in John Garraty, ed., *Quarrels That Have Shaped the Constitution*, pages 88–89).

In general, it should be noted, biblical law is evolutionary, not revolutionary; indeed, this is most likely why the Torah did not outlaw slavery in a world in which it was uniformly practiced. Nonetheless, this law indicates the Bible's discomfort with slavery, for in no other area does the Torah cavalierly permit depriving a person of his or her property. Because a slave is a human being, however, and therefore also created in God's image, his or her status could never be reduced to mere property. And because the Bible saw the desired state of man as free—that, after all, is the central message of the first half of the Book of Exodus—if a slave risked his master's wrath by fleeing, the Bible's sympathies were exclusively on one side, the slave's.

The contemporary upshot of this biblical verse is that democracies should be generous in granting political asylum to people fleeing dictatorships and totalitarian regimes. The most immoral thing to do would be to return "a runaway slave to his master."

BALANCING RITUAL OBSERVANCE WITH SENSITIVITY

Rabbi Israel Salanter was once invited by a former student to spend Shabbat with him. Knowing how strict his teacher was in observing the dietary laws, the student described in detail how careful he was in all matters of Jewish law. He added that in his house between each course of the Friday night meal, the participants engaged in discussions of Torah and Talmud, and sang *zmirot* (Sabbath songs).

Rabbi Salanter said that he would accept the invitation on the condition that the meal be shorter than usual. The student was surprised, but agreed, and the meal proceeded quickly. At its end, he asked Rabbi Salanter what it was about his normal way of conducting the meal that bothered him.

"I'll show you," replied the rabbi. He called over the

31

maid, a widow, and apologized to her for making her work faster than usual.

"On the contrary," the woman smiled. "I'm grateful to you. Friday night meals usually end very late, and I'm exhausted from the whole week's work. Tonight, I'll be able to catch up on some needed sleep."

After she left, Rabbi Salanter told his host that his customary Shabbat dinner sounded fine indeed, but it shouldn't come at the expense of his very tired maid.

—Based on Rabbi Zelig Pliskin, *Love Your Neighbor*, pages 219–220

A similar story tells of Rabbi Salanter eating a meal at another's house, and surprising everyone present by using a minimal amount of water in the ceremonial washing of the hands before the blessing over the bread. The others, who had lavishly poured water over their outstretched hands, asked him to explain his unusual behavior.

"I noticed that a maid brings the water up to the house in buckets drawn from the well. Those buckets are very heavy, and I don't want to perform *my mitzvah* on *her* shoulders."

4

MENSCH—NINE CHALLENGES A GOOD PERSON MUST MEET

Not all biblical verses have had an equal impact on Jewish life, and some are quoted in Jewish writings and among Jews far more frequently than others. For example, the most famous verse in the Bible, "Love your neighbor as yourself," has stimulated so many comments that it has its own section in this book (Chapter 23).

This chapter consists of a compilation of nine other representative biblical verses and laws which, over the millennia, have strongly influenced Jewish notions of how a *mensch*, a good person, should behave:

1. Do not stand by while your neighbor's blood is shed (literally, Do not stand upon your neighbor's blood).

—Leviticus 19:16

> How do we know that if one person pursues after another to kill him, the pursued person must be saved even at the cost of the pursuer's life? From the verse, "Do not stand by while your neighbor's blood is shed."
>
> —Babylonian Talmud, *Sanhedrin* 73a

Thus, if it is within one's power to kill a "pursuer," one is obliged to do so, but only if there is no other way to stop him.

> How do we know that if one sees someone drowning, mauled by beasts, or attacked by robbers, one is obligated to save him? From the verse, "Do not stand by while your neighbor's blood is shed."
> —Babylonian Talmud, *Sanhedrin* 73a

This talmudic quote brings to mind the infamous case of Kitty Genovese, a twenty-eight-year-old woman who was murdered over a period of thirty-five minutes on a New York City Street in March 1964. Thirty-eight witnesses watched from their windows; not one called the police. Her neighbors' indifference persisted despite the wounded woman's anguished shouts, "Oh, my God, he stabbed me! Please help me! Please help me!"

Among the excuses later offered by witnesses were: "I didn't want to get involved." "I was tired. I went back to bed." "Frankly, we were afraid."

While Jewish law does not oblige you to intervene if your own life would be endangered by so doing, at the very least, you must call the police or others who can help and, if necessary, pay money to one who can help save the endangered person's life.

But, if the risk to yourself is minimal, you are obliged to intervene. Thus, if someone is drowning, and you can barely swim, you are not obliged to jump in. However, if you are a good swimmer, and the risk appears small, you are obligated to help.

Although this imperative is a bedrock of biblical morality, it is rejected in American law. Harvard law professor Mary Ann Glendon notes that "generations of first-year law students have been introduced to basic elements of the law through one or another variant of the following hypothetical case: An Olympic swimmer out for a stroll walks by a swimming pool and sees an adorable toddler drowning in the shallow end. He could easily save her with no risk to himself, but instead he pulls up a chair and looks on as she perishes." Glendon writes that the object of this exercise is to prove to future lawyers that the athlete has violated no law, that indeed "there is no peg in our legal system on which to hang a duty to rescue another person in danger."

Nor, as Glendon documents, should this case be regarded as a hypothetical classroom exercise: "In a long line of [American] judicial rulings, bystanders consistently have been exempted from any duty to toss a rope to a drowning person, to warn the unsuspecting target of an impending assault, or to summon medical assistance to someone bleeding to death at the scene of an accident" (Mary Ann Glendon, *Rights Talk*, pages 78–80). From the perspective of Jewish law, such bystanders would be regarded as grievous sinners and evil people.

On a "macro" level, probably the most flagrant violation of "Do not stand by while your neighbor's blood is shed" was committed by the Allies during the Holocaust. Throughout 1944, Jewish groups urged the American and British air forces to bomb the railroad tracks transporting Jews to Auschwitz. Since the Allies then controlled the skies over Europe, the risk of a plane being shot down was minimal. In fact, during 1944, the Allies repeatedly bombed seven synthetic oil factories located within forty-five miles of the famous death camp, on many occasions flying over the railroad tracks leading there. Yet the Allied armies rejected requests to bomb the railroad tracks; when Allied planes finally did strike Auschwitz twice, they restricted their bombings to the rubber factories where Jews and other inmates performed forced labor. (The story of the Allies' indifference is told in two important historical works: David Wyman, *The Abandonment of the Jews: America and the Holocaust 1941–1945,* and Martin Gilbert, *Auschwitz and the Allies.*)

To encourage people to actively help those whose lives are in danger, the Talmud decrees:

> If one chases after a pursuer in order to rescue the pursued, and breaks some utensils, whether of the pursuer, the pursued, or of any other person, he is not liable for payment. This should not be so according to strict law, but if you

will not rule in this manner, no man will save his neighbor from a pursuer [lest in doing so he cause damage for which he will have to pay].

—Babylonian Talmud, *Sanhedrin* 74a

This ruling was promulgated solely to motivate bystanders to intervene when they see a person threatened. The ruling's innovative nature is underscored by the fact that "If [the man who is being pursued] breaks articles belonging to other people, he is liable" (Maimonides, *Mishneh Torah,* "Laws of Wounding and Damaging," 8:13). Thus, one would think that the pursuer in our case would be liable as well. But unlike the pursued, who will do whatever is necessary to save his life, a bystander needs to be reassured that he will not be sued for trying to save another's life.

He [or she] who hears heathens or informers plotting to harm a person is obliged to inform the intended victim. If he is able to appease the perpetrator and deter him from the act, but does not do so, he has violated the law "Do not stand by while your neighbor's blood is shed."

—*Shulkhan Arukh, Hoshen Mishpat* 426:1

The biblical book of Esther records that when Mordechai overheard two men in King Ahasuerus's court plotting to kill him, he reported the matter to his cousin, Queen Esther, and the king's life was saved (Esther 2:21–23). This was one of the acts that later helped deter the king from carrying out Haman's genocidal plot against Mordechai and his fellow Jews.

British Rabbi Aryeh Carmell has written a powerful short story, "The Midnight Rescue," illustrating how observance of the command "Do not stand by while your neighbor's blood is shed" leads one also to fulfill the command "Love your neighbor as yourself":

It was past midnight. I was walking through the deserted city to my hotel on the other side of the river. The night was dark and foggy and I couldn't get a taxi. As I approached the bridge, I noticed a shabby figure leaning over the parapet. A "down-and-out," I thought. Then he disappeared. I heard a splash. My God, I thought, he's done it. Suicide!

I ran back under the bridge, onto the embankment, and waded into the river, grabbing him as he came past, borne by the current. I dragged him up onto the embankment. He was quite a young guy. He was still breathing. A couple of people noticed and I shouted to them to get an ambulance. They managed to stop a taxi and between us we half dragged, half carried the man into the taxi. . . . I got in and told [the driver] to drive to the nearest hospital emergency room. I waited until the man was admitted, gave my report and got a taxi back to my hotel at last.

I had ruined a good suit and knew I would have a terrible cold in the morning. I could feel it coming on. But anyway I had saved a life. I had a hot bath and got into bed but it still worried me. Such a young man! Why had he done it?

The next morning, as soon as I was free, I bought a large bunch of grapes and set off for the hospital. I was determined to find out what was behind this matter. Maybe I could help.

Why was I so interested in the guy? In this great city there were at least half a dozen would-be suicides every night. Their plight did not touch me. Then it dawned on me. Of course. First you *give*, then you *care*. I had given quite a lot. I had risked my life and gotten a bad cold in the bargain. I had invested something of myself in that man. Now my love and care were aroused. That's how it goes. First we *give*, then we come to love.

—Aryeh Carmell, *Masterplan: Judaism:*
Its Program, Meanings, Goals, pages 118–119

From where do we learn that if you are in a position to offer testimony on someone's behalf, you are not permitted to remain silent? From "Do not stand by while your neighbor's blood is shed."

—*Sifra Leviticus* on 19:16

From the perspective of Jewish law, whether or not a court subpoenas you to testify is irrelevant; all that matters is whether you know something that can advance justice. If you do, and refuse to tell what you know, you are guilty of a serious sin.

* * *

2. Do what is right and good in the sight of the Lord.
—Deuteronomy 6:18

> Rav Judah taught in Rav's name: If one takes possession [through payment of a land tax] of property lying between fields belonging to brothers or partners, he is an impudent man, yet cannot be removed. . . . [The rabbinic judges of] Neherdea ruled: He is removed from the land [i.e., forced to sell] . . . for it is written "Do what is right and good in the sight of the Lord."
> —Babylonian Talmud, *Bava Mezia* 108a

According to Jewish law, equity demands that people owning property adjacent to available land be given the first opportunity to acquire it. In the above case, the purchaser stepped in before the land's availability was known, and acquired it. Because of the principle enunciated in the biblical verse, the rabbis of Neherdea, a Babylonian city and a major center of Jewish religious life, forced the purchaser to sell the land.

Such logic flies in the face of most people's understanding of the capitalist ethic. But the Torah verse holds Jews to a standard of "what is right and good," not "what is profitable." As Mother Teresa has remarked in a different context: "God has not called me to be successful; He has called me to be faithful."

The following verse is similar to that from Deuteronomy cited above:

3. So follow the way of the good, and keep to the paths of the just.
—Proverbs 2:20

> Some employees negligently broke a barrel of wine belonging to Rabbah son of Bar Hanana, and he seized their

cloaks [when they failed to pay for the damage]. They went and complained to Rav.

"Return their cloaks to them," he ordered.

"Is that the law?" asked Rabbah.

"Yes," he answered, "for it is written 'So follow the way of the good.' "

He returned the cloaks to the porters. Then they complained [to Rav]: "We are poor men, we have worked all day, and are hungry, and we have nothing."

"Go and pay them," Rav ordered Rabbah.

"Is that the law?" he asked.

"Yes," he replied, "[for see the end of the verse], 'and keep to the paths of the just.' "

—Babylonian Talmud, *Bava Mezia* 83a

According to Jewish law, the negligent employees were responsible for the damage they wrought, and Rabbah was fully within his rights in confiscating their cloaks, and not paying them. Rav, however, ruled that applying the letter of the law in this case—in which the breakage resulted from negligence, not premeditation—would lead to injustice. He held Rabbah responsible to a higher standard, what is known as *lifnim me-shurat ha-din* (beyond the letter of the law).

This talmudic anecdote is frequently cited in encouraging an affluent person not to insist on the strict application of the law against a defendant of more limited means. A friend told me that he thought of this ruling when an itinerant window washer carelessly broke an expensive vase. His first instinct was to charge the man for the vase or, at the very least, not pay him for his work. When he recalled the talmudic ruling, however, he paid the man and accepted his apology for the broken vase.

*   *   *

4. Her ways [the ways of Torah] are pleasant, and all her paths, peaceful.

—Proverbs 3:17

The whole of the Torah is for promoting peace, as it is written, "Her ways are pleasant, and all her paths peaceful."

—Babylonian Talmud, *Gittin* 59b

The above verse from Proverbs provides guidance in instances where strict application of Torah law would lead to injustice. Under this verse's influence, the talmudic rabbis originated the doctrine of *darkei shalom* (the ways of peace), going so far as to alter certain laws so as to bring about more peaceful and equitable interpersonal relations.

For example, according to biblical law, ownership of property is not granted until one takes physical possession of the sought-after item. Normally, this creates no problems of equity. But what about a case, the Talmud asks, in which a poor man climbs to the top of an olive tree in the public domain and starts knocking down the olives, intending subsequently to pick them off the ground? Since the man does not acquire ownership until he picks up the olives, biblical law would permit a passerby to collect the olives off the ground and keep them.

Yet the Rabbis rule that *mipnei darkei shalom* (because of the ways of peace), the olives belong to the person who knocked them down. Anyone else who takes them is a thief, although biblical law technically would permit him or her to do so (Mishna *Gittin* 5:8).

A contemporary application of this principle would forbid one from stepping in when another has all but concluded a business deal (i.e., the contract has not yet been signed) to "steal" the business away for him- or herself.

The Talmud (*Gittin* 61a) also cites a universalistic example of *mipnei darkei shalom*: "We support the non-Jewish poor along with the poor of Israel, and visit the non-Jewish sick along with the sick of Israel and bury the non-Jewish dead along with the dead of Israel, for the sake of peace. . . ."

*　　*　　*

5. You shall be holy, for I, the Lord God, am holy.

—Leviticus 19:2

On this verse, the Talmud comments:

> Sanctify yourself through that which is permitted to you.
> —Babylonian Talmud, *Yevamot* 20a

Merely refraining from activities that the Torah prohibits will not, in and of itself, lead a person to holiness. For example, a person can restrict his or her eating to foods permitted by Jewish law and still "eat like a pig." Similarly, the way a person drinks, carries on business activities, and has sex might break no Jewish laws, but still be unholy. Thus, the Rabbis added the above admonition. In this way, no matter what the activity in which a person is engaged, he must ask himself whether he is fulfilling the biblical command "You shall be holy" (Leviticus 19:2).

The secular world, in contrast and by definition, lacks the concept of holiness.

*　　*　　*

6. Justice, justice you shall pursue.

—Deuteronomy 16:20

> They asked [Hasidic Rebbe Ya'akov Yitzhak, known as] the "holy Yehudi": "Why is it written, 'Justice, justice you shall pursue?' Why is the word 'justice' repeated?"
> He answered: "We ought to follow justice with justice, and not with unrighteousness." That means: The use of unrighteousness as a means to a righteous end makes the end itself unrighteous.
> —Hasidic Rebbe Ya'akov Yitzhak of Pzhysha (1766–1814),
> quoted in Martin Buber, ed., *Ten Rungs:*
> *Hasidic Sayings,* page 7

The Talmud understands "Justice, justice you shall pursue" as offering guidance in a case where two "rights" confront each other. In such instances, the Talmud explains that justice is served by both parties compromising. (For example, where two boats sailing on a river meet, if both attempt to pass simultaneously, both will sink; whereas if one makes way for the other, both can pass without mishap [Babylonian Talmud, *Sanhedrin* 32b]). The Talmud likewise understands the verse as obligating the party who will suffer less to yield to the party who will suffer more (a good guideline to follow in personal and family disputes as well):

> Two camels meet on the steep ascent to Beit-Horon; if they both ascend simultaneously, both will tumble down [into the valley]. If they ascend one after the other, both can go up safely. How should they act? If one is laden and the other unladen, the unladen camel should let the laden one go first.
>
> —Babylonian Talmud, *Sanhedrin* 32b

This somewhat obscure talmudic discussion became widely discussed in Israel in 1952. That fall, the country was rent by a religious/secular dispute over the government's right to draft women for national military service, a move the religious parties vigorously opposed. In the midst of the controversy, Prime Minister David Ben-Gurion traveled to Bnai Brak to meet the Hazon Ish (Rabbi Avraham Yeshayahu Karelitz, 1878–1953), the leader of Israel's ultra-Orthodox Jews. Ben-Gurion asked the religious sage how religious and secular Jews could live together in harmony. The Hazon Ish's response was based on the preceding talmudic discussion:

"The Talmud states: Two ships are traveling down a river; one is laden, the other is empty, and they meet. If they attempt to pass one another, both will sink. The empty ship must back up and allow the laden ship to pass. The ship of the religious Jews . . . which is laden with thousands of years of sanctification of the divine name, and of devotion to Torah, has encountered in the narrow straits of our era the empty ship of the secularists. There can be no compromise. There can be no harmony. The collision between the ships is inevitable. Therefore, whose ship ought to back up before whose? Should it not be your empty ship before our laden one?" (cited in Lawrence Kaplan, "The Hazon Ish: Haredi Critic of Traditional Orthodoxy," page 169).

Needless to say, Prime Minister Ben-Gurion heatedly denied the Hazon Ish's characterization of non-Orthodox Israeli society as empty. But anxious to avert a civil war, he exempted religious women from military service.

*   *   *

7. You shall not covet your neighbor's wife: You shall not crave your neighbor's house or his field . . . or his ox or his donkey, or anything that is your neighbor's.

—Deuteronomy 5:18; number 10 of the Ten Commandments

It is not wrong to want more than what you now have, but it is wrong to desire it at your neighbor's expense.

Although Torah law almost never attempts to regulate *thought,* only *deeds,* an exception is made in this case, because coveting represents a desire so strong that it inevitably leads to immoral actions. The Bible depicts two kings, men who presumably possessed more than almost any one else, as guilty of coveting. David coveted Bathsheba, Uriah's wife (II Samuel, chapter 11). As a result, he soon violated two other of the Ten Commandments: He committed adultery with her (the Seventh Commandment) and, when she became pregnant, had her husband killed to cover up the potential scandal (the Sixth Commandment).

More than a century later, King Ahab coveted the vineyard of a man named Navot (I Kings, chapter 21). When Navot refused to sell Ahab the land, the king went into a deep depression: His wife, Queen Jezebel, resolved to acquire the land for him by any means necessary. She arranged for false witnesses to testify that Navot had committed treason, which led to his execution, whereupon the king took possession of his field. Thus, what started with coveting ended up with violation of three more of the Ten Commandments—the Ninth Commandment, which forbids "bearing false testimony," the Sixth, which prohibits murder, and the Eighth, which forbids stealing.

A person cannot be a *mensch* unless he or she learns to control covetous impulses. One must remind oneself constantly that what belongs to another person is forbidden to him or her.

43

*　　*　　*

8. When you build a new house, you shall make a parapet for your roof, so that you do not bring bloodguilt on your house if anyone should fall from it.

—Deuteronomy 22:8

According to Jewish law, if your house has a flat roof, you must put up a railing strong enough so that a person can lean on it without falling (*Shulkhan Arukh, Hoshen Mishpat* 427:1,5). Similarly, if you dig a well or pit on your property, you must either make a railing around it or put a cover on it so that no one falls in (*Shulkhan Arukh, Hoshen Mishpat* 427:7; the various outgrowths of this biblical law are listed in Zelig Pliskin, *Love Your Neighbor*, pages 415–416).

The Rabbis also understand this biblical law as obligating one to remove anything from his property that could cause a fatal injury:

> From where do we learn that a man should not raise a vicious dog nor keep a rickety ladder in his house? From the verse, "so that you do not bring bloodguilt on your house."
>
> —Babylonian Talmud, *Ketubot* 41b

As this law makes clear, human beings are expected to foresee the injuries that can ensue from their actions or passivity:

> If one places a jug in a public domain, and a person trips on it and breaks it, the person who broke it is not responsible for the breakage, for people are not expected to be watching so carefully when they are walking. Indeed, if the person who tripped was injured, the owner of the jug is responsible for the injury.
>
> —Moses Maimonides, *Mishneh Torah*, "Laws Concerning Property Damage," 13:5

*　　*　　*

Finally, we come to the question posed by Cain to God, after he killed his brother Abel: It is no exaggeration to claim that the rest of the Bible is a resoundingly affirmative response to Cain's query:

9. Am I my brother's keeper?

—Genesis 4:9

5

HONESTY, DISHONESTY, AND THE "GRAY AREAS" IN BETWEEN

BUSINESS HONESTY

If one is honest in his business dealings and people esteem him, it is accounted to him as though he had fulfilled the whole Torah.

> —*Mekhilta, Vayeesa,* chapter 1 (see Lauterbach, Vol. II, page 96;
> see also page 3, and the teaching that the first question posed
> to a person after death concerns honesty in business)

Let your fellow man's property be as dear to you as your own.

> —*Ethics of the Fathers* 2:17

The shopkeeper must wipe his measures twice a week, his weights once a week, and his scales after every weighing.

> —Mishna *Bava Bathra* 5:10

In other words, let the *seller* beware!:

A vendor may not combine different grades of produce in one bin [in more familiar terms, one may not place the nicest, reddest strawberries on top if not all of them are

46

of the same quality] . . . a vendor whose wine has become diluted with water may not sell it unless he makes full disclosure to the customer, and in any event he may not sell it to another retailer, even if he makes disclosure, for fear that the second retailer will deceive *his* customers.

—Mishna *Bava Mezia* 4:11; I have followed the translation of, and included the annotations of, Gordon Tucker, "Jewish Business Ethics," page 35.

Concerning people who think of themselves as relatively honest, but who buy stolen merchandise, the Rabbis relate a parable:

There is the story of a ruler who used to put to death receivers of stolen property, but let thieves go. Everyone criticized him for not acting rationally. So what did he do? He had it proclaimed throughout the province, "All people to the arena!" Next, what did he do? He brought mice and placed before them portions of food. The mice took the portions and carried them to their holes.

The following day, he again had it proclaimed, "All people to the arena!" Again he brought mice and placed before them portions of food, but this time he stopped up the holes, so that when the mice took their food to the holes and found them stopped up, they returned the portions to where they had been. Thus the mice demonstrated that, but for the recipients of stolen goods, there would be no thievery.

—*Leviticus Rabbah* 6:2; I have followed, almost verbatim, the translation of William Braude in H. N. Bialik and Y. H. Ravnitzky, *The Book of Legends*, page 652.

In the course of a talmudic debate, Rabbi Joseph expressed the same view as the mythical ruler of this parable:

Not the mouse, but the hole is the thief.

His contemporary, Abbaye, challenged him for inadvertently exonerating the thief:

Nevertheless, if there were no mouse, how would the hole get filled with stolen goods?

—Babylonian Talmud, *Gittin* 45a

If you steal from a thief, you also have a taste of thievery.

—Babylonian Talmud, *Berakhot* 5b

THE WORST FORMS OF STEALING

It is worse to steal from the many than to steal from an individual; for one who steals from an individual can appease him by returning the theft: one who steals from the many, however, cannot [since he does not even know all the people from whom he stole].

—Tosefta, *Bava Kamma* 10:14

Because the act is irrevocable, defrauding the public becomes, like murder and slander, something of an unforgivable sin.

Those who have stolen from the public and wish to repent are advised to "pay back those whom they know they have defrauded, and devote the balance to public needs" (e.g., building a park or digging a well; Tosefta, *Bava Mezia* 8:26).

Stealing from a non-Jew is worse than stealing from a Jew because of the profanation of God's name.

—Tosefta, *Bava Kamma* 10:15

Thus, a Jew who steals from another Jew violates the biblical law against stealing, but that is his or her only offense. However, when a Jew steals from a non-Jew, he also brings Judaism and the Jewish people into disrepute, so that his sin is more severe. As the fifteen-year-old Anne Frank recorded in her diary, "What one Christian does is his own responsibility. What one Jew does is thrown back at all Jews" (*The Diary of a Young Girl*).

WHAT JUSTICE DEMANDS OF A THIEF

If one robs another of wood and makes it into utensils, or wool and makes it into garments, he is required to repay the value of the material at the time of the robbery.

If he robbed another person of a pregnant cow which subsequently gave birth to a calf [while in the robber's possession], or of a sheep bearing wool which he later sheared, he is required to repay the value of a cow which is about to give birth and of a lamb which is ready to be shorn.

If he stole a cow which became pregnant while with him and then gave birth, or a sheep which while with him grew wool which he sheared, he is required to repay the value of the animals at the time of the robbery.

This is the general rule: All robbers repay the value which the article had at the time of the robbery.

—Mishna *Bava Kamma* 9:1

At first reading, the Mishna's ruling seems illogical: Should not a thief who stole a pregnant cow be made also to repay the value of the calf that is subsequently born?

The Mishna's ruling is rooted in an unexpected calculation: rabbinic sympathy for the arduous labors performed by the thief. In the case of the cow that gives birth, the thief was obliged to care for the calf; in the case of the lamb, he was obliged to shear it.

In a case, however, where the damage inflicted by the thief is irrevocable, the Rabbis take great care to safeguard the interests of the victim:

> If a thief robbed another . . . of fruits and they rotted, or of wine and it became sour, he is required to repay their value at the time of the robbery.
>
> —Mishna *Bava Kamma* 9:2

In this case, repaying the goods' value at the time of the robbery is, of course, a disadvantage to the thief.

49

*   *   *

If one says to two people, "I have stolen from one of you or from the father of one of you [and the fathers are dead], and I do not know which," if the thief wishes to fulfill his duty in the sight of heaven (*lazeit y'dei shamayim*), he must pay to each one the amount stolen. However, his legal obligation is to restore only the amount stolen; they then divide it equally, as neither was aware there was a theft, and it was the thief who volunteered that he had stolen it.

— Moses Maimonides, *Mishneh Torah*, "Laws of Thievery and
Lost Objects," 4:10

This is a relatively rare instance in which rabbinic law offers would-be penitents a choice. But as Maimonides makes clear, fulfilling the legal obligation alone is insufficient if the thief wants fully to undo the damage he has done. For if he returns precisely what he stole and the two people divide it, one will still lack the 50 percent that would have been his had the thief not taken it.

BUSINESS ETHICS

One is forbidden to sell heathens weapons of war. Nor may one sharpen their spears, or sell them knives, handcuffs, chains, bears, lions or anything which can endanger the public. One may, however, sell them shields which are only for defense.

— Maimonides, *Mishneh Torah*, "Laws of Murder and Preservation of Life," 12:12, paraphrasing Babylonian Talmud,
Avodah Zara 15b

Rabbi J. David Bleich cited the above ruling in an open letter appealing to Isaac Goldstein (owner of the Dallas pawnshop where John Hinckley purchased the handgun with which he made his 1981 attempt to assassinate President Reagan) to stop selling handguns ("Should a Jew Sell Guns?," reprinted in *Listening to American Jews,* edited by Carolyn Oppenheim, pages 209–210). Jewish law holds that a person bears moral responsibility for the evil that ensues from his or her irresponsible actions.

Unlike American law, which is concerned with consumer rights but not obligations, Jewish law insists on both:

> Just as fraud pertains in buying and selling, so can it apply to spoken words. One may not say to a store owner, "How much does this item cost?," if one has no intention of buying it.
>
> —Mishna *Bava Mezia* 4:10

You are permitted to engage in comparison shopping if you are considering a purchase. But to raise the hopes of the salesperson, or to "steal" his time, just to satisfy your curiosity or to assure yourself that you "got a good deal" on an item bought elsewhere, is forbidden.

WHY HONEST PEOPLE MUST BE CAREFUL IN A DISHONEST WORLD

> What is meant by the verse in Job, "In the dark, thieves dig into houses which they had marked for themselves in the daytime"? (24:16). [Rava explained]: This verse teaches that when the people of Sodom cast envious eyes at wealthy men, they would entrust precious, scented oil [for safekeeping] to them. [The wealthy person would then store the costly oil with his own valuables.] At night, the Sodomites would [break into the man's residence], sniff out the oil like dogs . . . then steal all his valuables.
>
> Rabbi Yossi taught this explanation of the verse in Sepphoris (in northern Israel), and that night [after his lecture,] there were three hundred burglaries in the city.
>
> The townspeople reproved him angrily, "You taught a method to thieves."
>
> He replied, "How was I to know that thieves would come to my lecture?"
>
> —Babylonian Talmud, *Sanhedrin* 109a

51

It happened that a man who had deposited a hundred *denars* [a large sum] with Bar Telamion [a particularly sly and dishonest person] came to get them back. Bar Telamion said, "I have already turned over to you what you deposited with me." The man said, "Come take an oath."

What did Bar Telamion do? He took a cane, hollowed it out, put the hundred *denars* in it, and then leaned on it as if it were a walking stick. When he reached the synagogue, he said to the man, "Hold this cane in your hand, while I swear an oath to you." [Then he said,] "I swear by God that I have given back to you what you deposited with me."

In his rage, the man threw the cane on the ground, and the hundred *denars* began to roll out. As he bent down, Bar Telamion said, "Gather them, gather them, it's your own you are gathering."

—*Leviticus Rabbah* 6:3; with minor variations, I have followed
the translation of William Braude in H. N. Bialik and
Y. H. Ravnitzky, *The Book of Legends*, page 702.

WHAT IT MEANS TO BE FULLY HONEST

Whoever reports a saying in the name of its originator brings the world toward redemption.

Ethics of the Fathers 6:6

From Judaism's perspective, one who takes credit for a statement made by another is a double thief, misappropriating the credit that belongs to the statement's originator, while also deceiving listeners into thinking higher of his intelligence than he deserves.

But what does this have to do with the world's redemption? When a person contributes an unusually witty or insightful observation to a discussion, he or she might be motivated primarily by a desire to deepen the discussion or, alternatively, by the wish to make people conscious of how intelligent he or she is. However, when the person credits the statement to its originator, it becomes clear that his motive is more to impart truth than to win accolades. A world in which people have this motivation already is well on its way toward redemption.

> The Holy One hates him who says one thing in his mouth, and another in his heart.
>
> —Babylonian Talmud, *Pesachim* 113b

> Rabbi Meir used to say, "A man should not urge his friend to eat with him if he knows very well that he won't. Nor should he offer him any gifts if he knows that he won't accept them."
>
> —Babylonian Talmud, *Hullin* 94a

The dishonesty in this case is what the Rabbis call "stealing the mind," trying to curry favor with someone by convincing that person that you would do more for him or her than you intend to.

6

"YOU MUST PAY HIM HIS WAGES ON THE SAME DAY"

Between Employers and Employees

AN EMPLOYER'S OBLIGATIONS TO HIS OR HER EMPLOYEES

You shall not abuse a needy and destitute laborer, whether a fellow countryman [a Jew] or a stranger [a non-Jew]. . . . You must pay him his wages on the same day, before the sun sets, for he is needy and urgently depends on it; or else he will cry to the Lord against you and you will incur guilt.

—Deuteronomy 24:14–15

"For he is needy and urgently depends on it"—Why did this worker climb the ladder [to build a house], suspend himself from a tree [to pick fruit], and risk death? Was it not for his wages?

—Babylonian Talmud, *Bava Mezia* 112a

The above law applies to day laborers—in modern terms, to a domestic worker, handyman, or people doing similar work. Since such people are assumed to need their wages immediately, any delay in paying them is a serious sin. (Regarding those who are compensated by the week or month, Jewish law obligates the employer to pay them no later than nightfall on the last day of the week or month, unless the employer has entered into a previously agreed-upon arrangement.)

Unfortunately, many people disregard this law. In Leon Trotsky's autobiography, the only "good" thing he can say about his father is that he was an atheist, one who certainly considered himself bound by no biblical laws. He recalls how his father forced a poor peasant woman to come to him on foot twice, a distance of seven miles, to collect the one-ruble wage he owed her (see Hayim Greenberg, "Leon Trotsky," in his *The Inner Eye,* Vol. II, page 238).

People of finer character than Trotsky's father frequently sin in this regard. A friend was speaking to my mother of her impoverished Brooklyn childhood, during which her mother mended and sewed dresses, which her daughter, my mother's friend, would deliver. Although many of her mother's clients were affluent and some claimed to be "religious," she told my mother, "You would be shocked how often they would tell me that they didn't have the money ready, even when it was a small sum, and then tell me to come back a day or two later to collect it."

Significantly, none of these people offered to bring the money to the dressmaker's house themselves. Not only did they not pay on time, they also humiliated the girl by forcing her to make a return visit to collect money that was rightfully hers. "Do not say to your fellow," the Bible teaches, " 'Come back again; I'll give it to you tomorrow,' when you have it with you" (Proverbs 3:28).

The evil of not paying a needy person his or her wages promptly is underscored in a rabbinic parable:

> "For he is needy and urgently depends on it." It is like the case of a man who had bought a sheaf of corn which he placed upon his shoulder, and then walked in front of his donkey who was longing to eat it. But what did the owner do? When he reached home, he tied the sheaf high above the donkey, so that the animal could not reach it. People said to him, "You cruel man—the animal has been running the whole way for the sake of the sheaf, and now

55

you refuse to give it to him." So it is with the hired worker; the whole day he has been toiling and sweating, hoping for his wages, and you send him away empty-handed.

—*Tanhuma Mishpatim* #10

Along with financial honesty, Jewish law demands that an employer act fairly, even if this leads to tensions with his or her spouse:

Rabbi Issi's wife quarreled with her maid and, in the maid's presence, Rabbi Issi denied that his wife was right. When she asked him, "Why do you declare me wrong before my maid?," he answered, "Did not Job say, 'Did I ever brush aside the case of my servants, man or maid, when they made a complaint against me? What then shall I do when God arises; when he calls me to account, what should I answer Him?' " (Job 31:13–14).

—*Genesis Rabbah* 48:3

In other words, one who acts haughtily and unjustly toward his or her social inferior should expect to be treated with an equal lack of respect and justice by God, everyone's ultimate superior.

EMPLOYEES' OBLIGATIONS TO EMPLOYERS

A man must not plough with his ox at night and hire it out by day, nor must he himself work at his own affairs at night, and hire himself out by day. And he must not undertake fasts or other ascetic deprivations, because the ensuing weakness will diminish the amount of work he can perform for his employer.

Rabbi Yochanan went to a place, and found the school teacher was fatigued. He asked the cause. They said to him, "Because he fasts." He said to the man, "You are forbidden to act in this manner."

—Palestinian Talmud, *Demai* 7:4

Honesty requires that a worker who expects to be paid normal wages perform the workload of a normal employee. Thus, to come to work with a hangover or groggy from lack of sleep is a form of thievery from one's employer.

But if one informs his or her employer of one's extra workload, and the employer agrees, then there is no issue of dishonesty.

While Jewish law in principle recognizes the right of employees to quit a job at any time, "even in the middle of the day," it does restrict this right in practice:

> When does this principle [that a worker may quit at any time] apply? Only when the loss is not irreparable. But in a case of irreparable loss, as, for example, flax that needs to be hauled up from the steeping pond, or a donkey which has been hired to transport the pipes for a funeral or a wedding, and a similar circumstance, then neither a day-worker nor a contractor may quit the job, except because of an accident or a death in the immediate family.
> —*Shulkhan Arukh, Hoshen Mishpat* 333:3; I have followed, with
> minor variations, the translation of Norman Frimer,
> *A Jewish Quest for Religious Meaning*, page 103.

If the workers quit, and the employer is forced to pay those who replace them a higher wage, he may deduct the additional amount he was forced to pay from the wages owed the workers who quit. If, however, the employer is able to hire new workers at the same rate of pay, then the workers who quit are not penalized.

7

TRUTH, LIES, AND PERMISSIBLE LIES

It should come as no surprise that the Bible and Talmud favor truthfulness:

> Stay far away from falsehood.
>
> —Exodus 23:7

> Do not steal, do not deceive and do not lie to one another.
>
> —Leviticus 19:11

> Teach your tongue to say, "I do not know," lest you be led to lie.
>
> —Babylonian Talmud, *Berakhot* 4a

> One should not promise to give a child something and then not give it to him, because as a result, the child will learn to lie.
>
> —Babylonian Talmud, *Sukkah* 46b

WHEN HALF-TRUTHS AND WHITE LIES ARE ALLOWED

> Great is peace, seeing that for its sake even God modified the truth.
>
> —Babylonian Talmud, *Yevamot* 65b

The Talmud bases this teaching on an incident in Genesis, in which three angels come to visit Abraham and Sarah, who are, respectively, ninety-nine and ninety years old. They tell the patriarch that, within a year, his wife will give birth. Sarah, who is listening nearby, "laughed to herself, saying, 'Now that I am withered, am I to have enjoyment, with my husband so old?' " In the next verse, God says to Abraham, "Why did Sarah laugh, saying, 'Shall I in truth bear a child, old as I am?' " (18:12–13). God omits Sarah's reference to Abraham being too old to impregnate her, apparently fearing that Abraham would become incensed at his wife.

From this incident, the Rabbis conclude that when human feelings are at stake, it is permissible to relate less than the whole truth, even if doing so conveys a false impression. One of the Talmud's most famous arguments takes things one step further:

> Our Rabbis taught: How does one dance [and what words does one say] before a bride?
>
> The School of Shammai says, "The bride [is described] as she is."
>
> The School of Hillel says, "[Every bride is described as a] beautiful and graceful bride."
>
> The School of Shammai said to the School of Hillel, "If she was lame or blind, does one say of her, 'Beautiful and graceful bride'? Does not the Torah command, 'Stay far away from falsehood'?" (Exodus 23:7).
>
> But the School of Hillel answered the School of Shammai, "According to your words, if a person has made a bad purchase in the market, should one praise it to him or deprecate it? Surely one should praise it to him."
>
> Therefore, the Rabbis teach, "Always should one's disposition be pleasant with people."
>
> —Babylonian Talmud, *Ketubot* 16b–17a

As for praising a person's purchase when you really are unimpressed with it, the critical distinction is whether your opinion is solicited before or after the purchase is concluded. If before, the Rabbis would advise you to speak truthfully, since your words may be helpful. If after, it is better to help the person feel good.

Similarly, if someone preparing to go to a party in inappropriate attire asks your opinion, you should tell him or her your true feelings (you may save the person from embarrassment). But if you meet someone at a party inappropriately dressed, tell the individual he or she looks fine, since the truth would only make the person very uncomfortable.

In social settings, then, Judaism has a pragmatic attitude toward truth. Truths that inflict hurt without achieving a greater good are forbidden, which is why the School of Hillel's position has been accepted.

One final thought about the School of Shammai: It is difficult to believe that Shammai intended one to call out a bride's physical shortcomings. This would violate talmudic laws forbidding one to shame another. More likely, as one talmudic commentary (Tosafot) suggests, Shammai only intended that a person restrict his praise of the bride to that which was truly attractive, "her eyes or hands if they are pretty."

If this commentary is correct, however, Hillel's objection becomes even more understandable. For if instead of praising the bride's overall beauty, a person confines his praise to just one of her features (e.g., her eyes), that will just remind everyone of the unattractive features left unmentioned. Shammai's type of praise, therefore, runs the risk of becoming an insult.

According to the Rabbis, the noblest teller of "white lies" was Aaron, Moses' brother. Although the Torah tells us little about his personal life, rabbinic writings depict Aaron as obsessed with making peace between quarreling parties. He would say anything to help people reconcile:

> When two men had quarreled, Aaron would go and sit with one of them and say, "My son, see what your friend is doing! He beats his breast and tears his clothes and moans, 'Woe is me! How can I lift my eyes and look my companion in the face? I am ashamed before him, since it is I who treated him foully.' "
> Aaron would sit with him until he had removed all

anger [literally, jealousy] from his heart.

Then Aaron would go and sit with the other man and say likewise, "My son, see what your friend is doing! He beats his breast and tears his clothes and moans, 'Woe is me! How can I lift my eyes and look my companion in the face? I am ashamed before him, since it was I who offended him.' "

Aaron would sit with him also until he had removed all anger from his heart.

Later, when the two met, they would embrace and kiss each other.

—*The Fathers According to Rabbi Nathan*, chapter 12:3

A rabbinic colleague confided to me that he once had tried to resolve a conflict utilizing Aaron's strategy. Unfortunately, in this instance, the technique backfired. When the two aggrieved parties met, each acknowledged how happy he was that the other person now regretted his earlier behavior. The truth quickly emerged, and their quarrel resumed with renewed intensity.

SPEAKING TRUTH TO GOD

The seal [literally, the signature] of God is truth.

—Babylonian Talmud, *Shabbat* 55a

The one sin in the Ten Commandments which God pronounces unpardonable is the Third, speaking falsely in God's name; doing so, Rabbi Abraham Twersky has commented, renders one guilty of "forging His seal."

Even in prayer, where exultation of God is the norm, the Rabbis showed remarkable tolerance for those who refused to laud God with praises that defied their own experience of Him:

Why were the men [who served] in the Great Assembly [the leading body in Jewish life in the third century B.C.E.] called by that name?

Because they restored the praise of God to its ancient completeness. For Moses had said, "The great, the mighty

61

and the awesome God" (Deuteronomy 10:17).

But Jeremiah came and said, "Aliens are destroying His Temple. Where then are His 'awesome' deeds?" Hence [when Jeremiah described God] he omitted the attribute "awesome" (in Jeremiah 32:18, he describes God as "O great and mighty God").

Daniel came and said, "Aliens are enslaving his sons. Where are His 'mighty' deeds?" Hence [when Daniel spoke of God] he omitted the word "mighty" (in Daniel 9:4, he speaks of God as "O Lord, great and awesome God").

But the Men of the Great Assembly came and said, "On the contrary! . . . Therein lie His awesome powers; for was it not for the fear of Him, how could one [deeply hated] nation survive among the many nations?"

But how could the earlier rabbis [Jeremiah and Daniel] abolish an expression established by Moses? Rabbi Elazar said: "Since they knew that the Holy One, blessed be He, insists on truth, they would not ascribe false things to Him [and since in Jeremiah's lifetime, God had not revealed himself to be 'awesome,' and in Daniel's to be 'mighty,' they could not falsify themselves by using such an expression]."

—Babylonian Talmud, *Yoma* 69b

Several people with whom I have studied this passage have claimed that Jeremiah's and Daniel's omission of the words "awesome" or "mighty" reflects not rebelliousness but happenstance. Maybe, but it's unlikely! Moses' description of God was so well known that those who omitted parts of it presumably did so intentionally. Imagine an American president speaking publicly of the constitutional right to "life and the pursuit of happiness." Would we not assume that the omission of "liberty" was intentional?

Concerning God's love of truth, Francine Klagsbrun relates the following tale about an eighteenth-century rabbi:

The Hasidic rebbe, Elimelekh of Lyzhansk (d. 1786) said:
When I die and stand in the court of justice, they will

62

ask me if I had been as just as I should have been.

I will answer no.

Then they will ask me if I had been as charitable as I should have been.

I will answer no.

Did I study as much as I should have?

Again, I will answer no.

Did I pray as much as I should have?

And this time, too, I will have to give the same answer.

Then the Supreme Judge will smile and say:

"Elimelekh, you spoke the truth. For this alone you have a share in the world to come."

—Francine Klagsbrun, *Voices of Wisdom*, page 524

SHOULD ONE TELL THE TRUTH TO A PERSON WHO IS DYING?

According to most rabbinic authorities, one is to make a seriously ill person aware of his or her illness, without issuing any definitive pronouncements that will deprive him or her of hope:

When a man is about to die, we tell him to recite the *viduii* (confession of sins). We say to him, "Many have said the confession and then not died, and many have not said the confession and died."

—*Shulkhan Arukh, Yoreh Deah* 338:1

Rabbi Abraham Danzig's early-nineteenth-century code of Jewish law, *Hokhmat he-Adam*, reports that "the officers of the *Hevra Kadisha* in Berlin and a number of other communities would visit all sick persons on the third day of their illness. By assuring the one thus visited that *all* sick people were treated equally, regardless of the severity of their condition, they were then able to discuss matters pertaining to final preparations and death as a matter of community policy."

—Basil Herring, *Jewish Ethics and Halakhah for Our Time*, page 62

Rabbi J. David Bleich, a contemporary legal scholar, sees the practice of the Berlin community as "a model for present day physicians. The physician, when treating a patient suffering from what may possibly be a serious malady ... should make it clear to the patient that he offers identical advice to all of his patients, and that he does so routinely, not only when he fears the worst. In this way, the patient will neither be lulled with a false sense of security, nor will he perceive a cause for undue alarm" (*Judaism and Healing,* page 32).

FINAL REFLECTIONS ON LIARS AND TRUTH TELLERS

The Hasidic rebbe, Naftali of Rotchitz (d. 1827), remarked of a man who was a well-known liar, "Not only is what he says untrue, but even the opposite of what he says is untrue."

—Shmuel Avidor Ha-Cohen, *Touching Heaven, Touching Earth,* page 78

A liar's punishment is that even when he tells the truth, he is not believed.

—Babylonian Talmud, *Sanhedrin* 89b

A half-truth is a whole lie.

—Yiddish proverb

Truth never dies but it lives a wretched life.

—Yiddish proverb

8

"STICKS AND STONES" AND WORDS

The Ethics of Speech

Do not go about as a talebearer among your people.
—Leviticus 19:16

Perhaps the least observed of the Torah's 613 commandments, this law posits that it is forbidden to say something negative about another person, *even if it is true,* unless the person to whom you are speaking vitally needs the information (e.g., he or she is considering marrying, hiring, or going into business with the person about whom you are speaking). In Hebrew, such speech is known as *lashon hara* (literally, evil tongue). Jewish law also forbids slander, in Hebrew *motzi shem ra* (giving someone a bad name).

Among knowledgeable Jews, however, the term *lashon hara* is used as a generic reference to cover all negative talk about others. In *Operation Shylock,* Philip Roth describes the evil done by a malignant tongue in one of the most passionate and comprehensive delineations of *lashon hara* that I know:

> *Lashon hara:* the whispering campaign that cannot be stopped, rumors it's impossible to quash, besmirchment from which you will never be cleansed, slanderous stories

65

to belittle your professional qualifications, derisive reports of your business deceptions and your perverse aberrations, outraged polemics denouncing your moral failings, misdeeds, and faulty character traits—your shallowness, your vulgarity, your cowardice, your avarice, your indecency, your falseness, your selfishness, your treachery. Derogatory information. Defamatory statements. Insulting witticisms. Disparaging anecdotes. Idle mockery. Bitchy chatter. Malicious absurdities. Galling wisecracks. Fantastic lies. *Lashon hara* of such spectacular dimensions that it is guaranteed not only to bring on fear, distress, disease, spiritual isolation, and financial loss but to significantly shorten a life. They will make a shambles of the position that you have worked nearly sixty years to achieve. No area of your life will go uncontaminated. And if you think this is an exaggeration you really *are* deficient in a sense of reality.

—Philip Roth, *Operation Shylock*, page 397

In his memoirs, Israeli Prime Minister Yitzhak Rabin described how *lashon hara* was used to discredit and demoralize Israeli Prime Minister and Defense Minister Levi Eshkol in the days immediately preceding the 1967 Six-Day War (see page 593 for Golda Meir's and Abba Eban's comments on the same subject): "They mocked him and chipped away at his image and publicized his weaknesses and made false accusations and claimed that the country did not, in effect, have a defense minister in its most difficult hour. Eshkol was exhausted. The burden of the times and that slander campaign worked together to call his position into question. His authority was damaged in the eyes of a few ministers, and those of senior officers as well. . . . With his wings clipped and his authority curtailed, he lacked the power to impose his will on the government" (Yitzhak Rabin, *Service Book*, page 148).

The gossiper stands in Syria and kills in Rome.

—Palestinian Talmud, *Peah* 1:1

Unlike armaments, which can hurt only those within their immediate vicinity, verbal "shots" can inflict ruinous injuries from a distance. (In the modern world, the telephone makes it particularly easy to do so.)

This rabbinic dictum likewise brings to mind the late American car manufacturer Henry Ford, who, in the early 1920s, funded publication of *The International Jew,* a libelous series of books charging world Jewry with conspiring to cheat non-Jews and destroy their religions. As far as we know, no American Jews were killed because of Ford's antisemitic fulminations. But in Germany, Adolf Hitler had these writings translated and printed in massive editions. Although Ford did his dirty work in America, thousands of miles away, in Europe, his publications helped incite the Nazis to carry out the mass murder of European Jewry.

> If you say of a rabbi that he does not have a good voice and of a cantor that he is not a scholar, you are a gossip. But if you say of a rabbi that he is no scholar and of a cantor that he has no voice—you are a murderer.
>
> —Rabbi Israel Salanter

Because the damage wreaked by gossip often is irrevocable, several Jewish sources liken malicious gossip to murder. A famous Hasidic story tells of a man who went about his town slandering his rabbi. One day, realizing how vicious his comments had been, he went to the rabbi and asked for forgiveness. The rabbi told the man he would forgive him on one condition: that he went home, cut up a feather pillow, and scattered the feathers to the winds. The man did so, then returned to the rabbi.

"Am I now forgiven?" he asked.

"One more thing," the rabbi said. "Now go and gather all the feathers."

"But that's impossible," the man said.

"Precisely," the rabbi answered. "And although you sincerely regret the damage you have done me, it is as impossible to undo it as it is to recover all the feathers."

> Don't speak well of your friend, for although you will start with his good traits, the discussion might turn to his bad traits.
>
> —Babylonian Talmud, *Bava Bathra* 164b

Obviously, such an injunction is not meant to be observed all the time, but, as the Soncino commentary on this passage notes, "By pointing to a person's good actions or qualities, attention is inevitably directed to his bad actions and qualities also." Other Jewish laws admonish one to avoid praising one's friend in the presence of those who dislike the person; you won't change their minds, and they will start telling everyone present what they don't like about him or her. In other words, don't say things that are likely to provoke gossip.

> I can retract what I did not say, but I cannot retract what I already have said.
> —Solomon Ibn Gabirol (c. 1020–c. 1057), *Pearls of Wisdom*

> Words are the guides to acts; the mouth makes the first move.
> —Rabbi Leon da Modena (1571–1648)

> Only God can give us credit for the angry words we did not speak.
> —Rabbi Harold Kushner, *When All You've Ever Wanted Isn't Enough,* page 187

The Haffetz Hayyim, the rabbinic sage who wrote the standard Jewish text on the laws against gossip, once commented to a man who was speaking ill of others: "There are people in the adjoining room preparing a telegram. Notice how carefully they consider each word before they put it down. That's how careful we must be when we speak."

The Haffetz Hayyim's words bring to mind a late nineteenth-century Hasidic tale about a rebbe who told his followers, "Everything that has been created in God's world has a lesson to teach us."

Thinking that the rebbe was engaging in hyperbole, one of his followers called out, "And what can we learn from the train?"

"That because of being one minute late," the rebbe answered, "you can lose everything."

"And from the telegraph?"

"That for every word you pay."

"And from the telephone?"

"That what we say *here,* is heard *there.*"

> "Cursed be he who strikes his neighbor in secret" (Deuteronomy 27:24); this refers to the slanderer.
>
> —Targum Jonathan on this verse

One final piece of advice:

> Have you heard something? Let it die with you. Be of good courage: it will not burst you.
>
> —Apocrypha, *Ecclesiasticus* 19:10

9

ARGUING ETHICALLY

HOW TO ARGUE ETHICALLY

For three years there was a dispute between the School of Shammai and the School of Hillel, the former asserting "The law (*halakha*) is according to our view," and the latter asserting, "The law is according to our view." Then a voice issued from heaven announcing, "The teachings of both are the words of the living God, but the law is in agreement with the School of Hillel."

But [it was asked] since both are the words of the living God, for what reason was the School of Hillel entitled to have the law determined according to their rulings?

Because they were kindly and humble, and because they studied their own rulings and those of the School of Shammai, and even mentioned the teachings of the School of Shammai before their own.

—Babylonian Talmud, *Eruvin* 13b

The singularly ethical manner in which the School of Hillel conducted themselves during disputes also made them more likely than their opponents to reach truthful conclusions. For one thing, because they were "kindly and humble," their egos did not prevent them from acknowledging truth when stated by the other side. Second, they made a point of studying their opponents' positions, not just viewpoints with which they already agreed. This guaranteed that they reached a conclusion only after a thorough examination of all sides of an issue.

The School of Shammai, the Talmud implies, studied only one side. When they were in error, therefore, they were unlikely to self-correct, since they didn't expose themselves to opposing views.

Thus, the School of Hillel's way of arguing was not only more "kindly and humble," it also led to greater accuracy and truth.

An openness to truth from whatever the source likewise characterized the first-century Rabbi Joshua ben Hananiah, himself a follower of the School of Hillel. Rabbi Joshua claimed to have been bested in arguments only three times in his life: once by a woman who reproved him for imperfect manners, and the other times "by a little boy and a little girl."

> What happened in the case of the little girl? [he was asked]. I was once walking down a road, and there was a path that led through a [privately owned] field. I used that path. Then a little girl called out to me, "Master, is this not a field [and therefore forbidden for you to use without permission]?"
>
> "No," I replied, "it is obviously a well-trodden path."
>
> "Robbers like you have made it into such," she said to me.

As the little girl noted, the fact that a dishonest act is widely practiced does not render it permissible. A contemporary example that comes to mind is duplicating copyrighted software instead of buying the product.

> And what happened in the case of the little boy?
>
> Once again I was on a journey, and I noticed a little boy who was sitting at the crossroads. I asked him: "Which road does one take into the city?"
>
> He replied: "This road here is short but long. And that road there is long but short."
>
> I took the road that he described as "short but long." But when I approached the city, I saw that it was sur-

rounded by gardens and orchards [and that one could only get to the city by detours]. I therefore backtracked to the crossroads. When I saw the little boy, I said to him: "My son, did you not tell me that this road was short?"

"And did I not also tell you 'but long'?" he replied.

Then I kissed him on his head and exclaimed, "Happy are you, O Israel! For you are all wise, the young as well as the old."

—Babylonian Talmud, *Eruvin* 53b

From the little boy, Rabbi Joshua learned that advice, particularly when worded succinctly, should be analyzed carefully.

The boy's pithy advice reminds me of a characteristically Israeli story I heard from the late Jerusalem scholar and writer Rabbi Pinchas Peli.

A man was about to start up a hill when he noticed an old man nearby. He asked him, "How long will it take me to get up this hill?"

The old man said nothing.

The man asked the question again, this time in a louder voice.

Again, the old man said nothing.

Assuming that the old man was either deaf or senile, the man started up the hill. He had taken some ten steps when suddenly the old man called out, "About twenty minutes."

The man turned around. "Why didn't you say anything when I asked you?"

The old man answered, "Because until I saw the speed at which you were walking, how I could I possibly know how long it would take you to climb the hill?"

Every dispute that is for a heavenly cause will ultimately endure.

—*Ethics of the Fathers* 5:17

Unlike petty squabbles that are quickly forgotten, disputes "for the sake of heaven" will "ultimately endure" and be studied for generations. The nineteenth-century rabbi Israel Salanter, however, understood this dictum quite differently: "The greatest danger is to believe that your dispute is for a heavenly cause—for then it will endure and endure" (cited in Saul Weiss, *Insights,* page 204).

THE RABBIS "BEST" GOD

On that day, Rabbi Eliezer put forward all the arguments in the world, but the Sages did not accept them.

Finally, he said to them, "If the law is according to me, let that carob tree prove it."

He pointed to a nearby carob tree, which then moved from its place a hundred cubits, and some say, four hundred cubits.

They said to him, "One cannot bring a proof from the moving of a carob tree."

Said Rabbi Eliezer, "If the law is according to me, may that stream of water prove it."

The stream of water then turned and flowed in the opposite direction.

They said to him, "One cannot bring a proof from the behavior of a stream of water."

Said Rabbi Eliezer, "If the law is according to me, may the walls of the House of Study prove it."

The walls of the House of Study began to bend inward. Rabbi Joshua then rose up and rebuked the walls of the House of Study. "If the students of the wise argue with one another in matters of Jewish law," he said, "what right have you to interfere?"

In honor of Rabbi Joshua, the walls ceased to bend inward; but in honor of Rabbi Eliezer, they did not straighten up, and they remain bent to this day.

Then said Rabbi Eliezer to the Sages, "If the law is according to me, may a proof come from Heaven."

Then a heavenly voice went forth and said, "What have you to do with Rabbi Eliezer? The law is according to him in every place."

Then Rabbi Joshua rose up on his feet, and said, "It is not in the heavens" [a quote from Deuteronomy 30: 12].

What did he mean by quoting this? Said Rabbi Jeremiah, "He meant that since the Torah has already been given on Mount Sinai, we do not pay attention to a heavenly voice; for God Himself has written in the Torah, 'Decide according to the majority,' " [Exodus pages 23:2].

Rabbi Nathan met the prophet Elijah. He asked him, "What was the Holy One, blessed be He, doing in that hour?"

Said Elijah, "He was laughing and saying, 'My children have defeated me, my children have defeated me.' "
—Babylonian Talmud, *Bava Mezia* 59b

Haym Maccoby, who has translated this story in his singular anthology, *The Day God Laughed: Sayings, Fables and Entertainments of the Jewish Sages* (pages 141–142), notes that this narrative infuriated medieval Christian theologians. During the 1240 Disputation of Paris, at which the Talmud was put on trial and sentenced to be burned, this story was cited as an example of talmudic "imbecility." Indeed, its insistence that since the time the Torah was given, Jews should listen to no new voices from heaven undoubtedly was understood as an attack on Jesus.

Maccoby insists that this tale "strikes the key-note of the Talmud. God is a good Father, who wants His children to grow up and achieve independence. He has given them His Torah, but now wants them to develop it in their own way." Thus, while acknowledging the truth of God and of miracles, they insist that both "must give way to the demands of human discussion and rationality" (*The Day God Laughed*, page 142).

Maccoby's last point raises a crucial, and always contemporary, issue in interreligious discussions: miracles. Religious apologists often strive to prove the truths of their faith by citing the miracles recorded in their respective scriptures. On several occasions, ardent Christian proselytizers have wondered how I could disbelieve in Jesus' divinity, given that the New Testament records that he arose on the third day after he was crucified, and was seen by numerous witnesses. Such arguments seldom convince adherents of other faiths because these people already believe in the miracles claimed by their own belief systems, and usually reject those claimed by others. Thus, because every religion claims miracles, the only arguments worth presenting are those that appeal to a universal standard of reason and rationality.

A MALICIOUS ARGUER GETS HIS COMEUPPANCE

Caesar once said to Rabbi Tanchum: "Come, let us all become one people."

He replied: "Very well. But since we who are circumcised cannot become like you, you, then, should become circumcised and become like us."

"Well spoken," Caesar said. "But anyone who defeats the Emperor in an argument must be thrown to the lions" [literally, an arena of wild beasts].

They threw Rabbi Tanchum into the arena, but the lions did not eat him.

A certain heretic [who was standing nearby] said: "The only reason the animals did not eat him is because they were not hungry."

They therefore threw the unbeliever into the arena, and the lions devoured him.

—Babylonian Talmud, *Sanhedrin* 39a

10

THE OBLIGATION TO CRITICIZE, HOW TO DO SO, AND WHEN TO REMAIN SILENT

You shall not hate your fellow man in your heart. Reprove your kinsman but incur no guilt because of him.
—Leviticus 19:17

The medieval *Sefer ha-Hinnukh,* an explication of the Torah's 613 laws, explains that the observance of the above two commandments is the necessary prerequisite for establishing a peaceful society: "For when one man sins toward another and the offended party reproves him in secret, the offender will apologize to him, and the other will accept his apology and make peace with him. But if the other will not rebuke him, he will hate him in his heart, and will cause him harm either then or at some other time" (see commandment #239; vol. 3:81).

The final words of the commandment, "but incur no guilt because of him," can be understood in two ways:

1. Don't remain passive when you see another about to act evilly, lest you share in the guilt. Rather, reprove the person and, therefore, bear no responsibility for his actions.

Alternatively:

2. Although you are permitted to reprove another, don't commit a sin while doing so: Don't humiliate the person you are reproving, for to humiliate another, particularly in public, is itself a very serious offense. As Maimonides advises:

> He who rebukes another, whether for offenses against the rebuker himself or for sins against God, should administer the rebuke in private, speak to the offender gently and tenderly, and point out that he is only speaking for the wrongdoer's own good. . . . One is obligated to continue admonishing until the sinner assaults the admonisher and says to him, "I refuse to listen."
>
> —Moses Maimonides, *Mishneh Torah*, "Laws Concerning Character Development and Ethical Conduct," 6:7

> Whoever can stop the members of his household from committing a sin, but does not, is held responsible for the sins of his household. If he can stop the people of his city from sinning, but does not, he is held responsible for the sins of the people of his city. If he can stop the whole world from sinning, and does not, he is held responsible for the sins of the whole world.
>
> —Babylonian Talmud, *Shabbat* 54b

> Rabbi Tarfon said: "I wonder if there is anyone in this generation capable of accepting reproof. . . ." Rabbi Elazar ben Azarya said: "I wonder whether there is anyone in this generation who knows how to reprove" [without humiliating the one being criticized].
>
> —Babylonian Talmud, *Arakhin* 16b

> Love unaccompanied by criticism is not love. . . . Peace unaccompanied by reproof is not peace.
>
> —*Genesis Rabbah* 54:3

If people fear to offer criticism lest it lead to a rupture of peace, that in itself proves that the peace is false. Peace, if it is to last, must be based on truth and lack of fear.

WHEN TO SAY NOTHING

Just as one is commanded to say that which will be heeded, so is one commanded *not* to say that which will *not* be heeded.

—Babylonian Talmud, *Yevamot* 65b

Rabbi Israel of Vishnitz was in the habit of strolling with his *gabbai* [assistant] for a half hour every evening. On one such occasion, they stopped in front of the house of a certain wealthy bank manager. The man was known to be a *maskil*, a follower of the "Enlightenment" movement, i.e., anything but a follower of the rebbe. Rabbi Israel knocked on the door and, when a servant opened it, entered the house. The puzzled *gabbai*, without asking a word, followed the rebbe inside.

The bank manager received his distinguished guest respectfully and politely. The rebbe took the seat that was offered him, and sat for quite some time without saying a word. Knowing that protocol would deem it impertinent to ask the rebbe directly the reason for his visit, the host whispered his question to the rebbe's assistant, but the *gabbai* simply shrugged his shoulders. After a good while, the rebbe rose to leave, and bade his host farewell. The bank manager accompanied him to the door and, his understandable curiosity getting the better of him, asked: "Could you please explain to me, rebbe, why you honored me with a visit?"

"I went to your house in order to fulfill a mitzvah," the rebbe replied, "and thank God I was able to fulfill it."

"And which mitzvah was that?" asked the confused bank manager.

"Our Sages teach that 'Just as one is commanded to say that which will be listened to, so is one commanded not to say that which will not be listened to.' Now if I remain in my house and you remain in yours, what kind of mitzvah is it that I refrain from telling you 'that which will not be listened to'? In order to fulfill the mitzvah properly, one obviously has to go to the house of the person who will not listen, and *there* refrain from speaking to him. And that is exactly what I did."

"Perhaps, rebbe," said the bank manager, "you would be so good to tell me what this thing is? Who knows, perhaps I *will* listen?"

"I am afraid you won't," said the rebbe.

The longer the rebbe refused, the greater grew the curiosity of the other to know the secret: he continued to press the rebbe to reveal "that which would not be listened to."

"Very well," said the rebbe finally. "A certain penniless widow owes your bank quite a sum for the mortgage of her house. Within a few days, your bank is going to dispose of her house by public sale, and she will be out on the street. I had wanted to ask you to overlook her debt, but didn't, because of the mitzvah of 'not saying . . .' "

"But what do you expect me to do?" asked the bank manager in amazement. "Surely you realize that the debt is not owed to me personally, but to the bank, and I am only its manager, and not its owner, and the debt runs into several hundreds, and if . . ."

"It's exactly as I said all along," the rebbe interrupted, "that you would not want to hear."

With that he ended the conversation and walked away.

The bank manager went back into his house, but the rebbe's words found their way into his heart and gave him no rest until he paid the widow's debt out of his own pocket.

—Rabbi Shlomo Yosef Zevin, *A Treasury of Chassidic Tales on the Torah,* pages 189–191; I have based the above on Uri Kaploun's translation of Rabbi Zevin's rendering of the tale.

11

WHEN LIFE IS AT STAKE

You shall live by them, but you shall not die because of them.

—Babylonian Talmud, *Yoma* 85b

Basing themselves on the verse in Leviticus, "You shall live by them" (i.e., the laws of the Torah; 18:5), the Rabbis conclude that the Torah's laws are intended to enhance life, never to cause death. Thus, whenever observance of the law endangers life, the requirement to observe it is suspended.

However, there are three instances when the law takes precedence over life. If the only way one can stay alive is by committing murder, worshipping idols or committing adultery or incest, one should be prepared to die.

In cases of idolatry and unchastity, however, the specific application of the Talmud's ruling is not always clear (for example, a married woman, who, in the normal course of events, is forbidden to have sexual relations with anyone other than her husband, is not expected to resist a rapist if doing so will endanger her life).

But when it comes to murder, the law allows no exceptions: A person cannot save his own life, or the life of someone dear to him, if it means killing an *innocent* person:

A man came to [the fourth-century Rabbi] Rava and said to him: "The governor of my town has ordered me to kill someone and, if I refuse, he will have me killed. [What shall I do?]"

Rava said, "Be killed and do not kill; do you think that your blood is redder than his? Perhaps his blood is redder than yours."

—Babylonian Talmud, *Pesachim* 25b

What Rava neglected to add was that the man had every right to kill the governor, since it was he, not his designated victim, who was endangering his life. In such cases, the Talmud mandates: "If someone comes to kill you, kill him first" (Babylonian Talmud, *Sanhedrin* 72a). Killing the man designated by the governor, however, would be murder.

What does Jewish law rule, however, in a case where a life can be saved only by the *indirect* killing of an innocent? The Talmud discussed this question almost two millennia ago:

A group of people are walking along a road when they are stopped by heathens, who say to them, "Give us one of you and we will kill him. If not, we will kill all of you."

Let them all be killed, and let them not surrender one soul from Israel. But if the heathens single out one name, as was the case with Sheba ben Bichri, that person may be surrendered to them, so that the others may be saved.

Rabbi Simeon ben Lakish said, "Only someone who is under a death sentence, the way Sheba ben Bichri was, may be turned over." But Rabbi Johanan said, "Even someone who is not under sentence of death like Sheba ben Bichri" [but anyone whose name has been specified may be turned over].

—Palestinian Talmud, *Terumot* 8:10

Sheba ben Bichri had led a treasonous revolt against King David, and thus was under a death sentence. He fled to a small city, which David's troops soon besieged. Realizing that many innocent people would be killed if David's troops invaded, a prominent woman in the town had Sheba killed and his head thrown over the city's wall (II Samuel, 20:21–22).

According to Simeon ben Lakish, turning over a person to be killed is permissible only when the person already deserves to die, as did Sheba. Otherwise, it is tantamount to an act of murder, which, as noted, Jewish law forbids even when life is at stake.

Rabbi Johanan differs. Turning the designated party over to be killed does not taint the survivors with the guilt of murder, since not doing so would not save his life; it would guarantee only that all would be killed along with him (see *Tosefta Terumot* 7:20).

Jewish law never has reached a definitive ruling on this issue, although Maimonides, the most important codifier of medieval Jewish law, ruled according to Simeon ben Lakish, that unless the person designated is guilty of a capital offense, "they should all die rather than hand him over" (*Mishneh Torah*, "Laws of the Basic Principles of the Torah," 5:5).

Unfortunately, the Nazis forced Jewish law to consider this question anew. When Rabbi Zvi Hirsch Meisels, who survived incarceration in Auschwitz, compiled *Mekadshe Ha-Shem* (*Those Who Sanctified God's Name*, a book of *responsa*, which consists of questions asked of a rabbi, and the responses), he included a question asked of him in Auschwitz on a day when the Germans had rounded up fourteen hundred teenage boys and locked them in an enormous cell. Word quickly spread that they were to be murdered the following evening.

Throughout the day, relatives and friends bargained with the *kapos,* the Jewish guards, in an attempt to have their loved ones released. One father who had the means to bribe the guards realized the terrible moral dilemma such "bargaining" involved:

A simple Jew from Oberland approached me and said, "Rabbi, my only son, who is dearer to me than the pupil of my eye, is among the boys destined to be burned. I have the necessary means to redeem him, but I know without doubt that the *kapos* would take another in his place. I ask you, Rabbi, to give me a ruling according to the Torah: Am I permitted to save my son? Whatever you will tell me I will do."

When I heard the question, I began to tremble and I answered him, "My dear man, how can I give you a clear ruling on such a question? Even in the days when the Temple was standing, questions that dealt with matters of life and death would be brought before the Sanhedrin [the Jewish high court]. And here I am in Auschwitz, without a single book on Jewish law, with no other rabbis, and without peace of mind because of the terrible troubles and tragedies here."

[Meisels then describes the internal debate going on in his mind]: If the system of the *kapos* had been first to free one boy and then substitute another, I might have had room to maneuver. I might have been able to reason that it was not certain that each boy released would be replaced by another. The *kapos* were, after all, Jewish, and Jewish law so strongly forbids taking one life in order to save another. Perhaps, I might have argued, at the last moment their Jewish consciousness might be awakened, and they would not violate this important law. . . .

Unfortunately, I knew with certainty that the *kapos'* method was always to seize a replacement first and then to release a redeemed child. In that way, they protected themselves and kept the number constant. So I had no way to get around the situation.

The man kept after me: "Rabbi, you must make a decision for me," he insisted. Again, I pleaded with him, "My dear man, don't ask me because I cannot give you an answer or even half an answer without studying a single book, and in a matter as terrible as this . . ."

Finally, when he saw that I would not decide the issue for him, the man said to me with great emotion, "Rabbi, I have done what the Torah commanded me. I have asked my rabbi for a decision, and there is no other rabbi with whom I can consult. If you cannot tell me that I should go ahead and save my son, that's a sign that according to the law you were not able to find a reason to permit it, for if it were permitted, you would certainly have told me so. I take it for granted, then, that according to Jewish law, I must not save my son. That's enough for me. My

only child will be burned in fulfillment of the Torah. I
accept this decision. . . ."

—Rabbi Zvi Hirsch Meisels, *Mekadshe Ha-Shem*, Vol. 1, page 8;
I have followed, with minor variations, the translation in H. J.
Zimmels, *The Echo of the Nazi Holocaust
in Rabbinic Literature*, pages 112–114.

Jewish law considers yet another case wherein one person's
death might be attributed to the passive complicity of another. Here,
the Rabbis are divided:

Two men are travelling together [in the desert], and one
has a pitcher of water. If both drink the water, they will
both die, but if only one drinks, he can reach civilization
and survive. [What should the man with the water do?]
[Rabbi] Ben Petura taught, "It is better that both should
drink and die, rather than one of them look on while his
comrade dies." But Rabbi Akiva came and taught, "[The
verse in the Torah] 'that your brother may live with you'
(Leviticus 25:36) means [only if he can live with you must
you share the water, but in cases of conflict] your life takes
precedence over his."

—Babylonian Talmud, *Bava Mezia* 62a

The Talmud does not express a preference between Bar Petura's
and Rabbi Akiva's opinions, although Akiva's preeminence in Jewish law has prompted most rabbinic authorities to interpret the law
according to him. In a lecture about Rabbi Akiva, Elie Wiesel cited
the above discussion, then concluded, "Rabbi Akiva was very hard,
very hard on the survivor."

Wiesel's terse comment illuminated something I had never previously understood; why many Holocaust survivors seem to suffer
from feelings of overwhelming guilt. Logically, those who survived
the concentration camps were the one group of people who should
not have suffered from guilt: The Germans should have felt guilty,
as should the Europeans who passively acquiesced in the Holocaust,
and the American, British, and other leaders who refused to admit
refugees. What, then, was the source of the survivors' guilt? Those

who survived concentration camps, Wiesel was suggesting, sometimes had to make the decision of Rabbi Akiva, not to share their meager rations with others who were dying.

Jesus, who was of course a first-century Jew, suggested a third option: that the person with the water act as a martyr and give the water to his companion—"Greater love hath no man than this, that he would lay down his life for a friend" (John 15:13). But while Jewish law acknowledges martyrdom as a heroic act, it never made it obligatory. For if A was commanded to give his water to B when B was extremely thirsty, then B would be commanded to return it to A when A was in the same circumstance, until such time as rescuers would discover two bodies in the desert, a large water jug lying between them.

> The saving of life supersedes the Sabbath.
> —Babylonian Talmud, *Shabbat* 132a

The Sabbath is the only ritual law mentioned in the Ten Commandments; its sanctity is so great that many Jews once assumed they were commanded to die rather than violate it. Around 167 B.C.E., the Book of Maccabees records, a group of pious Jews in revolt against Antiochus were attacked by the Syrian emperor's troops on the Sabbath. They refused to fight back, and all were slaughtered, "men, women and children, up to a thousand in all."

Immediately thereafter, Mattathias, the founder of the Maccabees, ruled: "If we all do as our brothers have done, if we refuse to fight the gentiles for our lives as well as for our laws and customs, then they will soon wipe us off the face of the earth." The Book of Maccabees concludes: "That day they decided that, if anyone came to fight against them on the Sabbath, they would fight back, rather than all die as their brothers ... had done" (see I Maccabees, 2:3–41).

Since then, all Jewish sources have ruled that saving human life takes precedence over observing the Sabbath. Indeed, Maimonides rules that in those instances when the Sabbath must be violated, it is preferable to have an adult and scholarly Jew, not a minor or non-Jew, do so, "to teach that the purpose of the laws of the

Torah ... is to bring mercy, loving-kindness and peace upon the world" (*Mishneh Torah*, "Laws of the Sabbath," 2:3).

In accordance with Maimonides' ruling, a remarkable organization of largely learned, Orthodox Jews called Hatzolah (Rescue) has been established in New York City to provide emergency first-aid treatment and to bring very ill people to hospitals. Hatzolah operates seven days a week and on all Jewish holidays.

Questions concerning violations of Jewish law when life is at stake also often focus on the Yom Kippur fast. The great scholar Rabbi Hayyim Soloveichik of Brisk was known for being lenient in permitting very sick people to eat on Yom Kippur. When challenged about this, Rabbi Hayyim responded, "I am not at all lenient about allowing sick people to eat on Yom Kippur: I am just very strict in matters involving endangerment of life (in Hebrew, *pikuakh nefesh*)."

Jewish law goes even further, permitting its most sacred rituals to be violated where there is only a *potential* endangerment of life. This is illustrated by a famous case in Vilna in 1848, where a cholera epidemic had broken out. Local doctors advised the city's leading rabbi, Israel Salanter, that not only should those already sick eat on the holy day, but everyone else should as well, since the twenty-four-hour fast would lower people's resistance, and make them more susceptible to the life-threatening disease.

Rabbi Salanter issued a public proclamation that all Jews should eat on Yom Kippur. When he learned that many Jews were ignoring his ruling because of their awe of the holy day, he went up to the pulpit of the Great Synagogue of Vilna at the end of the morning service, took out wine and cake, recited the appropriate blessings, then drank and ate in front of the entire congregation. Witnessing the most pious figure in Vilna eating on Yom Kippur freed others from their inhibitions about also doing so. Although some rabbis criticized Salanter's behavior, he maintained until the end of his life that he felt privileged to have helped save many lives.

ENDANGERMENT OF LIFE AND ITS POLITICAL IMPLICATIONS

The Palestinian Talmud rules (*Yoma* 8:5) that if one stops to ask a rabbi whether it is permissible to desecrate the Sabbath and Yom Kippur in order to save a life, this delay is a form of murder. While he is busy asking the question, the patient might die. When a life is at stake, haste is required.

—Rabbi Ovadia Yosef, former Sephardic Chief Rabbi of Israel

Rabbi Yosef's words were written in the context of a responsum affirming that Israel had a right to cede territories conquered in the Six-Day War of 1967, if such a concession could bring about peace with the Arabs. Normally, Jewish law would forbid giving up any part of the land of Israel but, as Rabbi Yosef explains, since "the saving of a life takes precedence over all the commandments in the Torah, even the commandment to bring the Messiah and achieve the redemption . . ." therefore, there is no bar to returning territories in order to avoid a probable war [in which case people would definitely die]. (A section of Rabbi Yosef's responsum has been translated and published in Arthur Hertzberg, ed., *Judaism,* pages 231–232.)

While the late Rabbi Joseph Soloveitchik, one of the giants of American Orthodox Judaism, advocated a position strikingly similar to that of Rabbi Yosef, several prominent rabbis on the political right have issued legal rulings forbidding Israel to cede any land to non-Jews. Regarding Rabbi Yosef's argument concerning the "endangerment of life," they simply argue that the ceding of any land will weaken Israel's security, and therefore lead to greater loss of life.

12

"IT IS AS IF HE SAVED THE ENTIRE WORLD"

The Infinite Value of Each Human Life

Whoever saves one life, it is as if he saved the entire world.
—Mishna *Sanhedrin* 4:5

According to the Talmud, the proof of the infinite value of human life is that God originally created only one human being, Adam. Thus, had Adam been killed, all humanity would have been destroyed, and conversely, had he been saved, so would the entire world.

From Judaism's perspective, that each human is of supreme importance has many implications. For one thing, it means that one who murders an innocent person has committed the ultimate crime; murdering ten more people increases the crime's magnitude, but not its severity.

This teaching also has social, political, and economic implications as well. As Rabbi Irwin Kula has said, "In light of this talmudic statement, we must try to figure out what we must do to fashion a world in which each person is treated as if he or she has infinite value. Indeed, what does it mean to say that every human being is infinitely valuable when people die for lack of a dollar's worth of food a day?"

The same passage in the Mishna proceeds to draw other moral and theological lessons from Adam's creation:

> [Only one person was originally created] for the sake of peace among human beings, so that a man should not say to his fellow, "My father is greater than your father. . . ."
>
> And also to proclaim the greatness of the Holy One, praised be He. If a human being stamps several coins with the same die, they all resemble one another. But the King of kings of kings, the Holy One, praised be He, stamps all human beings with the die of the first man; and yet not one of them is identical with another.
>
> Therefore every individual is obliged to say, "For my sake was the world created!"
>
> —Mishna *Sanhedrin* 4:5

Sadly, one proof of the distinctive stamp of every individual is today primarily known to criminologists; that every human being has his/her own fingerprints and genetic imprints.

> One who sees 600,000 Jews together recites the following blessing: Blessed are you, Lord, our God, Ruler of the Universe, Wise One, Who knows everyone's innermost thoughts [i.e., Who appreciates each human being's uniqueness].
>
> —*Shulkhan Arukh, Orakh Chayyim* 224:5

The perspective of the *Shulkhan Arukh,* the standard code of Jewish law, is counterintuitive. Most people's reactions when they see an enormous crowd is to view it as one enormous collectivity, a mob, rather than to focus on the individuality of each person present.

The Talmud likewise cautions a person amid a large gathering to remember the intellectual distinctiveness of each person present:

The mind of each is different from that of the other, just as the face of each is different from that of the other.

—Babylonian Talmud, *Berakhot* 58a

THE MANY SIDES OF EACH INDIVIDUAL

Everyone must have two pockets, so that he can reach into the one or the other, according to his needs. In his right pocket are to be the words: "For my sake was the world created," and in his left: "I am dust and ashes."

—A Hasidic saying quoted by Martin Buber, *Ten Rungs,*
page 106

If I try to be like him, who will be like me?

—Yiddish proverb

The Hasidic rebbe Zusha (d. 1800) used to say: "When I die and come before the heavenly court, if they ask me, 'Zusha, why were you not as great as Abraham?' I will not be afraid. I will say that I was not born with Abraham's intellectual capabilities. And if they ask me, 'Zusha, why were you not Moses?' I will say that I did not have Moses' leadership abilities. But when they ask me, 'Zusha, why were you not Zusha?' for that I will have no answer."

The Hasidic rebbe Menachem Mendel of Kotzk (d. 1859) insisted that one's singularity shine through in every encounter, and that a person should never alter his essence to please the person to whom he or she is speaking:

If I am I because I am I, then I am I and you are you. But if I am I because you are you, and you are you because I am I, then I am not I and you are not you.

90

13

"ALL JEWS ARE RESPONSIBLE ONE FOR ANOTHER"

Communal Responsibilities

All Jews are responsible one for another.
—Babylonian Talmud, *Shevuot* 39a

This widely known talmudic aphorism helps account for the wide-ranging charitable activities within the Jewish community; Jews are indeed commanded to feel responsible for each another.

The Hebrew word used for "responsible," *ah-reivin,* literally means "surety," one who makes himself responsible for another, either as a sponsor, godparent, or guarantor of a loan.

Judah is the biblical model of a surety. In Egypt, when Joseph, whose identity is unknown to his brothers, informs them that he will sell them food only if they return with their remaining brother, Benjamin, their father Jacob forbids it. At first, the other brothers accede to Jacob's resistance. But as the famine in Canaan intensifies, they conclude that they must convince their father to let them take Benjamin. Finally, Judah says to Jacob, "Send the boy in my care. . . . I myself will be surety for him; you may hold me responsible; if I do not bring him back and set him before you, I shall stand guilty before you forever" (Genesis 43:8–9).

Later, Judah proves that he was not just uttering a platitude. A cup from Joseph's court is found hidden amid Benjamin's possessions, and Joseph announces that he will take Benjamin as a slave, while letting the other brothers go free. Judah steps forth to plead with Joseph: "Now your servant [i.e., I] has made himself a surety for the boy to my father, saying, 'If I do not bring him back to you, I shall stand guilty before my father forever.' Therefore please let your servant remain as a slave to my lord instead of the boy, and let the boy go back with his brothers" (Genesis 44:32–33).

The willingness of Judah, the very brother who seventeen years earlier had suggested selling Joseph as a slave, to himself serve as one in lieu of Benjamin impels Joseph to fully forgive the evil his brothers once did him. A midrash suggests that in reward for this selfless behavior, all Jews are subsequently named for Judah (the word for Jew in Hebrew is *yehudi,* which comes from his name, *Yehudah*).

In addition to making Jews responsible for other Jews' physical safety and well-being, this aphorism is also understood by some to mean that all Jews ultimately are responsible for the behavior of all other Jews. Thus, some Orthodox Jews quote this statement to underscore their personal sense of obligation to influence non-Orthodox Jews to become observant, while politically active Jews are motivated by this statement to try to alter the political and social behavior of their coreligionists.

> Whoever can stop ... the people of his city from sinning, but does not ... is held responsible for the sins of the people of his city. If he can stop the whole world from sinning, and does not, he is held responsible for the sins of the whole world.
>
> —Babylonian Talmud, *Shabbat* 54b

From the rabbinic perspective, individual acts potentially influence the whole world's fate:

Our Rabbis taught: A person should always see himself as being equally balanced between his good and his evil deeds. Fortunate is he who performs one commandment, for he has tipped the scales in his favor. Woe unto him if he has performed one evil deed, for he has tipped the scales toward his guilt. . . . Rabbi Elazar ben Simeon said: Because the world is judged on the basis of its majority, and the individual is judged on the basis of the preponderance of his actions, fortunate is one who fulfills a commandment, for he has tipped the scales in his own favor and in favor of the world. Woe to him who violates one commandment, for he has tipped the scales against himself and against the world.

—Babylonian Talmud, *Kiddushin* 40a–40b; with minor variations,
I have followed the translation of Ben Zion Bokser,
The Talmud: Selected Writings, page 173.

In light of this passage, small wonder that Jews became a guilt-ridden people!

Do not separate yourself from the community.
—*Ethics of the Fathers* 2:4

The above implicitly criticizes Jews who believe that they will be immune from problems confronting other Jews. When Queen Esther tells Mordechai that she cannot intervene with King Ahasuerus to annul Haman's decree of destruction against all Jews, Mordechai warns her: "Do not imagine that you, of all the Jews, will escape with your life by being in the king's palace. On the contrary, if you keep silent in this crisis, relief and deliverance will come to the Jews from another quarter, while you and your father's house will perish. And who knows, perhaps you have attained to royal position for just such a crisis?" (Esther 4:12–14). Esther, of course, does intervene and saves the Jews.

However, the prohibition against separating from the community is not absolute. Maimonides warns:

If one lives in a country where the customs are pernicious, and the inhabitants do not act in an honest way, he should leave for a place where people are righteous and act like good people.

—*Mishneh Torah,* "Laws of Character Development and Ethical Conduct," 6:1

However, the Rabbis usually reserved great scorn for those who distanced themselves from their brethren during crises:

When the community is in trouble, a person should not say, "I will go to my house and I will eat and drink and be at peace with myself."

—Babylonian Talmud, *Ta'anit* 11a

Our Rabbis have taught: When Jews are in trouble and one separates himself from them, then the two angels who accompany every person come and place their hands upon his head, and say, "So and so who separated himself from the community shall not witness its deliverance.... [But, the passage continues,] one who shares in the distress of the community will merit to witness its deliverance."

—Babylonian Talmud, *Ta'anit* 11a

Moses is the archetypical Jew who took upon himself his community's pain. Because he lived in Pharaoh's palace, he easily could have ignored the Hebrew slaves' sufferings. Yet "he went out to his kinsfolk and witnessed their labors." And when he saw an Egyptian overseer beating a Hebrew slave, he struck him down. This is one of the three incidents described in the Bible that convinced God to appoint Moses to lead the Hebrews from slavery to freedom (Exodus 2:11–19).

The wicked son [at the Passover Seder is so designated because he] excludes himself from the community.

—*Mekhilta* commenting on Exodus 13:8

94

In the Passover Haggada, the wicked son comments, "What does this service mean to *you?*" making it clear that it means nothing to him.

> A fast in which no Jewish sinners participate is no fast.
> —Babylonian Talmud, *Kritot* 6b

The Jewish community should never become so elitist that it excludes sinners. Thus, the thirteenth-century Rabbi Meir of Rothenburg composed a formula which is still recited in synagogues as the prelude to the *Kol Nidre,* Yom Kippur's opening prayer: "With the approval of God and with the approval of the congregation, both in the Court in heaven and in the Court on earth, we declare it lawful to pray together with those who have [grievously] sinned."

I have added "grievously," because without it, the statement makes no sense, since everyone is assumed to have committed some sins. We know that Rabbi Meir composed this formula specifically to include Jews who had been excommunicated because of their defiance of communal regulations (see Saul Weiss, *Insights,* page 212).

> Some people were sitting in a ship, when one of them took a drill and began to bore a hole under his seat.
>
> The other passengers protested to him, "What are you doing?"
>
> He said to them, "What has this to do with you? Am I not boring the hole under my own seat?"
>
> They retorted, "But the water will come in and drown us all."
>
> [Such is the fate of the Jews; one sins and all suffer.]
> —*Leviticus Rabbah* 4:6

As a minority, Jews often are identified collectively with their most troublesome or evil members. Thus, antisemites who were also anticommunist invariably noted that Karl Marx was a Jew, although he was converted to Christianity at age six and was himself fiercely antisemitic (see pages 472–473). The Soviet Union, a government established on Marxist principles, was also antisemitic.

* * *

[A third-century prayer which Rabbi Hisda recited when starting out on a perilous journey]: "May it be Your will, O Lord my God, to conduct me in peace, to direct my steps in peace, to uphold me in peace, and to deliver me from every enemy and ambush on the road. Send a blessing upon the work of my hands, and let me obtain grace, loving-kindness and mercy in Your eyes and in the eyes of all who behold me. Blessed are You, O Lord, Who listens to men's prayers."

[But Abbaye objected to the wording and commented]: "One should always associate himself with the community when praying. How should one pray? 'May it be Your will, O Lord *our* God, to direct *our* steps in peace, etc.' "
—Babylonian Talmud, *Berakhot* 29b–30a

Almost no prayers in the Jewish prayer book are recited in the first person; they almost always are offered in the plural. For if people prayed in the first person, their prayers might well be directed either against others or, alternatively, against others' interests. Thus, when a person prays that he receive a job for which he has applied, in effect, he also is praying that the other applicants be rejected. Only when people address God in the plural are they likely to pray for that which is universally beneficial.

Finally, the Rabbis teach that the selfish, who profit at the expense of the community, will in the end suffer for their greed:

Our Rabbis taught: A man should not remove stones from his ground and throw them onto public grounds. A certain man was throwing stones from his ground onto public grounds, when a pious man said to him, "Fool, why do you remove stones from ground which is not yours and throw it onto ground which is yours?" The man laughed at him. After a time, the man had to sell his field, and when he was walking on that public ground he stumbled over those stones. He then said, "How well that pious man put it. 'Why do you throw stones from ground which is not yours to ground which is yours?' "

—Babylonian Talmud, *Bava Kamma* 50b

THE INTERCONNECTEDNESS OF THE INDIVIDUAL AND THE COMMUNITY

Hasidic rebbe Shlomo of Karlin (1738–1792) taught: A man once saw a precious object very high up. Wanting to fetch it down he asked a number of people to make a "tower" so that the topmost person could reach for the object. Supposing one of them, the lowest, for instance, had said, "What's the point of my being here? After all, I'll never reach up so high in any case!" and, so saying, had jumped aside, his action would have been extremely foolish and would have endangered the lives of the others. We are all equally necessary—the highest and the lowest. If so much as one person fails, the whole will not reach the desired goal.

—Jiri Langer, *Nine Gates to the Chasidic Mysteries*, page 99

If I am not for myself, who is for me?
And if I am only for myself, what am I?

—Hillel, *Ethics of the Fathers* 1:14

Professor Louis Kaplan, formerly of the Baltimore Hebrew College, has noted that Hillel's choice of words suggests that a person who is concerned only with himself or herself ceases to be a "who," and becomes instead a "what."

We are one.

—Former United Jewish Appeal campaign slogan

The Jewish support for the various UJA campaigns to bring oppressed Jews to Israel underscores how intensely many Jews feel a familial commitment to their brethren throughout the world. Thus, among the rescue campaigns the UJA has organized over the past forty-five years, campaigns that have raised well over a billion dollars, are Operation Magic Carpet (the Jews of Yemen), Operation Moses and Operation Solomon (both on behalf of Ethiopian Jewry), and Operation Exodus (Soviet Jewry).

> Jews alone are vulnerable. . . . But Jews must not be alone.
> —Elie Wiesel; Wiesel articulated this view as a mission
> statement for the New York-based National Jewish
> Center for Learning and Leadership (CLAL).

14

MODELS OF LEADERSHIP

[When Moses shepherded the flocks of Jethro], he used to stop the bigger sheep from grazing before the smaller ones, and let the smaller ones loose first to feed on the tender grass; then he would let the older sheep loose to feed on the grass of average quality; lastly he let the strong ones loose to feed on the toughest. God said, "Let . . . him who knows how to shepherd the flock, each according to its strength, come and lead My people."

—*Exodus Rabbah* 2:2

When Noah came out of the ark, he opened his eyes and saw the whole world completely destroyed. He began crying for the world and said, "Master of the World! If You destroyed Your world because of human sins or human fools, then why did You create them? One or the other You should do: either do not create the human being, or do not destroy the world! . . ."

The Blessed Holy One answered him, "Foolish shepherd! I lingered with you [before the flood] and spoke to you at length so that you would ask mercy for the world! But as soon as you heard that you would be safe in the ark, the evil of the world did not touch your heart. You built the ark and saved yourself. Now that the world has been destroyed you open your mouth to utter questions and pleas."

—*Zohar: The Book of Enlightenment,* translated by Daniel Chanan Matt, pages 57–58

When God told Abraham that He intended to destroy Sodom and Gomorrah because of the cities' many sins, the patriarch argued with God, and even entered into negotiations with Him in an effort to have the order of destruction rescinded. He even called into question God's moral perfection, "Shall not the judge of all the earth act justly?" (Genesis 18:25).

Noah, on the other hand, heard God's decree about the coming great flood, yet neither argued with God nor warned his fellow citizens. Consequently, Jewish tradition regards Abraham as the model of a good leader, and Noah as the sort of leader from whom one should learn how not to act, for he lacked moral assertiveness.

HOW LEADERSHIP CAN ENDANGER ONE'S CHARACTER

[Rabbi Judah ben Tabbai] said: If anyone had said to me before I entered high office, "Assume that office," my only wish would have been to hound him to death. Now that I have entered high office, if anyone were to tell me, "Give it up," I would pour a kettle of boiling water on his head. Because to high office it is hard to rise, yet . . . it is even harder to give it up. For so we find in the case of [King] Saul. When he was told, "Rise to kingship," Saul hid, as the Bible says, "And the Lord answered [after the Israelites had been told that Saul would be their king, and they could not find him], 'Behold, he is hiding among the baggage'" (I Samuel 10:22); but when Saul was told, "Give up the kingship," he hunted after David [his designated successor] to kill him.
—*The Fathers According to Rabbi Nathan*, chapter 10:3; a similar expression of a leader's inability to relinquish leadership is found in the Babylonian Talmud, *Menahot* 109b, where the same sentiment is attributed to Rabbi Joshua ben Perakhia.

THE TOLL OF POLITICAL AND COMMUNAL LEADERSHIP

Woe to authority, which buries its possessor, for there is not a single prophet who did not outlive four kings.

—Babylonian Talmud, *Pesachim* 87b

For example, Isaiah's opening verse reveals that he prophesied during the reigns of Uzziah, Jotham, Ahaz, and Hezekiah.

OF PRINCES AND ROOSTERS

Once there was a prince who fell into the delusion of thinking he was a rooster. He took off all his clothes, sat under the table, and refused to eat any food but corn seeds. The king sent for many doctors and many specialists, but none of them could cure him.

Finally a wise man appeared before the king and said: "I think that I can cure the prince." The king gave him permission to try.

The wise man took off his clothes, crawled under the table and began to munch on corn seeds. The prince looked at him suspiciously, and said: "Who are you, and what are you doing here?"

The wise man answered: "Who are you, and what are you doing here?"

"I am a rooster," answered the prince belligerently.

"Oh, really? So am I," answered the wise man quietly.

The two of them sat together under the table until they became accustomed to each other. When the wise man felt that the prince was used to his presence, he signaled for some clothing. He put on the clothing, and then he said to the prince: "Don't think that roosters can't wear clothing if they want to. A rooster can wear clothes and be a perfectly good rooster just the same."

The prince thought about this for a while, and then he too agreed to put on clothes.

Another time, the wise man signaled to have food put under the table. The prince became alarmed and said: "What are you doing?"

The wise man reassured him: "Don't be upset. A rooster can eat the food that human beings eat if he wants to, and still be a good rooster." The prince considered this statement for a time, and then he too signaled for food.

Then the wise man said to the prince: "Do you think that a rooster has to sit under the table all the time? A rooster can get up and walk around if he wants to and still be a good rooster." The prince considered these words for a time, and then he followed the wise man up from the table, and began to walk. After he began dressing like a person, eating like a person, and walking like a person, he gradually recovered his senses and began to live like a person.

> —Rabbi Nachman of Bratslav (1771–1810); retold from the Hebrew and Yiddish sources by Jack Riemer. Nachman of Bratslav was a Hasidic rebbe who died in 1810 at the age of thirty-eight. He taught primarily through parables and stories, which his followers still study.

Howard Schwartz, who has reprinted this parable in his *Gates to the New City: A Treasury of Modern Jewish Tales* (page 458), quotes Rabbi Nachman's own comment on his tale: "In this way must the genuine teacher go down to the level of his people if he wishes to raise them up to their proper place" (page 45). Schwartz himself observes that, from a modern reader's perspective, "the wise man is an archetype for the psychiatrist, who, according to the theories of R. D. Laing, among others, must share his patients' madness so as to fully comprehend what it is they are experiencing, in order to lead them away from that place" (page 699).

In short, if you wish to transform and elevate people, sympathy and preaching are not enough, because both compel the listener to concede the falseness of how he has been living until now. The first requirement is empathy. Only when a person senses that you identify with his/her circumstances and understand his/her truth, will he or she be open to change.

MISCELLANEOUS

Finally, I conclude with a quote from a non-Jew, an American presidential candidate addressing the annual convention of a Zionist organization:

> The Jewish people, ever since David slew Goliath, have never considered youth as a barrier to leadership.
> —John F. Kennedy addressing the ZOA (Zionist Organization of America) during the 1960 American presidential campaign. During the speech, the forty-three-year-old Kennedy, soon to be the youngest person ever elected president, also noted that Theodor Herzl was only thirty-seven when he proclaimed the "inevitability" of a Jewish state's "triumphant reality" (cited in I. L. Kenen, *Israel's Defense Line,* page 156).

15

"LISTEN TO HER VOICE"

Conflicting Biblical and Talmudic Views of the Character of Women

> Whatever Sarah has said to you, listen to her voice.
> —God to Abraham, Genesis 21:12

Concerning women, there is a fundamental, if seldom commented upon, conflict between biblical law and biblical narrative. The Bible's laws favor men (e.g., only they can initiate divorce and, in most instances, only they can inherit), but its narratives portray women as operating on a level of relative domestic equality.

In the above verse, Abraham is instructed by God to follow his wife's wishes, although they strongly conflict with his own. A generation later, Genesis 27 makes it clear that Rebecca has far better insight than Isaac into the character of their two sons, Esau and Jacob.

Exodus's opening two chapters depict one heroic and noble woman after another. First, two midwives, Shifra and Puah, are the only people we know of in Egypt who resist Pharaoh's order to murder all male Hebrew babies at birth. Later, Moses' mother, not father, plays the key role in hiding him when he is born. His sister, Miriam, not his brother, Aaron, watches over him when he is put afloat in the Nile (although, to be fair to Aaron, he was only three at the time). Finally, Pharaoh's compassionate daughter saves Moses from drowning, raises him in her father's house, and thus sets the stage for the Jewish slaves' liberation from Egypt. Decades later, in one of the most cryptic passages in the Torah, Moses' wife Tzipporah saves his life (Exodus 4:24–26).

In the Book of Samuel, Hannah, a childless wife who beseeches God to make her fertile, serves as a talmudic model for how *all* Jews are to pray (I Samuel 1:10–17; see Babylonian Talmud, *Berakhot* 31a and *Yoma* 73a). Hannah's prayers are answered, and the child born to her becomes the prophet Samuel.

Centuries later, when Haman plots genocide against the Jews of Persia, the Jewish Queen Esther, aided by her cousin Mordechai, saves them.

Despite these examples, the thrust of many later, particularly talmudic, teachings about women (with significant exceptions; see pages 115–116) are condescending and demeaning. Some talmudic statements, particularly, as we shall soon see, those of the influential second-century Rabbi Eliezer ben Hyrcanus, are misogynistic. But it should come as no surprise to realize that even the most sublime texts also reflect the period in which they were written.

WOMEN IN THE TALMUD; PATRONIZING AND/OR NEGATIVE COMMENTS

> In what lies the merit of women? In bringing their sons to study at the synagogue, in letting their husbands study at the *Beit Ha-Midrash,* and in waiting for them to return home from the *Beit Ha-Midrash* [men would often stay away from home for long periods to pursue Torah study].
>
> —Babylonian Talmud, *Berakhot* 17a

Rabbi Eliezer Berkovits, the renowned late Orthodox scholar, points out that while these activities certainly are worthy of appreciation, the cumulative effect of this statement is to limit women to serving as assistants to those whose work, Torah study, is what really is important (*Jewish Women in Time and Torah,* page 7). Lest one argue that the Talmud's statement in no way presumes a diminished status for woman, consider how pleased most men would be had the Jewish tradition stated:

> In what lies the merit of men? In bringing their daughters to study at the synagogue, in letting their wives study at the *Beit Ha-Midrash,* and in waiting for them to return home from the *Beit Ha-Midrash.*

The perception that the most noble woman is one who enables her husband to study is underscored in the story of Rabbi Akiva and his wife:

> Rabbi Akiva was a shepherd of Ben Kalba Sabua. When his daughter saw how modest and noble Akiva was, she said to him, "If I become betrothed to you, would you go away to study at the academy?"
>
> "Yes," he replied.
>
> She became secretly betrothed to him, and sent him off. When her father heard of it, he drove her from his house, and vowed that she should have no benefit from his possessions.
>
> Akiva went and stayed twelve years at the academy. When he returned home, he was accompanied by twelve thousand disciples. He heard an old man saying to his [i.e., Akiva's] wife, "How long will you live a life of living widowhood?"
>
> "If he would listen to me," she replied, "he would stay away in the academy another twelve years."
>
> Then Akiva thought, "I would be doing it with her permission."
>
> So he departed and stayed in the academy another twelve years. When he finally returned, he brought with him twenty-four thousand disciples.
>
> When his wife heard of his coming, she went out to meet him. Her neighbors said to her, "Borrow some respectable clothes and dress up in them."
>
> She replied, "The righteous man knows the soul of his beast" (Proverbs 12:10).
>
> When she came to him, she fell upon her face and

kissed his feet. His disciples began to push her away, but he said, "Let her be, mine and yours are hers."

When her father heard that a learned man had come to the city, he said, "I will go to him, and perhaps he will annul my vow."

He came to Akiva, and Akiva said to him, "If you had known that he was a learned man, would you have made your vow?"

He said, "If he had only known even one chapter or one *halakha* [law], I would not have made the vow."

Then Akiva told him, "I am the man."

Ben Kalba Sabua fell down and kissed Akiva's feet, and gave him half his wealth.

—Babylonian Talmud, *Ketubot* 62b–63a

Several things stand out in this story. Noble as Akiva's wife is— and it is clear that the Talmud has the highest regard for her—this talmudic tale never bothers to tell us her name. She is referred to as either the daughter of Ben Kalba Sabua or the wife of Rabbi Akiva (elsewhere in the Talmud we learn that her name was Rachel).

Also, the very biblical verse with which Akiva's wife refers to herself, "The righteous man knows the soul of his beast," hardly reflects a wonderful self-image. Her friends' suggestion that she *borrow* some respectable clothes reveals the dire poverty in which she was living, which probably had damaged her self-esteem as well.

Finally, when Ben Kalba Sabua renounces his vow, he gives half of his wealth to Rabbi Akiva; one might have thought his daughter to be the more deserving and natural recipient.

There is talmudic evidence to suggest that there was a great love between Rabbi Akiva and his wife. Most notably, the Palestinian Talmud (*Sotah* 9:16) tells us that in his days of poverty, Akiva promised Rachel a golden tiara with an engraving of Jerusalem on it (a piece of jewelry known as "Jerusalem of Gold"), a promise he later fulfilled. Similarly, Akiva's statement, "Who is wealthy? . . . He who has a wife comely in deeds" (Babylonian Talmud, *Shabbat* 25b) undoubtedly referred to his wife.

Nonetheless, one wonders how Rachel must have reacted when

she heard of her husband's ruling in opposition to the School of Shammai that "[A man may divorce his wife] if he finds another woman more beautiful than she is" (Mishna *Gittin* 9:10).

[A man asked] Rabbi Eliezer: "If my father and mother each ask me to bring them a glass of water, to whom should I bring the water first?"

"Leave your mother's honor and fulfill the honor due to your father," he replied, "for you and your mother are both required to honor him."
—Babylonian Talmud, *Kiddushin* 31a

One elaboration on this text: If the parents are divorced, then the father no longer takes precedence over the mother; the child's obligation to honor their wishes is equal.

Women are temperamentally light-headed.
—Babylonian Talmud, *Kiddushin* 80b

The Talmud records this dictum in expressing its belief that women, being "light-headed," are easily seduced. Thus, rabbinic law rules that a man is forbidden to be alone with two women, since it will be easy for him to lure both of them into sleeping with him. On the other hand, one woman is permitted to be alone with two men, since they allegedly will be too embarrassed in one another's presence to have sexual relations with her.

Yet despite the Talmud's assumptions about women's weak will, it requires unwarranted optimism about human nature to assume that one woman will necessarily be safe with two men, while *ménages à trois* ("threesomes") involving two females occur far more often in male fantasies than in real life.

The world cannot exist without males and females, but happy is he whose children are sons and woe to him whose children are daughters.
—Babylonian Talmud, *Bava Bathra* 16b

108

A child's birth is such a significant, joyful event in its parents' lives. Imagine telling them to regard the birth of a child of the "wrong" sex as a curse. How painful to them—and how cruel to the newborn child! Throughout Jewish history, who knows how many young girls suffered from being raised by parents who were frustrated and disappointed that their child was of the "wrong" sex?

That such a comment affected how some Jews reacted to the birth of a girl, *even in the twentieth century,* is suggested by an autobiographical reminiscence of Bertha Pappenheim, an early-twentieth-century German-Jewish activist: "The old Jews offered congratulations only when a boy was born; the response to the question of the baby's sex if it was female was 'Nothing, girl,' or 'Only a girl' " (cited in Naomi Shepherd, *A Price Below Rubies,* page 229).

Such sentiments notwithstanding, it must be emphasized that, among the Jews' neighbors in the ancient world, the exposure of infant children, particularly those who were handicapped or were female, was widely practiced. In the ancient world, Jewish law alone forbade infanticide and regarded it as murder.

Parallel negative reactions to the birth of a daughter persist in many cultures. Norwegian actress Liv Ullman, who was born in Tokyo, writes in the preface to her autobiography, *Changing,* that immediately after she was born, a Japanese nurse bent down and whispered apologetically to her mother, "I'm afraid it's a girl. Would you prefer to inform your husband yourself?"

A British scholar, Rabbi A. Cohen, has offered the following apologetic for the above talmudic passage: "Sons were preferred because they were a support in old age and might fulfill their parents' ambition of becoming renowned scholars" (A. Cohen, *Everyman's Talmud,* pages 171–172). If his explanation is correct, the contemporary entry of significant numbers of women into the professions and into academia should help eliminate this sexist preference.

THE DISTURBING TEACHINGS OF RABBI ELIEZER

Rabbi Eliezer, one of the Talmud's foremost legal scholars, of whom it was said, "When Rabbi Eliezer died, the Torah scroll was hidden away" (a tribute to his great learning; Babylonian Talmud, *Sotah* 49b)—spoke of women with withering contempt:

> He who teaches his daughter Torah teaches her lewdness.
>
> —Mishna *Sotah* 3:4

To understand how teaching a woman the Bible can be compared to instructing her in lewdness, one first must understand the mind-set of a man who has a very low regard for women. Rabbi Eliezer believed that women would use their cunning to pervert the words of Torah and find a way to commit adultery without being caught. His words bring to mind the Virginia legislators who, in response to the 1831 Nat Turner slave rebellion, ruled that it was forbidden to teach blacks how to read and write.

> A matron asked Rabbi Eliezer [to explain a biblical verse that appeared to her inconsistent]. He responded, "There is no other wisdom for a woman except at the spindle." ...His son Hyrcanus said to him, "Your refusal to answer her one question from the Torah will cost me [a gift of] three hundred *kor* of tithes which she used to give me every year." Rabbi Eliezer answered him, "Let the words of Torah be burned rather than entrusted to women."
>
> —Palestinian Talmud, *Sotah* 3:4

Given that almost two thousand sages are quoted in the Talmud, Rabbi Eliezer's words might be dismissed as just one view among many. However, he was not just another sage, but among the pre-eminent talmudic scholars. In one of the Talmud's most famous passages, Rabbi Eliezer stands stubbornly alone in disputing dozens of other sages, until a heavenly voice reproves the other sages, "Why do you dispute Rabbi Eliezer, with whom the *halakha* (the law) always agrees?" (Babylonian Talmud, *Bava Mezia* 59a; see pages 73–74). Thus, it is no surprise that his hostile statements about women, particularly the one dismissing women's Torah study as

110

lewdness, frequently are quoted in medieval and even modern rabbinic writings.

My mother, Helen Telushkin, has commented about this and similar passages: "How could good men say such things? Didn't they have mothers? Is this what they thought of the mothers who had raised them, that teaching such women Torah would be like teaching them lewdness?"

A final passage offers unparalleled insight into how Rabbi Eliezer felt about those whom he regarded as his social inferiors, in this case a person who had the "double stigma" of being both a slave and a woman:

> When Rabbi Eliezer's female slave died, his disciples came to console him. As soon as he saw them, he withdrew into an upper chamber, but they went up after him. He then went into the bathhouse, and they followed him there. He then went into the dining hall, and they followed him there. Finally, he said to them, "I thought that lukewarm water would be enough to 'scald' you, but I see that you are not even scalded with boiling hot water [i.e., I should have thought my earlier, evasive actions would have made it obvious that I have no desire to receive consolation]. Have I not taught you that no row of mourners is formed at the death of male and female slaves . . . nor is condolence offered? What then do you say about them? The same as you say to a man whose ox or donkey has died, 'May the Almighty replenish your loss.' So, too, when a man's male or female slave dies, you should say to him, 'May the Almighty replenish your loss.' "
>
> —Babylonian Talmud, *Berakhot* 16b

That Rabbi Eliezer compared the death of a human being created in God's image to the death of an animal is shocking enough; that he was speaking about a woman who had spent years of her life serving him is both deeply disturbing and depressing.

Rabbi Eliezer's extraordinary rabbinic scholarship notwithstanding, his colleagues regarded him as so ornery and stubborn that near the end of his life they felt compelled to put him under the very rare ban of excommunication, an ostracism that remained in force until his death.

THE TWO GREATEST RELIGIOUS TEACHERS OF MEDIEVAL JEWISH LIFE, RASHI AND MAIMONIDES, ON WOMEN

[The following is a talmudic passage on which Rashi comments]: Rabbi Judah used to say, A man is bound to say the following three blessings daily:

"[Blessed are You . . .] who has not made me a heathen," ". . . who has not made me a woman," ". . . who has not made me a brutish person."

Rabbi Aha ben Jacob once overheard his son saying ". . . who has not made me a brutish person," whereupon he said to him, "And this too!" [i.e., this blessing smacks of conceit]. Said his son, "Then what blessing should I say instead?"

He replied, "Who has not made me a slave."

"And is not a slave the same as a woman?" [the Talmud asks].

"A slave is more contemptible."

—Babylonian Talmud, *Menaḥot* 43b–44a

[Comments Rashi on the question, "And is not a slave the same as a woman?"]: "For a woman is a servant to her husband like a slave is to his master. . . . Nevertheless, the status of a slave is still more contemptible."

The eleventh-century Rashi's teachings about the Bible and Talmud have remained the most important Jewish commentaries ever written. The above text, albeit a commentary, is particularly surprising given that Rashi had three daughters (but no sons), all of whom were reputed to be very knowledgeable Jewishly.

That the analogy between a wife and a slave was not a singular, and unfortunate, aberration, is suggested by Rashi's gloss on the Babylonian Talmud, *Kiddushin* 23b: "For a wife is like a slave in that her husband is entitled to the work of her hands and whatever she may find [just as the master possesses all the acquisitions of a slave]."

Although the status and rights of women in Jewish law was of course far higher than that of slaves, the repeated comparisons drawn between them could only have served to lessen respect for women.

Maimonides, whose influence on Jewish thought is as profound as Rashi's, had a generally low regard for women. Thus, in elaborating on Rabbi Eliezer's teaching that a girl should not be taught Torah, he ruled:

> Our sages commanded that one should not teach one's daughter Torah because the minds of most women are incapable of concentrating on learning, and thus, because of their intellectual poverty, they turn the words of Torah into words of nonsense.
>
> —Moses Maimonides, *Mishneh Torah,*
> "Laws of Torah Study," 1:13

Of the marital relationship, Maimonides writes:

> And thus our sages have commanded that a man should honor his wife more than himself and love her as himself; that if he has money, he should increase his generosity to her according to his wealth; that he should not cast excessive fear upon her. . . . And thus they have also commanded the wife that she honor her husband exceedingly, that the fear of him should be upon her, and that all her actions should be done in accordance with his instructions; he should be in her eyes like a prince or a king, while she behaves according to his heart's desire, and keeps away from anything that is hateful to him.
>
> —*Mishneh Torah,* "Laws of Marriage," 15:19–20

Rabbi Eliezer Berkovits, himself a devoted student of Maimonides, notes his perplexity at this ruling: "It is difficult to understand why Maimonides did not see the contradiction between these two

113

commands. How can a husband who loves and honors his wife, as indicated, want her to fear him, to look up to him as if he were a prince simply because he happens to be her husband? . . . The truth is that the two principles are mutually exclusive; either you love your wife as yourself and honor her more than yourself, or you demand that she regard you as her lord and master, and serve you accordingly" (*Jewish Women in Time and Torah*, page 56).

When studying Maimonides' writings concerning women, one should remember that he lived in a Muslim society, one in which the status of women was quite low, and still is. Thus, in contemporary Saudi Arabia—the country with Islam's two holiest cities, and one ruled by Islamic law—women are not allowed to drive a car, marry whom they want without permission of a male guardian, or travel without written permission from a male guardian (see Ann Louise Barach, "Tearing Off the Veil," *National Times*, January 1994, page 10).

> It is unseemly for a woman to be constantly going outside and into the streets. A husband should prevent his wife from doing this and not allow her to go out more than once or twice in a month, as the need may arise [e.g., if she needs to visit her father's house, or pay a condolence call, or attend a wedding]. For the beauty of a woman consists in her staying in a corner of her home, for this is how it is written, "All the honor of a king's daughter is within [her home; Psalms 45:14]."
>
> —*Mishneh Torah*, "Laws of Marriage," 13:11

Maimonides's rulings concerning women were not uniformly restrictive. In one ruling, which is particularly significant, given that Jewish law does not permit women to initiate divorce, Maimonides writes:

> A woman who refuses to have intercourse with her husband is called *moredet* (rebellious). She is asked the reason for her rebellion. If she says, "I find him disgusting and am unable to have sexual relations with him willingly,"

the husband is compelled to divorce her. She is not like a prisoner who has to live with one whom she detests.
—*Mishneh Torah*, "Laws of Marriage," 14:8

Elsewhere (see page 170), Maimonides rules that a man who refused to grant a divorce to a woman entitled to it should be whipped until he does so.

WOMEN AND THEIR TRAITS: POSITIVE VIEWS

Until now, many of the statements cited reflect a disapproving evaluation of women's intelligence and/or character, and exerted a negative effect on women's status in Jewish law.

However influential they may have been, these quotes do not tell the whole story. The Jewish tradition contains other statements and laws reflecting a more positive understanding of women (Chapter 16, on marriage, likewise reflects rabbinic concern with the loving treatment of one's wife):

Honor your father and mother.
—Fifth of the Ten Commandments, Exodus 20:12

You shall each revere [alternatively, fear] his mother and father.
—Leviticus 19:3

My son, heed the discipline of your father, and do not forsake the instruction [literally, the Torah] of your mother.
—Proverbs 1:8

These three biblical verses all suggest the equality of the father and the mother in raising a child; indeed, the verse from Proverbs focuses far more on the mother than the father as teacher. Jewish law also teaches that the child's religious identity follows that of the mother, not the father.

Women are tender-hearted.

—Babylonian Talmud, *Megillah* 14b

The Holy One, Blessed be He, endowed women with more insight than men.

—Babylonian Talmud, *Niddah* 45b

It once happened that a pious man married a pious woman, and they did not produce children. They said, "We are of no use to the Holy One, Blessed be He," and they arose and divorced each other. The man went and married a wicked woman, and she made him wicked, while the woman went and married a wicked man, and she made him righteous. This proves that all depends on the woman.

—*Genesis Rabbah* 17:7

Women thus were assumed to exert a powerful moral influence, a view reflected in another midrash:

The Holy One, Blessed be He, said to Moses, "Go speak to the daughters of Israel [and ask them] whether they wish to receive the Torah." Why were the women asked first? Because the way of men is to follow the opinion of women.

—*Pirkei d'Rabbi Eliezer,* chapter 41

HENRIETTA SZOLD AND THE KADDISH

Among traditional Jews, it generally has been assumed that only sons need recite the *Kaddish* prayer for deceased immediate family members. This practice had the unfortunate effect of diminishing the significance of girl children. In Eastern Europe, when a couple's first boy was born, he was referred to as "the *kaddishl*"; prior to his birth, a couple felt that there would be no one to memorialize them after they died.

In 1916, the mother of Henrietta Szold, the founder of Hadassah, died. Her friend Haym Peretz offered to recite the *Kaddish* on her mother's behalf. Szold wrote to thank him effusively for his offer: "It is impossible for me to find words with which to tell you how deeply I was touched. . . . It is beautiful what you have offered to do—I shall never forget it." However, she went on to explain, she could not accede to his offer:

> I cannot ask you to say *Kaddish* after my mother. The *Kaddish* means to me that the survivor publicly and markedly manifests his wish and intention to assume the relation of the Jewish community which his parent had, and that so the chain of tradition remains unbroken from generation to generation. . . . You can do that for the generations of your family, I must do that for the generations of my family.
>
> I believe that the elimination of women from such duties was never intended by our law and custom—women were freed from positive duties when they could not perform them, but not when they could. It was never intended that, if they could perform them, their performance of them would not be considered as valuable and valid as when one of the male sex performed them. And of the *Kaddish* I feel sure this is particularly true.
>
> My mother had eight daughters and no son; and yet never did I hear a word of regret pass the lips of either my mother or my father that one of us was not a son. When my father died, my mother would not permit others to take her daughters' place in saying the *Kaddish,* and so I am sure I am acting in her spirit when I am moved to decline your offer. But beautiful your offer remains nevertheless, and, I repeat, I know full well that it is much more in consonance with the generally accepted Jewish tradition than is my or my family's tradition.
>
> —Henrietta Szold to Haym Peretz, September 16, 1916, in Marvin Lowenthal, *Henrietta Szold: Life and Letters*

16

"IT IS NOT GOOD FOR MAN TO BE ALONE"

Jewish Perspectives on Marriage

IT IS NOT GOOD FOR MAN TO BE ALONE

The Lord God said, "It is not good for man to be alone . . ."

—Genesis 2:18

"Loneliness," the sixteenth-century John Milton noted in *Tetra-chordon,* "was the first thing which God's eye named not good."

The nineteenth-century Bible commentator Jacob Zvi Meklen-burg writes: " 'It is not good for man to be alone,' means that man's inner capacity for goodness can never be realized unless he has some-one upon whom to shower his affections" (*Ha-Ketav ve-Ha-Kabbalah*).

In *Naked Nomads,* a study of single males, George Gilder re-peatedly demonstrates why this biblical verse should be understood literally; it is truly not good, and certainly not healthy, for man to be unattached. Among the statistics Gilder cites are the following: The death rate for late-middle-aged single men is more than twice as high as that for married men (page 16), single men are six times more likely to die from accidental falls (page 4), and bachelors are twenty-two times more likely to be committed for mental illness (page 19), three times more likely to suffer from insomnia (page 16), and far more likely to commit suicide.

It is similarly not good for society when men stay single. While single men comprise some 13 percent of the population over age fourteen, they commit about 90 percent of major and violent crimes.

> Therefore shall a man leave his father and mother and cleave to his wife, and they become one flesh.
>
> —Genesis 2:24

This verse implies that, after marriage, a man's primary loyalty should be transferred from his parents to his wife.

The total fusion of the life experiences of a marrying couple is suggested by an ancient talmudic tradition:

> It was the custom [in ancient Israel] that when a boy was born a cedar tree was planted and when a girl was born a pine tree. When they grew up and married, the wedding canopy was made of branches taken from both trees.
>
> —Babylonian Talmud, *Gittin* 57a

> Forty days before a child is born, a voice from heaven (*bat kol*) announces: "The daughter of this person is destined for so-and-so."
>
> —Babylonian Talmud, *Sotah* 2a

Some Jews understand this talmudic teaching quite literally: in the Orthodox world, people sometimes refer to a spouse as one's *bashert,* one's fated or destined partner.

Unfortunately, the enormous rise in divorce rates in recent years—a rise that also has been felt, although to a lesser extent, in traditional Jewish communities—has made it more difficult for many to believe that there exists a "destined" mate for everyone. But to a person like me, who didn't get married until he was thirty-nine, this talmudic teaching provided great comfort. And, lo and behold, I really did meet and marry my *bashert.*

119

Another rabbinic passage indicates that the sages were well aware that many people lived in awful marriages. If they invoked God as the ultimate marriage broker, it was because they felt that anything less than divine wisdom was inadequate:

> A Roman matron asked Rabbi Yossi ben Halaphta: "In how many days did God create the world?"
>
> He answered: "In six days, for so it is written [in Exodus 31:17], 'In six days the Lord made heaven and earth.'"
>
> "And what has He been doing since then?"
>
> "He has been arranging marriages: The daughter of such and such to so and so. . . ."
>
> "But that is something even I can do," said the matron. "I own many male servants and female servants, and I can couple them easily."
>
> Rabbi Yossi replied: "Arranging marriages may be a trivial matter in your eyes. Yet for God this task is as difficult as the splitting of the Red Sea."
>
> After Rabbi Yossi left the matron, she arranged for a row of one thousand menservants to be placed alongside a row of one thousand maidservants. Then, she commanded: "So-and-so is going to marry so-and-so, and so-and-so is going to marry so-and-so." The marriages were performed that very night.
>
> In the morning, the newly paired couples appeared before the matron, one with a cracked skull, another with a missing eye, a third with a broken leg. This one said, "I don't want that woman!" That one said, "I can't stand this man!"
>
> The Roman matron sent for Rabbi Yossi, and told him, "Your Torah is right, and what you have told me is absolutely true."
>
> Rabbi Yossi replied: "That is precisely what I have been telling you. You might think the arranging of marriages is an easy task. But for God it is as difficult as the splitting of the Red Sea."
>
> —*Pesikta d'Rav Kahana* 2:4

Given the Roman matron's unhappy experience, the Rabbis understandably opposed anyone, even a parent, arranging other people's marriages without input from the parties involved:

> A father is forbidden to marry off his daughter while she is a minor. He must wait until she is grown up and says, "I want so-and-so."
>
> —Babylonian Talmud, *Kiddushin* 41a

Many Jews to whom I have related this ruling express shock that the Talmud expresses such a sentiment. They long have been taught that religious Jews in Eastern Europe arranged marriages for their children, and that the intended partners met only briefly, shortly before marrying. True, such behavior was common, but it clearly violated the Talmud's wishes. Indeed, the above ruling's very wording presupposes a society in which unmarried men and women mixed; a woman thus would have had enough exposure to a potential groom to be able to tell her father, "I want so-and-so."

In an infrequently quoted passage, the Talmud damns those who arrange inappropriate marriages:

> One who marries his daughter to an old man, or takes a wife for his young son . . . concerning him, the Torah teaches . . . "the Lord will not pardon him."
>
> —Babylonian Talmud, *Sanhedrin* 76a, basing itself on Deuteronomy 29:19

The Talmud also provides instructions to would-be grooms:

> A man is forbidden to marry a woman until he first sees her, lest he later find her objectionable and she becomes repulsive to him.
>
> —Babylonian Talmud, *Kiddushin* 41a

POLYGAMY

[The son of Rabbi Judah the Prince] spent twelve years in study apart from his wife. By the time of his return, she had become sterile. On hearing of this, Rabbi Judah said, "How shall we act? If my son divorces her, people will say that this poor woman waited all those years in vain. If he takes a second wife, people will say that the second woman is his wife, and the other his harlot!" He prayed on her behalf and she was healed.

—Babylonian Talmud, *Ketubot* 62b

Although the Bible permitted polygamy, and some of its greatest figures had more than one wife (most notably Jacob, who had four wives), virtually every one of its polygamous marriages generated unhappiness. Thus, Genesis (29:30) tells us that Jacob "loved Rachel more than Leah." Needless to say, this made Leah miserable, and a few years later her embittered sons led the way in selling Joseph, Rachel's oldest son and their own half brother, into slavery. The very wording of Deuteronomy 21:15 assumes that multiple marriages often will generate multiple miseries: "If a man has two wives, the one beloved, and the other hated . . ."

This lesson was not lost on the Rabbis. Although the Talmud continued to permit polygamy (Jewish law formally outlawed it around 1000 C.E.), apparently none of the almost two thousand Rabbis it cites had more than one wife. One sage, Rabbi Isaac, ridiculed the problems of a man who decided to take a second, much younger wife:

A man had two wives, a young one and an old one. The young wife pulled out his white hair, and the old one pulled out his black hair. In the end, the poor man was left with no hair at all.

—Babylonian Talmud, *Bava Kamma* 60b

AN IMMORAL REASON FOR MARRYING

Whoever marries a woman for her money will have disreputable children.

—Babylonian Talmud, *Kiddushin* 70a

In other words, the children will be like him.

Over the years, quite a few people have told me that their parents raised them with axioms such as "You shouldn't marry for money, but then again it's just as easy to fall in love with a rich girl [or rich boy] as a poor one." The long-standing contempt in Jewish sources for such thinking is evident not only in the above passage, but in a thirteenth-century work of Jewish law and lore:

> A youth need not obey his parents if they urge him to marry not the girl he wants, but another with money, for they are not acting properly.
>
> —*Sefer Hasidim*, paragraph 953

Marrying for money often leads to misery not only for the rich partner who married under the erroneous assumption that he or she was loved, but for the unscrupulous spouse as well. As the late Rabbi Wolfe Kelman used to say, "Whoever marries for money ends up paying for it."

FIRST LOVE

> When a man's first wife dies during his lifetime, it is as though the Temple had been destroyed in his lifetime. . . . When a man's wife dies in his lifetime the world becomes dark for him.
>
> —Babylonian Talmud, *Sanhedrin* 22a

The talmudic Rabbis perceived the Temple's destruction with the same horror that Jews today perceive the Holocaust. Thus, the anguish with which they regarded the death of the "wife of one's youth" is evident.

> When a man marries a woman after his [dead] first wife, he remembers the deeds of the first.
>
> —Babylonian Talmud, *Berakhot* 32b

123

While there is little humor in this psychologically astute talmudic observation, it makes me recall a favorite story of America's wittiest president, Abraham Lincoln: "In the course of [a] sermon, the preacher asserted [that Jesus] was the only perfect man who had ever appeared in this world, also that there was no record in the Bible, or elsewhere, of any perfect woman having lived on this earth. Whereupon there arose in the rear of the Church a persecuted-looking personage who said, 'I know a perfect woman, and for the last six years.' 'Who was she?' asked the minister. 'My husband's first wife,' replied the afflicted female" (quoted in *Abraham Lincoln: The War Years* by Carl Sandburg).

INSTRUCTIONS TO HUSBANDS AND WIVES

> A man must always be exceedingly careful to show honor to his wife.
>
> —Babylonian Talmud, *Bava Mezia* 59a

The same page of the Talmud offers men several more behavioral guidelines. Most important, a man should be extremely careful not to hurt his wife with sharp words, since women are more apt than men to cry when insulted. Need one add how many spouses, when angry, seek out precisely the words that will cause their partner the most hurt!

The Talmud notes that one way of showing proper respect is to consult one's wife about all important decisions. "If your wife is short, bend down and whisper to her [and get her opinion]" is the colloquial way it expresses this thought: In other words, just because you are physically larger than your wife, don't assume you are greater than she.

> A man should love his wife as himself and honor her more than himself.
>
> —Babylonian Talmud, *Yevamot* 62b

Since "love his wife as himself" is simply a restatement of the biblical command to "Love your neighbor as yourself" (Leviticus

124

19:18), why did the Rabbis go out of their way to specify one's wife? Professor Reuven Kimelman, a Talmud scholar, explains that love in marriage is not always expressed as delicately as in other relationships. At social gatherings, one sometimes hears a man say things about his wife that he would not say about his business partner if he intended to continue working with him. Yet, if you ask him, "Why do you speak so harshly of your wife?" he responds, "Oh, she knows that I love her."

Kimelman suggests that the proof of whether or not you have carried out the command to "Love your neighbor [in this case, your wife] as yourself" is not whether *you* feel you have fulfilled it, but whether your wife feels that you love her as you love yourself.

One who properly fulfilled this commandment was the Israeli Rabbi Aryeh Levin, a modern saint. Once, when his wife, Hannah, was in pain, he accompanied her to Dr. Nahum Kook, and told the physician, "My wife's foot is hurting us" (Simcha Raz, *A Tzaddik in Our Time,* page 150).

Obviously, a wife is similarly obligated to "love her husband as herself." Indeed, Hannah Levin, Rabbi Aryeh's wife, shocked him one day with an unusual confession:

> "Aryeh, I must tell you that I am jealous of this-and-this woman, our neighbor." Reb Aryeh was puzzled: His good wife hardly knew what jealousy was. What reason had she to envy her neighbor? And who was this neighbor anyway?
>
> He soon found out:
>
> There was a rich man in Jerusalem, a person of standing in the community, who lost all his wealth. Creditors took everything he had, until he was forced to move to the Mishk'not section of Jerusalem, where Reb Aryeh lived. This was a poor, impoverished neighborhood, where there were not even bathrooms in homes, but only outhouses in the courtyards. To support his family, this formerly rich man had to go climbing up on a scaffold to work as a repairman on the exteriors of buildings, fixing defects, all in order to earn a small daily wage. Yet every evening, the neighbors noticed his wife going out in the

street dressed up in pretty clothes and finery.

The neighbors were amazed to see this, and began talking and gossiping about her. . . . Some time later, Hannah happened to be talking to the woman, and the reason behind her behavior became clear. "You see," said this neighbor, "when my husband returns home from work, his heart is just paralyzed. He is like a dead man. To think of it! He used to be so wealthy, and now he has to work like a common laborer! When I realized how downtrodden his spirit was, I decided that I must make myself attractive and go wait for him out there on Agrippas Street when he comes home from work—so that I can welcome him with a smiling face, and raise his morale."

"Nu," said Hannah to Reb Aryeh, "of that woman I am jealous. I have not reached her level of devotion."

—Simcha Raz, *A Tzaddik in Our Time*, page 62

*　　　*　　　*

Rabbi Simeon ben Gamliel said: If a man forbade his wife to do any work at all, he must divorce her and pay her *ketuba* [the amount promised in the marriage contract], for idleness leads to insanity.

—Mishna *Ketubot* 5:5

A man is not to see his wife merely as a plaything, and forbid her to have any area of expertise or responsibility. This reminds me of Walter Lippmann's comment in *A Preface to Morals:* "Lovers who have nothing to do but love each other are not really to be envied; love and nothing else very soon is nothing else."

MARRIAGE AND ITS DISCONTENTS

Among those who will never behold the face of hell (*gehennom*) is he who has a bad wife.

—Babylonian Talmud, *Eruvin* 41b

In other words, one who stays in a bad marriage endures such suffering that, by the time he dies, all his sins have been expiated.

126

Presumably, the same would apply to a woman married to a bad husband, but the Talmud characteristically addressed most of its teachings to men.

> Before you marry, make sure you know whom you are going to divorce.
> —Yiddish proverb, quoted in Hanan Ayalti, *Yiddish Proverbs*

Finally, a lighter note from a contemporary comic:

> We sleep in separate rooms, we have dinner apart, we take separate vacations—we're doing everything we can to keep our marriage together.
> —Rodney Dangerfield

17

"FOR LOVE IS
AS STRONG AS DEATH"

Romantic Love

A woman of valor who can find?
    For her value is far above rubies.

              —Proverbs 31:10

Among traditional Jews this verse initiates a love poem which a husband is expected to recite to his wife every Friday evening before the Sabbath dinner. The poem is written as an acrostic, each verse starting with a succeeding letter of the Hebrew alphabet. Among the traits that characterize a woman of valor: "She gives generously to the poor, her hands are stretched out to the needy. . . . Her mouth is full of wisdom, her tongue with kindly teaching."

The Hebrew for "a woman of valor" is "*aishet khayyil*"; to this day, this term is applied to any admirable Jewish woman. Thus, in the dedication to one of my earlier books I wrote: "For my wife Dvorah, concerning whom I would rephrase the verse from Proverbs to read, 'A woman of valor I have found.' "

> When our love was strong, we could have made our bed
> on the blade of a sword. Now that our love is no longer
> strong, a bed sixty cubits wide is not large enough.
>   —Babylonian Talmud, *Sanhedrin* 7a

128

Love is as strong as death.
—Song of Songs 8:6

Many waters cannot quench love, neither can floods drown it.
—Song of Songs 8:7

Rabbi Akiva said. . . . All the writings [in the Bible] are holy, but Song of Songs is the Holy of Holies.
—Mishna *Yadayim* 3:5

When determining which books to include in the Bible, some Rabbis apparently argued that Song of Songs should not be included; its vivid descriptions of male-female love, in their view, made the book anything but a holy text. Some fifty to a hundred years later, however, Rabbi Akiva claimed that there never could have been such a debate concerning the book's status since its sanctity was so obvious.

Rabbi Akiva's statement notwithstanding, the article on Song of Songs in the *Encyclopedia Judaica* (15:143–152) clearly suggests the book's unusual character: "The Song of Songs is unique in the Bible, for nowhere else within it can be found such a sustained paean to the warmth of love between man and woman. It is completely occupied with that one theme. No morals are drawn: no prophetic preachments are made. God receives no mention, and theological concerns are never discussed. While the Book of Esther also fails to mention God, an unmistakable spirit of nationalism permeates its pages; but the Song of Songs lacks even this theme."

The Rabbis of the Talmud claimed that Song of Songs was allegorical in nature, that it used the model of a man and a woman to explain the love between God and the Jewish people. The very use of such a model suggests the high regard Judaism had for male-female love and sexuality. This was not the case throughout the ancient world; in the Greco-Roman world, for example, women were commonly seen as vehicles for procreation, while sexual affection between males was understood to be a deeper form of love (e.g., in *Symposium*, Plato, who never married, makes it clear that it was fully acceptable to seduce a young lad, while in Edward Gibbon's *History of the Decline and Fall of the Roman Empire,* the author notes that Claudius was the only one of the first fifteen Roman emperors "whose taste in love was entirely correct" (i.e., not homosexual; see Dennis Prager, "Judaism, Homosexuality, and Civilization," *Ultimate Issues,* April–June 1990, page 5).

And, finally, the classic statement of romantic lovers from the Song of Songs:

I am my beloved's and my beloved is mine.

—Song of Songs 6:3

18

SEX: THE COMMANDED, THE PERMITTED, THE FORBIDDEN

THE POWER OF THE MALE SEX DRIVE: TALMUDIC REFLECTIONS

A man's sexual impulse is out in the open [his erection stands out and he embarrasses himself in front of his fellows]. A woman's sexual impulse is within and no one can recognize her [arousal].

> —Babylonian Talmud, *Ketubot* 64a; I have followed the
> translation of Rachel Biale, which incorporates into the
> first bracketed comment Rashi's explanation; see Biale's
> *Women and Jewish Law*, page 22.

There is a small organ in a man. If he starves it, it is satisfied. If he feeds it, it whets his appetite for more.

> —Babylonian Talmud, *Sukkah* 52b

Recognizing the power of the sex drive, the Rabbis advocated early marriage: for men at eighteen; for women, even earlier—any age, it would appear, past puberty:

A man who passes the age of twenty and is not yet married spends all his days in sin. In sin? Is that really so? Rather

131

say, he spends all his days in sinful thoughts.

—Babylonian Talmud, *Kiddushin* 29b

With considerable realism, the Rabbis saw sexual thoughts as omnipresent: Rabbi Isaac comments: "Even during the time a man is in mourning, his impulse is apt to overcome him" (Babylonian Talmud, *Kiddushin* 80b). In a much later period, a man is reputed to have asked the eighteenth-century Baal Shem Tov, the founder of Hasidism, how a person could discern a true religious leader from a false one. The Baal Shem Tov answered, "Ask him if he knows a way to prevent impure thoughts. If he says he does, he's a charlatan."

Similarly, the Talmud never associated saintliness with a dormant libido: "The greater a man, the greater his evil inclination" (Babylonian Talmud, *Sukkah* 52a), evil inclination here specifically connoting sex drive. The following is one of several talmudic tales depicting great rabbis struggling with their sexual passions:

> Several captive women [had been redeemed] and were brought to Nehardea [at night], where they were taken to an attic in the house of Rabbi Amram the Pious. The ladder to the attic was then removed. As one of the women walked by, the light [of her beauty] could be seen through the skylight. Seeing her, Rabbi Amram grabbed the ladder, which ten men could not lift, and set it up unaided. He started to climb up. After he had gone halfway, he forced himself to stand still and cried out, "A fire is burning in Rabbi Amram's house!" His disciples came running [and found him halfway up the ladder]. They told him, "You have made us put you to shame [for we see what you were intending to do]." Rabbi Amram answered, "Better that you shame Amram in this world than be ashamed of him in the next."
>
> —Babylonian Talmud, *Kiddushin* 81a

If a man sees that his evil impulse is conquering him, let him go to a place where he is unknown, put on black clothes, wrap himself in a black cloak, and do what his

132

heart desires, but let him not publicly profane God's name.
—Babylonian Talmud, *Kiddushin* 40a

Black clothes, Rabbi A. Cohen suggests, are worn "as a sign of mourning; it might achieve the purpose of sobering him" (*Everyman's Talmud*, page 92).

> There was a case where a certain man set his eyes on a certain woman and his heart became [so] consumed with burning desire [that his life was endangered]. When doctors were consulted, they said, "His only cure is that she submit to him." The sages responded, "Let him die rather than have her yield."
>
> "Then let her stand naked before him," [the doctors said].
>
> "Let him die rather than that she stand naked before him."
>
> "Then let her at least talk to him from behind a fence."
>
> "Let him die rather than that she talk to him from behind a fence."
>
> —Babylonian Talmud, *Sanhedrin* 75a

This passage, one of the most misunderstood in the Talmud, has led more than a few people to conclude that the sages were so puritanical that they deemed it preferable that an unmarried man die rather than converse with an unmarried woman.

However, this narrative has little to do with illicit sexual behavior: it really concerns emotional blackmail. Imagine the societal damage that would ensue if whenever one person's will was thwarted by another, the rejected party said he [or she] would die if the other party did not grant whatever he or she wished. Ultimately, the fact that this man is obsessed with this woman is *his* problem, and his alone (the Talmud provides no indication that the woman had led him on); thus, he is not entitled to make demands of her. As Hyam Maccoby insightfully notes: "What the story is really telling us is that no woman is required to sacrifice her status or dignity for the sake of a madman."

What makes this case so unusual is the doctors' claim that the man's life is at stake. Normally, when such a diagnosis is made, Jewish law permits a whole range of otherwise forbidden activities (see Chapter 11). For example, if the doctors had said the man must eat unkosher food lest he die, the Rabbis would have permitted it. But Jewish law never permits imposing unreasonable demands *on others,* even when a life is at stake. Thus, if the same man should insist that his cure is conditional on other people's eating unkosher food, this would not be permitted (see Hyam Maccoby, "Halakha and Sex Ethics," pages 141–142). Standards of behavior in Jewish life cannot be determined by the insane or the intransigent.

A WOMAN'S SEXUAL DRIVE AND NEEDS

If a man forbids himself by vow from having intercourse with his wife, the School of Shammai says [she must go along with the vow] for up to two weeks [if it lasts longer, the court can compel him to divorce her], but the school of Hillel says for [only] one week.

—Mishna *Ketubot* 5:6

Because the Rabbis considered women to be more inhibited than men in expressing sexual needs, they prescribed a minimum schedule of sexual relations based on their husband's professions (which in turn affected the men's availability):

For men of independent means, every day. For laborers, twice weekly. For donkey drivers, once a week. For camel drivers, once every thirty days. For sailors, once every six months.

—Mishna *Ketubot* 5:6

[Commentary of the fifteenth-century Rabbi Obadiah of Bartenura on this passage]: If someone was originally employed in a trade near his home and wished to change to a trade in which he would have to travel far from home, his wife may prevent him from changing, on the grounds that their sexual relations would become less frequent.

Thus, a man cannot on his own volition change from being a laborer to a camel driver, since "a woman would rather have one bushel and enjoyment with her husband than ten bushels and her husband away" (Babylonian Talmud, *Ketubot* 62b). In another passage, "A woman prefers little food and sexual indulgence to much food and continence" (Mishna *Sotah* 3:4).

The Talmud's understanding and acceptance of women's sexual nature suggests the antithesis of the stereotype of Jewish women conveyed in JAP jokes. While Jewish-American Princess jokes depict Jewish women as sexually cold and inordinately materialistic, the Talmud assumes a woman cares more about having her husband near her than about being rich.

In an extraordinary, and unexpected, combination of male chauvinism and openness to female sexuality, the Rabbis offered the following advice on how to guarantee the birth of a male child:

> Those who restrain themselves during intercourse to enable their wives to have orgasms first, their children shall be male [by implication, if the man has his orgasm first, the woman will give birth to a female].
> —Babylonian Talmud, *Niddah* 31b

TWO CONTRASTING JEWISH AND NEW TESTAMENT ATTITUDES ON SEXUALITY

On the desirability of sexual relations

Be fruitful and multiply.
> —God's command to Adam and Eve (Genesis 1:28);
> see pages 143–146.

One who [willfully] does not engage in propagation of the race is like someone who has shed blood . . . and as one who diminished the Divine Image [since having children increases the number of people created in the image

135

of God, and not having children decreases the number of people in God's image].

—Babylonian Talmud, *Yevamot* 63b

Paul, however, writes: "It is well for a man not to touch a woman, but because of the temptation to immorality, each man should have his own wife and each woman her own husband. . . . I say this by way of concession, not command. I wish that all were as I am [celibate]. . . . To the unmarried . . . I say that it is well for them to remain single as I do. But if they cannot exercise self-control, they should marry. For it is better to marry than to burn with passion" (I Corinthians 7).

In contrast to Paul's exaltation of celibacy, when Jephtah's daughter learns that she will be sacrificed in two months because of a monstrous vow her father has taken, the Bible reports that she went off into the hills to bewail her virginity (Judges 11:37).

On adultery

Jesus taught: "You have heard that it was said, 'You shall not commit adultery,' but I say to you that every one who looks at a woman lustfully has already committed adultery with her in his heart" (Matthew 5:27–28).

Jesus' comment became famous, even among non-Bible scholars, during the 1976 American presidential campaign, when Democratic candidate Jimmy Carter confessed in a *Playboy* interview that he had often lusted after women in his heart and so considered himself guilty of being an adulterer (indeed, by Jesus' standard, there never have been more than a handful of heterosexual males who are not adulterers).

Judaism's attitude is that the deed, not the thought, is what counts. That's why the Seventh of the Ten Commandments legislates, "You shall not *commit* adultery" (Exodus 20:13).

HOW SEXUAL RELATIONS DIFFER FROM OTHER COMMANDMENTS

A rabbinic midrash imagines David thinking the following about his father:

> Did my father Jesse really intend to bring me into the world? Why, he had only his own pleasure in mind. . . . As soon as he and my mother satisfied their desires, he turned his face to one side and she turned her face to the other side. It was You who then led every drop [of semen] to its proper place.
>
> —*Leviticus Rabbah* 14:5

Rabbi Michael Gold comments: "[Since] it is all but impossible to begin the sexual act with only holiness in mind, accordingly, the Rabbis did not ordain a blessing before the sexual act as they did before other *mitzvot* (commandments)" (*Does God Belong in the Bedroom?*, page 15).

ON PREMARITAL SEX: A CONTEMPORARY, AND DECIDEDLY NON-ORTHODOX, GUIDELINE

> Living in a world where we cannot [practically] advocate either ideal sex or no sex as the alternatives, what we must begin to evolve is a sliding scale of sexual values. . . . At the top of this scale would stand the fully knowing and loving relationship . . . while rape—fully unconsenting . . . sexuality—would stand at the bottom. Somewhere near the middle of the scale, neither glorified nor condemned, would be the relationship of two consenting persons, treating one another with decency, fulfilling the biological aspects of one another's love needs, while making no pretense at deeper intimacy. Given such a scale, a Jew might begin to judge his/her own sexual behavior in terms of a series of changes which s/he might want to address.
>
> —Arthur Green, "A Contemporary Approach to Jewish Sexuality," page 99

Rabbi Green's view summarizes the thinking about premarital sex most common among non-Orthodox Jews. Within Orthodoxy, an absolute ban against premarital sexual relations, indeed against any physical intimacy between an unmarried couple, remains in force.

This prohibition is linked to the Bible's stringent laws against sexual relations during and after the time a woman is menstruating. Subsequent to her period, she is expected to immerse herself in a *mikveh* (ritual bath) and only after doing so is she permitted to have intercourse. In theory, an unmarried woman who goes to a *mikveh* is permitted to have sex; "in theory," because in Orthodox circles, unmarried women are not permitted to go to a *mikveh*—to ensure that premarital sex does not ensue.

Although the Bible outlaws adultery and incest, it never forbids sexual relations between two unmarried partners. Nonetheless, one rabbinic proponent of the double standard, Rabbi Eliezer, taught, "An unmarried man who had intercourse with an unmarried woman with no matrimonial intent renders her thereby with the status of a *zonah* (prostitute)," and thereby forbidden to marry a Jew of priestly descent. Nonetheless, Jewish law rules against him (Babylonian Talmud, *Yevamot* 61b; see Maimonides, *Mishneh Torah,* "Laws of Forbidden Sexual Relations," 17:13).

> For Judaism, the value in human sexuality comes only when the relationship involves two people who have committed themselves to one another and have made that commitment in a binding covenant recognized by God and society. The act of sexual union, the deepest personal statement that any human being can make, must be reserved for the moment of total oneness.
>
> —Rabbi Maurice Lamm, *The Jewish Way in
> Love and Marriage,* page 31

FORBIDDEN SEX

Adultery

You shall not commit adultery.
—The Seventh of the Ten Commandments; Exodus 20:13

The Bible regards adultery as an act of betrayal against both one's spouse and against God. Thus, when Joseph worked as a slave for Potiphar in Egypt, and Potiphar's wife tried to seduce him, he said to her: "How can I do this most wicked thing, and sin before God" (Genesis 39:9).

Biblical law both rejected and enshrined the double standard. On the one hand, when a man, single or married, slept with a *married* woman, both parties were condemned as adulterers. On the other, because biblical law permitted polygamy, a married man committed adultery only when he slept with a woman who was forbidden to him, i.e., a married woman. If he slept with an unmarried woman, this was not regarded as adultery since he was permitted to take her as his wife, whether or not he ever intended to do so. Thus, in determining whether or not adultery had been committed, the woman's marital status was what was decisive. A married woman who slept with anyone other than her husband always committed adultery, while an unmarried woman never did.

Although the Bible designated adultery as a capital offense (Leviticus 20:10), the Torah and Talmud imposed so many judicial requirements for conviction (e.g., requiring two witnesses who had warned the couple in advance) that the law, in effect, became a dead letter.

Yet when adultery clearly had occurred, two lesser, but very severe, penalties were imposed:

1. The adulteress was both prohibited from remaining married to her husband (even if he was willing to forgive her) and forbidden to marry her lover.

2. A child who ensued from the adulterous relationship was characterized as a *mamzer* (bastard), and forbidden to marry other Jews besides *mamzerim*. (Significantly, the offspring of a relationship between two unmarried people was not regarded as either a "bastard" or "illegitimate.")

These two laws' severity caused many tenderhearted Rabbis to deny that adultery had occurred even in instances where it clearly had. Thus, the sixteenth-century Code of Jewish Law, the *Shulkhan Arukh*, ruled that if a woman gave birth to a child up to a full year after her husband had gone off to sea, we simply assume that she had a very long pregnancy (*Even ha-Ezer* 4:14). Rabbi Michael Gold has observed, "[The Rabbis] were willing to ignore biological facts to avoid ending the marriage and imposing the stigma of 'bastard' on the newly born child" (*Does God Belong in the Bedroom?*, page 54).

Rape

If a man comes upon a virgin who is not engaged and he seizes her and lies with her, and they are discovered, the man who lay with her shall pay the girl's father fifty [shekels of] silver, and she shall be his wife. Because he has violated her, he can never have the right to divorce her.

—Deuteronomy 22:28–29

In the ancient world, virginity was considered so important a prerequisite for a woman hoping to marry that a rape victim probably would never find a husband. However, the Talmud made it clear that the rapist is compelled to marry his victim only if she consents.

If the raped woman already is legally engaged or married, the rapist incurs a death sentence.

Regarding marital rape:

A man should never force himself upon his wife and never overpower her, for the Divine spirit never rests upon one whose sexual relations occur in the absence of desire, love and free will. . . . The Talmud tells us that just as a lion tears at his prey and eats it shamelessly, so does an ignorant man shamelessly strike and sleep with his wife (Babylonian Talmud, *Pesachim* 49b). Rather act so that you will warm her heart by speaking to her charming and seductive words.

—*Iggeret ha-Kodesh*, attributed to the thirteenth-century
Bible scholar Moses Nachmanides

OBSCENITY

Said Rabbi Hanan, the son of Rav: Everybody knows why the bride enters the bridal chamber, but if anyone speaks obscenely about it, even if seventy years of happiness have been decreed and sealed for him on High, the decree is changed for him into evil.

—Babylonian Talmud, *Ketubot* 8b

My friend Rabbi Jack Riemer of Miami likewise expresses great exasperation at the obscene jokes that frequently are told by people attending a circumcision. Turning the sacred ceremony through which a male Jewish baby enters the covenant into a source for ribald humor demonstrates how obscenity can desecrate the sense of the sacred. For if entering the covenant is turned into a source of jokes, then the covenant itself eventually will be treated as a joke.

HOMOSEXUALITY

Do not lie with a male as one lies with a woman; it is an abomination.

—Leviticus 18:22; Leviticus 20:13 designates
the offense as capital.

"You shall not copy the practices of the land of Egypt where you dwelt, or of the land of Canaan to which I am taking you" (Leviticus 18:3). . . . What did they do? A man would marry a man and a woman would marry a woman.

—*Sifra Leviticus* on 18:3

In recent years, Judaism's categorical rejection of homosexuality has come under strong attack. In 1972, the Reform movement ac-

cepted a gay-oriented synagogue into the Union of American Hebrew congregations; eighteen years later, the Central Conference of
American [Reform] Rabbis ruled that avowed homosexuals could
serve as rabbis. Although hundreds of articles have appeared on
both sides of this issue, the following quotations pretty well summarize the positions of the two sides:

> In my view, the Jewish condemnation of homosexuality is
> the work of human beings—limited, imperfect, fearful of
> what is different and, above all, concerned with ensuring
> tribal survival. In short, I think our ancestors were wrong
> about a number of things, and homosexuality is one of
> them.
>
> —Rabbi Janet Marder, "Jewish and Gay"; Rabbi Marder has
> served as rabbi of Beth Chayyim Chadashim,
> a gay synagogue in Los Angeles.

While Marder's focus is on the narrowness of the Torah and
Talmud's concern with "ensuring tribal survival" [through an emphasis on family life], this is precisely the issue that motivates Dennis
Prager, a prominent contemporary Jewish political and social critic,
to oppose ordaining homosexuals:

> Even if . . . it is proven that some people are geneti-
> cally homosexual, the Jewish principle of exalting
> marriage and family life would still have to remain
> intact. Would this be unfair to the born homosexual
> who wished to be a rabbi? Yes, it would. But for the
> sake of society, life is filled with unfairness to indi-
> viduals. Stutterers, no matter how brilliant, cannot be
> radio commentators or talk-show hosts, because no
> matter how insightful and witty, they cannot do the
> job right. . . . Avowed homosexuals, no matter how
> Jewishly knowledgeable and personally kind, cannot
> become rabbis because they cannot do the job of be-
> ing a Jewish role model right.
>
> —Dennis Prager, "Judaism, Homosexuality, and Civilization"

19

"BE FRUITFUL AND MULTIPLY"

The Duty to Have Children

THE DUTY TO HAVE CHILDREN

Then God blessed them [Adam and Eve] and said: Be fruitful and multiply and fill the earth.

—Genesis 1:28

This is the first of the Torah's 613 commandments. The Talmud understood this commandment as obligating only males (Babylonian Talmud, *Yevamot* 65b). Rabbi Meir Simkha of Dvinsk (1843–1926) explains why:

The Torah freed the woman from the religious obligation to "be fruitful and multiply [because] . . . the woman endangers her life in pregnancy and childbirth [and hence cannot be obligated to have children]. . . . But for the sake of the preservation of the species did God so form woman's nature that her yearning to have children is stronger than the man's."

—Rabbi Meir Simkha of Dvinsk, *Meshech Hokhmah* commenting on Genesis 9:1

Thus, because the pain and danger of childbirth was particularly great in the premodern world, the Rabbis did not make propagation obligatory for women, since it would be immoral to obligate a person to do something that causes enormous hardship and endangers life. Indeed, the Rabbis assumed that during the most painful moments of delivery, almost all birthing women would swear never to have sexual relations again. Consequently, when the Temple was standing, new mothers brought a sacrifice to free them from such a vow.

Ironically, the Torah's first commandment is one of the less observed among contemporary American Jews, who have fewer children than the national average. Among Orthodox Jews, however, the average number of children per couple is much higher, and among ultra-Orthodox Jews it is common to find families with six or more children.

> [Let not the fear of bad offspring deter you]. . . . You do your duty and the Holy One will do what pleases Him.
> —Babylonian Talmud, *Berakhot* 10a

This is the Talmud's conclusion to an imagined conversation between the prophet Isaiah and King Hezekiah. One of the kingdom of Judah's eminent monarchs, Hezekiah sired Manasseh, who sired Amon, two of the most evil kings ever to rule the Jews. According to this talmudic dialogue, Hezekiah, while still childless, explained to Isaiah that he had no intention of propogating since he had seen in a vision that evil children would spring from him. To this, Isaiah responded with the statement quoted above.

While obvious exceptions come to mind (if only Hitler's mother had practiced birth control!), the contemporary implication seems to be that would-be parents should not look for excuses not to bring children into the world.

> It happened once that a man who made out his will specified: "My son shall inherit nothing of mine until he acts like a fool." Rabbi Yossi ben Judah and Rabbi [Judah] went to Rabbi Joshua ben Korcha to get his opinion re-

garding the meaning of this unusual provision. When they found [Rabbi Joshua], they saw him crawling on his hands and knees, a reed sticking out of his mouth, and being pulled along by his young son.

Seeing this, the two rabbis withdrew and went to his house. When they asked him about the provision in the will, he began to laugh, and said: "As you live, this business you are asking about [acting like a fool] could apply to me only a few moments ago." And he went on to say, "When a person has children, it is not unusual for him to act like a fool [when it comes to his children]."

—*Midrash Psalms* 92:13

HOW MANY CHILDREN SHOULD A COUPLE HAVE?

A man may not refrain from fulfilling the commandment, "Be fruitful and multiply," unless he already has children.

The School of Shammai ruled that he must have [a minimum of] two sons [to be considered as having fulfilled the commandment].

The School of Hillel ruled: a son and a daughter, for it is written, "Male and female He created them" (Genesis 5:2).

—Mishna *Yevamot* 6:6

Jewish law rules according to the School of Hillel. A couple, where possible, should at least replace themselves (i.e., they should have at least one child of each sex).

No marital relations in years of famine.

—Babylonian Talmud, *Ta'anit* 11a

Since the Talmud does exclude people who have not yet had any children from this provision, the contemporary application might well be that couples who already have children, and who are undergoing great financial hardship (i.e., comparable to "years of famine"), are not required to have more children.

145

ADOPTION

Whoever brings up an orphan in his home is regarded by
the Bible as though the child had been born to him.
—Babylonian Talmud, *Sanhedrin* 19b

The Talmud bases this conclusion on the story of Michal, the
daughter of King Saul. While one verse in the Bible informs us that
Michal was childless (II Samuel 6:23), another verse describes her
as the mother of five sons (II Samuel 21:8). The Talmud notes that
the five sons were actually born to her sister, Merab, and that subsequent to Merab's early death, Michal raised them, and was credited as being their mother.

The high status of adoptive parents is reflected in a passage concerning one of the Talmud's greatest scholars:

[Abbaye's father died when his mother conceived him, and
his mother died when she bore him]. But that is not so,
for Abbaye used to say, "My mother told me." That was
his adoptive mother.
—Babylonian Talmud, *Kiddushin* 31b

20

BETWEEN PARENTS
AND CHILDREN

WHAT CHILDREN OWE PARENTS

Honor your father and mother.
> —Exodus 20:12; the Fifth of the Ten Commandments

The often confused mixture of emotions that children feel for parents perhaps accounts for the peculiar fact that while the Bible legislates love of neighbor (Leviticus 19:18), the stranger (Leviticus 19:34), and God (Deuteronomy 6:5), it does not do so for parents. In so vital and intense a relationship, love is too volatile an emotion to be commanded; therefore, the Bible demands a standard of honor and respect that can remain in force even in times of estrangement.

You shall each revere [alternatively, fear] his mother and father.
> —Leviticus 19:3

Our Rabbis taught: What is "revere" and what is "honor"? "Revere" means that a child must neither stand nor sit in his [father's] place, nor contradict his words, nor tip the scale against him [by siding with his opponents in a dispute].

"Honor" means that a child must give him [i.e., his parents] food and drink, clothe and cover him, and lead

147

him in and out [when they are old and need a helping hand].

—Babylonian Talmud, *Kiddushin* 31b

If a father unwittingly transgresses a Torah law, his child should not say to him, "Father, you have transgressed a Torah law." He should say, "Father, is that what it says in the Torah?" But aren't both expressions equally insulting? So what he should really say is, "Father, the Torah says such-and-such" [and let the father draw his own conclusions].

—Babylonian Talmud, *Sanhedrin* 81a

*　　*　　*

The love of parents goes to their children, but the love of these children goes to their children.

—Babylonian Talmud, *Sotah* 49a

In his novel, *The Conversion of Chaplain Cohen,* the late Rabbi Herbert Tarr tells the story of David, an orphaned young man raised by a loving aunt and uncle. In one scene, as he goes off to enter the American army as a chaplain, they escort him to the train station:

David grabbed their rough peddler's hands in his smooth student ones. "How can I ever begin to repay you for what you've done for me!" Uncle Asher spoke gently: "There's a saying, 'The love of parents goes to their children, but the love of these children goes to their children.'"

"That's not so!" David protested. "I'll always be trying to—"

Tante Dvorah interrupted. "David, what your Uncle Asher means is that a parent's love isn't to be paid back; it can only be passed on."

—Herbert Tarr, *The Conversion of Chaplain Cohen*

In a poignant passage, a contemporary Orthodox scholar meditates on the difference between the love of children and the love of parents:

A person loses his father. It is very sad. A time for retrospection and repentance. How does the son feel, however, when he suddenly hears that his father in passing left an enormous inheritance for him? . . . With the sadness, there is nonetheless still some joy. The grief can be pushed aside for a bit of materialistic joy. But, when the contrary happens, and the son passes away and leaves behind more wealth than the world has ever seen . . . the father doesn't care [at all] for the money. He cares for his son. . . . He says, "Let the world have the money! What is money to me, alas, I have lost my blessed son! I would rather be the poorest man in the world if I could only have my dearest child." When Absalom died, David reacted with fierce cries of pain. He cried, "My son! My son!" seven times. Even though Absalom had tried to kill his own father, still David cried, "*B'nee! B'nee!* My son! My son!." . . . Imagine! A murderer so fierce, that he was out to kill his own father, and yet David cried, "My son! My son! I have lost you forever." Father and son. Who emotionalizes more for whom?

—Mordechai Menachem Reich, *The Crown of Wisdom*,
Vol. II, pages 298–299

WHEN CHILDREN AND PARENTS DISAGREE

The Torah teaches: "You shall each revere his mother and father, and keep My Sabbaths: I am the Lord your God" (Leviticus 19:3).

The Talmud comments: "From where do we learn that if one's father told him: . . . 'Do not return a lost object' [or, alternatively, to desecrate the Sabbath] that the son should not listen to him? From the verse, 'You shall each revere his mother and father, and keep my Sabbaths'— you are all [your parents no less than you] obligated to honor Me."

—Babylonian Talmud, *Bava Metzia* 32a

In other words, one does not owe one's parents control over one's conscience. As a popular nineteenth-century code of Jewish law, the *Kitzur Shulkhan Arukh*, rules:

If a child is told by his father not to speak to, or forgive, a certain person with whom the child wishes to be reconciled, he should disregard his father's command. . . .

—*Kitzur Shulkhan Arukh* 143:11

The father's command would be justifiable only if the person was a particularly malevolent sinner. Otherwise, it is wrong to hate another person, and by commanding his son to act in a hateful manner, the father is in effect commanding him to violate the words of the Torah.

Jewish educator Steven Brown notes that the "admonition that a child not listen to a parent who tells him not to forgive or reconcile with a certain person is profoundly important in a world of increasing family tensions and often devastating breaks in the nuclear family structure" ("Parents As Partners with God," page 44).

WHEN PARENTS GROW OLD OR BECOME MENTALLY DISTURBED

When a father gives to his son, both laugh. When a son gives to his father, both cry.

—Yiddish proverb

A son must not dishonor his father in his speech. How so? For example, when the father is old and wants to eat early in the morning, as old men do because they are weak . . . and the son says, "The sun is not yet up, and already you're up and eating."

Or when the father says, "My son, how much did you pay for this coat [which you have given me]?" And the son says, "What do you bother yourself for? I bought it and I have paid for it, it is no business of yours to ask about it!"

Or when he thinks to himself, saying: "When will this old man die so that I can be free of what he costs me?"

—Rabbi Israel ben Joseph Alnakawa (died as a martyr in 1391),
Spanish rabbi, *Menorat ha-Maor*, chapter 4; cited in
Francine Klagsbrun, *Voices of Wisdom*, page 191

A man may feed his father fattened chickens and inherit hell, and another may put his father to work treading a mill and inherit the Garden of Eden.

How is it possible for a man to feed his father fattened chickens and inherit hell?

There was a man who used to feed his father fattened chickens. Once his father said to him, "My son, where did you get these?" He answered, "Old man, old man, shut up and eat, just as dogs shut up when they eat." Such a man feeds his father on fattened chickens but inherits hell.

How is it possible for a man to put his father to work in a mill and still inherit the Garden of Eden?

There was a man who worked in a mill. The king ordered that millers be brought to work for him. Said the man to his father, "Father, you stay here and work in the mill in my place [and I will go to work for the king]. For if insults come to the workers, I prefer that they fall on me and not on you. Should floggings come, let them beat me and not you." Such a man puts his father to work in a mill yet inherits the Garden of Eden.

—Palestinian Talmud, *Kiddushin* 1:7

A man once came to Rabbi Hayyim of Brisk (an early 20th-century sage) with the following question: He had heard that his father was ill, and felt obliged to visit him. But since Jewish law rules that a child need not spend money honoring parents, perhaps he was not obliged to make the journey, since he would be forced to purchase a train ticket. Rabbi Hayyim answered tersely: "Correct, you are not obliged to spend the money. Walk!"

—Based on Gerald Blidstein, *Honor Thy Father and Mother: Filial Responsibility in Jewish Law and Ethics*, page 72

If one's father or mother become mentally disordered, [the child] should try to indulge the vagaries of the stricken parent, until they are pitied by God [and die]. But if he finds he cannot endure the situation because of their extreme madness, let him leave and go away, and appoint others to care for them properly.

—Moses Maimonides, *Mishneh Torah*, "Laws Concerning Rebels," 6:10

151

Once he [Dama the son of Netinah] was seated among the
great men of Rome, dressed in a silken gold garment, when
his mother came and tore the garment from him, slapped him
on the head, and spat in his face. But he did not shame her.

—Babylonian Talmud, *Kiddushin* 31a

The Rabbis told many stories about Dama, a non-Jew; almost
all revolve around his exemplary respect for his parents. It is remarkable how willing they were to learn the proper way to observe
the Fifth Commandment from the behavior of this righteous gentile.

It is natural for old people to be despised by the general
population when they can no longer function as they once
did, but sit idle, and have no purpose. The commandment,
"Honor your father and mother" was given specifically for
this situation.

—Gur Aryeh ha-Levi, a seventeenth-century commentator, on the
Fifth Commandment, in his *Melekhet Mahshevet;* cited in
Francine Klagsbrun, *Voices of Wisdom,* page 198

Among the storks, the old birds stay in the nests when
they are unable to fly, while the children fly . . . over sea
and land, gathering from every quarter provisions for the
needs of their parents. . . . With this example before them,
should not human beings who take no thought for their
parents deservedly hide their faces in shame . . . ?

—Philo, first century, *On the Decalogue,* sections 116–118;
translation by F. H. Colson, *Philo,* Vol. 7, pages 67–69

The difficulties experienced in many parents' older years might
have been behind this unexpected reflection:

[Rabbi Shimon bar Yohai said that] the most difficult [to
observe] of all the [613] commandments is "Honor your
father and mother."

—*Tanhuma, Ekev,* 2; the word Rabbi Shimon uses for difficult,
hamur, can alternatively be translated as "serious."

A man should honor his father and mother more for the moral instruction they gave him, than for their having brought him into this world. For in bringing him into this world, their own pleasure was their motive.

—Rabbi Israel ben Joseph Alnakawa,
Menorat Ha-Maor, chapter 4

WHAT PARENTS OWE CHILDREN

The father is obliged to circumcise his son, to redeem him [if he is a firstborn; see Numbers 18:15–6], to teach him Torah, to find him a wife, and to teach him a trade or profession.

—Babylonian Talmud, *Kiddushin* 29a

Rabbi Judah says: Whoever does not teach his son a trade or profession teaches him to be a thief.

—Babylonian Talmud, *Kiddushin* 29a

The Talmud explains that because an uneducated child is not equipped to earn a living honestly, he will end up engaging in illegal activities.

Some say he must also teach him how to swim. . . . What is the reason? His life may depend on it.

—Babylonian Talmud, *Kiddushin* 30b

In the ancient world, where so much travel occurred over bodies of water, swimming was a necessary survival skill. In contemporary terms, this obligation means that parents are required to teach their children analogous skills, i.e., obeying traffic signals, driving carefully, CPR.

An adult should make an effort to provide for the needs of his children, and the next generation in general, even after he or she dies:

Once the emperor Hadrian was walking along the road near Tiberias in the Galilee, and he saw an old man working the soil to plant some fig trees.

"If you had worked in your early years, old man," he said, "you would not have to work now so late in your life."

"I have worked both early and late," the man answered. "And what pleases the Lord, He has done with me."

"How old are you?" asked Hadrian.

"A hundred years old," the man answered.

"A hundred years old, and yet you stand there breaking up the soil to plant trees!" said Hadrian. "Do you expect to eat the fruit of the trees?"

"If I am worthy, I will eat," said the old man. "But if not, as my father worked for me, I work for my children."

—*Leviticus Rabbah* 25:5

COMMONSENSE PARENTING

The rule that "a father may forgo the honor due him" applies to his honor. But he may not allow himself to be struck or cursed.

—Rabbi Ahai, *She'iltot* 60

Rav was [constantly] tormented by his wife. If he asked her to cook lentils for him, she would cook peas. If he asked for peas, she would cook lentils.

When his son Hiyya grew up, he gave her his father's messages, but reversed what his father had told him (i.e., if his father wanted lentils, he would say that he wanted peas).

One day, Rav said to his son, "Your mother has improved."

Said Hiyya, "[That is because] I reversed your messages."

Said Rav, "That is what people say, 'your own offspring teach you reason.' Nevertheless, do not do so anymore, for the [Bible is a higher authority than the people, and the] Bible says, 'They have taught their tongues to speak lies' " (Jeremiah 9:4).

—Babylonian Talmud, *Yevamot* 63a

In Rav's view, a parent's obligation to raise a child to be truthful overrides any convenience that might accrue to the parent from the child's lies. The contemporary upshot from this two-thousand-year-old story? It's wrong to accustom a child to telling lies, whether they be to unwanted telephone callers ("Tell them Mommy's not home") or to ticket agents at movie theaters ("Tell them 'I'm only eleven,' ") in cases where a twelve-year-old is charged as an adult). Need it be added that a parent also should not lie to a child:

> One should not promise a child something, and then not give it to him, because as a result, the child will learn to lie.
>
> —Babylonian Talmud, *Sukkah* 46b

In addition, parents should refrain from being menacing or otherwise inducing fear in their children:

> A man should never impose an overpowering fear upon his household.
>
> —Babylonian Talmud, *Gittin* 6b

Many people suffer when the head of a household has a bad temper, including him- or herself. The Talmud records that it was great fear of Rabbi Hanina ben Gamliel's rage that caused his servant to feed him unkosher food after kosher foodstuffs suddenly disappeared (ibid., 7a).

A bad-tempered head of the house, the Talmud also claims, will even cause death, given that members of his household will flee his wrath and, in their haste, meet with fatal accidents (ibid., 6b).

In most cases, however, it is the children who suffer most when the house has a bad-tempered parent:

> A young child from Bnai Brak broke a bottle on the Sabbath. His father threatened to box his ears, and the boy, afraid, killed himself in a [deep] pit. They came and con-

155

sulted Rabbi Akiva, who said: "No mourning rites whatever are to be withheld" [because Jewish law regards
suicide as a form of murder, certain religious rites are supposed to be withheld in such cases].

As a result of this [and similar] incident[s], the Rabbis
said: A person should not threaten a child even with [as
small a thing as] boxing his ears. Rather, he should punish
him immediately, or say nothing.

—Babylonian Talmud, the minor talmudic
tractate of *Semakhot* 2:5–6

If one can claim to have a least favorite verse in the Bible, mine
is the advice proffered in Proverbs (13:24): "He that spares the rod
hates his son." Building on the spirit of this teaching is a verse from
the apocryphal book *Ecclesiasticus* (30:1): "A man who loves his
son will whip him often so that when he grows up, he may be a joy
to him."

A great deal of cruelty has been committed in the name of these
verses, both by parents and teachers. The great Hebrew poet, Hayim
Nahman Bialik, offered bitter autobiographical recollections of the
elementary school in which he studied, particularly how his life was
made wretched by teachers who believed in the verse from Proverbs:
"[They] knew only to hurt, each one in his own way. The *rebbe*
used to hit with a whip, with his fist, with his elbow, with his wife's
rolling pin, or with anything else that would cause pain. But his
assistant, whenever my answer to his question was wrong, would
advance toward me, with the fingers of his palm extended and bend
before my face and seize me by my throat. He would look to me
then like a leopard or a tiger or some other such wild beast and I
would be in mortal dread. I was afraid he would gouge out my eyes
with his dirty fingernails and the fear would paralyze my mind so
that I forgot everything I had learned the previous day."

This description of horrendous behavior certainly does not reflect a uniform pattern in Jewish thinking. No less characteristic,
and infinitely sweeter, is the advice offered in the Talmud: "If you
must strike a child, hit him only with a shoelace" (Babylonian Talmud, *Shabbat* 10b).

156

A man should never single out one of his children for favored treatment, for because of two extra coins' worth of
silk, which Jacob gave to Joseph and not to his other sons,
Joseph's brothers became jealous of him, and one thing
led to another until our ancestors became slaves in Egypt.
—Babylonian Talmud, *Shabbat* 10b

The Talmud is referring here to the silk coat of many colors that
Jacob bestowed on Joseph, the second-to-last of his twelve sons, and
his favorite. Unfortunately, the patriarch made no effort to conceal
his partiality. Given this, coupled with Joseph's propensity for tat-
tling to his father about his brothers' misdeeds, and for sharing with
his brothers dreams that depicted them as bowing down to him, it
is no wonder that the brothers came to hate him. Eventually, they
sold him as a slave into Egypt, and told Jacob that he had been
killed by a wild animal (Genesis 37). How ironic that the very coat
through which Jacob expressed his special love for Joseph made him
hated by other family members.

While parents often feel different emotions for different children,
the Rabbis regard it as repugnant to treat children differently as a
result. That is one reason Rabbi Samuel admonished Rabbi Judah
to do whatever was in his power to dissuade parents from disinher-
iting a "bad son" to benefit a good one for, among other reasons,
"one never knows what issue will come from the bad son" (see
Babylonian Talmud, *Bava Bathra* 133b and *Ketubot* 53a).

When parents who refused to support their children were
brought before Rabbi Hisda, he would say: "Turn a mor-
tar upside down in public, and have the delinquent father
stand on it and declare: 'Even a raven cares for its young,
but I do not care for my young.'"
—Babylonian Talmud, *Ketubot* 49b

Your son is at five your master, at ten your servant, at
fifteen your double, and after that, your friend or foe, de-
pending on his bringing up.
—Hasdai ibn Crescas, c. 1230

In a similar vein, a twentieth-century Yiddish writer has advised:

The best security for old age: respect your children.

—Sholem Asch

PARENTAL INFLUENCE

What the child says in the street is his father's words or his mother's.

—Babylonian Talmud, *Sukkah* 56b

Rabbi Huna, citing Rabbi Yochanan, told the parable of a man who opened a perfume shop for his son on a street inhabited by prostitutes. The prostitutes plied their trade, the perfume store owners plied theirs [prostitutes were constant users of perfume], and the boy, like any young man, indulged his natural inclination, and fell into depraved ways. When the father came and caught him with a prostitute, he began to shout, "I'll kill you!" But the father's friend was there, and he said: "You yourself ruined your son, and now you are yelling at him! You ignored all other occupations and taught him to be a perfumer; you ignored all other streets and deliberately opened a shop for him in the street of prostitutes!"

—*Exodus Rabbah* 43:7; a very condensed and somewhat different version of the story is found in the Babylonian Talmud, *Berakhot* 32a.

BITTERSWEET REFLECTIONS ON PARENTS AND CHILDREN

Concerning children who grow up and give their parents grief, a talmudic Rabbi ruminated:

Rabbi Judah ben Rabbi Nahmani said: "It is like a man who bought a knife to cut meat. The knife slipped and cut his finger. He said: 'I bought a knife with which to cut

158

meat—did I buy it to cut my finger?' So, too, a man produces offspring to honor him, and they curse him."

—*Midrash Samuel* 7:1

One father can support ten sons; ten sons cannot support one father.

—Medieval Jewish proverb

TWO MODERN REFLECTIONS ON ADULT CHILDREN AND THEIR PARENTS

Parents give you advice and never stop to think of what you think of what they turned out to be.

—Harold Brodkey, *First Love and Other Sorrows*

A Jewish man with parents alive is a fifteen-year-old boy, and will remain a fifteen-year-old boy until they die.

—Philip Roth, *Portnoy's Complaint*

Roth's comment brings to mind the joke about the Jewish mother who charges into her son's room. "You've got to get up for school, Bernie."

Bernie pulls the blanket over his head. "I don't wanna go to school."

"You have to go," the mother says.

"I don't wanna. The teachers hate me, and all the kids make fun of me."

The mother pulls the blanket down. "Bernie, you don't have any choice. You have to go to school."

"Yeah," Bernie says. "Give me one good reason."

"You're fifty-two years old, and you're the principal."

THE MOST BEAUTIFUL BLESSING IN THE TALMUD

When Rabbi Nahman and Rabbi Isaac were about to part, Rabbi Nahman asked Rabbi Isaac to bless him. Rabbi Isaac replied: "Let me tell you a parable. To what may this be compared? To a man who was traveling in the desert. He was hungry, tired and thirsty, when suddenly he came upon a tree whose fruits were sweet, its shade pleasant, and a stream of water was flowing beneath it. The man ate of the tree's fruits, drank of the water, and sat in the tree's shade. When he was about to continue his journey, he turned to the tree and said: 'Tree, O Tree, with what shall I bless you? Shall I say to you may your fruits be sweet? They are already sweet. That your shade be pleasant? It is already pleasant. That a stream of water flow by you? A stream of water already flows by you. Therefore, this is my blessing, "May it be God's will that all the shoots planted from you be just like you." '

"So it is with you," [Rabbi Isaac said to Rabbi Nahman]. "With what shall I bless you? Shall I wish you Torah learning? You already have learning. Wealth? You already have wealth. Children? You already have children.

"Therefore, this is my blessing: May it be God's will that your offspring will be like you."

—Babylonian Talmud, *Ta'anit* 5b–6a

21

IF THE FETUS IS NOT
A LIFE, WHAT IS IT?

Judaism and Abortion

When men fight, and one hurts a pregnant woman and a
miscarriage results, but no other injury, the assailant shall
be fined as the woman's husband may exact from him and
as the judges determine. But if other damage ensues [that
is, if the woman dies from the assailant's attack], then you
shall punish him life for life.

—Exodus 21:22–23

As this passage makes clear, whatever value the fetus has, the
Torah does not grant it the status of a human life. If it did, the
punishment for killing the fetus would not be a monetary fine, but
the same as that for killing the woman, i.e., death. Hence, whatever
the offense of abortion might be in Jewish law, it definitely is not
murder.

The above is the Torah's only verse that deals with a fetus's legal
status. Two talmudic passages make it clear that the fetus does have
legal standing and should not be destroyed with impunity:

If a woman is in hard labor [and her life is in danger],
they cut up the fetus within her womb and remove it limb

161

by limb, because her life takes precedence over that of the fetus. But if the greater part was already born, they may not touch him, for one may not set aside one person's life for that of another [in other words, one is designated a person only after "the greater part was already born"].

—Mishna *Ohalot* 7:6

The permission granted by the Mishna to dismember the fetus because the life of the mother "takes precedence over that of the fetus" suggests that if the mother's life were not at stake, such permission would not be granted. Some observant Jews cite this Mishna to argue that abortion should be permitted, therefore, only when the mother's life is in danger. Others, of a more lenient view, argue that endangerment of life can be broadened to include mental anguish as well.

While the lenient view sounds suspiciously modern, its proponents point to another talmudic case, in which abortion is permitted in order to spare the mother mental anguish:

[In the case of a] woman [convicted of a capital offense] who goes forth to be executed [and who, after the verdict has been issued, is found to be pregnant], we do not wait for her to give birth [but execute her immediately].

—Mishna *Arakhin* 1:4

During many years of teaching, I have found that this passage offends almost everyone, pro-life and pro-choice advocates alike. Therefore, a word of explanation: Since a Jewish high court was the only tribunal empowered to sentence a prisoner to death, there was no higher court to which the prisoner could appeal his or her sentence. (It would be as if death sentences in the United States could be affirmed only by the Supreme Court.) The sentence was carried out on the day after the conviction, since the Rabbis believed that it was a form of "torture" to the prisoner to delay the execution.

As this probably theoretical ruling (there is no evidence that such a case ever happened) makes clear, the Rabbis regard the fetus's life as subservient not only to the life of the mother but also to her great mental anguish.

Still, whenever I have taught this text, people ask, "Why execute a pregnant woman at all?" Indeed, the societies that surrounded the Jews—the Egyptians, Greeks, and Romans—all postponed execution in such cases until after the birth. Why not the Jews?

About seventy years ago, Jewish scholar Viktor Aptowitzer examined this issue in a pathbreaking study, "The Status of the Embryo in Jewish Criminal Law." Aptowitzer argued that the calculation made by Greek and Roman jurists not to execute the woman was a utilitarian, not a moral, one. From their perspective, the woman was a useless piece of machinery, fit only to be discarded. But the fetus, because it might someday be useful to the state, remained a cog to be jealously guarded.

Jewish law's perspective, however, is moral. The convicted woman is still a person entitled to compassion. Just as the fetus is sacrificed to save the mother's physical life, so too is it sacrificed to save her spirit from further torture and suffering.

But couldn't one argue precisely the opposite, that Egyptian, Greek, and Roman justices were more moral, that it was they, not the Rabbis of the Talmud, who exhibited greater respect for the value of life? No, Aptowitzer answered, because all three differed from Jewish law in another instance as well. They all permitted infanticide, the killing of children who were born with physical defects or other "abnormalities" (perhaps they were just not the sex the parents wanted).

Alone in the ancient world, Jewish law regarded infanticide as murder; once a baby was born, he or she had all the rights of any other human being. The Jewish opposition to infanticide was radical in the ancient world (the first-century Roman historian Tacitus ridiculed this Jewish practice); given reports of the murder of female infants in China, it might also be regarded as radical in parts of the contemporary world.

There is yet one more proof that Jewish law does not regard the fetus as an independent human being, but as part of the mother's body: When a pregnant woman converts to Judaism, the child to whom she subsequently gives birth is Jewish, and does not need to convert. But if she converts subsequent to giving birth, her child, even if only one day old, does not become Jewish.

> The embryo is considered to be mere water until the fortieth day [of pregnancy].
> —Babylonian Talmud, *Yevamot* 69b

Thus, aborting a fetus younger than six weeks apparently is not forbidden by Jewish law, even for a very weak reason.

> [A woman] differs from "mother earth" in that she need not nurture seed implanted within her *against her will;* indeed, she may "uproot" seed illegally sown.
> —Rabbi David Feldman summarizing nineteenth-century Rabbi Yehuda Perilman's ruling that a raped woman has the right to abort (*Birth Control in Jewish Law,* page 287)

In recent years, a number of prominent Orthodox rabbis have ruled that, even in cases of rape, the woman should not have the right to abort. These rabbis wish to restrict abortion solely to instances when the mother's life is physically endangered. It seems to me that, in effect, they demonstrate less compassion for a woman who has been violated than the talmudic Rabbis did toward a woman who had committed a capital offense.

CONTEMPORARY JEWISH VIEWS ON ABORTION: CONSERVATIVE, ORTHODOX, AND REFORM

> If a ... probability exists that a child may be born defective and the mother would seek an abortion on grounds of pity for the child whose life will be less than normal, the Rabbi would decline permission. ... If, however, an abortion for that same potentially deformed child were sought on the grounds that the possibility is causing severe *anguish to the mother*, permission would be granted. The fetus is unknown, future, potential, part of "the secrets of

God"; the mother is known, present, alive, and asking for compassion.

—Rabbi David Feldman, *Birth Control in Jewish Law*, pages 291–292

Feldman's statement reflects the views of the most traditional forces within Conservative Judaism and the most liberal voices within Orthodoxy, which, while generally restrictive on abortion, would be open to it in instances of Down Syndrome and Tay-Sachs.

Most Orthodox spokesmen today tend to be much more restrictive in granting permission for abortions. As Dr. Fred Rosner, an Orthodox physician and a leading authority on Jewish medical ethics, summarizes the recent trend of Orthodox responsa:

[Permitting abortions in cases of incest or rape] "is a minority viewpoint. [In addition], only a very small group of Rabbinic Responsa regard the possibility of a deformed child being born to prey so much on the mother's mind as to constitute impairment of her health [and therefore grounds for permitting an abortion]."

—Fred Rosner, "The Jewish Attitude Toward Abortion," page 75

Rabbi J. David Bleich, an Orthodox scholar, opens his survey of "Abortion in Halakhic Literature" with the following citation from the Zohar, the primary text of Jewish mysticism:

There are three who drive away God's presence from the world, make it impossible for the Holy One to fix His abode in the universe, and cause prayer to go unanswered. . . . [The third is] he who causes the fetus to be destroyed in the womb, for he destroys the artifice of the Holy One, and His workmanship. . . . For these abominations, the Spirit of Holiness weeps.

—Zohar on Exodus 36

The Reform position is that the mother (presumably with input from the father) should make decisions concerning abortion, and need not consult with a rabbi. As Rabbi Balfour Brickner, speaking

165

several years ago on behalf of the Union of American Hebrew Congregations, testified before a congressional subcommittee:

> It is precisely because of this regard for that sanctity [of life] that we see as most desirable the right of any couple to produce only that number of children whom they feel they can feed and clothe and educate properly, only that number to whom they can devote themselves as real parents.
>
> —Brickner's testimony is printed in Menachem Kellner, *Contemporary Jewish Ethics,* pages 279–283

Nevertheless, I suspect that Brickner would not have a high regard for parents who aborted a child that was revealed by ultrasound or amniocentesis to be of the "wrong" gender.

When I interviewed the fundamentalist minister Reverend Jerry Falwell a number of years ago, he pinpointed the issue that makes abortion-on-demand problematic for many people: I've never heard of a woman who was planning to have a baby speak about "the fetus" in her womb. She'll always call it a "baby." The word "fetus" is invariably used by people who support abortion, and who want to disguise from themselves the evil of what they are doing. (I have paraphrased Reverend Falwell since I have no verbatim record of his comment.)

The above statements notwithstanding, it would be wrong to assume that Jewish "pro-life" and "pro-choice" positions can invariably be predicted simply by knowing a rabbi's denominational affiliation. What follows are two admittedly unrepresentative views on the subject, the first by Rabbi Ben Zion Uziel, an Orthodox rabbi and the late Sephardic Chief Rabbi of Israel (1939–1953); the second by Rabbi Marc Gellman, a contemporary Reform rabbi in Dix Hills, Long Island, and, I believe, one of the few non-Orthodox rabbis who, on ethical grounds, believes that abortion rights should be restricted.

> It is clear that abortion is not permitted without reason. That would be destructive and frustrative of the possibility

of life. But for a *reason,* even if it is a *slim reason (ta'am kalush),* such as to prevent the pregnant woman's *nivul* [disgrace, as in the case of the pregnant woman who is to be executed], then we have precedent and authority to permit it.

—Rabbi Ben Zion Uziel, *Responsa Mishp'tei Uziel,* Vol. III,
Hoshen Mishpat, No. 46

In a short memoir describing his shift from left-wing politics during the 1960s, Rabbi Gellman explains his unhappiness with liberalism's almost uniform support for abortion rights:

Many of the pro-life people were moved by their faith to take this position. I could not say that about the pro-choice people I knew. The pro-life people spoke of rights and wrongs, while the pro-choice people spoke of rights and laws. The former language was . . . far closer to my sense of how God wants us to make religion real in the world. . . . This struggle smells like a fight to keep women and men from accepting the consequences of sexual promiscuity. How narrow and selfish that seems to me now. . . .

[As for the charge made by pro-choice activists that religious opposition to abortion represents an effort by religious groups to impose their sectarian views on America, Gellman writes]: "I had never apologized for being pro-civil rights on the basis of the Bible; why should I apologize for being pro-life on the basis of the Talmud. . . .

"I am still uncertain about how my view on abortion ought to be translated, if at all, into public policy, but I know that the killing of a fetus is a not a morally neutral act. . . . "

—Rabbi Gellman's untitled essay is published in David Dalin, ed.,
American Jews and the Separationist Faith, pages 53–56.

22

"EVEN THE ALTAR SHEDS TEARS"

Divorce

Although Jewish sources are not famous for their romantic sensibilities, the subject of divorce prompts a surprising number of romantic meditations and anecdotes:

> Rabbi Elazar said, If a man divorces his first wife, even the altar sheds tears. . . .
>
> —Babylonian Talmud, *Gittin* 90b

The Talmud generally assumes the husband to be at fault because, until the tenth century, Jewish law permitted a man to divorce a woman against her will (a wife could never initiate a divorce). This is based on the Torah, which devotes a total of four verses to the subject of divorce, only one of which is generally relevant today:

> If a man takes a wife and possesses her, but she fails to please him because he finds something obnoxious in her, then he shall write her a bill of divorcement, hand it to her, and send her away from his house.
>
> —Deuteronomy 24:1

Although this verse hardly will please modern sensibilities, it should be noted that imposing on the man the obligation to write and execute a legal document of divorce had a restraining and delaying effect. Compare this with societies surrounding the Jews, in which a man could divorce a woman solely by oral declaration, a procedure that has remained legal to this century among many Arab Muslims (in Islam, the man can effect divorce by saying "I divorce you" three times in succession).

Shortly before the Common Era, the Rabbis ruled that when marrying, a man must give his bride a *ketuba* (marital contract), in which he guarantees her a substantial financial settlement in the event he divorces her:

> Why did the Rabbis institute that the husband give his wife a *ketuba* at the time of their marriage? So that it might not be an easy matter for him to divorce her.
> —Babylonian Talmud, *Ketubot* 39b

The Talmud debates whether a man needs any grounds for divorcing his wife. The positions taken by the various participants are somewhat surprising: The most conservative, Rabbi Shammai and his followers, greatly limit the instances in which divorce can take place, while Rabbi Hillel and his followers, and Rabbi Akiva, all of whom are generally known for their humanistic approach to legal problems, rule that a man can divorce his wife for any reason:

> The School of Shammai say: A man should not divorce his wife unless he has found her guilty of sexual misconduct. . . .
> The School of Hillel say: [He may divorce her] even if she has merely spoiled his food. . . .
> Rabbi Akiva says: [He may divorce her] even if he finds another woman more beautiful than she is. . . .
> —Mishna *Gittin* 9:10

While some Jewish apologists deny evidence of sexism in the School of Hillel and Akiva's arguments ("A woman should not have to go on living with a man who finds other women more attractive than she" is how I heard one rabbi explain Akiva's statement), I doubt that many men would countenance being treated in a similar fashion. Imagine how this passage might read were the right to divorce vested in the woman's hands:

> The School of Shammai says: A woman should not divorce her husband unless she has found him guilty of sexual misconduct. . . .
> The School of Hillel says: She may divorce him even if he has not brought home a large enough paycheck. . . .
> Rabbi Akiva says: She may divorce him even if she finds another man more handsome than he. . . .

Because the Rabbis were conscious of the inherent unfairness in divorce laws, over the centuries they established new laws to protect women. The tenth-century Rabbi Gershom, who also issued a decree against polygamy, legislated that it was illegal to divorce a woman against her will, a law that has remained in effect since. During the twelfth century, Maimonides ruled that if a man refused to grant a divorce to a woman who was entitled to it, he was to be whipped without mercy until he did so (*Mishneh Torah,* "Laws of Divorce," 2:20). The legal precedent for his ruling was the talmudic law, "If a man refuses to give a woman a divorce, he is forced until he declares, 'I am willing' " (Babylonian Talmud, *Ketubot* 50a). That Maimonides was willing to accept as *voluntary* a statement elicited by a whipping indicates how anxious he was to assist a woman who was being mistreated.

In Jewish law today, if both partners want a divorce, no other grounds are necessary. On the other hand, it sometimes happens that a man refuses to grant his wife a *get* (Jewish divorce), or demands a large sum of money for doing so. (It sometimes, although less often, happens that a woman who refuses to accept a *get* imposes a similar sort of blackmail.) Without the *get,* the woman remains married to him (in Hebrew, she is called an *agunah,* a chained woman), and forbidden to any other man. In the 1950s, the Conservative movement dealt with this issue by inserting a clause into the *ketuba* that, in effect, obligates the man to issue a *get* in the event of a civil divorce, and obligates the woman to accept it. Orthodox scholars rejected the Conservative *ketuba,* arguing that the wording of the clause did not meet their understanding of the requirements of Jewish law; currently, however, some prominent Orthodox rabbis are composing a different prenuptial agreement that, they hope, will achieve the same effect.

TWO UNEXPECTED RABBINIC STORIES ABOUT DIVORCE

[The verse in Isaiah], "Do not hide yourself from your own flesh" (58:7) refers to the duty one owes to one's divorced wife [as we learn from the case of Rabbi Yossi].

Rabbi Yossi's wife used to subject him to much suffering and ridicule.

Rabbi Elazar came to him and said, "Master, divorce her, she does not accord you the respect due you."

Rabbi Yossi replied, "I cannot afford to pay her the money specified in the *ketuba.*"

Rabbi Elazar replied, "I will give you the money for the settlement, so divorce her."

Rabbi Elazar gave him the money, and Rabbi Yossi divorced her.

She then went and married the town watchman. Some time later, the watchman lost all his money and became blind, and his wife would lead him by the hand begging for charity. Once she led him through the whole city but no one gave them anything. He asked her, "Is there no other neighborhood in the city where we can go?"

She replied, "There is one other neighborhood, but my first husband lives there, and I am too embarrassed to go there."

He beat her until she took him to Rabbi Yossi's neighborhood.

Just then, Rabbi Yossi passed by. He saw how the husband was abusing her, and he provided them with a house and with food for the rest of their lives.

Nevertheless, the divorced wife was overheard saying, "It was better for me to suffer pain on the outside of my body, than what I now suffer inside [because of being supported by my ex-husband]."

—Palestinian Talmud, *Ketubot* 11:3; I have followed the
commentary of the *Korban Ha-Eida;* another
version is found in *Genesis Rabbah* 17:3.

It once happened that a certain woman in Sidon lived with her husband for ten years, but they had no children. [Following the law that, in those days, governed such matters] they went to Rabbi Shimon bar Yohai and requested a divorce.

He said to them, "By your lives, just as you had a festive banquet when you got married, so you should now begin your separation with a festive banquet."

They followed his advice and prepared a great banquet.

During the meal, the woman gave her husband more to drink than usual. When he was in high spirits, he said to his wife, "My beloved [in addition to your divorce settlement], you may take with you out of my house whatever you like best, and then return to the house of your father."

What did she do?

After he fell asleep, she told her servants to take him and the bed upon which he was sleeping to her father's house.

In the middle of the night, he awoke, and when his intoxication wore off, he looked around in astonishment. "My beloved," he said, "where am I?"

"In my father's house," she replied.

"But what business do I have in your father's house?"

She said, "Don't you remember telling me last night that I should take with me whatever I like best when I return to my father's house? There is nothing in the world I like more than you."

They went back again to Rabbi Shimon bar Yohai, who prayed for them, and the woman became pregnant.

—*Song of Songs Rabbah* 1:4; I have followed, with some changes,
the translation of Jakob Petuchowski,
Our Masters Taught, pages 92–93.

Rabbinic law insisted on divorce if a couple had no children after ten years. However, the onus of infertility attached to neither partner. Both were encouraged to remarry in the hope that they would become fertile with a different spouse. Yet some rabbis, Rabbi Shimon apparently among them, saw divorce in these circumstances as tragic. Thus, the above story, I believe, constitutes a sort of literary romantic protest against this law, and helped set the stage for the law eventually being changed. Divorce is no longer demanded in cases of childlessness; several great rabbis of recent Jewish history have been childless.

A FINAL THOUGHT

The late Rabbi Samuel Katz, an Orthodox rabbi in Los Angeles and a man who supervised many religious divorces, commented to a friend of mine about the explosive rise in divorces in the United States: "In America, too many people get divorced. In Europe, too few people got divorced."

23

"LOVE YOUR NEIGHBOR"

Love your neighbor as yourself.

—Leviticus 19:18

Strangely enough, most Christians, and many Jews, believe that this principle was first formulated by Jesus (Matthew 22:39); they don't realize that he was simply quoting the Torah.

Although this verse simply states only one of the Torah's 613 commandments, the Talmud's greatest teachers long recognized that this law had special status (see Hillel's summary of Judaism, page 6). Rabbi Akiva, one of the greatest scholars and teachers of the entire talmudic era, taught:

"Love your neighbor as yourself," this is the major principle of the Torah.

—Palestinian Talmud, *Nedarim* 9:4

Regarding the eminently reasonable objection, "How can one love another as dearly as one loves himself?" Israel Baal Shem Tov (1700–1760), the founder of Hasidism, suggested a practical guideline on carrying out this command by putting particular emphasis on the words "as yourself."

Just as we love ourselves despite the faults we know we have, so should we love our neighbors despite the faults we see in them.

—Israel Baal Shem Tov

This pragmatic guideline was the standard guiding the Rabbis when they explained how one was to fulfill all such seemingly impossible commandments. For example:

Let your fellow man's honor be as dear to you as your own (*Ethics of the Fathers* 2:15). Is it possible [to be as concerned about another person's honor as about one's own? Rather] this teaches that just as one looks out for his own honor, so should he look out for his fellow man's honor. Just as he desires that there should be no smear on his good name, so must he be anxious not to smear the reputation of his fellow man.

—*The Fathers According to Rabbi Nathan* 15:1

*   *   *

Some people are foul-weather friends, able to empathize and sympathize only with those who are experiencing difficulties. The Talmud asks people to reach for a higher standard, to rejoice in the others' successes:

One in whom people take pleasure, God also takes pleasure; one in whom people do not take pleasure, God does not take pleasure.

—*Ethics of the Fathers* 3:13

I once commented to my friend Dennis Prager how much pleasure I got when I saw my two little daughters playing lovingly with each other.

"Doesn't it give you more pleasure," he asked, "than if one of your daughters said 'I love you, Daddy' but didn't act nicely to her sister?"

"Of course," I answered.

"I imagine God is the same way," Dennis said. "He derives

greater pleasure when people are good to each other than when they are 'good' to Him but not to each other."

Along similar lines, the Hasidic rebbe Levi Yitzchak of Berditchev (d. 1809) taught: "Whether a man really loves God can be determined by the love he bears toward his fellow man," who is of course created in God's image.

While obvious exceptions to this statement come to mind (dissidents in totalitarian regimes seldom have been popular among their neighbors), this teaching remains a generally applicable guideline. God commands us to love our neighbors, and if we find that we rarely are loved in return, we probably are expressing an emotion other than love.

> Rabbi Moshe of Leib of Sassov (d. 1807) said: How to love men is something I learned from a peasant. He was sitting in an inn along with other peasants, drinking. For a long time he was silent as all the rest, but when he was moved by the wine, he asked one of the men seated beside him: "Tell me, do you love me or don't you love me?" The other replied: "I love you very much." But the first peasant replied: "You say that you love me, but you do not know what I need. If you really loved me, you would know." The other had not a word to say to this, and the peasant who had put the question fell silent again. But I understood. To know the needs of men and to bear the burden of their sorrow—that is the true love of men.
>
> —Martin Buber, *Tales of the Hasidim—Later Masters*, page 86

WHEN NEIGHBORS BEAR GRUDGES

While "Love your neighbor as yourself" might be the most famous of the Torah's 613 commandments, the verse in which it appears begins with two other commandments: "Do not take revenge or bear a grudge against a member of your people" (Leviticus 19:18). The Rabbis explain how this law is to be actualized in daily life:

> What is revenge and what is bearing a grudge? If A says to B, "Lend me your sickle," and B says, "No," and the

next day, B says to A, "Lend me your ax," and A replies, "I will not, just as you refused to lend me your sickle," that is revenge [and is forbidden by the Torah].

And what is bearing a grudge? If A says to B, "Lend me your ax," and B says, "No," and the next day B says to A, "Lend me your garment," and A replies, "Here it is. I am not like you, who would not lend me what I asked for," that is bearing a grudge.

—Babylonian Talmud, *Yoma* 23a

Admittedly, this standard of behavior borders on the saintly, particularly the demand that we stifle the self-righteous impulse to point out to B that we are not acting in the same selfish manner in which he or she did. In family life, however, if every member were to remind others of every slight committed against him or her by a spouse, parent, child, or sibling, the family would rapidly disintegrate. The Torah seems to be instructing us to strive to broaden that family feeling beyond our immediate families.

On the other hand, I know of no Jewish source that delineates how often one is obligated to fulfill this Torah commandment vis-à-vis the same person. Thus, if even after the above incident, B continues to refuse to lend A what he or she needs, is A obligated to continue lending items to B without making a comment? I don't know.

GOD'S DEEPEST HOPE

This is what the Holy One said to Israel: My children, what do I seek from you? I seek no more than that you love one another and honor one another.

—*Tanna d'Bai Eliyahu*, medieval rabbinic work,
most likely dating from the tenth century

24

"EITHER FRIENDS OR DEATH"

Friendship

The Bible depicts two great friendships, one between two women, the other, two men:

> But Ruth replied [to Naomi], "Do not urge me to leave you, to turn back and not follow you. For wherever you go, I will go; wherever you lodge, I will lodge; your people shall be my people, and your God my God. Where you die, I will die and there I will be buried. Thus and more may the Lord do to me if anything but death parts you from me now."
>
> —Ruth 1:16–17

> Jonathan's soul became bound up with the soul of David. . . . Jonathan and David made a pact, because [Jonathan] loved him as himself. Jonathan took off the cloak and tunic he was wearing and gave them to David. . . .
> —I Samuel 18:1, 3–4; the description of Jonathan's feelings brings
> to mind the biblical verse, "And you shall love
> your neighbor as yourself."

Jonathan said to David, "Whatever you want, I will do it for you."

—I Samuel 20:4

After Jonathan was killed, along with his father and two brothers, in a battle with the Philistines, David lamented:

I grieve for you, my brother Jonathan. You were most dear to me. Your love was wonderful to me, more than the love of women.

—II Samuel 1:26

The friendships of Ruth and Naomi, and of David and Jonathan, were pure and, given their contexts, surprising. Naomi was Ruth's mother-in-law, a relationship that is not always associated with intense love; furthermore, their friendship grew *after* Ruth's husband died. Exacerbating matters even more was that Ruth came from Moab, a nation known for having hostile relations with ancient Israel. However, her devotion to Naomi led to her becoming a Jew: "your people shall be my people, and your God my God."

David and Jonathan's friendship survived far greater tensions. As King Saul's son, Jonathan was the presumed heir to the throne, whereas David was the leading soldier in Saul's army, and the popular choice to become king. But Jonathan expressed no jealousy; instead, he told David, "You are going to be king over Israel and I shall be second to you" (I Samuel 23:17). Jonathan ultimately risked his father's wrath and his life to protect his friend from his father's efforts to kill him.

QUALITIES TO BE VALUED IN A FRIEND

Once, one of the great Torah scholars from another land asked Rabbi Kook [then Chief Rabbi of Palestine], "What is the reason you are so fond of Reb Aryeh Levin?"

The Chief Rabbi answered, "I have not one reason but three. For twenty years he has been frequenting my house, and in all that time (1) he has never flattered me . . . and

if he ever saw me do anything which he did not understand, he questioned it or commented on it; (2) he never
once told me of anything said by my fierce opponents, who
were continually denigrating and defaming me [see page
224]; (3) and whatever he asked of me, it was never a
favor for himself, but only for others."

—Simcha Raz, *A Tzaddik in Our Time*, pages 85–86

"EITHER FRIENDS OR DEATH": THE HUMAN NEED FOR COMPANIONSHIP

Philosopher Martin Buber claimed that, had you asked him in his
early years whether he preferred to have dealings only with people
or with books, he would have answered books. In later years, he
changed his mind, and challenged anyone who claimed to feel as he
once did with the following "infallible test":

Imagine yourself in a situation where you are alone,
wholly alone on earth, and you are offered one of the two,
books or men. I often hear men prizing their solitude but
that is only because there are still men somewhere on earth
even though in the far distance. I knew nothing of books
when I came forth from the womb of my mother, and I
shall die without books, with another human hand in my
own. I do, indeed, close my door at times and surrender
myself to a book, but only because I can open the door
again and see a human being looking at me.

—Martin Buber, *Meetings*, page 61

Buber claimed that it was a specific incident that motivated him
to value human over intellectual and spiritual encounters: "One afternoon [after a morning of spiritual, and solitary, study], I had a
visit from an unknown young man, without being there in spirit. I
certainly did not fail to let the meeting be friendly. . . . I conversed
attentively and openly with him, only I omitted to guess the questions which he did not ask. Later, not long after, I learned from one
of his friends—he himself was no longer alive—the essential content

of these questions; I learned that he had come to me not casually, but borne by destiny, not for a chat but for a decision. He had come to me; he had come in this hour. What do we expect when we are in despair and yet go to a man? Surely a presence by means of which we are told that nevertheless there is meaning. Since then . . . I possess nothing but the everyday out of which I am never taken" (*Meetings,* pages 45–46). As a result of this experience, Buber usually made himself accessible to those who wished to meet with him.

> Woe to him who is alone and falls with no companion to raise him.
>
> —Ecclesiastes 4:10

> Either friends or death.
>
> —Babylonian Talmud, *Ta'anit* 23a

This was a popular proverb in ancient Israel that the Rabbis associated with Choni, a scholar who awoke from a seventy-year sleep only to discover that he had no peers, and no friends (see pages 259–260). Choni prayed to God to release him from his misery, and his wish was granted.

Finally, a simple guide for knowing what your friend probably feels about you:

> What is in your heart about your fellow man is most likely in his heart about you.
>
> —*Sifre Deuteronomy*, piska 24

25

"WHEN I WAS YOUNG, I ADMIRED CLEVER PEOPLE. NOW THAT I AM OLD . . ."

Kindness and Compassion

When I was young I admired clever people. Now that I
am old, I admire kind people.
>   —Rabbi Abraham Joshua Heschel (1907–1972)

For I desire kindness, not sacrifice.
>   —Hosea 6:6; speaking in the name of God

*   *   *

To Jews, compassion is the keystone of being a *mensch,* and so
basic a requirement of being human that the Talmud's Rabbis were
willing (at least in theory) to read an unkind person out of the Jewish
community:

> Jews are compassionate children of compassionate par-
> ents, and one who shows no pity for fellow creatures is
> assuredly not of the seed of Abraham, our father.
>>   —Babylonian Talmud, *Betzah* 32a

182

From Judaism's perspective, an unkind person is presumably a nonbeliever. How could anyone who believes in the God of the Bible treat his or her fellow human beings, all of whom are created in God's image, with less than compassion?:

> Have we not all one Father?
> Did not one God create us?
> How then can we deal treacherously each man with his brother? . . .
>
> —Malachi 2:10

An ancient Jewish folktale depicts a man visiting hell, and being amazed to find its inhabitants all seated at long tables, with fancy tablecloths, beautiful silverware, and bountiful food in front of them. Yet no one was eating, and all of them were wailing. When he looked closely, he saw that none of them could bend their elbows; thus, although they could touch the food, no one could bring it to his mouth.

The visitor then went to heaven, where the scene was identical, long tables, fancy tablecloths, beautiful silverware, and bountiful food. And here as well, people could not bend their elbows, yet no one was wailing—because each person was serving his neighbor.

> —I have heard this tale orally, but have been
> unable to find a source for it.

Once, when Abba Tahnah the Pious was entering his city on Sabbath eve at dusk, a bundle slung over his shoulder, he came upon a man afflicted with boils lying [helplessly] at a crossroads.

The man said to him, "Master, do an act of kindness for me. Carry me into the city."

Abba Tahnah replied, "If I abandon my bundle, how shall I and my household support ourselves? But if I abandon a man afflicted with boils, I will forfeit my life!"

What did he do? He let his good inclination overpower his evil inclination [set down his bundle on the road], and carried the afflicted man into the city. Then he returned for his bundle and reentered the city with the last rays of the sun. Everybody was astonished [at seeing so pious a man carrying his bundle when the Sabbath was about to begin, and during which it is forbidden to carry], and exclaimed, "Is this really Abba Tahnah the Pious?"

He too felt uneasy at heart and said to himself: "Is it possible that I have desecrated the Sabbath?"

At that point, the Holy One caused the sun to continue to shine [thereby delaying the Sabbath's beginning].

—*Ecclesiastes Rabbah* 9:7

Let a good man do good deeds with the same zeal that the evil man does bad ones.

—Hasidic saying attributed to the Belzer Rebbe,
Shalom Rokeakh (1779–1855)

THREE UNEXPECTED TALMUDIC HEROES: THE SAINTLY DEEDS OF SEEMINGLY ORDINARY PEOPLE

Rabbi Beroka of Hoza used to frequent the marketplace in Be Lefet [a city in Persia], where Elijah often appeared to him. Once, Rabbi Beroka asked him, "Is there anyone in this marketplace who has a place in the World-to-Come?"

Elijah replied, "No."

In the meantime, there walked by a man wearing black shoes, who had no ritual fringes (*tzitzit*) on the corners of his garment.

"This man [Elijah declared] is destined for the World-to-Come."

Rabbi Beroka ran after the man, and asked him what his occupation was.

The man replied, "Go away today and come back tomorrow."

Next day, he asked him again, "What is your occupation?"

He replied, "I am a jail guard, and I keep the men and women apart. I place my bed between the men and women, so that they should not come to do that which is forbidden; when I see a Jewish girl upon whom the Gentile wardens are casting their eyes, I risk my life and save her.

"One day, there was a betrothed girl prisoner upon whom the Gentiles were casting their eyes. I took dregs of red wine and threw them on the lower part of her skirt and said to them that she was menstruating [the wardens would find it repulsive to have relations with a menstruating woman]."

Rabbi Beroka asked the man, "Why have you no fringes on your garment and why do you wear black shoes?"

He replied, "In order that I can come and go among the Gentiles and they not recognize me as a Jew. That way, when a harsh decree is to be enacted against Jews [I can hear about it and] I can inform the rabbis, who can then pray to God to have the decree annulled."

He further asked him, "When I asked you what is your occupation, why did you say to me, 'Go away today and come back tomorrow'?"

He answered, "They had just issued a harsh decree and I said to myself I would first go and inform the Rabbis of it so that they might pray to God."

In the meantime, two others walked by. Elijah remarked, "These two also have a share in the World-to-Come."

Rabbi Beroka asked them, "What is your occupation?"

They replied, "We are comedians. When we see people who are depressed, we cheer them up; also, when we see two people quarreling, we strive hard to make peace between them."

—Babylonian Talmud, *Ta'anit* 22a

The only depressing element in these inspirational stories is how few people Elijah seems to feel are destined for the World-to-Come.

The Talmud's emphasis on the jail guard's greatness clearly was intended to remind all Talmud students not to judge the worthiness of their fellow Jews solely on the basis of their outer garments.

*　　*　　*

Finally, the words of fifteen-year-old Anne Frank, a year before she died in a Nazi concentration camp:

> Give of yourself. . . . you can always give something, even if it is only kindness. . . . No one has ever become poor from giving.
>
> —*The Diary of a Young Girl,* March 1944

26

"WHAT DOES A GOOD GUEST SAY?"

Good Manners

It was said of Rabbi Yochanan ben Zakkai that no man ever greeted him first, even a gentile in the marketplace.
—Babylonian Talmud, *Berakhot* 17a

Shammai said: Receive all people cheerfully.
—*Ethics of the Fathers* 1:15

Human beings cannot necessarily control *what* they are feeling, but they can control *how* they express themselves. Your being in a bad mood does not entitle you to inflict that mood on another, or even to be curt, cool, or dismissive toward him or her.

GRATITUDE AND INGRATITUDE

Ben Zoma used to say: What does a good guest say? "How much trouble has my host gone to for me. How much meat he set before me. How much wine he brought me. How many cakes he served me. And all this trouble he has gone to for my sake!"

But what does a bad guest say? "What kind of effort

did the host make for me? I have eaten only one slice of bread. I have eaten only one piece of meat, and I have drunk only one cup of wine! Whatever trouble the host went to was done only for the sake of his wife and children."

—Babylonian Talmud, *Berakhot* 58a

Have you ever noticed how often people leave a house where they have dined and immediately engage in cutting character analysis of the very people who just hosted them? This constitutes a grotesque violation of an important Jewish ideal, *ha-karat ha-tov* (the command to remember and recognize all acts of goodness, even a minor favor which another has done for you). Within talmudic Judaism's hierarchy of values, ingratitude is a singularly loathsome, if very common, characteristic.

Rabbi Ben Zoma seems to have specialized in the *mitzvah* of expressing gratitude. The sight of large crowds of people, which provoke some to misanthropic observations, incite in Ben Zoma gratitude:

Ben Zoma once saw a crowd on the steps of the Temple Mount. He said . . . "Blessed is He who has created all these people to serve me." For he used to say: "What labors did Adam have to carry out before he obtained bread to eat? He plowed, he sowed, he reaped, he bound the sheaves, threshed the grain, winnowed the chaff, selected the ears, ground them, sifted the flour, kneaded the dough, and baked. And only then did he eat. Whereas I get up and find all these things done for me. And how many labors did Adam have to carry out before he obtained a garment to wear? He had to shear the sheep, wash the wool, comb it, spin it, weave it, and only then did he have a garment to wear. Whereas I get up and find all these things done for me. All kinds of craftsmen come to the door of my house, and when I rise in the morning, I find all these things ready for me."

—Babylonian Talmud, *Berakhot* 58a

One who learns from his companion a single chapter, a single law, a single verse, a single expression, or even a single letter, should accord him respect.

—*Ethics of the Fathers* 6:3

The Palestinian Talmud (*Bava Mezia* 2:11) records that when Rab heard that his earliest childhood teacher had died, he tore his garment as a sign of mourning.

The above ruling notwithstanding, people often express ingratitude to those from whom they have learned. Sanford Pinsker, writing in Toronto's *Idler* magazine, records a humorous recollection of ingratitude recounted to him by the late Nobel Prize–winning novelist Isaac Bashevis Singer:

Singer was once invited to read a story to a group of Yiddishists in Brooklyn. They begged him to come, even though they were too poor to be able to pay him. But, their spokesman argued, at least he would be among *landsmen,* people who understand Yiddish, not like when he visits fancy-shmanzy colleges and people make fun of his accent.

"What could I do?" Singer told me. "These are old people, so I went. The cab ride to Brooklyn cost me $35. And when I finally arrived, who was there? Maybe 12 people all together. So I read them a new story. No sooner am I finished than the first person gets up and says the following: This is not a good story. This is not a Zionist story. I spit on your story. And he proceeded to spit on the floor in anger, and then to sit down.

"At that point the next person gets up and says: This is not a good story. This is not an Orthodox story. This is a dirty story, so I also spit on your story. And like the first man, he spat on the floor in anger and sat down.

"Others objected that the story was not a socialist story or a nice story or even a properly Yiddish story; but about one thing they agreed: it was definitely not a good

story. In fact, one man spat on the story twice—once because it was not a Zionist story and once because it was
not an Orthodox story. So from 12 people I collected 13
spits."

—Cited in a letter from David Frum in William F. Buckley, Jr.,
In Search of Anti-Semitism, page 133

27

"IF YOU SEE YOUR ENEMY'S DONKEY"

A Jewish Alternative to Jesus' Command: "Love Your Enemies"

> If you see your enemy's donkey lying down under its bur-
> den, and would refrain from raising it, you must never-
> theless raise it with him.
>
> —Exodus 23:5

The Torah demands that we struggle against natural, but unkind, human tendencies. The fact that you dislike someone does not
entitle you to ignore his or her animal's sufferings, let alone those
of the person's family members.

In addition, two *midrashim,* one written in the third century, the
other a 1991 anecdotal retelling of the first, show how observing
this law can transform one's relationship with one's antagonist.

> Rabbi Alexandri said: Two donkey drivers who hated each
> other were walking on a road when the donkey of one lay
> down under its burden. His companion saw it, and at first
> he passed on. But then he reflected: Is it not written in the
> Torah, "If you see your enemy's donkey lying down under
> its burden . . . ?" So he returned, lent a hand, and helped

191

his enemy in loading and unloading. He began talking to his enemy: "Release a bit here, pull up over there, unload over here." Thus peace came about between them, so that the driver of the overloaded donkey said, "Did I not suppose that he hated me? But look how compassionate he has been." By and by, the two entered an inn, ate and drank together, and became fast friends. [What caused them to make peace and to become fast friends? Because one of them kept what is written in the Torah].

> —*Tanhuma, Mishpatim* #1; with minor variations,
> I have followed the translation of William Braude in
> Hayim Nahman Bialik and Yehoshua Ravnitzky, eds.,
> *The Book of Legends, Sefer Ha-Aggadah*, page 459.

I was driving along a somewhat deserted country road when I saw old Harry working on his car. He obviously had a flat tire. He had a jack in his hands and was trying to insert it into the side of the car without success. . . .

Now I never did like old Harry. Couldn't stand him in fact. Always avoided him like the plague. Hadn't spoken to him for years. He had been very nasty to me sometime ago. I decided to drive past pretending I hadn't noticed. After all, he had gotten himself into this mess. It was nothing to do with me.

Then I remembered. We had just learned it last week, "If you see your enemy's donkey lying down under its burden, and would refrain from raising it, you must nevertheless raise it with him." This was it. I couldn't just drive past. "I don't have to speak to him," I told myself. "I'll just change his tire and drive off."

I parked my car a little way up the road and walked back. Without saying anything I took the jack from his hands and started adjusting it to fit into the leverage point. I couldn't keep it up, however. Changing a tire goes better as a cooperative enterprise. I soon had to speak to him to get things moving. Eventually we did the job together, more or less. Anyway, I worked and he helped.

When it was finished, he was extremely grateful. He got out a cold drink and two plastic cups from his picnic case and we drank together. His gratitude seemed to me very sincere. "Perhaps he's not such a bad guy after all," I thought to myself.

"I don't know how to thank you," he said again.

"That's quite all right, Harry," I said. "Any time."

I walked back to my car. Before I got in I turned around. "All the best," I called out. "Be well."

"Extraordinary thing, this Torah," I thought to myself. "It tells you to help your enemy, and then it turns out you haven't got an enemy. Extraordinary!"

—Aryeh Carmell, *Masterplan: Judaism:
Its Programs, Meanings, Goals,* pages 140–141

According to the New Testament, Jesus teaches: "Love your enemies and pray for those who persecute you . . . for if you love those who love you, what right have you to claim any credit?" (Matthew 5:44, 48).

Judaism does not command a person to love his enemies (although it is untrue to claim, as the Gospel of Matthew does [5:43] that Judaism commands one to hate his enemies). For example, a Jew is not commanded to love a Nazi, as Jesus' statement implies; however, he or she is commanded to act justly, fairly, and, in some instances, even compassionately toward enemies:

If your enemy is hungry, give him bread to eat.

—Proverbs 25:21

SHOULD ONE SHOW MERCY TOWARD AN ENEMY WHO IS EVIL?

Jesus' command to love one's enemy and to pray for one's persecutor have deeply influenced Christian and Western notions of right and wrong. In 1981, the world was shocked by Ali Agca's attempted assassination of Pope John Paul II. Yet just four days after the shooting, the pope announced that he forgave his attacker, even though

Agca himself (who previously had murdered another person) had not asked for forgiveness. Jewish teachings oppose such an attitude:

> He who is merciful when he should be cruel will in the end be cruel when he should be merciful.
> —*Midrash Samuel* (Jewish rabbinic text from early Middle Ages)

The discussion about cruelty and mercy on which the above quote is based occurs in a commentary on I Samuel. In chapter 15, God commands King Saul to kill his prisoner Agag, the murderous king of Amalek. He does not do so because of a combination of mercy and respect for a fellow monarch.

As punishment, God instructs the Prophet Samuel to replace Saul with David. When Saul realizes that he will lose his kingdom, he becomes furious. The king, who was too merciful to slay the murderer Agag, proceeds to murder eighty-five innocent priests of the city of Nob for giving David a night's lodging (chapter 22).

The biblical story is one of many instances in which misplaced mercy led to cruelty. In March 1917, Alexander Kerensky helped to overthrow the czar and establish the first democratic government in Russian history. Kerensky permitted Lenin and the Bolsheviks to operate freely, although their contempt for, and opposition to, democracy was widely known.

Lenin repaid Kerensky's kindness by overthrowing his government in November. Kerensky fled to New York where he lived out his life in exile. It was the Russian people, who had to live under more than seventy years of Communist rule, who paid the price for Kerensky's well-intended but misplaced mercifulness.

> A man is only as good as what he loves.
> —Saul Bellow, *Seize the Day*

Bellow's words should be kept in mind when we hear of "good" people who remain friendly with vicious people, or who support immoral political movements. A reader of biographies of Adolf Hitler, for instance, might easily form the impression that the woman who loved and lived with him, Eva Braun, was an essentially sweet, if politically naive, woman. Yet the single most revealing thing that we know about Eva Braun is that she loved Adolf Hitler.

> "Hate the sin, love the sinner," is often correct, but those who love Hitler are less likely to fight him than those who hate him.
>
> —Dennis Prager

28

THE TERRIBLE TOLL
OF HATRED

Why was the first Temple destroyed [in 586 B.C.E.]? Because of three offenses committed [by the Jews of that pe-
riod]: idolatry, sexual immorality, and murder. . . . But
why then was the second Temple destroyed [in 70 C.E.],
given that the Jews of that time studied Torah, kept the
commandments, and performed acts of charity? Because
groundless hatred was prevalent. This teaches us that the
offense of groundless hatred is the equivalent of the three
sins of idolatry, sexual immorality, and murder.

—Babylonian Talmud, *Yoma* 9b

Groundless hatred brought down more than divine wrath upon
the Jews: The terrible rivalries and hatreds within their community
also militarily weakened the Jews vis-à-vis the Romans. Thus, at the
very moment that Rome's army was besieging Jerusalem, warring
Jewish factions burned the city's food supplies. Starving people cannot fight, so shortly thereafter, the Roman army broke through Jerusalem's walls and set the Temple ablaze.

When I was studying at Yeshiva University, Rabbi Aaron
Kreiser, a professor of Talmud, once posed the following question:
Why is it that the first Temple was destroyed as punishment for the
most heinous crimes, yet nonetheless was rebuilt within seventy

years, while the second Temple was destroyed because of a much lesser sin, yet still has not been rebuilt?

He proposed this answer (since I heard his lecture twenty-five years ago, I am paraphrasing): When people commit terrible crimes, such as those committed by the generation of the First Temple, and an enormous punishment comes upon them, they step back, recognize the evil they have done, and repent. But people guilty of "groundless hatred" never acknowledge that they have committed a sin. Ask them if they think it is wrong to hate their opponents and they will tell you why their adversaries are worthy of being hated. Consequently, although their sin seems to be of a lesser dimension, they never repent of it. That is why we are still not worthy of having the Temple rebuilt in our time.

> The Second Temple was destroyed because of causeless hatred. Perhaps the Third will be rebuilt because of causeless love.
>
> —The first Ashkenazic Chief Rabbi of Israel,
> Abraham Isaac Kook

> Love blinds us to faults, hatred to virtues.
> —Moshe ibn Ezra (c. 1055–after 1135), *Shirat Yisrael*

> Hatred makes the straight crooked.
>
> —Hebrew proverb

People who hate don't "see straight." Describe to them a good act performed by a person they despise, and they will formulate theories explaining why it really is evil, or motivated by evil intentions. For example, Voltaire, the leading figure of the eighteenth-century French Enlightenment, wrote passionately on the subject of torture. He devoted much of his life to campaigning against such forms of violent coercion as Church torture of suspected heretics.

When he learned that Jewish law had always outlawed torture (see page 410)—indeed, the Jews were the only nation in the ancient world to do so—one might have expected Voltaire to express admiration. Unfortunately, because he was a fierce antisemite (e.g., he labeled the Jews "the most abominable people in the world," and claimed that they ritually murdered non-Jews), news that Judaism outlawed torture incited not admiration but sarcasm: "What is very odd is that there is never any mention of torture in the Jewish books. It is truly a pity that so gentle, so honest, so compassionate a nation did not know this means of finding out the truth. The reason for this, in my opinion, is that they did not need it. God always made . . . [the truth] known to them as His cherished people . . . thus torture cannot be in use with them. This was the only thing lacking in the customs of this holy people" (cited in Leon Poliakov, *The History of Anti-Semitism: From Voltaire to Wagner*, page 491, note 38).

THE DESTRUCTIVE EFFECTS OF HATRED

Rabbi Joshua said: An evil eye, the evil inclination and hatred of people remove a man from the world.

—*Ethics of the Fathers* 2:11

The "evil eye" refers to a person who is distraught at his/her neighbor's success.

Regarding "hatred of people," a medieval Jewish story, whose source I have been unable to locate, indicates its self-destructive nature: An angel appeared to a man and told him that he would return in thirty days. At that time, the man could express one wish, which would be granted. "But," the angel added, "whatever you choose to receive, your next-door neighbor will receive double." The man hated his neighbor, and the thought that the neighbor would receive a double portion frustrated and infuriated him. When the angel returned after thirty days and asked what he wished, the man answered, "I want you to put out one of my eyes."

29

GOOD ADVICE ON FIFTEEN SUBJECTS

FROM RELIGIOUS TEXTS

Eating healthy: Two men entered a shop. One ate coarse bread and vegetables, while the other ate fine bread, fat meat, and drank old wine, and partook of an oily sauce and came out feeling ill. The one who ate fine food suffered harm, while the one who had coarse food escaped harm. Similarly, have you ever seen a donkey or a camel in convulsions [because of stomach upset? People and animals who live on simple diets are more apt to be healthy].

—*Ecclesiastes Rabbah* 1:18

Gifts: If one gives a gift to a friend, he must inform him [and not give the gift anonymously].

—Babylonian Talmud, *Shabbat* 10b

The Rabbis apparently believed that a person should always know who it is who loves him. Thus, the *Ethics of the Fathers* note, when God created man, it was "a special act of love that He informed man that he was created in His image" (3:18).

Guarding your valuables: A man should not put all his money in one corner.

—*Genesis Rabbah* 76:2

The Rabbis derived the idea of not putting "all your eggs in one basket" from an incident involving Jacob. When threatened by Esau's army, Jacob divided his family and servants into two camps, "thinking, if Esau comes to the one camp and attacks it, the other camp may yet escape" (Genesis 32:8–9).

> **Neighbors:** Keep far away from an evil neighbor, and don't become friendly with the wicked.
> —*Ethics of the Fathers* 1:7

Bad neighbors generally exert a more powerful influence than good ones. Thus, one more often hears of teenagers influenced to snort cocaine by their peers than of "coke" snorters who go "cold turkey" because of their friends' influence.

Don't delude yourself into thinking that you are one of those who will be unaffected, the Rabbis warn; rather, stay away from bad people, period.

> **Real estate:** Spend according to your means on food, less than you can afford on clothing, but more than you can afford on a home.
> —*Genesis Rabbah* 20:12

Good investment advice, since food and clothing are perishable, while real estate endures.

> **Self-improvement:** First improve yourself, then improve others.
> —Babylonian Talmud, *Bava Mezia* 107b

The Talmud preaches righteousness, not self-righteousness. Elsewhere it cautions, "A fault that you have, don't go about pointing out in other people" (Babylonian Talmud, *Bava Mezia* 59b).

> If you won't be better tomorrow than you were today, then what need do you have for tomorrow?
> —Rabbi Nahman of Bratslav (1772–1811)

Speech: Say little but do much.

—*Ethics of the Fathers* 1:15

People who make extravagant pledges often fail to carry them out; for such people, it seems, words themselves take the place of deeds.

Maimonides comments on this rabbinic admonition: "The wicked say much and do not even do little." By example, he cites the case of Ephron the Hittite who, after the death of Sarah, speaks to Abraham as if he will give him a beautiful burial site as a gift, but who then proceeds to exact a very high price (Genesis 23:10–16).

Torah study: Do not say, "When I have leisure, I will study." Perhaps you will have no leisure.

—*Ethics of the Fathers* 2:4

How often have you deferred working on an important project until you were less busy, only to find that you never became less busy? Because Torah study is so important, you should make the time available now.

A man once asked Rabbi Israel Salanter: "I have only fifteen minutes a day available for study. Should I devote it to studying Torah and Talmud, or to studying a *mussar* (pietistic) text?"

"Study the *mussar* text," Salanter counseled, "and it will soon make you realize that something is terribly wrong with your life if you only have fifteen minutes a day to study."

Worry: Rabbi Yehiel maintained that he had learnt from his teachers never to worry about two things—what can be corrected and what cannot be corrected. What can be corrected should be corrected at once, without any worry. And as for what cannot be corrected, worrying will not help.

—Rabbi Shmuel Avidor Ha-Cohen, *Touching Heaven, Touching Earth*, page 108

MODERN ADVICE

Economics: When Nobel Prize–winning economist Milton Friedman served as an adviser to the late Israeli Prime Minister Menachem Begin, he delivered a speech on economics to the Knesset. After his talk, Shlomo Lorincz, a Knesset member, said to him, "In the Talmud, Hillel summarized Judaism in one sentence: 'What is hateful to you, do not do to your neighbor: this is the whole Torah. The rest is commentary.' Could you summarize economics in one sentence?"

"Yes," replied Friedman. "There is no such thing as a free lunch."

Envy and jealousy: A man must always be considerate of the feelings of his neighbors. . . . So, for instance, if I went out to the fair . . . and did well, sold everything at a good profit, and returned with pockets full of money . . . I never failed to tell my neighbors that I had lost every cent and was a ruined man. Thus, I was happy and my neighbors were happy. But if, on the contrary, I had really been cleaned out at the fair . . . I made sure to tell my neighbors that, never since God made fairs, had there been a better one. You get my point? For thus, I was miserable and my neighbors were miserable.
—Sholem Aleichem (1859–1916), cited in Francine Klagsbrun,
Voices of Wisdom, page 35

Goodness: It is better for my enemy to see good in me than for me to see evil in him.
—Yiddish proverb

Living wisely: I have only one life, and it is short enough. Why waste it on the things I don't want most?
—Justice Louis Brandeis (1856–1941)

Public speaking: If after twenty minutes you don't strike oil, stop boring.

—Rabbi Joseph Lookstein to a Yeshiva University homiletics class

Simplicity: Everything should be made as simple as possible—but not simpler.

—Albert Einstein (1879–1955)

PART II

PERSONAL ISSUES

Judaism and the Quest for Meaning

30

HUMAN NATURE—
A SOMBER LOOK

THE INCLINATION TOWARD EVIL

The tendency of man's heart is towards evil from his
youth.

—Genesis 8:21

This early biblical assessment of human nature frequently is mis-
interpreted as a precursor of the New Testament's concept of original sin, according to which a person is born in a state of sin
irrespective of anything he has done, which cannot be changed by
his actions. Yet Genesis really is suggesting that evil and selfishness
are more natural to people than goodness and altruism. Children
are born selfish and have to be educated to generosity. As a friend
of mine once pointed out: "When was the last time you heard a
mother yelling at her three-year-old son, 'Johnny, stop being so selfless and giving all your toys away to the other children?' "

In Western society since the Enlightenment, the biblical belief
that evil comes from within human beings has largely been rejected
in favor of the Enlightenment view that human beings are born good
and corrupted by society. That is why there are so many organizations trying to change societal institutions, and so few devoted to
changing people.

Society, however, certainly humanizes people as much as it corrupts them. Ask parents whose children are retarded, fat, short, or ugly who is most likely to taunt them—adults or other children? Children, of course.

So, evil must come from within human beings. Once, when I was attacked for asserting this, I answered: "If human beings are naturally good, then when their minds are free to wander their thoughts should be kind ones. Yet how many people would be pleased to have the fantasies that run through their minds before they fall asleep at night made known to the world? Most of us, I suspect, don't fantasize about how to reduce world hunger."

> Once a man has committed a sin once and then a second time . . . it [appears to him that it] is permitted.
> —Babylonian Talmud, *Yoma* 86b

Most of us are quite uncomfortable the first time we commit an illegal or immoral act, less uncomfortable the second time, and by the third, as Rabbi Nosson Scherman has commented, "It becomes one more facet of normal behavior." Furthermore, we're likely to think that people who don't act as we do are naive.

> There are three sins which no person avoids committing every day: sinful (i.e., lustful) thoughts, expecting one's prayers to God to be answered immediately, and slander.
> Slander? How can one say such a thing? [Surely it is possible to avoid slandering another person for twenty-four hours.]
> What is meant is the dust of slander.
> —Babylonian Talmud, *Bava Bathra* 164b–165a

The above acts usually are regarded as minor, even inevitable, but sins nonetheless. Thus, one should try to curb lustful thoughts, for indulging in them can lead, among other things, to violating more serious commandments, such as the Seventh Commandment, which prohibits adultery, and the Tenth Commandment, which prohibits coveting one's neighbor's spouse (Exodus 20:14). Still, the Talmud's reassurance that everyone commits this offense can relieve a person of some of the guilt that so often attaches to offenses connected to sexual desire and behavior.

Similarly, it seems to be human nature to expect God to respond, hopefully immediately, to one's prayers. An old Yiddish joke tells of a struggling businessman who prays, "God, You help complete strangers, so why don't You help me?"

As for slander, the truth is that many, perhaps most, people cannot go a day without saying something nasty, or at least unpleasant, about somebody else. If you are confident that this talmudic dictum does not apply to you, monitor yourself for the next twenty-four hours and see if you pass this time without saying anything unpleasant about another.

Yet because the Rabbis recognize that some saintly people really do avoid slandering others, they focus on the sin of "the dust of slander." This involves suggesting something ugly about another person without saying it outright (e.g., shrugging your shoulders or making a face when the person's name is mentioned), or encouraging others to slander a person (e.g., raising the name of a specific person in the presence of those who dislike him or her).

*   *   *

The greater the man, the greater his evil inclination.
—Babylonian Talmud, *Sukkah* 52a

While there are saints who seem to have almost no evil inclinations, the Rabbis believe that a person of extraordinary abilities has more temptations and opportunities to use those abilities for wrong than do his less talented brethren. The Talmud, in fact, reaches the above conclusion after telling this anecdote about one of its greatest rabbinic scholars:

"Abbaye once heard a certain man saying to a certain woman, 'Let us arise and travel together.'

" 'I will follow them,' thought Abbaye, 'and keep them from sinning with one another.'

"He followed them across the meadows. When they were about to separate, he heard one of them say, 'Your company was pleasant, and now the way is long.'

" 'If it had been me,' Abbaye thought, 'I could not have restrained myself.'

"In deep despair he went and leaned against a lamppost. An old man came up to him and taught him, 'The greater the man, the greater his evil inclination.' "

*   *   *

Ten people join together to steal a beam, and are not ashamed in each other's presence.
—Babylonian Talmud, *Kiddushin* 80b

Mob scenes are notorious for loosening people's moral constraints. This talmudic aphorism brings to mind photographs and films taken during riots that show people helping each other remove stolen items from stores.

When a thief has nothing to steal, he regards his "virtue" as real.
—Babylonian Talmud, *Sanhedrin* 22a; I have followed the
translation of Rabbi William Braude, translator of
The Book of Legends: Sefer Ha-Aggadah by H. N. Bialik and
Y. H. Ravnitzky, page 654.

ENVY

A man is apt to envy everyone, *except* his son and his disciple. His son, as shown by the example of Solomon, and his disciple, as shown by Elisha saying to Elijah, "Let a double portion of your spirit pass on to me" (II Kings 2:9).
—Babylonian Talmud, *Sanhedrin* 105b

The Rabbis were struck by the congratulations David's courtiers offered him when his son, Solomon, was anointed king in his stead: "May God make the renown of Solomon even greater than yours, and may He exalt his throne even higher than yours" (I Kings 1: 47). Clearly, the courtiers had no fear that David would resent their blessing, any more than Elisha feared that his mentor, Elijah, would resent his request to be granted a "double portion" of Elijah's spirit.

"You have asked a difficult thing," Elijah responds, but says that if Elisha sees him when he is taken away, that is a divine sign that Elisha's request will be granted. Moments later, Elisha witnesses a fiery chariot bear Elijah heavenward in a whirlwind.

THE DESIRE FOR FAME

> If Reuben had known that the Holy One, Blessed be He, would have it written of him, "But when Reuben heard it, he tried to save [Joseph] from them" (Genesis 37:21), he would have carried Joseph on his shoulders back to his father. And if Boaz had known that the Holy One, Blessed be He, would have it written of him, "He handed [Ruth] roasted grain, and she ate her fill" (Ruth 2:14), he would have given her fatted calves to eat.
>
> —*Leviticus Rabbah* 34:8

Publicity generally has one of two positive effects on people: deterring them from bad deeds or stimulating them to perform good ones. Charitable organizations know that they often procure larger donations when donors' names and the size of their gifts are announced.

Thus, the Bible tells us that Reuben urged his brothers not to murder their younger sibling Joseph, but to throw him in a pit, intending all the while to return later and restore his brother to their father. But Reuben didn't rush back, and by the time he returned to the pit, the brothers had pulled Joseph out and sold him into Egyptian slavery. Had Reuben known that his failure to save his brother would be recorded in the most widely read book ever written, he undoubtedly would have argued much more forcefully, and might well have stayed at Joseph's side by the pit to ensure that his brother was saved. Don't we all wish to be known as heroes?

Boaz acted in a kind manner toward Ruth, providing the poor widow roasted grain. But had he known his gift would be recorded for all posterity, who knows what generous victuals he might have offered?

The prospect of publicity likewise also can deter people from bad deeds. A friend of mine told me about a prescient piece of advice his mother once offered him. "Whenever you are tempted to get involved in a venture that you think might be wrong, but aren't sure, imagine that your involvement will be headlined in the next morning's *New York Times*. If that thought doesn't worry you, then go ahead with your plans."

REACTIONS TO ONE'S NEIGHBOR'S PAIN

The students of Rabbi Zeira asked him . . . : "In virtue of what have you reached such a good old age?" [In response, Rabbi Zeira lists several traits, the most remarkable of which is], "I never rejoiced in my neighbor's shame."

—Babylonian Talmud, *Ta'anit* 20b

That Rabbi Zeira understood this to be a rare personal distinction indicates how common is the tendency, even among otherwise good people, to take pleasure in others' misfortunes. The summer of 1992 found three books on the same subject dominating the *New York Times* best-seller list: the collapsing marriage of Prince Charles and Princess Diana. Most of the books' purchasers presumably derived a certain morbid satisfaction from reading about the deep pain of the "rich and famous." People likewise derive perverse pleasure in seeing their neighbors "brought down a peg."

THE PROPENSITY FOR EVIL

God did not build Auschwitz and its crematoria. Men did. . . . The Holocaust may make faith in God difficult, but it makes faith in man impossible.

—Dennis Prager and Joseph Telushkin, *The Nine Questions People Ask About Judaism*, page 35

As the British psychiatrist R. D. Laing has written, "Normal men have killed perhaps 100,000,000 of their fellow normal men in the last fifty years." Goethe described the ambivalence in man's nature most succinctly: "The unnatural—that too is natural."

> Mankind on the average, and taken by and large, are a wretched lot.
>
> —Sigmund Freud (1856–1939); quoted in Ernst Freud, ed., *The Letters of Sigmund Freud and Arnold Zweig*, page 3

One of the main factors that influenced Freud to adopt this grim view was the variety and virulence of Jew-hatred: "With regard to antisemitism . . . I feel a strong inclination to surrender my affects in this matter and find myself confirmed in my wholly nonscientific belief that mankind on the average . . .'"

HARNESSING THE EVIL INCLINATION FOR GOOD

> "And God saw everything that He had made, and found it very good" (Genesis 1:31). [Rabbi Nahman said in the name of Samuel: "The words 'very good'] refer to the *yetzer ha-ra*, the evil inclination."
>
> "But is the evil inclination a very good thing?" [Rabbi Nahman was challenged]. "What an astonishing thing to say!"
>
> "Were it not for the evil inclination," he answered, "men would not build homes, take wives, have children, or engage in business."
>
> —*Genesis Rabbah* 9:7

Because pure and beautiful things can be created even when the motives for them are mixed (e.g., a couple's motives for mating may be lust, a scientist's motive for discovering the cure to a disease might be to become wealthy), the Rabbis urge people to worship God with their evil inclination no less than with their good. Thus, while the desire for fame, for example, springs more from ignoble than noble motives, if a person finds him- or herself overwhelmed by such a need, let that person try to become famous for doing good, e.g., by donating the funds for a hospital building to be named for him or her.

> A person's nature can be recognized through three things:
> his cup, his purse, and his anger.
> —Babylonian Talmud, *Eruvin* 65b

In other words: by how a person acts when he drinks liquor, by how much charity he dispenses, and by how well he controls himself when provoked. Unfortunately, the English translation loses the Hebrew's alliterative quality; the Hebrew words are *koso* (cup), *kiso* (purse), *ka'aso* (anger). The Talmud then adds on a fourth criterion, "by what he does for pleasure."

> Rabbi Judah said in the name of Rav: [In ethical areas], you should never intentionally test yourself.
> —Babylonian Talmud, *Sanhedrin* 107a

The Talmud explains this statement through a legend that tells of King David challenging God to test him, just as he had tested the Patriarchs (i.e., challenging Abraham to offer up his son as a sacrifice). God answers: "I will test you, and even grant you a special privilege, for I did not inform [the Patriarchs of the nature of their trial beforehand], yet I inform you that I will try you in a matter of adultery." Immediately thereafter, the Talmud relates, David committed the greatest sin of his life, when he slept with Batsheva, who was married, and then arranged to have her husband killed. "Would that a bridle had fallen into [my mouth] so that I had never spoken as I did," the Talmud imagines David later saying.

The notion of not intentionally testing yourself is, of course, widely known to recovering addicts, whether they be former alcoholics, smokers, gamblers, or compulsive womanizers. A human being must know his or her areas of weakness, and shy away from those areas as much as possible.

People never leave this world with half their cravings satisfied. If they have a hundred, they want two hundred, and if they have two hundred, they want four hundred.

—*Ecclesiastes Rabbah* 3:12

Further exacerbating the problem of insatiable human desire is that people not only want more than they have, they also want more than anybody else has.

31

THE HUMAN CONDITION

Four Parables and a Bushel of Quotes

For two and a half years, the House of Shammai and the House of Hillel disputed. The House of Shammai argued that it would have been better [alternatively, easier] for man had he not been created, and the House of Hillel argued that it was better for man to have been created.

In the end, a vote was taken, and it was decided: "It would have been better for man not to have been created, but now that he has been created, let him examine his deeds." Others say, "Let him consider his future actions."
—Babylonian Talmud, *Eruvin* 13b

This is perhaps as sober an assessment of the human condition as one can imagine. Indeed, later Jewish scholars were concerned that sinners might cite talmudic comments such as the above in their defense, arguing that it is unfair to punish them for violating laws imposed upon them while living a life they never requested. In anticipation of such an argument, or the variants thereof, the eighteenth-century rabbi Yaakov Kranz of Dubno, popularly known as the Dubno Maggid (preacher of Dubno) offered this parable:

There was once a couple who had lived in peace and harmony for a good many years. The husband was ugly and always had been deaf; the wife was a shrew and had been blind from childhood. Being blind, the wife never knew how ugly her husband really was, while he, being deaf, was not troubled at all by his wife's sharp tongue.

One day, they learned of a physician of whom it was said that he could work miraculous cures, and they decided to go and see whether he could heal them of their handicaps. They agreed in advance to pay whatever amount of money the physician might charge them.

And it happened that the physician was successful, so that the wife was blind no more and the husband no longer deaf. Unfortunately, this amazing cure also spelled the end of the couple's domestic felicity. The husband now heard his wife's constant scolding and soon lost his patience with her, while his wife, clearly seeing his ugly features for the first time, could not bear to look at him. Therefore, when the physician presented them with his bill, they refused to pay. In fact, they told him, it was he who owed them compensation for having ruined their happy marriage.

When he saw that he could not prevail upon his two patients to pay for his services, he sighed and said: "If it is really true that I have made you unhappy by my cure, I will attempt to restore your happiness to you. If you wish, sir, I can make you deaf again, and you, madam, can easily be returned to your former state of blindness, and then your life will be as happy and peaceful as it was before you met me."

To this, however, both the man and his wife objected most strenuously.

"Well," replied the physician, "if you are unwilling to return to your former state, then it is obvious my skill must have made you happier than you were before. Hence it is only fair that you pay me for my services."

"Let this be a lesson," the Dubno Maggid concluded, "for those who refuse to accept responsibility for their actions. If life, once given to human beings, is so dear that they will not relinquish it voluntarily, it stands to reason that they must pay for the privilege of living. And what

form must this payment take? Responsibility before God
for their deeds."

—Benno Heinemann, *The Maggid of Dubno
and His Parables,* pages 161–162

A non-Jew asked Rabbi Joshua ben Korcha, "Do you not
claim that God sees into the future?"

"Yes," he replied.

The man said, "But it is written in your Torah, 'And
the Lord regretted that He had made people on earth, and
His heart was saddened' " [Genesis 6:6; if God knew be-
forehand that He was going to regret creating humankind,
why did He do it?].

Rabbi Joshua asked him: "Has a son ever been born
to you?"

"Yes," the man replied.

"And what did you do [when he was born]?"

He answered, "I rejoiced and made everyone else joyous."

The rabbi asked, "And did you not know that some
day the child would die?"

He answered, "At the time when one should be joyous, be joyous. And when it is time to mourn, mourn."

The rabbi said, "So, too, with the Holy One, blessed
be He."

—*Genesis Rabbah* 27:4

THE LIMITS OF WEALTH

"As a man came out of his mother's womb, so must he
depart at the end, naked as he came. He can take nothing
of his wealth to carry away with him" (Ecclesiastes 5:14).

The Rabbis comment: Man's life can be compared to
a fox who found a vineyard, fenced in on all sides. There
was one little hole in it, through which the fox wanted to
get in. But it was too narrow, and he did not succeed.
What did he do? He fasted for three days until he became
thin and frail, and then entered through the hole. Once
inside, the fox ate the grapes and grew fat. When he

wanted to leave, however, he was again unable to fit through the hole. So once more he fasted for three days until he was thin and frail, and he went out.

Once outside, he turned towards the vineyard and said, "Vineyard, vineyard, how good is your fruit! All that is within you is beautiful and worthy of praise. But of what use are you? Just as one enters you, so one must come out."

So too with this world!

—*Ecclesiastes Rabbah* 5:14

On the same verse in Ecclesiastes, Rabbi Meir offers yet another image:

A baby enters the world with hands clenched, as if to say, "The world is mine; I shall grab it." A man leaves with hands open, as if to say, "I can take nothing with me."

—Ibid.

THE LIMITS OF HAPPINESS

The nineteenth-century Hasidic rebbe Hanokh of Aleksandrov explained a talmudic saying [comparing the world to a wedding hall] through a parable: A man came to an inn in Warsaw. In the evening, he heard sounds of music and dancing coming from the next house.

"They must be celebrating a wedding," he thought to himself.

But the next evening he heard the same sounds, and again the evening after that.

"How can there be so many weddings in one family?" the man asked the innkeeper.

"That house is a wedding hall," answered the innkeeper. "Today one family holds a wedding there, tomorrow another."

"It's the same with this world," said Rabbi Hanokh. "People are always enjoying themselves. But some days it's

219

one person and the other days it's another. No single person is happy all the time."
—Retold in Francine Klagsbrun, *Voices of Wisdom,* page 8

THE OFTEN PUZZLING NATURE OF HUMAN FATE

It is not in our power to explain either the prosperity of the wicked or the sufferings of the righteous.
—*Ethics of the Fathers* 4:15

One man wants to live but can't, another man can, but doesn't want to.

—Yiddish proverb

People say to the bee [alternatively, hornet], "I don't want your honey, I don't want your sting."
—*Numbers Rabbah* 20:10

A man is what he is, not what he used to be.
—Yiddish proverb

Once the Angel [of Destruction] is permitted to begin his work [literally, to harm], he does not distinguish between the righteous and the wicked.
—*Mekhilta* (Lauterbach, Vol. 1, page 85)

Expecting the world to treat you fairly because you are a good person is like expecting the bull not to charge you because you are a vegetarian.
—Rabbi Harold Kushner, paraphrasing Rabbi Mordechai Kaplan (1881–1983), in *When All You've Ever Wanted Isn't Enough,* page 91

THE HARD LIFE OF GOODNESS

[The Hasidic rebbe] Moshe of Kobryn once looked at the Heavens and cried: "Angel, little angel! It is no great trick to be an angel up there in the sky. You don't have to eat

and drink, beget children, and earn money. Just you come
down to earth and worry about eating and drinking, about
raising children and earning money, and we shall see if
you keep on being an angel. If you succeed, you may
boast—but not now."

—Martin Buber, *Tales of the Hasidim,* Vol. II, page 161

This brings to mind Dr. Albert Schweitzer's words: "You don't
have to be an angel in order to be a saint."

THE EVER-CHANGING HUMAN PREDICAMENT

According to ancient Jewish folktale, King Solomon com-
missioned a jeweler to make for him a ring with an inscription, the words of which would be meaningful to him
whatever his mood, happy or sad. The jeweler brought
him one with the words, "This too shall pass."

32

ON SUFFERING

Rabbi Yochanan once became ill, and Rabbi Hanina went to visit him. He asked him, "Are your sufferings welcome to you?" Rabbi Yochanan replied, "Neither they nor their reward."

—Babylonian Talmud, *Berakhot* 5b

Rabbi Hiyya bar Abba said: If someone should say to me, "Sacrifice your life for the sanctification of God's name," I would be ready to do so, but only on condition that I be put to death at once. But I could not endure the tortures of [Hadrian's] great persecution.

—*Song of Songs Rabbah* 2:7

To stifle Jewish resistance, Hadrian's soldiers would heat iron balls in fire, then wedge them into a person's armpit until he or she died.

As Rabbi Hiyya bar Abba makes clear, the Rabbis believed that torture could cause the most righteous people to succumb far more than the fear of death. Thus, of Hananiah, Mishael, and Azariah, who accepted being thrown into a public furnace rather than worship Nebuchadnezzar's statue, they write:

If they had lashed Hananiah, Mishael and Azariah, they would have worshipped the statue.

—Babylonian Talmud, *Ketubot* 33b

Jewish law, it should be noted, was the only premodern legal system with which I am familiar that did not permit torturing prisoners (see page 410).

SUFFERING AND THE UNKNOWABLE WILL OF GOD

It was taught in the name of Rabbi Akiva: A man should always accustom himself to say, "Whatever God does is for good." Once, while Rabbi Akiva was traveling, he came to a certain town and looked for lodgings but was everywhere refused. He said, "Whatever God does is for good," and went and spent the night in a field. He had with him a cock, a donkey, and a lamp. A wind came and blew out the candles, a cat came and ate the cock, and a lion came and ate the donkey. He said, "Whatever God does is for good." The same night some soldiers came and carried off the inhabitants of the town. Rabbi Akiva said to his companions, "Did I not say to say, 'Whatever God does is for good.' "

—Babylonian Talmud, *Berakhot* 60b–61a

*   *   *

A man is not held responsible for what he says in the hour of his distress.

—Babylonian Talmud, *Bava Bathra* 16b

If a person curses God while he or she is in extreme agony, Jewish law does not regard that person as guilty of blasphemy. Similarly, if, while in terrible pain, a person curses the members of his family or makes ludicrous accusations against them, they should not take his words personally, much less reject the person on that account.

SUFFERING CAUSED BY INSULTS

They who are insulted but do not insult, who hear them-
selves cursed and do not reply . . . the Bible says of them . . .
"[They will be] as the sun rising in might" (Judges 5:31).
—Babylonian Talmud, *Shabbat* 88b

Two of the greatest figures of twentieth-century Jewish life were
Rabbi Abraham Isaac Kook, the first Chief Rabbi of Palestine, and
his good friend and companion, Rabbi Aryeh Levin. Kook was
fiercely hated in certain ultra-Orthodox anti-Zionist circles because
of his passionate support for the *chalutzim* (Zionist pioneers), most
of whom were nonreligious.

One morning at a synagogue service, Rabbi Levin was accosted
by an anti-Zionist extremist, who cursed him and almost tore the
tefillin off his head. When the other worshippers present remained
silent, Rabbi Levin left quietly, and never returned to this synagogue.

Later, one of those who had been present asked him, "Do you
know perhaps *why* you were punished by that man's actions and
words of deep insult? Do you know the underlying reason?"

"It may be that I sinned toward God."

"Oh, no," said the other man, himself one of the extremists. "It
is because you are so close and friendly with *that* rabbi." [He didn't
deign to mention Rabbi Kook by name.]

"Tell me," said Reb Aryeh, "was I right to keep silent and say
nothing?"

"Certainly," the other answered. "That is a very fine quality you
have. You know what our sages said, 'They who are insulted but do
not insult, who hear themselves cursed and do not reply . . . the Bible
says of them . . . "[They will be] as the sun rising in might." ' "

"Well, you should know," said Reb Aryeh, "that I learned *this*
trait from *that* rabbi" (Simcha Raz, *A Tzaddik in Our Time,* page 96).

Indeed, Rabbi Kook was known to write letters to doctors who
admired him, asking them to treat free of charge impoverished family members of the very people who defamed him.

224

33

"ONE DOES MORE, AND ONE DOES LESS"

Humility

Be very humble in spirit, because in the end you will be eaten by worms.

—*Ethics of the Fathers* 4:4

Let man contemplate that all snow begins pure white and turns into slush, and he too, with all his beauty, will change into a small heap of corrupted matter.

—*Sefer Hasidim* (*Book of the Pious*), paragraph 305

The test of humility is your attitude to subordinates.

—Anonymous, *Orhot Tzaddikim*, chapter 2

Let a man always strive to be one of the persecuted rather than one of the persecutors.

—Babylonian Talmud, *Baba Kamma* 93a

The above teaching is applicable only when there is no alternative. Ideally, one should be sufficiently strong to prevent others from persecuting him or her, without turning into a persecutor himself.

Rabbi Irving Greenberg articulates one important lesson Jews should learn from the Holocaust: "Never again should Jews be so weak that their very weakness tempts others to oppress them."

FALSE HUMILITY

My grandfather, Nissen Telushkin, was a rabbi for over sixty years. He once told me about a certain wealthy man who had a high standing in the community, and thus was entitled to sit in a prominent seat at the front of the synagogue. However, he insisted on sitting in the back, where he would carefully watch all who entered to see if they noticed that he had chosen to sit in so humble a location. Finally, my grandfather said to him, "It would be better if you sat up front, and thought that you should be seated in the back, rather than to sit in the back, and think the whole time you should be seated in the front."

WHEN HUMILITY BECOMES PARALYZING OR HARMFUL

One of Rabbi Israel Salanter's disciples told him, "Rebbe, I am in very serious financial trouble, because I don't have a job."

"Why not become a rabbi?" asked Rabbi Israel.

"Rebbe, I am afraid that I might give an incorrect ruling."

"Who then should become a rabbi?" said Rabbi Israel. "One who is not afraid of ruling incorrectly?"

—Cited in Shmuel Himelstein, *A Touch of Wisdom, a Touch of Wit,* page 172

A RABBINIC APPRECIATION OF ONE'S FELLOW MAN

A favorite saying of the Rabbis of Yavneh was: I am God's creature and my fellow man [referring in this instance to one who is not learned] is God's creature. My work is in the town, and his work is in the field. I rise early for my work and he rises early for his work. As he does not seek to do my work, I do not seek to do his work. And should you say, I do much [study of Torah] while he does little, we have learnt: One does more and one does less. What matters is that one directs his heart towards Heaven.

—Babylonian Talmud, *Berakhot* 17a

Rabbi Zvi Ehrman comments: "Not the volume of learning matters, but the spirit of it" (The *El-Am Talmud, Berakhot* page 392).

When a king and a bridal party meet, the bridal party must make way for the king. Nevertheless, [the first-century] King Agrippa made way for a bride, and the sages praised him. When they asked him, "What made you do so?" he replied, "I wear a crown every day; she will wear her crown but a brief hour."

—Babylonian Talmud, minor tractate *Semakhot* 11:6

AGAINST ARROGANCE

Adam was created [last of all beings] on the eve of the Sabbath. Why? . . . So that if a person becomes too proud, one can say to him, "The gnat was created before you."

—Babylonian Talmud, *Sanhedrin* 38a

*　　*　　*

Because Jewish tradition places such extraordinary emphasis on Torah learning, there always is a danger that scholars will become arrogant. A number of talmudic anecdotes strongly criticize this tendency, and emphasize that a scholar should always be conscious that goodness matters more than intellect:

Rabbi Yannai was taking a walk, and he saw a man of impressive appearance [who appeared to be a scholar].
　　Rabbi Yannai said to him, "Would you be my guest?"
　　He said, "Yes."

So Rabbi Yannai took him to his house, and gave him food and drink. He spoke to him of talmudic matters and found that the man knew nothing; then he spoke about the Mishna, the Aggadah and the Bible, and saw that the man was ignorant of them all. Then he said to him, "Take the wine cup and recite the blessing."

The man said, "Let Yannai make the blessing in his own house."

Rabbi Yannai said, "Can you repeat what I say to you?"

He said, "Yes."

"Then say, 'A dog has eaten Yannai's bread.' "

The man jumped up, seized Yannai, and said, "You have my inheritance, which you are withholding from me."

Yannai said, "What inheritance of yours do I have?"

The man answered, "Once I passed a school, and I heard the voices of the children reciting, 'The Law which Moses commanded us is the inheritance of the congregation of [all the children of] Jacob (Deuteronomy 33:4)'; they did not say, 'the inheritance of the congregation [only] of Yannai.' "

Then Rabbi Yannai said, "What merit have you [i.e., what good deeds have you done] that you should eat at my table?"

The man said, "I never heard malicious gossip and repeated it [particularly not to the person being spoken of], nor did I ever see two people quarreling without making peace between them."

Said Rabbi Yannai, "You have such fine qualities (*derekh eretz*), and I called you a dog."

—*Leviticus Rabbah* 9:3

The twentieth-century writer John Rich wisely suggests the dangers of living in a society that snobbishly values intellectual achievement at the expense of other accomplishments: "If everybody contemplates the infinite instead of fixing the drains, many of us will die of cholera."

The Talmud also contains the following advice as an antidote to scholarly arrogance:

> Rabbi Yochanan ben Zakkai said: Do not give yourself great airs if you have learned much Torah, because for this purpose you were created.
>
> —*Ethics of the Fathers* 2:8

34

"DID YOU SEE MY ALPS?"

Against Asceticism

In the future world, a man will have to give an accounting for
every good thing his eyes saw, but of which he did not eat.
—Palestinian Talmud, *Kiddushin* 4:12

Although some individual rabbis have been ascetics, the talmudic
Rabbis, and most subsequent Jewish scholars, believed that God put
human beings on this world to enjoy it. True, because of the laws
of *kashrut,* certain foods were forbidden, but all those that were not
forbidden should be eaten. Indeed, the above talmudic passage goes
on to note that "Rabbi Elazar paid particular attention to this statement, setting aside money so that he could eat every kind of food
at least once a year."

Of course, the Jewish tradition acknowledges pleasures other
than the culinary. For example, when Rabbi Simeon ben Gamliel
saw a particularly beautiful woman, he exclaimed, "How great are
your works, O Lord" (from Psalm 104:24; see Babylonian Talmud,
Avodah Zara 20a).

The great leader of nineteenth-century German Orthodoxy, Samson Raphael Hirsch, surprised his disciples one
day when he insisted on traveling to Switzerland. "When
I stand shortly before the Almighty," he explained, "I will

230

be held answerable to many questions. . . . But what will I say when . . . and I'm sure to be asked, 'Shimshon, did you see my Alps?' "
—Martin Gordon, *Journal of Jewish Thought,* 1985, page 123

It is not enough what the Torah has forbidden you, but you wish to forbid yourself more things? [The Talmud's response to a person who forbids himself things permitted by the Torah, such as drinking wine].
—Palestinian Talmud, *Nedarim* 9:1

In commenting on a verse in Ecclesiastes, "Be not overrighteous" (7:16), Maimonides writes, "No one should, by vows and oaths, forbid to himself the use of things otherwise permitted" ("Laws of Character Development and Ethical Conduct," 3:1).

Although sobriety long has been an honored value among Jews, even the prohibition of drunkenness never has been absolute:

A person should become so drunk on Purim that he cannot tell the difference between "Cursed be Haman," and "Blessed be Mordechai."
—Babylonian Talmud, *Megillah* 7b

To the Rabbis, this represents the deepest level of drunkenness imaginable, comparable to a person today not knowing the difference between "Cursed be Hitler," and "Blessed be Anne Frank."

Yalta said to Rabbi Nahman [her husband]: For everything that God prohibited to us, an equivalent was permitted. We are forbidden to eat blood, but permitted to eat liver [which is rich in red blood corpuscles]. . . . Pork is prohibited, but the brains of the *shibuta* [a fish which tastes like pork] is permitted. . . . A married women is prohibited, but marrying a divorcée [whose former husband is alive] is permitted. . . . Therefore, [Yalta concluded,] I would like to eat milk and meat together [i.e., where is its equivalent?].

Rabbi Nahman instructed the butchers: "Grill her a

cow's udder" [which presumably imparts a milk flavor to the meat].

—Babylonian Talmud, *Hullin* 109b

THE DANGERS OF ASCETICISM

A rich Hasid came to Rabbi Dov Baer and asked for his blessing. The rebbe started to engage him in conversation. "I'm curious to learn how a man of your great wealth conducts his household," the rebbe asked him. "For example, what do you eat every day?"

"Oh, we live very simply," the man answered. "I myself eat nothing more than dry bread and salt."

The rebbe became incensed. "Dry bread and salt are not sufficient for a man of your riches! You should be eating meat, wine, and fresh bread." He continued chiding the rich man until he finally consented to eat tastier, more luxurious, food. After he left, Dov Baer's surprised disciples questioned him: "What does it matter to you if that man eats stale bread with salt or meat with wine?"

"It matters a great deal," Dov Baer answered. "If he feasts on meat and wine, he will understand that the poor need at the very least stale bread with salt. But if he himself eats nothing more than stale bread with salt, he will imagine that the poor can satisfy themselves with stones."

—Based on Louis Newman, *The Hasidic
Anthology*, pages 467–468

Where there is no bread, there is no Torah.

—*Ethics of the Fathers* 3:17

People whose bodies are screaming for food will lack the presence of mind to focus on their studies. Strangely enough, I have come across a parallel thought in the writings of a Hindu master, Vivekananda (1863–1902): "First bread, and then religion. No dogmas will satisfy the cravings of hunger."

When the Second Temple was destroyed, many in Israel became ascetics, committing themselves not to eat meat or drink wine. Rabbi Joshua approached them and said, "My children, why do you eat no meat nor drink wine?"

They answered, "Shall we eat meat which used to be offered on the altar as a sacrifice, now that the altar has ceased to exist? Shall we drink wine, which used to be poured as a libation on the altar, now that it is poured no longer?"

He said to them, "In that case, we should stop eating bread, since the meal offerings have ceased."

"We will get by on fruit," [they answered].

"But we cannot eat fruit," [Rabbi Joshua said], "because the offering of the first fruits has ceased."

"We will eat the other kinds of fruit [which did not require an offering at the Temple]."

"But in that case we ought not to drink water because the pouring of the water on the altar [during the holiday of Sukkot] has ceased."

They were silent.

He then said to them, "My children, come and let me advise you. Not to mourn at all is impossible, because of the destruction which has befallen us. But to mourn too much is also impossible, because we are forbidden to impose a decree on the community that the majority will find unbearable."

—Babylonian Talmud, *Bava Bathra* 60b

The asceticism here was occasioned not by a philosophical rejection of material pleasure, but by the anguish of those who had lived through the failed revolt against Rome and the destruction of the Second Temple. The crushing of the Great Revolt, which was accompanied by an enormous loss of life, was a tragedy of epic proportions, comparable in its impact on first-century Jewry to the Holocaust's impact today.

Although Rabbi Joshua empathized with the depth of the ascetics' pain, he understood that their attitude would lead to the end of the Jewish people, and so was untenable. A nation cannot go on existing for generation after generation in perpetual mourning; at the very least, most of its members will choose to assimilate to a more joyful way of life.

The mind-set of such ascetics, however, still strikes a responsive chord within some. At a rabbinic conference several years ago, one participant advocated that Jews commemorate the Holocaust every Sabbath lunch by eating a meal modeled on the diet offered in Auschwitz: inadequate portions of moldy bread, thin soup, and the like. In responding to the suggestion, I recalled the words of Rabbi Joshua, "to mourn too much is also impossible," and argued that such a ritual, instead of increasing Holocaust awareness, would lead rather to a diminution of Sabbath observance.

In fulfillment of Rabbi Joshua's words, "Not to mourn at all is impossible," the Talmud records three symbolic acts of deprivation ordained on all Jews by the Sages; unfortunately, I know few Jews today who observe these restrictions:

> A man may plaster his house, but he should leave a small
> space unfinished. A man can prepare a full-course banquet,
> but he should omit a few dishes. . . . And when a woman
> puts on her jewelry, she should omit an item or two.
> —Babylonian Talmud, *Bava Bathra* 60b

Thus, in lieu of asceticism, the Rabbis ordained symbolic reminders that we live in an unredeemed world.

ASCETIC TENDENCIES WITHIN JUDAISM

While the above statements reflect, I believe, the main thrust of the Jewish tradition, there have been Jewish teachers, and even movements, that have encouraged a rejection of the pleasures of this world:

> [On his deathbed, Rabbi Judah the Prince, the leader of
> his generation and a wealthy man, raised both hands and
> declared before God]: "It is known to You that I have not

enjoyed the pleasures of this world even with my little finger."

—Babylonian Talmud, *Ketubot* 104a

This is the way [to acquire knowledge] of the Torah: You must eat bread with salt and drink water measure by measure, and you must sleep on the ground and you must endure a life of deprivation while you toil in the Torah.

—*Ethics of the Fathers* 6:4

One of the Talmud's most famous rabbis, Shimon bar Yohai, was known as a vigorous opponent of Roman rule in Israel, and the Romans issued a death sentence against him. Rabbi Shimon and his son went "underground," and during their years in hiding, they became ascetics.

Shimon and his son hid themselves in the House of Study. Every day, his wife would bring them a loaf of bread and a jug of water. But when the persecutions increased [they became afraid that she would be tortured to reveal their identity and] they hid in a cave.

There, a miracle happened to them. A carob tree grew for them, and a spring of water welled up for them.

They undressed and sat up to their necks in the sand. They studied the Torah the whole day long. Only for the times of prayer did they get dressed, and after having prayed, they removed their clothes again, in order not to wear them out. In this manner, they remained in the cave for twelve years.

Then the prophet Elijah came, stood at the entrance of the cave and called out, "Who will make known to Shimon bar Yohai that the Emperor has died and that his decree has been annulled?"

Hearing this, they left the cave. They saw farmers plowing and sowing, and they became angry and said, "Those people are neglecting [the study of Torah which leads to] eternal life, and are busying themselves with mundane matters" [trying to earn a living and eat well].

Everything upon which they gazed was immediately consumed by fire.

Then a heavenly voice was heard saying, "Have you come out of the cave in order to destroy My world? Go back to your cave!" [The two men returned to the cave for another year, and when they came out they were more tolerant of people's desire to earn a livelihood and live well].

—Babylonian Talmud, *Shabbat* 33b

Compare the ascetic Rabbi Shimon, who believed Torah study to be the sole path to holiness, with the no less learned Rabbi Hillel, who saw the potential for holiness in everyday acts:

Once, when Hillel had concluded a class with his disciples, he left the House of Study with them.

The disciples asked him, "Master, where are you going?"

He replied: "To fulfill a religious obligation."

"What is this religious obligation?" the disciples wanted to know.

He replied: "I am going to the bathhouse in order to have a bath."

The disciples were astonished, and they asked, "Is that really a religious obligation?"

He answered: "Yes! If somebody who is appointed to scrape and clean the statues of the king that stand in the theaters and circuses is paid for the work and even associates with the nobility, how much more should I, who am created in the image and likeness of God . . . take care of my body?"

—*Leviticus Rabbah* 34:3

As the case of Rabbi Shimon bar Yohai should make clear, although most Jewish texts discourage asceticism, some of Judaism's most distinguished rabbis did preach extreme self-denial. I suspect, however, that this represented individual personality inclinations more than a Jewish imperative. The eighteenth-century Rabbi Elijah, popularly known as the Gaon (genius) of Vilna, was the most famous Jewish ascetic. To this day, his name is used among religious Jews as a synonym for "genius" (e.g., "If he applies himself to his studies, who knows, he could be another Vilna Gaon"). Although the Gaon knew almost all major texts of Judaism by heart by his Bar-Mitzvah, he continued to learn Torah and Talmud sixteen to eighteen hours a day. He and his family lived on a pittance: "He often sold all his furniture to assist the poor or gave away his last meal," one biographical essay about the Gaon informs us (Louis Ginzberg, "The Gaon, Rabbi Elijah Wilna," page 143).

What such asceticism must have meant for his family is suggested by the Gaon of Vilna's commentary on Proverbs (23:30):

> True heroes are men of noble heart . . . who constantly perform the commandments and meditate on the Torah day and night, even though their home be without bread and clothing, and their families cry out: "Bring us something to support and sustain us, some livelihood." But he pays no attention at all to them nor heeds their voice . . . for he has denied all love except that of the Lord and His Torah.
>
> —Rabbi Elijah, the Gaon of Vilna

Jews of less ascetic temperament might characterize a man who ignores his family's pleas for food and clothing as something other than a "true hero."

The thirteenth-century *Hasidei Ashkenaz,* the "Saints of Germany," practiced the most extreme, and in some ways unprecedented, manifestations of asceticism. Louis Jacobs has persuasively argued that their practices did not derive from the Jewish tradition, but rather from the Christian monastic orders and the ascetic mood then "in the air" in their part of Europe (*What Does Judaism Say About?,* page 46). In penance for sins, the Hasidei Ashkenaz would engage in prolonged fasts, submit to floggings, and roll in the snow naked in winter. In the summer, some would sit naked in fields, their bodies smeared with honey so that they would be stung by bees.

Once such extreme actions were introduced, they continued to influence some people with ascetic inclinations. The Hasidic movement, which originated in the mid-eighteenth century, emphasized joy in serving God and tried to wean Jews away from self-mortification. A well-known Hasidic story tells of a young man who came to Rabbi Israel of Rizhyn (d. 1850), boasting that he drank only water, rolled in the snow, wore nails in his shoes, and allowed himself to be flogged regularly. Rabbi Israel took the young man to the window, and pointed to a horse in the yard: "He too wears nails in his shoes, rolls in the snow, drinks only water, and is flogged regularly. Yet he is still only a horse!"

A FINAL BIT OF BIBLICAL ADVICE ON THE WORLD'S PLEASURES

Go, eat your bread in gladness and drink your wine in joy, for your action was long ago approved by God. Let your clothes always be freshly washed and your head never lack ointment. Enjoy happiness with a woman you love all the fleeting days of life that have been granted you under the sun. . . . Whatever it is in your power to do, do with all your might.

—Ecclesiastes 9:7–10

35

"WHAT HAVE I IN COMMON WITH JEWS?"

Alienation

What have I in common with Jews? I have hardly anything in common with myself and should stand very quietly in a corner, content that I can breathe.
> —Franz Kafka (1883–1924), *Diaries;* cited in Robert Alter,
> *After the Tradition,* page 17

In a "Letter to His Father," Kafka described the process by which his father's meager efforts to pass on some Jewish feeling within his family failed:

> You really had brought some traces of Judaism with you from the ghetto-like village community. It was not much and it dwindled a little more in the city and during your military service; but still, the impressions and memories of your youth did just about suffice for some sort of Jewish life [for you]. . . . But it was too little to be handed on to the child; it all dribbled away while you were passing it on.

* * *

The people I can pray with, I can't talk to, and the people
I can talk to, I can't pray with.

—Ernst Simon (1899–1988)

When Simon, an early associate of Martin Buber, became an
observant Jew, he found that the political and intellectual concerns
that he retained did not seem to interest his religious compatriots,
while his religious concerns bored his secular friends.

Even some aspects of Zionism, the Jews' return to their own
land and to the Hebrew language, were capable of generating an
alienation from the Jewish past:

> "I want to state," Yudka spoke with an effort in low, tense
> tones, "that I am opposed to Jewish history. . . . I would
> simply forbid teaching our children Jewish history. Why
> the devil teach them about our ancestors' shame? I would
> just say to them: Boys, from the day we were exiled from
> our land we've been a people without a history. Class dis-
> missed. Go out and play [soccer]."
>
> —Haim Hazaz, *Ha-Derashah* ("The Sermon"), translated by Ben
> Halpern, *Partisan Review* 23 (1956), pages 171–187

Hazaz represented one particular current in Zionist thinking,
shlilat ha-golah, "negation of the diaspora," which in effect means
rejection of one's grandparents and all other ancestors.

The stultifying limits such an approach can inflict on the very
boys told to "Go out and play soccer" is underscored in the comment of a character in an important Israeli War of Independence
novel:

> My grandfather, whom I never knew, was a scholar; all
> he did was study his Torah and his books; his life was
> whole and he was firmly rooted in all his relationships.
> Fine. My father tore himself away and came here and
> planted himself again. Now I and my friends are *segatiles.*
> Plants sprouting by the roadside. No longer scholars of
> the Torah, and not yet wise with any new wisdom. . . .
> Fellows without forefathers. Only fathers. And anything

before your father's imagination—darkness.
—S. Yizhar, *The Days of Ziklag;* I have followed the translation
of Robert Alter, *After the Tradition,* page 218.

While Simon, Hazaz, and Yizhar are speaking of an alienation from the Jewish past and present, a contemporary historian of Jewish life in the American South recalls his grandmother's expression of the isolation she felt in the midst of her non-Jewish neighbors:

The lonely days were Sundays—Sundays when I watched the town people going to church, while we stayed upstairs in our apartment. Then I would feel like an outsider in this little community. I would have hunger in my heart for my own people. I would visualize a Utopia—a village like this of all Jews—going to temple on the Sabbath.
—Jennie Nachamson, recalling life in the American South
in the early 1900s; cited in Eli Evans, *The Lonely Days
Were Sundays: Reflection of a Jewish Southerner,* on
unnumbered page following the dedication

ALIENATION AND CONTEMPT

The Jews have produced only three originative geniuses, Christ, Spinoza and myself.
—Gertrude Stein (1874–1946), quoted in
James Mellow, *Charmed Circle*

In Stein's rather egocentric view of history, the only brilliant Jews seem to be those whom the world does not think of as Jews at all.

Why do you come to me with your special Jewish sorrows? I feel just as sorry for the wretched Indian victims in Putamayo, etc. . . . I cannot find a special corner in my heart for the ghetto. I feel at home in the entire world wherever there are clouds and birds and human tears.
—Revolutionary Rosa Luxembourg (1871–1919) in a letter to
Mathilde Wurm, February 16, 1917. Luxembourg,

co-founder with Karl Liebknecht of the German Communist
party (KPD) in 1918, was killed during an abortive
antigovernment uprising in 1919.

Born in Poland to a committed Jewish family, Luxembourg not
only felt indifferent to Jewish sufferings, but to those of her family
as well. Indeed, her indifferent response to the death of her mother
prompted her anguished father to write: "An eagle soars so high he
loses sight of the earth below. . . . I shall not burden you any more
with my letters."

According to Israeli scholar Naomi Shepherd, the absurdity of
Luxembourg's claiming to "feel at home in the entire world" while
indifferent to Jewish sorrows resembles "her claim to have been
'making the whole world happy' rather than dealing with the special
sorrows of her family" (*A Price Below Rubies: Jewish Women as
Rebels and Radicals,* pages 112–113).

36

"A PERSON IS *ALWAYS* LIABLE FOR HIS ACTIONS"

Free Will and Human Responsibility

A person is always liable for his actions, whether awake
or asleep.

—Babylonian Talmud, *Bava Kamma* 3b

According to Jewish law, a person who breaks another's property unintentionally, e.g., while sleepwalking, still is obligated to pay
for the damage. If this seems unfair, consider the alternative: The
victim would remain uncompensated for his loss.

The Talmud's insistence that human beings always are liable for
the damage they cause sharply contrasts with an emerging norm in
contemporary American life, in which people often are not held responsible even when they *intentionally* cause damage. In *A Nation
of Victims*, Charles Sykes documents numerous instances of this new
type of "enlightened" thinking.

- In Pennsylvania in 1987, an FBI agent embezzled two thousand
  dollars, then lost the money gambling in Atlantic City. He
  promptly was fired but won reinstatement after a court ruled that
  the man's pressing need to gamble with other people's money
  should be regarded as a "handicap." Firing him, therefore, vio-

lated federal laws protecting the handicapped (*Rezza* v. *United States Department of Justice et al.,* No. 87–6732, May 12, 1988, U.S. District Court, Eastern District of Pennsylvania).

- In San Francisco in 1978, Supervisor Dan White murdered Mayor George Moscone and Supervisor Harvey Milk. At White's trial, his lawyer offered the "Twinkie defense," arguing that an addiction to junk food had clouded White's mind and caused him to commit the murders. The jury sympathized, and sentenced White to only six years in prison.

- In an incident in New York City in the 1980s, a man attempting suicide jumped in front of an oncoming subway train. After he didn't die, but was badly maimed, the man sued the city and was awarded $650,000 because the train had not stopped in time.

According to the FBI agent and Dan White, external factors were responsible for the evil acts they had committed; thus, they should not be punished (ironically, they probably felt that they should be credited for whatever good acts they had done). While common sense dictates that many aspects of human achievements are limited by heredity (I could practice ten hours a day, and still not play tennis as well as the late Arthur Ashe) and/or environment (the most accomplished African American or Jew could not hope to be elected president in nineteenth-century America), the Jewish tradition firmly believes that morality is one realm of human existence where choices always exist:

> Rabbi Hanina bar Papa explained: The angel in charge of conception is called *lailah* [Hebrew for "night"]. [When conception occurs], he takes the drop of semen and brings it before God, and says: "Master of the universe, what shall be the fate of this drop? Will it develop into a strong person or a weak one? A wise person or a fool? A wealthy person or a poor one?" Whether the person will be wicked or righteous, this he does not ask.
>
> —Babylonian Talmud, *Niddah* 16b

Free will also is central in the thinking of Moses Maimonides, the foremost medieval Jewish philosopher. Indeed, if human beings lack free will, Maimonides argues, then it follows that the Almighty is unjust:

> If God decreed that a person should be either righteous or wicked, or if there was some force inherent in his nature which irresistibly drew him to a particular course . . . how could God have commanded us through the prophets, "Do this and do not do that, improve your ways, and do not follow your wicked impulses," when, from the beginning of his existence a person's destiny had already been decreed? . . . What room would there be for the whole of the Torah? By what right or justice could God punish the wicked or reward the righteous? "Shall not the judge of all the earth act justly?" (Genesis 18:25).
>
> —Moses Maimonides, *Mishneh Torah*, "Laws of Repentance," 5:4

Maimonides's comment ". . . if there was some force inherent in his nature which irresistibly drew him to a particular course . . ." brings to mind Justice Louis Brandeis's bon mot: "The irresistible is often only that which is not resisted."

Elsewhere in the same chapter, Maimonides asserts that free will in the moral realm is absolute:

> Every human being may become righteous like Moses our Teacher, or wicked like Jeroboam [the king who reintroduced idolatry into Israel; see I Kings 12:26–33]; . . . merciful or cruel, miserly or generous, and so with all other qualities.
>
> —Moses Maimonides, *Mishneh Torah*, "Laws of Repentance," 5:2

Louis Jacobs, a contemporary Jewish theologian, believes that Maimonides's "no ifs, ands or buts" espousal of free will caused him to seriously underrate environmental influences on people. This does not mean that individuals utterly lack free will, Jacobs argues, only that it might be more limited than Maimonides suggests: "It may well be that the child reared by thieves is compelled to steal by his upbringing and training. He will not see stealing as wrong and for him free will does not operate in this area. But he, too, can come to see, for instance, that it is wrong to do violence while stealing, and his area of choice may be confined to whether or not he will do violence" (*Principles of the Jewish Faith,* page 332).

Until quite recently, Judaism's condemnation of people who act wickedly paralleled the prevailing thinking in Western society. How then do we explain recent changes? Sykes attributes the turnaround to "the triumph of therapeutic thinking," in which psychological explanations are utilized to excuse people from responsibility for immoral acts. Thus, embezzling money becomes as much a "hand-icap" as being physically crippled, and should, therefore, inspire neither guilt nor punishment.

Not surprisingly, one of the earliest champions of this new thinking was America's most famous criminal defense lawyer, Clarence Darrow (1857–1938). In arguing against the death penalty, Darrow posited that free will does not exist: "All people are products of two things, *and two things only*—their heredity and their environment. And they act in exact accord with the heredity which they took from all the past, and for which they are in no wise responsible, and the environment, which reaches out to the farthest limits of all life that can influence them. We all act from the same way (i.e., influences)" (emphasis mine; Darrow's speech is printed in *Lend Me Your Ears: Great Speeches in History,* selected and introduced by William Safire, pages 327–335).

The point of view espoused by Darrow is by now so "ingrained in modern American [university] attitudes as hardly to be challenged," writes Professor James Deese. "I once tried to dissuade an intelligent young undergraduate student in a seminar on ethics and psychology from the belief that anyone who committed a murder was *ipso facto* 'sick.' I failed" (*American Freedom and the Social Sciences,* page 31).

In contrast, Judaism argues that human nature is ambivalent at its core (see pages 207–215). Thus, to label all murderers as "mentally ill" makes no more sense than labeling all people who risked their lives to save Jews from the Nazis as mentally unbalanced people who felt compelled to become martyrs. A person's decision to murder is less likely rooted in sickness than in a freely-arrived-at decision to commit an evil act.

In stark contrast to the amoral premises of much contemporary psychological and criminological writing, the reflections of two prominent psychiatrists who were inmates in Nazi concentration camps are particularly illuminating:

> Blaming others, or outside conditions for one's own mis-behavior may be the child's privilege; if an adult denies responsibility for his own actions, it is another step to-wards personality disintegration.
>
> —Bruno Bettelheim

In 1938, Dr. Bettelheim was imprisoned for a year in Buchen-wald and Dachau. He later wrote of his experiences, and the impli-cations he drew from them, in *The Informed Heart,* a study of human behavior under extreme circumstances. Bettelheim's ordeal led him to conclude that a concentration camp inmate's personality disintegration became apparent the moment he or she started justi-fying utterly improper behavior as caused by outside oppression.

Parallel to Bettelheim's opinion is the conclusion reached by Vik-tor Frankl in *Man's Search for Meaning* (an account of his experi-ences as a concentration camp prisoner) that human beings always retain a certain degree of freedom:

> We who lived in concentration camps can remember the men who walked through the huts comforting others, giv-ing away their last piece of bread. They may have been few in number, but they offer sufficient proof that every-thing can be taken away from a man but one thing: the last of the human freedoms—to choose one's attitude in any given set of circumstances, to choose one's own way.

OLD AGE

Anguish and Opportunities

> You shall rise before the aged and show deference to the
> old: You shall fear your God.
>
> —Leviticus 19:32

The verse's first words are posted in Israeli buses to encourage
people to offer their seats to the elderly. I have seen Israeli bus drivers specifically request seated passengers to do so.

Although some Torah precepts were deemed applicable only to
fellow Jews, the Talmud rules that this law also applies to non-Jews:

> "You shall rise before the aged" means any aged. . . .
> Rabbi Yochanan used to rise in the presence of aged non-
> Jews, saying, "How many experiences have happened to
> these people!"
>
> —Babylonian Talmud, *Kiddushin* 33a

Note that the Torah concludes the verse ordaining deference to
the old with the words, "You shall fear your God," a biblical phrase
that invariably follows commandments obliging just treatment of
society's weakest members. For example, a few verses earlier, the
Torah ordains: "You shall not place a stumbling block in front of

a blind man: You shall fear your God" (Leviticus 19:14); elsewhere it decrees: "You shall not rule [over your servant] with vigor: You shall fear your God" (Leviticus 25:43).

> Show respect to an old man who has forgotten his learning through no fault of his own, for we have learned that the fragments of the old tablets [of the Ten Commandments which Moses shattered] were kept alongside the new tablets in the Ark of the Covenant.
>
> —Babylonian Talmud, *Berakhot* 8b

This is a relatively uncommon, and poignant, instance of poetic metaphor in the Talmud. As Rabbi Avi Ehrman explains: "A scholar who has lost his intellectual [abilities] and is thus intellectually 'broken' is compared to the broken tablets of the Law," and should be shown the respect that they were (El-Am Talmud, *Berakhot*, 153).

THE WISDOM OF THE OLD

> Ask your father and he will tell you, your elders and they shall instruct you.
>
> —Deuteronomy 32:7

In traditional societies, elders are respected for their ties to the past and for the wisdom they transmit. In today's secular, scientific society, where knowledge in many fields is doubling every decade, we are prone to view the wisdom of the old as out-of-date or "out of touch." Today's heroes generally are actors, rock stars, and sports figures; small wonder that there is a poor regard for those who are often physically deteriorating. Yet this prejudice toward old age, which is underscored by the desperate need of so many Americans to look much younger than they are, is ultimately self-destructive. Since we who are not elderly already hope to become old, it surely is in our self-interest to cultivate respect for the future condition we will share. Probably the reason that we don't is that old age is viewed like death: something we know happens to everyone, but which, in our "heart of hearts," we don't believe will happen to us—until it actually does.

> In answer to young people who told him that he could not understand their problems, Fritz Kortner, the German-Jewish actor, responded: "You were never as old as I am; on the other hand, I was as young as you are now."
>
> —Quoted in Lore and Maurice Cowan,
> *The Wit of the Jews,* page 92

> As regards scholars, the older they become the more wisdom they acquire.... But as regards the ignorant, the older they become, the more foolish they become.
>
> —Babylonian Talmud, *Shabbat* 152a

WAYS TO ACHIEVE OLD AGE

Jewish tradition understood long, healthy years to be a blessing granted by God. Several biblical and talmudic statements enumerate the specific behavior that moves God to bestow this blessing. The Torah lists long life as the reward for fulfilling three of its 613 commandments—honoring one's parents (Exodus 20:12), sending away a mother bird before capturing her young (Deuteronomy 22:7), and using honest weights in business (Deuteronomy 25:15). But the Talmud counsels a far more demanding list of ethical and ritual requirements for attaining a long life:

> The students of Rabbi Zeira, and some say Rabbi Adda bar Ahavah, asked him: "In virtue of what have you reached such a good old age"
> He said to them: "In all my days,
> I never showed impatience in my house,
> I never walked in front of any person greater than me,
> I never thought about Torah matters while walking in filthy alleys,
> I never walked four paces without musing over the Torah or without wearing *tefillin* (phylacteries),
> I never slept in the *Beit ha-Midrash* (house of study), ei-

ther a full night's sleep or even a nap,
I never rejoiced in my neighbor's shame, and
I never called my fellow by a nickname [which he might
resent or be embarrassed by].

—Babylonian Talmud, *Ta'anit* 20b

Ideally, Jewish tradition considers it a blessing to live to a great old age. Thus, some Jews start correspondence with the inscription "Dear so-and-so, *amush*," a Hebrew acronym for *ad meah v'esrim shana*, "may you live to one hundred and twenty years." A hundred and twenty became the ideal age because the Bible describes Moses as having reached that age, with "his eyes undimmed and his vigor unabated" (Deuteronomy 34:7). The Talmud likewise teaches that several of its greatest sages, including Hillel, Yochanan ben Zakkai, and Akiva lived until one hundred and twenty, and likewise remained intellectually and physically vital until the end.

The blessing of "one hundred and twenty years" frequently is offered people on their birthdays. One Jewish joke has it that a man greeted his friend on his birthday with the wish "May you live and be well until one hundred and twenty-one." When asked why he had changed the blessing's wording, the man answered, "God forbid, I don't want you to die suddenly."

Yet the *Ethics of the Fathers* questions whether an unusually long life is a blessing for most people. In enumerating the stages of a person's life, it teaches, "and one who is a hundred, it is as if he died and has passed from the world" (5:21).

THE AGONIES OF OLD AGE

The most haunting biblical verse concerning old age, from Psalms, summons up the fear that torments almost every elderly person:

Do not cast me off in old age;
when my strength fails me, do not forsake me!

—Psalms 71:9

This verse forms part of the High Holy Day liturgy, and I have long noticed that whenever it is chanted, one hears scattered sobs throughout the congregation, an indication of how universal is the fear, and reality, of rejection when one becomes old and weak. Other biblical verses note the varieties of physical deterioration that almost invariably accompany long years:

> And Barzillai said to King [David, who had invited the old man to journey with him to Jerusalem] . . . "I am now eighty years old. . . . Can I taste what I eat and drink? Can I still listen to the singing of men and women? Why then should I continue to be a burden to my lord the king?"
>
> —II Samuel 19:35–36

In addition to losing a sense of taste and hearing, many very old people suffer from physical infirmities. The Bible tells us that during David's final years, his servants used to cover his body with blankets, but "he never felt warm" (I Kings 1:1), while Isaac became blind when he was old (Genesis 27:1).

One talmudic sage, Rabbi Yossi ben Kisma, expressed the hardships of old age through a bitter riddle: "Two are better than three, and woe for the one thing that goes and does not return."

Several commentaries note that the "two" refers to the two legs of youth, which are superior to the three (the two legs plus a walking stick) that old people often need.

And "the one thing that goes and does not return," a talmudic sage explains, is one's youth (Babylonian Talmud, *Shabbat* 152a).

Although old people today frequently bemoan a deterioration of their physical power, the situation of elderly people today is far better than in ancient times. One finds many people in their eighties who can still enjoy what they "eat and drink," and who lead self-sufficient lives. On the other hand, because of medical advances, many old people with extremely incapacitating infirmities (people who would have died in earlier times) live in pain and with a sense of futility for many years.

*   *   *

When we were young, we were treated as men [in other words, told to act like adults]; now that we have grown old, we are looked upon as babies.

—Babylonian Talmud, *Bava Kamma* 92b

If a person has reached the "age of strength" [eighty], a sudden death is like dying from a kiss [i.e., as if the God took back the soul through a kiss].

—Babylonian Talmud, *Moed Kattan* 28a

We do not seat as a judge in the Sanhedrin [the Jewish High Court] an old man or a eunuch or one who is childless.

—Babylonian Talmud, *Sanhedrin* 36b

Two medieval explanations of this passage: Rashi says: "An old man is excluded because he has already forgotten the pain and anxiety of raising children, and therefore is no longer compassionate."

Along similar lines, Maimonides explains: "We do not appoint to the Sanhedrin a very aged man, or a eunuch, because they tend to lack tenderness" (*Mishneh Torah*, "Laws of the Sanhedrin," 2: 3). The late Israeli legal scholar, Rabbi Shlomo Yosef Zevin, observes that Maimonides only disqualifies one who is "very aged"; otherwise, "old age is a recommendation for membership in the Sanhedrin" (see Rabbi Zevin's, "The Old," page 130). This is in line with the previously cited teaching, "As regards scholars, the older they become, the more wisdom they acquire."

WHAT IS EXPECTED OF THE OLD?

Every Jew is obligated to study Torah, whether he is poor or rich, in sound health or ailing, in the vigor of youth or very old and feeble. . . . Until what period in life ought one to study Torah? Until the day of one's death.

—Moses Maimonides, *Mishneh Torah*, "Laws of Torah Study," 1:8,10

Older Jews, like others, are commanded to carry out all *mitzvot* (commandments) which they are physically capable of fulfilling. There is no retirement age when it comes to carrying out the commandments. Thus, in many synagogues, elderly, retired people make up a disproportionately high percentage of those attending the daily morning services. Rabbi Dayle Friedman observes that rather than seeing these continuing obligations as burdens, we should view them as bestowing dignity on the lives of individuals who have been freed from so many other responsibilities:

> To tell older adults that they are as bound to *mitzvot* as any other Jew is to tell them that something is expected of them, that their actions [still] matter. . . .
> —Rabbi Dayle Friedman, "The Crown of Glory: Aging in the Jewish Tradition," pages 215–216

38

"THE ANNIVERSARY OF A DEATH, *THAT* A JEW REMEMBERS"

Death and Mourning

If God didn't conceal from each person the day of his death, no one would build a house or plant a vineyard; each person would think rather, "Tomorrow I will die, why should I work for others?"

Thus, God concealed the day of a person's death, so that he will build and plant. If he merits [a long life] he will enjoy the fruit of his labors. If he doesn't, others will benefit from his work.

—*Yalkut Shimoni* on Ecclesiastes, #968

Among Jews, a birthday is no holiday, but the anniversary of a death, *that* a Jew remembers.

—Mendele Mokher Seforim (1835–1917), pen name of the Hebrew and Yiddish writer Jacob Abramowitz

While most modern Jews do celebrate birthdays, doing so is a relatively recent practice, one most likely adopted from the Jews' neighbors. The Bible itself mentions only one birthday, that of Pharaoh, a non-Jew (Genesis 40:20).

The anniversary of a death, known by the Yiddish word *yahr-zeit,* is a very special day. Close relatives light a twenty-four-hour candle, and the *Kaddish* prayer is recited in the synagogue. Perhaps there is greater emphasis on the day of death because only when a person dies do we know if he or she led a worthwhile life. At the time of birth, we know nothing:

> Commenting on the verse in Ecclesiastes [7:1], " . . . the day of death [is] better than the day of birth," Rabbi Levi explained: "This can be compared to two ocean-going ships, one leaving the harbor, and the other entering. Everybody is celebrating the departing ship, but only a few are rejoicing at the ship that is arriving. A wise man, seeing this, said, 'I see here an irony. People should not celebrate the departing ship, since they have no way of knowing what conditions she will meet, what seas she will encounter, and what winds she will have to face. People should rejoice rather over the ship that is entering the harbor, because it has safely returned from its voyage.' "
>
> —*Exodus Rabbah* 48:1

> With the death of a husband [or wife] you lose your present; with the death of a parent you lose your past, and with the death of a child you lose your future.
>
> —Norman Linzer, *Understanding Bereavement and Grief*

DEATH'S INEVITABILITY AND IRREVERSIBILITY

> I shall go to him, but he shall not return to me.
>> —II Samuel 12:23; David's lament on the death of
>> the newborn son he had conceived with Bathsheba

While Judaism, as we shall soon see, offers unique insights and laws on mourning, its reflections on death's inevitability and irreversibility resemble those of other societies: It is fascinating to compare the similarity of responses in different cultures:

To the men who told Socrates, "The Thirty Tyrants have condemned you to death," he replied, "And nature, them."

—Michel de Montaigne (1533–1592)

Wouldn't you think a man a prize fool if he burst into tears because he didn't live a thousand years ago? A man is as much a fool for shedding tears because he isn't going to be alive a thousand years from now.

—Seneca (c. 4 B.C.E.–65 C.E.), *Epistles*

That the end of life should be death may sound sad; yet what other end can anything have?

—George Santayana (1863–1952), *Some Turns of Thought in Modern Philosophy*

As opposed to the American philosopher, Judaism regards death as the end of life on this earth, but not the end of all existence (see Chapter 40, on afterlife).

After the game, the king and the pawn go into the same box.

—Italian proverb

Movie mogul Samuel Goldwyn once criticized Dorothy Parker: "Your stories are too sad, Dorothy. What the public wants are happy endings."

"Mr. Goldwyn," she responded. "Since the world was created, billions and billions of people have lived, and not a single one has had a happy ending."

WHEN LIVING BECOMES PAINFUL, AND NOTHING MORE

Although Jewish law opposes euthanasia, it recognizes that survival is not always a blessing. In three poignant passages, the Talmud describes great scholars whose quality of life deteriorated so significantly that death came as a blessing. The sufferings of Rabbi Judah

257

the Prince were physical; those of Rabbi Yochanan and Choni were social. The people closest to them had died, and they had no desire to go on living in what, to them, had become a friendless world:

On the day that Rabbi Judah was dying, the Rabbis declared a public fast, and offered prayers that God have mercy [and spare him]. . . . Rabbi Judah's maid went up to the roof of his house and offered this prayer: "The angels in heaven desire Rabbi Judah to join them, and the mortals on earth desire him to remain with them. May it be the will of God that the mortals overpower the angels." However, when she saw how much Rabbi Judah was suffering [literally, how often he had to go to the bathroom, each time painfully taking off his *tefillin* and putting them on again], she offered a second prayer: "May it be the will of God that the angels overpower the mortals." As the Rabbis continued their incessant prayers, she took a jar and threw it down from the roof. [It made a great noise and] for a moment the Rabbis ceased praying, and the soul of Rabbi Judah departed.

—Babylonian Talmud, *Ketubot* 104a

Discussions of this passage in numerous Jewish sources make it clear that the maid's action was commended.

[Resh Lakish, the closest friend and study partner of Rabbi Yochanan, died, and Rabbi Yochanan was plunged into deep grief.] Said the Rabbis, "Who shall go and take his mind away from his grief? Let Rabbi Eleazar ben Pedat go, for he has a very subtle mind."

Rabbi Eleazar went and sat before Rabbi Yochanan. Every time Rabbi Yochanan uttered an opinion, he said, "There is a *baraita* [a rabbinic source] which supports your opinion."

Said Rabbi Yochanan, "You are not like the son of Lakish. Whenever I stated an opinion, the son of Lakish used to make twenty-four objections, to which I was compelled to give twenty-four answers, and so the understanding of the Law was broadened. You, however, say, 'There

258

is a *baraita* which supports you.' Do I not know myself that what I have said is correct?"

He continued to tear his garments and weep, saying, "Where are you, son of Lakish?" Eventually, he lost his reason; so the Rabbis prayed for him and he died.

—Babylonian Talmud, *Bava Mezia* 84a

Strangely enough, the Talmud records that at the time of Resh Lakish's death, he and Yochanan had just had a bitter personal fight, and were not on speaking terms. The very intensity of the fight caused Resh Lakish to become ill, but when Resh Lakish's wife begged Rabbi Yochanan to forgive him, Yochanan refused, and Resh Lakish died almost immediately thereafter. Thus, Yochanan's subsequent mental decline might have been due to belated guilt feelings, as well as to the loss of so dear a friend and study partner.

A third story, legendary in character, tells of a rabbi named Choni who saw a man planting a carob tree:

"How many years does it take until this carob tree will bear fruit?" he asked the man.

"Seventy years."

Choni said to him, "Do you think you will live seventy more years?" [i.e., does it make sense for you to work at a task that cannot possibly benefit you in any way?]

The man replied, "I found a world containing fully grown carob trees, and just as my ancestors planted those trees for me, so too, will I plant them for my children."

Immediately thereafter, Choni sat down and ate some bread. Drowsiness soon overcame him, and he fell asleep. Some rocks rose to cover him, and he became hidden from sight. He slept for seventy years, and when he woke up, he saw what looked to be the same man picking fruits from the carob tree he had planted.

Choni asked him, "Are you the man who planted this tree?"

He answered, "No, I am his grandson."

Choni said, "It seems that I have slept for seventy years . . . " [and walked away].

He went to his house, and asked there, "Is the son of Choni still alive?"

The people there told him, "His son is no longer alive, but his grandson is."

He said to them, "I am Choni."

They didn't believe him.

He left and went to the study house, where he heard a rabbi saying, "These teachings are as clear to us as they were during the time of Choni," for it was known that whenever Choni came to the study house, whatever problems the rabbis had encountered in their studies, Choni would resolve.

Choni said to them, "I am Choni."

They did not believe him, and did not treat him with the honor due him [undoubtedly, they thought he was crazy].

Choni became anguished, and prayed for heavenly mercy, and died.

Rava said, "This is an example of the popular adage, 'either friends or death.'"

—Babylonian Talmud, *Ta'anit* 23a

The ArtScroll translation and commentary on this tractate notes: "Without the respect of his colleagues, Choni could no longer fulfill his life's task of teaching Torah, or participate in the work of a new generation. He did not wish to live beyond the normal life span of people if there was no longer a task left for him to accomplish."

In short, the Talmud recognized that long years are worthwhile only if they are fulfilling.

WHEN LIFE ENTERS ITS FINAL STAGES

If a person is near death, it is forbidden to leave him, so that he should not die alone. (And it is a *mitzvah* to stand by a person at the moment of death.)

—*Shulkhan Arukh, Yoreh De'ah* 339:4; the comment in parenthesis is by Rabbi Moses Isserles (1525–1572).

During the last year of Rabbi Israel Salanter's life, he was ill, and the Jewish community hired a guardian to accompany him. The guardian was a good-natured but simple man. Late one night, when Rabbi Salanter felt that his death was imminent, he spent the final moments of his life explaining to the guardian that he shouldn't fear, or be nervous about, being alone in a room with a corpse.

—Dov Katz, *T'nuat Ha-Mussar (The Mussar Movement)*, Vol. 1, page 376

THE DIFFERENT STATUS ACCORDED THE LIVING AND THE DEAD

For a day-old infant, the Sabbath is desecrated; for David, King of Israel, dead, the Sabbath must not be desecrated.

—Babylonian Talmud, *Shabbat* 151b; the Talmud is referring, of course, to an infant whose life is endangered.

FUNERALS

One who sees a corpse [en route to burial] and does not accompany it is like one who mocks the poor and deserves excommunication. He should accompany the corpse for a distance of at least four cubits [i.e., four steps].

—*Shulkhan Arukh, Yoreh Deah* 361:3

At one time, funerals in Israel became so costly that the expense was harder for some relatives to bear than the death itself. Some relatives even abandoned the corpse and ran away. Such desertions ended when Rabbi Gamliel [the preeminent leader of his generation, and a wealthy man] left orders that his body be carried to the grave in a simple linen garment [the costly garments in which dead people were interred had been one of the largest funeral expenses. Since coffins were not used then in Jewish funerals, all passersby could see the simple garment in which Rabbi Gamliel was interred.] From then on, everyone followed

Rabbi Gamliel's example. . . . Said Rabbi Papa: And now it is the general practice to carry out the dead even in rough cloth worth only a *zuz*.

—Babylonian Talmud, *Ketubot* 8b

The problem of costly funerals that Rabban Gamliel wished to counteract is still with us, as suggested by the experience of Ed Koch, the feisty former mayor of New York. In his autobiography, Koch writes of his mother's death from cancer, and of the humiliating pressures the funeral director immediately imposed on him and his father:

We needed to pick out a casket. We told the director we were looking for something in the Orthodox tradition, and he ushered us into a room with a twenty-five-hundred-dollar casket. . . . He knew that we were looking for something simple, but he figured he'd work his hard sell on us just the same. He took us into several rooms, and in each room the caskets cost less. He didn't skip a room. Probably he thought our resolve would weaken and we would be shamed into buying an expensive one. Finally, he took us into the basement, where he showed us two pine boxes, which is what we had told him we wanted in the first place. My mother would not have appreciated an expensive casket . . . besides, an Orthodox funeral requires a simple wooden casket without nails or ornament. . . . Yet . . . even here in the basement, he wanted to sell us the more expensive of the two pine caskets. . . . We were so humiliated by the ordeal that we said yes to [the more expensive one]. We could resist no further. I've never forgotten that. That man made us feel cheap, and we succumbed.

—Edward Koch with Daniel Paisner, *Citizen Koch: An Autobiography*, pages 60–61

*   *   *

The *halakha* [Jewish law] did not like to see the dead interred in silent indifference. It wanted to hear the shriek of despair and to see the hot tear washing away human cruelty and toughness. [As the Bible says], "And Abraham came to mourn for Sarah and to weep for her" (Genesis 23:2).

—Rabbi Joseph Soloveitchik, at eulogy for
Rebecca Twersky, January 30, 1977

While Western society extols "keeping a stiff upper lip," as epitomized by the quiet dignity Jacqueline Kennedy demonstrated at her husband's 1963 funeral, Jewish law encourages the deceased's close relatives and friends to express openly the deep pain they are feeling.

The funeral orator's goal is to make those present aware of the great loss that they have suffered. As Rabbi Soloveitchik says elsewhere in the same eulogy, "The *hesped* [eulogy] . . . seeks first of all to make people weep."

Some years ago, I was invited to speak at the funeral of a non-Jewish man I deeply loved. My eulogy followed the traditional Jewish approach; I recalled specific episodes of his generosity and love for others, and people began weeping. I was struck when the Protestant minister who followed me spoke in a very different manner. "This is not a sad day," he declared, "but a happy one. For Rolf is now in a far better world. We should not cry, therefore, but rejoice."

CONSOLING THE MOURNERS

Do not attempt to console a person whose dead relative still lies before him.

—*Ethics of the Fathers* 4:18

When Job's children died, his three closest friends came to visit him: "They sat with him on the ground seven days and seven nights. None spoke a word to him for they saw how great was his suffering" (Job 2:13).

While the behavior of Job's friends became the model for how Jews are to act in a house of mourning (one is to wait until the mourner speaks before saying anything), some Rabbis apparently

insisted on offering consolation even when the mourner did not seem
ready to hear it:

> When Rabbi Yochanan ben Zakkai's son died, his disci-
> ples came to comfort him. Rabbi Eliezer entered, sat down
> before him, and said to him, "Master, with your permis-
> sion, may I say something to you?"
> "Speak," he replied.
> Rabbi Eliezer said, "Adam had a son who died, yet he
> allowed himself to be comforted concerning him. And how
> do we know that he allowed himself to be comforted? For
> it is said, 'And Adam knew his wife again' [and they had
> another son; Genesis 4:25]. You, too, let yourself be com-
> forted."
> Said Rabbi Yochanan to him, "Is it not enough that I
> grieve over my own son, that you remind me of the grief
> of Adam?"
> [The process continued: Rabbi Joshua entered and
> asked him to be comforted as was Job. Rabbi Yochanan
> responded, "Is it not enough that I grieve over my own
> son, that you remind me of the grief of Job?" Rabbi Yossi
> reminded him that Aaron allowed himself to be comforted
> over the death of his two sons, and Rabbi Simeon men-
> tioned how David was comforted when his son died.]
> Rabbi Elazar ben Arakh entered. As soon as Rabbi
> Yochanan saw him, he said to his servants, "Take my
> clothing and follow me to the bathhouse, for he is a great
> man and I shall be unable to resist him."
> Rabbi Elazar entered, sat down before him, and said
> to him, "I shall tell you a parable. To what may your
> situation be compared? To a man to whom the king en-
> trusted an object to be carefully guarded. Every day the
> man would weep and cry out, 'Woe is me! When shall I
> be freed of this trust, and again be at peace?' You too,
> Master. You had a son, he studied the Torah, the Proph-
> ets, the Holy Writings, he studied Mishna, Halakha, Ag-
> gada, and he left this world without sin. Now that you
> have returned that which was entrusted to you, it is ap-
> propriate for you to be comforted."

Said Rabbi Yochanan to him, "Rabbi Elazar, my son, you have comforted me the way people ought to give comfort."

—*The Fathers According to Rabbi Nathan* 14:6; the final section of this narrative largely follows the translation of Danny Siegel, *Where Heaven and Earth Touch*, page 41.

A generation later, Beruriah, the wife of Rabbi Meir and the Talmud's most learned woman, broke the most terrible news to her husband in a touchingly similar manner:

While Rabbi Meir was teaching in the house of study on a Sabbath afternoon, his two sons died. What did their mother do? She left them lying on their couch and spread a sheet over them. When the Sabbath ended, Rabbi Meir returned. "Where are my two sons?" he asked.

"They went to the house of study," Beruriah answered.

"I looked for them but did not see them."

She gave him the cup of wine for *havdalah* [the prayer ushering out the Sabbath and other holy days] and he pronounced the blessing. Again he asked, "Where are my two sons?"

"They must have gone elsewhere and will return soon."

She brought food for him, and after he ate, she said, "I have a question to ask you."

"Ask it," he said.

"A while ago, a man came and left with me an item to watch for him. Now he has returned to claim what he left. Shall I return it to him or not?"

"Is not one who holds a deposit required to return it to its owner?" Rabbi Meir asked.

"Still, without your opinion," Beruriah said, "I would not give it back to him."

What did she do then?

She took him by the hand, led him up to the children's room, and brought him to the couch. She pulled off the sheet, and he saw that both boys were dead. He burst into tears. . . .

Then Beruriah said to him, "Did you not tell me that we are required to restore a pledge to the owner?"

To which he replied, " 'The Lord has given and the Lord has taken away; Blessed be the name of the Lord' " (Job 1:21).

> —*Midrash Proverbs* 31:10; I have followed, with minor varia-
> tions, the translation of Burton Visotzky, *The Midrash on
> Proverbs*, page 121.

Powerful as this story is, I have long doubted that it happened precisely as this account describes. For one thing, it is hard to imagine Beruriah maintaining her calm demeanor throughout this extended dialogue with her husband; more likely, she would have broken down the moment she began talking to him. Furthermore, the two boys' sudden death is very puzzling. Clearly, they had been in good health only a few hours earlier, which is why Rabbi Meir was looking for them at the house of study. Indeed, if they both died in the abrupt manner described in this story, Beruriah's measured response seems even more incredible.

Nonetheless, both these stories underscore the same lesson: Parents are only the guardians of their children's souls; if the children die early, the one consolation for the parents is the knowledge that their souls have been returned to God in a state of purity. Rabbi Yochanan's warm response to Rabbi Elazar notwithstanding, such a consolation usually works its effect only after much time has elapsed.

> May God comfort you among all those who mourn for Zion and Jerusalem.
> —Traditional formula recited when departing from mourners

By alluding to the ancient destruction of Jerusalem, this formulaic expression helps put the individual's suffering in perspective. However, these words are recited only during *shiva,* the week of mourning that follows the funeral. Prior to that, when the deceased has not yet been buried, we are commanded to be silent: It would be cruel at that point to ask the person to view his or her suffering in such a long-term perspective.

> A person who meets a mourner after a year and speaks words of consolation to him then, to what can he be compared?
> To a physician who meets a person whose leg had been broken and healed, and says to him, "Come to me, and let me break your leg again, and reset it, to convince you that my treatment is good."
> —Rabbi Meir, Babylonian Talmud, *Mo'ed Kattan* 21b

Rabbi Meir speaks of one who offers consolation "after a year" because Jewish tradition holds that this is the time limit for mourning. "Consoling" the mourner once the time for grieving has passed is cruel rather than comforting, since it prevents him or her from getting on with life.

Despite Rabbi Meir's words, however, some mourning clearly does last far longer than a year, particularly when the deceased has met an unnatural death or succumbed at an early age. Consider Jacob, who was tricked into believing that his favorite son, Joseph, had been killed by a beast. The Bible informs us that "All his sons and daughters sought to comfort him, but he refused to be comforted, saying, 'No, I will go down mourning my son till my death'" (Genesis 37:35).

While prolonged grieving normally is associated with parents mourning the loss of a child, one of the most anguished letters in Jewish literature was written by Moses Maimonides, whose younger brother, David, drowned while on a business trip. Maimonides clearly related to his brother as a son (at this point in his life, he did not yet have a child). As the letter's conclusion makes clear, he identified with the inconsolable Jacob:

> The greatest misfortune that has befallen me during my entire life, worse than anything else, was the demise of [my brother] the saint . . . who drowned in the Indian sea. . . .

On the day I received that terrible news I fell ill and remained in bed for about a year, suffering from boils, fever, and depression, and was almost given up.

About eight years have since passed, but I am still mourning and unable to accept consolation. And how should I console myself? He grew up on my knees, he was my brother, he was my student; he traded on the markets and earned money so that I could sit safely at home.... My joy in life was to look at him. Now, all joy has gone. He has passed away and left me disturbed in my mind in a foreign country. Whenever I see his handwriting or one of his letters, my heart turns upside down and my grief awakens again. In short, "I will go down mourning my son till my death."

—Moses Maimonides in letter to Japhet ben
Eliyahu of Acco, 1176

MOURNING

One should not grieve too much for the dead, and whoever grieves excessively is really grieving for someone else. [The Torah has set limits for every stage of grief]: three days for weeping, seven for lamenting, and thirty for abstaining from laundered garments and from cutting the hair.

Whoever does not mourn as the law has prescribed is considered callous....

—*Shulkhan Arukh, Yoreh De'ah,* 394:1,4

*   *   *

Yitgadal ve-Yitkadash Shmei Rabbah, Magnified and sanctified be His great name throughout the world which He has created according to His will.

—Opening words of the *Kaddish* prayer recited for the dead

Along with the *Sh'ma,* the *Kaddish* probably is the best-known Jewish prayer. Yet many Jews don't know its meaning (perhaps because it is written in Aramaic, not Hebrew), and are surprised when they learn that it never alludes to death. Instead, the *Kaddish* is a paean to God, expressing the hope that His majesty will be accepted by the entire world.

Why was the *Kaddish* chosen as the memorial prayer for the dead? Probably because the greatest testament to the deceased is that he or she has left behind descendants who attend synagogue and pledge themselves to work toward perfecting the world under the rule of God.

EULOGIZING AND REMEMBERING THE DEAD

From Moses to Moses there was none like Moses.
—Tombstone inscription over the grave of Moses Maimonides

But who is now my comforter? To whom shall I pour out my soul? Where shall I turn? All my life my beloved companion harkened to my troubles, and they were many, and comforted me so that somehow they would quickly vanish. But now . . . I am left to flounder in my woe.
—Gluckel of Hameln, a seventeenth-century Jewish woman
lamenting the death of her husband; Marvin Lowenthal, trans.,
The Memoirs of Gluckel of Hameln, page 150

You can't tell the size of an evergreen until it is cut down.
—Rabbi Jacob J. Weinstein eulogizing the Zionist activist and
philosopher Hayim Greenberg. Weinstein knew this
expression from his native Oregon. (See the posthumously
published *The Inner Eye,* Vol. II,
by Hayim Greenberg, page 18.)

Hayim Nahman Bialik, perhaps the greatest twentieth-century Jewish poet, composed his own eulogy, one that underscores the totality of the rupture imposed by death:

After I am dead
Say this at my funeral:
There was a man who exists no more.
That man died before his time
And his life's song was broken off halfway.

O, he had one more poem
And that poem has been lost
For ever.

> —Hayim Nahman Bialik, "After My Death," published in S. Y.
> Penueli and A. Ukhmani, *Anthology of Modern Hebrew Poetry,*
> Vol. 1, pages 33–34

* * *

On my father's memorial day
I went out to see his mates—
All those buried with him in one row,
His life's graduation class

I already remember most of their names,
Like a parent collecting his little son
From school, all of his friends.

My father still loves me, and I
Love him always, so I don't weep.
But in order to do justice to this place
I have lit a weeping in my eyes
With the help of a nearby grave—
A child's. "Our little Yossi, who was
Four when he died."

> —Yehuda Amichai, "My Father's Memorial Day," in his book of
> poems, *Amen*, page 57

A FINAL THOUGHT

Two men came to Rabbi Moshe Yitzchak of Ponovezh.
They had both bought plots in the cemetery, and each
wanted the better of the two. After they had argued back
and forth for some time, Rabbi Moshe Yitzchak rendered
his verdict: "Whoever dies first gets the better plot."

Never again did they argue the issue.

> —Shmuel Himelstein, *A Touch of Wisdom,*
> *a Touch of Wit*, page 185

39

"A SENTINEL WHO HAS DESERTED HIS POST"

Suicide

A suicide is a sentinel who has deserted his post.
—Bahya ibn Pakuda, *Duties of the Heart*, chapter 4

Jewish law decrees that a suicide is to be buried at the outskirts of a cemetery and denied normal mourning rites. But the Rabbis apparently enacted such rulings mainly to discourage would-be suicides. In practice, Jewish law rarely ruled a self-inflicted killing to be suicide (usually pronouncing it an accident or due to momentary insanity), because it recognizes that imposing such a stigma would punish only the bereaved family, not the suicide.

The codes of Jewish law actually encourage rabbis to search for any rationale to avoid declaring a person a willful suicide:

> Who is ruled to be a willful suicide? Not one who climbs to the top of a tree or to the top of a roof and falls to his death. Rather, it is one who says, "I am climbing the roof, or the tree, and I am going to throw myself to my death," and others see him climb to the top of the tree or to the top of the roof and fall to his death. Such a person is presumed to be a suicide and no mourning rites whatso-

271

ever should be observed. A man found strangled or hanging from a tree or lying dead on a sword is presumed not
to have committed suicide willfully, and none of the
mourning rites are withheld from him.

—Babylonian Talmud, minor tractate *Semahot* 2:2–3

The essential principle is that when dealing with a case of
suicide, we ascribe his actions to any [extrinsic] motive we
can find, as for example, to terror, despondency, insanity
. . . or to a motive similar to these.

—Rabbi Yechiel Epstein, *Arukh ha-Shulkhan, Yoreh Deah* 345:5

*   *   *

The closer the relationship between the killer and the
killed, the more heinous the crime [and man is closest to
himself].

—Bahya ibn Pakuda, *Duties of the Heart,* chapter 4

Compassion for family members of suicides notwithstanding, the
eleventh-century philosopher Bahya implies that suicide is, if anything, worse than murder. While I have found no support for this
view among other Jewish scholars (the more characteristic rabbinic
teaching is that of Rabbi Akiva: "Leave him to his oblivion: Neither
bless him nor curse him," Tractate *Semahot* 2:1), there are similar
arguments advanced by some Catholic theologians. Saint Augustine
taught, "Parricide is worse than homicide, but suicide is the most
wicked of all" (*On Patience*), while the twentieth-century Catholic
writer G. K. Chesterton reached an even more extreme conclusion:
"The man who kills a man, kills a man. The man who kills himself,
kills all men, as far as he is concerned, he wipes out the world" (*On
Orthodoxy*).

On the basis of logic, however, most people reject the argument
that suicide is more evil than murder. In the case of suicide, the dead
person wanted to be dead; in the case of murder, the victim wished
to live.

OCCASIONS WHEN JUDAISM PERMITS SUICIDE

[King] Saul said to his arms-bearer, "Draw your sword
and run it through me, so that the uncircumcised [Philis-
tines] may not run it through and make sport of me." But
his arms-bearer, in his great awe, refused; whereupon Saul
grasped the sword and fell upon it.

—I Samuel, 31:4

Saul's killing himself, after it became apparent that the Philistines had defeated his army, is the most famous suicide in the Bible.
The medieval Bible commentator David Kimhi (c. 1160–c. 1235),
known by the acronym Radak, comments:

Saul did not sin in killing himself . . . because he knew that
in the end he was bound to die in that war. . . . It was,
therefore, better for him to take his own life, rather than
have the uncircumcised make sport with him.

—Radak on I Samuel 31:4

Indeed, it was probably Saul's example that prompted Rabbi
Judah to conclude that King Zedekiah, during whose reign the Ju-
dean revolt against Babylonia failed and the Temple in Jerusalem
was destroyed (586 B.C.E.), was a fool for not ending his life, even
when the alternative was not death:

"For these things I weep" (Lamentations 1:16); for Zedekiah's lack of sense . . . said Rabbi Judah. How could
Zedekiah, knowing that his eyes would soon be put out,
not have had the sense to dash his head against the wall
until his life left him?

—*Lamentations Rabbah* 1:51

Other Jewish sources also justify suicide, even in cases where
death will not necessarily result, but where individuals would be
forced to live a shameful existence. The following talmudic tale dates
from the period following the failure of the first Jewish revolt against
the Romans (around 70 C.E.):

273

Four hundred boys and girls were carried off for immoral purposes [to be used as prostitutes in Rome]. They understood why they were wanted, and they asked, "If we drown in the sea, will we enter the World-to-Come?" The eldest among them cited the verse, "The Lord said: . . . I will bring them back from the depths of the sea" (Psalms 68:23) and interpreted it as meaning "I will bring them back [to eternal life] from the depths of the sea." When the girls heard this, they jumped up and leaped into the sea. The boys then reasoned regarding themselves, "If they, for whom being mounted for the sexual act is natural [sic] [prefer death to submission], we, for whom being mounted is unnatural [should more certainly prefer death to submission]." At that, they also leaped into the sea. Of them, the Bible says, "It is for Your sake that we are slain all day long, that we are regarded as sheep to be slaughtered" (Psalms 44:23).

—Babylonian Talmud, *Gittin* 57b

The 960 Jews who killed themselves and their families at Masada in 73 C.E. comprise the most famous suicides in Jewish history. Their motives seem to have been a combination of what prompted King Saul and the young men and women in the above story. Like Saul, they knew that the Romans would kill off many of them as soon as they captured Masada; like the young men and women, they realized that those who survived the massacre, particularly women and children, would be sold off in Roman markets as prostitutes and slaves.

The first-century historian Flavius Josephus set down the [supposed] final words of Elazar, the leader of Masada, urging the Jews to kill themselves rather than surrender:

We were the very first that revolted from them, and we are the last that fight against them; and I cannot but esteem it as a favor that God has granted us, that it is still in our power to die bravely, and in a state of freedom. . . .

Let our wives die before they are abused, and our children before they have tasted of slavery; and after we have slain them, let us bestow that glorious benefit upon one another mutually.

—Elazar's speech is reprinted in Yigal Yadin,
Masada, pages 232–237

At the conclusion of Elazar's speech, ten men were chosen by lot to kill the others. They then killed each other, and the final survivor killed himself.

Josephus claims to have learned the content of Elazar's speech from two Jewish women who hid themselves in an underground cavern and did not commit suicide.

Finally, a sardonic, if life-affirming Yiddish perspective on suicide:

Your health comes first—you can always hang yourself later.

—Yiddish proverb

40

THE AFTERLIFE

In the World-to-Come, there will be no eating, or drinking, or procreation, or business, or jealousy or hatred or competition, but the righteous will sit with crowns on their heads feasting on the radiance of the *shekhina,* the divine presence.

—Babylonian Talmud, *Berakhot* 17a

For most believers, the major issue of faith is God's existence, not whether there is an afterlife. For once one believes that there is a good and all-powerful God, it follows that there must be a life beyond this one. The only possible explanation for God allowing so much suffering and injustice is that there is another dimension of existence where there is redress.

Strangely, the Torah contains no reference to an afterlife. Perhaps this is because these five books were written in the aftermath of Hebrew slavery in Egypt. The Egyptian experience had taught the children of Israel how dangerous an obsession with afterlife could become. Consider that the major achievement of many Pharaohs was to have built an enormous tomb, a pyramid, for themselves; for this purpose, thousands of slaves were worked to death. The Egyptians' holiest work, *The Book of the Dead,* reflects their obsession with afterlife.

Perhaps the Bible did not raise the issue of afterlife because it recognized that when it becomes central to religion, it diverts people's attention from their responsibilities in *this* world.

*　　*　　*

All Israel have a portion in the World-to-Come.
—Mishna, *Sanhedrin* 10:1

The righteous among the nations of the world will have a share in the World-to-Come.
—Tosefta *Sanhedrin* 13:2

Despite talmudic Judaism's categorical assertion of an existence beyond this one, opinion polls about Americans' religious beliefs repeatedly have discovered that a far smaller percentage of Jews than Christians believe in an afterlife. Doubts about "the next world" are common even among non-Orthodox rabbis. Dennis Prager has written of attending a funeral conducted by one of America's most prominent Conservative rabbis. At the grave site, the rabbi commented, "Judaism does not believe in a life after death. Rather, we live on in the good works we do and in the memories of those we leave behind." Among other things, Prager reasons, such a statement is a particularly poor, thoughtless attempt at solace "to the six million Jews, nearly all of whose loved ones also died. If this life is all there is, and people live on solely through the memories of loved ones, then most of the six million died as forgotten smoke . . ." ("Is This Life All There Is?," *Ultimate Issues*, Spring 1987, page 2).

For Prager, the Holocaust in particular underscores the importance of an afterlife, particularly for anyone who claims to believe in God:

> If there is nothing after this life, then the Nazis and the Jewish children they threw alive into Auschwitz furnaces have identical fates. If I believed such a thing, I would either become an atheist or hate a God who had created such a cruelly absurd universe.
> —Dennis Prager, ibid.

Judaism's classic work of mysticism, the Zohar, offers a parable that conveys how consoling a belief in afterlife can be:

A king has a son whom he sends to a village to be educated until he shall have been initiated into the ways of the palace. When the king is informed that his son is now come to maturity, the king . . . sends the matron his mother to bring him back to the palace, and there the king rejoices with him every day. . . . The village people weep for the departure of the king's son from among them. But one wise man said to them: Why do you weep? Was this not the king's son, whose true place is in his father's palace and not with you?

—Gershom Scholem, trans., *Zohar, The Book of Splendor*, pages 72–73

41

"WHO IS RICH?"

Who is rich? One who is happy with what he has.
—*Ethics of the Fathers* 4:1

A sage was asked: "Who do you believe are greater, the wise or the rich?"

"The wise," he answered.

"But if that is the case, why do you find more of the wise at the doors of the wealthy than wealthy at the doors of the wise?"

The sage answered: "Because the wise appreciate the value of riches, but the rich do not similarly appreciate the value of wisdom."
—Solomon Ibn Gabirol (c. 1020–c.1057), *Pearls of Wisdom*

Told that a certain man had acquired great wealth, a sage asked: "Has he also acquired the days in which to spend it?"
—Ibn Gabirol, ibid.

Many men hoard for the future husbands of their wives.
—Ibn Gabirol, ibid.

Riches, of course, can carry us only so far because, as an old Yiddish proverb notes, "Shrouds have no pockets."

PART III

BETWEEN PEOPLE AND GOD

What God Wants from Us

42

GOD

FAITH AND DOUBT

If only God would give me some clear sign! Like making a large deposit in my name at a Swiss bank.

—Woody Allen

Even if evil were a total mystery on which theology could not make so much as a dent, [faith in God] . . . would still be indicated. For, at the worst, it leaves less unexplained than does its alternative. If the believer has his troubles with evil, the atheist has more and graver difficulties to contend with. Reality stumps him altogether, leaving him baffled not by one consideration but by many, from the existence of natural law through the instinctual cunning of the insect to the brain of the genius and the heart of the prophet. This, then, is the intellectual reason for believing in God: that, though this belief is not free from difficulties, it stands out, head and shoulders, as the best answer to the riddle of the universe.

—Milton Steinberg, *Anatomy of Faith*
(edited by Arthur Cohen), page 91

If I knew God, I would be God.

—Medieval Jewish proverb

God may have had His own reasons for denying us certainty with regard to His existence and nature. One reason

283

apparent to us is that man's certainty with regard to anything is poison to his soul. Who knows this better than
moderns, who have had to cope with dogmatic Fascists,
Communists and even scientists?

—Rabbi Emanuel Rackman in *The Condition of
Jewish Belief*, page 179

Many today have doubts about God's existence, but they
live their lives as if God does not exist. They are agnostics,
but live as atheists. . . . You may be agnostic in theory, but
in practice you live either a religious or a secular life.

—Dennis Prager and Joseph Telushkin, *The Nine Questions
People Ask About Judaism*, page 39

In the final analysis, for the believer there are no questions,
and for the non-believer there are no answers.

—The Haffetz Hayyim

PROOF OF THE EXISTENCE OF GOD

A characteristic feature of some works of medieval Jewish, and particularly Christian, philosophy was an attempt to prove God's existence. Obviously, if any medieval thinkers had succeeded in doing
so, the word "faith" would no longer be used to describe people's
relationship to God, since we use this term specifically because we
lack definitive evidence. One of the most common medieval proofs
for God's existence was the "argument from design":

Do you not realize that if ink were poured out accidentally
on a sheet of paper, it would be impossible that proper
writing should result, or legible lines such as written with
a pen? . . . Now, if we find it impossible to reconcile ourselves to the idea that written forms can make themselves,
how is it possible to say, when we see something more
subtle in form [and] more difficult to create . . . that it was

284

made without the purpose, power and wisdom of a mighty designer?

—Bahya ibn Pakuda, *Duties of the Heart* (*Hovot ha-Levavot*),
Chapter 1; I have combined elements of the translation
of M. Hyamson and Menahem Mansoor's more recent
translation, *The Book of Directions to the Duties of
the Heart*, page 121.

SEEKING GOD

Rabbi Levi said: The Holy One appeared to [Israel at Sinai] as though He were a statue with faces on every side. A thousand people might be looking at the statue, but it would appear to each to be looking directly at him. So, too, when the Holy One spoke, each and every person in Israel could say, "The Divine Word is addressing me." . . . The Divine Word spoke to each and every person according to his particular capacity.

—*Pesikta d'Rav Kahana* 12:25

This is definitely one of the most powerful, if peculiar, midrashic texts. As the contemporary American Rabbi Irwin Kula writes, "In order to convey an insight about God, Rabbi Levi compares God to an idol! Using this almost blasphemous metaphor, Rabbi Levi teaches that at Sinai, people experienced God so individually that standing there one might have said, 'God is addressing me! [and me alone].' Because of people's different temperaments, personalities, and life experiences, no single image of God is appropriate for every person, or for that matter, for every moment in a person's life. Kula concludes that 'Sometimes, God is Father, King, Husband, Friend, Mother . . . or, for Rabbi Levi, a statue with thousands of faces' " (Irwin Kula in *Wisdom of the Ages,* page 36).

The episode in Exodus 3:2 in which God speaks to Moses through a bush that is burning and not consumed, prompted a query from a perplexed non-Jew:

A non-Jew asked Rabbi Joshua ben Korcha, "Why did God choose to speak to Moses through a [common] thorn bush? [Why not out of a greater tree?]"

The rabbi answered, "Were it a carob tree or a syca-
more tree, you would have asked the same question, but
to dismiss you without any reply is not right, so I will tell
you why. To teach us that there is no place devoid of
God's presence, not even a thorn bush."

—*Exodus Rabbah* 2:5

A parallel notion is suggested by an exchange between the Hasidic Kotzker rebbe and his disciples:

"Where does God exist?" the rebbe asked several of his
followers.

"Everywhere," the surprised disciples responded.

"No," the rebbe answered. "God exists only where
man lets him in."

This is a remarkable statement of the power God has ceded to people, the ability either to keep Him out of their lives or to let Him in.

ARGUING WITH GOD

(I have no doubt that you are the Almighty and that whatever you do is for the best, but it is impossible for me to
obey the commandment, "You shall love your God." No,
I cannot, Father, not in this life.

—The character of Jacob in Isaac Bashevis Singer's
novel *The Slave*

Jacob, a deeply religious man whose wife and children have been
murdered in the Chmelnitzki massacres of 1648, is ruminating about
one of the most difficult of the Torah's 613 commandments, to love
God (Deuteronomy 6:5). In the same century in which Singer's novel
is set, the Catholic philosopher Blaise Pascal wrote, "The knowledge
of God is very far from the love of Him."

Lord of the universe! I saw an ordinary Jew pick up his
tefillin (phylacteries) from the floor and kiss them; and

You have let your *tefillin*, the Jewish people, lie on the ground for more than two thousand years, trampled by their enemies. Why do you not pick them up? Why do You not act as a plain Jew acts? Why?

—Hasidic Rebbe Levi Yitzhak of Berditchev (d. 1809)

"Why do they pray to Me? Tell them to thunder against Me. Let them raise their fists against Me and claim recompense for their shame."

—Hayim Nahman Bialik, "In the City of Slaughter" (1904)

"In the City of Slaughter," a bitter poetic response to the 1903 Kishinev pogrom, expresses fury not only at the Russian government that sanctioned the pogrom and the mobs who carried it out but also at those Jews who, instead of fighting their oppressors, prayed for God's intervention. In the above line, Bialik imagines God's furious response to the Jews' prayers. (Regarding Jewish arguments with God since the Holocaust, see pages 303–315.)

SUBMISSION TO GOD

A person is obligated to bless God for the evil that befalls him just as he blesses Him for the good.

—Mishna *Berakhot* 9:5

Thus, one who hears of a death is instructed to say, *Barukh dayan emet* (Blessed is the true judge). In accordance with this mishnaic teaching, the Talmud also advises, "A man should always accustom himself to say, 'Whatever God does is for the best'" (Babylonian Talmud, *Berakhot* 60b; see story of how Rabbi Akiva practiced this principle on pages 320–321).

GOD'S ROLE IN JEWISH HISTORY

Evidence of God I have found in the existence of [the people] Israel.

—Edmund Fleg, *Why I Am a Jew*

In *The Nine Questions People Ask About Judaism*, Dennis Prager and I similarly argue that the riddle of Jewish survival is most satisfactorily explained by positing God's existence: "The history [and] survival . . . of the Jews cannot be explained by the criteria applied to any other nation's fate. . . . In all of world history, only the Jews have survived for nearly four thousand years with their culture intact. Only the Jews have had their homeland destroyed (twice), been dispersed throughout the world for two thousand years, endured hatred wherever they have lived, survived the most systematic attempt in history to destroy an entire people, and been expelled from nearly every nation among whom they have lived. Yet the Jews still live, studying about their ancestors who lived around 1600 B.C.E., having the same homeland as in 1000 B.C.E., speaking there the same language as their ancestors did over three thousand years ago, and worshipping the same God" (page 29). For the Jews, their survival against all odds is due to God's involvement in their history.

> Other nations of antiquity, when they were defeated, acknowledged that their gods had been defeated. The Jews always saw in their defeat the *triumph* of their God.
> —Rabbi Abba Hillel Silver, *World Crisis and Jewish Survival*, page 51

When nations in the ancient world were defeated in war, their citizens usually converted to their conquerors' religion, believing that their god had triumphed. Perhaps this is why almost no ancient Near Eastern religions, with the exception of Judaism, survived into the modern era.

But precisely because the ancient Jews believed that God had sent their enemies to punish them for their sins (e.g., this is how Jeremiah explained Nebuchadnezzar's destruction of Judea in 586 B.C.E.), they were never tempted to accept their victors' gods. Instead, they remained loyal to the God of Israel, confident that, if they repented, He would return them to Israel and restore their glory.

This very loyalty prompted an intellectually puzzled Sigmund

Freud to write in *Moses and Monotheism:* "Why the people of Israel adhered to their God all the more devotedly the worse they were treated by Him, that is a question we must leave open."

FEAR OF GOD

May your fear of God be as strong as your fear of men.
—Rabbi Yochanan ben Zakkai's deathbed advice to his students;
Babylonian Talmud, *Berakhot* 28b

Rabbi Yochanan, perhaps the Talmud's most commonsensical figure, was not trying to be coy or blasphemous. He simply acknowledged a seldom-noted truth: Most human beings fear other people far more than they fear God. When they prepare to act unethically or violate a Jewish ritual, they usually are careful to make sure that no human witnesses are present, but rarely are fearful that God will see what they are doing. If people feared God as much as they do other humans, they would perform almost no evil acts.

During the same meeting, Rabbi Yochanan told his disciples of his fear at being judged by One "Whom I cannot appease with [flattering] words nor bribe with money" (Babylonian Talmud, *Berakhot* 28b).

Fear only two: God, and him who fears not God.
—The early twentieth-century Yiddish preacher,
Judah Leib Lazerov

A FINAL THOUGHT

God is of no importance unless He is of supreme importance.
—Abraham Joshua Heschel (1907–1972), *Man's Quest for God,*
page xiii

43

IS GOD NECESSARY
FOR MORALITY?

In the nineteenth century the problem was that God was
dead; in the twentieth century the problem is that man is
dead.

—Erich Fromm, *The Sane Society*

A popular argument against religion is that many evils have been
perpetrated in its name. But it seldom is noted that the two most
murderous societies in history, the Nazis and the Soviet Communists, were aggressively atheist. Hitler declared his life's mission the
destruction of the "tyrannical God of the Jews," while during its
seventy-three-year history, the Soviet Union made it a crime to advocate belief in God.

The "death of God" to which Fromm refers was a notion first
articulated by the late-nineteenth-century philosopher Friedrich Nietzsche. At about the same time, Feodor Dostoevsky wrote in *The
Brothers Karamazov*, "If there is no God, all is permitted."

From Judaism's perspective, Dostoevsky's comment is a logical
conclusion: If there is no God, who is to say that anything should
be prohibited? To this day, there is ultimately no philosophically
compelling answer to the question "Why was Hitler wrong?" aside
from "Because God said so."

Bertrand Russell, this century's most prominent secular philosopher, himself articulated the dangers of a God-free subjective

ethics: "I cannot see how to refute the arguments for the subjectivity of ethical values, but I find myself incapable of believing that all that is wrong with wanton cruelty is that I don't like it."

Although Russell lived well into his nineties, he never was able to produce a more compelling argument against wanton cruelty than that he didn't like it. Unfortunately, a considerable number of people do.

*   *   *

A philosopher asked Rabbi Reuven, "Who is the most hateful person in the world?"

"The person who denies his creator," Rabbi Reuven replied.

"Why is that?"

The rabbi answered: "Honor your father and mother; you shall not murder . . . ; you shall not steal; you shall not bear false witness against your neighbor . . . ; behold, a person does not repudiate any of these laws until he repudiates the root of them [God]."

—Tosefta *Shevuot* 3:6

*   *   *

The attempt made in recent decades by secularist thinkers to disengage [the moral principles of Western civilization] from their [scripturally based] religious context, in the assurance that they could live a life of their own as a "humanistic" ethic, has resulted in what one writer has called our "cut-flower culture." Cut flowers retain their original beauty and fragrance, but only so long as they retain the vitality that they have drawn from their now severed roots; after that is exhausted, they wither and die. So with freedom, brotherhood, justice, and personal dignity—the values that form the moral foundation of our civilization. Without the life-giving power of the faith out of which they have sprung, they possess neither meaning nor vitality. Morality ungrounded in God is indeed a house built upon sand, unable to stand up against the vagaries of impulse and the brutal pressures of power and self-interest.

—Will Herberg, *Judaism and Modern Man*, pages 91–92

[Those of us in the Western world who are secular] have found ourselves baffled by the Nietzschean challenge: if God is really dead, by what authority do we say that any particular practice is prohibited or permitted? Pure reason alone cannot tell us that incest is wrong (so long as there are no offspring). . . . Pure reason cannot tell us that bestiality is wrong; indeed, the only argument against bestiality these days is that, since we cannot know whether animals enjoy it or not, it is a violation of "animal rights."
—Irving Kristol, "Afterword," in David Dalin, ed.,
American Jews and the Separationist Faith, page 161

An ancient Yiddish maxim that I first heard as a child from my great-grandmother: "When you are riding in a horse and wagon and pass the door of a church, if the driver does not cross himself, get off immediately."
—J. David Bleich in David Dalin, ed., *American Jews and the Separationist Faith*, page 29

Bleich explains: "That admonition had nothing to do with theology and everything to do with safety and survival. The Jew understood that his own security demanded that the non-Jew profess a religion, and that for such purposes, any religion is better than none. Voltaire, a doctrinaire atheist himself, believed that atheism was safe only for intellectuals. He is reported to have said, 'I want my lawyer, tailor, valets, even my wife to believe in God. I think that if they do I shall be robbed less and cheated less.' "

Sigmund Freud shared Voltaire's confidence that intellectually inclined atheists could be trusted to be moral even without believing in God. Writing in Vienna in 1927, he argued that while people of low intellectual achievement might need religion to guarantee their morality, "Civilization has little to fear from educated people. . . . In them, the replacement of religious motives for civilized behavior by other, secular motives [will] proceed unobtrusively" (*The Future of an Illusion*, page 39).

Within ten years of this rare instance of Freudian optimism about human nature, Freud himself witnessed that civilization had as much to fear from educated people as from the uneducated. His fellow Austrian and German intellectuals exhibited no greater moral insight, strength, or courage than any other group of their fellow citizens; in fact, many of them, doctors and professors alike, participated in Nazi atrocities. For example, after World War II, the twenty-four *Einsatzgruppen* leaders put on trial for their wholesale rounding up and murdering of more than one million Soviet Jews included nine lawyers, two economists, an architect, a professor, banker, high-school teacher, and dentist. (See Irving Greenberg's article in Eva Fleischner, ed., *Auschwitz: Beginning of a New Era?*, page 442, footnote 16.)

44

IDOLATRY AND ITS ATTRACTIONS

Their idols are . . . the work of men's hands.
They have mouths, but cannot speak,
eyes, but cannot see;
they have ears, but cannot hear,
noses, but cannot smell. . . .
Those who fashion them, all who trust in them, shall become like them.

—Psalms 115:4–6, 8

The Jewish elders in Rome were asked: "If your God has no desire for idolatry in this world, why does He not destroy the idols?"

They replied: "If people worshipped things unnecessary to the world, He would do so; but they worship the sun, the moon, the stars and the planets. Should He destroy this universe on account of fools?"

They said to the elders: "If so, let Him destroy what is unnecessary for the world and leave whatever is essential."

"If He did that," they replied, "it would only strengthen the faith of those who worship [the sun, the moon, the stars, the planets and other] idols, because they will say, 'Since these were not destroyed they are definitely deities.'"

—Mishna *Avodah Zara* 4:7

In commenting on this Mishna, the Talmud offers another illustration of why God does not destroy all objects of idolatry:

> Suppose a man stole a measure of wheat and went and sowed it in the ground. Justice dictates that it should not grow, but the world pursues its natural course. [As regards those who worship the sun and stars the world pursues its natural course], and as for the fools who act wrongly, they will have to render an account [before God].
>
> —Babylonian Talmud, *Avodah Zara* 54b

IDOLATRY'S POWERFUL ATTRACTION

During a public lecture, Rav Ashi (c. 335–c. 427) once made fun of the idol-worshipping King Manasseh (see II Kings, chapter 21; among other outrages, Manasseh had his own son burned as an idolatrous offering). That night, the king appeared to him in a dream, and asked him a difficult question of Jewish law. Rav Ashi did not know the answer, whereupon Manasseh told it to him. Rav Ashi asked him:

> "Since you are so wise, why did you worship idols?"
> Manasseh replied, "Had you been living in my time, you would have picked up the skirt of your garment, and run after me."
>
> —Babylonian Talmud, *Sanhedrin* 102b

From Rav Ashi's perspective, more than a millennium after Manasseh, it was difficult to imagine an intelligent person attracted to idolatry, just as today many find it hard to believe that otherwise intelligent people believed in Nazism, Communism, or witches. Yet when these movements were in their prime, they evoked powerful support and passions.

IDOLATRY IN THE MODERN WORLD

Many people who conceive of idolatry as the worship of statues and totem poles assume that it no longer exists. From Judaism's perspective, however, idolatry occurs when one holds any value higher than God and morality. A person who says "My country right or wrong" and, on this basis, acts unjustly, is an idolater. By regarding his country's demand to do wrong as more binding than God's demand to do right, such an individual makes it clear that he or she regards country as higher than God.

Unfortunately, the idolatries that tempt modern man often are of great value, i.e., the nation, art and literature, even education. It is only when one ascribes to them *supreme* value that they turn into "gods." For example, the people who agitated to have fascist propagandist Ezra Pound released from incarceration because he was a great poet (see page 477) apparently believed that great literary figures are beyond good and evil, and therefore should not be punished for doing evil. Good literature is wonderful, but such an attitude is idolatrous.

Evil can ensue when one so elevates a good ideology that it becomes a form of idolatry, e.g.:

> I think it is necessary to state here, Zionism is above everything.
>
> —Yitzchak Gruenbaum, a member of the Jewish
> Agency Executive in Palestine during World War II,
> and later Minister of the Interior in the Israeli cabinet
> (see Tom Segev, *The Seventh Million*, page 102).

In January 1943, as reports about the Holocaust were reaching Palestine, the Zionist leadership discussed whether funds intended for the development of the *Yishuv* (Jewish community inside Palestine) should be diverted to efforts to rescue European Jews. Rabbi Yitzchak Itshe Meir Levin, a leader of the ultra-Orthodox Agudat Yisrael party, pleaded at a meeting of the Zionist Executive Committee: "Won't you halt the work in Palestine during such a period, when they are murdering and slaughtering Jews by the hundreds of thousands, even millions? Don't establish new settlements; take the [Jewish National Fund] money for those needs."

Gruenbaum responded that because "Zionism is above everything," he would not divert any funds to rescue efforts.

Yosef Sprinzak, a future Israeli cabinet official, disagreed: "What do we need at this moment? Not a Zionist program but something very simple: *a varm Yiddish hartz* [Yiddish for 'a warm Jewish heart']. That's what we must have. . . . "

"They will say that I am an antisemite. . . . " Gruenbaum responded, "that I don't have *a varm Yiddish hartz*. . . . Let them say what they want. I will not demand that the Jewish Agency allocate a sum of 300,000 or 100,000 pounds sterling to help European Jewry. And I think that whoever demands such a thing is performing an anti-Zionist act."

Had Gruenbaum argued that the money should not be appropriated because there was no effective way to use it to save Jews, there could have been a moral, hence nonidolatrous, dimension to his argument. But apparently he would have opposed appropriating money even were he convinced that it could be used to save lives. He thus committed a form of idolatry by viewing Zionism as more important than anything else.

*   *   *

The essence of Judaism is the denial of false gods. According to the Talmud, anyone who shares this point of view shares automatic kinship with Jews:

> Whoever repudiates idolatry is called a Jew.
> —Babylonian Talmud, *Megillah* 13a

45

CHOSEN PEOPLE

A Beautiful, but Often Misunderstood, Concept

> Blessed are You, Lord our God, King of the universe, who
> has chosen us from among all the nations and given us
> His Torah. Blessed are You, God, giver of the Torah.
> —Blessing recited by one receiving an *aliyah* to the Torah

Because all bar mitzvah boys and, among non-Orthodox Jews,
bat mitzvah girls, receive an *aliyah* (are called up to bless the Torah),
this blessing, which affirms the doctrine of Jewish chosenness, is
widely known among Jews.

It also is well known among non-Jews; thus, it was sufficient for
Chaim Potok to title his 1967 best-seller *The Chosen,* for people to
immediately understand that it was a novel about Jews.

> You alone have I singled out of all the families of the earth.
> That is why I will visit upon you all your sins.
> —Amos 3:2

Antisemites often have claimed that, because of the concept of
chosenness, Jews consider themselves superior to non-Jews. In truth,
*chosenness has nothing in common with doctrines of "racial" or
ethnic superiority*. While racists such as the Nazis regarded Aryans

as superior to all other people, and thus entitled to exploit and kill their inferiors, the verse from Amos demonstrates that chosenness obligates Jews to a higher, not lower, morality.

Chosenness could never have evolved into a racist doctrine because Jews are not a race, and anyone can become a Jew by converting. The biblical book of Ruth describes how its protagonist, a Moabite pagan, converts to Judaism and becomes so highly esteemed that she is rewarded by becoming a progenitor of King David, from whom the Messiah will descend. Imagine a Nazi, a Ku Klux Klan member or a follower of Reverend Louis Farrakhan claiming that his or her greatest leader will descend from a member of a different race. Jews could assume such a belief because what renders one a member of the Chosen People is belief, not blood.

> We therefore affirm, not that we are better, but that we ought to be better.
>
> —Morris Joseph (1848–1930),
> *Judaism as Creed and Life,* page 117

> We learn to drive, to swim, to throw a football, or to play the piano not by reading a book about how to do it, but by watching people do it correctly and trying to imitate them. . . . The Jewish people were [chosen by God] to be a "pilot project," a demonstration community. God would give them explicit instructions about how to carry on the God-centered life. If they did it . . . they would bring the other peoples of the world to see how satisfying it is to live that way.
>
> —Harold Kushner, *To Life,* page 31

> I the Lord . . . have summoned you . . . and appointed you a covenant people, a light of [or a light unto] nations. Opening eyes deprived of light, rescuing prisoners from confinement.
>
> —Isaiah 42:6–7

Missionizing Christians often have seen their sole responsibility as bringing people to faith in Jesus. My understanding of Isaiah's words is that God's summons should lead Jews specifically into this-worldly, sometimes very political, activities.

A HISTORICAL PROOF OF JEWISH CHOSENNESS

> It becomes obvious that we are not discussing a dogma incapable of verification, but the recognition of sober historical fact. The world owes Israel the idea of the One God of righteousness and holiness. . . . Clearly God used Israel for this great purpose.
> —Louis Jacobs, *A Jewish Theology,* page 274

Jews have always claimed that they were chosen to carry out a specific task: to make God and His moral law known to the world. Today, the billions of people who do acknowledge the God of the Bible also acknowledge that God originally became known through the Jews.

An almost two-thousand-year-old rabbinic reflection on the subject underscores how Jews have understood the task imposed upon them by chosenness:

> Commenting on the verse in Isaiah [43:10]: "You are My witnesses," Rabbi Shimon bar Yohai says, "Only when you are My witnesses, am I God, but when you are not My witnesses, then I—if one dares speak in such a manner—am not God."
> —*Pesikta d'Rav Kahana,* piska 12:6

In other words, if Jews in antiquity had not fulfilled their task of making God known to humankind, God would have remained unknown. His existence would have exerted no impact on civilization, and it would have been as if there were no God.

> We are God's stake in human history.
> —Abraham Joshua Heschel, *The Earth Is the Lord's,* page 109

JEWISH OPPOSITION TO THE DOCTRINE OF CHOSENNESS

Modern-minded Jews can no longer believe that the Jews constitute a divinely chosen people.
—Preface to Mordechai Kaplan's *Sabbath Prayer Book,* page xxiv

Kaplan, founder of Reconstructionism, the small but influential "fourth denomination" in American-Jewish life, eliminated the concept of chosenness from the 1945 prayerbook his movement published. Besides his belief that modern categories of thinking precluded so primitive a doctrine as God's choosing of one particular nation, Kaplan justified this deletion as "the best way . . . to answer the charge that the chosen people doctrine has been the model for theories of national and racial superiority" (*The Condition of Jewish Belief,* page 121).

While understandable, this second rationale strikes me as both wrong and naive. It is understandable because of the large number of Judaism's critics who have linked chosenness to racism. For example, shortly after the Nazis gained power, George Bernard Shaw, perhaps the most noted literary figure of his time, claimed that their doctrine of Aryan racial superiority was merely an imitation of the Jewish doctrine of chosenness. As recently as 1971, *Religion in Life,* a liberal Methodist journal, printed the view that "it is not surprising that Hitler retaliated against the chosen race by decreeing that it was not the Jewish but the Aryan race that was chosen" (Summer 1971, page 279).

But I dispute Kaplan because I believe in Jewish chosenness, and consider him naive, because I find it unlikely that the sort of people who charge the chosen people doctrine as being the model for doctrines such as Nazism will suddenly become Jew-lovers if Jews would only drop this belief. People who draw such outrageous equations do not do so because *chosenness* offends them; rather, *Jews* offend them. Were Jews to eliminate this belief, such people would seek another aspect of Judaism to attack.

In recent years, many Reconstructionist Jews have broken with their movement's founder over the issue of chosenness; some have reinserted the prayers that affirm it. Their rejection of Kaplan's view is certainly as understandable as his decision to drop the doctrine. For without a sense that Jews have a special mission in the world, the case for Jewish survival, and certainly for passionate Jewish commitment, is greatly weakened.

Finally, a bit of Yiddish irony, given the painful history of the Jews:

> "Thou has chosen us from among all nations"—what, O God, did You have against us?
>
> —Old Yiddish joke

46

JEWS AND GOD AFTER THE HOLOCAUST

ANGER WITH GOD AFTER THE HOLOCAUST

A Jew can be Jewish with God, against God, but not without God.

—Elie Wiesel

The best-known writer on the Holocaust, Wiesel also is the most famous fighter with God of this generation. In assuming this role, he is part of a long Jewish tradition in which it is believers who express their rage and disappointment, as well as their love, to God. This unique tradition goes back to biblical figures. The prophet Habakkuk laments, "How long, O Lord, shall I cry out and You not listen" (Habakkuk 1:2). The Psalmist demands, "Awake, why do You sleep, O Lord. . . . Why do You hide Your face, and forget our suffering and oppression?" (Psalms 44:24–5). And a stark passage in Job observes, "From out of the city the dying groan, and the soul of the wounded cry for help; yet God pays no attention to their prayers" (Job 24:12).

Hundreds of years later, the Talmud recorded the reaction of the school of Rabbi Ishmael to God's inaction as the Romans destroyed Jerusalem: "Who is like You among the mute?" (Babylonian Talmud, *Gittin,* 56b).

In all these cases, the writer's anger stems from the belief that

God has responsibilities, just as man does, and is to be criticized when He fails to meet them. This attitude goes back to Abraham, who challenged God: "Shall not the judge of all the earth act with justice?" (Genesis 18:25). All these examples strikingly suggest the intimate relationship these believers had with God.

Indeed, the very intimacy that encouraged believers to express anger and hurt also sometimes moved them to express "pity" for God, if one can use such a term. Rabbi Abraham Joshua Heschel describes a trip a religious friend, S. Z. Shragai, took to Poland a few years after the Holocaust. Seated in the luxurious compartment of a train, Shragai invited a poor Jew whom he met to share the compartment:

> My friend tried to engage him in conversation, but he would not talk. When evening came, my friend . . . recited the evening prayer, while the other fellow did not say a word of prayer. The following morning my friend took out his prayer shawl and phylacteries and said his prayer; the other fellow, who looked so wretched and somber, would not say a word and did not pray.
>
> Finally, when the day was almost over, they started a conversation. The fellow said, "I am never going to pray anymore because of what happened to us in Auschwitz. . . . How could I pray? That is why I did not pray all day."
>
> The following morning, it was a long trip from Warsaw to Paris, my friend noticed that the fellow suddenly opened his bundle, took out his prayer shawl and phylacteries, and started to pray. He asked the man afterward, "What made you change your mind?"
>
> The fellow said, "It suddenly dawned upon me to think how lonely God must be; look with whom He is left. I felt sorry for Him."
>
> —Abraham Joshua Heschel, *A Passion for Truth*, pages 302–303

*   *   *

During the Holocaust, a story was told of a rabbi in Auschwitz who said to his followers, "There is a possibility that God is a liar." His disciples, shocked at the blasphemy, demanded that he explain himself. "Because when God looks down at Auschwitz, He says, 'I am not responsible for this.' And that is a lie."

In 1979, Yaffa Eliach, herself a survivor, served on a fact-finding mission for President Carter's Commission on the Holocaust, during which she and other commission members visited Auschwitz. That evening was the night of *Tisha Be'Av,* the Jewish fast that commemorates the destruction of both Temples, and commission members attended services at the ancient Rema Synagogue in Cracow. One member, Miles Lerman, the sole survivor of a large family, banged on the table at the front of the synagogue and announced that he was summoning God to a *Din Torah* (a Jewish court). Lerman then proceeded to state his grievances:

> God! How could you stay here when next door [is] Auschwitz?. . . . Where were you when all over Europe your sons and daughters were burning on altars? What did You do when my sainted father and mother marched to their deaths? When my sisters and brothers were put to the sword?
>
> —Miles Lerman

Lerman, who knew that Eliach had seen her own mother murdered in front of her eyes, walked over to her: "Do you want to say a few words?" he asked. Eliach refused to speak, and later confided to her diary why:

> I have no quarrel with God, only with men! I, too, want a trial, but not at the Rema Synagogue. . . . I would put on trial each Western university and library, for harboring millions of malicious words written against an ancient people, words like murderous daggers hiding beneath the cloak of science and truth. . . . I want to bring to trial the pulpits of countless churches where hate was burning like eternal lights. . . . I want to try . . . the train conductors with their little red flags for conducting traffic as usual. I want to bring to trial the doctors in their white coats who

killed so casually. . . . I want to bring to trial a civilization for whom man was such a worthless being. But to bring God to trial? On what charges? For giving men the ability to choose between good and evil?

—Yaffa Eliach, *Hasidic Tales After the Holocaust*, pages 212–213

THE DEBATE WITHIN ORTHODOXY OVER GOD'S ROLE DURING THE HOLOCAUST

U'mipnei chata-einu galeenu me-artzainu—And because of our sins we were exiled from our land.

> —Jewish prayer recited at the beginning
> of each month, and on festivals

As the above prayer reflects, traditional Jewish theology often has understood Jewish suffering as punishment for Jewish sins. Since the Holocaust, *some* Orthodox thinkers have claimed that God inflicted the Holocaust as a punishment. However, unlike the above prayer's author, who speaks of *"our* sins," these new writers emphasize that the sins that prompted the Holocaust were those committed by Jews other than themselves.

Perhaps the first rabbinic figure to express this view regarding the Nazis was Rabbi Hayyim Elazar Shapira, a Slovakian Hasidic rebbe with a large following. In 1933, shortly after the Nazi rise to power, Shapira wrote:

When [the Nazis] imposed the boycott in Germany against Jewish businesses, I thought this was certainly not a reason to ordain a fast. For nearly all [of the Jews] in Germany profane the Sabbath publicly by [keeping] their stores [open]. Now they are being paid back measure for measure [i.e., the closing down of their stores]. . . .

> —Rabbi Hayyim Elazar Shapira of Munkacs, Slovakia, 1933;
> the responsa from which the above is quoted
> is translated and annotated in Robert Kirschner,
> *Rabbinic Responsa of the Holocaust Era*, pages 24–25.

On April 1, 1933, the newly governing Nazis initiated a boycott of all German-Jewish businesses. Nazi guards stood in front of Jewish-owned stores and offices, discouraging non-Jews from entering. Most Germans acquiesced to the Nazi demand, which is why German Rabbi Leo Baeck later termed the boycott "the day of the greatest cowardice. Without that cowardice, all that followed would not have happened."

At the time, Rabbi Shapira was asked to sign a declaration supporting an international Jewish fast day in sympathy with the plight of German Jewry. He refused, arguing that most German Jews were religiously nonobservant, and kept their businesses open on the Sabbath. Thus, it would be appropriate to fast on their behalf only *after* they began keeping the commandments and acknowledged that the root cause of their suffering was "the finger of God" punishing them, "measure for measure," for their Sabbath desecrations.

Rabbi Shapira's words suggest that, at some level, he regarded the boycott—which other Jews viewed as having been instigated by their arch-enemy Adolf Hitler—as having been brought about by God Himself. Thus, because German Jews violated Jewish law by keeping their stores open on the Sabbath, God punished them "measure for measure" by sending the Nazis to keep business away from their stores on Saturday and throughout the week.

Of course, such reasoning can be used to justify even "harsher" conclusions. Some ten years after Rabbi Shapira wrote his opinion, almost all his followers were sent to Nazi concentration camps. Could one not argue that because they refused to fast in sympathy with Germany's suffering Jews, God decided to impose on them the concentration camps' fastlike diet? I certainly don't believe that—indeed, I find such an idea vile—but might not Rabbi Shapira's logic be employed to arrive at just such a conclusion?

After the Holocaust, the late Rabbi Yoel Teitelbaum (1888–1979), the Satmar rebbe and a long-standing enemy of Zionism, became the most famous proponent of the view that the Nazis were God's instrument for punishing Jews. Rabbi Teitelbaum argued that the Holocaust was a punishment for the Zionists' sins, for instead of waiting for the messiah, they had rebelled against God by interfering in His divinely preordained plan of messianic redemption. At times, Rabbi Teitelbaum went further, arguing that the Zionists actually *willed* a catastrophe for European Jewry, hoping thereby to hasten the creation of a Jewish state. The fact that Zionist leaders helped save Jewish lives from the Nazis made little impression on Rabbi Teitelbaum, who dismissed such activities with the following parable:

> There was once a very evil, vengeful and hateful man who desired to burn down the house of an acquaintance of his. He hired for this purpose an expert in such matters and instructed him to do his dastardly work so that no one would sense who caused the destruction. Knowing that the victim was a very hospitable type, this expert presented himself as a wanderer who needed a place to stay. The gentleman immediately granted his request. In the middle of the night, the evildoer—having ascertained that the entire household was fast asleep—silently went and lit the house on fire and quickly returned to his bed and pretended to be asleep. A little later on, when the flames had spread, the entire household was awake and, seeing the terror that was upon them, tried desperately to salvage whatever they could from the fire. But due to their panic and sudden shock they were disorganized and unable to undertake an effective rescue action. The cunning guest who had started the entire fire also pretended to awake in shock and went immediately to "help" the landlord. Since he was emotionally settled and saw that his activities had yielded their fruit, he was able to act more effectively and save a few token items from the flames. The next morning the landlord related his bitter experiences to his friends. But along with recounting the misfortunes, he paid tribute to the importance of fulfilling the obligation of hospitality; for thanks to his own fulfillment of that imperative, God sent him a wonderful guest who "saved" much of his household. . . . The parable is evident. For these evil Zionists cause by their sinfulness and forbidden political activities all of the trials and tribulations of our people, only to take on later the appearance and role of the saviors of

our nation, and they succeed in this deception.

—Rabbi Yoel Teitelbaum, the Satmar rebbe,
Va'Yoel Moshe, Vol. I, No. 110, translated by Allan Nadler
and published in his article, "Piety and Politics:
The Case of the Satmar Rebbe," *Judaism*, Spring 1982, page 149

Along with exonerating themselves and their forebears from any responsibility for the Holocaust, writers such as Rabbi Teitelbaum also deliver a singularly odious message to their tens of thousands of followers: "It is because of the sins of *those* Jews that *your* parents, grandparents and brothers and sisters were murdered in the Holocaust."

A historical postscript regarding those who claim the Holocaust was God's punishment for Zionism: Among the few European Jews who escaped the Holocaust were Zionists who emigrated to Palestine.

But on the upsurge of the greatest defection from Torah in history, which was expressed in Poland by materialism, virulent anti-nationalism, and Bundism (radical antireligious socialism), God's plan finally relieved them of all free will and sent Hitler's demons to end the existence of these communities before they deteriorated entirely.

—Rabbi Avigdor Miller, *Rejoice, O Youth*, page 279

The logical, let alone moral, absurdity of such a statement would seem self-evident. As I have written elsewhere, "Aside from the fact that suffocating a small child in a gas chamber seems an excessive response to the Sabbath violations of that child's parents, such a view makes no sense on other grounds. However irreligious European Jewry was in the 1930s and 1940s, the percentage of Jews in the United States who were religiously nonobservant was much higher. Yet American Jewry was spared the Holocaust and has had a very prosperous history" (*Jewish Literacy*, page 554).

While it is Orthodox rabbis such as Rabbis Teitelbaum and Miller who offer such defaming explanations of the Holocaust, it is Orthodox rabbis as well who have passionately refuted them. To these rabbis, an unbridgeable gap exists between the wrathful God of Rabbis Shapira, Teitelbaum, and Miller, and the loving, compassionate God in Whom they believe:

> To point an accusing finger at European Jewry . . . is an unparalleled instance of criminal arrogance and brutal insensitivity. How dare anyone even suggest that any "sin" committed by any significant faction of European Jewry was worthy of all the pain and anguish and death visited upon them by Hitler's sadistic butchers?
>
> —Rabbi Norman Lamm, "The Face of God: Thoughts on the Holocaust," in *Theological and Halakhic Reflections on the Holocaust,* edited by Bernard Rosenberg and co-edited by Fred Heuman, pages 122–123; Dr. Lamm is the president of Yeshiva University.

> Now that [the victims of the Holocaust] have been cruelly tortured and killed, boiled into soap, their hair made into pillows and their bones into fertilizer, their unknown graves and the very fact of their death denied to them [by Holocaust deniers], the theologian would inflict on them the only indignity left: that is, insistence that it was done because of their sins.
>
> —Rabbi Irving Greenberg, "Cloud of Smoke, Pillar of Fire: Judaism, Christianity and Modernity After the Holocaust," in *Auschwitz: Beginning of a New Era,* edited by Eva Fleischner, page 25

Given polemicists' unfortunate tendency to use the Holocaust to justify positions in which they already believe, Irving Greenberg has offered this guideline for Holocaust discussants:

> No statement, theological or otherwise, should be made that would not be credible in the presence of the burning children.
>
> —Rabbi Irving Greenberg, ibid., page 23

WHAT KIND OF FAITH IN GOD CAN JEWS HAVE AFTER THE HOLOCAUST?

Can one still speak to God after Auschwitz? Can one still, as an individual and as a people, enter at all into a dialogue relationship with Him? Dare we recommend to the survivors of Auschwitz, the Jobs of the gas chambers, "Call to Him, for He is kind, for His mercy endures forever"?

—Martin Buber, "Dialogue Between Heaven and Earth," in Will Herberg, ed., *Four Existentialist Theologians*, page 203

We learned in the crisis that we were totally and nakedly alone, that we could expect neither support nor succor from God nor from our fellow creatures. Therefore, the world will forever remain a place of pain, suffering, alienation and ultimate defeat.

—Richard Rubenstein, *After Auschwitz*, pages 128–129

A principal teaching of the Hebrew Bible is that God, Who created the world, intervenes in history. Thus, when Pharaoh enslaved the ancient Hebrews, God acted to free them. (His intervention, however, came only after two centuries of slavery.)

God's inaction during the Holocaust led Rubenstein to conclude in *After Auschwitz* that, contrary to the Exodus story, there is no God Who acts in history. His work is among the bleakest and most disturbing Jewish books ever written. The alternate position (articulated by Rabbi Avigdor Miller, among others), that the Holocaust represented not God's inaction but rather his punishing of the Jewish people for their sins, was rejected by Rubenstein as repugnant: "If indeed such a God holds the destiny of mankind in His power, His resort to the death camps to bring about His ends is so obscene that I would rather spend my life in perpetual revolt than render Him even the slightest homage" (*Power Struggle*, page 11).

With the publication of *After Auschwitz*, Rubenstein became identified with the mid-1960s "death of God" movement. But while the movement's radical Protestant thinkers (e.g., Thomas Altizer, author of *Radical Theology and the Death of God*) saw God's so-called "death" as a fortunate event that would liberate human beings from God's "heavy hand," Rubenstein, who has a bleak estimation of human nature, found it a cause for despair. Because the Holocaust has already happened once, he argued, similar acts of mass murder are more, not less, likely to recur, to Jews or to other people (see his *The Cunning of History*).

While empathizing with Rubenstein's pain, two other Jewish thinkers, Eliezer Berkovits and Emil Fackenheim, view his conclusion that there is no God Who acts in history as representing an unintentional triumph for Hitler:

> What, on account of the Jewish experience at Auschwitz, attempts to emerge as a Jewish version of a death-of-God theology has both an ironic and a tragic aspect. Its starting point is the problem of faith raised by the German barbarism of the Nazi era. In search of a solution to the problems, it arrives at a position from which one may not only not reject Nazism, but, indeed, find a "moral" validation for it as one of the man-created truths. [For if there is nothing higher in the universe than man, who is to judge which man-made truth is higher than another?] This is the bitterest irony . . . and presents us with one of the truly great triumphs of the Nazi position. It is of the very essence of [Rubenstein's] proposition that there is no personal God who is concerned with justice, morality, or human suffering. . . .
>
> —Eliezer Berkovits, *Faith After the Holocaust,* page 72

> There emerges what I will boldly term a 614th commandment: the authentic Jew of today is forbidden to hand Hitler yet another, posthumous victory. . . .
>
> We are, first, commanded to survive as Jews, lest the Jewish people perish.
>
> We are commanded, second, to remember in our very guts and bones the martyrs of the Holocaust, lest their memory perish.

We are forbidden, thirdly, to deny or despair of God, however much we may have to contend with Him or with belief in Him, lest Judaism perish.

We are forbidden, finally, to despair of the world as the place which is to become the kingdom of God, lest we help make it a meaningless place in which God is dead or irrelevant and everything is permitted.

To abandon any of these imperatives, in response to Hitler's victory at Auschwitz, would be to hand him yet other, posthumous victories.

—Emil Fackenheim, *The Jewish Return into History,* pages 22–24

The Torah, of course, ordains 613 commandments. While Fackenheim directs his "614th commandment" to all Jews, his primary concern seems to be those who have lost their faith in, and commitment to, Judaism because of the Holocaust.

Fackenheim argues that if Jews lose faith in God and stop living Jewish lives because of Auschwitz, then much as they might hate Hitler, they will be carrying out his will. For the Nazi Führer wanted nothing more than to end Judaism and the Jewish people. Thus, Jews who assimilate grant Hitler a "posthumous victory."

Fackenheim's formulation comes closer than any other to explaining the fervor of post-Holocaust Jewry's commitment to Soviet Jewry, Ethiopian Jewry, and most important, Israel. World Jewry's response to Hitler's decimation of Jewish life has been to do everything in its power to save endangered Jewish communities.

Still, Fackenheim's 614th commandment can be compelling for one or, at most, two generations. Ultimately, whether or not Jews decide to live Jewish lives will be, *must be,* based on their appreciation of Judaism's value, not on a desire to defy Hitler.

It is now about fifty years since the Holocaust ended. As its memory begins to recede, intermarriage rates among American Jews have sharply increased, so that they now exceed 50 percent. Most of those intermarrying are not committed to raising their children as Jews. Should they eventually decide to do so, that will more likely occur because of a belief in Judaism and its values, rather than out of a desire to defy Hitler.

The most cogent, if coolly rational, critique of Fackenheim's 614th commandment was delivered by the Orthodox Jewish philosopher Michael Wyschogrod:

> Let us imagine that there arises a wicked tyrant who sets as his goal, for his own depraved and psychotic reasons, the extermination of all stamp collectors in the world. It is clear that it would be the duty of every decent person to do everything in his power to frustrate the scheme of that tyrant. Let us further imagine, however, that before the tyrant is made harmless, he succeeds, in fact, in murdering a large proportion of the world's stamp collectors. Does it not follow [according to Fackenheim's 614th commandment] that subsequent to the tyrant's demise it becomes the duty of the remaining stamp collectors not to lose interest in their stamp collecting so as not to hand the tyrant a posthumous victory? . . . Would it be a posthumous victory for the tyrant were stamp collecting to disappear from the world as long as this disappearance is due, not to force, but to free choice? I cannot see why, if I am a secular, non-believing Jew, it is incumbent upon me to preserve Judaism because Hitler wished to destroy it. What was incumbent upon me was to destroy Hitler, but once this is accomplished, the free choice of every individual is restored and no further Hitler-derived burdens rest on the non-believing Jew.
>
> —Michael Wyschogrod, "Faith and the Holocaust,"
> a review of Emil Fackenheim's *God's Presence
> in History, Judaism,* Summer 1971 (20:3), pages 288–289

For Wyschogrod "the Holocaust was a totally destructive event which makes my remaining a Jew infinitely more difficult than it has ever been." He can only marvel at Fackenheim's attempt to deduce a commanding voice out of Auschwitz.

Having repeatedly reread both Fackenheim's description of the 614th commandment and Wyschogrod's critique, I am reminded of an old Jewish joke: Two men come before a rabbi with an argument. After the first person presents his arguments, the rabbi says, "You're right." When he hears the second man's side, he again says, "You're right." The rabbi's wife challenges him: "How can you tell one man he's right, then tell his opponent that he's right?" The rabbi ponders a moment, then turns to his wife, "You're also right."

Rabbi Irving Greenberg represents a position close to Berkovits and Fackenheim, but one that also acknowledges Rubenstein's despair. According to Greenberg, the Holocaust has blurred the boundary lines between believers and nonbelievers, perhaps permanently:

> After Auschwitz, faith means that there are times when faith is overcome. . . . We now have to speak of "moment faiths" . . . interspersed with times when the flames and smoke of the burning children blot out faith, although it flickers again. . . . The difference between the skeptic and the believer is frequency of faith, and not certitude of position.
> —Irving Greenberg, "Cloud of Smoke, Pillar of Fire: Judaism, Christianity and Modernity After the Holocaust," page 27

47

HOW DOES ONE SANCTIFY GOD'S NAME? HOW DOES ONE DESECRATE IT?

You shall not carry God's name in vain, for the Lord God will not forgive one who carries His name in vain.
—Exodus 20:7; the Third of the Ten Commandments

If you are familiar with the Ten Commandments and the above version sounds unfamiliar, that may be because I have translated the verse literally from the original Hebrew. The Third Commandment usually is translated as "You shall not take God's name in vain." People usually are taught that this means that one has to write God's name as "G-d," or that is blasphemous to use God's name in a curse. However, it is unclear why these offenses are so heinous that they would be included in the very document that forbids murder, adultery, thievery, and idolatry.

The literal translation, however, suggests that what is forbidden is to use "God" to justify selfish and/or evil causes. To cite two egregious historical examples:

The medieval Crusaders often murdered in the name of God. In 1209, a Crusader army occupied the French city of Beziers, which contained, according to a bishop's report, 220 Christian heretics known as Cathars. Unable to ferret them out, the Crusaders asked the papal commander, Arnaud Amalric, "What shall we do? We cannot distinguish the good from the wicked." Pope Innocent III's representative responded: "Kill them all. God will recognize His own." Fifteen thousand people were murdered in the ensuing one-day slaughter; the Church had conveniently assured the Crusaders in advance that all their sins would be forgiven (see Otto Friedrich, *The End of the World,* pages 75–78).

Similarly, many nineteenth-century American clergy cited the God of the Hebrew Bible as their authority for slavery. While it is true that the Torah, which was written some three thousand years ago, did allow slavery, it prescribed so many restrictions as to markedly differentiate it from the slavery practiced in the American South. Murdering a slave was a capital offense (Exodus 21:20), while a master who punished a slave so that he or she lost a limb, or even a tooth, had to set him or her free (Exodus 21:26–27).

It also was forbidden to return a runaway slave to his or her master (Deuteronomy 23:16), a biblical ordinance that the Supreme Court ignored in the infamous Dred Scott decision of 1857. According to biblical law, the kidnapping of people and their subsequent enslavement (which is how slaves were originally procured in the United States) is a capital crime: "He who kidnaps a person, whether he sold him or is still holding him, shall be put to death" (Exodus 21:16). In other words, more than twenty-five hundred years ago, a slave under Jewish law had far greater rights than slaves in the United States a little over a century ago. Thus, there are few more hideous violations of the Third Commandment than some nineteenth-century clerics' attempts to use the Bible to justify their practice of slavery.

The Third Commandment is the only one concerning which God says, "for the Lord God will not forgive him who carries His name in vain." The reason is now clear: When a person commits an evil act, he discredits him- or herself. But when a religious person does so in the name of God, he or she also discredits God and alienates people who otherwise might have become religiously observant. Consequently, God pronounces this sin unpardonable.

And you shall love the Lord your God (Deuteronomy 6:5); this means that you should cause God to be loved

317

through your acts. Thus, if a person studies Bible and Mishna . . . and is honest in his business dealings, and speaks gently to people, what do people say about him? "Happy is the father who taught him Torah. Happy is the teacher who taught him Torah. Woe unto those who haven't learned Torah. This man studied Torah; see how noble his ways are, how good his actions. . . . " But when a person studies Bible and Mishna . . . but is dishonest in business, and does not speak gently with people, what do people say of him? "Woe unto him who studies Torah. . . . This man studied Torah; look how corrupt are his deeds, how ugly his ways."

—Babylonian Talmud, *Yoma* 86a

Rabbi Samuel . . . went to Rome. The Empress lost a bracelet and he happened to find it. A proclamation was issued throughout the land that if anyone returned it within thirty days, he would receive such-and-such a reward but if, after thirty days, he did not do so, he would lose his head. He did not return it within the thirty days but thereafter.

She said to him: "Were you not in the province?"

He replied: "Yes, I was here."

She said: "But did you not hear the proclamation?"

"I heard it," said he.

"What did it say?" she asked.

He replied: "If anyone returns it within thirty days, he will receive such-and-such a reward, but if he returns it after thirty days, he will lose his head."

She said: "In that case, why did you not return it within the thirty days."

He said: "Because I did not want anyone to say that I returned it out of fear of you, whereas, in fact, I returned it out of fear of the All-merciful."

She said to him: "Blessed is the God of the Jews."

—Palestinian Talmud, *Bava Mezia* 2:5; I have followed almost verbatim the translation of Louis Jacobs, *Jewish Law,* page 50.

Jews must . . . not lie to a Jew or non-Jew, and not mislead anyone in any matter. . . . For if Jews cheat non-Jews, they will say, "Look how God chose for His people a nation of thieves and deceivers." . . . Indeed, God dispersed us among the nations so that we could gather converts to Judaism, but if we behave deceitfully towards others, who will want to join us?

—Rabbi Moshe of Coucy, thirteenth-century French author of a code of Jewish law known as *Semag*, page 152b. Rabbi Moshe's advice was offered at a time when Christian Crusaders were murdering Jews, and Jews lacked equal rights throughout Europe.

Rabbi Moshe intuited that it is a minority's fate to be judged by its worst members. Almost no one has ever spent time contemplating the fact that President John F. Kennedy's murderer, Lee Harvey Oswald, was born into a white Protestant family. But had the president's assassin been named Lee Harvey Goldberg or been an African American, his ethnicity or racial identity almost certainly would be many people's first association upon hearing his name.

A Jew who acts badly in God's name alienates people from God—and from other Jews. Conversely, a Jew who acts nobly, as Rabbi Moshe of Coucy suggests, will encourage people to feel affection for Jews and Judaism. Thus, among the righteous gentiles who saved Jews during the Nazi era were many who had had earlier, positive experiences with Jews.

"Sanctifying God's name," in Hebrew, *Kiddush ha-Shem,* also refers to one who dies as a martyr: See the following chapter.

48

MARTYRS

Those Who Died al Kiddush ha-Shem (to Sanctify God's Name)

According to Albert Camus, "There is only one really serious philosophical problem; and that is suicide."

May I differ and suggest that there is only one really serious problem; and that is martyrdom. Is there anything worth dying for?

— Abraham Joshua Heschel, *Who Is Man?,* page 92

IN THE ANCIENT WORLD

My son, go and say to Abraham your father, "You erected one altar [on which you were prepared to sacrifice Isaac], I have erected seven altars."

— Hannah, whose seven sons were murdered by the Syrian emperor Antiochus, for refusing to worship idols, c. 170 B.C.E.

Hannah directed these words to the last of her murdered sons, who was three years old. Immediately after he was killed, she climbed on a roof, hurled herself down, and died.

Rabbi Akiva, who was publicly tortured to death by the Romans in 135 C.E., was the most famous of all Jewish martyrs to die with the words *Sh'ma Yisra'el, Adonai Eloheinu Adonai Ekhad* (Hear, O Israel, the Lord is our God, the Lord is One) on his lips. Akiva had helped inspire Bar-Kochba's anti-Roman revolt, and had continued teaching Torah after the Romans made it a capital offense to do so:

> When Rabbi Akiva was taken out for execution, it was the time to recite the [morning] *Sh'ma*, and as he did so [literally, took upon himself the yoke of heaven], the Romans flayed his skin with iron combs. His disciples said to him, "Our teacher, even at this point [you continue to recite the *Sh'ma*]?"
>
> He said to them, "All my life I have been troubled by the verse [in the first paragraph of the *Sh'ma*, which says, 'You shall love the Lord your God . . .] with all your soul,' which I understood as meaning even if he takes your soul. I asked myself, when shall I have the opportunity to fulfill this verse? Now that I have the opportunity, shall I not fulfill it?"
>
> —Babylonian Talmud, *Berakhot* 61b

While reciting the *Sh'ma*, Akiva prolonged the final word *ekhad*, "one," and died while pronouncing it. To this day, it is customary to prolong "*ekhad*" when reciting the *Sh'ma* as a symbolic statement of the reciter's willingness to offer his or her soul, if need be, for God.

The Talmud tells of another rabbi whom the Romans executed at about the same time:

> Rabbi Hanina ben Teradion was found by the Romans studying Torah, publicly holding gatherings of pupils, and keeping a scroll of the Torah next to his heart.
>
> They wrapped him in the scroll, placed bundles of branches around him, and set it all on fire. Then they bought tufts of wool that had been soaked in water and placed them near his heart so that he should not die quickly. . . .

His disciples called out to him, "Rabbi, what do you see?"

He answered, "The parchments of the Torah are being burned, but the letters are soaring on high."

"Open your mouth, so that the fire will penetrate you," they said.

He answered, "Let Him who gave me my soul take it away, but no one should injure himself."

> —Babylonian Talmud, *Avodah Zara* 18a; I have followed the translation of Francine Klagsbrun, *Voices of Wisdom*, page 484.

In other words, an individual Torah and an individual Jew can be destroyed, but the Torah's words are eternal.

The Talmud relates that the Roman guard supervising his execution was so impressed by his courage and piety that he said to him, "Rabbi, if I raise the flame and take away the tufts of wool from over your heart, will you guarantee that I will enter the World-to-Come?"

"Yes," Rabbi Hanina replied.

"Swear to me!" the executioner urged him.

He swore unto him. The executioner raised the flame and removed the tufts of wool from over Rabbi Hanina's heart, and his soul departed speedily. The executioner then threw himself into the fire.

A voice from heaven announced, "Rabbi Hanina ben Teradion and the executioner have been assigned to the World-to-Come."

When Rabbi Judah heard this, he wept and said, "One man acquires eternal life in a single hour, another after many years" (Babylonian Talmud, *Avodah Zarah* 18a).

IN THE MIDDLE AGES

In 1348–1349, Europe was struck by the "Black Death," which is estimated to have wiped out as much as a third of the continent's population. Antisemites accused the Jews of having caused the plague by poisoning the wells. In communities throughout Europe, Jews were offered the choice of conversion to Christianity or death.

Tens of thousands of Jews refused to convert, and were murdered, including six thousand Jews in Mainz, Germany, and two thousand in Strasbourg, France (who were burned on a wooden scaffold in the Jewish cemetery). A medieval chronicler's account describes the manner in which the martyrs of Nordhausen, Germany, met their deaths:

> They asked the burghers to permit them to prepare themselves for martyrdom; permission having been given . . . they joyfully arrayed themselves in their prayer shawls and shrouds, both men and women. They [the Christians] dug a grave at the cemetery and covered it with wooden scaffolding. . . . The pious ones [among the Jews] asked that a musician be hired to play dancing tunes so that they should enter the presence of God with singing. They took each other by the hand, both men and women, and danced and leapt with their whole strength before God. Their teacher, Rabbi Jacob, went before them; his son, Rabbi Meir, brought up the rear to see that none should lag behind. Singing and dancing they entered the grave, and when all had entered, Rabbi Meir jumped out and walked around to make certain that none had stayed outside. When the burghers saw him, they asked him to save his life [by apostasy]. He answered: "This now is the end of our troubles, you see me only for a while, and then I shall be no more." He returned to the grave; they set fire to the scaffolding. They died all of them together and not a cry was heard.
>
> —*Sefer Minhagim* of Worms; quoted in H. H. Ben-Sasson,
> *Trial and Achievement*, pages 255–256

*　　　*　　　*

A poor man in search of a lost bag of pennies passed through a city where he found fame and fortune. Do you suppose he would resume his search for the missing pennies?

—Count Valentine Potocki before his execution, 1749

Potocki, a Polish nobleman, was sentenced to death for converting to Judaism, a capital crime in eighteenth-century Poland. The above was his response when he was offered clemency if he returned to Christianity.

At about the same time in Germany, Suss Oppenheimer served as the Duke of Württemberg's finance minister. After the duke's sudden death, Oppenheimer's enemies had him arrested on trumped-up charges and sentenced to death. A Pastor Rieger promised Oppenheimer that he would save his life if he converted to Christianity. Though hardly an observant Jew, Oppenheimer refused the offer: "I am a Jew and will remain a Jew. I would not become a Christian even if I could become an emperor. Changing one's religion is a matter for consideration by a free man; it is an evil thing for a prisoner." When he died, the words of the *Sh'ma* were on his lips.

DURING THE HOLOCAUST

> Let my death be an energetic cry of protest against the indifference of the world which witnesses the extermination of the Jewish people without taking any steps to prevent it. In our day and age, human life is of little value; having failed to achieve success in my life, I hope that my death may jolt the indifference of those who, perhaps even in this extreme moment, could save the Jews who are still alive in Poland.
>
> —From the suicide note of Shmuel Zygelboim, May 12, 1943

Zygelboim, a Polish Jew, had escaped to England, where he tried to rouse support for his country's Jews, who were being murdered by the Nazis. He committed suicide shortly after the failure of the Warsaw Ghetto revolt (it had started on April 19). Despite Zygelboim's hope that his death would jolt the world from its indifference, it didn't.

*　　*　　*

In the Janowska Road Camp, a particularly harsh Nazi work camp, one foreman of a work brigade was a Jew from Lvov, Poland, named Schneeweiss, who was known to be both antireligious and cruel. Yet the afternoon before Yom Kippur, Israel Spira, a Hasidic rebbe, approached Schneeweiss and requested that a group of religious Jews be exempted from the thirty-nine categories of work that Jewish law forbids on that day, so that they could thereby minimize the transgression of working on Yom Kippur. To the rabbi's amazement, the request moved Schneeweiss, and he assured the rebbe that he would do whatever he could.

The following morning, Schneeweiss took a group of Hasidim to the SS quarters, and told them, "You fellows will shine the floor without any polish or wax. And you, Rabbi, will clean the windows with dry rags so that you will not transgress any of the thirty-nine major categories of work."

As the Jews started their work, they chanted the Yom Kippur prayers, which they knew by heart. Some thirty years after the event, Rabbi Spira recalled what happened next:

> At about twelve o'clock noon, the door opened wide and into the room stormed two angels of death, S.S. men in their black uniforms. . . . They were followed by a food cart filled to capacity. "Noontime, time to eat bread, soup and meat," announced one of the two S.S. men. The room was filled with an aroma of freshly cooked food, such food as they had not seen since the German occupation: white bread, steaming hot vegetable soup, and huge portions of meat.
>
> The tall S.S. man commanded in a high-pitched voice, "You must eat immediately, otherwise you will be shot on the spot!" None of them moved. The rabbi remained on the ladder, the Hasidim on the floor. The German repeated the orders. The rabbi and the Hasidim remained glued to their places. The S.S. men called in Schneeweiss. "Schneeweiss, if the dirty dogs refuse to eat, I will kill you along with them." Schneeweiss pulled himself to attention, looked the German directly in the eyes, and said in a very quiet tone, "We Jews do not eat today. Today is Yom Kippur, our most holy day, the Day of Atonement."
>
> "You don't understand, Jewish dog," roared the taller of the two. "I command you in the name of the Führer and the Third Reich, *fress*!" (a vulgar word, meaning to

devour food as animals do, as opposed to the polite *essen,* used for humans).

Schneeweiss, composed, his head high, repeated the same answer. "We Jews obey the law of our tradition. Today is Yom Kippur, a day of fasting."

The German took out his revolver from its holster and pointed it at Schneeweiss's temple. Schneeweiss remained calm. He stood still, at attention, his head high. A shot pierced the room. Schneeweiss fell. On the freshly polished floor, a puddle of blood was growing bigger and bigger.

The rabbi and the Hasidim stood as if frozen in their places. They could not believe what their eyes had just witnessed. Schneeweiss, the man who in the past had publicly transgressed against the Jewish tradition, had sanctified God's name publicly and died a martyr's death for the sake of Jewish honor.

"Only then, on that Yom Kippur day in Janowska," said the rabbi to his Hasidim, "did I understand the meaning of the statement in the Talmud: 'Even the transgressors in Israel are as full of good deeds as a pomegranate is filled with seeds'" (Babylonian Talmud, *Eruvin* 19a).

—The story of Schneeweiss is told in a remarkable compilation of true stories from the Holocaust, *Hasidic Tales of the Holocaust* by Yaffa Eliach, pages 155–159.

*   *   *

In 1943, when the large majority of the more than half-million Jews crammed into the Warsaw Ghetto had already been murdered, Poland's Catholic hierarchy made it known that they were willing to smuggle out and save the remaining rabbis in the Ghetto. The only three still alive, Rabbis Menahem Zemba, Shimshon Stockhammer, and David Shapiro, met to consider the life-saving offer. For a long time, no one spoke. Rabbi Shapiro finally broke the silence:

I am the youngest and therefore what I have to say does not obligate the two of you. We know well that we can no longer help our fellow Jews in any way. However, merely by being with them, by not leaving them, we encourage and strengthen them. It is the last possible encouragement that we can still give to the last Jews. I simply don't have the strength to leave these unfortunate people.

All three rabbis refused to be saved: only Rabbi Shapiro survived the war.

Rabbi Shapiro's opening sentence, "I am the youngest . . . " was based on the protocol practiced by the Sanhedrin, the Jewish high court in ancient Jerusalem. When passing judgment in a life-and-death matter, the youngest justices spoke first: otherwise, it was feared, they would be overawed by the opinions expressed by their seniors.

*   *   *

Perhaps the least-known martyr to have his words recorded here is Itzik Rosenzweig, a poultry farmer from Slovakia, who was murdered by the Nazis. Crowded with hundreds of other Jews into a cattle car bound for Auschwitz, and surrounded by hostile and jeering Polish neighbors, Rosenzweig turned to them: "Please, go to my house and give water and food to the poultry. They have had nothing to eat or drink all day." Eliezer Berkovits, who concludes his book *Faith After the Holocaust* with Rosenzweig's story, writes: "Because of what man did to Itzik Rosenzweig, I have no faith in man; because of Itzik, in spite of it all, I have faith in the future of man" (pages 168–169).

A TWENTIETH-CENTURY STORY OF AN ALMOST MARTYR WITH A HAPPY ENDING

Five years ago I submitted my application for an exit visa to Israel. Now I am further than ever from my dream. This would seem to be cause for regret. But it is absolutely otherwise. I am happy. I am happy that I lived honestly, in peace with my conscience. I never compromised my soul, even under the threat of death. . . . For more than two thousand years the Jewish people, my people, have been dispersed. But wherever they are, wherever Jews are found, each year they have repeated, "Next year in Jerusalem." Now, when I am further than ever from my people, from Avital [my wife], facing many arduous years of imprisonment, I say, turning to my people, my Avital: Next year in Jerusalem! And I turn to you, the court, who were required to confirm a predetermined sentence: to you I have nothing to say.

—Anatoly (Natan) Sharansky's last speech (July 14, 1978) before the Soviet court that sentenced him to thirteen years' imprisonment on a false accusation of spying for the United States. (The charge had carried with it the possibility of a death sentence.) Sharansky was incarcerated for sixteen months before his trial, and despite being subjected to psychological and physical torture, he refused to confess. Until Sharansky's release from prison in February 1986 (in response to tremendous international efforts largely organized by Avital), many Jews read Sharansky's final statement to the court at their Passover seders. Sharansky's entire speech is reprinted in his remarkable autobiography, *Fear No Evil* (pages 224–225).

49

MITZVAH (COMMANDMENT) AND SOME OF THE DISTINGUISHING CHARACTERISTICS OF JUDAISM

Greater is one who is commanded to do something and does it, than one who is not commanded to do something and does it.

—Babylonian Talmud, *Kiddushin* 31a

Since most people regard a voluntary act as morally superior to an obligatory one, this rabbinic dictum seems puzzling. A major reason the Rabbis so valued people acting from a sense of obligation may well have been their belief that such individuals will behave with greater consistency than those who perform commandments voluntarily. The latter will usually stop doing so when they grow tired of them, whereas those who feel obligated will be deflected neither by tiredness nor by a sense of burden.

This dictum, which the Talmud attributes to Rabbi Hanina, makes considerable psychological sense when analyzed in light of two types of diets. A large percentage of Americans diet, and usually do so for two reasons: to be both more attractive and healthier. As powerful as these motivations are, very few Americans adhere to their diet for three months or more without breaking it at least once.

Compare this statistic with the experience of individuals who observe the Jewish dietary laws known as *kashrut*. They can go a lifetime without eating such foods as shellfish or pork, solely because Jewish law forbids them, not because refraining from them leads to greater physical attractiveness and/or health. If only the American government mandated putting pork into all chocolate products, I easily could shed twenty pounds!

> A man should always occupy himself with Torah and the commandments, even if not for their own sake, for even if he does them with an ulterior motive, he will eventually come to do them for their own sake.
> —Babylonian Talmud, *Pesachim* 50b

In his *The Rector of Justin,* the contemporary novelist Louis Auchincloss has articulated a similar insight: "Keep doing good deeds long enough and you'll probably turn out a good man. In spite of yourself."

ADVICE ON FULFILLING THE COMMANDMENTS

> If a commandment comes your way, don't delay.
> —Mekhilta, *Bo*

If you have the opportunity to do something worthwhile, do it immediately. Thus, if you feel impelled to donate money to a poor person or to a worthwhile cause, don't procrastinate; if you do, you might end up not doing it at all.

> Make a fence about the [laws of the] Torah.
> —*Ethics of the Fathers* 1:1

The Rabbis believed that it is not enough to refrain from doing what the Torah forbids: One also should keep far from anything that might lead to violating a biblical or rabbinic statute. For ex-

330

ample, since the Torah forbids making a fire on the Sabbath, Jewish law insists that one not handle matches on that day, since that might lead to their being lit.

Similarly, in the case of a Nazirite (a person who has vowed not to cut his hair, drink wine, or eat grapes, as a way of achieving a higher spiritual state), the Talmud advises: "Take a circuitous route, Nazirite, but do not approach the vineyard" (Babylonian Talmud, *Shabbat* 13a). A contemporary application of this principle would be to warn a recovering alcoholic against meeting someone at a bar, even if he or she intends to drink only nonalcoholic beverages.

> Run to perform a light commandment as you would to perform the most important. Flee from sin, for one commandment leads to another commandment, and one sin brings about another.
>
> —*Ethics of the Fathers* 4:2

> It is forbidden to fulfill a commandment through a transgression.
>
> —Babylonian Talmud, *Sukkah* 30a

What is an example of a commandment fulfilled through a transgression? A person who steals money and then gives some of it to charity. Indeed, if anyone is to be credited for the charitable contribution, it should not be the giver (it wasn't his money to give), but the person whose money was stolen.

The above talmudic observation is made as part of a legal discussion about the status of a person who steals a *lulav* (the palm branch used during the Sukkot rituals) and then recites a blessing to God over it. The Rabbis conclude that when a thief acts in this way, it is really as if he had cursed, not blessed, God.

While a thief blessing a stolen item occurs rarely, people often break one law while fulfilling another. More than a century ago, Rabbi Israel Salanter cautioned: "It is not infrequent for an energetic individual to rise in the middle of the night [to offer the *Selikhot* prayers, recited at dawn in the weeks before the New Year] and make such noise in rising from the bed that he wakes the entire household. . . . He is blissfully unaware that his loss outweighs his gain" (cited in Dov Katz, *T'nuat ha-Musar* Vol. 1, page 355). Better he had stayed in bed, and not deprived other people of their sleep.

TWO OPPOSING TALMUDIC VIEWS ON WHETHER THE PERFORMANCE OF COMMANDMENTS IS REWARDED IN THIS WORLD

Those on a mission to perform a commandment will not suffer any harm, neither on their way there, nor on the way back.

—Babylonian Talmud, *Pesachim* 8b

The belief that God will protect a person trying to fulfill a commandment has led to a widely observed Jewish custom which, unfortunately, is little known in the non-Orthodox world: When a person departs on an arduous, possibly dangerous, journey, his relatives and friends give him money to distribute as charity upon arrival at his or her destination. Jews who observe this custom refer to it as "*shaliakh mitzvah gelt*" (money for a messenger to do charitable deeds). Their underlying belief is that God will protect a person en route to performing such an important commandment throughout his or her journey.

On the other hand:

There is no reward for following the commandments in this world.

—Babylonian Talmud, *Kiddushin* 39b

While we would all like to believe that people who do good deeds should lead lives devoid of suffering, the world does not, indeed cannot, work that way. As I once heard Rabbi Harold Kushner ask, "Would you really prefer if a good person could go outside in a terrible snowstorm without an overcoat and not become sick?" Indeed, if good deeds were always rewarded and evil deeds punished in this world, then we would no longer have freedom of choice. Who would choose to do anything bad under those circumstances?

Therefore, as this dictum suggests, if observance of the commandments is to be rewarded, that reward will come in the afterlife.

ARE THE TORAH'S 613 LAWS DIVINE FIATS, OR ARE THEY ROOTED IN REASON?

There is a group of human beings who consider it a grievous thing that causes should be given for any law; what would please them most is that the intellect would not find a meaning for the commandments and prohibitions. What compels them to feel thus is a sickness that they find in their souls. . . . For they think that if those laws were useful in this existence and had been given to us for this or that reason, it would be as if they derived from the reflection and understanding of some intelligent being. If, however, there is a thing for which the intellect could not find any meaning at all and that does not lead to something useful, it indubitably derives from God: For the reflection of man would lead to no such thing.

—Moses Maimonides, *Guide to the Perplexed* 3:31

That Jewish laws have to be reasonable seems axiomatic, since the Torah teaches that their observance "will make you wise and profound in the eyes of the nations, who on hearing all these laws will say, 'Surely this great nation is a wise and discerning people' " (Deuteronomy 4:6). If such laws were merely divine decrees without a deeper rationale, Maimonides asks, then why would non-Jews think Jews "wise and discerning" for observing them? In his *Guide to the Perplexed,* the great medieval philosopher attempts to explain the social and religious rationale for the 613 laws in the Torah.

On the other hand:

A person should not say, "I loathe pig's meat. . . . " but he should say, "I do desire it, but what can I do since my Father in heaven has decreed that it is forbidden."

—*Sifra, Leviticus*

This is one of the most uncharacteristic Jewish statements about the pig, which usually is described as a loathsome and dirty animal. The Jewish attitude toward the pig influenced the Western world toward a generally low regard for this creature. (The New Testament coined the expression "Do not throw pearls before swine," Matthew 7: 6.) To this day, I know of no Western or Muslim society in which comparing a human being to "a pig" is not an insult.

Presumably, all this should make pigs very happy. A cartoon I once saw showed a number of pigs grazing contentedly in a field, with one saying to the others, "Don't you wish the whole world were Jewish?"

> Rabbi Isaac said: Why were the reasons of [most] biblical laws not revealed? Because in two verses reasons were revealed, and they caused the greatest in the world to stumble.
> —Babylonian Talmud, *Sanhedrin* 21b

"The greatest in the world" refers to King Solomon who, according to Jewish tradition, was the wisest man of his time. Nonetheless, although the Torah commanded that a king "shall not have many wives, lest his heart go astray" (Deuteronomy 17:17), Solomon, the Talmud teaches, reasoned to himself, "I will take many wives, and not let my heart be perverted." Yet we learn, "In his old age, his wives turned away Solomon's heart after other gods" (I Kings 11:4).

Thus, of the very king who during his early years built the Great Temple (*Beit Ha-Mikdash*) in Jerusalem, the Bible records that he followed the Phoenician goddess Ashtoreth and the Ammonite god Milcom, going so far as to build idolatrous shrines "for all his foreign wives who offered and sacrificed to their gods" (I Kings 11:5, 7–8).

Similarly, the Torah, reflecting the experience of Jewish slavery in Egypt, commanded that the king "not keep many horses or send people back to Egypt to add to his horses, since the Lord has warned you, 'You must not go back that way again' " (Deuteronomy 17: 16). Again, Solomon reasoned, "I will multiply horses, but will not cause Israelites to return to Egypt." But we learn that he subsequently engaged in extensive horse trading with Egypt, which involved Israelites going there often (I Kings 10:29).

This oft-cited talmudic teaching underscores that people's *certainty* about the reason for a commandment is apt to cause them to ignore it and follow their own reasoning instead (confident that even if they violate "the letter of the law," they are adhering to its "spirit"). Thus, although traditional Jewish law forbids traveling on the Sabbath and making a fire on that day, I have occasionally heard Jews argue that because they understand the purpose of the Sabbath to be a time for relaxation and revitalization they spend it camping out and barbecuing, activities that may satisfy their understanding of the Sabbath's purpose, but which are forbidden by Jewish law.

> For what does it matter to the Holy One, Blessed be He, whether or not the Jews carry out the laws of *kashrut?* It is clear, then, that the commandments were given solely for the purpose of training [literally, involving] people.
> —*Midrash Tanhuma, Shmini 7*

This passage suggests that some ritual commandments, such as *kashrut*, were given to train people in self-control. My friend Dennis Prager, who grew up in a kosher home, recalls that when he was six years old, the first words he learned to read in English were "pure vegetable shortening only" (lest he eat something containing non-kosher animal fat). He comments: "It's not a bad thing to learn at the age of six, that you can't have every candy bar in the candy store." Indeed, this might not be the least significant lesson learned from observing the ritual commandments.

50

STUDYING TORAH

THE TORAH'S INFLUENCE

The Patriarchs' deeds are a sign for the children [i.e., all their descendants, forever].
—Jewish proverb based on *Midrash Tanchuma, Lekh Lekha* 9,
which suggests that "everything that happened to [Abraham]
happened to his descendants."

When Jews read the Torah portion each week, they extract both positive and negative lessons for daily living. For example, Genesis records that because Jacob favored Joseph above his other sons, he made him a beautiful coat of many colors (37:3). This infuriated his brothers, leading the Rabbis to conclude (as was noted in the chapter on parent/child relations): "A man should not single out one of his children for special treatment, for because of two coins' worth of silk [the added value of Joseph's special coat], Joseph's brothers became jealous of him, and one thing led to another until our ancestors became slaves in Egypt" (Babylonian Talmud, *Shabbat* 10b).

Jews studied the lives of the Patriarchs, the Matriarchs, and even their servants, for guidance on dealing with their own families' important events and crises. For example, Genesis records that Abraham sent his servant Eliezer to find a wife for his son, Isaac. Besides instructing Eliezer not to choose a wife from the Canaanite women, Abraham was sparse in detailing the criteria his servant should consider.

Eliezer decides that the determinative factor should be kindness: "Let the maiden to whom I say," he prays to God at one point, " 'Please lower your jar that I may drink,' and who replies, 'Drink, and I will also water your camels,' let her be the one whom You have decreed for your servant Isaac" (24:14). Almost immediately, Rebecca makes exactly that response and soon becomes Isaac's wife, and Judaism's second Matriarch.

> Turn it over and over again, for one can find everything in it [i.e., the Torah].
>
> —*Ethics of the Fathers* 5:22

As Harold Kushner has written: "Jews read the Bible the way a person reads a love letter. When you read a love letter, you don't just read it for content. You try and squeeze every last little bit of meaning out of it, e.g., Why did he sign it 'Yours' instead of 'Love'? (*To Life,* page 40).

TORAH AS THE JEWISH PEOPLE'S LIFEBLOOD

Our Rabbis taught: The wicked [Roman] government once issued a decree forbidding the Jews to study the Torah. But Pappus ben Judah found Rabbi Akiva teaching Torah to public assemblies. Pappus said to him, "Akiva, are you not afraid of the government?"

Akiva replied: "I will answer you with a parable. A fox was once walking alongside a river, and he saw fishes anxiously swimming from place to place. He said to them, 'From what are you fleeing?'

"The fishes answered, 'From the nets cast for us by men.'

"The fox said, 'Why do you not come up and find safety on land, so that you and I can live together [in peace] . . . ?'

"But the fishes replied, 'Are you the one they call the most clever of animals? You are not clever, but foolish. If we are afraid in the one element in which we can live, how much more would we have to be afraid in the element in which we would certainly die?'

"So it is with us [said Akiva]. If we are in such danger when we sit and study the Torah, of which it is written, 'For thereby you shall have life and shall long endure' (Deuteronomy 30:20), how much worse our situation will be if we were to neglect the Torah!"

Soon afterwards, Rabbi Akiva was arrested and thrown into prison, and Pappus ben Judah was also arrested and imprisoned next to him. He said to him, "Pappus, for what sin were you brought here?"

He replied, "Happy are you, Rabbi Akiva, that you have been arrested because of Torah! Woe to Pappus who was arrested for worthless reasons."

—Babylonian Talmud, *Berakhot* 61b

At times, Torah study has waned greatly among Jews, but a few leading sages and teachers always worked hard and heroically to revive it. Thus, a little before 200 C.E., during a period of widespread ignorance of Torah in Israel, one such sage, Rabbi Hiyya, dedicated himself to spreading Judaism's teachings:

"To make sure the Torah would not be forgotten in Israel, what did I do?

"I sowed flax, and from the flax cords I made nets. With the nets I trapped deer, giving their meat to orphans to eat, and from their skins prepared scrolls.

"On the scrolls, I wrote the five books of Moses. Then I went to a town that had no teachers and taught the five books to five children, and the six orders of the Mishna to six children.

"I instructed them, 'Until I return, teach each other the Torah and the Mishna.' And that is how I kept the Torah from being forgotten in Israel."

—Babylonian Talmud, *Bava Mezia* 85b

Of Rabbi Hiyya's accomplishment, the Talmud was later to write: "When the Torah was forgotten from Israel, Ezra came up

338

from Babylonia and established it. When [some of] it was once more forgotten, Hillel the Babylonian came up and established it. When [some of] it was once more forgotten, Hiyya and his sons came up and established it" (Babylonian Talmud, *Sukkah* 20a).

THE PREEMINENCE OF STUDY

Rabbi Tarfon and the other rabbis were once staying . . . in Lydda when the question was raised before them: "Is study greater or practice?" Rabbi Tarfon said, "Practice is greater." Rabbi Akiva said, "Study is greater." Then they all answered and said, "Study is greater for it leads to deeds."

—Babylonian Talmud, *Kiddushin* 40b

This story seems the Jewish equivalent of "Give a man a fish, and you feed him for a day. Teach him how to fish, and you feed him for a lifetime." One good deed, the Rabbis are saying, does not a good life make. Because right actions require knowledge, people lacking that knowledge will not know the proper way to behave.

Thus, study takes precedence over action not because it is more important, but because without it, right behavior will not be maintained for long.

WHO SHOULD STUDY TORAH?

Every Jew [literally, every Jewish man] is required to study Torah, whether poor or rich, healthy or ailing, young or old and feeble. Even a man so poor that he is maintained by charity or goes begging from door to door, as also a man with a wife and children to support, is under the obligation to set aside a definite period during the day and night for the study of the Torah. . . . Until what period in life is one obligated to study Torah? Until the day of one's death.

—Moses Maimonides, *Mishneh Torah*, "Laws of Torah Study," 1:8,10

[A parent must not ignore his own study of Torah], for just as it is a commandment to educate his child, so, too, is the parent commanded to educate himself.

—Moses Maimonides, ibid., 1:4

*   *   *

When did Rabbi Akiva begin to study Torah? It was said that he was forty years old and had not yet learned anything. Once, while he was standing by the mouth of a well, he asked, "Who cut a hole in this rock?"

They told him, "The water that kept falling on it every day. . . . "

Rabbi Akiva immediately began to reason in the following manner: "If something so soft can cut something so hard, then certainly the words of Torah, which are as hard as iron, can engrave themselves on my heart, which is only flesh and blood."

He and his son then went to a teacher of little children. He said, "My teacher, teach me Torah!"

Rabbi Akiva held one end of the slate, and his son the other. The teacher wrote "Aleph, Bet" ["A, B"] for him, and he learned it. "Aleph, Taf" [the entire alphabet] and he learned it. The Book of Leviticus [with which teachers traditionally began Torah study], and he learned it. He just kept studying and studying until he learned the entire Torah. . . .

Rabbi Akiva began to study Torah at age forty, and thirteen years later he was teaching Torah to crowds of people.

—*The Fathers According to Rabbi Nathan,* chapter 6:1; with minor variations, I have followed Danny Siegel's lyrical translation, *Where Heaven and Earth Touch,* pages 202–204.

That the Rabbis understood the obligation to study Torah as devolving on every Jew is illustrated in three talmudic anecdotes that anticipate the most common excuses for not doing so:

Our Rabbis taught: A poor man, a rich man and a sensual [literally, evil] man come before the heavenly court.

340

They ask the poor man, "Why did you not study To-rah?"

If he answers, "I was poor and worried about earning my living," they will ask him, "Were you poorer than Hillel?"

For it was told of Hillel that every day, he used to work and earn one *tropaik* [a small amount], half of which he would give [as tuition] to the doorkeeper at the House of Learning; the other half he would spend on his and his family's needs. One day, he was unable to earn anything and the doorkeeper would not permit him to enter the House of Learning. So he climbed up to the roof and sat upon the window to hear the words of the Living God out of the mouths of [Rabbis] Shmaya and Avtalion. That day was a Friday in the middle of the winter, and snow fell down upon him from the sky.

When the dawn rose, Shmaya said to Avtalion, "Brother Avtalion, every day, this house is light and today it is dark. . . . They looked up and saw the figure of a man in the window. They went up and found Hillel covered by four feet of snow. They brought him downstairs, bathed and anointed him, and placed him in front of the fire. . . ."

They ask the rich man, "Why did you not study To-rah?"

If he answers: "I was rich and preoccupied with my possessions," they say to him, "Do you mean to say you were richer than Rabbi Eleazar?"

Of Rabbi Eleazar ben Harsom it is reported that his father left him an inheritance of one thousand cities on land and a thousand ships on sea. Yet every day he would take a sack of flour on his shoulder and go from city to city and province to province for the sole purpose of study-ing the Torah. . . .

They ask the sensual person, "Why did you not study Torah?"

If he says, "I was so good-looking and was too busy just keeping my passions under control," they will ask him, "Do you mean to say you were better-looking than Joseph?"

It was told of Joseph the virtuous that every day Potiphar's wife tried to seduce him with [both] words [and actions]. The dresses she put on for him in the morning, she did not wear in the evening; those she put on in the evening, she did not wear the next morning. She said to him, "Yield to me!" He said, "No." She said, "I shall have you imprisoned" [if you don't]. . . . [Finally] she offered him a thousand pieces of silver if only he would lie with her, but he refused. . . .

Thus, the poor who do not study Torah stand condemned by the example set by Hillel. The rich who do not study Torah stand condemned by the example set by Rabbi Eleazar ben Harsom. And the sensual who do not study Torah stand condemned by the example set by Joseph.

—Babylonian Talmud, *Yoma* 35b; with some variations,
I have followed the translation of Jakob Petuchowski,
Our Masters Taught, pages 46–48.

TECHNIQUES FOR MAKING STUDY BOTH HABITUAL AND PRODUCTIVE

Make your study of Torah a fixed, habitual activity.
—*Ethics of the Fathers* 1:15

Among Eastern European Jews, a very devoted student of Torah was called a *masmid*. Although the term normally was applied to one who studied ten or more hours a day, Rabbi Israel Salanter argued that this usage was erroneous: "A *masmid* is not one who studies continuously, but one who studies every day. This is proved by the use of the word *tamid* [from which *masmid* derives; in Hebrew *tamid* means 'continually'] to describe the daily sacrifice, even though it was offered only twice during the day."

When my father, Shlomo Telushkin, became very busy with his accounting work, my grandfather, Rabbi Nissen Telushkin, fearful that his son would neglect Jewish learning, urged him to learn two laws from the Mishna every morning. Adhering to this schedule for the rest of his life, my father succeeded in studying the entire Mishna several times.

> A foolish student will say, "Who can possibly learn the whole Torah . . . ?" A wise student will say, "I will learn two laws today, and two tomorrow, until I have mastered the whole Torah."
>
> —*Song of Songs Rabbah*, 5:11

> He who repeats what he has learned one hundred times cannot be compared to one who repeats it a hundred and one times.
>
> —Babylonian Talmud, *Hagigah* 9b

As my friend David Szonyi notes, "This suggests that relearning something many, many times, rather than being a repetitive, and perhaps boring, intellectual experience, can lead one to a deeper and fresher understanding."

> One who is bashful will never learn.
>
> —*Ethics of the Fathers* 2:5

The Rabbis had no desire to deprecate shy people; they simply were noting that those who are too timid to ask questions will never gain a deep understanding of a subject.

> A student should not be embarrassed if a fellow student has understood something after the first or second time and he has not grasped it even after several attempts. If he is embarrassed because of this, it will turn out that he will come and go from the house of study without learning anything at all.
>
> —*Shulkhan Arukh, Yoreh De'ah* 246:11

343

A hot-tempered [alternatively, overly demanding] person cannot teach.

—*Ethics of the Fathers* 2:5

Students are afraid to ask questions of a teacher who is irascible. Maimonides warns teachers of fiery temperament to restrain themselves, and urges students not to be intimidated by them: "When a teacher is teaching, and the students do not understand, he should not be angry at them or become upset, but rather he should go over the material again and again, even many times, until they understand the depth of the law. Similarly, a student should not say, 'I understand,' if he has not understood. He should ask again, many times if necessary. And if the teacher becomes angry and disturbed, the student should say, 'My teacher, this is Torah, and I must learn it, but my capacities are limited' " (*Mishneh Torah,* "Laws of Torah Study," 4:4; translation is by Danny Siegel, *Where Heaven and Earth Touch,* page 250).

An ignoramus cannot be a [fully] pious person.

—*Ethics of the Fathers* 2:5

An ignorant person's insufficient piety is not necessarily due to a lack of good intentions. Rather, true piety demands right action, not just right intentions, and that requires study and knowledge.

Lot, Abraham's nephew, had a good heart, and when the citizens of Sodom wished to rape the visitors who had come to his house, he did everything possible to dissuade them. But after his arguments failed, he offered his daughters, in lieu of the visitors, for the Sodomites to rape (Genesis 19:8). A person of such moral ignorance cannot be regarded as "pious" without doing severe damage to the word.

SOME FINAL ADVICE

If you truly wish your children to study Torah, study it yourself in their presence. They will follow your example. Otherwise, they will not themselves study Torah but will simply instruct their children to do so.

—Rabbi Menahem Mendel of Kotzk

51

"HOW CAN WE TELL WHEN A SIN WE HAVE COMMITTED HAS BEEN PARDONED?"

On Repentance and Sin

Who needs to repent? Everyone.
What motivates repentance? Anything.
When should one repent? Always.

WHO NEEDS TO REPENT?

For there is no man so righteous on earth who does only good and never sins.

—Ecclesiastes 7:20

WHAT MOTIVATES REPENTANCE?

The removal of the ring [which King Ahasuerus gave to Haman] had a greater effect [on the Jews] than the forty-eight prophets and seven prophetesses whom God sent to Israel, for all these were not able to turn the Jews to a better course, whereas the removal of the ring did influence them to repent.

—Babylonian Talmud, *Megillah* 14a

The Book of Esther records that when Haman proposed to King Ahasuerus the murder of every Jew in the Persian Empire, Ahasuerus "removed his signet ring from his hand, and gave it to Haman. . . . And the king said to Haman, 'The money and the people are yours to do with as you see fit.' . . . The orders were issued . . . and sealed with the king's signet" (Esther 3:10–12). A few verses later, the Bible describes Mordechai tearing his clothes and putting on sackcloth and ashes, while the Jews of Shushan fasted for three days and nights.

Rabbi Saul Weiss succinctly summarizes the rabbinic comment: "The exhortations [criticisms and condemnations] of all the prophets did not cause the Israelites to repent whereas the impending disaster, symbolized by the 'removal of the ring,' did" (*Insights: A Talmudic Treasury,* page 83).

While antisemitism often constitutes a catalyst for repentance, what might be the most inelegant story in the entire Talmud "shows how small a thing can set a man on the road to repentance, even a prostitute's [passing gas]" (Hyam Maccoby, *The Day God Laughed,* pages 66–67):

> It was said of Rabbi Eleazar ben Dordai that he did not omit having intercourse with any prostitute in the world. Once, on hearing that there was a certain prostitute in one of the towns by the sea who accepted a purse of *denarii* [valuable coins] for payment, he took a purse of *denarii* and crossed seven rivers to reach her.
>
> As he was with her, she passed gas and commented, "Just as this gas will never return to its place, so will the repentance of Eleazar ben Dordai never be accepted."
>
> He went and sat between two hills and mountains, and said, "Mountains and hills, plead with God to have mercy on me."
>
> They replied, "Before we pray for you, we must pray for ourselves, for Scripture says, 'For the mountains shall depart and the hills be removed' " (Isaiah 54:10).

He said, "Heaven and Earth, ask God to have mercy on me."

Said the Heaven and Earth, "Before we pray for you, we should pray for ourselves, for Scripture says, 'For the heavens shall melt away like smoke, and the earth wear out like a garment' " (Isaiah 51:6).

He said, "Sun and Moon, ask God to have mercy on me."

Said the Sun and Moon, "Before we pray for you, we should pray for ourselves, for Scripture says, 'Then the moon shall be ashamed and the sun abashed' " (Isaiah 24:23).

He said, "Stars and Constellations, ask God to have mercy on me."

Said the Stars and Constellations, "Before we pray for you, we should pray for ourselves, for Scripture says, 'And all the hosts of heaven shall wither' " (Isaiah 34:4).

He said, "Then the matter depends on me alone." He placed his head between his knees, and groaned and wept until his soul departed.

A heavenly voice went forth and said, "Rabbi Eleazar ben Dordai has been summoned to the life of the World-to-Come."

Rabbi Judah the Prince, when he heard of this, wept, and said, "One person may gain the World-to-Come by the toil of many years, and another gains it in one hour." And, he added, "It is not enough for those who repent that they are accepted; they are called 'Rabbi' too!"

—Babylonian Talmud, *Avodah Zara* 17a

WHEN SHOULD ONE REPENT?

Rabbi Eliezer said, "Repent one day before your death."

His disciples asked him, "But does a person know on what day he [or she] is going to die?"

"All the more reason, therefore, to repent today, lest

347

one die tomorrow. In this manner, one's whole life will be spent in repentance."

—Babylonian Talmud, *Shabbat* 153a

A man cannot say to the Angel of Death, "Wait till I make up my accounts."

—*Ecclesiastes Rabbah* 8, commenting on verse 8

THE UNEQUALED POWER OF REPENTANCE

In the place where a repentant sinner stands, a thoroughly righteous person is not entitled to stand.

—Babylonian Talmud, *Berakhot* 34b

The Rabbis believed that it is a much greater struggle for a person to repent and give up acts formerly permitted him or her than it is for one who has always been righteous to go on being so. Understandably so: A person addicted to extramarital affairs who decides to remain monogamous will presumably feel a greater, more constant temptation to "slip" than one who has never strayed; thus, his or her repentance is valued more highly.

As for the thoroughly righteous, they too have areas where they are not so righteous, and if they refrain from sinning in those areas they will gain merit accordingly.

TRUE REPENTANCE

How is one proved to be a true penitent? Said Rabbi Judah: If the opportunity to commit the same sin presents itself on two occasions, and he does not yield to it.

—Babylonian Talmud, *Yoma* 86b

What constitutes complete repentance? When one is confronted by the identical situation wherein he previously sinned and it is within his power to commit the sin again, and he nevertheless does not succumb because he wishes to repent, and not because he is afraid or physically too weak [to repeat the sin]. For example, if he had relations

> with a woman forbidden to him and, after some time, he
> is alone with her, still in the throes of his passion [literally,
> his love] for her, and his virility is unabated, and [they
> are] in the same place where they previously sinned; if he
> [or she] abstains and does not sin, this is a true penitent.
>
> —Moses Maimonides, *Mishneh Torah,* "Laws of Repentance," 2:1

Maimonides's emphasis on the man's continued virility as one
reason for commending his "complete repentance" brings to mind
Saint Augustine's words: "To abstain from sin when a man cannot
sin is to be forsaken by sin, not to forsake it."

> There were some criminals in Rabbi Meir's neighborhood
> who caused him much trouble, and he prayed that they
> should die. His wife Beruriah said to him: "What are you
> thinking? (i.e., How could you possibly believe that such
> a prayer is even allowed?). Do you justify it on the basis
> of the verse [in Psalms 104:35], 'May sinners disappear
> from the earth, and the wicked be no more'? But the word
> that you take to mean 'sinners' [Hebrew: *hot-tim*] can also
> be read as 'sins' [*hatta-im*; in other words, 'Let *sins* dis-
> appear from the earth']. Furthermore, look at the end of
> the verse, 'and the wicked be no more.' Once the sins will
> cease, they will no longer be wicked men! Rather pray that
> they repent, and there will be no more wicked people
> around." Rabbi Meir did pray for them, and the criminals
> repented.
>
> —Babylonian Talmud, *Berakhot* 10a

This not only is one of the Talmud's sweetest stories, it also
provides one of the rare instances in the Talmud in which a woman
defeats a man in a religious dispute. Unfortunately, Beruriah's good
wishes aside, praying for other people to repent usually does not
impel them to do so. Still, the story serves as a corrective to the
common human instinct to pray that those who have hurt you be
punished; pray instead that they no longer hurt you or anybody else
and, therefore, no longer be deserving of punishment.

WHEN REPENTANCE IS USELESS

The Day of Atonement atones for sins against God, not for those against man, unless the injured party has been appeased.

—Mishna *Yoma* 8:9

In the mid-1960s, Rabbi Abraham Joshua Heschel, one of the great teachers of twentieth-century Jewry, was invited to speak before a group of American businessmen, to explain Jewish perspectives on modern issues. At the end of his talk, one non-Jewish attendee asked him, "Don't you think it's about time you and the Jewish people forgave the rest of the world for the Holocaust?"
Rabbi Heschel responded with this story:

Over fifty years ago, [Hayyim Soloveitchik] the rabbi of Brisk, a scholar of extraordinary renown, revered also for his gentleness, entered a train in Warsaw to return to his hometown. The rabbi, a man of slight stature, and of no [strikingly] distinctive appearance, found a seat in a compartment. There, he was surrounded by traveling salesmen, who, as soon as the train began to move, started to play cards.

As the game progressed, their excitement increased. The rabbi remained aloof and absorbed in [the book he was reading]. Such aloofness was annoying to the others. One of them finally suggested that the rabbi join in the game. He answered that he never played cards. As time passed, the rabbi's aloofness became even more irritating, until one man said to him, "Either you join us, or leave the compartment." Shortly thereafter, he took the rabbi by the collar and pushed him out of the compartment. For several hours, the rabbi had to stand until he reached his destination, the city of Brisk.

Brisk was also the salesmen's destination. When the rabbi left the train, he immediately was surrounded by admirers welcoming him and shaking his hands. "Who is that man?" asked the salesman [who had pushed him out of the compartment].

"You don't know? It's the famous rabbi of Brisk."

The salesman's heart sank. He had not realized whom he had offended. He quickly went over to the rabbi to ask forgiveness.

The rabbi declined to forgive him: "I would like to forgive you," he said, "but I can't."

In his hotel room, the salesman could find no peace. He went to the rabbi's house and was admitted to the rabbi's study. "Rabbi," he said. "I am not a rich man. I have, however, savings of three hundred rubles. I will give them to you for charity if you will forgive me."

The rabbi's answer was brief: "No!"

The salesman's anxiety was unbearable. He went to the synagogue to seek solace. When he shared his anxiety with some people in the synagogue, they were deeply surprised. How could their rabbi, so gentle a person, be so unforgiving? Their advice was for him to speak to the rabbi's eldest son and to tell him of the surprising attitude taken by his father.

When the rabbi's son heard the story, he could not understand his father's obstinacy. Seeing the man's anxiety, he promised to discuss the matter with his father.

It is not proper, according to Jewish law, for a son to criticize his father directly. So the son entered his father's study and began a general discussion of Jewish law and turned to the laws of forgiveness. When the principle was mentioned that a person who asks for forgiveness three times should be granted forgiveness, the son mentioned the name of the man who was in great anxiety. Thereupon the rabbi of Brisk answered:

"I cannot forgive him. He never insulted me. He did not know who I was. Had he had any idea who I was, he never would have acted as he did. He wants forgiveness? Let him go find a poor anonymous Jew sitting on a train reading a book and ask him for forgiveness."

"No one can forgive crimes committed against someone else," Rabbi Heschel concluded. "It is therefore preposterous to assume that any Jew alive can grant forgiveness for the suffering of any one of the six million people who perished.

"According to Jewish tradition, even God Himself can only forgive sins committed against Himself, not against man."

—I originally heard this story from Rabbi Wolfe Kelman,
who heard the episode from Rabbi Heschel immediately
after it happened; in the main, I have followed the
version of Heschel's response printed in Simon Wiesenthal,
The Sunflower, pages 130–131.

As Rabbi Heschel's response makes clear, not all acts lend themselves to forgiveness.

But while the act of murder cannot be undone or pardoned, even a murderer can try to make his subsequent life worthwhile in other ways. The most powerful story about repentance I know concerns Ernst Werner Techow, one of three German right-wing terrorists who assassinated Walter Rathenau, Germany's Jewish foreign minister in 1922. The killers' motivations were both political extremism and antisemitism. When the police caught the assassins, two committed suicide; Techow alone survived. Three days later, Mathilde Rathenau, the victim's mother, wrote to his mother:

"In grief unspeakable, I give you my hand—you of all women the most pitiable. Say to your son that, in the name and spirit of him he has murdered, I forgive, even as God may forgive, if before an earthly judge your son makes a full and frank confession of his guilt . . . and before a heavenly judge repents. Had he known my son, the noblest man earth bore, he would have rather turned the weapon on himself. May these words give peace to your soul. Mathilde Rathenau."

Techow was released from prison for good behavior after five years. In 1940, when France surrendered to Nazi Germany, he smuggled himself into Marseilles where he helped over seven hundred Jews escape to Spain with Moroccan permits. While some had money, most were penniless, and Techow arranged their escapes for nothing.

Shortly before his activities in Marseilles, Techow met a nephew of Rathenau, and confided that his repentance and transformation had been triggered by Mathilde Rathenau's letter: "Just as Frau Rathenau conquered herself when she wrote that letter of pardon, I have tried to master myself. I only wished I would get an opportunity to right the wrong I've done."

—The story of Techow was first told by George Herald, "My Favorite Assassin,"
Harper's, April 1943; an extraordinarily powerful dramatization of the story,
which appeared on the radio program *Eternal Light,* is printed in
Jack Riemer, ed., *The World of the High Holy Days,* pages 179–190.

To the question, therefore, Can a murderer ever be forgiven? the Talmud observes: When a condemned murderer was ten cubits [about fifteen feet] away from the place of execution, the court officials instructed him to say, "May my death be an expiation for all my sins" (Mishna *Sanhedrin* 6:2). In other words, although there is no full forgiveness for murder in this world, there might be in the next.

THREE GUIDES TO REPENTANCE

The repentant sinner should strive to do good with the same faculties with which he sinned. . . . With whatever part of the body he sinned, he should now engage in good deeds. If his feet had run to sin, let them now run to the performance of the good. If his mouth had spoken falsehood, let it now be opened in wisdom. Violent hands should now open in charity. . . . The trouble-maker should now become a peace-maker.

—Rabbi Jonah Gerondi, *The Gates of Repentance* (thirteenth
century)

It is told that once there was a wicked man who committed all kinds of sins. One day he asked a wise man to teach him an easy way to repent, and the latter said to him: "Refrain from telling lies." He went forth happily, thinking that he could follow the wise man's advice, and still go on as before. When he decided to steal, as had been his custom, he reflected: "What will I do in case somebody asks me, 'Where are you going?' If I tell the truth, 'To steal,' I shall be arrested. If I tell a lie, I shall be violating the command of this wise man." In the same manner he reflected on all other sins, until he repented with a perfect repentance.

—Rabbi Judah ben Asher (fourteenth century)

Think about three things and you will not be overcome by the desire to sin: Know what is above you; an eye that sees, an ear that hears, and all your actions are recorded in a book.

—*Ethics of the Fathers* 2:1

People drive more carefully when they see a police car nearby; from a religious person's perspective, God the Judge always is nearby, and watching.

FINAL REFLECTIONS

Rabbi Simha Bunam of Pzysha once asked his disciples, "How can we tell when a sin we have committed has been pardoned?"

His disciples gave various answers but none of them pleased the rabbi.

"We can tell," he said, "by the fact that we no longer commit that sin."

—Martin Buber, *Tales of the Hasidim: Later Masters,* page 253

The same sort of commonsense approach to repentance and forgiveness (not to make it too difficult to attain) is reflected in a talmudic ruling: If one who has stolen a beam and used it to build a house wishes to repent, he is not required to tear down the house in order to return the beam. It is sufficient that he compensate the owner for the beam, either with money or with another beam. Although, in theory, the owner can argue that he wants his own beam back, the Rabbis rule that he has to be satisfied either with monetary compensation or a different beam, since they do not wish to unfairly burden, and thereby discourage, the would-be penitent (Babylonian Talmud, *Gittin* 55a).

> If a man has beheld evil, he may know that it was shown to him in order that he learn his own guilt and repent; for what is shown to him is also within him.
>
> —Rabbi Israel Baal Shem Tov,
> eighteenth-century founder of Hasidism

One of my favorite comments on repentance comes from the non-Jewish nineteenth-century American humorist Josh Billings (1818–1885):

> It is much easier to repent of sins that we have committed than to repent of those we intend to commit.

52

PRAYER

THE SHORTEST PRAYER IN THE BIBLE

Please God, make her well.
—Numbers 12:13; Moses' five-word (*el na, refah na lah*) plea to
God to heal his sister, Miriam, who had been stricken with sud-
den leprosy, apparently for speaking against him. God heeds
Moses' prayer, so that Miriam is subsequently healed.

Moses' prayer is petitionary, the kind most often offered when
people pray spontaneously. Although entreating God might be most
people's primary association with prayer, Rabbi Hayim Donin notes
three additional types of prayer: *thanksgiving* (as in saying "Thank
God" after a crisis ends); *praise* (e.g., the Psalmist's statement "O
Lord, how great are Thy works!" 104:24) and *confession and introspection* (e.g., the repetition of sins to which Jews confess on Yom
Kippur; see *To Pray as a Jew,* page 5).

HOW TO APPROACH GOD

Rabbi Elazar would first give a coin to a poor man, and
then pray.

—Babylonian Talmud, *Bava Bathra* 10a

If you are going to beseech God for mercy, first show it to others.
Inspired by Rabbi Elazar's example, most synagogues pass around

a *pushke* (collection box) at the daily morning service; congregants are expected to put in something every day (except on the Sabbath and most holidays, when Jewish law forbids handling money).

> The pious men of ancient times used to spend an hour [meditating before praying], then pray, so that they could direct their heart towards their Father in Heaven.
> —Babylonian Talmud, *Berakhot* 30b

While few people today might be willing to invest so much time in their prayers, Jewish tradition encourages everyone to meditate briefly before reciting the *Sh'ma*. One is supposed to close one's eyes (or cover them with one's hands) and meditate on God's Oneness, and one's obligations and gratitude to God, before saying the prayer.

A SMALL SELECTION OF THE DIFFERENT TYPES OF JEWISH PRAYERS

Praise of God

Ain kei'loheinu—
There is none like our God,
There is none like our Master,
There is none like our King,
There is none like our Redeemer.

One of the best known songs chanted during the service, the theme of *Ain kei'loheinu* is simple: God is both unique and wonderful.

> *Sh'ma Yisra'el, Adonai Eloheinu, Adonai Ekhad*, Hear, O Israel, the Lord is Our God, the Lord is One.
> —Deuteronomy 6:4

These six Hebrew words come the closest to constituting Judaism's basic credo; the equivalent of Christianity's statement that Jesus is the son of God who died to atone for humankind's sins, and of Islam's declaration that "There is no God but God, and Mohammed is his prophet."

The most traditional Jews recite the *Sh'ma* four times a day; twice in the morning service, once in the evening service, and before going to sleep.

Rabbi Akiva, the most famous martyr in Jewish history, died with the *Sh'ma* on his lips. Throughout history, all Jews, not only martyrs, have been encouraged to emulate his example.

Rabbi Irving Greenberg once told me of a man he knew who hung a small bell on the rearview mirror in his car: "When I drive on the road," he told Greenberg, "and I hit a bump, the bell tinkles. That tinkle reminds me there are *mitzvot* [commandments] I can fulfill just by thinking about them, like 'and you shall love the Lord your God.' And if, God forbid, I suddenly lose control of the car, and start going over the side of the road, the last sound I will hear will be the tinkle of the bell, and I'll be reminded to say, '*Sh'ma Yisra'el, Adonai Eloheinu, Adonai Ekhad.*' At least that way, I'll leave this world with a blessing, rather than a curse."

In the Torah, the *Sh'ma* refers not only to the first six words, but encompasses the following paragraph as well. It is recited twice daily during services:

> And you shall love the Lord your God, with all your heart, with all your soul and with all your might. And these words which I command you this day, teach them to your children, and talk about them, when you are at home, when you are away, when you lie down, and when you rise up. Bind them as a sign upon your hand, and let them be a symbol between your eyes. Inscribe them on the doorposts of your home and on your gates.
>
> —Deuteronomy 6:5–9

Six of the Torah's 613 commandments are commanded in this paragraph. The Babylonian Talmud explains that "You shall love the Lord your God" obligates a Jew to "cause God to become beloved through you" (*Yoma* 86a). "With all your soul" is understood as obligating a Jew to be willing to give up his or her soul (i.e., life), if need be, on behalf of God (see pages 320–321 for the story of Rabbi Akiva's martyrdom), while "with all your might" means with all your possessions, an instruction to be generous with what God has bestowed on you, and to be willing to lose everything if God so decrees.

This paragraph also obligates parents to teach their children about God and Torah, and thus is the ultimate source of Jews' age-old veneration of education. Already two thousand years ago, the Talmud prohibited Jewish parents from moving to a city that lacked teachers for their children.

"Talk about them . . . when you lie down, and when you rise up" is the basis for the commandment that all Jews should recite the *Sh'ma* at least twice daily, in the morning and again at night.

"Bind them as a sign upon your hand, and let them be a symbol between your eyes" is understood to oblige Jewish males to put on *tefillin* (phylacteries) every weekday morning, one on their arms, the other on their foreheads (many religious authorities regard each of these acts as a separate commandment).

"Inscribe them on the doorposts of your home and on your gates" refers to the *mezuzah* that Jews are expected to put on the doorposts of their homes.

An introspective prayer (with a little petition)

My God, keep my tongue from evil, and my lips from speaking deceitfully. Help me ignore those who curse [or slander] me, and let me be humble before all. . . . Frustrate the designs of those who plot evil against me, and make nothing of their schemes. . . . May the words of my mouth and the meditations of my heart be acceptable in Your sight, my Rock and my Redeemer.

—Concluding paragraph appended to the *Amidah* prayer, which is recited at all three daily services. With minor variations, I have followed the translation of *Siddur Sim Shalom*, edited by Rabbi Jules Harlow, page 121.

I know of no prayers that beseech God to help one observe the Sabbath, give charity, or honor one's parents. But Mar, son of Ravina, the fourth-century rabbi who composed this prayer (see Babylonian Talmud, *Berakhot* 17a) understood how hard it is for a person to control sins of the mouth. He or she, Mar realized, needs nothing less than God's help to always avoid speaking wrongly or otherwise unfairly of others (see Chapter 8 on *lashon hara*, gossip).

A petitionary prayer

May God make you like Ephraim and Menashe.
May God make you like Sarah, Rebecca, Rachel, and Leah.

—Parental blessing bestowed, respectively,
on sons and daughters at the beginning of the Sabbath

Ephraim and Menashe were Joseph's two sons, while Sarah, Rebecca, Rachel, and Leah were biblical Judaism's four matriarchs. Praying that a child become like them is to request, in effect, that the child become a great Jew and a great human being.

Traditionally, parents place their lips on the child's forehead, and hold him or her while reciting this blessing. Herbert Weiner, an American Reform rabbi, who witnessed an elderly North African Jew dispensing blessings at a small synagogue in Safed, Israel, was moved to write: "I could not help but think of successful suburban fathers who had made comfortable provisions for their children, yet would never receive the honor and respect that had fallen to the lot of the old North African Jew who could offer only blessings" (9 1/2 *Mystics,* page 257).

UNUSUAL PRAYERS

From the twelfth century B.C.E.

O Lord God! Please remember me, and give me strength just this once, O God, to take revenge of the Philistines, if only for one of my two eyes.

—Samson in the book of Judges 16:28

A man of superhuman strength, Samson repeatedly attacked the Philistines, who were ruling and oppressing Israel. He was betrayed by his Philistine lover, Delilah, who informed Philistine authorities that his strength was rooted in his uncut hair. The Philistines then cut Samson's locks as he lay sleeping on Delilah's lap. They immediately gouged out both his eyes, and set him to work as a mill slave.

Sometime later, as thousands of Philistines gathered in a stadium to offer a sacrifice to their god, Dagon, Samson was fetched to dance before a jeering crowd. After he finished, he was placed between two of the stadium's pillars. Samson then offered the above prayer to God, to restore his strength, if only for a moment. God did so, and with the shout, "Let me die with the Philistines!" Samson brought down both pillars, and collapsed the stadium on top of his tormentors. According to the biblical account, "Those who were slain by him as he died outnumbered those who had been slain by him when he lived" (Judges 16:30).

From the eleventh century B.C.E.

[The opening chapter of the First Book of Samuel tells the story of Hannah, an infertile woman who comes to the Temple at Shilo to beseech God to grant her a child]: "O Lord, if You will look upon the suffering of Your maidservant and will remember me and not forget Your maidservant, and if You will grant Your maidservant a male child, I will dedicate him to the Lord for all the days of his life; and no razor shall ever touch his head."
—I Samuel 1:11

Samuel, the child born to Hannah, became one of Israel's foremost prophets and leaders. The Rabbis of the Talmud, however, not satisfied with the terse prayer recorded in the Bible, imagined some other remarks Hannah might have addressed to God:

Master of the Universe, of all that You created in woman, there is not one part without its purpose—eyes to see, ears to hear, a nose to smell, a mouth to speak, hands to work with, legs to walk with, breasts to give suck. The breasts

You placed over my heart, what are they for? Are they not to give suck? Give me a son that I may give him suck with them.

—Babylonian Talmud, Berakhot 31b

From the thirteenth century

There was a certain man who was a herdsman, and he did not know how to pray. But it was his custom to say every day, "Lord of the world! It is . . . known to You, that if You had cattle and gave them to me to tend, although I take wages from all others, from You I would take nothing, because I love You."

Once, a learned man was going his way and came upon the herdsman, who was praying thus. He said to him, "Fool, do not pray thus."

The herdsman asked him: "How should I pray?"

Thereupon, the learned man taught him . . . the *Sh'ma* and the prayer service, so that in the future he would not say what he was accustomed to say.

After the learned man had gone away, the herdsman forgot all that had been taught him, and did not pray. And he was even afraid to say what he had been accustomed to say, since the righteous man had told him not to.

But the learned man had a dream, and in it he heard a voice saying, "If you do not tell him to say what he was accustomed to say before you came to him, know that misfortune will overtake you, for you have robbed Me of one who belongs to the World-to-Come."

At once the learned man went to the herdsman and said to him, "What prayer are you offering?"

The herdsman answered, "None, for I have forgotten what you taught me, and you forbade me to say, 'If you had cattle.' "

Then the learned man told him what he had dreamed, and added, "Say what you used to say."

—Sefer Hasidim, paragraphs 5–6; I have followed,
with minor variations, the translation of Nahum Glatzer,
A Jewish Reader, pages 88–89.

This medieval herdsman's prayer reflects a common motif in Jewish folklore, the special holiness of prayers offered by the simple. In a Hasidic tale related five or six centuries later, a young shepherd who can recite the Hebrew alphabet but does not know how to read, sits in synagogue and recites the alphabet over and over, while saying to God, "I know only the letters. You, please, rearrange them into the right words."

In another Hasidic tale, an illiterate shepherd boy enters the synagogue of the Baal Shem Tov, the founder of the Hasidic movement, on Yom Kippur. Unable to pray, he starts to whistle, the one thing he knows he can do beautifully; he offers his whistling as a gift to God. The other worshippers are horrified and want to expel the boy from the synagogue, but the Baal Shem Tov stops them: "Until now, I could feel our prayers being blocked as they tried to reach the heavenly court. This young shepherd's whistling was so pure, however, that it broke through the blockage and brought all of our prayers straight up to God."

From the late fifteenth century

Lord of the universe: You are doing much to make me desert my faith. But I assure You that—even against the will of . . . heaven, a Jew I am and a Jew I shall remain. And neither the sufferings that You have brought upon me, nor that which You shall yet bring upon me, will be of any avail.

—Words of a Jew exiled from Spain in 1492,
after he was "put ashore in some uninhabited place," and
witnessed the deaths of his wife and two children; Solomon
ibn Verga, *Shevet Yehuda* (fifteenth–sixteenth century), chapter 52

Some four hundred and fifty years after this defiant statement of faith, writer Zvi Kolitz placed a similar thought into the mouth of a Jew who died during the Warsaw Ghetto Revolt. Kolitz titled his piece "Yossel Rakover's Appeal to God." Yossel Rakover was the actual name of a Hasidic Jew who perished in the Holocaust. Familiar with the destruction of the whole Rakover family, Kolitz tried to imagine how such a Jew would have responded to God's apparent desertion of the Jews during World War II. "How would a Hasid," Kolitz asked himself, "a pious Jew of Eastern Europe filled with the spirit of men like Levi Yitzhak of Berditchev [see next prayer], how would such a Jew address himself to God [as he prepared to die]?":

God of Israel . . . You have done everything to make me stop believing in You. Now lest it seem to You that You will succeed by these tribulations to drive me from the right path, I notify You, my God and the God of my father, *that it will not avail You in the least*! You may insult me, You may castigate me, You may take from me all that I cherish and hold dear in the world, You may torture me to death—I shall believe in *You*, I shall love You no matter what You do to test me.

And these are my last words to You, my wrathful God: nothing will avail You in the least. You have done everything to make me renounce You, to make me lose my faith in You, but I die exactly as I lived, a *believer*. . . .

Hear, O Israel, the Lord is our God, the Lord is One. Into your hands, O Lord, I consign my soul.

—Zvi Kolitz, "Yossel Rakover's Appeal to God,"
printed in full in Albert Friedlander, *Out of the Whirlwind:
A Reader of Holocaust Literature*, pages 390–399

From the eighteenth century

Good morning to You, Lord of the world!
I, Levi Yitzhak, son of Sarah of Berditchev, am coming to You in a legal manner concerning Your people of Israel.
What do you want of Israel?
It is always, "Command the children of Israel."
It is always, "Speak unto the children of Israel."

Merciful Father! How many people are there in the world?
Persians, Babylonians, Edomites!
The Russians, what do they say?
Our emperor is the emperor.
The Germans, what do they say?
Our kingdom is the kingdom.
The English, what do they say?
Our kingdom is the kingdom.
But I, Levi Yitzhak, son of Sarah of Berditchev, say:
Glorified and sanctified be His great name.
And I, Levi Yitzhak, son of Sarah of Berditchev, say:
I shall not go hence, nor budge from my place
until there be a finish
until there be an end of exile—
Glorified and sanctified be His great name.
> —Nahum Glatzer, *A Jewish Reader,* pages 94–95

In addition to his several recorded quarrels with God on the Jews' behalf, Levi Yitzhak also was known as a great optimist. When he announced his son's forthcoming marriage, the invitation read: "The wedding will take place in Jerusalem on such and such a date, and at such and such a time. But if, by chance, the Messiah will not yet have arrived, the wedding will take place on the same date and at the same time here in Berditchev."

From the twentieth century

I pray that my mother and father may look from heaven and see that their son is Bar Mitzvah today, and may they know that my sister and I have remained good Jews, and will always remain so.
> —The words of Shmuel, a young boy, during an improvised Bar
> Mitzvah ceremony in a displaced persons' camp in Germany
> shortly after the Holocaust; see Nahum Glatzer, *The Language of
> Faith,* page 78, and the footnote on page 121

COMMUNAL PRAYER

A man [or woman] to whom a calamity has occurred should make it known to the public, so that many people may entreat God's mercy for him.
—Babylonian Talmud, *Hullin* 78a

Sometimes, when I speak to a friend who has not been in touch for a while, he will tell me, "I was going through some hard times, and I just wasn't in the mood to speak to anyone." Jewish law does not want one who is suffering to react in this manner, and cut him- or herself off from all contact with others.

That is, perhaps, one reason that it insists that certain prayers, such as the *Kaddish* for the dead, can be recited only in the presence of a *minyan* of ten adult Jews. In the absence of such a law, many people who lose a parent, spouse, or child might withdraw into their own world, and say *Kaddish* privately. Because of this law, mourners are compelled three times a day to join a community of praying Jews. This helps ensure that they continue to interact with others. Similarly, Jewish law insists that during the *shiva*, the seven days following the death of a very close relative, people visit the mourning family; this guarantees that the mourners are not alone.

One who is standing outside Israel [when praying], should direct his [or her] heart toward the Land of Israel.
—Babylonian Talmud, *Berakhot* 30a

This is the source of the Jewish tradition that Jews face east, in the direction of Jerusalem, when praying (a Jew in Tokyo or elsewhere east of Jerusalem would, however, face west). For this reason, the Torah Ark in synagogues, which Jews face while praying, is built on the eastern wall.

One who says, "Let good people [and only good people] bless You," is considered to have spoken heresy.
—Mishna *Megillah* 4:9

Ovadiah Bartenura, the fifteenth-century author of the standard commentary on the Mishna, explains that such a prayer must be silenced because of its implication that the congregation should consist only of the righteous. Basing himself on a passage in the Babylonian Talmud (*Kritot* 6b), Bartenura explains this point metaphorically: The recipe for the sacred incense offered in the Temple in Jerusalem included *chelbana* (galbanum), a foul-smelling chemical.

Along similar lines, the word for congregation in Hebrew, *tzibbur,* consists of an acronym, the *tz* standing for *tzaddik,* the righteous, the *b* for *beinoni,* those in the middle, and the *r* standing for *rasha,* the evil.

INAPPROPRIATE PRAYER

Then the Lord said to Moses, "Why do you cry out to Me? Tell the children of Israel to go forward" (Exodus 14: 15). According to Rabbi Eliezer, the Holy One said to Moses: There is a time to be brief and a time to be lengthy. My children are in great distress, the sea is enclosing them, the enemy is in pursuit, and you stand here praying away! [Instead], "Tell the children of Israel to go forward."

—*Exodus Rabbah* 21:8

Almost immediately after the Israelites fled Egypt, they found themselves caught between the Red Sea on one side, and Pharaoh's rapidly approaching troops on the other. Panicking, the people cursed Moses for leading them toward death in the desert. He turned to God, who responded in the words of the above verse from Exodus. In what is probably the best-known miracle in the Bible, God arranged for the sea to temporarily part, although the Egyptian troops who pursued after the Israelites drowned.

The moral: When circumstances are very desperate, if your only choice is between praying and doing something—even if that "something" is a very "long shot"—do it. A statement I have heard attributed to Napoleon advises: "When you fight, fight as if everything depended on you. When you pray, pray as if everything depended on God."

> To petition God regarding events that have already happened is to utter a vain prayer. For example, if a man's wife is pregnant, and he says, "May it be God's will that my wife give birth to a boy," he utters a vain prayer. If, upon returning from a journey, he hears a cry of distress in the town and says, "May it be God's will that there is nothing wrong in my house," he utters a vain prayer.
> —Babylonian Talmud, *Berakhot* 54a

The Rabbis believed that it is wrong to take God's name in vain, which is why invoking God in a prayer to alter the past is futile, hence pointless and "vain." If a catastrophe has *already* happened, what point is there in praying that it did not happen to one's family? It either occurred or it didn't; in addition, there is something inappropriate about praying that the catastrophe befell one's neighbor, not oneself.

Although this advice is wise and eminently logical, it is difficult for most people—myself included—to always follow. Imagine telling a person who has just heard that a plane on which his or her close relative was scheduled to travel had exploded in midair not to pray, "I hope he missed the flight," or "I hope she was saved when the plane exploded." Such prayers seem to come automatically, unthinkingly, into one's minds and onto one's lips. Of course, it is this very illogicality that caused the Rabbis to discourage them.

> I see and hear old Kuhn praying aloud, with his beret on his head, swaying backwards and forwards violently. Kuhn is thanking God because he has not been chosen [to be in the next group condemned to be gassed].
> Kuhn is out of his senses. Does he not see Beppo the Greek in the bunk next to him, Beppo who is twenty years old, and is going to the gas chambers the day after tomorrow and knows it and lies there looking fixedly at the light without saying anything and without even thinking

anymore? Can Kuhn fail to realize that the next time it will be his turn? Does Kuhn not understand that what has happened today is an abomination, which no propitiatory prayer, no pardon, no expiation by the guilty, which nothing at all in the power of man can ever clean again? If I was God, I would spit at Kuhn's prayer.

—Primo Levi, *Survival in Auschwitz,* pages 151–152

WHAT PRAYER DOES GOD OFFER?

Rabbi Yochanan said in the name of Rabbi Yossi.... God, the Holy One, Blessed be He, prays.... What is God's prayer?

Rabbi Zutra says in the name of Rav, [God prays as follows]: May it be My will that My mercy overcome My anger, and My loving qualities override My strict traits; that I treat My children with the quality of mercy and that I always deal with them beyond the letter of the Law.

—Babylonian Talmud, *Berakhot* 7a

This remarkable rabbinic imagining contradicts the popular, petitionary, image of prayer. Rabbi Irving Greenberg comments: "Most of us associate prayer with being weak or in need: When we are in trouble, we turn to God ('there are no atheists in foxholes')." But this passage depicts God, the acme of self-sufficient might, praying that He use His strength properly.

Human beings, Greenberg adds, must learn from this prayer how to pray:

"The celebrity should pray: May my integrity and creativity override my desire for fame and fortune."

"The businessman should pray: May my drive for success and wealth be guided by my ethical character and concern for people."

"We all need to pray: May my generosity overcome my self-centeredness. May my charitableness and care for others override my need for conspicuous consumption" (*Wisdom of the Ages,* page 28).

Finally, two examples of proverbial Yiddish whimsy, the first, a prayer of a struggling businessman, the second about the Jewish proclivity for misfortune:

God, You help complete strangers, so why don't You help me?

If a Jew breaks a leg, he thanks God he did not break both legs; if he breaks both, he thanks God he did not break his neck!

53

RABBIS

A rabbi whom they don't want to drive out of town is no rabbi.

    And a rabbi who lets himself be driven out is no man.

—Rabbi Israel Salanter

It takes twice as much spiritual strength to be an honest businessman as to be an honest rabbi, but if you have that much spiritual strength, why waste it on business?

—Salanter to a student who felt himself unworthy
of serving as a rabbi

As the rabbi must inspect periodically the slaughtering knives of the ritual slaughterers in his town, to see that they have no defect [which would render the meat unkosher], so must he go from store to store to inspect the weights and measures of the storekeepers.

—Rabbi Israel Salanter

When Rabbi Hayyim Soloveitchik, one of the twentieth-century's greatest Talmud scholars, was asked what a rabbi's function is, he replied: "To redress the grievances of those who are abandoned and alone, to protect the dignity of the poor, and to save the oppressed from the hands of the oppressor."

—Cited in Rabbi Joseph Soloveitchik, *Halakhic Man* (translation by Lawrence Kaplan), page 91. Soloveitchik goes on to note that "neither ritual decisions nor political leadership constitutes the main task of halakhic man."

Rabbi Joseph Soloveitchik, Rabbi Hayyim's grandson, relates a characteristic incident that happened during his grandfather's tenure as rabbi of Brisk:

> Once two Jews died in Brisk on the same day. In the morning a poor shoemaker who had lived out his life in obscurity died, while about noontime a wealthy, prominent member of the community passed away. According to the *halakha* [Jewish law], in such a case the one who dies first must be buried first. However, the members of the burial society, who had received a handsome sum from the heirs of the rich man, decided to attend to him first . . . for who was there to plead the cause of the poor man? When Rabbi Hayyim was informed about the incident, he sent a messenger . . . to warn the members of the burial society to desist from their disgraceful behavior. The members of the burial society, however, refused to heed the directive of Rabbi Hayyim and began to make the arrangements for the burial of the rich man. Rabbi Hayyim then arose, took his walking stick, trudged over to the house of the deceased, and chased all the attendants outside. Rabbi Hayyim prevailed—the poor man was buried before the rich man. Rabbi Hayyim's enemies multiplied and increased.
> —Rabbi Joseph Soloveitchik, *Halakhic Man*, page 95

WHY IT'S HARD TO BE A RABBI

Rabbi Harold Kushner, a veteran of several decades in the pulpit, was invited to address the graduating class of a rabbinical seminary. "There will be Friday evenings," he warned the young rabbis about to embark on their careers, "when you will rush your family through dinner so that you can get to services on time to give a sermon about the Sabbath as uninterrupted family time. There will be days when you will leave a sick child at home or a child studying for a test, while you go to teach religious values to the Temple youth group. There will be Sundays when you will cancel plans for a family picnic to officiate at a funeral, where you will praise the deceased as a man who never let his business interfere with his obligations to his family. And worst of all, you won't even realize what you are doing as you do it."

—Rabbi Harold Kushner, *When All You've Ever Wanted Isn't Enough,* page 24

54

"YOUR PEOPLE SHALL BE MY PEOPLE"

Converts

Your people shall be my people, your God my God.

—Ruth 1:16

When Ruth, a Moabite woman whose Jewish husband had died, decides to become a Jew, she makes this declaration to Naomi, her Jewish mother-in-law. Ever since, her words have defined the essence of Judaism: "Your people shall be my people," i.e., "I wish to join the Jewish nation"; "Your God shall be my God," i.e., "I wish to accept the Jewish religion."

The acceptance of only one of these principles is insufficient to make a Jew of a non-Jew, for Judaism is a fusion of religion and peoplehood.

> Rabbi Elazar ben Pedat taught: The Holy One, Blessed be He, exiled Israel among the nations only for the purpose of gaining converts.
>
> —Babylonian Talmud, *Pesachim* 87b

Given that the Jews' exile from Israel by the Romans was one of the worst events in Jewish history, it is remarkable that so prominent a rabbi could find something good that derived from it. Even more surprising is that despite this talmudic teaching, most modern Jews believe that Judaism is uninterested in, even opposed to, gentiles becoming Jews.

It is true that Judaism never claimed, as Christianity long did—and as fundamentalist Christians still do—that one must believe in its doctrines to attain salvation. According to Jewish teachings, ethical non-Jews are righteous in God's eyes and will be rewarded by God.

But if non-Jews can achieve righteousness without becoming Jews, why does Judaism care if people convert? For the same reason that idealistic political conservatives and liberals want "converts" to their points of view, in the belief that the more active adherents they have, the better it is for the individual and for the society.

> If a man wishes to convert to Judaism, but says, "I am too old at this time, I cannot be a convert," let him learn from Abraham, who, when he was ninety-nine years old, entered God's covenant.
>
> —*Tanhuma B, Lekh Lekha* 40b

A Jewish male enters God's covenant through circumcision: according to Genesis 17:24, Abraham was one year shy of a century when he circumcised himself.

This teaching is once again reflective of rabbinic Judaism's openness to converts. Of the more than thirty statements on the subject in rabbinic literature, four are negative and the rest positive.

> The masses have long since shown a keen desire to adopt our religious observances, and there is not one city, Greek or barbarian, nor a single nation, to which our custom of abstaining from work on the seventh day has not spread, and where the feasts and lighting of candles and many of our prohibitions in the matter of food are not observed.
>
> —Flavius Josephus, the first-century Jewish historian,
> *Contra Apion* 2:39

While one might suspect the proudly Jewish Josephus of exaggerating the number of conversions to Judaism, many other sources support his statement. Enough non-Jews converted in the first century to motivate the renowned Roman writer Juvenal to compose an angry satire (14:96–99) about Roman fathers who observe the Sabbath, eat no pork, worship only the heavenly God, and whose sons undergo circumcision, despise Roman law, and study the Jews' Torah.

In the same century, the Stoic philosopher Seneca bewailed the irony of Rome's having conquered Judea militarily, only to discover decades later that "the vanquished have given their laws to their victors." As they say in Yiddish, *"Halevai"* (If only it were true). Both Juvenal's and Seneca's comments are cited in Louis Feldman, *Jew and Gentile in the Ancient World,* pages 346–347.

The Gospel of Matthew likewise reports that the Jews would "sail the seas and cross whole countries to win one convert" (23:15).

* * *

> One may do something advantageous for a person in his absence.
>
> —Babylonian Talmud, *Ketubot* 11a

Although this juridical principle is seemingly unrelated to converts, the talmudic Rabbis introduce it while debating whether or not adopting parents are permitted to convert a minor child to Judaism. The issue's resolution hinges on a fundamental issue: Is it advantageous or disadvantageous to be Jewish? If the former, then one is permitted to convert a minor because it is permitted to do something beneficial for a person in his absence (e.g., buy a lottery ticket as a gift for a person without informing him, since he or she will be pleased if it pays off). If the latter, it is forbidden to convert a minor, since it would be wrong to impose a disadvantage on someone without his consent (e.g., listing a person as a loan guarantor without consulting him).

Into which category does conversion to Judaism fall? On the one hand, there are some distinct disadvantages to being Jewish. Non-Jews are obligated to follow only the laws of Noah, seven basic precepts of morality, while Jews are obligated to observe the Torah's 613 laws, and the Talmud's thousands of elaborations on them. Jews also have long been persecuted, so converting a child to Judaism might subsequently subject him or her to oppression, even death.

Yet since traditional Jewish theology believes Judaism to be the best way of life known to humankind (because the Torah and its laws come directly from God), what greater favor could one do a child than to bestow upon him or her such a gift?

The Rabbis finally conclude it is more of an advantage to convert the child to Judaism, and since "one may do something advantageous for a person in his absence," adopting parents should convert a child to Judaism.

However, the Talmud adds an unusual proviso: A person converted as a child may, at the age of Bar or Bat Mitzvah (thirteen for boys, twelve for girls), disavow the conversion and reject Judaism. If the adolescent chooses to accept his or her status as a Bar or Bat Mitzvah, he or she is Jewish forever. Incidentally, minors who have been converted to Judaism are the only Jews whose right to renounce Judaism is recognized in Jewish law.

Still, the serious political and social liabilities in being Jewish impelled the Rabbis to warn potential converts of the risks to which they were subjecting themselves:

> Our Rabbis taught: If at the present time a person desires to convert to Judaism, he or she is to be addressed as follows: "What reason do you have for wanting to become a convert? Do you not know that Jews at the present time are persecuted and oppressed, despised, driven from place to place, and overcome with hardships?" If he or she replies, "I know, and yet am unworthy [of the privilege of becoming a Jew]," he or she is accepted immediately, and is taught some of the minor and some of the major commandments.
>
> —Babylonian Talmud, *Yevamot* 47a

This sobering counsel is countered, however, with a depiction of the glory of being Jewish. Then, on the very next page, the Talmud calibrates a precise balancing act in formulating Judaism's attitude toward would-be converts: "He is not, however, to be persuaded or dissuaded too much." Once, however, the person does convert, "he [or she] is deemed to be a Jew in all respects."

Because conversion to Judaism entails difficulties and subjects the convert to many dangers, the Rabbis expressed a special affection for converts, one they attribute to God as well:

> Said Resh Lakish: The convert is dearer than the Jews who stood before Mount Sinai. Why? Because had they [the Jews] not seen the thunder and the lightning and the mountains quaking and the sounds of the horn, they would not have accepted the Torah. But this one, who saw none of these things, came, surrendered himself to the Holy One and accepted upon himself the kingdom of heaven. Could any be dearer than he?
>
> —*Tanhuma B, Lekh Lekha 6*

> The Holy One, Blessed be He, loves converts greatly.
> To what may this be compared? To a king who had a flock which went out to the fields every morning, and came in again in the evening. One day, a stag came in with the flock. He went along with the goats and grazed with them, and the king was told, "A stag has joined the flock and is grazing with them every day. . . . " The king felt great affection for the stag, and when he saw him going out to the fields, he gave orders, "Let the stag graze in whatever pasture he likes: let no man beat him, and let everyone treat him with great care." When the stag returned from the fields with the flock, the king would order, "Give him water to drink."
> The king's servants said to him, "My Lord, although you possess so many rams, sheep and goats, you give us no special instructions about them. Yet when it comes to this stag, every day you give us special commands. Why?"
> The king answered: "It is natural for the flock to graze in the field all day and to sleep in the yard at night. But

stags sleep in the wilderness; it is not their nature to enter the places cultivated by men. Shall we not be pleased with this stag who has left behind the broad, vast wilderness . . . and has come to stay in this yard?"

In the same way, should we not be grateful to the convert who has left behind his family, his nation and all the other peoples of this world, and has chosen to come to us? Therefore, God has given him special protection.

—Numbers Rabbah 8:2

A high regard for converts is so marked in Jewish sources that Jewish tradition bestows one of its greatest honors upon one. According to the Talmud, the Messiah will be a direct descendant of Ruth (the great-grandmother of King David), a Moabite woman who converted to Judaism, and for whom a biblical book is named.

Given this strong a bias in favor of converts, why do most modern Jews assume Judaism opposes the seeking of converts? History, more than theology, is one key. In the fourth century, shortly after the Roman Empire became Christian, its emperor decreed conversion to Judaism to be a capital offense, both for the convert and for the Jews involved in the conversion. This regulation was periodically reaffirmed throughout the Christian world and, later, in Muslim countries as well. Consequently, medieval Jews, who were frequently struggling to avoid persecution and expulsion, came to regard would-be converts as endangering their already tenuous status. A leading sixteenth-century European Talmud scholar ruled:

Under the present conditions, when we live in a country that is not ours, like slaves under the rod of a master, if a Jew encourages someone to convert to Judaism he becomes a rebel against the government, subject to the death penalty. . . . Therefore, I caution anyone against being a party to such activity when the law of the state forbids it, for he thereby forfeits his life.

—Rabbi Solomon Luria (1510–1573),
commentary to Babylonian Talmud, Yevamot 49a

Why has the Jewish reluctance to seek converts persisted in America's far more tolerant climate? One reason may well be inertia.

379

A millennium-long communal attitude is not easily broken. A second, perhaps more important reason is that many, if not most, American Jews are more secular and ethnic than religious; they hardly are prone to encourage conversion to a religion which they themselves seldom practice.

Hillel Halkin, the secular Jewish author of the widely hailed *Letters to an American Jewish Friend: A Zionist's Polemic*, observes: "A Jewish girl whom I knew was thinking of marrying a non-Jewish boy and wanted him to become a Jew. She asked me if I would talk to him; I agreed. . . . His first question was, 'Tell me, apart from my future mother-in-law's feelings, why should I become a Jew?' . . . And there wasn't a single reason I could think of. . . . This encounter happened with a non-Jew, but had it been with an assimilated Jew or with a Jew who wished to know why he should feel more committed to his Jewishness than he did, I could not have answered any differently. I don't know why one should be a Jew" (pages 239–240).

* * *

While the Rabbis hoped that a non-Jew, ideally, would be motivated to convert by attraction to Judaism rather than romantic ties to an individual Jew, they understood that the two reasons frequently are intertwined. This rabbinic realization forms the background for the Talmud's single most romantic story, which, understandably, was never taught in the Jewish day school I attended as a child:

> A certain man, who scrupulously observed the law of *tzitzit* [ritual fringes], heard of a prostitute in a far-off land who demanded four hundred gold coins as her price. He sent her four hundred gold coins, and set a date to meet her.
>
> When the day arrived, he waited by the prostitute's door. Her maid came and told her, "The man who sent you four hundred gold coins is waiting at the door." The woman replied, "Let him come in." When he entered . . . the prostitute went to her bed and lay down upon it naked.

He too started toward her bed when, all of a sudden, the four ritual fringes on his garment flew up and struck him across the face; at that point, he moved away from her and sat down on the ground.

The prostitute stepped down from her bed and sat down on the ground, opposite him. "By the head of the Roman Emperor," she swore, "I will not leave you alone until you tell me what blemish you saw in me [that caused you to leave my bed]."

He replied, "Never have I seen a woman as beautiful as you are, but there is a commandment which the Lord our God has commanded us. It is called *tzitzit*." [He goes on to explain to her that the fringes are intended to remind people to observe God's commandments: Indeed, the Lord will reward those who keep His commandments, and punish those who violate them.] "Now the four fringes of the *tzitzit* appeared to me as four witnesses [testifying before God about the sin I was about to commit with you]."

The prostitute said: "I will not let you leave here until you tell me your name, the name of your town, the name of your teacher, and the name of the school in which you study Torah." He wrote all this down and put it in her hand. Thereupon [the man departed for home] and the woman divided her estate into three parts, one third to the Roman government, one third to be distributed among the poor, and the final third she [converted into jewelry and cash and] took with her. The linens on her bed, however, she kept. She then traveled to the yeshiva headed by Rabbi Hiyya, and said to him, "Master, instruct the rabbis to convert me to Judaism."

"My daughter," he replied. "Perhaps you have set your eyes on one of my students?"

She took out the paper the young man had given her, and handed it to Rabbi Hiyya. "Go," said he, "and enjoy your acquisition." [The woman was quickly converted, and immediately married the young man. And so, the Talmud concludes:] The very linens she had spread for him for an illicit purpose, she now spread out for him lawfully.

—Babylonian Talmud, *Menakhot* 44a

55

"YOU SHALL REJOICE IN YOUR FESTIVAL"

A Few Scattered Thoughts on Jewish Holidays

THE SABBATH

Remember the Sabbath day to keep it holy.
—Exodus 20:8; the Fourth of the Ten Commandments

Despite the popular misconception that the Sabbath is primarily a day of rest (which has led many nonobservant Jews to regard it primarily as merely a day of leisure), the Bible makes it clear that its ultimate goal is holiness. The acts Jewish law commands on this day, including lighting candles, reciting the *Kiddush* over wine, blessing one's children, and reading the weekly Torah portion, all are aimed at infusing the day with a sacred sense.

More than the Jews have kept the Sabbath, the Sabbath has kept the Jews.
—The early Zionist leader and theoretician,
Ahad Ha'am (1856–1927)

Jews have observed the Sabbath, the only holiday mentioned in the Ten Commandments, for over three thousand years; in fact, we know of no Jewish community in history that did not "remember" it. (If such communities existed, they didn't survive.)

When some nineteenth and early-twentieth-century German and American Reform rabbis tried to move the holiday's celebration from Saturday to Sunday, Rabbi Leopold Stein of Germany warned: "If we transfer the Sabbath to Sunday, we will bury Judaism on Friday evening to permit it to be resurrected on Sunday morning as another religion" (David Philipson, *The Reform Movement in Judaism,* page 210).

> The Sabbath is . . . the greatest wonder of religion. Nothing can appear more simple than this institution . . . . Yet no legislator in the world hit upon this idea! To the Greeks and Romans it was an object of derision, a superstitious usage. But it removed with one stroke a contrast between slaves who must labor incessantly and their masters who may celebrate continuously.
> —Benno Jacob, "The Decalogue," *Jewish Quarterly Review,*
> 1923, xiv, page 165

As Jacob notes, several prominent Roman writers, including the first-century Stoic philosopher Seneca, ridiculed the Sabbath for "wasting" one seventh of a person's life, while the historian Tacitus charged the Jews with laziness (*Histories* 5:4:3; see Louis Feldman, *Jew and Gentile in the Ancient World,* page 166). In fact, what underlay the theology of the Sabbath was the radical notion that human beings have worth even when they are not working or otherwise productive.

THE THREE PILGRIMAGE HOLIDAYS THE TORAH COMMANDS

You shall rejoice in your festival, with your son and daughter . . . the stranger, the fatherless and the widow in your communities.

—Deuteronomy 16:14

While this biblical commandment (the 488th of the 613 commandments, according to the enumeration in the medieval *Sefer ha-Hinnukh*) is specifically enjoined concerning the harvest holiday of Sukkot, Jewish law applies it to all three of the Torah's pilgrimage festivals (when Jews are commanded to go up to Jerusalem: Passover, Shavuot, and Sukkot).

Characteristically, both the Talmud and the medieval Jewish legal codes do not allow the command to "rejoice" to pass without some elaboration. After all, does one fulfill the commandment by walking around with a wide smile? Dancing in the streets? Feeling a deep inner peace? All three? Drawing on talmudic texts, and his own knowledge of human nature, Maimonides offers different examples of how to make the holidays joyful:

Children should be given parched ears [of corn], nuts and other dainties, women should have clothes and pretty jewelry bought for them according to one's means, and men should eat meat and drink wine, for there can be no real rejoicing without meat to eat and wine to drink . . .

One who locks the doors to his courtyard and eats and drinks with his wife and children, without giving anything . . . to the poor and bitter in soul—his meal is not "the joy of the commandment," but the joy of his stomach . . . . Rejoicing of this kind is a disgrace.

—Moses Maimonides, *Mishneh Torah*,
"Laws of the Festivals," 6:18

When the Talmud was compiled, only the wealthy could afford to eat meat daily, so that doing so on a holiday became equated with a sense of luxury and ease, comparable to the once-popular

384

male American tradition of relaxing with a good cigar after a meal. A Jewish vegetarian, however, is not obligated to eat meat if such an act will mar his or her holiday; the same applies to wine in the case of a recovering alcoholic.

> In each generation, every person is obliged to feel as though he or she personally came out of Egypt.
> —Mishna *Pesachim* 10:5, and part of the Passover *Haggadah*

> *Mah nishtana ha-lie-lah ha-zeh mee-kol ha-leilot*—Why is this night different from all other nights? On all other nights we may eat either leavened or unleavened bread, but on this night we eat only unleavened bread . . . .
> —Mishna *Pesachim* 10:4; and part of the Passover *Haggadah*

The Passover Seder's goal is nothing less than assuring the Jewish people's continuity by having parents teach their children how God freed their ancestors from slavery and forged them into a nation.

For that reason, much of the Seder is designed to involve the children, since they will carry on Judaism into the next generation. To ensure that they remain awake throughout the Seder, children are encouraged to "steal," and then hide the *afikomen* (a piece of matza without which the Seder cannot be concluded), and then offer it back in exchange for a gift. Most important, the telling of the going forth from Egypt commences when the youngest child present chants the *Mah Nishtana*'s four questions. For most Jewish children, this constitutes their first public performance, and is something they rarely forget.

> Our Rabbis taught: On the sixth day of the month [of *Sivan*], the Ten Commandments were given to Israel.
> —Babylonian Talmud, *Shabbat* 86b

The holiday which commemorates this event (the giving of the Torah and the Ten Commandments at Mount Sinai) is *Shavuot*. While the Talmud speaks of the revelation of the Ten Commandments on this day, many Jews believe that Jewish tradition teaches that Moses received the entire Torah at Mount Sinai. This, of course, would be impossible, since the revelation at Sinai occurred a mere seven weeks after the Exodus, while the last three and a half of the Torah's five books describe the forty years of desert wandering that followed this revelation (e.g., the story of Korakh's revolt against Moses that occurred many years later; Numbers 16). As the Babylonian Talmud teaches elsewhere, the rest of the Torah was revealed to Moses scroll by scroll during the sojourn in the desert (*Gittin* 60a).

The Torah teaches that Moses carried down from Sinai the tablets containing the Ten Commandments. On *Shavuot*, Jews commemorate this beginning of the Torah's revelation. A popular way the holiday has long been celebrated is with a *tikkun;* people get together for the entire night and study small selections from the various sacred Jewish writings, e.g., the Torah, the rest of the Bible, Mishna, Talmud, and Midrash.

> "You shall dwell in booths seven days" (Leviticus 23:42). This means that you should consider the sukkah as a fixed dwelling for these days. This statement led the Rabbis to say that one should consider the sukkah permanent and the home temporary for these seven days of Sukkot. How? One should transfer the finest furniture and beds to the sukkah, eat and drink in the sukkah and study in the sukkah.
>
> —Babylonian Talmud, *Sukkot* 28b

Although the Talmud clearly commands people to sleep in sukkot (plural of sukkah) throughout the seven-day holiday, Diaspora Jews are exempt from this requirement if they live in intemperate climates. This is in keeping with the previously cited injunction, "You shall rejoice in your festival" (Deuteronomy 16:4): That Jewish law suspended the obligation to dwell in the sukkah when doing so causes discomfort renders this commandment "unique among commandments. The *halakha* does not recognize discomfort, inconvenience, or even financial loss as an excuse not to eat kosher or observe Shabbat. But joy is so central to the sukkah experience that if one carries out the mitzvah in pain or serious inconvenience it is not a fulfillment of the spirit of the holiday" (Irving Greenberg, *The*

Jewish Way, pages 103–104). However, on Sukkot's first night, regardless of how hard it might be raining, the tradition is to wait until midnight before resigning oneself to not entering the sukkah, in the hope that one will yet be able to eat in it.

ROSH HASHANA AND YOM KIPPUR

In the seventh month, on the first day of the month, you shall observe complete rest, a sacred occasion proclaimed with loud blasts.

—Leviticus 23:24–25

Of course, the "loud blasts" refer to the shofar, the ram's horn that is blown exactly one hundred times during the Rosh Hashana service. Maimonides explains the ritual's rationale:

Although the sounding of the shofar on Rosh Hashana is [observed because it is] a decree of the Torah, still it has a deep meaning, as if saying: "Wake up from your deep sleep, you who are fast asleep . . . search your deeds and repent; remember your Creator . . . examine your souls, mend your ways and deeds. Let everyone give up his evil ways and bad plans."

—Moses Maimonides, *Mishneh Torah,*
"Laws of Repentance," 3:4

On Rosh Hashana it is written and on Yom Kippur it is sealed: How many shall leave this world and how many shall be born into it,
who shall live and who shall die,
who shall live out the limits of his days and who shall not,
who shall perish by fire and who by water,
who by sword and who by beast,
who by hunger and who by thirst,
who by earthquake and who by plague,
who by strangling and who by stoning,
who shall rest and who shall wander,
who shall be at peace and who shall be tormented,

who shall be poor and who shall be rich,
who shall be humbled and who shall be exalted.
But penitence, prayer and good deeds can annul the severity [alternatively, the bitterness] of the decree.
> —The *U-ne-taneh Tokef,* the most famous prayer of Rosh Has-
> hana; I have followed the translation of Rabbi Jules Harlow,
> *Mahzor for Rosh Hashana and Yom Kippur,* page 241.

The Lord alone is God.
> —I Kings 18:39; this prayer is called out seven times by every
> congregant at the conclusion of the Yom Kippur service. The
> prayer underscores the basic Jewish proclamation to the world.

Israel had no happier days than the fifteenth day of the
month of Av and Yom Kippur.
> —Babylonian Talmud, *Ta'anit* 26b

Because Yom Kippur is a fast day, one on which Jews also are
commanded to refrain from sexual pleasure and bathing, most people regard it as a sad or "heavy" day. But the Talmud's insistence
on classifying it as happy is more in keeping with the day's spirit,
for Yom Kippur is a day of reconciliation between people and God
(see Leviticus 16:30) and between one person and another. When
observed properly, it leaves participants with a deep feeling of joy
and renewal.

Few Jews today are aware of the fifteenth of Av, the other holiday the Talmud commends so highly. This was a sort of Jewish
Sadie Hawkins Day, during which single women wooed, and sometimes proposed marriage to, single men.

To help create an "even playing field," the Rabbis ruled that all
maidens, including those from wealthy families, should dress in simple white garments, so as not to embarrass those less well off. According to the Talmud, the unmarried women would dance in the
vineyards, where the unmarried men would go to meet them.

He who says, "I will sin and repent, and sin and repent
again," will be given no opportunity to repent. He who

388

says, "I will sin and Yom Kippur will effect atonement," Yom Kippur effects no atonement. Yom Kippur atones for sins against God, not for those against man, unless the injured party has been appeased.

—Mishna *Yoma* 8:9

Whose sin does God forgive?
He who forgives sins [against himself].

—Babylonian Talmud, *Rosh Hashana* 17a

Rabbi Chaim of Sanz was approached for a ruling on Yom Kippur.

He was asked what should be done for one who was ravenously thirsty, and was sick as a result.

"Give him a teaspoon of water," Rabbi Chaim ordered.

They did so, but soon came back to report that the man's thirst was still unquenched.

"You may tell him," said Rabbi Chaim, "that he may drink as much as he wants, but he is to donate one hundred kopeks to charity for each spoonful that he drinks."

When he heard the condition, the man suddenly no longer felt thirsty.

—Shmuel Himelstein, *A Touch of Wisdom, a Touch of Wit,*
page 271

For more information on Jewish holidays, and particularly the post-Torah ones such as Purim and Hannuka, see *Jewish Literacy*, pages 561–605.

PART IV

BETWEEN PEOPLE AND THE WORLD

Jewish Values Confront Modern Values

56

"PEOPLE WOULD SWALLOW EACH OTHER ALIVE"

Against Anarchy

Judges and officers you shall appoint in all your cities . . .
and they shall judge the people with righteous judgment.
—Deuteronomy 16:18

Pray for the welfare of the government, for were it not for
the fear of it, people would swallow each other alive.
—*Ethics of the Fathers* 3:2

While obvious exceptions come to mind (people would not be
obliged to pray for the government's welfare in Nazi Germany or
in the Soviet Union), this rabbinic advice reflects the dominant trend
of Jewish thinking, and is rooted in Judaism's considerable skepticism about human nature. Followers of the nineteenth- and early-
twentieth-century philosophical and political ideology known as
anarchism called for eliminating government precisely because they
believed in people's essential goodness, and saw government as the
cause of most of the evil in the world.

Judaism disputes anarchism's premise; it views human nature as
neither good nor bad but neutral, with some strong proclivities toward evil (see pages 207–210). Therefore, the problem isn't that

people are good and governments evil, but that governments act immorally because the human beings running them aren't moral. For that very reason, one must be wary in one's dealing with governmental officials:

> Be cautious in your dealings with the government, for they do not make advances to a man except in their own interest. They seem like friends at the time when it is advantageous for them, but they do not stand by a man when he is in trouble.
>
> —*Ethics of the Fathers* 2:3; I have followed the translation of Louis Jacobs, *Religion and the Individual*, page 34.

Yet if there were no ruling authority at all, conditions probably would be worse. Many people may complain about police brutality and corruption, but would they be willing to leave their houses unarmed if their town or city's police department went on strike? Indeed, it is likely that if such a strike persisted, they would choose to move to a city with a strong municipal government.

Rabbinic Judaism's skepticism about human nature is conveyed in a comment on a verse in Habakkuk (1:14), "You have made mankind like the fish of the sea":

> As it is with the fishes of the sea, the one that is larger swallows the others, so it is with humankind. Were it not for the fear of the government, everyone greater than his fellow would "swallow" him.
>
> —Babylonian Talmud, *Avodah Zara* 4a

Hundreds of years before the Talmud was compiled, the Babylonian Empire suppressed a revolt in Judea (586 B.C.E.), destroyed Solomon's Great Temple, and exiled tens of thousands of Jews from Jerusalem to Babylon. If ever there was a government for whose "welfare" Jews might *not* be expected to pray, it was Babylon's. Yet the leading prophet of the day offered this advice to his fellow Jews as they went into exile there:

> Seek the welfare of the city to which I [God] have exiled
> you and pray to the Lord on its behalf, for in its prosperity
> you shall prosper.
>
> —Jeremiah 29:7

Jeremiah's concluding words are instructive. More than he could possibly have known, the prophet intuited that it is precisely in economically struggling states, and during unprosperous times, that antisemitism is likely to turn most menacing.

Even in the United States, a society with relatively little bigotry against Jews, the Jewish community immediately becomes anxious about the possibility of widespread antisemitism during a recession. Thus, during the 1974–1975 severe economic downturn prompted by the Arab oil boycott, Jews expressed fear that they would be blamed for the decline. (One heard numerous, largely unsubstantiated, reports, of people who allegedly had seen bumper stickers reading BURN JEWS NOT OIL.)

During the recession of the early 1990s, Jewish fears focused in large part on the former American Nazi leader David Duke who, in his bid to become governor of economically depressed Louisiana, received the support of more than half of the state's white voters.

> The law of the state is law.
>
> —Babylonian Talmud, *Bava Kamma* 113a; this well-known
> dictum is mentioned five times in the Talmud.

Jews are obligated to observe state laws so long as they are not immoral and/or antisemitic. In Europe and the Arab world, where Jews were long subjected to special, discriminatory legislation, they were under no moral, or Jewish legal, obligation to fulfill these laws, given that the laws of the state itself were unethical. In societies such as the United States, where Jews have equal rights, Jewish law obligates them to obey the laws of the state.

※   ※   ※

In those days there was no king in Israel; everyone did as
he pleased.
> —Concluding sentence of book of Judges 21:25, describing the
> anarchy prevailing in ancient Israel, c. 1100 B.C.E.

A reading of the chapters immediately preceding this verse reveals the Bible's strong disapproval of a society in which "everyone
did as he pleased." Judges 19–20 describes a bitter, protracted quarrel between the tribe of Benjamin and the rest of Israel. In the absence of centralized leadership to adjudicate the dispute, the other
tribes overwhelmed Benjamin and murdered a large majority of its
members, including, apparently, almost every woman.

They then decided to exterminate Benjamin permanently by having all Israelites swear not to give their daughters in marriage to one
of its members.

Concurrently, the other tribes decided to murder everyone, children included, of the city of Jabesh-Gilead as punishment for not
sending troops to participate in the war of extermination against
Benjamin.

In the interim, however, they decided it was wrong to wipe out
a tribe; in an act of "mercy," they chose to spare four hundred
virgins in the city of Jabesh-Gilead, whom they then turned over to
the Benjaminite men so that they could acquire wives without the
other Israelites having to violate their oath. But the Benjaminites
soon complained that four hundred women were not enough.

The other tribes advised them to go to the annual feast at Shiloh,
"lie in wait in the vineyards," and then kidnap the girls attending
the feast and spirit them back to Benjaminite territory. Thus they
would again acquire wives, without the other tribes having broken
their oath not to "give" their daughters in marriage to Benjamin.

It is after this description of one disgusting act of immorality
after another that the Bible concludes, "In those days there was no
king in Israel; everyone did as he pleased."

On a literary level, the Bible might well have intended to contrast
this verse with a verse from Deuteronomy (12:8), "You shall not do
. . . every man whatever is right in his own eyes."

THE SEVEN NOAHIDE LAWS (JUDAISM'S BASIC PRINCIPLES OF MORALITY FOR A NON-JEWISH SOCIETY)

1. Not to deny God (i.e., idolatry)
2. Not to blaspheme God
3. Not to murder
4. Not to engage in forbidden sexual activities (e.g., incest)
5. Not to steal
6. Not to eat a limb torn from a living animal
7. To set up courts to ensure obedience to the other six laws

—See Babylonian Talmud, *Sanhedrin* 56a

Significantly, the sole positive commandment addressed to non-Jews ordains the establishment of courts, to ensure that the other laws are properly implemented and observed. That this is the one positive commandment among the seven is yet another indication of how much Judaism fears anarchy.

57

"LET THE LAW CUT THROUGH THE MOUNTAIN"

Jewish Principles of Justice

GUIDING PRINCIPLES FOR JUDGES

Let the law cut through the mountain.
—Babylonian Talmud, *Sanhedrin* 6b

The above is a poetic expression of the Talmud's belief that, inside the courtroom, justice must override all other considerations, even those of mercy. Thus, although judges are instructed to encourage litigants at the outset of a case to arbitrate and compromise, once a verdict is announced, "the judge is no longer permitted to allow arbitration, but he must let the law cut through the mountain" (Maimonides, *Mishneh Torah,* "Laws of the Sanhedrin," 22:4).

*   *   *

You shall not render an unfair decision: do not favor the poor nor show deference to the rich; judge your kinsmen fairly.
—Leviticus 19:15

The eleventh-century Bible commentator, Rashi, relying on an earlier rabbinic source, explains:

398

" 'Do not favor the poor.' [What does this mean?] You shall not say, 'This is a poor man, and the rich man in any case is obliged to help support him. Therefore, I will rule in the poor man's favor and he will thereby obtain some support in a respectable fashion.'

" 'Or show deference to the rich.' [What does this mean?] You shall not say, 'This is a rich man, or a man of noble descent, how can I shame him or be witness to his shame?' . . . It is for this reason that the Torah states, 'nor show deference to the rich.' "

The above brings to mind a possibly apocryphal story about New York City Mayor Fiorello La Guardia (1933–1945). At one time during the Depression, he was serving as a night-court judge when a woman appeared before him who had stolen food to feed her children. Desiring to satisfy the demands of both justice and mercy, La Guardia told the woman, "I fine you ten dollars for stealing, and I fine everyone else in this courtroom, myself included, fifty cents each for living in a city where a woman is forced to steal to feed her children." The money was immediately collected, the fine paid, and the extra money given to the woman.

*   *   *

Keep far from falsehood.

—Exodus 23:7

And how do we know that a judge who knows that a plea is false [in an instance where the judge cannot himself disprove the witnesses' testimony, but it is, nonetheless, apparent to him that they are speaking untruthfully or are in error] should not say, "Since the witnesses have testified, I will rule according to their testimony, and let the chain of guilt hang around their necks?" Because it says [in the Torah], "Keep far from falsehood."

—Babylonian Talmud, *Shevuot* 30b–31a

This biblical admonition has had a far-reaching impact on Jewish law. It sometimes mandates overriding the respect a disciple is

399

required to show his teacher, determines which testimony a judge can and cannot hear, and even influences the attire litigants wear in the courtroom:

> How do we know that a disciple sitting before his master, who sees that the poor man is right and the wealthy man wrong, should not remain silent [if his teacher comes to the opposite conclusion]? Because it is said, "Keep far from falsehood."
>
> —Babylonian Talmud, *Shevuot* 31a

> How do we know that a judge should not hear the words of one litigant before the other litigant arrives? Because it is said, "Keep far from falsehood."
>
> —Babylonian Talmud, ibid.

This advice is applicable to us all. Experience has taught me (unfortunately, again and again) how unwise it is to reach a conclusion after hearing only one side of a story.

I remember as a child that my favorite feature in my mother's *Ladies' Home Journal* was "Can This Marriage Be Saved?" Every month, the magazine would publish an account of a troubled couple, followed by the advice of a marriage counselor. First, one would read the husband's or wife's side of the story. Invariably, when I finished this section, I was certain that the person whose side I had read was totally in the right, and that the other spouse had acted miserably and, usually, indefensibly. Of course, when I read the other spouse's version, I usually would come to an altogether different conclusion.

The tendency to be swayed by one side of a story is so common that Jewish law permits a judge to hear one litigant's version of the events only when the other litigant is present to dispute the testimony and offer his or her version of what happened.

> How do we know that, if two people come into court, one clothed in rags, and the other in garments worth a hundred

manehs, that the court should say to the well-dressed man, "Either dress like him, or dress him like you." Because it is said, "Keep far from falsehood."

—Babylonian Talmud, ibid.

The Rabbis knew that judges, being human, are apt to have a lower regard for a poorly dressed litigant.

*　　*　　*

When one claims something in his neighbor's possession, the burden of proof lies on the claimant.

—Babylonian Talmud, *Bava Kamma* 35a

This is the talmudic equivalent of the popular dictum, "Possession is nine-tenths of the law." However, as the following case makes clear, the Rabbis were willing to suspend this law when following it would lead to injustice:

[A man who said he was] the brother of Mari ben Isak came from the city of Be Hozai [in Persia], and said, "Divide [our father's estate] with me."

"I don't know you," said Mari [who had not seen his brother in many years].

They went to Rabbi Hisda. "Mari might be speaking the truth," he said, "for it is written in the Torah, 'And Joseph knew his brothers but they did not recognize him' (Genesis 42:8), because when he left them he had no beard, and now he appeared before them with one. [So too, Mari may not recognize you, even if you are his brother.] Go and bring witnesses that you are his brother."

"I have witnesses," said the brother, "but they are afraid to testify because Mari is a man of violence."

Rabbi Hisda said to Mari, "Then you go and bring witnesses that he is not your brother."

"Is this the law?" Mari answered. "According to the law, the one who claims something in his neighbor's possession is the one who must bring the proof."

"This is my judgment in your case," answered Rabbi Hisda, "and for all men of violence like you."
—Babylonian Talmud, *Bava Mezia* 39b; with minor variations, I have followed the translation of Aaron Kirschenbaum, *Equity in Jewish Law,* pages 59–60.

Rabbi Hisda ignored Mari's challenge that his ruling violated basic norms of justice because, to the rabbi, justice meant fairness, not blind obedience to an abstract legal principle. As Professor Aaron Kirschenbaum wrote regarding this passage, "Elementary justice requires that men of violence not be allowed to abuse the formal rules of procedure for their own benefit." He went on to observe that the Mari case has served as a precedent for Jewish judges throughout the centuries not to allow violent people to utilize legal technicalities to thwart justice (*Equity in Jewish Law,* pages 61ff).

*　　*　　*

A judge must be guided only by what his own eyes actually see.
—Babylonian Talmud, *Sanhedrin* 6b

"An eye for an eye" (Exodus 21:24). But not an eye and a life for an eye.
—Babylonian Talmud, *Ketubot* 38a

Although the Torah demands "an eye for an eye," Jewish tradition understood this verse as meaning that the assailant must pay a fine rather than have his own eye extracted. Why? Because of the demands of justice:

Now if you assume that actual retaliation is intended, it could sometimes happen that both eye and life would be taken [in payment for the eye], as, for instance, if the offender died as he was being blinded.
—Babylonian Talmud, *Bava Kamma* 84a

Thus, although one who intentionally blinds another deserves, on moral grounds, to be blinded, in practice the assailant pays compensation, lest the court commit the greater injustice of killing as well as blinding him.

> The sword comes into the world because of justice delayed and because of justice perverted.
>
> —*Ethics of the Fathers* 5:8

Justice delayed, in other words, is justice denied, and justice denied will lead to bloodshed.

THE QUALITIES REQUIRED OF THOSE APPOINTED AS JUSTICES TO THE SANHEDRIN, THE JEWISH HIGH COURT

> Only a person who [is so subtle that he] can prove from the Bible that a reptile is clean may be appointed to the Sanhedrin.
>
> —Babylonian Talmud, *Sanhedrin* 17a

According to biblical law, the reptile's carcass renders one whom it touches ritually impure (Leviticus 11:29–38).

The Rabbis, aware that many defendants and litigants appearing before the Sanhedrin would advance intricate, shrewd, even sly, arguments, had no desire to seat naive people as justices. They wanted judges *intelligent* enough to be able to "prove" the opposite of what the Bible teaches, and *honest* enough to recognize that their "proofs" were untrue.

A modern analogue to one who could both "prove" the untrue, yet still recognize truth, was Samuel Leibowitz (1893–1978), long regarded as one of America's most effective criminal-defense lawyers. Leibowitz influenced many jurors to acquit murderers on the basis of farfetched, but persuasively presented, arguments.

Having secured acquittals for many of America's leading gangsters, including Bugsy Siegel, Leibowitz later became a Brooklyn criminal-court judge, and soon became known as a "hanging judge." "I was tough with hardened criminals," he declared upon retiring from the bench, "toughness is all they understand." Because he himself had spent many years constructing arguments on behalf of criminals (defenses as subtle and farfetched as proving that a reptile's carcass is ritually clean), Leibowitz was better able than other judges to recognize the deceits in many pleas and alibis now presented before him. (For a brief account of Leibowitz, see Carl Sifakis, *The Encyclopedia of American Crime*, pages 417–418.)

> We only appoint to the Sanhedrin those who are men of
> stature, wisdom, impressive appearance, and mature years;
> they must have a knowledge of witchcraft, and be conver-
> sant with [the world's] seventy languages, in order that the
> court should have no need of an interpreter.
> —Babylonian Talmud, *Sanhedrin* 17a

Although the Torah strictly forbids witchcraft, a judge must understand this belief system if he is to fairly judge one accused of this offense. Lest this sound like a farfetched requirement, consider that, had the judges at the 1692 Salem witchcraft trials had a better understanding of what witches supposedly did, they might have recognized the falsity of the charges made against nineteen innocent people and refrained from sentencing them to death.

If interpreted literally, the obligation to be "conversant with the world's seventy languages" strains credulity. Perhaps different dialects were subsumed within these many languages; more likely, the number seventy symbolically represents the need to know many different languages, not just one's own.

In addition to freeing the judges from relying on interpreters, this requirement guaranteed that they were cosmopolitan people with wide-ranging knowledge of the cultures around them.

> We do not appoint as members of the Sanhedrin an aged
> man, a eunuch, or one who is childless. Rabbi Judah in-
> cludes also a cruel man.
> —Babylonian Talmud, *Sanhedrin* 36b

Since the Jewish tradition normally associates age with wisdom, the reference to an "aged man" is to one who is very old.

The law excludes eunuchs and the childless because they are presumed to lack paternal tenderness, while the very old are presumed to have forgotten the pain of raising children, and become unduly severe as a result.

Rabbi Judah's exclusion of the cruel should be, but unfortunately isn't, self-evident: History offers ample evidence of evil wreaked by sadists wearing judicial robes; the Nazi justices who sentenced many people to death constitute a recent example.

A RABBINIC SATIRE ON INJUSTICE

Alexander of Macedon visited [the mythical] King Katzya, who displayed to him enormous quantities of gold and silver.

Alexander said to him, "I have no need of your gold and silver. I only came here to see your customs, how you administer justice."

While they were talking, a man came before the king with a case against his neighbor from whom he had bought a field and in it had discovered a bundle of coins.

The purchaser argued, "I bought the field, but not the treasure buried in it," and the seller contended, "I sold the field and all it contained."

While they were arguing, the king turned to one of them and asked, "Have you a son?"

"Yes," he replied.

He asked the other, "Have you a daughter?"

"Yes," he answered.

"Let them marry, and give them the treasure," the king ruled.

Alexander began to laugh, and King Katzya asked him, "Why do you laugh? Did I not judge well? Suppose such a case came before you, what would you have ruled?"

Alexander replied, "I would have put them both to death, and confiscated the treasure."

"Do you then love gold so much?" asked Katzya.

[Immediately thereafter] Katzya made a feast for Alexander and served him golden cutlets and golden poultry.

"I do not eat gold," Alexander exclaimed.

The king retorted, "If you do not eat gold, why do you love it so much?" He then asked him, "Does the sun shine in your country?"

"Certainly," Alexander answered.

"Does rain fall in your country?"

"Of course."

"Are there small animals in your country?"

"Of course," Alexander again replied.

" . . . You are only permitted to live then because of the merit of those animals," Katzya retorted.

—Palestinian Talmud, *Bava Mezia* 2:5; with minor variations, I have followed the translation of Ben Zion Bokser, *The Talmud: Selected Writings,* pages 179–180.

Louis Jacobs's comments that the moral of the story is "When man is not just, he is less than the beasts" (*Jewish Law,* page 51).

58

MURDER AND THE DEATH PENALTY

The Conflicting Views of the Bible and Talmud

Whoever sheds the blood of man, by man shall his blood be shed, for in His image did God make man.

—Genesis 9:6

Because man is created in God's image, murdering a human being is also considered a crime against God.

He who fatally strikes a man shall be put to death. [That this law only applies to premeditated murderers is indicated by the following verse]: If he did not do it by design . . . I will assign you a place to which he [the killer] can flee.

—Exodus 21:12–13

You may not accept a ransom for the life of a murderer who is guilty of a capital crime; he must be put to death.

—Numbers 35:31

The societies surrounding the ancient Hebrews permitted the victim's family to accept money from the murderer in return for their agreeing not to prosecute or wreak vengeance. As Maimonides explains, the Bible forbids this practice because "the soul of the victim is not the property of [his family members] but the property of God" (*Mishneh Torah*, "Laws of Murder and Preservation of Life," 1:4).

The Bible offers two rationales for executing murderers and those who commit other particularly odious crimes (e.g., a witness who falsely testifies that someone has committed a capital offense, and one who kidnaps another and enslaves or sells him):

> 1. So that others will hear and be afraid, and such evil things will not again be done in your midst.
> —Deuteronomy 19:20

In short, the Bible offers the argument that capital punishment serves as a deterrent. In recent years, opponents of the death penalty have argued that there is no reason to believe that capital punishment serves this function. Judge Robert Bork, the former U.S. Solicitor General, has sarcastically responded: "The assertion that punishment does not deter runs contrary to the common sense of the common man and is perhaps, for that reason, a tenet fiercely held by a number of social scientists."

> 2. And you shall burn the evil out from your midst.
> —Deuteronomy 19:19 and 24:7

The Bible obliges its followers to hate evil (although not necessarily people who do evil; see page 349), and destroy those who have committed grotesquely evil acts. In the final analysis, the Allies hanged Nazi leaders at Nuremberg and Israel executed Adolf Eichmann (see Chapter 78) not because they thought doing so would deter future murderers or because they feared that these people might murder again if released. Rather, they believed that the Nazis' evil was so enormous that it deserved a corresponding punishment;

in the words of the Rabbis, *middah k'negged middah*, measure for measure.

However, lest one argue that the Bible would sanction capital punishment only in the case of mass murderers, Jewish teaching insists that every innocent human life is of infinite value. Hence, the murder of one innocent person is the ultimate evil; the murder of ten more increases the magnitude, not the evil (pages 88–90).

In fact, the Rabbis believe that many instances in which a single person has been killed constitutes a kind of mass murder, a view based on an episode in Genesis (4:10). When Cain murders his brother Abel, God calls out to him, "Your brother's blood cries out to Me from the earth." The word God uses, *d'mai*, literally means "bloods." The Rabbis ask, " Why does it say 'your brother's *bloods*?' and not 'your brother's blood?' " They answer, "His blood and the blood of all his descendants [who will never be born]" (Mishna *Sanhedrin* 4:5). Thus, a murderer bears guilt for the victim's unborn children and all of their descendants until the end of time.

The Bible does place an enormous restriction on the death sentence: it insists that it can be carried out only if there were at least two witnesses to the crime (Deuteronomy 17:6).

THE TALMUDIC VIEW OF THE DEATH SENTENCE

There are few areas in Jewish law where the biblical and talmudic view so conflict as in the matter of capital punishment. The dominant, although not exclusive, line of argument proffered in the Talmud opposes the death sentence, even in the case of premeditated murder. It places so many restrictions on the judicial authorities that very few, if any, murderers would be convicted were these restrictions enforced.

Among the talmudic restrictions:

1. PROHIBITION OF CONFESSIONS IN CAPITAL CASES

A man cannot bear witness against himself [literally, a man does not depict himself as evil].

—Babylonian Talmud, *Sanhedrin* 9b

Because of this talmudic injunction, Jewish courts did not accept confession in capital cases. Drawing on his medical as well as rabbinical knowledge, Maimonides speculated that confessions might have been prohibited because of the danger that they might be prompted by emotional illness: "Perhaps he was one of those who are in misery, bitter in soul, who long for death. . . . Perhaps this was the reason that prompted him to confess to a crime he had not committed, in order that he might be put to death" (*Mishneh Torah,* "Laws of the Sanhedrin," 18:6).

The Talmud's rejection of confession led to Jewish courts being the only ones in the ancient and medieval world to prohibit torture. (In monetary cases, Jewish law permits confession, since a person has the right to do whatever he wants with his money; his life, however, is not his to destroy.) Because Roman, Catholic, and almost all other judicial systems considered evidence from confessions to be the most reliable, they sanctioned torture against those believed guilty. Jewish courts were never tempted to do so, since a confession would be judicially worthless.

This talmudic injunction long raised the moral stature of Jewish courts above their neighbors'. Today, however, it is questionable whether outlawing confessions in societies that outlaw torture is still necessary. Police officials to whom I have recounted the talmudic ban have told me that prohibiting confessions would lead to a precipitous decline in the number of murders solved.

2. ABSOLUTE PROHIBITION OF CIRCUMSTANTIAL EVIDENCE

Our Rabbis taught: What is meant by [not convicting on the basis of] circumstantial evidence? The judge says to

410

the witnesses, "Perhaps you saw the defendant running after the other fellow into a ruin, you pursued him, and found him with sword in hand and blood dripping from it, while the victim was writhing in agony. If that is what you saw, you saw nothing."

—Babylonian Talmud, *Sanhedrin* 37b

According to the Rabbis, the only evidence that can convict a murderer is that of two witnesses who simultaneously see the crime, including the immediate events leading to it, from beginning to end.

A contemporary Orthodox legal scholar, Rabbi J. David Bleich, notes that, from the perspective of Jewish law, "fingerprints, forensic evidence and the like must be relegated to the category of circumstantial evidence" ("Capital Punishment in the Noachide Code," page 117), and thus are judicially worthless.

One can speculate, of course, if the Rabbis would have ruled in this manner had they known, two thousand years ago, that each individual has unique fingerprints and genetic imprints.

3. THE WITNESSES MUST REVEAL THEMSELVES TO THE WOULD-BE MURDERER AND WARN HIM OF THE PUNISHMENT HE WILL FACE

The Talmud also insists that the two witnesses must warn the would-be killer that he will be executed, and the would-be murderer must acknowledge this warning. Law professor Helene Schwartz offers a hypothetical case wherein the Rabbis would agree that the death sentence could be inflicted:

Zvi and Samuel are standing next to each other in the street. They see Moshe approach with Laban. Neither Zvi nor Samuel is related to Laban nor otherwise ineligible to serve as a witness. As Moshe and Laban walk towards Zvi and Samuel, Laban draws his knife and prepares to kill Moshe.

"Stop," says Zvi within Samuel's hearing. "It is against the law intentionally to kill, and if you do, you may be condemned to death by decapitation." The required warning has been given, together with the correct death penalty for the crime.

411

"I know murder is a crime, and that the death penalty is decapitation," Laban replies, indicating that he has understood the warning. Laban then raises his knife and, in the presence of Zvi and Samuel, plunges it into Moshe's heart.

—Helene Schwartz, *Justice by the Book*, page 16

"Assuming that Zvi and Samuel can withstand the rigorous interrogations at the trial," Schwartz concludes, "Laban may be convicted of murder and executed. The scenario is an unlikely one."

Indeed, in this case, one might question the justice of capital punishment, since the murderer would so clearly be of unsound mind, just the sort of person encompassed in Maimonides's ruling, "one of those who are in misery, bitter in soul, [and] who long for death." Why else would one commit a murder in the presence of witnesses, when merely waiting for a more propitious time would free the killer from the death sentence?

The general range of rabbinic views concerning the death penalty is expressed in the following Mishna:

A Sanhedrin [Jewish high court] which executed one person in seven years is called "murderous." Rabbi Elazar ben Azarya says once in seventy years.

Rabbi Tarfon and Rabbi Akiva say that "if we had been on the Sanhedrin, no one would ever have been executed."

Rabbi Simeon ben Gamliel says that they would thereby multiply shedders of blood in Israel.

—Mishna *Makkot* 1:10

Rabbi Akiva and Rabbi Tarfon never sat on the Sanhedrin because it had ceased to exist before their time. It was the only Jewish court authorized to order executions, a right apparently lost under Roman rule around 30 C.E. The Talmud explains that they would have ensured that no death sentences were carried out by subjecting the witnesses to such searching cross-examination that, inevitably, there would be questions they couldn't answer (the questions would have been along the lines of "How many of the defendant's shirt buttons were buttoned and which were not?"). Akiva and Tarfon would have used the witnesses' inability to answer as the rationale for not sentencing the defendant to death (Babylonian Talmud, *Makkot* 7a). Gerald Blidstein has rightly noted that the "source of their opposition was not a fear of killing the innocent but a reluctance to kill the guilty" (see his "Capital Punishment—The Classic Jewish Discussion," page 319).

Rabbi Simeon ben Gamliel's response, that Akiva and Tarfon's behavior would have caused an increase in murder, reflects, of course, the view that the death sentence is a deterrent.

To me, it seems that the impossible range of restrictions the Rabbis placed on judicial authorities constituted a form of protest against Roman rule, for the Romans executed whomever they wanted, for whatever offense, based on the flimsiest evidence. While the world today knows only the case of Jesus, the Romans executed between fifty and one hundred thousand Jews during the first 150 years of the Common Era. Rabbi Akiva himself was later executed by the Romans for the "crime" of disseminating knowledge of the Torah (see pages 320–321). In such a society, the Rabbis undoubtedly were right to insist that it would be morally better to allow no executions at all.

Two additional talmudic rulings have convinced me that the Rabbis realized the impracticality of the standards upon which they were insisting. First, they added a clause that, in times of emergency, these extreme precautionary measures could be suspended, a ruling subsequently incorporated into Maimonides's code and the *Shulkhan Arukh,* the standard code of Jewish law (*Hoshen Mishpat* 2:1; see also Babylonian Talmud, *Sanhedrin* 46a).

Some Jews who favor the death penalty believe that contemporary American society should be regarded as a society going through a long-term emergency. Currently, one out of every hundred and thirty-three Americans will die from being murdered, and the rates are rising. This seems to me a period of emergency.

One who murders without clear proof [that he is the murderer, i.e., there were not two witnesses] or without warning [having been administered by the witnesses] ... the king has authority to execute him and to perfect the world in accordance with what the hour requires. . . . [The king is empowered to take the measures necessary] to inspire fear, and to break the hands of the world's evil people.

—Moses Maimonides, *Mishneh Torah,* "Laws of Kings," 3:10

Second, the Talmud ruled that if it was clear to the court that a defendant had committed murder, but one of the technical factors had not been fulfilled, then the courts were empowered to impose their own form of capital punishment:

Mishna: One who commits murder without witnesses is placed in a cell and fed with bread of adversity and waters of affliction.

The Talmud comments: How do we know he committed the murder? [A variety of responses is offered, among them] Samuel said, [There were witnesses] but they did not warn him. Rabbi Hisda said ... [He was convicted] through witnesses who were disproved on the minor circumstances of the crime, but not on the vital points. . . . [The Talmud says that the murderer is placed by the court in a cell] and fed with barley bread until his stomach bursts.

—Babylonian Talmud, *Sanhedrin* 81b

Thus we come to one of the ironic results of the utopian and impracticable standards the Rabbis imposed on the judiciary. For even in those limited instances where talmudic law permitted executions, it insisted that the defendant be killed in the quickest manner possible (which is why Jewish law always forbade crucifixion, the goal of which was to prolong and intensify the death agony). But by tying the judges' hands, and so creating the possibility that murderers literally would "get away with murder" (no prison system comparable to ours existed in the ancient world), the Rabbis permitted modes of indirect execution that should have been prohibited on grounds of excessive cruelty.

Rabbi Harold Kushner has suggested another reason for the Talmud's widespread opposition to capital punishment: the rabbinic belief that God would punish *in this world* any murderers who could not be convicted. The Rabbis were not terribly concerned, therefore, if a murderer walked free out of court, since they were confident that God would rectify the injustice. In fact, the Talmud relates several stories of murderers who would have gone free under the Talmud's guidelines, but who nevertheless received a divinely inflicted death sentence:

> It has been taught: Rabbi Simeon ben Shetach said, "May I never live to see [the] comfort [of the ultimate redemption] if I did not once see a man pursuing his fellow into a ruin, and when I ran after him and saw him, sword in hand with blood dripping from it, and the murdered man writhing, I exclaimed to him: 'Wicked man, who murdered this man? It is either you or I. But what can I do, since your blood does not rest in my hands, for it is written in the Torah, "A person shall be put to death only on the testimony of two or more witnesses" (Deuteronomy 17: 6).' " [Rabbi Simeon then cursed the man] "May He who knows a person's thoughts exact vengeance from this one who murdered his fellow!" It is said that before they moved from the place, a serpent came and bit the man so that he died.
>
> —Babylonian Talmud, *Sanhedrin* 37b

The Talmud continues this discussion with the claim that now that Jewish courts can no longer impose the four modes of execution, God Himself brings them about. One who is worthy of being stoned, for example, either falls from a roof or is trampled to death by a wild beast; one who deserves strangulation drowns in a river or suffocates.

Thus if, as Kushner argues, the Rabbis were confident God would personally wreak punishment on murderers, one can better understand their apparent nonchalance about whether or not the courts did so.

Unfortunately, such a pattern of thinking is unhelpful today. By all accounts, Adolf Eichmann was leading a relatively normal life in Buenos Aires when Israeli agents kidnapped him and brought him to trial in Israel in 1960. There is no reason to believe that, had Israel not done so, God would have punished Eichmann in this world.

A FINAL REFLECTION ON THE DEATH SENTENCE AND THE SOUL OF THE MURDERER

When a life has been deliberately taken, the death of the murderer is the only means of atonement for him as well as for society.

—David Novak, *Jewish Social Ethics,* page 177

Novak bases this comment on the procedure described in the Mishna immediately prior to execution: "They say to him, 'Confess, for such is the way of those convicted to die, and whoever confesses [and is then executed] has a portion in the World-to-Come. . . . ' " (*Sanhedrin* 6:2). "In other words," Novak concludes, "by performing justice in this world, we also provide the convicted criminal with the opportunity to be worthy of divine mercy in the other world."

59

"MUST THE SWORD DEVOUR FOREVER?"

Jewish Reflections on War

MILITARY DEFERMENTS: THE BIBLICAL VIEW

When you take the field against your enemies . . . the officials shall address the troops as follows, "Is there anyone who has built a new house but has not dedicated it? Let him go back to his home, lest he die in battle and another dedicate it.

"Is there anyone who has planted a vineyard but has never harvested it? Let him go back to his home, lest he die in battle and another initiate it.

"Is there anyone who has become betrothed to a woman but who has not yet married her? Let him go back to his home lest he die in battle and another marry her."

The officials shall go on addressing the troops and say, "Is there anyone afraid and disheartened? Let him go back to his home, lest his brothers' hearts melt as his heart."

—Deuteronomy 20:1, 5–8

The biblical laws are a combination of common sense and mercy. It would be cruel to draft a person who has just married or started a business, only to have the person perish in war, and another walk away with his spouse or source of livelihood. Deuteronomy also ruled that a newly married husband should not be drafted during the first year of his marriage (24:5).

Regarding the final ground for exemption, both mercy and common sense dictate that an army rid itself of very fearful soldiers, since cowardice usually is contagious. Because a certain amount of fear before battle is natural, the Talmud delineates what constitutes one who is "afraid and disheartened":

> If he hears the sound of the trumpets and is terrified, or the crash of shields and is terrified, or beholds the flashing of swords and water drips upon his knees [i.e., he urinates from terror], he returns home . . . because it is written "lest his brothers' hearts melt as his heart."
>
> —Babylonian Talmud, *Sotah* 44b

When Israel (or any country in which Jews have equal rights) is invaded, all deferments, with the exception of the fainthearted, are suspended:

> In a war of self-defense [literally, an obligatory war] all go out to do battle, even a groom from his room, and the bride from under the wedding canopy.
>
> —Mishna, *Sotah* 8:7

The commentaries explain that this does not imply that women served as combatants; rather, they supplied food for the troops.

ANTIWAR STATEMENTS

> I wanted to build a House for the name of the Lord my God. But the words of the Lord came to me, saying, "You have shed much blood and fought great battles; you shall not build a House for My name for you have shed much blood on the earth in My sight."
>
> —King David in I Chronicles 22:7–8

Since one finds no divine criticism of David's military campaigns in the two books of Samuel, where his life story is told, this statement from Chronicles suggests that fighting, even in justified wars, is detrimental to one's soul. God's words to David bring to mind a comment by Russian poet Yevgeny Yevtushenko: "The hand that strikes often loses its capacity for tender touches."

Similar thinking informs a midrashic comment on Genesis 32:8, which informs us that "Jacob was greatly afraid and distressed" when he heard that his brother, Esau, who had once threatened to kill him, was advancing toward him with his personal army. The Rabbis ask:

> Are not fear and distress identical? [Why then does the Torah specify both?] The meaning, however, is that "he was *afraid*" lest he be slain, "and was *distressed*" lest he should slay. For Jacob thought: "If he prevails against me, will he not slay me? While if I am stronger than he, will I not slay him?"
>
> —*Genesis Rabbah* 76:2

*   *   *

> And they shall beat their swords into plowshares and their spears into pruning hooks. Nation shall not lift up sword against nation, neither shall they learn war anymore.
>
> —Isaiah 2:4

This is perhaps the most famous verse from the prophetic books of the Bible: The last sentence adorns the Isaiah Wall across the street from the United Nations building in New York. Jewish tradition, which considers universal peace an essential component of the messianic age, views Jesus' inability to usher in an end to bloodletting as proof that he was not the Messiah.

As much as the prophets longed for peace, they hardly viewed all war as wrong. In a far less well-known biblical passage, the prophet Joel, writing of a time when the Jews needed to forcefully confront their enemies, reversed Isaiah's words: " . . . Prepare for battle, arouse the warriors. . . . Beat your plowshares into swords, and your pruning hooks into spears. . . . " (Joel 4:9–10).

*　　*　　*

> A person may not go out on the Sabbath with a sword, bow, shield, club, or spear. . . . Rabbi Eliezer says they are considered adornments [and hence one should be allowed to carry them on the Sabbath]. But the sages say they are really degrading.
>
> —Mishna *Shabbat* 6:4

Jewish law rules according to the sages, not Rabbi Eliezer.

> Renunciation of chemical and biological warfare, and humane treatment for prisoners of war . . . are certainly marks of civilized peoples, but on a more fundamental level such matters are little different from a convention requiring cannibals to eat with knives and forks. "Civilized warfare" is inherently a self-contradiction.
>
> —Rabbi J. David Bleich, *Contemporary Halakhic Problems*,
> Vol. II, pages 159–160

WHEN FIGHTING AND BLOODSHED ARE NECESSARY

In probably no other area of ethics are the differences between Judaism and the New Testament as pronounced as on issues of self-defense, and responses toward evil people. Both Jesus (in his Sermon on the Mount) and the Talmud articulate their positions unequivocally:

> If anyone hits you on the right cheek, offer him the other as well.
>
> —Matthew 5:38–39

The early Zionist essayist, Ahad Ha'am, comments: "If I practice love to the extent that when you smite me on the right cheek, I offer you the left also, I am thereby encouraging injustice. I, like you, am then guilty of the injustice that is practiced." In an argument with the pacifist writer Leo Tolstoy, Thomas Masaryk (1850–1937), the great (non-Jewish) humanist and founding president of Czechoslovakia, expressed a similar notion: "If someone attacks me with the intention of killing me, I shall defend myself, and if I cannot avoid it, I shall kill the attacker. If one of us two must be killed, let the one be killed who has the bad intentions." Indeed, Masaryk's words sound as if they came straight out of the Talmud:

> If someone comes to kill you, kill him first.
>
> —*Sanhedrin* 72a

A thousand years before the Talmud, the Torah likewise legislated that one need not wait until an opponent had begun his violent attack. Strong circumstantial evidence of murderous intentions constituted sufficient provocation; thus, "If a thief is seized while tunneling his way [into a house during the nightime] and is smitten so that he die, there is no bloodguilt. . . . " (Exodus 22:1).

Although the Bible offers no rationale to justify the killing of a would-be thief, the Talmud does. In an admittedly speculative passage, it tries to enter into the mind-set of the kind of burglar who tunnels into an occupied house (had the house been empty, he would have entered in a less arduous way, e.g., through the door or window). Such a thief, the Talmud reasons, is fully aware that he might encounter resistance, yet makes the following calculation: "If the owner fights me and tries to prevent me from taking his property, I will fight back, and if need be, kill him" (Babylonian Talmud, *Sanhedrin* 72a). The Talmud concludes that that is why the Torah permits the homeowner to take preemptive action.

What additional guidelines do the Hebrew Bible and the New Testament offer for dealing with a violent attack? Again, Jesus' teaching seems blunt and unequivocal: "Offer the wicked man no resistance" (Matthew 5:38–39).

In contrast, the Hebrew Bible repeatedly reiterates that one should offer the evildoer forceful opposition. On several occasions, the Torah enjoins: "You shall burn the evil out from your midst"

(Deuteronomy 7:17). It also describes Moses' killing of an Egyptian taskmaster who was beating a Jewish slave (Exodus 2:12).

While a few Christian sects such as the Jehovah's Witnesses still hold themselves bound by Jesus' pacifism, almost every nation with a large Christian population has chosen to disregard or reinterpret his words. Indeed, Jesus' foremost twentieth-century disciple on this issue has turned out to be not a religious Christian, but a devout Hindu, Mahatma Gandhi. During the Second World War, when it appeared that Nazi Germany might overwhelm England, Gandhi offered the British the following advice: "I would like you to lay down the arms you have as being useless for saving you or humanity. You will invite Herr Hitler and Signor Mussolini to take what they want of the countries you call your possessions. . . . If these gentlemen choose to occupy your homes you will vacate them. If they do not give you free passage out, you will allow yourselves, man woman and child to be slaughtered, but you will refuse to owe allegiance to them" (*Non-Violence in Peace and War*).

A few years earlier, in the final months before World War II erupted, Gandhi had offered German Jews similar wisdom for overcoming Nazi antisemitism:

> I am as certain as I am dictating these words that the stoniest German heart will melt [if only the Jews] . . . adopt active non-violence. Human nature . . . unfailingly responds to the advances of love. I do not despair of his [Hitler's] responding to human suffering even though caused by him.
>
> —Mahatma Gandhi (in his newspaper *Harijan*,
> December 17 and 24, 1938, and January 7, 1939).
> I have drawn these quotes of Gandhi from Gideon Shimoni's
> far-reaching analysis, *Gandhi, Satyagraha and the Jews;*
> see, in particular, pages 46, 51–52, and 59.

Jews reacted to Gandhi's words with pain, scorn, and incredulity. The philosopher Martin Buber, referring to the link between Jesus' and Gandhi's teachings, responded to Gandhi in an open letter:

We did not proclaim, as did Jesus, the son of our people, and as you do, the teaching of nonviolence, because we believe that a man must sometimes use force to save himself or, even more, his children.

Six years and six million murdered Jews later, Gandhi offered some postmortem wisdom to the dead Jews:

Gandhi [in a June 1946 conversation with his biographer, Louis Fischer]: "Hitler killed five million [sic] Jews. It is the greatest crime of our time. But the Jews should have offered themselves to the butcher's knife. They should have thrown themselves into the sea from cliffs."
Fischer: "You mean that the Jews should have committed collective suicide?"
Gandhi: "Yes, that would have been heroism."

A FINAL REFLECTION ON FIGHTING ON BEHALF OF THOSE WHO ARE PURSUED

Every Jew is commanded to save a person being pursued for his life, even if it means killing the pursuer, and [even if] the pursuer is a minor.

Thus, if warning is issued and he continues to pursue, the pursuer can be killed even without his acknowledging the warning. But if the pursuer can be stopped by disabling part of his body, by striking him with an arrow, a stone, or a sword . . . then that should be done.

And this is a negative commandment, i.e., not to have mercy on the life of a pursuer.

—Moses Maimonides, *Mishneh Torah,* "Laws of Murder
and Preservation of Life," 1:6–7, 9;
I have followed the translation of Basil Herring,
Jewish Ethics and Halakhah for Our Time, Vol. II, 137.

While Maimonides's statement refers to taking action against one individual who is threatening another, the same logic applies to one nation fighting a war against an aggressor state. Terrible as war may be, the alternative often is worse. Had Gandhi convinced the English to lay down their arms, Nazism would have conquered Europe, if not the world, democracy would have come to an end, and not a single Jew might be alive today. Similarly, if Israel had not been willing to fight wars of self-defense, it would long ago have been destroyed, and its citizens killed. Thus war, while always unfortunate, is not always evil; sometimes, fighting a war is the most moral thing to do.

60

AGAINST UTOPIANISM

> It is not your obligation to complete the task [of perfecting the world], but neither are you free to desist [from doing all you can].
>
> —*Ethics of the Fathers* 2:16

Rabbi Tarfon's statement, my favorite talmudic quote, forbids one to point to the world's imperfectibility as an excuse not to fight evil. Albert Camus (1913–1960), the great French novelist and humanist, expressed a similar idea in more concrete terms: "Perhaps we cannot prevent this world from being a world in which children are tortured. But we can reduce the number of tortured children" ("The Unbeliever and Christians").

My friend Professor David Shatz notes that this dictum likewise underscores the inability of one human being acting alone to fulfill the task of perfecting the world.

*   *   *

> Rabbi Yochanan ben Zakkai used to say, "If there is a sapling in your hand when they say to you, 'Behold, the Messiah has come!' complete planting the sapling, and then go and welcome the Messiah."
>
> —*The Fathers According to Rabbi Nathan*, version B #31

The first-century rabbi was registering his profound mistrust of the frequent "messiahs" and messianic movements that arose during his lifetime, claiming to redeem people and history.

*   *   *

Concerning those who hold Israel to standards of morality that they apply to no other country (see page 319), a contemporary American rabbi has quipped:

> If we Jews are five percent better than the rest of the world, we can be a "light unto the nations." If we are twenty-five percent better than the rest of the world, we can bring the Messiah. If we're fifty percent better than the rest of the world, we'll all be dead.
>
> —Rabbi Irving Greenberg

*   *   *

The calf and the lion shall lie down together but the calf won't get any sleep.

> —Woody Allen

61

"POVERTY WOULD OUTWEIGH THEM ALL"

The Curse of Poverty

> They that are slain with the sword are better than they that are slain through hunger.
>
> —Lamentations 4:9

The above verse long has puzzled Bible commentators. Jeremiah (author of Lamentations) does not say, "They that are slain with the sword are *better off* than they that are slain with hunger" (presumably because death from the sword is quick, while death from hunger is protracted), but suggests that the former somehow are *better people* than the latter.

The Hasidic rebbe and Holocaust survivor Israel Spira, the Grand Rabbi of Bluzhov, claims that only in the Nazi work camp of Janowska did he come to understand this verse. Imprisoned with him and thousands of other Jews were young twin brothers, whose family were among the rabbi's followers. The three helped each other whenever possible.

One day, when the inmates were taken to work, Rabbi Spira, one twin, and a third inmate were told to remain in the barracks and to clean it. During the day, a German guard sadistically shot the twin in one leg, ordered him to stand, then shot him in the other

427

leg, ordered him to stand again and, when he couldn't, emptied his revolver into the young boy. Rabbi Spira and the other inmate were instructed to carry the dead boy's body over to the pile of corpses that accumulated daily at the camp. While carrying him, the rabbi shed tears; he later recalled that one thought dominated him:

How will he tell the other twin about his brother's death? How will he break the terrible news to one of two souls that were so close to each other?

"Tell him that his twin brother is very sick," the other Jew advised the rabbi.

Evening came. The inmates returned to camp. "Chaim'l, your brother is very sick, his life is in danger. It is quite possible that he is no longer alive," said the Rabbi of Bluzhov, trying to avoid the boy's eyes.

The brother began to cry. "Woe unto me! What am I going to do now?"

The rabbi tried to comfort the boy, but he refused to be comforted. "Today was his turn to watch over the bread. I left all the bread with him, now I don't have a single piece of bread left."

The rabbi was shocked but continued his ruse, saying that the other twin had sent him Chaim'l's share. With a trembling hand, he took from under his coat a small piece of bread which was his ration for the day and gave it to the boy. Chaim'l glanced at the small piece of bread and said, "It's missing a few grams. The piece I left with him was a much larger one."

"I was hungry and ate some of it. Tomorrow I will give you the rest of the bread," replied the Rabbi of Bluzhov.

When Rabbi Israel Spira finished telling the story [in 1976, more than thirty years after the event] he said, "Only on that day in Janowska did I understand the verse in the Scriptures, 'They that are slain with the sword are better than they that are slain with hunger.'"

—Yaffa Eliach, *Hasidic Tales of the Holocaust*, pages 153–155

Nothing in the world is more grievous than poverty, the most terrible of all sufferings. . . . For one who is crushed by poverty is like one to whom all the troubles of the world cling and upon whom all the curses of Deuteronomy (28:15–68) have descended.

Our Rabbis said: If all the sufferings and pain in the world were gathered [on one side of a scale] and poverty was on the other side, poverty would outweigh them all.

—*Exodus Rabbah* 31:12 and 31:14

Like animals, human beings have basic physical needs. But unlike the rest of the animal kingdom, they also are also created "in the image of God"; that is humankind's glory. However, poverty forces a human being to focus his or her attention exclusively on fulfilling physical needs (most obviously, eating), and therefore, dehumanizes more than other types of suffering.

When the bread basket is empty [literally, when the barley is gone from the jar], strife comes knocking at the door.

—Ancient Jewish proverb quoted by Rabbi Papa
in the Babylonian Talmud, *Bava Mezia* 59a

This two-thousand-year-old proverb still is applicable. Studies have repeatedly shown that money problems are a major cause of marital strife.

A poor man's wisdom is scorned,
And his words are not heeded.

—Ecclesiastes 9:16

In addition to the other indignities the poor suffer, they are assumed to be less intelligent than those better off. A popular American aphorism declares: "If you're so smart, why aren't you rich?" In *Fiddler on the Roof,* Tevye longs for wealth because, among its benefits is the fact that others will then seek his counsel: "When you're rich, they think you really know."

Rabbinic Judaism tried to counter the natural tendency to demean the poor by telling stories of impoverished rabbis who were extraordinarily wise (Hillel and Akiva in their youth, as well as

Rabbi Joshua, who earned his living as a charcoal burner). It also warned communal authorities to make certain that poor children receive a free, high-quality education: "Neglect not the children of the poor, for from them shall come forth Torah" (Babylonian Talmud, *Nedarim* 81a).

> When a poor man eats chicken, one of them is sick.
> —Yiddish proverb

> God must hate a poor man, else why did he make him poor.
> —Sholem Aleichem, *Tevye the Dairyman*

Sholem Aleichem's bitter reflection notwithstanding, the Talmud, thousands of years earlier, implored those who suffer not to see themselves as cursed by God. In a remarkable, infrequently quoted passage, Rava denies the commonly expressed religious sentiment that whatever happens in this world must be God's will:

> Length of life, children, and sustenance depend not on one's merit, but on one's *mazal* [literally, constellation, or luck]. Consider [the third-century scholars] Rabbah and Rabbi Hisda. Both were saintly sages: when one prayed for rain, it came; when the other prayed for rain, it also came. Yet Rabbi Hisda lived to the age of ninety-two, but Rabbah only to age forty. In Rabbi Hisda's house, sixty wedding feasts were celebrated; in Rabbah's house sixty bereavements. In Rabbi Hisda's house, there was bread of the finest flour even for dogs, and it went to waste; in Rabbah's house, barley bread was served to human beings [barley normally was used as fodder for animals], and even that was hardly to be had.
> —Babylonian Talmud, *Moed Kattan* 28a; I have followed the translation of William Braude, translator of *The Book of Legends, Sefer Ha-Aggadah*, edited by Hayim Nakhman Bialik and Yehoshua Ravnitzky, page 604.

TWO MODERN JEWISH POEMS ON POVERTY

Family of Eight

Only two beds
for a family of eight.
Where do they sleep
when the hour is late?

Three with the father
and three with the mother—
small feet and fingers
entwined with each other.

And when it came time
to prepare for the night,
then Mama starts wishing
her death were in sight.

And what is the wonder
she'd rather be gone?
The grave's narrow too
but you lie there alone.

—Abraham Reisin (1876–1953); translated from the Yiddish by
Marcia Falk

Finally, another poet's bitter reflection about the poverty that
poisoned the lives of the first generation of Eastern European Jews
in America:

Mein Yingele (My Little Son)

I have a little boy, a fine little son.
When I see him, it seems to me I own the whole world.
But I seldom see him, my little son, when he is awake.
I always meet him when he sleeps.
I only see him at night.
My work drives me out early and makes me come home
late.

Strange to me is my own flesh and blood.
Strange to me is the look of my child.

When I come home shattered, wrapped up in darkness,
then my pale wife tells me how nicely our child plays,
how sweetly he chatters, how cleverly he asks:
"O Mother, good Mother, when will he bring me a penny,
   my good, good father?"
I listen and yes, it must, yes, yes, it must happen!
Father love blazes up in me. My child, I must see him.
I must stand by his cot and see and hear and look.
A dream stirs his lips: "O where is Daddy?"
I kiss the little blue eyes.
They open, O child! They see me and quickly they close.
There stands your father, dearest, there you have a penny!
A dream stirs his lips: "O where is Daddy?"
I become sad and oppressed, bitterly I think,
when you finally wake, my child,
you won't find me anymore.
   —Morris Rosenfeld (1862–1923); reprinted in Lionel Blue and
Jonathan Magonet, *How to Get Up When Life Gets You Down,*
pages 126–127

62

"A PHYSICIAN WHO HEALS FOR NOTHING IS WORTH NOTHING"

Medicine and Doctors

When men quarrel and one strikes the other with stone or fist, and he does not die but has to take to his bed . . . the assailant . . . must pay for his idleness and his cure.
—Exodus 21:18–19

[On this verse, the Talmud comments]: From this we learn that authorization was granted to the physician to heal.
—Babylonian Talmud, *Bava Kamma* 85a

That three thousand years ago the Torah mandated medical care perhaps helps explain the long-standing, oft-noted Jewish attraction to the art of healing. Well before the modern era, Jews served as physicians in courts throughout Europe and the Middle East; in fact, Maimonides and other of Judaism's foremost philosophers and rabbinic sages (see the *Encyclopedia Judaica* 11:1178–1211) were doctors.

In the absence of biblical support for medicine, Jews might have been drawn to the sort of thinking that characterizes Christian Scientists and Jehovah's Witnesses: that illness or any physical suffering must be cured by God without human intervention.

Judaism never has taught that all ailments that afflict mankind are divinely ordained. In the above biblical case, for example, the man is confined to his bed because his neighbor assaulted him. To assume that God instigated the neighbor to do so would be to deny one of Judaism's most basic tenets: that human beings have free will. While it certainly is true that God, if He so chooses, can cure the injured man, Jewish law *forbids* Jews to rely on such thinking:

> One may not rely on a miracle.
> —Babylonian Talmud, *Pesachim* 64b

Thus, common sense, Talmud style, forbids a person to depend on God to cure him or her when alternative treatments are available.

The same commonsensical approach characterizes a talmudic maxim about doctors:

> A physician who heals for nothing is worth nothing.
> —Babylonian Talmud, *Bava Kamma* 85a

While the Rabbis reserve singular praise for doctors who take no payment from the poor [see the following passage], this maxim has legal implications. As Maimonides rules: "[Thus], if one who injures another person says to him, 'I will heal you, or I have a physician who will treat you for nothing,' we pay no attention to him; but he must bring a competent physician to treat him for a fee" (*Mishneh Torah*, "Laws Concerning Wounding and Damaging" 2:18).

A SENSITIVE SURGEON

Abba the surgeon [i.e., bloodletter] used to receive a daily greeting from the Heavenly Academy [the commentaries explain that a voice from heaven would call out to him, "*Shalom aleikhem,*" "Peace unto you"].

But [the great scholar] Abbaye received such a greeting only every Friday.

And [the great scholar] Rabba received it only once a year, on the eve of Yom Kippur.

Abbaye felt slighted because Abba the surgeon received the higher distinction. But Abbaye was informed: "You cannot perform the kind of deeds performed by him."

What were the deeds of Abba the surgeon?

When he performed the operation of bloodletting, he had two separate consulting rooms, one for men and one for women. . . .

When a female patient would come to him, he would have her put on a garment with many slits so that he did not look upon her exposed body. Outside his consulting room he had placed a box into which his patients deposited the fees. Those who had money paid there. Those who did not have money could leave the house without being embarrassed.

—Babylonian Talmud, *Ta'anit* 21b

CYNICISM ABOUT DOCTORS

Amid such a plethora of praise for physicians, one comes across a truly shocking quote:

[Even] the best of physicians is destined for hell.
—Mishna, *Kiddushin* 4:14

This example of talmudic hyperbole, as demoralizing as it may be to doctors, is intended to underscore the life-and-death significance of their work. A parallel: If a person has led an exemplary life but drives carelessly one night and kills someone, the evil of what he or she has done overshadows the good. From the victim's perspective, or that of his/her family, the person's only relevant activity is his or her negligent driving. Similarly, although a physician heals many people, he or she undoubtedly will make errors, sometimes fatal ones, in the course of a lifetime's practice, and/or refuse treatment to a poor person who might die of his ailment.

The former Israeli Chief Rabbi Isaac Herzog likewise sees this statement as hyperbolic: "Much, rather too much, has been made of [this] statement. . . . [In examining other rabbinic dictums] we see that judges and schoolmasters are subjected to the same categoric condemnation. Physicians thus find themselves in good company! . . . In reality all [that this statement]amounts to is a severe criticism of contemporary physicians, many of whom fail to maintain that high level of devotion to duty which the healing art, precisely because of the great responsibilities it entails, demands from the practitioner" (*Judaism: Law and Ethics,* page 157).

Despite Rabbi Herzog's eloquent explanation, doctors have been the objects of no small amount of criticism, some of it so extreme as to be humorous:

> It was difficult for the Angel of Death to kill everybody in the whole world so he appointed doctors to assist him.
>
> —Rabbi Nahman of Bratslav

> Anyone who goes to a psychiatrist ought to have his head examined.
>
> —Samuel Goldwyn (1882–1974)

ADVICE TO DOCTORS

A thirteenth-century plea for preventive medicine

> Who is a wise doctor? He who knows to warn his patient how to avoid becoming sick. Whereas he who does not know how to forewarn [though he heals] is not a wise doctor.
>
> —Medieval *Sefer Hasidim,* section 592

> The more you demand for your service . . . the greater will it appear in the eyes of the people. Your art will be looked upon as insignificant by those whom you treat for nothing.
>
> —Isaac Israeli, tenth-century Egyptian physician and philosopher,
>
> *Doctor's Guide*

Comfort the sufferer by the promise of healing, even when you are not confident, for thus you may assist his natural powers.

—Isaac Israeli, ibid.

About a millennium later, George Bernard Shaw expressed more humorously a similar thought in his play *Misalliance*: "Optimistic lies have such immense therapeutic value that a doctor who cannot tell them convincingly has mistaken his profession."

63

"FOR THERE WILL BE NO ONE TO REPAIR IT AFTER YOU"

Toward a Jewish Ecology

When God created Adam, He led him around the Garden of Eden and said to him: "Behold my works! See how beautiful they are, how excellent! All that I have created, for your sake did I create it. See to it that you do not spoil and destroy my world; for if you do, there will be no one to repair it after you."

—*Ecclesiastes Rabbah* 7:13

BAL TASHKHIT, THE BIBLICAL LAW THAT FORBIDS UNNECESSARY DESTRUCTION

When you besiege a city . . . you shall not destroy its [fruit] trees. . . . You eat of them,g do not cut them down; for man's life depends on the trees of the field.

—*Deuteronomy* 20:19

In wartime, people are prone to ignore moral issues, let alone ecological ones. But even war does not justify needless destruction of the environment.

438

When there is a significant reason to destroy some trees (e.g., an economic motive), Jewish law permits doing so. Maimonides rules that it is permitted to cut down a fruit tree if it is harming more valuable plants, damaging another person's property, or if its wood has become more valuable than the fruit it produces. Because the Torah forbids only *pointless* destruction, it also is permitted to cut down a tree that yields neither edible fruit nor nuts (*Mishneh Torah,* "Laws of Kings," 6:8–9).

> [The Midrash comments on Exodus 36:20, which commands that the Tabernacle be built of an acacia tree]: God set an example for all time, that when a man is about to build his house from a fruit-producing tree, he should be reminded: If when the supreme King of kings commanded the Temple to be erected, His instructions were to use only such trees as are not fruit-bearing—even though all things belong to Him—how much more should this be so in your case?
>
> —*Exodus Rabbah* 35:2

The principle of *bal tashkhit* (literally, not to destroy), is rooted in the notion that "The earth is the Lord's and the fullness thereof" (Psalms 24:1). It is broadened in rabbinic law to include any gratuitous act of destruction:

> Not only one who cuts down food trees, but also one who [purposely and impulsively] smashes household goods, tears clothes, demolishes a building, stops up a spring, or destroys food violates the command, "You must not destroy . . . " (Deuteronomy 20:19).
>
> —Moses Maimonides, *Mishneh Torah,* "Laws of Kings," 6:10

Among other things, Maimonides's law justifies the age-old battle of parents to stop their children from engaging in food fights.

Among pious, particularly mystically inclined, Jews, all creation reflects God's will, and so must be regarded reverently. Rabbi Aryeh

Levin, a lifelong friend of Abraham Isaac Kook, the first Israeli Chief Rabbi, recalls an episode from the very first day he met Rav Kook:

> With God's grace, in the year 5665 [1904/5], I visited Jaffa ... and went to pay my respects to its Chief Rabbi [who was then Rabbi Kook]. He received me warmly ... and after the afternoon prayer, I accompanied him as he went out into the fields, as was his habit, to concentrate his thoughts. As we were walking, I plucked some flower or plant; he trembled, and quietly told me that he always took great care not to pluck—unless it were for some benefit—anything that could grow, for there was no plant below that did not have its *mazal* [literally, constellation, but also understood as "guardian angel"] above. Everything that grows says something, every stone whispers some secret, all creation sings.
>
> —Aryeh Levin, *Lahai Roi* (Hebrew), pages 15, 16; Rabbi Levin claimed that this particular encounter with Rabbi Kook taught him what it means to show compassion to all creatures.

Another implication of *bal tashkhit,* even for those who lack Rabbi Kook's reverence toward all creation, is to prohibit the destruction of something that can be useful to others:

> One should be trained not to be destructive. When you bury a person, do not waste garments by burying them in the grave. It is better to give them to the poor than to cast them to worms and moths. Anyone who buries the dead in an expensive garment violates the negative command of *bal tashkhit.*
>
> —Moses Maimonides, *Mishneh Torah,* "Laws of Mourning," 14:24

Similarly, people who throw out used clothing without making an effort to place them in the hands of the needy are not only being thoughtless, they also are violating a specific biblical directive.

The talmudic declaration that people should be compelled not to act in the manner of the citizens of Sodom (Babylonian Talmud, *Ketubot* 103a) also underscores the commandment not to waste things that can be beneficial to others. According to the Rabbis, one of the evils of the Sodomites was their refusal to help others, even when doing so cost them nothing.

Rabbi Aaron Lichtenstein suggests a few modern examples in which people frequently refrain from helping others, usually because of laziness. Thus, people who have tickets for a play or concert, but are unable to attend, frequently discard the tickets without attempting to find a friend who could use them. Similarly, people who move out of an apartment discard their keys without offering them to the incoming tenants.

RESPECT FOR THE ENVIRONMENT

... Graveyards and tanneries [which emit foul odors] are located at least 50 cubits [75 feet] outside a city. A tannery can only be operated on the east side of a city [i.e., that side of the town which will carry the bad odor away from the residential area].

—Mishna *Bava Bathra* 2:9

Our Rabbis taught: The pious ones of old used to hide their thorns and broken glass in the midst of their fields at a depth of three handbreaths [approximately eleven inches] below the surface, so that even a plow could not be hindered by them. Rabbi Sheshet used to throw them into the fire. Raba threw them into the Tigris River.

—Babylonian Talmud, *Bava Kamma* 30a

Traditional Jewish law already recognized the desirability of zoning, i.e., of separating business and residential neighborhoods:

If a person desires to open a shop in the courtyard, his neighbor may stop him because he [or she] will be kept awake by the noise of people going in and out of the shop.

—Babylonian Talmud, *Bava Bathra* 20b

Some eight hundred years ago, Maimonides (a doctor as well as rabbi)—in a passage that should give Jewish environmentalists great *nakhas*—noted the sharp contrast between urban and rural air:

> The quality of urban air compared to the air in the deserts and forests is like thick and turbulent water compared to pure and light water. And this is because in the cities with their tall buildings and narrow roads, the pollution that comes from their residents, their waste, cadavers, and offal from their cattle, and the stench of their adulterated food, makes the entire air malodorous, turbulent, reeking and thick . . . although no one is aware of it.
>
> —Moses Maimonides, *The Preservation of Youth: Essays on Health*, pages 70–71

A JEWISH ECOLOGY: WHAT MAKES IT DIFFERENT

> Judaism, in contradistinction to paganism [editor's note: and to some radical contemporary ecologists as well], refuses to ascribe . . . holiness to nature and natural objects as such. . . . The God of the Bible is beyond, not within, nature: "In the beginning, God created heaven and earth."
>
> —Norman Lamm, "Ecology in Jewish Law and Theology," page 173

Within Judaism's hierarchy of values, human beings are above the animal and vegetative worlds. Thus Jewish law sanctions animal experimentation when the results can help reduce illness among people, as well as the depletion of natural resources when there is a compelling reason to do so.

> A Jewish ecology . . . [is] not based on the assumption that we are no different from other living creatures. It [begins] with the opposite idea: We have a special responsibility precisely because we *are* different, because we know what we are doing.
>
> —Rabbi Harold Kushner, *To Life!,* page 59

442

A summing up:

Two people were once fighting over a piece of land. Each claimed ownership, and each bolstered the claim with apparent proof. After arguing for a long time, they agreed to resolve their conflict by putting the case before a rabbi.

The rabbi . . . listened carefully, but could not reach a decision. Both parties seemed to be right. Finally, the rabbi said, "Since I cannot decide to whom this land belongs, let us ask the land."

The rabbi put an ear to the ground, and after a moment stood up. "My friends, the land says it belongs to neither of you—you belong to it."

—Traditional Jewish folktale retold in David Stein, ed., *A Garden of Choice Fruit:200 Classic Jewish Quotes on Human Beings and the Environment,* page 54. This book is a particularly rich collection of source material on Judaism and the environment.

64

"HIS MERCY IS UPON ALL HIS WORKS"

Jewish Ethics Toward Animals

Few Jews are aware that the Ten Commandments include a law legislating kind treatment of animals: the Fourth Commandment, which ordains the Sabbath, mandates that:

> " . . . the seventh day is a Sabbath unto the Lord your God: you shall not do any work, you, your son or daughter, your male or female servant, or your *cattle* . . . "
>
> —Exodus 20:10

Given that, until the end of the nineteenth century, employees in this country sometimes were expected to work seven days a week, this three-thousand-year-old concern for animals is remarkable. Among the Torah's 613 commandments, several others call for the compassionate treatment of animals:

> You shall not plow with an ox and mule harnessed together [since both animals, being of unequal size and strength, will suffer].
>
> —Deuteronomy 22:10

> If along the road, you come upon a bird's nest . . . with fledglings or eggs and the mother sitting over the fledglings or on the eggs, do not take the mother together with her young. Let the mother [fly away], and only [then] take the young. . . .
>
> —Deuteronomy 22:6–7

> No animal . . . shall be slaughtered on the same day with its young.
>
> —Leviticus 22:28

On these last two verses, Maimonides waxes eloquent:

> It is prohibited to kill an animal and its young . . . in such a manner that the young is slain in the sight of its mother, for the pain of the animals under such circumstances is very great. There is no difference in this case between the pain of man and the pain of other living beings, since the love and tenderness of the mother for her young ones . . . exists not only in man but in most living beings. . . .
>
> The same reason applies to the law that obligates us to let the mother fly away when we take the young. . . . If the law provides that such grief not be caused to cattle or birds, how much more careful must we be not to cause grief to our fellow man.
>
> —*The Guide to the Perplexed* 3:48

Maimonides's concern with animals' suffering also is reflected in his legal code:

> If one encounters two animals, one crouching under its burden and the other unburdened because the owner needs someone to help him load, he is obligated to first unload the burdened animal because of the commandment to prevent suffering to animals.
>
> —Maimonides, *Mishneh Torah*, "Laws of Murder and Preservation of Life," 13:13

The Talmud assumes that animals suffer more than human beings from hunger, presumably because an unfed animal (like an infant) has no idea if it ever will be fed. Thus:

> A person is prohibited to eat until he first feeds his ani-
> mals.
>
> —Babylonian Talmud, *Berakhot* 40a

Initiated at a time when many Jews were farmers, this law is
still in force: A Jew is expected to feed his pets before he or she sits
down to breakfast. Elsewhere, the Talmud rules that a man is forbidden to acquire a domestic animal or bird unless he has sufficient
means to provide it with suitable food.

Because animals, particularly smaller, nonaggressive ones, often
depend on human beings, how a person treats them becomes an
important touchstone in assessing his or her goodness. A famous
rabbinic midrash claims it was the kind treatment of animals that
motivated God to designate Moses to lead the Jews from Egypt:

> Once, while Moses was tending the flock of his father-in-
> law, Jethro, one young sheep ran away. Moses ran after
> it until the sheep reached a shady place, where he found
> a pool of water and began to drink. When Moses reached
> the sheep, he said: "I did not know you ran away because
> you were thirsty. Now, you must be exhausted [from run-
> ning]." Moses put the sheep on his shoulders and carried
> him [back to the herd]. God said, "Because you tend the
> sheep belonging to human beings with such mercy, by
> your life I swear you shall be the shepherd of My sheep,
> Israel."
>
> —*Exodus Rabbah* 2:2

Similarly, the most famous image of God's compassion in the
Book of Psalms is as a tender of sheep: "The Lord is my shepherd,
I shall not want" (23:1).

A good man does not sell his beast to a cruel person.

—Medieval *Sefer Hasidim*, summary of paragraph 142

Although Jewish law permits slaughtering animals and the eating of meat, the Rabbis were severely critical of those who lacked mercy toward animals. Of no less a figure than Rabbi Judah the Prince (editor of the Mishna, and the preeminent rabbi of the early third century), it is told:

> The sufferings of Rabbi Judah came to him because of a certain incident, and left him in the same way. What was the incident that led to his suffering?
>
> A calf was once taken to be slaughtered. It [escaped, and] ran to Rabbi Judah, where it hid its head under his cloak, and cried.
>
> Rabbi Judah, however, [pushed it away, and] said, "Go. It was for this that you were created."
>
> It was then said [in heaven], "Since he has no pity, let us bring suffering upon him." [For the next thirteen years, Rabbi Judah suffered from various painful ailments.]
>
> And how did his sufferings end?
>
> One day, his maid was sweeping the house, and she came upon some young rats. She was about to sweep them out of the house, when Rabbi Judah stopped her, "Let them be. As it is written in Psalms, 'His mercy is upon all His works'" [145:9].
>
> It was then said [in heaven], "Since He is merciful, let us be merciful to him" [and he was immediately healed].
>
> —Babylonian Talmud, *Bava Mezia* 85a

*   *   *

In general, the extraordinary emphasis the Rabbis placed on intellectual achievement limited their esteem for the animal kingdom. Yet one unusual talmudic passage attributes various moral virtues to different animals:

> If the Torah had not been given [at Sinai], we could have learned modesty from the cat, honesty from the ant, chas-

447

tity from the dove, and good manners from the rooster, who first coaxes, then mates.

—Babylonian Talmud, *Eruvin* 100b

Rashi, the eleventh-century Talmud commentator, explains that the cat does not defecate in people's presence, and covers its excrement. Ants do not steal from each other, and the dove always is monogamous.

HUNTING

The laws of kosher slaughter guaranteed that an animal was permitted as food only if it was slaughtered with one quick stroke that caused instantaneous death. Any prolongation of the animal's death agony rendered its meat *treif* (forbidden). A ritual slaughterer (*shochet*) thus had both an economic and a moral incentive to hasten the animal's death.

All animals killed through hunting were unkosher. This prohibition impressed itself upon the Jewish psyche; today, hunting remains a singularly unpopular sport among Jews, even among those who don't observe *kashrut*.

Two centuries ago, a Jew who had extensive social dealings with non-Jews asked Rabbi Ezekiel Landau of Prague (1713–1793) if he was permitted to hunt with his gentile friends, as long as he did not eat of the killed animal's meat. The rabbi's blunt response is frequently cited as establishing Jewish law's attitude toward hunting:

> But how can a Jew kill a living thing without any benefit to anyone, and engage in hunting merely to satisfy "the enjoyable use of his time"?
>
> For according to the Talmud, it is permitted to slay wild animals only when they invade human settlements, but to pursue them in the woods, their own dwelling place, when they are not invading human habitations, is prohibited. Such pursuit simply means following the desires of one's heart. [Rabbi Landau seems to be echoing the verse in Genesis 8:21, "The tendency [alternatively, desires] of

man's heart is toward evil from his youth."]

In the case of one who needs to do this and who derives his livelihood from hunting, we would not say that hunting is necessarily cruel, as we slaughter cattle and birds and fish for the needs of man. . . . But as regards one whose hunting has nothing to do with earning his livelihood, this is sheer cruelty.

—Responsa *Nodeh B'Yehuda,* on *Yoreh Deah* 2:10

When a Jew says he is going hunting to amuse himself, he lies.

—Walter Rathenau (1867–1922), foreign minister in the Weimar Republic, in a conversation with Albert Einstein

The moral and psychological reasons for this opposition were articulated more than a century ago by the Jewish-born German writer Heinrich Heine (1797–1856): "My ancestors did not belong to the hunters as much as to the hunted, and the idea of attacking the descendants of those who were our comrades in misery goes against my grain."

VEGETARIANISM

The Bible contains two descriptions of paradise: the Garden of Eden in the distant past, and Isaiah's prophecy of a messianic age in the future. Although the "book of books" does not provide much information about either, it does disclose that the world once was, and again will be, herbivorous.

God said [to Adam and Eve]: "See, I give you every seed-bearing plant that is upon all the earth, and every tree that has seed-bearing fruit; they shall be yours for food."

—Genesis 1:29

God also restricted animals to a meatless diet: To them He gave "all the green plants for food" (Genesis 1:30).

The wolf shall dwell with the lamb,
The leopard lie down with the kid.
And the lion, like the ox, shall eat straw.
>   —Isaiah 11:6,8, prophesying about life in the messianic age

Regarding God's motives for initially forbidding meat, a medieval Jewish philosopher comments:

> In the killing of animals there is cruelty . . . and the accustoming of oneself to the bad habit of shedding innocent blood.
>   —Joseph Albo, *Sefer Ha-Ikkarim*, Vol. III, chapter 15.
> I came across this quote, as I did many others in this section,
> in Richard Schwartz's comprehensive and passionately
> argued book, *Judaism and Vegetarianism*.

My wife, Dvorah, who worked for many years as a translator, editor, and assistant to Isaac Bashevis Singer, the Nobel Prize–winning novelist and a strict vegetarian, recalls that he often said, "There will be no end of wars in the world until people stop killing animals. Slaughter and justice cannot dwell together."

Just as God is depicted as initially forbidding meat to humans, so too it is He who later permitted it. Generations after the Garden of Eden, the world had turned evil, and God annihilated all of humanity except for Noah and his family. He then permitted them and their descendants to eat meat:

> Every creature that lives shall be yours to eat. . . . You must not, however, eat flesh with its blood in it.
>   —Genesis 9:3–4

How to account for God's turnabout? The Bible doesn't explain it. But as a result of this dispensation, the nature of the human-animal relationship changes: Beasts now dread people (Genesis 9:2).

With the permission to eat meat, however, the Bible now imposes an absolute prohibition against consuming blood. Biblical scholar Jacob Milgrom notes that "none of Israel's neighbors possessed this absolute and universally binding blood prohibition. Blood is everywhere [else] partaken of as food. . . . Man has a right to nourishment, not to life. Hence the blood, which is the symbol of life, must be drained, returned to the universe, to God" ("The Biblical Diet as an Ethical System," *Interpretation,* July 1963).

Based on this enactment, the laws of kosher slaughter require that after an animal is slaughtered, its blood must be fully drained. What eventually became a Jewish obsession with not eating any creature's blood (i.e., salting the meat so that every drop of blood is removed) helped to produce a general Jewish abhorrence of bloodshed. Thus, Jews have committed fewer violent crimes than their non-Jewish neighbors in every society with which we are familiar.

KASHRUT AND THE VEGETARIAN IDEAL

A man should not eat meat unless he has a special craving for it.
—Babylonian Talmud, *Hullin* 84a, basing itself on the wording of
Deuteronomy 12:20, which permits one
to eat meat when "you have the urge to eat meat"

The laws of *kashrut* come to teach us that a Jew's first preference should be a vegetarian meal. If, however, one cannot control a craving for meat, it should be kosher meat, which would serve as a reminder that the animal being eaten is a creature of God, that the death of such a creature cannot be taken lightly, that hunting for sport is forbidden, that we cannot treat any living thing callously, and that we are responsible for what happens to other beings (human or animal) even if we did not personally come into contact with them.
—Pinchas Peli, *Torah Today,* page 118

The dietary laws are intended to teach us compassion and lead us gently to vegetarianism.
—Rabbi Shlomo Riskin, *The Jewish Week* (New York),
August 14, 1987, page 21

While Jewish scholars long have noted that one important out-growth of *kashrut* was limiting gratuitous pain to slaughtered animals, Richard Schwartz, a committed Jewish vegetarian, argues that *kashrut* laws today sometimes are perverted to permit cruelty to animals:

> [How are veal calves raised?] After being allowed to nurse for only one or two days, the veal calf is removed from its mother, with no consideration of its need for motherly nourishment, affection and physical contact. The calf is locked in a small slotted stall without enough space to move around, stretch or even lie down. To obtain the pale tender veal desired by consumers, the calf is purposely kept anemic by giving it a special high-calorie, iron-free diet. The calf craves iron so much that it would lick the iron fittings on its stall and its own urine if permitted to do so; it is prevented from turning by having its head tethered to the stall. . . . The calf leaves its pen only when taken for slaughter.
>
> —Richard Schwartz, *Judaism and Vegetarianism,* page 28

Defenders of eating veal claim that there are farms where veal is not raised in this cruel manner. The next time you are offered this meat, think about Schwartz's description and ask the person offering it whether he or she is certain that the animal was raised on the kind of farm that did not practice such cruelty.

For those who believe that vegetarians manifest too much sympathy for "dumb creatures," it is worth remembering the moral test posed by British philosopher Jeremy Bentham (1748–1832). The test of our behavior toward animals must be "not can they reason, not can they talk, but *can they suffer?*" (quoted in *The Extended Circle,* edited by Jon Wynne-Tyson, page 28).

TWO TWENTIETH-CENTURY REFLECTIONS ON JEWS, VEGETARIANISM, AND THE ANIMAL WORLD

Now I can look at you in peace; I don't eat you anymore.
—Franz Kafka, ruminating in front of some fish at an aquarium; cited in Richard Schwartz, *Judaism and Vegetarianism*, page 153

When asked if he was a vegetarian for health reasons, Isaac Bashevis Singer answered: "Yes, for the chicken's health."

PART V

MODERN JEWISH EXPERIENCE

Major Themes

65

ANTISEMITISM

In the warmest of hearts there is a cold spot for the Jews.
—Irving Howe (1920–1993)

[For the Jews] the world is divided into places where they
cannot live, and places which they cannot enter.
—Chaim Weizmann, 1936

Weizmann, the "father" of the Balfour Declaration, who later
served as Israel's first president, made this statement three years after
Hitler's rise to power. Indeed, other countries' unwillingness to offer
refuge to Jews hoping to flee Germany helped convince the German
leader that he had international support for his anti-Jewish acts.

Some thirty-five years earlier, the British-Jewish novelist Israel
Zangwill had expressed a similar frustration: "Homicides had more
cities of refuge in ancient Palestine than the Rumanian Jews have in
the whole world." Zangwill was referring to an unusual provision
in Numbers 35:16ff., which designated six cities of refuge in ancient
Israel to which perpetrators of manslaughter (but not murderers)
could flee, and where they would be protected from retribution by
their victims' families.

If my theory of relativity is proven successful, Germany
will claim me as a German and France will declare that I
am a citizen of the world. If my theory should prove to be

457

untrue, then France will say I am a German, and Germany will say I am a Jew.

> —Albert Einstein, *The New York Times,* February 16, 1930,
> quoting from a speech given by Einstein
> at the Sorbonne, in December 1929

In 1817, a German-Jewish political essayist and champion of Jewish emancipation expressed a similar combination of weary realism and biting sarcasm:

> On Sundays [the Jews] were prohibited from leaving the ghetto, to spare them from being beaten up by drunkards. . . . On public holidays, they had to reenter the ghetto by six sharp lest overexposure to the sun ruin their complexion. . . . Then, too, a great many of the streets, because their bumpy pavement was bad for the feet, were altogether closed to them.
>
> —Ludwig Boerne (1786–1837)

> Since my little son is only half-Jewish, would it be all right if he went into the pool only up to his waist?
>
> —Groucho Marx (1895–1977), in a telegram to a country club
> that had barred his son from entering; attributed

> An antisemite is a person who hates Jews more than is absolutely necessary.
>
> —Jewish proverb

*   *   *

THE WORLD'S FIRST TWO ANTISEMITES: PHARAOH AND HAMAN

A new king arose over Egypt . . . and he said to his people, "Look, the Israelite people are much too numerous for us. Let us deal shrewdly with them, so that they may not increase; otherwise, in the event of war, they may join our enemies in fighting us." [Pharaoh then went on to enslave the Hebrews, but still their numbers increased.] Then

458

Pharaoh charged all his people saying, "Every boy that is born [to the Hebrews] you shall throw into the Nile, but let every girl live."

—Exodus 1:8–10, 22

There is a certain people, scattered and dispersed among the other peoples in all the provinces of your realm, whose laws are different from those of any other people and who do not obey the King's laws; and it is not in Your Majesty's interest to tolerate them. If it please Your Majesty, let an order be made in writing for them to be exterminated.

—Haman advising King Ahasuerus in Esther 3:8–9

The themes sounded by the world's first recorded antisemites have been echoed ever since by their spiritual descendants: The Jews are too numerous, they are a traitorous fifth column, their religion is contrary to the interests of the state, and ultimately, "the Jewish problem" should be solved by killing them.

WHY THE JEWS?

Two conflicting explanations are commonly offered for the "why?" of antisemitism. The first is that there is no "why"; that Jews are hated for no particular reason, and those who hate them simply manufacture reasons to justify their feelings. The French philosopher Jean-Paul Sartre (1905–1980), author of the most widely read study of antisemitism, *Anti-Semite and Jew,* is the leading exponent of this view:

The Jew only serves [the antisemite] as a pretext; elsewhere his counterpart will make use of the Negro or the man of yellow skin.

—*Anti-Semite and Jew,* page 54

According to Sartre, Judaism and the Jewish people exist *only* because of antisemitism:

459

The Jew is one whom other men consider a Jew. It is the anti-Semite who makes the Jew. . . . It is neither their past, their religion, nor their soil, that unites the sons of Israel. . . . The sole tie that binds them is the hostility and disdain of the societies which surround them.

—*Anti-Semite and Jew,* pages 13, 67, 91

In an unintentionally insulting explanation of Jew-hatred, Sartre concludes: "We [non-Jews] have created this variety of men who have no meaning [except as scapegoats]" (page 135).

Thus, according to Sartre, antisemitism has nothing to do with the Jewishness of the Jews. In recent years, Konstantyn Jelenski, a Polish poet and literary critic, discussing his own country's long history of Jew-hatred, has sarcastically noted the extraordinary naïveté of such a theory:

Poles have never come out against Jews "because they are Jews," but because Jews are dirty, greedy, mendacious, because they wear earlocks, speak jargon, do not want to assimilate, and *also* because they *do* assimilate, cease using their jargon, are nattily dressed, and want to be regarded as Poles. Because they lack culture and because they are overly cultured. Because they are superstitious, backward and ignorant, and because they are damnably capable, progressive, and ambitious. Because they have long, hooked noses, and because it is sometimes difficult to distinguish them from "pure Poles." Because they crucified Christ and practice ritual murder and pore over the Talmud, and because they disdain their own religion and are atheists. . . . Because they are bankers and capitalists and because they are Communists and agitators. But in *no* case because they are Jews.

—Konstantyn Jelenski in the Parisian journal *Kultura,* May 1968

A more moderate, and less offensive, understanding of antisemitism than Sartre's was offered by Max Nordau, Herzl's closest ally in the founding of the Zionist movement:

460

"If you have to drown a dog," says the proverb, "you must first declare him to be mad." All kinds of vices are falsely attributed to the Jews, because people want to prove to themselves that they have a right to detest them. But the primary sentiment is the detestation of the Jews.

—Max Nordau (1849–1923), in a speech before the
First Zionist Congress, August 1897

*　　*　　*

Sigmund Freud, Jewish writers Maurice Samuel and Dennis Prager, and Catholic theologian Jacques Maritain are among those who offer an alternative understanding of the reason for antisemitism, i.e., that it involves hatred of the Jews' ideas:

We must not forget that all the people who now excel in the practice of anti-Semitism became Christians only in relatively recent times, sometimes forced to it by bloody compulsion. One might say they all are "badly christened"; under the thin veneer of Christianity they have remained what their ancestors were, barbarically polytheistic. They have not yet overcome their grudge against the new religion which was forced on them. . . . The hatred for Judaism is at bottom hatred for Christianity.

—Sigmund Freud, *Moses and Monotheism,* pages 116–117

To say that a man has hallucinations when he is hungry makes sense. To say that a man has hallucinations only about Jews when he is hungry does not.

—Maurice Samuel (1895–1972), *The Great Hatred*

Nobody loves his alarm clock.

—Maurice Samuel

The Jews are the world's miner's canary. Canaries are taken down to mines because they quickly die upon exposure to noxious fumes. When the miner sees the canary dead, he knows there are noxious fumes to be fought [or he too will die]. So it is with the Jews. Noxious moral

461

forces often focus first on the Jews. But their ultimate tar-
gets are the moral values that the Jews represent. Non-
Jews who share Jews' values . . . make a fatal error when
they dismiss antisemites as the Jews' problem.

—Dennis Prager, "What Bitburg Revealed About the Jews," *Ultimate Issues,* Summer 1985, page 1

Moral non-Jews who fail to counter antisemites often suffer because of them. For example, during the 1930s, American isolationists regarded Nazi antisemitism as an unpleasant feature of a country
that was otherwise highly civilized. Throughout the 1930s and early
1940s, they refused to see Hitler and the Nazis as dangerously evil,
and urged Americans not to fight them. Indeed, the leading isola-
tionist, Charles Lindbergh, warned American Jews against fomenting anti-Nazi feelings in the United States (pages 488–490). But had
Hitler been confronted earlier—when his evil was primarily expressed through his antisemitism—not only would six million Jewish
lives have been saved, so too would fifty million non-Jewish ones.

During the 1970s, the Ugandan dictator Idi Amin sent a message
to the United Nations announcing his admiration for Adolf Hitler's
"Final Solution." At the time, only Jews and the American ambassador to the U.N. protested. Fortunately, Amin was in no position
to carry out his evil designs against the Jews. But several hundred
thousand Ugandan Christians whom Amin later butchered suffered
from his evil nature, which should have been universally apparent
from his antisemitic utterances.

When Ayatollah Ruhollah Khomeini assumed power in Iran, his
first act was to occupy the Israeli embassy in Teheran, which he
immediately turned over to the PLO. The world dismissed this as
the Jews' problem, until the Iranians took over the American embassy less than a year later, and held over a hundred people hostage.

Finally, widespread hatred of Israel in the Arab world is often
dismissed mainly or entirely as a Jewish problem, one that reveals
little about the Arab or Islamic states. But clearly, the Arab world's
hatred for Jewish nationhood is not an unrepresentative quirk of
otherwise tolerant lovers of democracy. Rather, it is a quite precise
moral indicator, as evidenced by the Christians of Lebanon, who

have suffered far worse from Muslim hatred than have Israel's Jews. As Dennis Prager and I have written, "There is often a direct correlation between the ferocity of a Muslim leader's hatred of the Jewish state, and his hatred of democracy and other Western values. Iran's Khomeini, Libya's Qaddafi and Iraq's Hussein are three such examples. Conversely, Arab and other Middle Eastern Muslim societies that are less characterized by despotism and wanton cruelty, such as Tunisia and Turkey, are also characterized by a greater tolerance of the Jews" (*Why the Jews?*, pages 197–198).

Thus, moral non-Jews who do not heed the universal implications of antisemitism should realize that they, and certainly their values, may be its victims as well.

> Israel . . . is to be found at the very heart of the world's structure [teaching] the world to be discontented and restless as long as the world has not God. . . . It is the vocation of Israel which the world hates.
>
> —Jacques Maritain (1882–1973), *A Christian Looks at the Jewish Question*, pages 29–30

*　　*　　*

ANTISEMITISM: THE UNAPPEASABLE HATRED

> A Jew passed in front of Hadrian [the second-century Roman emperor] and greeted him. The king asked, "Who are you?" He answered, "I am a Jew." Hadrian exclaimed, "How dare a Jew pass in front of Hadrian and greet him?" and ordered, "Off with his head!" Another Jew passed and, seeing what happened to the first man, did not greet him. Hadrian asked, "Who are you?" He answered, "A Jew." He exclaimed, "How dare a Jew pass in front of Hadrian without giving a greeting?" and again ordered, "Off with his head!" His senators said, "We cannot understand your actions. He who greeted you was put to death, and he who did not greet you was put to death!" Hadrian replied, "Do you dare to advise me how I am to deal with those I hate?"
>
> —*Lamentations Rabbah* 3:9 commenting on verse 3:58

463

Hadrian acknowledged what most antisemites deny: Their hatred of Jews is unassuageable by any Jewish behavior. Thus, antisemites who fault Jews for "pushing in where they are not wanted" presumably would find no fault with those Jews who ghettoize themselves and remain within their own community. Yet studies have shown that the very antisemites who despise Jews for their "incursions" into the majority culture also are apt to denounce them for "clannishly sticking together."

Antisemites frequently reach for the argument that sounds most plausible. Thus, Jew-haters in the former Soviet Union long focused on Jews as capitalists who were subverting communism, while American antisemites accused Jews of being communists and subverting capitalism.

It is useless to try to reason with these disciples of Hadrian. As the nineteenth-century German historian Theodore Mommsen noted: "You are mistaken if you believe that anything at all can be achieved by reason. In years past I thought so myself and kept protesting against the monstrous infamy that is antisemitism. But it is useless, completely useless" (cited in Deborah Lipstadt, *Denying the Holocaust*, page 1).

ANTISEMITISM: THE DOUBLE STANDARD

The fellows who say to you, "I expect more of the Jews," don't believe them. *They expect less.* What they're really saying is, "Okay, we know you're a bunch of ravenous bastards, and given half the chance you'd eat up half the world, let alone poor Palestine. We know all these things about you, and so we're going to get you now. And how? Every time you make a move, we're going to say, 'But we expect *more* of Jews, Jews are supposed to behave *better.*'"

Jews are supposed to behave better? After all that has happened? I would have thought that it was the *non-Jews* whose behavior could stand a little improvement. Why are we the only people who belong to this wonderful exclusive moral club that's behaving badly?

—Philip Roth, *The Counterlife*, pages 178–179

CHRISTIAN ANTISEMITISM

And the people, to a man, shouted back, "His blood be
on our heads and the heads of our children."
                                                    —Matthew 27:25

According to Matthew, each year on Passover, the Roman procurator (in this case, Pontius Pilate), offered the Jews gathered in a
Jerusalem square the opportunity to save the life of a prisoner condemned to death. That year, the choice offered was between a brig-
and and anti-Roman revolutionary named Barabbas and Jesus.
According to Matthew, the Jews without exception chose Barabbas,
and shouted the above. (Obviously, it was important to Matthew
that *all* the Jews shouted this response; that way, all their descendants could be implicated in their ancestors' supposed crime.)

However, every element in this story (Matthew 27:11–26), including the mob's cry, can be shown to be replete with historical
inaccuracies and incongruities:

First, Matthew asserts that although Pilate offered the Jews a
choice between Jesus and Barabbas, his own desire was to save Jesus.
In that case, as the late Israeli Supreme Court Justice Haim Cohn
asked in *The Trial and Death of Jesus*, "Why then did he not pardon
him?" (page 165). Pilate functioned in Judea as a dictator; his power
was only limited by the Roman emperor. Even had the Jews had the
privilege of demanding that he release one prisoner, they certainly
had no right to compel Pilate to crucify a man he wanted to save.

Second, it defies everything that we know about the Roman
Empire to believe that Roman procurators granted their subjects the
right to save a prisoner condemned to death. No Roman or Jewish
source of the period mentions such a privilege. If it existed, would
we not find a record of its application in some earlier or later year?
In addition, we never hear of such an opportunity offered in even
the empire's more subservient regions. Finally, the notion that an
occupied people could secure the release of someone accused of se-
dition, especially in light of the frequent rebelliousness that existed
in Judea, seems, at the very least, to be farfetched.

Furthermore, as Justice Cohn asks, even if such a privilege existed, "[Why] were the multitudes that happened to be present [at that moment in a Jerusalem square] its incumbents?" (page 165).

Justice Cohn poses yet a third question: Even if such a choice existed, "Why was the choice confined to either Jesus or Barabbas?" (page 165).

Limiting the choice to two people is an effective literary device to heighten dramatic tension, and to magnify the Jews' evil (see Hyam Maccoby's discussion of this point in his *Revolution in Judaea*). Since the New Testament portrays Barabbas as a brigand, the instigator of a large riot, and a murderer (Luke 23:19), the Jews' choice of him over the saintly Jesus indicates how deeply evil they must be.

After long study of the Barabbas story, Professor S.G.F. Brandon, a Christian historian of the rise of Christianity, concluded that this incident never happened. To cite just one of the incongruities that convinced him that the story was a fiction: "The outcome of Pilate's amazing conduct was that he condemned to death one he knew to be innocent, and released a popular resistance fighter, probably a Zealot who had just proved how dangerous he could be" (*Jesus and the Zealots,* page 262).

Given that the Barabbas story opposes what we historically know to be true, what was its purpose?

There appear to be two: First, to prove to later Roman leaders that, although their government had crucified Jesus, he was no enemy of Rome; the Roman procurator himself wished to exonerate him. Therefore, Jesus was crucified only because the Jews "forced" Pilate to do so. Consequently, there was no real reason for the Romans to regard Jesus as an enemy, and to ban the religion based on his teachings (a ban that existed in the Roman Empire at the time the gospels were written).

Second, by showing the Jews to be Jesus' betrayers, the early Church could more justifiably argue that they had forfeited their position as the "chosen people," and that, in fact, Christianity had "superseded" Judaism. For this reason, the story depicts *all* the Jews clamoring for Jesus' blood. To invalidate the Jews for all time, it was insufficient to implicate the high priest and elders alone in Jesus' execution. Much better to have a large Jewish mob all calling for Jesus' death. That way their very curse would "biologically" implicate their descendants in the crime of murdering God.

Thus, the gospel's authors bear considerable, if indirect, responsibility for the hundreds of thousands of Jews who were murdered by people who read this narrative and, from it, learned to hate Jews. Of course, the bulk of the responsibility falls on the murderers themselves.

> The history of the daughter religions of Judaism is one uninterrupted series of attempts to commit matricide.
> —Moritz Steinschneider (1816–1907),
> German-Jewish bibliographer and historian

> What a shame it is that they should be more miserable under Christian princes than their ancestors were under Pharaoh.
> —Pope Innocent IV, *Letter in Defense of the Jews,* 1247

The pope's noble declaration perhaps was an apology for his predecessor, Pope Innocent III, who had written in 1208: "The Jews, against whom the blood of Jesus calls out . . . must remain vagabonds upon the earth, until their faces be covered with shame and they seek the name of Jesus Christ the Lord."

> It's their own bloody fault—they should have left God alone.
> —Hilaire Belloc (1870–1953), British writer and poet.
> A member of parliament, Belloc later became known
> as an outspoken Roman Catholic apologist.

The belief that Jesus Christ was God and that the Jews killed him fueled antisemitism. Fear lay at the heart of this hatred because, if the Jews had killed God, they must possess superhuman and demonic powers.

While this may well be the psychological basis of much antisemitism, the charge that the Jews killed Jesus of course is historically wrong. Crucifixion, the Roman punishment for rebels, was expressly forbidden by Jewish law. Jesus was one of between fifty and one hundred thousand Jews crucified as anti-Roman rebels in the first century.

Historian Hyam Maccoby has written: "The cross became as much a symbol of Roman oppression as nowadays the gas chamber is a symbol of German Nazi oppression. . . . Associating the guilt of the cross with the Jews rather than the Romans is comparable to branding the Jewish victims . . . with the guilt of using gas chambers instead of suffering from them" (*Revolution in Judaea: Jesus and the Jewish Resistance,* page 36).

> I was once asked at a public lecture: "Doesn't the history of the Jews' wandering and low status prove that they are being cursed for rejecting Jesus?"
>
> I answered, "No, not at all, because the people who predicted that the Jews would suffer are the same people who persecuted them. It would be as if I predicted that that window would break, and then threw a rock through it. That would say more about my propensity for violence than it would about my gift of prophecy."
>
> —Harold Kushner, *To Life!,* page 269

The claim of Christian antisemites that Jewish suffering proves that they are being punished for rejecting Jesus, a line of argument popular in the Middle Ages, seems particularly odd given the horrible fate to which Jesus himself was subjected.

*   *   *

> Not long ago, I was reading the Sermon on the Mount with a rabbi. At nearly every verse he showed me very similar passages in the Hebrew Bible and Talmud. When we reached the words, "Turn the other cheek," he did not say this too is in the Talmud, but asked with a smile, "Do the Christians obey this command?" I had nothing to say in reply, especially as at that particular time, Christians, far from turning the other cheek, were smiting the Jews on both cheeks.
>
> —Leo Tolstoy (1828–1910), *My Religion*

A strikingly similar sentiment is expressed in the writings of another Russian religious thinker, Nikolai Berdyaev: "Perhaps the saddest thing to admit is that those who have rejected the Cross have to carry it, while those who welcomed it are as often engaged in crucifying others" (*Christianity and Anti-Semitism,* page 12).

*   *   *

> They should have come out with a very simple statement: We have been guilty of antisemitism for two thousand years. Forgive us.
>
> —Edward Keating

Keating, a Catholic writer, was referring to Vatican II's declaration in 1965: "What happened in His [Jesus'] passion cannot be blamed upon all the Jews then living without distinction, nor upon the Jews of today." Although the declaration both irritated (because of its lack of apology) and pleased the Jewish community, the pleasure predominated. Pope John XXIII, the moving force behind Vatican II, apparently wished to apologize to the Jews. Shortly before his death he composed this prayer:

> We realize now that many, many centuries of blindness have dimmed our eyes, so that we no longer see the beauty of Thy Chosen People and no longer recognize in their faces the features of our first-born brother. We realize that our brows are branded with mark of Cain. Centuries long has Abel lain in blood and tears, because we have forgotten Thy love. Forgive us the curse which we unjustly laid on the name of the Jews. Forgive us, that with our curse, we crucified Thee a second time.
>
> —Pope John XXIII (1881–1963)

Occasionally, some of the most philosemitic and antisemitic statements have been made by the same person. Early in his career, Martin Luther (1483–1546) hoped that the Jews would join him in his protests against the Catholic Church, and convert to his brand of Christianity. During this period, Luther wrote in his pamphlet, *That Jesus Christ Was Born A Jew:*

> Our fools and jackasses, our priests, bishops, sophists, and monks have treated the Jews in such a manner, that if one wished to become a true Christian he might better become a Jew.

Less than two decades later, after his outreach to the Jewish community failed to garner converts to Christianity, Luther turned against the Jews with fury, advocating the community's destruction:

> I shall give you my sincere advice [about what to do with the Jews]
>   —to set fire to their synagogues or schools
>   —that their houses also be razed and destroyed . . . instead they might be lodged under a roof or in a barn . . .
>   —that all their prayer books and talmudic writings, in which such idolatry, lies, cursing, and blasphemy are taught, be taken from them
>   —that their rabbis be forbidden to teach, henceforth on pain of loss of life and limb
>   —that safe conduct on the highways be abolished completely for the Jews
>   —that usury be prohibited to them, and that all cash and treasure of silver and gold be taken from them
>   But if we are afraid that they might harm us . . . then eject them forever from the country.
> —Martin Luther, *On the Jews and Their Lies,* advising German rulers on the treatment of Jews; see Jeremy Cohen, "Traditional Prejudice and Religious Reform: The Theological and Historical Foundations of Luther's Anti-Judaism," pages 81–102. A selection from Luther's positive and negative writings about the Jews is found in Jacob Marcus, ed., *The Jew in the Medieval World,* pages 166–169.

I would threaten to cut their tongues out from their throats if they refuse to accept the Christian proof that God is a trinity, not a plain unity.

—Martin Luther; cited in Marie Syrkin, ed.,
Hayim Greenberg Anthology, page 114

Some four hundred years later, Adolf Hitler claimed, "He [Luther] saw the Jew as we are only beginning to see him today" (Friedrich Heer, *God's First Love,* page 286).

When you baptize a Jew, hold his head under water for five minutes.

—Bulgarian proverb

INFAMOUS MODERN QUOTES ABOUT THE JEWS

Jewish priests have always sacrificed human victims with their sacred hands.

—Voltaire, in the 1770 appendix to his entry on the Jews in the
Dictionnaire Philosophique

The French Enlightenment's most prominent thinker, an avowed secularist, infused new life into the libel that Jews sacrificed human beings and drank their blood, a leitmotif of ancient pagan and medieval Christian antisemitism. Voltaire's unremitting hostility to the Jews did much to advance modern antisemitism. For example, he described Jews as "the most abominable people in the world," although with characteristic Enlightenment "tolerance," he added: "Nevertheless, they should not be burned at the stake."

Unfortunately, Jews were one of Voltaire's obsessions. "During Hitler's domination of Europe," the French-Jewish historian Leon Poliakov has written, "a history teacher, Henri Lebrou, had no difficulty in compiling a 250-page book of Voltaire's anti-Jewish writings" (*The History of Anti-Semitism: From Voltaire to Wagner,* page 87).

The contemporary American-Jewish historian Arthur Hertzberg has documented, in *The French Enlightenment and the Jews,* how

471

Voltaire served as the major intellectual link between classical pagan and modern antisemitism. His writings established in the minds of many enlightened Europeans (the very people who should have been the most active proponents of Jewish emancipation) that Jews who wished to enter Western society should be willing to abandon their religion.

An influential early Zionist writer argued that the infamous blood libel provided the Jews with one unexpected psychological benefit: It helped immunize them against internalizing the world's hostile portrayal:

> This [blood libel] accusation is the solitary case in which the general acceptance of an idea about ourselves does not make us doubt whether all the world can be wrong, and we right, because it is based on an absolute lie. Every Jew who has been brought up among Jews knows as an indisputable fact that throughout the length and breadth of Jewry there is not a single individual who drinks human blood for religious purposes. . . . "But," you ask, "is it possible that everybody can be wrong and the Jews right?" Yes, it is possible: the blood accusation proves it possible.
> —Ahad Ha'am (1856–1927)

> Grant them civil rights? I see no other way of doing this except to cut off all their heads on one night and substitute other heads without a single Jewish thought in them.
> —Johann Fichte (1762–1814), a leading philosopher of the German Enlightenment, and first rector of the University of Berlin

*   *   *

> Money is the jealous God of Israel before whom no other gods are allowed to stand.
> —Karl Marx (1818–1883), "On the Jewish Question"

Marx was born into a Jewish family—indeed, he was the grandson of two rabbis—but his father baptized him at age six. From his earliest published writings, Marx's hostility to Jews was vicious and unremitting. No less an antisemite than Adolf Hitler claimed him as

472

a mentor: "It is quite enough that the scientific knowledge of the danger of Judaism is gradually deepened and that every individual on the basis of this knowledge begins to eliminate that Jew within himself, and I am very much afraid that this beautiful thought originates from none other than a Jew" (cited in Julius Carlebach, *Karl Marx and the Radical Critique of Judaism,* pages 355–356).

Hitler's allusion to Marx's "Jewishness" summarizes one problem he has long caused Jews: Most non-Jews view the founder of communism as a Jew because he was born one. Few are aware of his childhood conversion and subsequent hatred for Jews and Judaism. Indeed, in "On the Jewish Question," Marx defines "practical real Judaism," as an obsession with "haggling," and with "money," concluding his essay with the startling assertion that mankind will be fully liberated only when it emancipates itself from "the spirit of Judaism."

In later writings, Marx dismissed impoverished Polish-Jewish refugees as "the filthiest of all races." He claimed that all that united them with their affluent German-Jewish brethren was their "passion for greedy gain," a singularly vicious and ironic charge from a man who depended on other people's financial support during his entire adult life (see Paul Johnson, *Intellectuals,* pages 74–75).

During the 1850s, Marx ridiculed efforts by Baron Rothschild and British civil libertarians to secure the House of Commons seat that Rothschild had won in repeated elections, but which he was denied for failing to swear to a Christian oath: "It is doubtful whether the British people will be very much pleased by extending electoral rights to a Jewish usurer."

At about the same time as Marx, Pierre Joseph Proudhon (1809–1865) was spreading a revolutionary political and economic message throughout France. Along with strong doses of socialist and anarchist rhetoric (Proudhon believed that as people matured politically, government and law would one day no longer be needed), came vicious Jew-hatred:

> The Jew is the enemy of the human race. One must send this race back to Asia or exterminate it. . . . By fire or fu-

sion or expulsion, the Jew must disappear.... Tolerate
the aged, who are no longer able to give birth to offspring.
—*Carnets de P. J. Proudhon,* December 1847;
cited in George Lichtheim, "Socialism and the Jews," in his
Collected Essays, page 425

*   *   *

If saving an innocent Dreyfus involves any injury to the
French state, everything should be done to make Dreyfus
guilty, so that France may remain unstained.
—André Gide in a letter to a friend concerning
the "Dreyfus Affair," 1898

Gide, who subsequently achieved fame as one of France's great
writers, was then in an ultranationalist phase. Perhaps that is the
reason he failed to understand that it was the persecution of an
innocent man that was staining France's honor, not the fact of Dreyfus's innocence becoming known. That Gide was willing to accept
Dreyfus's continued incarceration in horrific conditions on Devil's
Island demonstrates the moral depths to which nationalistic chauvinism can lead.

*   *   *

Even in the best educated circles ... we hear today the cry,
as from one mouth, "The Jews are our misfortune."
—Heinrich von Treitschke, "A Word About Our Jewry," 1879

Because von Treitschke, Germany's leading historian in the late
nineteenth century, had a vast scholarly and political following, this
particular "witticism" immediately became widely known. Fifty
years later, "The Jews are our misfortune" was turned into the Nazis' slogan.

Today, von Treitschke's defenders note that he opposed physical
violence against Jews, and so definitely would not have condoned
the Holocaust. This defense reminds me of a nineteenth-century parable critics of Hegelian political philosophy told to explain how Hegelian thought could be used to justify great evils. A man once saw

a large sign in a store window, "Pants pressed here." He brought in his pants to be pressed, but was told, "We don't press pants here. We only make signs."

> We are fighting against the most ancient curse that hu-manity has brought upon itself. Against the so-called Ten Commandments, against them we are fighting.
>
> —Adolf Hitler (1889–1945), in conversation with Hermann Rauschning; cited in Rauschning's preface to Armin Robinson, ed., *The Ten Commandments*, pages ix–xiii. Hitler told Rauschning that his mission in life was to destroy the "tyrannical God of the Jews," and His "life-denying Ten Commandments."

Although the fifteen-year-old Anne Frank had no way of know-ing of Hitler's comment, she intuitively understood the basis of Nazi antisemitism. In her diary entry of April 11, 1944, she wrote: "Who knows, it might even be our religion from which the world and all peoples learn good, and for that reason and that reason only do we now suffer."

*   *   *

TWENTIETH-CENTURY LITERARY ANTISEMITISM

> The silent man in mocha brown
> Sprawls at the window-sill and gapes;
> The waiter brings in oranges
> Bananas, figs and hothouse grapes;
> The silent vertebrate in brown
> Contracts and concentrates, withdraws;
> Rachel nee Rabinovitch
> Tears at the grapes with murderous paws.
>
> —T. S. Eliot, "Sweeney Among the Nightingales," in *T. S. Eliot: Collected Poems 1909–1935*, pages 65–66

Although Eliot later moderated his antisemitism, this 1920s ex-ample presents an ugly picture of Jews as wealthy people who pub-licly feast in the presence of the poor. Given the well-known Jewish propensity for charitable giving, Eliot's singling out of Jews as those who mock the poor suggests an antisemitism that ran deep. Indeed, in an ugly reprisal of medieval Jew-hatred, Eliot fails to see Jews as normal human beings; instead of hands, they have "murderous paws."

Jewish hands seemed to have had a particular fascination for the poet. In a 1919 poem with a distinctly antisemitic theme, "Burbank with a Baedeker, Bleistein with a Cigar," Bleistein is described in terms of "a saggy bending of the knees, And elbows, with the palms turned out, Chicago Semite Viennese" (ibid., page 47). In the same poem, Eliot delivers himself of a line that, after the Holocaust, probably sounds more malevolent than even he intended: "The rats are underneath the piles. The jew [sic] is underneath the lot. Money in furs."

> It becomes increasingly difficult to discuss American affairs except on a racial basis. . . . Sometime the Anglo Saxons may awake to the fact that the Jewish kahal (community) . . . [does] not shove Aryan or non-yiddish nations into wars in order that those said nations may win wars. The non-Jew nations are shoved into wars in order to destroy themselves, to break up their structures, to destroy their populations.
> —Ezra Pound (1885–1972), from broadcast #32, delivered during World War II from Rome, April 30, 1942 (published in Allan Gould, *What Did They Think of the Jews?*, pages 318–320)

The American-born Pound, author of *The Cantos* (a series of poems published over several decades), is generally regarded as one of the greatest twentieth-century poets. His attraction to fascism influenced him to move to Mussolini's Italy in 1925. In 1939, he wrote an article for the Italian press revealingly entitled, "The Jew, Disease Incarnate."

Pound spent the war years in Italy, where he broadcast pro-Axis propaganda over Italian radio. He accepted, and expounded, the Nazi notions that Jews care only about money, and that they so hate non-Jews that they plunge nations into war so as to kill off large numbers of gentiles.

Because the Axis powers lost the war, Pound's influence on the future course of antisemitism was limited. Had they won, the Nazis undoubtedly would have harnessed this internationally renowned poet's abilities to make virulent antisemitism intellectually respectable.

In 1945, the American army arrested Pound and returned him to the United States to be tried for treason. However, a judge ruled him mentally unfit to stand trial, and Pound was committed to a mental hospital in Washington, D.C., where he remained for twelve years. During this time, numerous prominent poets and other literary figures argued on his behalf that it was unjust to keep so great a poet confined to a mental asylum (in 1958, Pound was released). The vehemence of these protests brings to mind George Orwell's comment, "One has the right to expect ordinary decency even of a poet."

*   *   *

> The Jews could be put down very plausibly as the most unpleasant race ever heard of. As commonly encountered, they lack many of the qualities that mark the civilized man: courage, dignity, incorruptibility, ease, confidence. They have vanity without pride, voluptuousness without taste, and learning without wisdom. Their fortitude, such as it is, is wasted upon puerile objects, and their charity is mainly a form of display.
>
> —H. L. Mencken (1880–1956), *Treatise on the Gods* (1930),
> quoted in Heywood Broun and George Brett,
> *Christians Only*, pages 276–277

In 1926, Walter Lippmann wrote that Mencken, a journalist and linguist, was "the most powerful personal influence on this whole generation of educated people." Thus, antisemitic diatribes such as the above could have inflicted very real damage to Jews. Fortunately, Mencken generally confined his antisemitic sentiments to his private journal. Indeed, when his diaries were published posthumously, readers were shocked by the extent of their anti-Jewish comments. During Mencken's lifetime, his public pronouncements vis-à-vis Jews usually were far more positive and, on occasion, even philosemitic. In Mencken's final column for the *Baltimore Sun* on New Year's Day, 1939, for example, he pleaded for admitting European Jewish refugees to the United States:

> Either we are willing to give refuge to the German Jews, or we are not willing. If the former, then here is one vote for bringing them in by the first available ships, and staking them sufficiently to set them on their feet. That is the only way we can really help them, and that is the only way we can avoid going down into history as hypocrites almost as grotesque as the English.
>
> The initiative should be taken by the so-called Christians who are now so free with weasel words of comfort and flattery, and so curiously stingy with practical aid. In particular, it should be taken by the political mountebanks who fill the air with hollow denunciations of Hitler, and yet never lift a hand to help an actual Jew.
>
> —H. L. Mencken, quoted by Joseph Epstein,
> *Pertinent Players,* page 231

*   *   *

> So come for the rent, jewboys, or come ask me for a book, or sit in the courts handing down yer [sic] judgments, still I got something for you . . . then one day, jewboys, we all even my wig wearing mother gonna put it on you all at once.
>
> —Amiri Baraka, the former LeRoi Jones,
> *Black Magic: Collected Poetry 1961–1967,* page 154

Irving Howe, the late literary scholar and critic, commented on this and other writings of Baraka-Jones: "When I read LeRoi Jones calling for 'dagger poems in the slimy bellies of their owner jews,' . . . then I know I am in the presence of a racist hoodlum, inciting people to blood. And I am not going to be deflected from that perception by talk about rhythm, metaphor and diction" (*The Critical Point: On Literature and Culture,* page 177).

Baraka now claims that he is no longer antisemitic, but still insists Israel has no right to exist. Professor of literature Guy Stern of Wayne State University comments: "Even if one were willing to accept the distinction between the two phobias [antisemitism and anti-Zionism], it is doubtful that Mr. Jones' retraction can vitiate the effect of his murderous lyrics" ("The Rhetoric of Anti-Semitism in Postwar American Literature," page 297).

A FINAL THOUGHT

Antisemitism is, unfortunately, not only a feeling which all Gentiles at times feel, but also, and this is what matters, a feeling of which the majority of them are not ashamed.
—W. H. Auden (1907–1973)

66

ANTISEMITISM AND THE AMERICAN-JEWISH EXPERIENCE

ULYSSES GRANT AND ORDER NO. 11

The Jews as a class, violating every regulation of trade established by the Treasury Department, and also [military] department orders, are hereby expelled from the department [of Tennessee] within twenty-four hours from the receipt of this order.

—General Ulysses Grant, Order No. 11, December 17, 1862

Grant's order represents the only expulsion of Jews in American history. The general's ire had been aroused by reports that a number of Jewish traders were engaging in illegal sales in territory occupied by the Union Army. However, the order of expulsion was not limited to them; it applied to *all* Jews, including women, children, and men engaged in legal work, thereby encompassing approximately 2,500 people.

Within days, Cesar Kaskel, a leader of the Jewish community of Paducah, Kentucky, accompanied by a Congressman Gurley of Ohio, met with President Lincoln at the White House. Until then unaware of Grant's order, Lincoln immediately rescinded it, and a telegram to Grant, informing him of the president's decision, was sent.

480

Grant never apologized for his behavior: When he was elected president in 1868, many Jews feared for their well-being. It turned out, however, that the act of expulsion had been an aberration, for President Grant engaged in no antisemitic activities. He offered Joseph Seligman, the well-known banker, the position of secretary of the treasury, the first time a Jew had been offered a Cabinet position (Seligman declined), served as godfather at the circumcision of his friend Simon Wolf's son, and after an outbreak of government-encouraged anti-Jewish attacks in Romania, appointed Benjamin Franklin Peixotto, a Jew, to serve as American consul in Bucharest. Grant dispatched Peixotto to his post armed with a presidential letter denouncing religious discrimination. The Romanian government was discomfited by the American president's action, so much so that physical assaults against Jews declined dramatically during Peixotto's five-year tenure.

*   *   *

JOSEPH SELIGMAN AND THE GRAND UNION HOTEL

Mr. Seligman, I am required to inform you that Judge Hilton [administrator of the Grand Union Hotel] has given instructions that no Israelites shall be permitted in the future to stop at this hotel.

—Desk clerk to Joseph Seligman, one of the most prominent
American Jews of his time, 1877

Henry Hilton, a political crony of New York's corrupt Mayor Boss Tweed, and an antisemite, claimed that business at the luxurious Grand Union Hotel in Saratoga, New York, had been declining because of gentile unhappiness over Jewish guests.

Seligman turned the case into a cause célèbre, and the story made many newspapers' front pages. Hilton (no kin to Conrad Hilton, founder of the Hilton Hotels Corporation) did not care: "As the law yet permits a man to use his property as he pleases, I propose exercising that blessed privilege, notwithstanding Moses and all his descendants may object."

Historian Howard Morley Sachar notes that while initial public reactions favored Seligman, in time, "a vicious circle of Gentile restrictionism and ghetto resorts developed in the aftermath of the Grand Union Affair" (see Sachar's discussion of the incident in *A History of the Jews in America,* pages 98–101). Once started, the discrimination quickly extended from the social to the professional. Soon newspapers were publishing classified ads proclaiming, "Hebrews need not apply," or "Jews excluded even when of unusual personal qualifications" (ibid., page 101).

*   *   *

THE LEO FRANK CASE

> Two thousand years ago another Governor washed his hands of a case and turned over a Jew to a mob. For two thousand years that Governor's name has been accursed. If today another Jew were lying in his grave because I had failed to do my duty, I would all through life find his blood on my hands and would consider myself an assassin through cowardice.
>
> —Georgia Governor John Slaton, June 21, 1915, commuting the death sentence of Leo Frank to life imprisonment

In 1913, Leo Frank, a prominent Jewish Atlantan, was arrested and accused of murdering fourteen-year-old Mary Phagan, an employee in his pencil factory. Although the evidence against him was very weak, the prosecution insisted on trying Frank, carefully suppressing evidence pointing to his innocence.

Frank's arrest triggered an outbreak of antisemitism in Atlanta. Throughout his trial, the jury heard mobs outside the courtroom's open windows chanting, "Hang the Jew! Hang the Jew!" Subsequent to his conviction, "[a jury member confessed] to a northern reporter that he was not sure of anything except that unless Frank was found guilty the jurors would never get home alive" (Leonard Dinnerstein, "A Dreyfus Affair in Georgia," page 101).

482

Despite the clear miscarriage of justice (among other things, the "star" prosecution witness against Frank had confessed committing the murder to his own lawyer, information that the lawyer apparently passed on to the judge), the U.S. Supreme Court refused to intervene, so that the decision whether or not to execute Frank was left in Governor Slaton's hands. Although assured by the powerful anti-Frank forces of a Senate seat if he let Frank hang, Slaton carefully investigated the case and became convinced of Frank's innocence. In the prevailing turbulent political climate, he was afraid to pardon Frank, hoping apparently that that would be done a few years later. Therefore, Slaton commuted Frank's death sentence, an act that permanently ended his political career.

Several months later, Frank was dragged from his prison cell by a mob consisting of, among others, two retired superior court justices, a former sheriff, and a clergyman. They lynched Frank; for decades, a picture postcard depicting his hanged body was widely sold throughout the South.

In 1982, *sixty-nine years* after the trial, eighty-three-year-old Alonzo Mann, who had been an office boy in Frank's factory, admitted that he had seen Jim Conley, a black employee at the factory and the chief witness against Frank at the trial, dragging the girl's body into the factory's basement on the day of the murder. Mann's mother had pressured him not to get involved in the politically charged trial. In 1986, the state of Georgia granted Frank a posthumous pardon.

As I have noted elsewhere, "the Frank case brought about the development of two diametrically opposed organizations: the Anti-Defamation League of B'nai B'rith (Frank had been president of B'nai B'rith's Atlanta chapter), and the revived Ku Klux Klan" (*Jewish Literacy,* page 406).

*　　*　　*

ARE THERE TOO MANY JEWS AT HARVARD?

The idea that any shrewd boy that can, by cramming, "get by" on written examinations must thereby be automati-

cally admitted to college is anti-American.
—President Faunce, Brown University, 1922

Of course, "shrewd" is a code word antisemites long have used for Jews. Faunce denied that he favored discrimination against Jews; he only wished to "exclude the greedy and overbearing and inconsiderate and disloyal" (cited in Morton Rosenstock, "Are There Too Many Jews at Harvard?," pages 103–104; several citations in this section are drawn from that study).

By the early 1920s, Jewish representation at leading American universities had grown greatly. In 1922, for example, Jews made up 22 percent of the incoming class at Harvard, more than triple the 6 percent of 1909. Harvard's president, A. Lawrence Lowell, feared that the Jewish percentage would rise still higher; as a result, he pushed for the institution of quotas to limit the Jewish enrollment.

Lowell claimed to be acting in the interests of Jews, no less than Harvard: Since a large Jewish presence on a campus invariably provoked antisemitism, he argued, would not limiting Jewish numbers decrease antisemitism?: "If every college in the country would take a limited proportion of Jews . . . we should go a long way toward eliminating race-feeling among the students" (cited in Howard Morley Sachar, *A History of the Jews in America,* page 329).

Under Lowell's direction, the Harvard admission form instituted a new question: "What change, if any, has been made since birth in your own name or that of your father?"—a not-so-subtle way of determining Jewish, and other non–Anglo-Saxon, immigrants and their descendants.

Needless to say, American Jews were not taken in by Lowell's claim that quotas were good for them; they were well aware of the threat the quotas posed to their welfare in America:

If the Jew loses his fight to gain admission to the college campus, he is defeated in a far more significant battle, namely the right to entrance into the higher spheres of the professions and commerce.

—Rabbi Louis Newman

Jews wanted university admissions to be based on merit, not geography or ancestry. As Louis Marshall, president of the American Jewish Committee, expressed it: "The only tests that we can recognize are those of character and of scholarship."

Unfortunately, Jews lost the fight over quotas, which were instituted at Harvard and other Ivy League colleges (in some places formally, in others as a tacit policy). It is estimated that some seven hundred other liberal arts colleges soon followed Harvard's lead.

American Jewry's salvation was that many colleges and universities supported by public funds (e.g., the City College of New York, the "Jewish Harvard," as it came to be known) did not discriminate; thus, Jews qualified to study at the college level still could find institutions to accept them. Acceptance into the elite institutions, however, became more and more difficult. In 1923, before quotas, Jewish enrollment at Columbia University's College of Physicians and Surgeons exceeded 50 percent; by 1928, it was under 20 percent; by 1940, 6.4 percent. Dr. William Rappleye, the medical school's dean, explained, "The racial and religious makeup in medicine ought to be kept fairly parallel with the population makeup." During the same period, Cornell's Medical School instituted a rigid quota which reduced Jewish students from some 40 percent in 1920 to 5 percent in 1940 (Marcia Graham Synnott, "Anti-Semitism and American Universities," pages 251–252).

Universities disinclined to admit Jews as students similarly were averse to hiring them as faculty. As historian Howard Morley Sachar writes, "Altogether, throughout the 1920s, fewer than one hundred Jewish professors could be found in American faculties of arts and sciences. Years of study went for naught, intellects were wasted, careers blighted" (*A History of the Jews in America*, page 332).

In the post–World War II era, and particularly during the 1960s, the merit system began to prevail over quotas, and Jewish representation at America's elite schools, both as students and as faculty members, rose greatly. And while the 1920s push for quotas was associated with people on the political right, in contemporary America those advocating quotas usually represent the political left.

*   *   *

HENRY FORD

International financiers are behind all war. They are what is called the international Jew—German Jews, French Jews, English Jews, American Jews. I believe that in all those countries except our own the Jewish financier is supreme. . . . Here the Jew is a threat.

—Henry Ford in interview with J. J. O'Neill of the *New York World*, 1920 (Howard Morley Sachar, *A History of the Jews in America*, page 311)

Ford (1863–1947), the founder of Ford Motor Company and the developer of the "assembly line" mass-production technique, was among the most popular Americans of his time. A 1923 presidential preference poll conducted by *Collier's* magazine revealed that the auto magnate, who was not even a candidate, was the people's preferred choice, which made his deep-seated antisemitism particularly worrisome to Jews.

Ford owned the *Dearborn Independent,* a weekly newspaper widely distributed through his car dealerships. Starting in 1920, Ford used the paper to launch the most widespread antisemitic campaign in American history. For ninety-one successive issues, it chronicled "The International Jew: The World's Problem." Week after week, sections of the infamous forgery, *The Protocols of the Elders of Zion,* were rewritten and published in greatly expanded form. The thrust of the articles was that

- Jews throughout the world are united in a conspiracy to control world finance and politics;
- Jews are behind the evils of both capitalism and communism;
- Jews have a plan to destroy every religion in the world except Judaism;
- Jews have no loyalty to the societies in which they live, but only to other Jews.

The *Dearborn Independent*'s circulation, seventy thousand when Ford acquired it, grew tenfold by 1925. To ensure that millions of nonsubscribers would have access to its anti-Jewish articles, Ford authorized the publication of four volumes of *The International Jew*, containing reprints of the articles the paper had previously printed.

Although many prominent Americans, including President Wilson and former President Taft, denounced Ford's antisemitic calumnies, others, particularly in rural areas, were more sympathetic. Some Jew-hatred even spread to sources Jews would not have thought of as antagonistic: Historian Howard Morley Sachar notes that *The Christian Science Monitor*, later one of Israel's harshest critics (the *Monitor* was the only major American newspaper to condemn Israel's 1976 freeing of captive Jews in Entebbe), headlined a June 1920 editorial, "The Jewish Peril" (*A History of the Jews in America*, page 315).

For several years Jews were stymied on how to deal with Ford's defamations. A major problem was that American law protects individuals, but not groups, from libel. If an antisemitic journal published the medieval canard that Jews murder non-Jews and drink their blood at the Passover *seder*, the Jewish community could take no legal action. Only if the journal mentioned a specific Jew as having carried out this supposed "ritual" could that person seek damages. Thus, when the *Dearborn Independent* accused Aaron Sapiro, a Jewish lawyer, of plotting to take over all agricultural resources and production in America, Sapiro sued. The prolonged trial generated such adverse publicity for Ford that even his son, Edsel, pleaded with him to drop his antisemitic vendetta and negotiate a settlement. Ford did so, and even issued a letter of apology to the Jews. Louis Marshall, then the leading figure in American Jewish life, really wrote the missive, with the words:

> I deem it to be my duty as an honorable man to make amends for the wrong done to the Jews as fellow-men and brothers, by asking their forgiveness for the harm that I have unintentionally committed . . . and by giving them the unqualified assurance that henceforth they may look to me for friendship and goodwill.

Yet the damage done by the *Dearborn Independent*'s campaign proved irrevocable. Hitler, who regarded "Heinrich Ford" as his great ally in America, reissued a German translation of *The International Jew*. Years later, Ford himself confided to the American antisemite Gerald L. K. Smith that he expected to reissue it someday as well.

In addition, Ford's publications helped set the stage for America's 1924 restriction of immigration into the United States. (After the *Dearborn Independent*'s "revelations," who would want to admit such a plotting and disloyal people?)

> It is a paradox of Jewish history that the antisemitism propagated in the United States after the First World War wrought more damage to the European Jews than to the American Jews. The restriction of immigration in accordance with the national-origins quota prevented hundreds of thousands of Jews from entering America in years to come when the difference was a difference between life and death.
>
> —Lucy Davidowicz, *On Equal Terms:*
> *Jews in America, 1881–1981*, page 93

*   *   *

CHARLES LINDBERGH

> The three most important groups who have been pressing this country towards war are the British, the Jews, and the Roosevelt administration. . . . Instead of agitating for war, the Jewish groups in this country should be opposing it in every possible way, for they will be among the first to feel its consequences.
> —Charles Lindbergh, September 11, 1941, addressing an overflow
> America First rally in Des Moines, Iowa

Lindbergh (1902–1974), the first pilot to fly solo across the Atlantic (May 1927), was among the most popular Americans of his age. After the outbreak of World War II, Lindbergh emerged as the most prominent figure in the America First Committee, an organization that urged American neutrality in the war between Germany and England. Lindbergh's defenders make the dubious argument that he was motivated solely by fear of Germany's strength, not by pro-Nazi leanings. But there is ample reason to suspect that Lindbergh admired the Nazis. In addition to excoriating those who wanted to fight them, he also refused to return a medal awarded him by Nazi leader Hermann Göring. Lindbergh would routinely refer to the prisoner-of-war camps in which the British incarcerated captured Nazi soldiers as "concentration camps," whereas he referred to Auschwitz and other German death camps as "Nazi prison camps" (Leonard Mosley, *Lindbergh: A Biography,* page 273). "If only the United States would be on the *right* side of an intelligent war," he cried out at President Roosevelt's efforts to aid the British in their fight against Hitler's army (ibid., pages 282–283).

Historian William O'Neill has concluded, "In promoting appeasement and military unpreparedness, Lindbergh damaged his country to a greater degree than any other private citizen in modern times" (*A Democracy at War,* page 49).

Lindbergh was particularly incensed at the Jews, many of whom wanted the United States to join, or at least support, the Allies. His thinly veiled threat that if America did enter the war, the Jews "will be among the first to feel its consequences," terrified many Jews; it apparently was one of the factors that later discouraged American Jewry from more actively pressing the Allies to bomb the train tracks leading to the Nazi death camps, for they did not want World War II to be spoken of as "the Jews' war." Significantly, Lindbergh's wife, the renowned poet Anne Morrow Lindbergh, herself sympathetic to many of her husband's political notions, pleaded with him not to give his Des Moines speech. According to her diary (September 14, 1941), she told him, "I would prefer to see this country at war than shaken by violent anti-Semitism" (ibid., page 49). Lindbergh, normally responsive to his wife's advice, ignored her.

Elsewhere in the same speech, Lindbergh targeted Jewry as representing a major danger to America:

> The greatest danger to this country lies in [the Jews'] large
> ownership and influence in our motion pictures, our radio
> and our government.

489

Lindbergh's imputation of excessive Jewish power evoked, probably intentionally, *The Protocols of the Elders of Zion,* the antisemitic forgery that Lindbergh's friend, and later employer, Henry Ford, had helped propagate.

When Japan attacked Pearl Harbor three months later, America joined the war, and the America First Committee "closed up shop." (Lindbergh then became highly unpopular, and Henry Ford offered him a job as a technical consultant, which he accepted; Leonard Mosley, ibid., page 315.) It was subsequently revealed that Nazi agents, and other pro-fascists, had been among its members (see Howard Morley Sachar's discussion of Lindbergh in his *A History of the Jews in America,* pages 521, 657, and 876). By then, however, Lindbergh's charge that the Jews were dragging America into war had already poisoned millions of minds.

*　　　*　　　*

BUCHANAN AND FARRAKHAN: ANTISEMITISM FROM THE FAR RIGHT AND LEFT

There are only two groups that are beating the drums . . .
for war in the Middle East—the Israeli Defense Ministry
and its amen corner in the United States.
　　　　　—Patrick Buchanan, 1990, on *The McLaughlin Group,*
　　　　　　　　　　　　　　　　　　　　a television program

Buchanan, who held high positions in both the Nixon and Reagan administrations, and was a 1992 Republican presidential candidate, seemed to have modeled himself (intentionally or not) on Charles Lindbergh. Like Lindbergh, Buchanan liked to speak of himself as favoring America First. And like the noted aviator, he focused on Jews as a group trying to drag America into war—in this instance against Iraq, which, in August 1990, had occupied Kuwait.

After the above statement was attacked, Buchanan denied that it was in any way antisemitic. However, shortly thereafter, he wrote a newspaper column in which he pinpointed four individuals as prime forces trying to push America into a "needless war": A. M. Rosenthal, a *New York Times* columnist and the paper's former managing editor; Richard Perle, former assistant secretary of defense; columnist Charles Krauthammer, and former secretary of state Henry Kissinger. In a later column—and in obvious juxtaposition to these four names—Buchanan wrote that the people who would die in such a war would be "kids with names like McAllister, Murphy, Gonzales, and Leroy Brown."

To political conservative William Buckley, these last two statements seemed to establish a considerable depth of anti-Jewish hostility in Buchanan. Why else would he pin support for war against Iraq—support which was widespread throughout the United States—on four people, all of whom have Jewish names? As Buckley put it: "A. M. Rosenthal, columnist, was no more belligerent on the Hussein issue than James Jackson Kilpatrick, also a columnist; Richard Perle no more than Frank Gaffney, his former colleague; Charles Krauthammer no more than George Will; and Henry Kissinger no more than one of his successors as Secretary of State, Alexander Haig. Four Christians" (*In Search of Anti-Semitism,* page 28).

Just as Buchanan lied by omission in mentioning only American Jews as supporting war against Iraq, so too did he lie by omission in specifying Israel as the one country supporting what would become the Gulf War. If anything, Saudi Arabia and Egypt were far more outspoken than Israel in making their unhappiness with Saddam Hussein's (Iraq's murderous dictator) invasion of Kuwait widely known. Why then single out "the Israeli Defense Ministry and its amen corner in the United States"?

Obviously, not because they were the only group pushing for war.

Support for Buchanan's attack was generally confined to the far left and far right, groups normally perceived as opposing each other, but which generally are united in their dislike for Israel and for Jews. Thus, the left-wing *Nation,* a periodical normally about as prone to write sympathetically of Buchanan as of Ronald Reagan, argued that the lesson to be learned from the furor over his comments was "that journalists need to be just as vigilant in addressing the smear of anti-

Semitism as they are in seeking to expose the disease itself" (cited in Joshua Muravchik, "Patrick J. Buchanan and the Jews," *Commentary,* January 1991, page 29).

In striving to exonerate Buchanan from the charge of antisemitism, the *Nation* had its own agenda. Five years earlier (March 1986), in a special 120th anniversary commemorative issue, the most widely discussed article, "The Empire Lovers Strike Back," was an antisemitic attack by the best-selling historical novelist Gore Vidal. Much of Vidal's essay was an attack on American neoconservatives Midge Decter and Norman Podhoretz: "Of course I like my country," he wrote in a mocking response to a critique by Midge Decter. "After all, I'm its current biographer. But now that we're really leveling with each other, I've got to tell you that I don't much like your country, which is Israel." Despite vehement protests, the *Nation*'s editor, Victor Navasky, himself a Jew, refused to concede that there was anything antisemitic in Vidal's suggestion that American Jews who supported Israel should be regarded as Israelis and not Americans.

During the 1990s, hatred of Israel, and by implication of American Jews who support it, remained one of the few issues that could unify the far left and right. Thus, when the far-right-wing columnist and Israel-basher Joseph Sobran (whose animus toward Israel was so extreme that William Buckley refused to permit him to write on the subject for *National Review*) found an American Jew he could admire, it turned out to be Noam Chomsky, the far-left-wing M.I.T. professor who once called the U.S. Defense Department "the most hideous institution on earth" ("On Resistance," *The New York Review of Books,* December 1967), and who defended the publication of neo-Nazi Robert Faurisson's book which claimed that the Holocaust was a hoax made up by Zionists (see page 554). Because Chomsky shared in both Sobran's opposition to war against Iraq and his hostility to Israel, Sobran wrote of him: "To my mind he represents something deeper and more honorable in the Jewish character than the Jewish chauvinists do. He's a true Israelite, in whom there is no guile" (Sobran in a letter to William Buckley; cited in Buckley's *In Search of Anti-Semitism,* page 17).

As of this time, it would appear that the major danger to Amer-

ican Jewry, as far as antisemitism is concerned, comes from the far
left of the Democratic party and the far right of the Republican.

*   *   *

> Judaism is a gutter religion.
>> —Reverend Louis Farrakhan, Muslim minister and the Nation of
>> Islam's leader, June 1984, during a radio broadcast.
>> During the same broadcast, Farrakhan charged that Israel
>> and its supporters are "engaged in a criminal conspiracy"
>> (see Milton Himmelfarb and David Singer, eds.,
>> *American Jewish Year Book, 1986,* page 66).

> You suck the blood of the black community, and you feel
> we have no right now to say something about it.
>> —Farrakhan addressing Jews in the audience at a speech at
>> Michigan State University, February 1990; cited by Nat
>> Hentoff, *Free Speech for Me but Not for Thee,* page 171. In
>> April 1988, during an appearance at the University of Pennsylvania,
>> Farrakhan blamed Jews for instituting black slavery in America.

Currently, Reverend Farrakhan is not only the most popular
speaker before black student groups on campuses, he also was invited (in 1993), along with other black leaders, to enter into a "covenant" with the Congressional Black Caucus.

More than any other contemporary American antisemite, Farrakhan and his followers have tried to resurrect the most damaging
antisemitic libels:

> We know that Jews are the most organized, rich and pow-
> erful people, not only in America but in the world. . . .
> They are plotting against us even as we speak.
>> —Farrakhan, speaking in Harlem, January 24, 1994; reported in
>> New York *Daily News,* January 28, 1994

> The AIDS epidemic is a result of doctors, especially Jewish
> ones, who inject AIDS into blacks.
>> —Steve Cokely, aide to Chicago Mayor Eugene Sawyer, in a 1988
>> address to the Nation of Islam. Mayor Sawyer hesitated almost a

493

week before firing Cokely; only three of Chicago's eighteen black aldermen had called for his dismissal; see David Singer, ed., *American Jewish Year Book, 1990,* page 223.

You see everybody always talks about Hitler exterminating six million Jews. That's right. But don't nobody ever ask what did they do to Hitler? . . . They went in there, in Germany, the way they do everywhere they go, and they supplanted, they usurped, they turned around and a German, in his own country, would almost have to go to a Jew to get money. They had undermined the very fabric of the society.

—Khalid Abdul Mohammad, Nation of Islam National Spokesman, at Kean College, New Jersey, November 29, 1993; printed in *Forward,* January 28, 1994, page 18. In the same speech, Mohammad charged that the Federal Reserve is "owned by the Jews." In an earlier speech to blacks at Columbia University, Mohammad began his talk with the statement: "My leader, my teacher, my guide is the honorable Louis Farrakhan. I thought that should be said at Columbia *Jew*niversity." After the Anti-Defamation League took out newspaper ads printing excerpts of the Kean College speech, Farrakhan criticized the tone of the remarks, while continuing to insist on their truthfulness. The Congressional Black Caucus announced that it was reconsidering its covenant with Farrakhan.

In *The Fatal Embrace,* Professor Benjamin Ginsberg argues that the increasing use of antisemitic rhetoric by radical black leaders has "played an important role in also making it possible for others to do the same" (page 182). Thus, the sort of anti-Jewish comments of a Pat Buchanan, suggesting that pro-Israel American Jews are pushing policies that will result in the deaths of non-Jews, would have once been regarded as professionally suicidal. But after accusations that Judaism is a "gutter religion," that Jews were responsible for black slavery, that Jewish doctors inject AIDS into blacks, or that the Holocaust victims brought that fate upon themselves, such views begin to sound almost moderate, and certainly within the bounds of legitimate discourse. Thus, while Farrakhan and his cohorts are unlikely to achieve political power and carry out anti-Jewish policies, their rhetoric has helped unleash forces that might one day come to do great damage to the Jews (see Ginsberg's discussion of this point, page 183).

Are American Jews currently in danger in America? The general consensus is that they are not. At this point, being designated an antisemite is still regarded as a liability to one's political future. Therefore, almost all public figures who are accused of antisemitism deny it. But if, at some future point, a justifiable accusation of antisemitism no longer damages one's political career, that would be a sign that Jewish security in America is endangered.

For statements from some prominent American philosemites, see the next chapter.

67

PHILOSEMITISM

Thousands of books have been written on antisemitism; precious few on philosemitism. In fact, many Jews don't even know that such a word, which means "love of Jews," exists.

Yet just as Jews have encountered fierce hatred, they also have prompted some powerful expressions of love, sometimes from unexpected sources. How many Jews, for example, would have predicted in the 1930s that Denmark's citizens would unite, as they did in 1943, to save their Jewish population from being murdered?

> I shall never believe I have seriously heard the arguments of the Jews until they have a free state, schools, universities, where they can speak and dispute without risk. Only then will we be able to know what they have to say.
> —Jean-Jacques Rousseau, *Emile* (published in 1762), translated by Allan Bloom, page 304

Rousseau argued that in the absence of such a state, and in the presence of European antisemitism, Jews were too apprehensive to say what they really felt: "These unhappy people feel that they are in our power; the tyranny they have suffered makes them timid."

> If hating Jews makes one a true Christian, then we all are outstanding Christians.
> —Desiderius Erasmus (1466–1536), Dutch humanist, scholar, and one of the Renaissance's most influential figures

In the fifties of the last [nineteenth] century every Slovak child in the vicinity of Goding was nurtured in an atmosphere of antisemitism; in school, church and society at large. Mother would forbid us to go near the Lechners because, as she said, Jews were using the blood of Christian children. I would therefore make a wide turn to avoid passing their house; and so did all my schoolmates. . . . The superstition of Christian blood used for Passover cakes had become so much part and parcel of my existence that whenever I chanced to come near a Jew—I wouldn't do it on purpose—I would look at his fingers to see if blood were there. For a long time I continued this practice. . . .

Would that I may unmake all that antisemitism caused me to do in my childhood days.

> —Thomas Masaryk (1850–1937), first president of Czechoslovakia, 1918–1935; recorded in Karel Capek, *President Masaryk Tells His Story*, page 28

*   *   *

May all my words perish if Dreyfus is not innocent. . . . I did not want my country to remain in lies and injustice. One day, France will thank me for having helped to save its honor.

> —Emile Zola, *L'Aurore*, February 22, 1898

In 1894, when it became known to French intelligence that a French soldier had betrayed military secrets to Germany, the army immediately accused Captain Alfred Dreyfus, a Jew, of being the spy, and a military court sentenced him to life imprisonment on Devil's Island. Dreyfus was accused simply because he was a Jew, and despite considerable evidence indicating that the real spy was a Colonel Esterhazy.

A number of valiant French intellectuals and activists, most notably the novelist Emile Zola, refused to let the case die. With the publication of a newspaper article entitled "J'accuse," in which he wrote the above, Zola initiated a national campaign on Dreyfus's behalf. Despite relentless opposition from the French army, government, and Catholic Church, Dreyfus's case was finally reopened. Twelve years after his arrest, he was exonerated and restored to his rank in the French army. Shortly after his rehabilitation, Marcel Proust wrote in a letter to a friend, "For once, contrary to habit, life is like a novel."

THREE AMERICAN PHILOSEMITES

In spite of . . . Voltaire [a vehement antisemite; see pages 471–472], I will insist that the Hebrews have done more to civilize men than any other nation. If I were an atheist, and believed in blind eternal fate, I should still believe that fate had ordained the Jews to be the most essential instrument for civilizing the nations. . . . I should believe that chance had ordered the Jews to preserve and to propagate to all mankind the doctrine of a supreme, intelligent, wise, almighty sovereign of the universe, which I believe to be the great essential principle of all morality, and consequently of all civilization.

—John Adams, in letter to FA. Van Der Kemp,
February 16, 1809

The Jews constitute but one percent of the human race. . . . Properly the Jew ought hardly to be heard of; but he is heard of, has always been heard of. He is as prominent on the planet as any other people. . . . He has made a marvelous fight in this world, in all the ages; and has done it with his hands tied behind him. . . . The Egyptian, the Babylonian, and the Persian rose, filled the planet with sound and splendor, then faded to dream-stuff and passed away; the Greek and the Roman followed, and made a vast noise, and they are gone; other peoples have sprung up and held their torch high for a time, but it burned out, and they sit in twilight now, or have vanished. The Jew saw them all, beat them all, and is now what he always was. . . . All things are mortal but the Jew; all other forces pass, but he remains. What is the secret of his immortality?

—Mark Twain (1835–1910), *The Complete Essays of Mark Twain*, Charles Neider, ed., page 249

While I was Police Commissioner [of New York City, in 1895], an antisemitic preacher from Berlin, Rector Ahlwardt, came over to New York to preach a crusade against the Jews. Many of the New York Jews were much excited and asked me to prevent him from speaking and not to give him police protection. This, I told them was impossible; and if possible would have been undesirable because it would have made him a martyr. The proper thing to do was to make him ridiculous.

Accordingly I detailed for his protection a Jew sergeant and a score or two of Jew policemen. He made his harangue against the Jews under the active protection of some forty policemen, every one of them a Jew.

—Theodore Roosevelt, *An Autobiography,* page 186; cited in
Allan Gould, ed., *What Did They Think of the Jews?,*
pages 285–286

THREE PHILOSEMITIC BRITISH PRIME MINISTERS

The treatment of the [Jewish] race has been a disgrace to Christendom, a disgrace which tarnishes the fair fame of Christianity even at this moment, and which in the Middle Ages gave rise to horrors which whoever makes himself acquainted with even in the most superficial manner, reads of with shuddering and feelings of terror lest any trace of blood-guiltiness then incurred should have fallen on the descendants of those who committed the deeds.

—Arthur James Balfour, prime minister of England, 1902–1905,
on May 2, 1905, during a debate in the British Parliament

Balfour's shame about Christians' mistreatment of Jews was an important factor in his later becoming the primary force behind the issuance of the 1917 Balfour Declaration (see page 580), which guaranteed British support for "the establishment in Palestine of a national home for the Jewish people."

Of all the bigotries that savage the human temper there is none so stupid as [antisemitism]. In the sight of these fanatics, Jews . . . can do nothing right.

If they are rich, they are birds of prey. If they are poor, they are vermin.

If they are in favor of war, that is because they want to exploit the bloody feuds of Gentiles to their own profit. If they are anxious for peace they are either instinctive cowards or traitors.

If they give generously—and there are no more liberal givers than the Jews—they are doing it for some selfish purpose of their own. If they don't give, then what would one expect of a Jew?

—David Lloyd George, British prime minister
(1916–1922) in 1923

*   *   *

A Hebrew proverb cautions, *"Kabdai-hu ve-hashdai-hu,"* ("Respect him and suspect him"). This seems to have characterized Winston Churchill's early attitudes toward Jews; he deeply esteemed certain Jewish characteristics, while fearing and deprecating others. In his later years, the esteem totally predominated.

And it may well be that this same astounding race may at the present time be in the actual process of producing another system of morals and philosophy, as malevolent as Christianity was benevolent, which, if not arrested, would shatter irretrievably all that Christianity has rendered possible. It would almost seem as if the gospel of Christ and the gospel of Antichrist were destined to originate among the same people; and that this mystic and mysterious race had been chosen for the supreme manifestations both of the divine and the diabolical.

—Winston Churchill, "Zionism Versus Bolshevism:
A Struggle for the Soul of the Jewish People,"
Illustrated Sunday Herald, February 8, 1920

Churchill's reference to the Jews as a race, odd as it sounds today, is not racist. Churchill was a lifelong pro-Zionist and opponent of antisemitism. Before the Holocaust, however, Jews commonly were referred to as a race, and sometimes referred to themselves that way.

Churchill was disturbed by the disproportionate involvement of Jews in communism, particularly in leadership roles. Three of the five top leaders of the new Soviet government that assumed power in 1917 were Jewish: Trotsky, Zinoviev, and Kamenev (the two non-Jews were Lenin and Stalin).

Although Churchill and most non-Jews regarded Jewish communists as Jews, in fact, their Jewishness usually went no deeper than their births. In terms of the pillars of Judaism—God, Torah, and peoplehood—Jewish communists rejected, or distanced themselves from, all three. Their Marxism committed them to atheism, so that they rejected God and the laws of the Torah. Their universalism and emphasis on economic class led them to reject Jewish peoplehood; hence, they almost always were unremitting opponents of Zionism.

Jewish communists thus constituted a complete liability for the Jewish community: they both incited antisemitism by causing non-Jews to associate Jews with communism, and did everything in their power to destroy Jews' commitment to Judaism and to their people.

A striking parallel to Churchill's comment, though significantly more hostile, is found in the writings of Ernest Renan (1823–1892), the nineteenth-century French historian:

> A peculiar people, in very truth, and created to present all manners of contrasts! This people have given God to the world, and hardly believe in Him themselves. They have created religion, and they are the least religious of peoples. They have founded the hopes of humanity in a kingdom of heaven, while all its sages keep repeating to us that we must only occupy ourselves with the things of this earth.
> —Quoted in "The Racial Motif in [Ernest] Renan's Attitude to Jews and Judaism," by Shmuel Almog, in Shmuel Almog, *Antisemitism Through the Ages,* page 258

Renan's listing of Jewish inconsistencies (influenced apparently by his encountering only secular, and few religious, Jews) brings to

mind a favorite joke told by the late Nobel Prize laureate Isaac Bashevis Singer:

In the 1920s, a Jew travels from his small Polish shtetl to
Warsaw. When he returns, he tells his friend of the wonders he has seen:
    "I met a Jew who had grown up in a yeshiva and knew
large sections of the Talmud by heart. I met a Jew who
was an atheist. I met a Jew who owned a large clothing
store with hundreds of employees, and I met a Jew who
was an ardent communist."
    "So what's so strange?" the friend asks. "There must
be a million Jews in Warsaw."
    "You don't understand," the man answers. "It was all
the same Jew."

A FINAL THOUGHT: THE LIMITS OF PHILOSEMITISM

I know that all the verse I wrote, all the positions I took
in the thirties, didn't save a single Jew from Auschwitz.
            —W. H. Auden in conversation with Allan Gould, editor of
            What Did They Think of the Jews?, page 479

68

ASSIMILATION AND INTERMARRIAGE

HOW JEWISH LAW REGARDS AN ASSIMILATED JEW

[A Jew] even if he sinned, remains a Jew.
—Babylonian Talmud, *Sanhedrin* 44a

According to Jewish law, there is no act by which a Jew can cease being a Jew. Thus, a Jew who adopts another religion, and subsequently wishes to return to Judaism, need not convert. However, during those years he or she practiced another faith, Jewish law regards the person as having sinned whenever he or she violated Judaism's laws.

This talmudic dictum aside, many Jews throughout history have left the Jewish community and become fully assimilated into surrounding societies.

ADVOCATES OF ASSIMILATION

Some Jews identify as such solely because of antisemitism. Although they do not believe in Judaism, they feel it would be dishonorable to leave the Jewish people as long as Jew-hatred exists. Of course, this argument is solely emotional; on logical grounds, one could easily make the opposite case: if one does not believe in Judaism, there is no reason to subject oneself or one's descendants to hatred and discrimination. This is precisely the argument advanced by Mischa Gordon, a character in Nobel Prize winner Boris Pasternak's most important novel, *Dr. Zhivago.*

> In whose interests is this voluntary martyrdom? Who stands to gain by keeping it going? So that all these innocent old men and women and children, all these clever, kind, humane people should go on being mocked and beaten up throughout the centuries? . . . Why don't the intellectual leaders of the Jewish people . . . dismiss this army which is forever . . . being massacred nobody knows for what? Why don't they say to them: "That's enough, stop now. Don't hold on to your identity, don't all get together in a crowd. Disperse. Be with all the rest."
>
> —Boris Pasternak, *Doctor Zhivago,* translated by Max Hayward and Manya Harari, pages 117–118

Even those with strong Jewish identities occasionally flirt with such views, as suggested by an outburst from the longtime editor of *Commentary,* one of American Jewry's most prestigious journals:

> In thinking about the Jews I have often wondered whether their survival as a distinct group was worth one single hair on the head of a single infant. Did the Jews have to survive so that six million innocent people should one day be burned in the ovens of Auschwitz?
>
> —Norman Podhoretz, "My Negro Problem and Ours," *Commentary,* February 1963, page 101

(Incidentally, Podhoretz's last sentence underscores how Auschwitz has become a symbol for the entire Holocaust. The six million Jews were murdered at different camps throughout Poland, and during large-scale roundups in Russia. Auschwitz was the largest camp, and approximately one and a half million Jews were murdered there.)

ON THE HIGH LEVELS OF JEWISH ASSIMILATION IN DEMOCRACIES

Referring to the striking fact that Jews were less likely to assimilate in societies where they suffered great discrimination than in such societies as France, Germany, and the United States, where they had equal rights, Zionist activist and philosopher Hayim Greenberg wrote:

> Ambassadors and consuls representing their countries in foreign lands do not constitute minorities and do not assimilate. The classical *galut* (diaspora) Jew felt like an ambassador or a consul of his kingdom of religion.
> —Hayim Greenberg, "The Eternity of Israel," in Marie Syrkin, ed., *The Hayim Greenberg Anthology*, page 309

*   *   *

INTERMARRIAGE

> You shall not intermarry with them: do not give your daughters to their sons or take their daughters for your sons. For they will turn your children away from Me to worship other gods.
> —Deuteronomy 7:3–4

Strictly speaking, the Torah only prohibited Jews from intermarrying with the seven Canaanite nations (listed in Deuteronomy 7:1), then resident in the land of Israel. In fact, many of the Bible's most prominent personalities did marry non-Jews: Samson took a Philistine wife (Judges 14:2–3), and King Solomon married scores of non-Jewish women. Unfortunately, the biblical rationale for prohibiting intermarriage, "for they will turn your children away from Me to worship other gods," portrays exactly what happened not only to some of Solomon's descendants, but to himself as well. Of the king who built the *Beit Ha-Mikdash* (the Great Temple in Jerusalem), the Bible records: "In his old age, his wives turned away Solomon's heart after other gods, and he was not as wholeheartedly devoted to the Lord his God as his father David had been. Solomon followed Ashtoreth the goddess of the Phoenicians, and Milcom the abomination of the Ammonites." This process of estrangement from monotheism apparently began when he built idolatrous shrines so that his non-Jewish wives would have a place to worship (see I Kings 11:3–10).

Early in Jewish history, Jewish law forbade intermarriage between Jews and non-Jews of any nationality; it has remained prohibited ever since. Obviously, in those cases where the non-Jewish partner chooses to convert to Judaism (see Chapter 54), the couple is not considered to be intermarried.

Throughout most of modern Jewish history, Jews who intermarried have been lost to the Jewish community. Even when the Jewish partner retained a Jewish identity, the couple's children usually identified with the majority religion in the surrounding society, e.g., in Europe, Christianity. Thus, in a society such as the contemporary United States, where intermarriage rates in some regions reach and exceed 50 percent, the Jewish community seems destined to decline significantly in numbers unless the non-Jewish partner becomes Jewish, or, in cases where the wife is non-Jewish, allows the children to be converted to Judaism. (Judaism's matrilineal principle dictates that a child of a Jewish mother is automatically Jewish, while the child of a Jewish father and non-Jewish mother must convert. Reform Judaism recognizes "patrilineal descent," i.e., the child of a Jewish father and non-Jewish mother is considered Jewish if he or she is raised with a Jewish identity.) However, both statistical data and common sense suggest that where one of the two parents remains non-Jewish, the home is likely to have a significantly less Jewish character than one in which both parents are Jews.

A riddle formulated by a contemporary Jewish political and social critic reflects the loss to the Jewish community of most children raised by intermarried couples:

> What do you call the grandchildren of intermarried Jews? Christians.
>
> —Milton Himmelfarb

69

A MISCELLANY

On Sports, Jewish Denominations, and Communism

SPORTS

The Irish didn't like it when they heard of Greenberg's
fame
For they thought a good first baseman should possess an
Irish name.
And the Murphys and Mulrooneys said they never
dreamed they'd see
A Jewish boy from Bronxville out where Casey used to
be. . . .
And with fifty-seven doubles and a score of homers made
The respect they had for Greenberg was being openly dis-
played.
But upon the Jewish New Year when Hank Greenberg
came to bat
And made two home runs off Pitcher Rhodes—they
cheered like mad for that.
Come Yom Kippur—holy fast day world wide over to the
Jews,
And Hank Greenberg to his teaching and the old tradition
true,

Spent the day among his people and he didn't come to
play.
Said Murphy to Mulrooney, "We shall lose the game
today!
We shall miss him in the infield and shall miss him at
the bat.
But he's true to his religion—and I honor him for that."
—Edgar Guest, printed in the Detroit *Jewish Chronicle*
October 5, 1934; quoted in Peter Levine, *Ellis Island to Ebbets
Field,* page 136

Granted, this poem hardly constitutes an essential Jewish quote.
But it does highlight what, in Jewish terms, was the most important
decision made by two well-known Jewish baseball players. Both
Hank Greenberg and Sandy Koufax, the most famous Jews to play
major-league baseball, chose to miss important games that fell on
Yom Kippur. The game Greenberg skipped occurred in 1934. Nine
days earlier, he had played on Rosh Hashana, hitting two home runs
in a game in which his Detroit Tigers beat the Boston Red Sox 2–
1. But nine days later, on Judaism's holiest day, he opted for the
synagogue over the ballpark.

Thirty-one years later, pitching great Sandy Koufax spent the
opening day of the 1965 World Series also observing Yom Kippur
in synagogue. His Los Angeles Dodgers lost to the Minneapolis
Twins 8–2. When pitcher Don Drysdale was taken out in the third
inning after giving up six runs, he told his manager, Walt Alston,
"I bet right now you wish I was Jewish too."

"Even in jest," comments sports historian Peter Levine, "the notion that being Jewish carried positive meaning reflected the real
progress Jews had made toward full [acceptance into American life]
by 1965" (*Ellis Island to Ebbets Field,* page 246).

JEWISH DENOMINATIONALISM AND ITS
DISCONTENTS

I don't care what denomination in Judaism you belong to,
as long as you're ashamed of it.
—Rabbi Irving "Yitz" Greenberg, President of CLAL,
the National Jewish Center for Learning and Leadership

Although worded as a quip, Greenberg's point is profound. Interdenominational acrimony is largely caused by various Jews' tendency to highlight their movements' perceived strengths and the others' weaknesses. Thus, Reform Jews commonly dismiss Orthodoxy as fanatical, and view their movement as the only truly tolerant, open-minded one. Orthodox Jews, meanwhile, often speak of themselves as the only ones sincerely trying to follow God's laws, and often view non-Orthodox Jews as irreligious people who change the Torah's meaning to conform to their own convenience.

But since all the movements have failed to fulfill Judaism's task of "perfecting the world under the rule of God," does it not behoove all of their adherents to speak more charitably of their "opponents," and more humbly of their own accomplishments?

Dennis Prager suggests two more meaningful divisions of Jews than Orthodox/Conservative/Reconstructionist/Reform: The first is between "serious" and "not serious" Jews. Alternatively, Prager argues:

> There is no authentic denomination; there are only authentic Jews.

ON THE WIDESPREAD ATTRACTION OF ALIENATED JEWS TO LEFT-WING POLITICS

> All Jews should set up a statue to Lenin for not being a Jew.
>
> —Israel Zangwill (1864–1926)

Zangwill was commenting on the well-known attraction of alienated Jews to communism, which contributed to antisemitism among many non-Jews. Thank God, Zangwill in effect was arguing, that the most famous twentieth-century communist was not Jewish, although many of his most important allies were.

> "Chaim, why do you want to leave the Soviet Union?" Yiddish writer David Bergelson asked Chaim Grade. "Is it

510

because you feel you won't be able to write the way we want you to write?"

"No," Grade answered. "It is much worse. I am leaving because I am afraid it will be too easy for me to learn to write the way you want me to write."

—Cited in Morton Reichik, "Chaim Grade,"
in Murray Polner, ed., *Jewish Profiles,* page 87

Grade, one of the twentieth century's foremost Yiddish writers, escaped Vilna ahead of the Nazis and fled to the Soviet Union, where he spent World War II. There he befriended many of Russia's foremost Yiddish writers, among them Bergelson. Although they pleaded with Grade to remain in the Soviet Union, he left as soon as possible, later immigrating to the United States.

On August 12, 1952, seven years after the above conversation, Bergelson and twenty-three other Russian-Jewish intellectuals were taken to Moscow's notorious Lubianka Prison and murdered on Stalin's orders.

In *Ashes Out of Hope,* an anthology of Soviet Yiddish fiction, Irving Howe and Eliezer Greenberg write of the irony of these Soviet Jewish writers' violent deaths: "Elsewhere in Europe, scores of Yiddish writers were destroyed by avowed enemies [during the Holocaust]; here in the Soviet Union a generation of gifted Yiddish novelists and poets came to its end in the prison cells or labor camps of the very state to which they had pledged themselves, sometimes with naive enthusiasm, sometimes with wry foreboding."

After their deaths, Grade was to write of Bergelson and the other Yiddish writers, "I weep for you with all the letters of the alphabet."

PART VI

THE
HOLOCAUST

70

THE HOLOCAUST

A Prologue

There is a story about Claire Boothe Luce complaining that she was bored with hearing about the Holocaust. A Jewish friend of hers said he perfectly understood her sensitivity to the matter; in fact, he had the same sense of repetitiousness and fatigue, hearing so often about the crucifixion.

> —Herbert Gold, *Selfish Like Me;* cited in
> Cynthia Ozick's prologue to Gay Block and
> Malka Drucker's *Rescuers: Portraits of Moral Courage in the Holocaust,* page xi

Elie Wiesel has expressed a similar thought, albeit in a less confrontational manner:

> One Jew was put to death in Jerusalem two thousand years ago and the non-Jewish world has not ceased to speak of his death. Do we [Jews] not have the right, the duty, to keep alive the memory of the six million dead?
>
> —Elie Wiesel, cited in Eva Fleischner,
> *Auschwitz: Beginning of a
> New Era,* page xi

O the chimneys
O the ingeniously devised habitations of death
When Israel's body drifted as smoke
Through the air.

—Nelly Sachs, title poem,
O the Chimneys

71

WHAT THE NAZIS SAID

ADOLF HITLER

I have often been a prophet in my life and was generally laughed at. During my struggle for power, the Jews primarily received with laughter my prophecies that I would someday assume the leadership of the state . . . and then, among many other things, achieve a solution of the Jewish problem. I suppose that the once resounding laughter of Jewry in Germany is now choking in their throats.

Today I will be a prophet once again. If international finance Jewry inside and outside of Europe should succeed once more in plunging nations into another world war, the consequence will not be the Bolshevization of the earth and thereby the victory of Jewry, but the destruction of the Jewish race in Europe.

—Adolf Hitler, January 30, 1939 (seven months before he
invaded Poland and launched World War II), in a speech
before the Reichstag (parliament) celebrating
the sixth anniversary of his achieving power

During World War II, Hitler referred on at least five occasions to this "prophecy." During a 1942 speech, after citing the last sentence from the above speech, he added: "At one time, the Jews of Germany laughed about my prophecies. I do not know whether they are still laughing or whether they have already lost all desire to laugh. But right now, I can only repeat: they will stop laughing

517

everywhere, and I shall be right also in that prophecy." (One of the striking aspects of both these speeches is Hitler's paranoiac fury at the Jews for supposedly laughing at him.)

Contemporary Holocaust scholars debate whether Hitler intended to murder the Jews from the beginning of his political career, or whether he resolved to do so only once World War II began. However, it already is apparent in the final chapter of his *Mein Kampf* (1925) that Hitler long had toyed with the idea of gassing large numbers of Jews:

> If at the beginning of the war [World War I] and during the war, twelve or fifteen thousand of these Hebraic corrupters of the nation had been subjected to poison gas . . . then the sacrifices of millions at the front would not have been in vain.
>
> —Adolf Hitler, *Mein Kampf*, page 984

> Above all I charge the leaders of the nation and those under them to scrupulously observe the laws of race and to mercilessly oppose the universal poisoner of all peoples, international Jewry.
>
> —Hitler's final "testament" to the German people, April 29, 1945, the day before he committed suicide

People who know little about antisemitism or about the Nazis commonly assume that, for Hitler, the Jews were scapegoats, that he blamed all of Germany's problems on them to achieve political power. The late historian Lucy Davidowicz, author of *The War Against the Jews,* convincingly argues the opposite: "Racial imperialism and the fanatic plan to destroy the Jews were the dominant passions behind [his] drive for power" (page 4). Thus, Hitler did not blame the Jews in order to gain power; he gained power, in large measure, to persecute the Jews. Hatred of Jews constituted his essence, rather than being a political strategy. Nothing proves this better than this final statement to the German people urging them, *"above all,"* to go on fighting the Jews.

JOSEPH GOEBBELS

Certainly the Jew is a human being. But then the flea is a living thing too; only not a pleasant one. Since the flea is not a pleasant thing, we are not obliged to keep it and let it prosper . . . but our duty is rather to exterminate it. Likewise with the Jews.

—Joseph Goebbels, 1929; Goebbels later served as Nazi Minister
of Propaganda; cited in C. C. Aronsfeld,
The Text of the Holocaust, page 12.

Note that Goebbels's comment about extermination was made four years before the Nazis achieved power. His openness about their intentions on democracy is apparent in yet another statement:

We will become members of the Reichstag in order to disable the Weimar order with its own acquiescence. . . . We come as enemies.

—Goebbels outlining Nazi political agenda prior to their attaining
power. The Weimar Republic to which he refers was Germany's
pre-Nazi (1919–1933) fragile, crisis- and strife-ridden democracy.

This blunt pronouncement of the Nazis' contempt for democracy raises anew the question of whether societies should grant political rights to those who use democratic means in attempts to destroy democracy. Such organizations as the American Civil Liberties Union assert that democratic governments never have the right to abridge their enemies' political freedom. Those who disagree argue that allowing democracy's enemies to use democratic elections to gain power is like permitting people who announce that they intend to rob banks to own guns. Indeed, the Nazis gained power largely through a democratic election, rather than a coup d'état.

The age of hairsplitting Jewish intellectualism is dead. . . .
The past lies in the flames.

—Goebbels, May 1933, at the Opera House opposite the
University of Berlin before a large crowd of book burners

Where one burns books, one will, in the end, burn people.
—Heinrich Heine, the nineteenth-century German-Jewish poet

[In Nazi Germany] the distance between burning books and burning people [was] eight years.
—Michael Berenbaum, *The World Must Know*, page 25.
(The above quotes and the details that follow are drawn from this book.)

Many people recalled Heine's words when thousands of German university students and professors removed tens of thousands of books from libraries and bookstores and threw them into vast bonfires. The works selected generally were either by Jews or by such non-Jewish anti-Nazi writers as Thomas Mann. In Frankfurt, the book burning was turned into a perverse kind of festival; thousands of volumes were brought to a huge bonfire in carts drawn by oxen, while a band played Chopin's "Funeral March."

HEINRICH HIMMLER ON THE "FINAL SOLUTION"

I also want to talk to you quite frankly on a very grave matter. Among ourselves it should be mentioned quite frankly and yet we will never speak of it publicly. I mean the evacuation of the Jews, the extermination of the Jewish race. . . . Most of you must know what it means when one hundred corpses are lying side by side or five hundred or one thousand. To have stuck it out and at the same time— apart from exceptions caused by human weakness—to have remained decent fellows, that is what has made us hard. This is a page in our history which has never been written and is never to be written.
—Heinrich Himmler, head of the SS, in a speech to SS and police leaders in Posen (October 1943), then part of Germany, now of Poland

"To have stuck it out and at the same time . . . to have remained decent fellows" is surely the most incredible, and unintentionally ironic, sentence in Himmler's speech.

520

Historian Richard Breitman, author of *The Architect of Genocide: Himmler and the Final Solution,* notes that although Himmler routinely camouflaged evidence of the Holocaust, this speech was tape recorded. In the course of his three-hour-and-ten-minute oration, Himmler defended the "Final Solution" as an act of self-defense: "We have the moral right, we had the duty with regard to our people, to kill this race that wanted to kill us" (pages 242–243).

Yet there were German leaders who were not persuaded—if only for "practical" reasons—that the Holocaust was justifiable. For example, on September 18, 1942, Nazi General Kurt Freiherr von Gienanth addressed a memorandum to government leaders outlining Germany's manpower difficulties and noting that Jewish slave laborers were performing much-needed work. He requested a slowing down in the murder of the Jews: "The principle should be to eliminate the Jews as promptly as possible without impairing essential war work."

Twelve days later, Himmler relieved Gienanth of his post and instructed "that steps be ruthlessly taken against all those who think it their business to intervene in the alleged interests of war industry, but who in reality want only to support the Jews and their businesses" (Lucy Dawidowicz, *A Holocaust Reader,* page 85).

A NAZI LEADER BEFORE AND AFTER THE WAR

> I ask nothing of the Jews, except that they should disappear. . . . We must destroy the Jews wherever we meet them and whenever opportunity presents offers.
>
> —Hans Frank, Nazi commandant of Poland,
> on December 16, 1941

> A thousand years will pass and the guilt of Germany will not be erased.
>
> —Frank, five years later, at the 1946 Nuremberg Trials
> of the Nazi leadership

72

THE EXPERIENCE OF THE "FINAL SOLUTION"

Six Stories out of Six Million

At the station, another girl I saw was about five years old. She fed her younger brother, and he cried. He cried, the little one; he was sick. Into a diluted bit of jam she dipped tiny crusts of bread and skillfully inserted them into his mouth. This my eyes were privileged to see, to see this mother, a mother of five years, feeding her child, to hear her soothing words. My own mother, the best in the world, had not invented such a ruse. But this one wiped his tears with a smile, injecting joy into his heart, this little girl of Israel. Sholem Aleichem could not have improved upon her.

They, the children of Israel, were the first in doom and disaster, most of them without father and mother. They were consumed by frost, starvation and lice. Holy Messiahs, sanctified in pain. Why, in days of doom, are they the first victims of wickedness, the first in the trap of evil, the first to be detained for death, the first to be thrown into the wagons of slaughter? They were thrown into the wagons, the huge wagons, like heaps of refuse, like the ashes of the earth. And they transported them, killed them, exterminated them, without remnant or remembrance.

The best of my children were all wiped out, woe unto
me, doom and desolation.

> —Yitzchak Katznelson, *Song of My Slaughtered People;*
> Katznelson, along with his oldest son, was murdered
> in Auschwitz in 1944; his wife and two younger sons had
> been killed earlier. His great prose poem, hidden in bottles
> and buried in the ground in a Nazi concentration camp in Vittel,
> France, was published after the war.

As Katznelson makes painfully clear, the Germans generally targeted Jewish children as their first victims, both because they were
too small to do forced labor and to ensure that they not grow up
and bring another generation of Jews into the world.

Between one and one and a half million children were among
the six million murdered Jews. In the death camps, German "effi-
ciency" consisted of tearing children away from parents about to
enter the gas chambers. Once the chambers were filled, the Germans
usually flung the children in over the adults' heads, thus maximizing
the number of Jews murdered. Later, when the Nazis decided it was
not worth "wasting" gas on children (it cost an average of less than
one cent per victim), SS men would sometimes throw living Jewish
children straight into the crematoria furnaces.

* * *

The Jews of Kelme, Lithuania, were already standing be-
side the pits which they had been forced to dig for themselves—standing ready to be slain for the Sanctification of
God's Name (*al Kiddush ha-Shem*). Their spiritual leader,
Rabbi Daniel [Movshovitz], asked the German officer in
command of the operation to allow him to say some part-
ing words to his flock, and the latter agreed but ordered
Rabbi Daniel to be brief. Speaking serenely, slowly, as
though he were delivering one of his regular Sabbath ser-
mons in the synagogue, Rabbi Daniel used his last minutes
on earth to encourage his flock to perform *Kiddush ha-
Shem* in the proper manner. Suddenly the German officer
cut in and shouted at the rabbi to finish so that he could
get on with the shooting. Still speaking calmly, the rabbi

concluded as follows: "My dear Jews! The moment has come for us to perform the precept of *Kiddush ha-Shem* of which we have spoken, to perform it in fact! I beg one thing of you: don't get excited and confused; accept this judgment calmly and in a worthy manner!" Then he turned to the German officer and said: "I have finished. You may begin."

—Yosef Gottfarstein, a chronicler of the Holocaust

The contemporary theologian Emil Fackenheim, who cites this story, comments: " 'I have finished. You may begin.' We search all history for a more radical contrast between pure, holy goodness and a radical evil utterly and eternally beyond all redemption. The German officer saw what he saw. He heard what he heard. So did his men. How then could even one go on with the shooting? Yet they all did" (Emil Fackenheim, "The Holocaust and the State of Israel: Their Relation," page 213).

*   *   *

Of course, not all victims acted heroically. Yet were it not for the Germans' fiendish cruelty, many would have lived out their lives without having to confront the ugliness and cowardice that emerged from within them during the Holocaust, sometimes only for an instant. The Polish writer Tadeusz Borowski recalls this scene from his years in Auschwitz:

> They go, they vanish. Men, women and children. Some of them know [that they are walking toward the trucks which will take them to the gas chambers].
>
> Here is a woman; she walks quickly but tries to appear calm. A small child with a pink cherub's face runs after her and, unable to keep up, stretches out his little arms and cries, "Mama! Mama!"
>
> "Pick up your child, woman!" [a guard shouts].
>
> "It's not mine, sir, not mine!" she shouts hysterically and runs on. . . . She wants to reach those who will not ride the trucks, those who will go on foot, those who will [do forced labor for the Nazis and] stay alive. She is

young, healthy, good-looking, she wants to live.

But the child runs after her, wailing loudly, "Mama, mama, don't leave me!"

"It's not mine, not mine, no!"

Andrei, a sailor from Sevastopol, grabs hold of her. His eyes are glassy from vodka and the heat. With one powerful blow he knocks her off her feet, then, as she falls, takes her by the hair and pulls her up again. His face twitches with rage.

"Ah, you bloody Jewess! So you're running from your own child; I'll show you, you whore!" His huge hand chokes her, he lifts her in the air and heaves her onto the truck, like a heavy sack of grain.

"Here! And take this with you, bitch!" and he throws the child at her feet.

"*Gut gemacht,* good work. That's the way to deal with degenerate mothers," says the S.S. man standing at the foot of the truck.

—Tadeusz Borowski, *This Way for the Gas,
Ladies and Gentlemen,* page 87

*　　　*　　　*

At Stolpce [Poland], on September 23, 1942, the ghetto was surrounded by German soldiers. Pits had been prepared outside a nearby village. The Germans entered the ghetto, shooting and searching. Eliezer Melamed later recalled how he and his girlfriend found a room in which to hide behind some sacks of flour. A mother and her three children followed them into the house. The mother hid in one corner of the room, the three children in another.

The Germans entered the room and discovered the children. One of the children, a young boy, began to scream, "Mama! Mama!" as the Germans dragged the children away. But another of them, aged four, shouted to his brother in Yiddish, "*Zog nit 'Mameh.' Men vet ir oich zunemen.*" ("Don't say 'Mama.' They'll take her too.")

The boy stopped screaming. The mother remained silent. Her children were dragged away. The mother was saved. "I will always hear that," Melamed recalled, "es-

pecially at night: '*Zog nit Mameh*'—'Don't say Mama.'
And I will always remember the sight of the mother [after]
her children were dragged away by the Germans. She was
hitting her head against the wall, as if to punish herself for
remaining silent, for wanting to live."

—Martin Gilbert, *The Holocaust,* page 465

While visiting Israel, Berel Wein, an American rabbi, came
across an American minister who started badgering him with hostile
questions and comments about Israel, and finally asked him, "What
is it that you Jews really want?"

Wein responded by telling the minister the above story, then
added, "What do we Jews really want? Well, I'll tell you what I
want. All I want is that my grandchildren should be able to call
'Mama.' All we want is that the world should leave us alone" (Dr.
James David Weiss, *Vintage Wein,* pages 171–172).

*   *   *

I shall tell the story of one day, an ordinary day, much
like any other. That day I worked cleaning out a shed. . . .
An umbrella had gotten stuck in a roof beam, and the SS
man Paul Groth ordered a boy to get it down. The boy
climbed up, fell from the roof and was injured. Groth punished him with twenty-five lashes. He was pleased with
what had happened and called over another German and
told him he had found "parachutists" among the Jews. We
were ordered to climb up to the roof one after another.
. . . The majority did not succeed; they fell down, broke
legs, were whipped, bitten by [the German shepherd] Barry
and shot.

This game was not enough for Groth.

There were many mice around, and each of us was
ordered to catch two mice. He selected five prisoners, ordered them to pull down their trousers, and we dropped
the mice inside. The people were ordered to remain at attention, but they could not without moving. They were
whipped.

But this was not enough for Groth. He called over a

Jew, forced him to drink alcohol until he fell dead. . . . We were ordered to lay the man on a board, pick him up and slowly march while singing a funeral march.

This is a description of one ordinary day. And many of them were even worse.

—Dov Freiburg describing life in the Sobibor concentration camp; cited in Yitzchak Arad, *Belzec, Sobibor, Treblinka: The Operation Reinhard Death Camps,* page 200. For other works describing what life was like in the concentration camps see Elie Wiesel, *Night;* Yaffa Eliach, *Hasidic Tales of the Holocaust;* Viktor Frankl, *Man's Search for Meaning;* Terence Des Pres, *The Survivor: An Anatomy of Life in the Death Camps;* and Benjamin Ferencz, *Less Than Slaves: Jewish Forced Labor and the Quest for Compensation.*

*   *   *

Three days after the liberation of Buchenwald, I became very ill with food poisoning. I was transferred to the hospital and spent two weeks between life and death.

One day I was able to get up, after gathering all my strength. I wanted to see myself in the mirror hanging on the opposite wall. I had not seen myself [since I was deported from the ghetto to the concentration camp].

From the depths of the mirror, a corpse gazed back at me. The look in his eyes, as they stared into mine, has never left me.

—Elie Wiesel, *Night*

527

73

BEFORE AND DURING THE HOLOCAUST

Reactions in the West

It is a fantastic commentary on the inhumanity of our time that for thousands and thousands of people a piece of paper with a stamp on it is the difference between life and death.

—Dorothy Thompson, American journalist, February 1939

Thompson's comment was made as part of an appeal to Congress to pass the Wagner-Rogers bill, which would have granted special permission to twenty thousand German-Jewish children under fourteen to enter the United States. The bill stipulated that financial support for them would be provided by private sources (Jewish organizations) so that no expenditure of public funds would be needed.

Although Senator Wagner and Congresswoman Rogers introduced their bill three months after the murderous pogroms of Kristallnacht, only a minority of Americans wanted to admit the children. One prominent organization, the American Legion, publicly opposed the bill on "moral" grounds, arguing that it was wrong to separate parents from children: "the American Legion therefore strongly opposes the breaking up of families, which would be done by the proposed legislation." This was a cruel mockery of the motives of the parents who wanted to save their children's lives. Apparently, as Eliezer Berkovits has written, the Legion's leadership regarded its morality as far superior "to the traditions of those cruel Jewish parents who were willing to part with their children rather than perish together with them in the bliss of family communion in the concentration camps" (*Faith After the Holocaust,* page 12).

President Franklin Delano Roosevelt, whom most Jews have mistakenly regarded as highly sympathetic to their needs, said not a word on the bill's behalf, despite his wife Eleanor's strong support for it. His silence, along with the isolationists' active opposition, ensured that Wagner-Rogers died in committee. The overwhelming majority of the twenty thousand Jewish children died in the gas chambers. Presumably, the Legion's leadership was relieved to learn that they died "together" with their parents.

Concerning F.D.R., historian Walter Laqueur has documented that, years later, after he knew for certain that Jews were being murdered, Roosevelt reassured his good friend the Jewish Supreme Court Justice Felix Frankfurter that there was no reason to worry about Jews being killed; deported Jews were being employed to build fortifications on the Soviet frontier. The president apparently hoped that this deception would defuse Jewish pressure on the Allies to act more aggressively against the Nazi genocide (*The Terrible Secret,* pages 94–95).

*   *   *

> "Are you a Jew?" asked one of the guards
> "Yes," answered the child at the barrier.
> "Jews not admitted," snapped the guard.
> "Oh, please let me in. I'm only a very little Jew."
> —Game played by Jewish children aboard the S.S. *St. Louis,*
> May 1939 (reported in Michael Berenbaum,
> *The World Must Know,* page 58)

Nine hundred thirty-seven German Jews, all holding Cuban visas, sailed on the S.S. *St. Louis* from Germany on May 27, 1939.

While en route, there was a change of government in Cuba, and its new leaders refused to honor the visas. Forced to set sail from the island nation, the ship headed toward territorial waters off Florida (less than one hundred miles away), where the Coast Guard fired a warning shot in its direction.

Eventually, after weeks at sea and intensive negotiations between the Joint Distribution Committee and four European countries (England, Belgium, Holland, and France), these nations agreed to accept the Jewish refugees. Yet because all but England later were occupied by the Germans, well over half of the Jews on the *St. Louis*'s "Voyage of the Damned" apparently died in the gas chambers.

*   *   *

> May God not punish me for my words, [but] the fact that in recent months Jews have not produced a substantial number of mentally deranged persons is hardly a symptom of health.
> —Hayim Greenberg, February 1943, writing of American Jewry in "Bankrupt" (reprinted in Marie Syrkin, ed., *Hayim Greenberg Anthology*, pages 192–203)

In "Bankrupt," written at the height of the Nazi murders, Labor Zionist leader Greenberg expressed his outrage and heartbreak at American Jewry's business-as-usual, even-tempered attitude, even as reports of the murder of two million European Jews were reaching them. With biting sarcasm, he called for a day of fasting and prayer, not for Europe's Jews but for the Jews of America who "have not done—and have made no effort to do—their elementary duty toward the millions of Jews who are captive and doomed in Europe."

Instead of uniting to press the American administration to adopt policies that could at least reduce the suffering's scope, Greenberg charged, the various Jewish organizations had engaged in petty squabbles and power plays. He recalled a session of the Jewish Labor Committee, where a Jew who had escaped from Poland rebuked the others present for their inactivity, only to be shouted down as a "hysteric." It was this incident that precipitated his denunciation of American's Jewry's lack of an appropriately outraged and active response.

Today, Greenberg's essay often is cited as proof that both the Western world and Western Jewry were aware—at least in general terms—of the Holocaust's horrors even as they were happening.

74

"LIKE LAMBS TO THE SLAUGHTER"

Why Did More Jews Not Fight Back?

Everywhere I turned, the question was fired at me: why did the Jews not rebel? Why did they go like lambs to the slaughter? Suddenly I realized that we were ashamed of those who were tortured, shot, burned. . . . Unconsciously, we have accepted the Nazi view that the Jews were subhuman. . . . History is playing a bitter joke on us: have we not ourselves put the six million on trial?

—Yoel Palgi, a Palestinian Jew who parachuted, along with
Hannah Senesh, into Hungary into 1944. When Palgi
returned to Palestine in June 1945, he went
to a veterans' club, where he encountered the above reaction.

The expression "like lambs to the slaughter" is taken from a verse in Psalms (44:23; see also Isaiah 53:7) in which the psalmist describes Jews dying for God's sake, and beseeches God not to hide His face from the Jews' affliction. These very words had been cited years earlier, when poet Abba Kovner called on his fellow Vilna Jews to revolt: "We will not be led like sheep to the slaughter. . . . Brothers! It is better to die fighting like free men than to live at the mercy of the murderers. Arise! Arise [and fight] with your last breath!" (January 1, 1942).

While a significant number of Jews did rebel, there are several reasons the overwhelming majority did not. The most important reason is that almost no Jews had weapons, and arms and legs are of little utility against machine guns and an organized army. (Indeed, while most American Jews support gun-control laws, the few Jews I know who oppose them invariably argue that had European Jewry been armed, many more Jews might have survived.) Few people realize that because of their lack of arms, almost none of the several million prisoners taken by the Germans fought back, including several million Russian soldiers, a large percentage of whom died in Nazi camps.

There also was a moral reason for the relatively low number of revolts: The Jews knew that other Jews would be the ultimate victims of any act of rebellion, even a successful one: The Germans would murder them in retaliation. A prominent Jewish philosopher has articulated the moral dilemma that would-be resisters confronted:

> Was it morally right to kill an S.S. officer if, as a consequence, hundreds and even thousands of men, women, and children would perish immediately?
> —Eliezer Berkovits (1910–1993),
> *Faith After the Holocaust,* page 30

In one notable case, Jewish fighters attacked a German police detachment in the old Jewish quarter of Amsterdam; the German response was terrible:

> Four hundred and thirty Jews were arrested in reprisal and they were literally tortured to death, first in Buchenwald and then in the Austrian camp of Mauthausen. For months on end they died a thousand deaths, and every single one of them would have envied his brethren in Auschwitz, and even in Riga and Minsk. There exist many things consid-

erably worse than death, and the S.S. saw to it that none of them was ever very far from their victims' minds and imagination.

> —K. Shabbetai, *As Sheep to the Slaughter? The Myth of Cowardice.* The survivors' sensitivity to charges of cowardice is underscored by the fact that Shabbetai's book was published by the World Federation of Bergen-Belsen Survivors' Association.

Yet many instances of Jewish resistance did still occur, the most famous in the Warsaw Ghetto:

> The dream of my life has become true. Jewish self-defense in the Warsaw Ghetto has become a fact. Jewish armed resistance and retaliation have become a reality. I have been witness to the magnificent heroic struggle of the Jewish fighters.
>
> —Mordechai Anielewicz, April 23, 1943, four days after the outbreak of the Warsaw Ghetto revolt, in a note to Yitzchak Zuckerman, a unit commander in the revolt

Only twenty-four years old when he helped organize the Warsaw Ghetto revolt, Anielewicz realized that the Germans intended to deport and murder every remaining Jew in Warsaw. The revolt was triggered by word that yet another Nazi deportation was imminent.

The Warsaw Ghetto fighters held out for about a month, longer than the Polish army withstood the 1939 Nazi invasion.

Yitzchak Zuckerman, the heroic unit commander to whom Anielewicz addressed the above note, was among the few Warsaw Ghetto fighters who survived the war. Some forty years later, he was interviewed by Claude Lanzmann for the movie *Shoah:*

> I began drinking after the war. It was very difficult. . . . You asked my impression. If you could lick my heart, it would poison you.

Despite the Warsaw Ghetto revolt and other acts of resistance, during the 1961 Eichmann trial it became fashionable among some

Jews and non-Jews alike to express shock and a certain contempt for those Jews who "failed to resist." Elie Wiesel responded:

> The Talmud teaches man never to judge his friend until he has been in his place. But, for the world, the Jews are not friends. They have never been. Because they had no friends they are dead. So learn to be silent.
>
> —Elie Wiesel, "A Plea for the Dead"

75

"THEN THEY CAME FOR ME, AND THERE WAS NO ONE LEFT"

Heroic Words and Tragic Quotes

RELIGIOUS RESPONSES

First they came for the socialists, and I did not speak out—because I was not a socialist. Then they came for the trade unionists, and I did not speak out—because I was not a trade unionist. Then they came for the Jews, and I did not speak out—because I was not a Jew. Then they came for me—and there was no one left to speak for me.

—Reverend Martin Niemoller, leader of the Confessional Church, an anti-Nazi group that condemned the regime's racial policies and anti-Christian teachings

In Reverend Niemoller's final sermon (June 27, 1937), delivered four days before he was arrested and sent to prison, then to Dachau, he declared:

No more are we ready to keep silent at man's behest when God commands us to speak. . . . We must obey God rather than man.

—Cited in Louis Snyder, *Encyclopedia of the Third Reich,* page

248. Snyder notes that Hitler followed Niemoller's speeches carefully and with growing fury, and was personally responsible for Niemoller's continued incarceration throughout the war.

Virtually identical words were repeated six years later in a different land:

> We must obey God before we obey man.
> —H. Fuglsand-Damgaard, the Lutheran bishop of Copenhagen,
> urging all Danes to resist the German order to deport the Jews

The bishop's efforts, as well as those of tens of thousands of lay people, were successful. In October 1943, as the Nazis prepared to deport Danish Jewry to concentration camps, Danes from all walks of life aided 7,720 Jews to escape on fishing boats to Sweden. The 464 Danish Jews who did not succeed in escaping were deported to the Theresienstadt concentration camp, where the Danish government made such strong, repeated representations on their behalf that, at war's end, all but fifty-one had survived.

> Our nation's infamy is bound to bring about Divine punishment.
> —Pastor J. von Jan, Swabia, Germany, November 16, 1938,
> one week after the Kristallnacht pogrom

When Pastor von Jan courageously denounced the Kristallnacht pogrom, a Nazi mob dragged him out of his Bible class and brutally beat him; his vicarage was smashed, and he was imprisoned (Martin Gilbert, *The Holocaust,* page 73).

> We stand before our God. . . . We bow to Him, and we stand erect before man.
> —Rabbi Leo Baeck (1873–1956), in a prayer to be read
> on Yom Kippur, 1938, that he distributed to synagogues
> throughout Germany

> In the past our enemies demanded our soul and the Jew
> sacrificed his body to sanctify God's name. Now, the en-
> emy demands the body of the Jew. That makes it imper-
> ative for the Jew to defend it and protect it.
> —Rabbi Yitzchak Nissenbaum (1868–1942) of Warsaw

Nissenbaum was alluding to the fact that throughout history, particularly during the Crusades, thousands of Jews who could have saved their lives by converting to Christianity refused to do so, and so died *al Kiddush ha-Shem* (to sanctify God's name). What was needed now, he argued, was *Kiddush ha-Hayyim,* the sanctification of life. The unprecedented attempt to murder every Jew made it imperative that Jews do all in their power to survive.

How ironic that some months later, when Nissenbaum was one of the last surviving rabbis in the Warsaw Ghetto, he felt compelled to refuse the Catholic Church's offer to save him and the ghetto's two other rabbis (for the reason for their refusal, see pages 326–327).

OTHER RESPONSES

> Wear the Yellow Badge with pride.
> —Robert Weltsch, April 1933

This constitutes the title of an editorial written by the German Zionist leader Robert Weltsch in response to the Nazi boycott of Jewish stores initiated soon after Hitler gained power. At the time, Jews did not yet have to wear a yellow badge, although the Nazis had painted large yellow Stars of David on the windows of most Jewish-owned stores. By 1941, however, the Nazis had made it a capital offense for Jews not to wear a yellow badge on their clothing.

Weltsch's editorial urged his fellow Jews to express pride in their Jewishness, rather than being demoralized by Nazi persecution. According to many accounts, his editorial lifted the morale of German Jewry.

Weltsch himself survived the war; in later years, he confided to friends that he regretted having written his famous words. Rather than urging Jews to retain their pride, he commented, he should have encouraged them to flee Germany. Of course, in April 1933, neither Weltsch nor any other Jew knew that the Germans and their collaborators eventually would attempt a "Final Solution" to Europe's "Jewish problem."

*   *   *

The SS wants me to kill children with my own hands.
> —Among the final words of Adam Czerniakow—the
> Nazi-appointed head of the Jewish community in the
> Warsaw Ghetto—before committing suicide on July 23, 1942

Many Warsaw Jews justifiably complained that Czerniakow cooperated with the Nazis. In the summer of 1942, when 300,000 Warsaw Jews were rounded up, the ghetto police supervised this operation under his direction. Czerniakow's defense was that if he refused to cooperate by turning over many Jews, all Jews would be killed.

In July 1942, Czerniakow learned that the Nazis had denied his request to exempt children in the Jewish orphanage from deportations. On July 23 (the Jewish fast of *Tisha Be'Av*, which commemorates the destruction of both Temples [586 B.C.E. and 70 C.E.]), Czerniakow swallowed cyanide.

Among the Jews long critical of him was Chaim Kaplan, a Warsaw Hebrew teacher and writer (Kaplan's diary was discovered in a kerosene can twenty years after the Warsaw Ghetto was destroyed). Yet when he learned of Czerniakow's suicide and the reason for it, he wrote, "He did not have a good life, but he had a beautiful death. May his death atone for his wrongs against his people. . . . There are those who earn immortality in a single hour. The President, Adam Czerniakow, earned his immortality in a single instant" (*The Warsaw Diary of Chaim Kaplan,* July 26, 1942; Kaplan's reference to earning immortality through one heroic act is a motif drawn from the Talmud; see page 322).

Czerniakow's refusal to carry out the terrible Nazi order should be contrasted with the behavior of Chaim Rumkowski, his Lodz Ghetto counterpart, who was unaffectionately known as "King of the Jews." Commanded by the Nazis to deliver all children under ten and all adults over sixty-five, Rumkowski ordered his fellow Jews to cooperate, arguing, "I love children as much as you do. [But] I have to perform this bloody operation myself. I simply must cut off the limbs to save the body itself. I have to take away children because otherwise others also will be taken, God forbid. . . . Fathers and mothers, give me your children" (see Martin Gilbert, *The Holocaust,* page 447).

Ultimately, almost every Jew in the ghetto was deported, including Rumkowski himself. When Soviet troops liberated Lodz in January 1945, 870 starving human beings remained from the ghetto's original 160,000 inhabitants. With good reason, Brian MacArthur, who has included Rumkowski's speech (September 4, 1942) in his *Penguin Book of Twentieth-Century Speeches* (pages 207–211), calls it "the most horrifying speech in this anthology."

And finally, the opening line of the most famous poem written by a remarkable young Jewish poet, twenty-three years old when she was executed:

> Blessed is the match that is consumed in kindling a flame.
> —Hannah Senesh (1921–1944)

A Hungarian-born Hebrew poet and fighter in the Haganah (the Jewish army in Palestine during the British Mandate), Senesh parachuted into Nazi-occupied Yugoslavia in March 1944, to rescue Allied prisoners-of-war and organize Jewish resistance. In June, as hundreds of thousands of Hungarian Jews were being deported to death camps, she decided to smuggle herself into Hungary to alert Jews there to the fate that awaited them. Well aware that she might be on a suicide mission, Senesh handed to her companion, Reuven Dafni, a crumpled piece of paper which contained the poem, "*Ashrei Ha-Gafrur*" ("Blessed Is the Match"), the first line of which is quoted above.

Inside Hungary, Senesh was quickly arrested by Hungarian police. Under torture, she revealed no names or other information to her fascist interrogators. On November 7, 1944, she was executed by a firing squad.

In 1950, Senesh's remains were brought to Israel and reburied on Mount Herzl, where Zionism's founder, Theodor Herzl, is interred. (See Marie Syrkin, *Blessed Is the Match,* for one of several biographies of Senesh.)

76

"LET THEM GO TO HELL"

Jewish Rage at the Nazis

> Oh, my God! How could you have created such filth in
> the world!
> —Yitzhak Katznelson, Hebrew poet murdered in Auschwitz

According to Eliezer Berkovits, Katznelson's anguished complaint reflected the mind-set of most religious victims of the Holocaust: "Far from inducing in them any sense of inferiority, the Holocaust kingdom revealed to them the polluted soul of a Nazified humanity. It filled them with radical contempt."

Berkovits observes that, conversely, the Germans' behavior often adversely affected assimilated Jews' self-image, because it derived "from the recognition they had received in the German or Austrian social structure." For example, Viktor Frankl, a psychiatrist who was imprisoned in a concentration camp, recalls how hurt he was when a German guard, instead of punishing him, threw a stone in his direction to remind him that he was merely a "domestic animal." Berkovits observes that "Yitzhak Katznelson would not have paid any attention to an incident of this kind. In his eyes, the ghetto and concentration camp guards were creatures with which you had so little in common that they could never insult you" (*With God in Hell*, pages 58–59).

*　　　*　　　*

> An elderly Jew passed the [Nazi] guards on Twarda Street
> [in the Warsaw Ghetto] and did not take off his hat in
> salute although the Jewish guards warned him. So [the
> Nazis] tortured him a long time. An hour later, he acted
> the same way. "They can go to hell," were his words.
>
> —Emanuel Ringelblum (1900–1944), *Notes from the Warsaw
> Ghetto: The Journal of Emanuel Ringelblum,* page 88

This elderly Jew's behavior brings to mind the actions of Mordechai who "would not kneel or bow low" before Haman (Esther 3:2). Although Jewish law would have permitted both Mordechai and the old Jew to show or feign subservience to save their lives, both refused out of a desire to deny their enemies control over how they were to behave.

> If the antisemites want to hate, let them hate, and let them
> go to hell.
>
> —Israeli Prime Minister David Ben-Gurion in a letter to an
> acquaintance who expressed fears that Israel's kidnapping
> and trying of Adolf Eichmann (1960–1961)
> would provoke antisemitism

> Forgive them not, Father, for they knew what they did.
>
> —A. M. Rosenthal, *New York Times* reporter (and later its
> managing editor), after an extended stay in Warsaw; see
> "Forgive Them Not, For They Knew What They Did," page 457

> While it is correct that only a handful of Germans knew
> all about the "Final Solution," very few knew nothing.
>
> —Walter Laqueur, *The Terrible Secret,* page 17

A distinguished historian, Laqueur notes that millions of people cannot be murdered without there being many participants and witnesses, as well as relatives and friends with whom many of them speak.

The German people cannot be proud of Beethoven and forget Hitler's crimes against humanity.

—Arthur Burns, former U.S. ambassador to Germany, during the 1985 Bitburg controversy (see pages 552–553)

And finally, and perhaps strangely, a joke:

Ever hear the one about the Jew in the German railway station? This poor Jew arrives at a station in Germany, carrying everything he owns in one battered old suitcase. Spotting an elderly gentleman studying the timetables, the Jew goes up to him and asks, "Excuse me, sir, are you an antisemite?"

The man is shocked. "How dare you ask me such a question?" he indignantly replies.

"No hard feelings," says the Jew and moves on to a woman standing nearby. "Excuse me, madam, are you an antisemite?" Her reaction is the same.

The scene repeats itself several times before the Jew finally meets up with a pleasant-looking, respectable couple and asks them the same question, "Pardon me, are you by any chance antisemites?"

"We certainly are," says the man. "We detest the Jews, the whole stinking lot of them."

"Ah," replies the Jew, "what a pleasure to meet such honest people. Would you mind keeping an eye on my suitcase for me?"

—Henry M. Broder in article printed in *Bitburg and Beyond,* edited by Ilya Levkov, page 294

77

"LET NOT THE MURDERERS OF OUR NATION ALSO BE ITS HEIRS"

The Debate over German Reparations

The 1952 debate over whether Israel should accept West German reparations proved emotionally wrenching and exceptionally bitter. The two sides were led by Prime Minister David Ben-Gurion, an ardent supporter of reparations, and future Prime Minister Menachem Begin, who argued that accepting money from the Germans constituted a betrayal of the six million.

> Let not the murderers of our nation also be its heirs.
> —David Ben-Gurion

The above appeal, the concluding sentence of Ben-Gurion's January 7, 1952, Knesset pro-reparations speech, brought to mind, perhaps intentionally, Elijah's bitter rhetorical question to King Ahab after he had murdered and then confiscated the property of Navot: "Have you murdered and also inherited?" (I Kings 21:19).

Ben-Gurion's position was in no way rooted in a willingness to forgive Germany for the Holocaust: "If I could take German property without sitting down with them for even a minute, but could go in with jeeps and machine guns to the warehouses and take it, I would do that. . . . But we can't do that."

His insistence on negotiating a financial agreement with Chancellor Konrad Adenauer was motivated by his belief that the Germans had no right to profit from property stolen from Jews, and by his awareness of Israel's desperate need for financial help in developing the new state (its population had doubled between 1948 and 1951).

Ben-Gurion's clearheaded analysis notwithstanding, the more emotionally powerful arguments were advanced by those who opposed taking money from the Germans:

> My little son came to me and asked, "How much shall we get for grandma and grandpa?"
> —Knesset member Elimelekh Rimalt, both of whose parents had
> been murdered by the Nazis; Rimalt was the first speaker
> to respond to Ben-Gurion.

> In the Vilna ghetto, when the winter temperature reached minus 39 degrees centigrade [−38 degrees Fahrenheit], when Jews died in the streets of cold and hunger, the Germans brought us the garments of hundreds of thousands of murdered Jews and told us, "Go ahead, take them. . . ."
> The Jewish representatives refused to accept clothing stained with their brothers' blood. I sat there then . . . and we [all] said we will not accept this . . . because they want to exploit us when we receive the clothes. . . . They wanted to take our pictures as we dressed in the garments of our [murdered] brothers and sisters.
> Yes, it was irrational.
> After the war, there was another irrational event. In the fields of Treblinka, gold hunters started to search for severed fingers and take the gold rings off them. The Jews of Poland went to the Polish government and asked that the practice be halted, and they fenced Treblinka in and did not touch the gold that was buried in the earth. That's the height of irrationality, but it is a moral and historic thing.
> —Knesset member and Holocaust survivor, Arieh Sheftel, cited in

Tom Segev, *The Seventh Million*, pages 207–208. The quotations in this section are drawn from Segev's book, an extraordinary account of the Holocaust's enduring impact on the Israeli mind.

We, who saw our fathers dragged to the gas chambers; we, who heard the clatter of the death trains; we, before whose eyes the elderly father was cast into the river . . . ; we, before whose eyes the elderly mother was murdered in the hospital; we, before whose eyes all these events unparalleled in history occurred—shall we fear risking our lives to prevent negotiations with our parents' murderers? . . . We are prepared to do anything, anything to prevent this disgrace to Israel.

—Knesset member Menachem Begin's response to Ben-Gurion during the January 7 debate

Begin's intense antipathy to the Germans—in his early years as prime minister, he refused private interviews to German journalists—seems to have temporarily unhinged his mind during the reparations debate. At one point, he addressed Ben-Gurion as if the Israeli prime minister himself was administering a Nazi-like state: "I know that you will drag me to the concentration camps. Today you arrested hundreds [of antireparation demonstrators]. Tomorrow you may arrest thousands. No matter, they will go, they will sit in prison. We will sit there with them. If necessary, we will be killed with them."

A similar paranoia punctuated Begin's speech the same day to a large crowd of anti-reparations demonstrators. He spoke of Germans in the same totalistic manner rabid antisemites often speak of Jews: "There is not one German who has not murdered our fathers. Every German is a Nazi. Every German is a murderer. Adenauer [who had been an anti-Nazi] is a murderer. . . . All his assistants are murderers." Begin proceeded to incorrectly inform his already highly inflamed audience that the Israeli police present were carrying German-made tear-gas grenades, with "the same gases that asphyxiated our parents."

Moments later, many demonstrators marched toward the Knesset and began throwing stones through the windows of the Israeli parliament; some tried to storm the building. By the time the demonstration ended, over two hundred demonstrators and police had been injured.

The Knesset subsequently suspended Begin for three months, and Ben-Gurion announced in a speech to the nation that he had succeeded in putting down "the first attempt . . . to destroy democracy in Israel."

TWO FINAL, AND CONFLICTING, THOUGHTS ABOUT REPARATIONS

> One should take care not to take ransom from a murderer even if he gives all the money in the world and even if the blood avenger wishes to let him go free, since the soul of the victim is not the property of the blood avenger but the property of God.
>
> —Moses Maimonides, *Mishneh Torah*, "Laws of Murder and Preservation of Life," 1:4

On the day of the Knesset debate, Begin's party newspaper ran this citation from Maimonides on its front page.

The "blood avenger" mentioned by Maimonides refers to a biblical law that enjoins an immediate family member to avenge the death of a relative who has been murdered: "The blood avenger himself shall put the murderer to death" (Numbers 35:19).

In contrast to the practice of the societies that surrounded ancient Israel, the Bible law forbade the "blood avenger" or other family members to enter into financial negotiations with the murderer. A fourteenth century B.C.E. letter written by the Hittite King Hattushilis to his Babylonian counterpart indicates how widely accepted this procedure was: "When someone is killed in Hittite land they seize the killer and hand him over to the brothers of the murdered man. His brothers take the monetary compensation for the murdered man. They then perform the expiatory ritual on the city in which the murder occurred" (cited in David Sperling, "Bloodguilt in the Bible and in Ancient Near East Sources," page 22).

The biblical verse on which Maimonides bases his ruling was in all likelihood directed precisely against this sort of practice: "You may not accept a ransom for the life of a murderer who is guilty of a capital crime; he must be put to death" (Numbers 35:31).

However, critics of this argument responded that "ransom" from an individual murderer is very different from reparations from the successor government to a once-murderous state; thus, they claimed, Maimonides's ruling was not relevant.

> Whoever wishes to make history is obligated to forget history.
>
> —Ernest Renan, nineteenth-century French historian

Renan's words were cited in a letter to the Israeli leadership from Michael Amir, Israel's consul in Belgium. Amir believed that it was shortsighted and self-defeating not to negotiate a reparations settlement with Germany: "To persist with the pariah and boycott policy [against Germany] is to persist with a nice and moral Don Quixote policy, but it means jousting with windmills. It is pretty and consistent, but it brings no benefit, only harm." He then cited Renan's line, although he added, "I do not forget, but we, in the State of Israel, are obligated to take a realistic political line" (quoted in Tom Segev, *The Seventh Million,* pages 195–196).

78

"AS YOUR SWORD HAS MADE WOMEN CHILDLESS . . ."

The Eichmann Trial

In 1960, Israeli agents in Argentina captured and brought to Jerusalem Adolf Eichmann, the chief administrator of the Nazis' "Final Solution." His 1961 trial, which was covered by journalists from throughout the world, became a turning point in Israel's history. After a four-month trial, Eichmann was convicted and subsequently hanged on May 31, 1962.

> As I stand before you, judges of Israel, to lead the prosecution of Adolf Eichmann, I am not standing alone. With me are six million accusers. . . . Their blood cries out but their voice cannot be heard.
> —Opening speech of Israeli Attorney General Gideon Hausner, prosecutor at the Eichmann trial, April 1961

> As your sword has made women childless, so shall your mother be childless among women.
> —I Samuel 15:33

Citing these words by the prophet Samuel before killing Agag, the murderous king of Amalek, Israeli President Yitzhak ben Zvi rejected Eichmann's petition for mercy to him.

Many other appeals for a commutation of the death sentence were addressed to Israel's leadership. Led by philosopher Martin Buber, an array of prominent Israeli intellectuals strongly opposed executing Eichmann. Had their arguments been rooted in a simple, unyielding opposition to capital punishment (which Israel had outlawed in all cases but those pertaining to the Holocaust), their opposition might have garnered greater support. But the very enormity of Eichmann's crimes motivated the opponents of execution to construct arguments of such subtlety that many Jews had trouble understanding them. For example, Buber's letter to President Ben Zvi, which was co-signed by nineteen others, most affiliated with the Hebrew University, argued, "Our belief is that concluding Eichmann's trial with his execution will diminish the image of the Holocaust and falsify the historical and moral significance of this trial."

With breathtaking optimism, the philosopher Shmuel Hugo Bergmann wrote, "I believe with perfect faith that clemency for this man will halt the chain of hatred and bring the world a bit of salvation. Equally certain am I that a death sentence . . . will help the devil with a great victory in the world."

Prime Minister Ben-Gurion convened a special cabinet meeting to discuss whether Eichmann's sentence should be commuted. The words of Attorney General Gideon Hausner, the prosecutor at the trial, carried the day: "We owe it to the Holocaust survivors to impose the punishment."

"THAT PLACE IS NOT YOUR PLACE"

Ronald Reagan and the Bitburg Controversy

> That place is not your place. Your place is with the victims of the SS.
>
> —Elie Wiesel, April 19, 1985, in a White House speech before President Ronald Reagan. Wiesel's entire remarks are found in Ilya Levkov, ed., *Bitburg and Beyond*, pages 42–44.

One of the most painful conflicts ever between the American-Jewish community and an American president occurred in April 1985. At that time, President Ronald Reagan announced that he would commemorate the fortieth anniversary of Nazi Germany's defeat by laying a wreath at the Bitburg military cemetery, where, among several thousand military graves, forty-seven officers of the SS (the units that helped carry out the Holocaust) were buried. The idea was not Reagan's but German Chancellor Helmut Kohl's; he hoped that the president's visit would establish in people's minds the belief that the dead Nazi soldiers should be regarded as ordinary soldiers.

Criticized for going forward with his trip even after learning that war criminals were buried there (to Kohl's discredit, the German chancellor never offered to have the SS officers' bodies removed and interred elsewhere), Reagan remarked at an April 18 press conference that the soldiers interred in Bitburg were "victims, just as surely as the victims in the concentration camps."

Coincidentally, the following day he awarded a Congressional Gold Medal to Elie Wiesel, who responded with a short speech containing the pointed words above.

Although visibly moved by Wiesel's words, the president went ahead with his visit to Bitburg, although he added a visit to the Bergen-Belsen concentration camp to his itinerary. Later that day (May 5), he spoke at the American Air Force Base in Bitburg, where he declared, "I am a Jew in a world still threatened by antisemitism."

> For heaven's sake, let him find another cemetery. There must be at least one in all of Germany which does not contain SS men.
> —Menachem Rosensaft, founding chairman of the International Network of Children of Jewish Holocaust Survivors

> When a friend makes a mistake, the friend remains a friend, and the mistake remains a mistake.
> —Israeli Prime Minister Shimon Peres's response to the president's visit to Bitburg. In similar fashion, Morris B. Abram, former president of Brandeis University and later chairman of the Conference of Presidents of Major American Jewish Organizations, wrote in *The New York Times* (May 10, 1985), "Bitburg was the mistake of a friend, not the sin of an enemy."

80

ON HOLOCAUST DENIERS

The great masses of the people will fall more easily victim
to a big lie than a small one.

—Adolf Hitler, *Mein Kampf*

The visual evidence . . . of starvation, cruelty and bestiality
were so overpowering as to leave me a bit sick. In one
room, where there were piled up twenty or thirty naked
men, killed by starvation, [General] George Patton would
not even enter. He said he would get sick if he did so. I
made the visit deliberately, in order to be in a position to
give firsthand evidence of these things if ever, in the future,
there develops a tendency to charge these allegations
merely to "propaganda."

—General Dwight Eisenhower (1890–1969), Supreme Commander
of the Allied armies in a letter to Chief of Staff George Marshall,
after visiting the Nazi concentration camp at Ohrdruf, Germany
(Harry James Cargas, *Shadows of Auschwitz*, page 157)

Compare the prescient comment of Eisenhower, who intuited as
early as 1945 that forces would arise to deny the Holocaust, with
the record of Noam Chomsky. The latter, the acclaimed M.I.T. linguist and left-wing polemicist, has aggressively defended the right of
Robert Faurisson, a French university professor, to teach that the
Holocaust never occurred and that Auschwitz contained no gas
chambers. One wonders whether Chomsky would similarly defend
the right of an M.I.T. professor to teach that slavery never existed

in America. As Bernard Baruch once stated: "Every man has a right to his own opinion. But no man has a right to be wrong in his facts."

> There is an obvious danger in assuming that because Holocaust denial is so outlandish, it can be ignored. The deniers' worldview is no more bizarre than that [of those who believe in the] *Protocols of the Elders of Zion,* a report purporting to be the text of a secret plan to establish Jewish world supremacy.
> —Deborah Lipstadt, *Denying the Holocaust,* page 24

A proven forgery, *The Protocols* were cited by the Nazis as one of their warrants for ridding Europe of Jews (see Norman Cohn, *Warrant for Genocide,* a history of this forgery and of the damage it did). Historian Lipstadt documents the growing acceptance of claims advanced by Holocaust deniers. In Italy, where many of their publications have appeared, a 1992 public opinion poll revealed that 10 percent of Italians believe the Holocaust never happened. In this country, a 1993 Roper poll question, "Does it seem possible or does it seem impossible to you that the Nazi extermination of the Jews never happened?" revealed that 22 percent of Americans believe it possible that the Holocaust is a hoax. Unfortunately, given Americans' common penchant for conspiratorial and revisionist history, we would probably have a more accurate perception of American attitudes had the questioner simply asked: "Do you believe the Nazi extermination of the Jews happened or did not?"

THE "METHODOLOGY" OF HOLOCAUST DENIERS

> It all follows a familiar American pattern of social science journalism. Professor X puts out some outrageous theory, such as the Nazis didn't really kill the Jews . . . or there is no such thing as cannibalism. Since facts are plainly against him, X's main argument consists of the expression, in the highest moral tones, of his own disregard for all available evidence to the contrary. . . . All this provokes Y and Z to issue a rejoinder. . . . X now becomes "the controversial Professor X" and his book is respectfully re-

viewed by non-professionals in *Time, Newsweek* and *The New Yorker*. There follow appearances on radio, TV and in the columns of the daily newspapers.

—Marshall Sahlins, *The New York Review of Books,*
March 22, 1979, page 47

An American anthropologist, Sahlins made this bitter comment in his essay-review of W. Arens's *The Man-Eating Myth* (Oxford University Press), which purported to prove that cannibals never existed. The thrust of Arens's argument is similar to that offered by Holocaust deniers: the lack of victims' testimony, supposedly the only kind of valid documentation according to Arens and the Holocaust deniers. By establishing a level of proof that always will be unattainable, deniers of both cannibalism and the Holocaust claim to have "proven" their hypothesis, or at least to have cast serious doubt on a widely accepted truth.

Sahlins concludes that it is a "scandal" for a publisher of Oxford's stature to print such a book. (For a discussion of the similarity between Arens's work and that of Holocaust deniers, see Pierre Vidal-Naquet, *Assassins of Memory: Essays on the Denial of the Holocaust,* pages 7–8.)

81

THE HOLOCAUST AND ITS MEANING FOR CHRISTIANS

In order to pacify the Christian conscience it is said that the Nazis were not Christians. But they were all the children of Christians.

—Eliezer Berkovits, *Faith After the Holocaust,* page 41

Regarding one major question that separates Jews and Christians—whether or not the Messiah has come—Elie Wiesel, reacting through the crucible of the Holocaust, has said:

If I told you that I believe in God, I would be lying.
If I told you that I did not believe in God, I would be lying.
If I told you that I believe in man, I would be lying.
If I told you I did not believe in man, I would be lying.
But one thing I do know: the Messiah has not come yet.

—Elie Wiesel, cited by Harry James Cargas,
Shadows of Auschwitz, page 161

It is not just a matter of deportation. You will not die there of hunger and disease. They will slaughter all of you there, old and young alike, women and children, at once; it is the punishment that you deserve for the death of our Lord and Redeemer, Jesus Christ. You have only one solution.

Come over to our religion and I will work to annul this decree.

—Slovakian Archbishop Kametko to Rabbi Dov Baer
Weissmandl. Weissmandl had asked the archbishop to plead
with Josef Tisso, his former employee and now head of the
Slovakian government, to spare Slovakia's Jews (1942).

Prior to the archbishop's cold and cruel comment, Rabbi Weissmandl had been unaware of the existence of gas chambers, and so had expressed concern at the deportation's effects on children, women, and old people.

In the fall of 1944, the rabbi was sent to a temporary camp, along with his family and hundreds of other Jews, prior to being deported to Auschwitz. Weissmandl escaped and made his way to the home of a high church official, whom he begged to intercede with Tisso. His request was curtly refused with the words: "This being a Sunday, it is a holy day for us. Neither I nor Father Tisso occupy ourselves with profane matters on this day."

When Weissmandl asked the man how he could regard the blood of infants and children as "profane matters," the priest answered: "There is no innocent blood of Jewish children in the world. All Jewish blood is guilty. You have to die. This is the punishment that has been awaiting you because of that sin [deicide]."

Thus, some two thousand years after a false quote was attributed to a group of first-century Jews—"His [Jesus'] blood be on our heads and the heads of our children" (Matthew 27:25; see page 465)—several highly positioned church officials concluded that God had sent Adolf Hitler to fulfill this New Testament curse.

There is nothing in these measures that can give rise to criticism from the viewpoint of the Holy See.

—The Vatican's response to an inquiry from the Vichy
government in France about its law of June 2, 1941, which
isolated the Jews and deprived them of rights and jobs
(Michael Marrus and Robert Paxton, *Vichy France and the Jews*,
page 201)

With several heartening exceptions, the future Pope John XXIII among them, the Vatican remained quite untouched by the Jews' fate. However, from the available data, it seems that it also did little on behalf of anti-Nazi Catholic priests who were deported to concentration camps.

When the War ended, however, several highly placed Vatican officials helped large numbers of Nazis to escape to South America and elsewhere. They included Franz Stangl, the commandant of the Treblinka death camp, who had supervised the gassing of one million Jews.

I have culled the above examples from Rabbi Irving Greenberg's remarkable lecture at a 1974 symposium on the Holocaust at New York's Cathedral of St. John the Divine ("Cloud of Smoke, Pillar of Fire: Judaism, Christianity and Modernity After the Holocaust," reprinted in *Auschwitz: Beginning of a New Era,* edited by Eva Fleischner, pages 7–55).

Following Greenberg's presentation, Professor Alan Davies, himself a minister of the United Church of Canada, responded:

> I would like some gifted Christian artist to paint a crucifix scene portraying Jesus as an Auschwitz Jew, including the yellow badge *Jude* on his body, against the barbed wire of a death camp. . . .
>
> [The painful truth about the reactions of Christians during the Holocaust] might raise the question, in radical form, as to whether it is morally possible to remain a Christian at all.
>
> —Professor Davies, ibid., page 64

During one of the final presentations at the same conference, Elie Wiesel shared an autobiographical reminiscence about his hometown of Sighet (then Hungary, now Romania) during the years before the Holocaust:

> As a child I was afraid of the Church to the point of changing sidewalks [when I came near a church]. In my town,

the fear was justified. Not only because of what I inherited—our collective memory—but also because of the simple fact that twice a year, at Easter and Christmas, Jewish schoolchildren would be beaten up by their Christian neighbors. Yes, as a child I lived in fear. A symbol of compassion and love to Christians, the cross has become an instrument of torment and terror to be used against Jews. I say this with neither hate nor anger. I say this because it is true. Born in suffering, Christianity became a source and pretext of suffering to others.

    —Elie Wiesel, in *Auschwitz: Beginning of a New Era,* page 406

Sensitive Christians long have been pained by the visceral and fearful reaction the cross inspires in so many Jews. One is Father Edward Flannery, author of *The Anguish of the Jews,* a pathbreaking history of Christianity and antisemitism. He notes that he was moved to write his book upon seeing a Jewish friend shuddering when she passed the large cross displayed in front of the Grand Central building in New York City during the Christmas season. Her reaction, Father Flannery wrote, "evoked many questions in me, not least of which was: How did the cross, the supreme symbol of universal love, become a sign of fear, of evil, for this young Jewess? . . . It was my first introduction to the problem of anti-Semitism" (Introduction, page xi).

In 1980, my friend Dennis Prager and I were guests of the Vatican. During an interview on Vatican Radio, Dennis, when asked our trip's purpose, responded: "For almost two thousand years, the cross has been a symbol of love to Christians, and a symbol of fear to Jews. We hope the pope can show to the Jews that it is a symbol of love for them as well."

82

"ONE, PLUS ONE, PLUS ONE"

Six Final Quotes on the Holocaust

When the Nazis came to power in Germany, there were two sorts of Jews living there: the optimists and the pessimists. The pessimists went into exile, the optimists went to the gas chambers.

—Bitter German-Jewish joke

German Jews long were known for their love affair with Germany; many could not believe that the country would long remain Nazi. The late Jakob Petuchowski, a German-born Reform rabbi and scholar, told me of his aunt, who visited Palestine in 1936, three years after the Nazis had come to power. She returned to Germany, explaining: "It's beautiful what the pioneers have done there, but it's not for us." A few years later, she and her family were murdered in a Nazi death camp.

* * *

The *Kapos* were concentration camp prisoners whom the Nazis appointed to supervise other prisoners. Many were cruel and brutal. Concerning the sort of people who assumed this position, Elie Wiesel has written:

[In the concentration camps there were Kapos] of German, Hungarian, Czech, Slovakian, Georgian, Ukrainian, French, and Lithuanian extraction. They were Christians, Jews and atheists. Former professors, industrialists, artists, merchants, workers, militants from the right and left, philosophers and explorers of the soul, Marxists and staunch humanists. And, of course, a few common criminals. But not one Kapo had been a rabbi.

—Elie Wiesel, *One Generation After,* page 189

*   *   *

To my wife, to my daughter
Martyrs

Killed by the Germans
Killed
Simply because they were called
ISAAC

—Jules Isaac, dedication of *Jesus et Israel*

*   *   *

I have been told you are a Jewish lawyer; I don't know whether you are young or old, but I can tell you one thing, and you can write it down and hang it up over your bed: A Jew may be stupid, but it's not obligatory.

—Nazi-hunter Simon Wiesenthal in a phone conversation with a Jewish lawyer for the ACLU who was defending the right of Nazis to march through Skokie, a Chicago suburb where several thousand Holocaust survivors live. Wiesenthal's angry retort was prompted by the lawyer's repeated, rather cold, response to his arguments: "The First Amendment permits it" (Simon Wiesenthal, *Justice Not Vengeance,* page 348).

*   *   *

When asked if she could forgive a seemingly truly penitent SS officer who, years earlier, had helped round up a group of Polish Jews and then set fire to the synagogue in which they were incarcerated, novelist and essayist Cynthia Ozick wrote:

"I forgive you," we say to the child who has muddied the carpet, "but next time don't do it again." Next time she will leave the muddy boots outside the door; forgiveness, with its enlarging capacities, will have taught her. Forgiveness is an effective teacher. Meanwhile, the spots can be washed away.

But murder is irrevocable. Murder is irreversible. . . . Even if forgiveness restrains one from perpetrating a new batch of corpses, will the last batch come alive again . . . ?

Forgiveness is pitiless. It forgets the victim. . . . It cultivates sensitiveness toward the murderer at the price of insensitiveness toward the victim. . . .

Let the SS man die unshriven.

Let him go to hell.

—Cynthia Ozick, in Simon Wiesenthal, *The Sunflower*, pages 186, 187, and 188

Ozick's view was informed by her realization that each of the Holocaust's victims was a unique, hence irreplaceable, human being. As a contemporary observer of how different countries remember and commemorate the Holocaust has observed:

We must remind ourselves that the Holocaust was not six million. It was one, plus one, plus one.

—Judith Miller, *One by One by One*, page 287

PART VII

ZIONISM AND ISRAEL

83

THE LAND OF ISRAEL IN THE BIBLE, THE TALMUD, AND JEWISH LAW

GOD'S PROMISE OF THE LAND

I assign the land you sojourn in to you and your offspring to come, all the land of Canaan, as an everlasting possession.

—God's promise to Abraham, Genesis 17: 8

God repeated this oath to Isaac (Genesis 26: 3) and then to Jacob, "The land that I assigned to Abraham and Isaac, I assign to you, and to your heirs to come will I assign the land" (Genesis 35: 12).

Bible scholar Harry Orlinsky has rightly underscored Israel's centrality in the relationship between God and the Jews:

Were it not for the Land that God promised on oath to Abraham and to Isaac and to Jacob and to their heirs forever, there would be no covenant. For be it noted that everything in the contract, all the blessings—economic, territorial, political, increase in population, and the like— all these would be forthcoming from God to Israel not in Abraham's native land in Mesopotamia . . . nor in Egypt, but in the Promised Land.

—Harry Orlinsky, "The Biblical Concept of the Land of Israel," page 34

Even the Fifth Commandment is linked to the land: "Honor your father and mother, that you may long endure on the land that the Lord your God is giving to you" (Exodus 20:12). The most extreme punishment threatened against the ancient Hebrews is captivity followed by exile from the land (e.g., Hosea 9:3, Amos 7:17). Significantly, the very prophets who threaten the Jews with this fate also promise that God will restore them to Israel (Hosea 11:11, Amos 9:11–15). This was an unusual prophecy, given that no other people ever had been exiled en masse from its homeland, and been restored. Indeed, a prophecy offered by Amos *twenty-eight hundred years ago* seems to foretell the Jews' late-nineteenth and twentieth-century return to Zion, even emphasizing Israel's agricultural revitalization:

I will restore my people Israel.
They shall rebuild ruined cities and inhabit them;
They shall plant vineyards and drink their wine;
They shall till gardens and eat their fruits.
And I will plant them upon their soil,
Nevermore to be uprooted
From the soil I have given them
Said the Lord your God.

—Amos 9:14–15

*   *   *

If I forget you, O Jerusalem,
let my right hand wither,
let my tongue stick to my palate
if I cease to think of you,
if I do not keep [the destroyed city of] Jerusalem in
   memory
even at my happiest hour.

—Psalm 137:5–6

This famous oath was composed during the Jews' first exile in Babylonia, in the sixth century B.C.E., and appears in the 137th

Psalm, which begins, "By the rivers of Babylon, there we sat and wept when we remembered Zion." Many Jews daily recite this psalm (except on the Sabbath and other holy days) at the beginning of the Grace After Meals.

In saying "If I forget you, O Jerusalem," a Jew asserts his or her ongoing loyalty to Israel and the Jewish people. At the Sixth Zionist Congress in 1903, when Theodor Herzl raised the possibility of trying to secure Uganda from the British as a temporary Jewish homeland (see pages 575–576), many delegates denounced him for betraying the land of Israel. Herzl was deeply stung; at the Congress's conclusion, he raised his hand in the manner of one taking an oath, and swore *"Im eshka-kheikh yerushalayim."* "If I forget you, O Jerusalem."

This oath is so well known that variations of it sometimes are offered by those wishing to convey the sacredness of an obligation they have assumed. In 1952, when Herut leader (and later prime minister) Menachem Begin spoke against Israel's negotiating a reparations agreement with Germany (see pages 547–548), he called on a crowd of protesters to raise their hands, and swear "in the name of Jerusalem . . . : If I forget the extermination of the Jews, may my right hand wither, may my tongue stick to my palate if I cease to think of you, if I do not keep the extermination of the Jews in memory even at my happiest hour" (cited in Tom Segev, *The Seventh Million*, page 216).

*   *   *

> *Mishna:* One may compel his entire household to go up with him to the Land of Israel, but none may be compelled to leave it. All of one's household may be compelled to go up to Jerusalem [from any other part of Israel], but none may be compelled to leave it. *The Talmud comments:* Our Rabbis taught: If the husband desires to go to live in Israel and his wife refuses, she may be pressured to go with him, and if she refuses, she may be divorced without being given the financial settlement promised in her *ketuba* (marriage contract). If she desires to go live in Israel and if he does not consent, he is pressured to go with her, and if he re-

fuses, he must divorce her and pay her the financial settlement promised in her *Ketuba*.

—Babylonian Talmud, *Ketubot* 110b

That the Rabbis were willing to permit divorce over the issue of living in Israel demonstrates not a callous disregard for the sacredness of marriage (indeed, Jewish law is known for its extraordinary regard for family life), but an even greater commitment to Jewish settlement in the land of Israel.

Involved, particularly religious, Diaspora Jews usually prefer to live in largely Jewish neighborhoods. However, the Talmud decrees:

> One should always live in the land of Israel, even in a city the majority of whose residents are not Jews, rather than live outside the land, even in a city the majority of whose residents are Jews.
>
> —Babylonian Talmud, *Ketubot* 110b

*   *   *

Rashi, the eleventh-century French biblical exegete whose Torah commentary still is studied in all traditional Jewish schools, also emphasizes Israel's centrality. Writing a thousand years after the Jews were exiled from Israel, he begins his commentary on Genesis 1:1 ("In the beginning God created the heaven and the earth") with immediate reference to Israel, and an implied expectation that the Jews would someday return there:

> Strictly speaking, the Torah should have commenced with the verse: "This month shall be to you the beginning of months" (Exodus 12:2), which is the very first commandment given to Israel. [Note: The commandment obligates the sanctifying of each month.] Why then, did the Torah begin with the account of the creation? To illustrate that God the Creator owns the whole world. So, if the peoples of the world shall say to Israel: "You are robbers in conquering the territory of the seven Canaanite nations," Is-

rael can answer them: "All the earth belongs to God—He created it, so He can give it to whomsoever He wills. When he wished He gave it to them, then when He wished He took it away from them and gave it to us."

—Rashi on Genesis 1:1; I have followed Chaim Pearl's translation, *Rashi: Commentaries on the Pentateuch*, page 31.

A MEDIEVAL ANTICIPATION OF ZIONISM; A MODERN REFLECTION ON IT

My heart is in the East, and I am in the furthermost West. How then can I taste what I eat? And how can food be sweet to me . . . while Zion is in fetters . . . and I am in Arab chains?

—Yehuda Halevi (c. 1075–1141), Hebrew poet and religious thinker who lived in Muslim Spain

*   *   *

Prior to World War II, many Orthodox leaders opposed Zionist efforts to reestablish a substantial and self-sufficient Jewish community in Palestine. They felt that a full scale Jewish restoration to Israel was something that needed to be achieved supernaturally, through the coming of the Messiah. Orthodox Rabbi Samuel Mohilever felt otherwise; in an epistle to the First Zionist Congress (1897), he unequivocally rejected any effort to turn the Jews into a passive, ahistorical people:

The resettlement of our country—that is, the purchase of land and the building of houses, the planting of orchards and the cultivation of the soil—is one of the fundamental commandments of our Torah; some of our ancient sages even say that it is equivalent to the whole Law, for it is the foundation of the existence of our people.

—Samuel Mohilever, "Message to the First Zionist Congress"; Mohilever's entire message is printed in Arthur Hertzberg, *The Zionist Idea*, pages 401–405.

84

THEODOR HERZL

Zionism's Founder

I have been pounding away for some time on a work of tremendous magnitude. I don't know even now if I will be able to carry it through. . . . For days and weeks it has saturated me to the limits of my consciousness; it goes with me everywhere, hovers behind my ordinary talk, peers at me over the shoulders of my funny little journalistic work, overwhelms and intoxicates me.

—The opening paragraph of Herzl's diaries,
late May or early June 1895

The work to which Herzl (1860–1904) alluded subsequently was published as *The Jewish State* (1896); it became the manifesto of the Zionist movement. Near the book's beginning, and again at its end, he repeated the same challenging words:

The Jews who will it shall achieve their state.

Later, Herzl wrote a second book, the novel *Altneuland* (Old-New Land), wherein he depicts two friends who visit Palestine at some point in the future and are amazed to find that it is a flourishing society. Haifa, the country's port of entry, is "the safest and most comfortable harbor in the Mediterranean"; the entire state consists of other prosperous cities, as well as successful industries and farms. Women have equal rights, free education is available to all, Jews and Arabs live together amicably, and modern medical facilities serve all the inhabitants. The novel's hero, Friedrich Lowenberg, a Jewish attorney from Vienna, wonders if what he is seeing is true or if it is just a fantasy. The novel closes with the words:

> But if you will it, it is no fantasy.

These words in Hebrew, *Im tirzu, ein zoh aggadah,* quickly turned into a Zionist slogan, and galvanized at least two generations of Jewish activists. The words' call to action helps explain the fervor with which early Zionist pioneers settled previously uncultivated swamplands, and persevered in turning them into fertile fields.

Zionist activists who worked for Hebrew's reestablishment as a modern, spoken language also cited Herzl's words. Prior to Hebrew, no other "dead language" ever had been resurrected. But the Hebraists' commitment to "If you will it, it is no fantasy" helped inspire its extraordinary revival.

From the 1900s to the 1940s, these five Hebrew words likewise helped motivate numerous Jewish leaders to continue lobbying non-Jewish statesmen to recognize the Jewish people's right to reestablish a homeland—then a state—in Palestine.

*   *   *

> If you are mad, then I am mad as well. I'm behind you, and you can count on me.
> —Max Nordau to Herzl, 1896

Many of Herzl's friends were convinced that his Zionist obsession was "crazy," and one suggested that he talk to Max Nordau, a prominent writer and social critic, as well as a doctor who specialized in treating emotional disorders. After offering the above diagnosis of Herzl's mental health, Nordau became Herzl's most important colleague and disciple. His stature helped attract to Herzl's cause such younger intellectuals as the French-Jewish so-

cialist thinker Bernard Lazare, and the British-Jewish writer and poet
Israel Zangwill.

> I am not better nor more clever than any of you. But I
> remain undaunted and that is why the leadership belongs
> to me.
>
> —Herzl in conversation with close friends;
> quoted in Walter Laqueur, A History of Zionism, page 90

Laqueur notes that the above statement was made during a low
ebb in Zionist fortunes. It was part of Herzl's genius as a leader that
even during Zionism's darkest periods, he confided his despair only
to his diary. "To the outside world," Laqueur writes, "he radiated
assurance and confidence."

*　　*　　*

THE FIRST ZIONIST CONGRESS

On August 29, 1897, Herzl convened the First Zionist Congress, a
gathering of 204 Zionist activists from nineteen countries, in Basel,
Switzerland. What until then had been tiny, often unconnected organizations coalesced in Basel into a unified political force.

A Zionist flag was hung at the entrance to the hall where the
Congress met, and Herzl's opening words made clear the grandiosity
of his vision:

> We are here to lay the foundation stone of the house which
> is to shelter the Jewish nation.

The Congress lasted three days. At its conclusion, the delegates
sang "Hatikvah" ("The Hope"), a Zionist poem written by Naphtali
Hertz Imber, which subsequently became Israel's national anthem.
When they finished singing, some younger delegates carried Herzl
on their shoulders through the hall.

Four days later, he confided to his diary:

If I were to sum up the Congress in a word—which I shall take care not to publish—it would be this: At Basel, I founded the Jewish state.

If I said this out loud today, I would be greeted with universal laughter. In five years perhaps, and certainly in fifty years, everyone will perceive it.

—Theodor Herzl, September 3, 1897

On May 15, 1948, fifty years and nine months after Herzl wrote the above, the Jewish state of Israel in fact came into existence. Thanks, first of all, to his vision, the "fantasy" had in fact become reality.

THE KISHINEV POGROM AND HERZL'S UGANDA PLAN

I do not understand; the rope is around their necks, and still they say, "No."

—Herzl's response when the two delegates from Kishinev voted
no to his Uganda Plan

On April 6–7, 1903, residents of the Russian city of Kishinev, in cooperation with the czarist police, organized a particularly vicious pogrom against local Jews. Forty-nine were murdered, hundreds more severely beaten, dozens of Jewish women were raped, and many Jewish homes and stores looted or destroyed. Outrage at this horror led to the formation of Jewish self-defense units throughout Russia, and to widely increased support for Zionism throughout the Jewish world.

Herzl, knowing that no immediate hopes existed for obtaining Palestine and fearing that Russian Jewry's days were numbered (the Kishinev pogrom was followed by others), entered into negotiations with the British government for a region within Uganda, then a British territory in Africa.

At the Sixth Zionist Congress (1903), when he raised the prospect of settling Jews in Uganda and asked the delegates to approve his negotiations with the British, a significant minority expressed outrage. This group, comprised largely of those from the more traditional Jewish communities of Eastern Europe, was certain that merely entering into negotiations about Uganda would lead to Palestine's being relinquished as the future Jewish homeland. When the vote was taken, Herzl was shocked when the two delegates from Kishinev itself voted against his proposal. According to Chaim Weizmann, although Herzl had long been an advocate of a Jewish homeland somewhere, he "became a Palestine Zionist the moment the Kishinev delegates said 'No' at the Uganda Congress."

*　　*　　*

[To a young French Jew who kept emphasizing to Herzl his "French nationality," Herzl responded]: "Don't you and I belong to the same nation [i.e., people]? Why did you wince when Lueger was elected? Why did I suffer when Captain Dreyfus was accused of high treason?"
—Herzl, *Diaries,* Vol. I, page 273 (November 1895)

Karl Lueger was the antisemitic Austrian politician who was elected mayor of Vienna in 1895, shortly after French army Captain Alfred Dreyfus was falsely convicted of having committed treason against France.

Lueger's landslide victory was particularly devastating to the many Austrian Jewish liberals who had exerted tremendous efforts to bring democracy to Vienna. Hitler later described him as "the best mayor we ever had" (see Conor Cruise O'Brien, *The Siege,* page 61).

*　　*　　*

If you come to Palestine and settle your people there, we shall have churches and priests ready to baptize all of you.
—Pope Pius X to Herzl, at a meeting in 1904;
see *Diaries,* Vol. IV, pages 1602ff

Herzl met with the pope in an attempt to secure Vatican support for Zionism. The pontiff was direct and coldly blunt: "The Jews have not recognized our Lord, therefore we cannot recognize the Jewish people."

576

ABOUT HERZL

Had Herzl been to a *heder* [a Jewish religious school],
never would the Jews have followed him. He charmed the
Jews because he came to them from the European culture.
—Chaim Weizmann

Weizmann, the prime Jewish mover behind the Balfour Declaration, and Israel's first president, was referring to the fact that Herzl
came from a largely assimilated Jewish background.

Historians and biographers often have commented on parallels
between his and Moses' life. While Moses' Jewish contemporaries
worked as slaves in Egypt, he was raised in Pharaoh's court. Perhaps
it was his free, affluent upbringing that led Moses to oppose so
strongly Israelite bondage. Other Jews seemed to suffer from a
"slave mentality" and could not imagine being free. Similarly,
Herzl's upper-middle-class upbringing caused him to feel a natural
revulsion at the second-class status Jews suffered in most of Europe,
a status many had come to take for granted.

Those who came before him carried the ideal [of Palestine]
in their hearts but only whispered about it in the synagogue. . . . Herzl brought us courage and taught us to
place our demands before the whole non-Jewish world.
—Zionist leader Menachem Ussishkin, upon Herzl's death of a
heart condition at the age of forty-four (1904)

Herzl's redeeming greatness was [that he] . . . removed the
Jewish problem from the waiting rooms of philanthropy
and introduced it into the chancellories of European di-
plomacy.
—Howard Sachar, *A History of Israel,* page 64

Sachar goes on to note that, because of Herzl, "the very term
'Zionism' soon fell naturally from the lips of world leaders and became an item on the agenda of prime ministers and princes."

The most remarkable of all things is when a man never gives up.

—Uncredited quotation on the front page of *The Diaries of Theodor Herzl,* edited and translated by Marvin Lowenthal. According to Lowenthal, Herzl's greatest achievement "was putting Zionism on the map."

The Austrian-Jewish writer Stefan Zweig attended Herzl's 1904 funeral in Vienna: decades later, he wrote of the experience in his memoirs:

> It was an unending procession. Vienna was suddenly made aware of the fact that this was not a mere author or mediocre poet who had died but one of those creators of ideas such as emerge only at the rarest of moments in the history of countries and peoples. At the cemetery . . . all semblance of order broke down, swamped by a kind of elemental and ecstatic mourning such as I have never seen before or since at a funeral. And this immense pain rising out of the depths of an entire people made me realize for the first time how much passion and hope this singular and lonely man had given to the world by the power of his idea.
>
> —Stefan Zweig, *Die Welt von Gestern,* page 133, translated in Ernst Pawel, *The Labyrinth of Exile: A Life of Theodor Herzl,* page 531

In Herzl's will, he requested that he be buried in Vienna alongside his father "until the Jewish people transfer my remains to Palestine." On August 17, 1949, a year after Israel came into existence, Herzl's remains, along with those of his parents and sister, were flown to the new Jewish state and reburied on Mount Herzl in Jerusalem.

85

CHAIM WEIZMANN AND THE BALFOUR DECLARATION

Chaim Weizmann (1874–1952) was the major Zionist leader after Herzl and Israel's first president.

> The story is told of Dr. Chaim Weizmann, the chemist who became the first president of modern Israel, at a time when he was lobbying British politicians to win their support for the Zionist effort to gain a Jewish homeland. One member of the House of Lords said to him, "Why do you Jews insist on Palestine when there are so many undeveloped countries you could settle in more conveniently?" Weizmann answered, "That is like my asking you why you drove twenty miles to visit your mother last Sunday when there are so many old ladies living on your street."
> —Harold Kushner, *To Life!*, pages 14–15

We don't know how the British politician to whom Weizmann addressed this remark was affected by it. But when he presented a subtly different analogy to Arthur Balfour in 1906, Weizmann set in motion a chain of thought that helped lead the British leader to issue the Balfour Declaration eleven years later:

"Mr. Balfour, supposing I were to offer you Paris instead of London, would you take it?"

He sat up, looked at me and answered: "But Dr. Weizmann, we have London."

"That is true," I said, "but we had Jerusalem when London was a marsh."

He leaned back, continued to stare at me and said two things which I remember vividly. The first was: "Are there many Jews who think like you?"

I answered: "I believe I speak the mind of millions of Jews whom you will never see and who cannot speak for themselves. . . . "

To this he said: "If that is so you will one day be a force."

—Chaim Weizmann, *Trial and Error*, page 111

THE BALFOUR DECLARATION, NOVEMBER 2, 1917

Dear Lord Rothschild,

His Majesty's Government view with favor the establishment in Palestine of a national home for the Jewish people, and will use their best endeavors to facilitate the achievement of this object, it being clearly understood that nothing shall be done which may prejudice the civil and religious rights of existing non-Jewish communities in Palestine, or the rights and political status enjoyed by Jews in any other country.

Although Balfour, by now the British foreign secretary, addressed this letter to Lord Lionel Rothschild, it is generally acknowledged that Weizmann played the key role in influencing him and the British government to issue this momentous document.

*   *   *

[For the Jews] the world is divided into places where they cannot live, and places into which they cannot enter.

—From Weizmann's testimony before the British appointed Peel Commission, November 25, 1936. (The Peel Commission

was appointed to try to resolve the increasingly violent
conflict between Arabs and Jews in Palestine.)

Weizmann's bitter comment was made after the Nazis had with-
drawn German Jews' citizenship, and as the Jewish political situation was deteriorating throughout Europe. Despite the virulence of
Nazi antisemitism, the United States, Great Britain, and other countries were reluctant to admit more Jews, even those in the most
desperate situations. When one high Canadian official was asked
how many Jewish refugees Canada could absorb, he responded,
"None is too many."

Weizmann's words bring to mind the brutally honest, if cynical,
words of one of the Hebrew language's greatest poets:

> Each people has as much heaven over its head as it has
> land under its feet.
> —Hayim Nahman Bialik (1873–1934)

Weizmann's testimony did not persuade the British to open Palestine to substantially more Jewish immigration. Three years later,
in 1939, just as German Jewry's situation was reaching new lows,
Britain issued its infamous "White Paper," which further limited
Jewish, but not Arab, immigration to Palestine. The White Paper
was enforced throughout the Holocaust. It was with such thoughts
in mind that Weizmann declared in Jerusalem before a 1946 Anglo-
American Commission of Inquiry on the situation of Holocaust survivors in DP (displaced persons) camps:

> I do not know how many Einsteins, how many Freuds,
> have been destroyed in the furnaces of Auschwitz and
> Maidenek. But there is one thing I know; if we can prevent
> it, it will never happen again.

In April 1948, as many Jews expressed fear that if Israel were
established as a state, the surrounding Arab armies would overrun
it, Weizmann pushed aggressively for a declaration of statehood.

Fear of the Arab armies did not overwhelm him, as he expressed in the presence of Abba Eban, soon to be appointed Israel's ambassador to the United States:

> The trouble with the Egyptian army is that their officers are too fat and their soldiers too thin.
>
> —Reported in Eban's autobiography, *Personal Witness,* page 139

Far more poignant are his words defining the sacrifices Jews would have to make to achieve statehood:

> A people does not get a country on a silver platter.
>
> —Chaim Weizmann

Weizmann's comment inspired Hebrew poet Natan Alterman to write one of Israel's best-known poems, *The Silver Platter,* in which he depicts a male and female soldier who died in the 1948 War of Independence, as the "silver platter" that enabled the Jewish people to regain sovereignty.

Some forty years later, Israeli General Yossi Peled, who spent the first years of his life hiding during the Holocaust, used Weizmann's words yet again: "In fact, this country was founded on a silver platter made of six million bodies" (Tom Segev, *The Seventh Million,* page 513).

Finally, it is interesting to recall an earlier comment of Weizmann's, his response to those of his critics who dismissed him as a "gradualist":

> I have heard critics of the Jewish Agency sneer at what they call the old "Lovers of Zion" policy of "another dunam and another dunam, another Jew and another Jew, another cow and another goat and two more houses in

Gederah." If there is any other way of building a house save brick by brick, I do not know it. If there is any other way of building up a country save dunam by dunam and man by man and farmstead by farmstead, again I do not know it.

—Chaim Weizmann, 1931

86

VLADIMIR JABOTINSKY

Jabotinsky (1880–1940) was the founder of the Revisionist party, a political group that represented Zionism's "maximalist wing." The Revisionists demanded that Britain grant the Jews sovereignty over both sides of the Jordan. Future Israeli prime ministers Menachem Begin and Yitzhak Shamir regarded Jabotinsky as their ideological and political godfather.

> We all realize, that of all the conditions necessary for national renaissance, the ability to know how to shoot is unfortunately the most important.
> —Vladimir Jabotinsky, 1933; *Ktavim* (collected writings),
> Vol. 11, page 90

In 1937, Jabotinsky was invited to testify before the British-appointed Peel Commission, then investigating the possibility of partitioning Palestine into separate Jewish and Arab states. At the time, German Jewry already had lived under Nazi rule for four years, while their three and a half million Polish brethren were suffering from widespread antisemitism.

Conscious of the urgent need to arrange for the emigration of large numbers from both communities, Jabotinsky explained to the commission why it was impossible for the Jews to make territorial compromises in Palestine:

584

I would remind you of the commotion which was produced . . . when Oliver Twist came and asked for "more." He said "more" because he did not know how to express it; what Oliver Twist really meant was this: "Will you just give me that normal portion which is necessary for a boy of my age to be able to live?" I assure you that you face here today, in the Jewish people with its demands, an Oliver Twist who has, unfortunately, no concessions to make. . . . We have got to save millions, many *millions*. . . . What can the concession be on the part of Oliver Twist? He is in such a position that he cannot concede anything; it is the workhouse people who have to concede the plateful of soup.

—Jabotinsky's entire speech before the Peel Commission can be found in Arthur Hertzberg, ed., *The Zionist Idea*, pages 559–570

During the same testimony, Jabotinsky responded to the Arab contentions that Palestine should be an Arab, not a Jewish, state:

It is quite understandable that the Arabs of Palestine would also prefer Palestine to be the Arab state no. 4, no. 5, or no. 6—that I quite understand; but when the Arab claim is confronted with our Jewish demand to be saved, it is like the claims of appetite versus the claims of starvation.

As of 1994, there are twenty-one Arab states in the world, and only one Jewish one. The Arab states' total landmass is 5,414,000 square miles, whereas Israel's is 8,290 square miles, (10,420 square miles if one includes the West Bank and Gaza). In short, the Arabs occupy 540 times as much land as the Jews.

JABOTINSKY AND THE HOLOCAUST

Liquidate the *Galut* [Diaspora] or the *Galut* will liquidate you.

—Popular expression coined by Jabotinsky prior to World War II

While no major Jewish figure actually predicted the Holocaust, Jabotinsky repeatedly warned Eastern European Jewry that it was in imminent danger, particularly if a war were to erupt in Europe. On August 10, 1938, on the Jewish fast day of *Tisha Be'Av,* just over a year before Hitler invaded Poland, he spoke to a gathering of Jews in Warsaw, few of whom were to survive the war:

> For three years, I have been imploring you, Jews of Poland, the crown of world Jewry, appealing to you, warning you unceasingly that the catastrophe is near. My hair has turned white and I have grown old over these years, for my heart is bleeding that you . . . do not see the volcano which will soon begin to spew forth its fires of destruction. . . . Time is growing short for you to be spared. . . . Listen to my words at this, the twelfth hour. For God's sake: let everyone save himself, so long as there is time to do so, for time is running short.
>
> —Vladimir Jabotinsky, cited in Benjamin Netanyahu,
> *A Place Among the Nations: Israel and the World,* page 364

For years, devotees of Jabotinsky have cited this speech and similar pronouncements as proof of his prophetic insight concerning the Nazis. But even Jabotinsky had no notion of the dimensions of the disaster that would soon overtake European Jewry. One indication of this is that his program to save Polish Jewry envisaged the transfer to Palestine of one and a half million of Poland's three and a half million Jews over the following *ten* years, a plan that obviously did not foresee "the scope nor the imminence of the tragedy" that would wipe out more than 90 percent of Polish Jewry in the coming seven years (Jacob Katz, "Was the Holocaust Predictable?," page 25).

Jabotinsky's sense of the devastation that lay ahead was limited because he believed Nazi rule to be rather fragile, and felt that it would crumble because of internal difficulties as soon as it confronted an external power.

Once Nazi Germany launched its successful invasion of Poland, Jabotinsky immediately understood the horrible reality now facing Polish Jewry. As news spread of the success of the Wehrmacht (Germany's army), he sadly and bitterly confided to his ideological opponent, the Labor Zionist leader Berl Katznelson: "You have won. You have America, the rich Jews. I had only poor Polish Jewry, and now it is gone" (Conor Cruise O'Brien, "Three Zionists: Weizmann, Ben-Gurion, Katznelson," page 264).

JABOTINSKY AS PROPHET

During the same somber speech in Warsaw, Jabotinsky offered a more optimistic, and singularly accurate, prophecy:

> And I want to say something to you on this day, the Ninth of Av: Those who will succeed in escaping this catastrophe will live to experience a festive moment of great Jewish joy: the rebirth and establishment of the Jewish state. I do not know whether I myself will live to see it—but my son will. I am certain of this, just as I am certain that the sun will rise tomorrow morning.

Within less than two years, Jabotinsky had died in the United States. Eight years after his death, the State of Israel was established, and Jabotinsky's son, Eri, served in Israel's first Knesset.

87

DAVID BEN-GURION

Ben-Gurion (1886–1973) was Israel's founding father and first prime minister.

> The difference between you and me is that you are ready
> to sacrifice immigration for peace, while I am not, though
> peace is dear to me. And even if I was prepared to make
> a concession, the Jews of Poland and Germany would not
> be because they have no other choice. For them, immigra-
> tion comes before peace.
> —David Ben-Gurion (March 1936) to Judah Magnes (chancellor
> of Hebrew University), a strong proponent of a conciliatory
> approach toward Palestinian Arabs (Shabtai Teveth,
> *Ben-Gurion: The Burning Ground, 1886–1948*, page 539)

Ben-Gurion's concern for bringing Polish and German Jews into Palestine was motivated as much by his iron-willed determination to establish a Jewish state as by his humanitarian concern for their welfare. In a meeting of the Jewish Agency Executive on December 6, 1942, he declared: "The extermination of European Jewry is a catastrophe for Zionism; there won't be anyone left to build the country with" (Tom Segev, *The Seventh Million*, page 97).

> We shall fight Hitler as though there were no White Paper,
> and we shall fight against the White Paper as though there
> were no Hitler.
> —David Ben-Gurion at beginning of World War II,
> September 1939

On May 17, 1939, England issued the White Paper, restricting immigration to Palestine to fifteen thousand Jews per year, after which further Jewish migration would be dependent on Arab approval. The extraordinary goodwill England previously had garnered throughout the Jewish world through issuance of the Balfour Declaration (November 1917) was almost entirely dissipated by the White Paper.

Because the more than three hundred thousand Jews then living in Germany were ruled by the most ferocious antisemite in history, the White Paper put the Palestinian Jewish community in an impossible situation: England forbade it to provide a haven for German Jewry. A few months later, Hitler invaded Poland, thus placing an additional three and a half million Jews under Nazi rule.

Unfortunately, although the "fight" against Hitler eventually succeeded, Ben-Gurion and the Jewish community's "fight" against the White Paper largely failed. Although thousands of illegal aliens were successfully smuggled into Palestine, they were but a small fraction of those who could have been saved had Palestine's borders been open. Unfortunately, the British never revoked the White Paper, even after they learned that Jews were being gassed in Nazi camps.

Ironically, England's rationale for this radically restrictive policy, her desire to gain allies among the Arabs (the Jews, it was assumed, would support England in any case, since the alternative was Hitler), also failed; with few exceptions, the Arab leadership supported Hitler. The most prominent Palestinian leader, Hajj Amin al-Husseini, the recently ousted mufti of Jerusalem, collaborated with Germany throughout the war, and recruited and helped train Muslim volunteers to serve in the Nazi army.

Yet even England's hostility, which had begun to emerge within a few years after the Balfour Declaration was issued, did not blind Ben-Gurion to the good England had formerly done the Jewish people. In a 1936 article (written before the White Paper), "Our Balance Sheet with the English," Ben-Gurion presented a remarkably measured assessment of Britain's achievements vis-à-vis the Jewish community in Palestine: "England allowed 350,000 Jews into the country. She built a harbor at Haifa, and Haifa became a city with a Jewish majority. She built roads connecting the Jewish settlements, and she supported, albeit not sufficiently, Jewish industry. The English are not a nation of angels, and I know only too well the terrible things done by them in Ireland and other places; but the English have also done many positive things in the countries under their rule. They are a great nation, with a rich culture, and not a people of exploiters and robbers. And to us, the English were far from being just bad. They recognized our historical right to this country—they were the first to do so—proclaimed our language an official language, permitted a large-scale immigration; and if we are to judge, let us judge justly and fairly" (*Mishnato shel David Ben-Gurion*, Vol. II, page 363; translated by Shlomo Avineri, *The Making of Modern Zionism*, page 212).

*　　*　　*

For a real peace, we should give up all the occupied territories except for Jerusalem and the Golan Heights.
　　—David Ben-Gurion in the aftermath of the 1967 Six-Day War

Although Israeli politics generally grew more hawkish after the Six-Day War, Ben-Gurion's politics turned dovish. During the war itself, he confided even more moderate views to his diary: "We have no need of the [Golan] Heights, because we won't remain there" (cited in Dan Kurzman, *Ben-Gurion: Prophet of Fire*, page 453).

Without Herut and the Communists.
　　—David Ben-Gurion, 1949, 1951, and on other occasions

Israel has so many political parties that none ever has won a majority of the 120 Knesset (parliament) seats, and ruled alone; every Israeli government has thus been composed of a multiparty coalition.

As prime minister, Ben-Gurion generally tried to draw as many parties as possible into his ruling coalition. However, starting with the 1949 elections to the First Knesset, he made it clear that, broad as his coalition might be, two parties would always be excluded: the Israeli Communist party, and Menachem Begin's Herut (the latter was the core of what later became the Likud party headed by Begin).

A lifelong socialist, Ben-Gurion despised the Communists, both for their support of totalitarianism and their opposition to Zionism. He also realized that if they entered his cabinet, confidential cabinet discussions might well be relayed back to the party's masters in the Soviet Union, and from there to Israel's Arab enemies.

As regards Herut, Ben-Gurion believed its leader (and the future prime minister), Menachem Begin, an enemy of democracy. Ben-Gurion had similarly disliked Begin's mentor, Vladimir Jabotinsky, and sometimes referred to him as Vladimir Hitler.

During a fiery Knesset debate in the early 1950s, Ben-Gurion asserted that if Begin came to power he would rule over Israel the way the Nazis had ruled over Germany, a vile comment that was disproved during Begin's years as prime minister (1977–1983).

The hatred between Ben-Gurion and Begin persisted until Ben-Gurion's last years. He undoubtedly was stunned when Begin urged him to come out of retirement and become prime minister during the frightening days before the 1967 Six-Day War. Apparently, even during the long years of ferocious animosity, Ben-Gurion's wife, Paula, had always admired Begin: Shortly before Ben-Gurion's death, Israel's founding father wrote his longtime political nemesis: "Paula . . . was for some reason an admirer of yours. I opposed your road . . . *but personally I never harbored any grudge against you,* and as I got to know you better . . . my esteem for you grew, and my Paula rejoiced in it" (emphasis mine, ibid., page 457).

Ben-Gurion, I suspect, might well have forgotten some of his earlier statements about Begin. Two quotes come to mind: "Anyone who believes you can't change history has never tried to write his memoirs." "After eighty, there are no enemies, only survivors."

BEN-GURION ON THE NEED FOR JEWISH STRENGTH

We Jews have been accused of many crimes. Yet our one indictable crime in history has been the crime of weakness. Be assured that we shall never be guilty of that crime again.

—Cited by Howard M. Sachar, *The New York Times Book Review*, March 6, 1994, page 20

What matters is not what the gentiles say, but what the Jews do.

—David Ben-Gurion

This is a characteristic Ben-Gurion statement; he believed that Jewish deeds—i.e., building up the Jewish state and army, and developing the Negev desert—and not gentile goodwill, would determine the Jews' future.

88

GOLDA MEIR

Meir (1898–1978) was the Israeli prime minister from 1969 to 1974.

> A leader who doesn't hesitate before he sends his nation into battle is not fit to be a leader.
> —Golda Meir, commenting on Levi Eshkol's ineffectual speech shortly before the Six-Day War of 1967

In the days immediately before the Six-Day War, Israel's Arab neighbors subjected her to continuing threats of annihilation (see below). When Prime Minister Levi Eshkol addressed the already frightened nation, he stumbled at one point in his speech, creating the impression that he was exhausted and near collapse. A wave of despair swept over the country and Eshkol was subjected to savage criticism, thus prompting Golda's comment.

Years later, Abba Eban revealed that Eshkol's stammering and hesitation had nothing to do with excessive nervousness. Rather, the speech he was delivering had been prepared for him. Because he had not had time to read it in advance, he was unaware that the speechwriter had inserted a rarely used word, "an unusual transitive verb for 'withdrawing.'" This word caused his infamous stumble. "It is hard to describe the alarm and despondency that swept through the country," Eban later wrote. "It must have been the only occasion in history in which a hesitant stutter resounded throughout the entire world" (*Personal Witness*, pages 399–400).

Kings and presidents can't mobilize their armies, attack another people, lose the battle, and then say it isn't nice to take something by force.

—Golda Meir on the hypocrisy of Arab leaders' demands for a return of territories they had lost in a war they had initiated

In May and June 1967, Egypt and Syria precipitated the Six-Day War with Israel, repeatedly proclaiming their intention to destroy the "Zionist entity." Egyptian President Gamal Abdel Nasser violated international law by closing the Gates of Tiran to Israeli ships. In Iraq, President Abdel Rahman Arif declared, "Our goal is clear—to wipe Israel off the map." Jordan, Israel's eastern neighbor, signed a military agreement with Egypt.

On June 5, Israel launched an attack against Egypt and Syria, and later against Jordan, which had opened fire on Jerusalem, Tel Aviv, and several Israeli airfields. During the six days of war, Israel conquered the West Bank from Jordan, the Golan Heights from Syria, and the Sinai Desert from Egypt.

Ever since, these three Arab countries, and the rest of the Arab world, have argued that Israel has no right to hold on to land it seized during war.

GOLDA MEIR'S CRITIQUE OF NASSER

Golda Meir's bête noire was Egyptian President Nasser (he ruled from 1952 to 1970), the Arab leader most responsible for fomenting hatred against Israel. Over the years, she attacked Nasser from many different perspectives, e.g.:

There was a man in a czarist Russian village who always knew in advance which night the horses were going to be stolen—because he was the *gonnif* (thief). When Nasser warns that there's going to be a war with Israel, how does he know? Because he's the *gonnif.*

*   *   *

Golda's not unreasonable conviction that Nasser had no love for his own people was powerfully conveyed twice between 1968 and 1970 (during Israel and Egypt's prolonged and bloody War of Attrition), when she was asked when there be might be peace with Egypt:

> I have given instructions that I be informed every time one of our soldiers is killed, even if it is in the middle of the night. When President Nasser leaves instructions that he be awakened in the middle of the night if an Egyptian soldier is killed, there will be peace.

> What we hold against Nasser is not only the killing of our sons, but forcing them, for the sake of Israel's survival, to kill the Arabs' sons.

*　　*　　*

When it came to intra-Jewish affairs, Golda possessed a decidedly down-to-earth, ironic Jewish sensibility:

> Let me tell you something we Israelis have against Moses. He took us forty years through the desert in order to bring us to the one spot in the Middle East that has no oil!

89

MENACHEM BEGIN

Begin was prime minister from 1977 to 1983; prior to statehood, he headed the Irgun, an underground, anti-British organization.

> We will not open fire. There will be no fraternal strife while the foe is at the gate.
>
> —Menachem Begin, 1948

In June 1948, the Irgun's supporters in Europe and America sent the *Altalena,* a ship loaded with weapons, to Israel. The arms were desperately needed because Israel was then under attack from all her Arab neighbors, and the victim of an almost universally observed arms boycott. However, when Begin insisted on retaining some 20 percent of the weapons for Irgun fighters, Ben-Gurion became convinced that he was planning to use the arms to stage a coup (an accusation Begin then and later denied), and ordered Israeli troops to fire on the ship. Twelve volunteers on the ship were killed; the *Altalena* itself was sunk, and all the armaments lost.

Begin was among the last to evacuate the ship. He fled the troops seeking to arrest him and, that night, speaking on an underground radio station, made the above declaration, urging his followers to take no retaliatory action. A potentially ruinous civil war was averted.

*　　*　　*

> These are not *occupied* territories. You've used this ex-
> pression for ten years, but from May 1977, I hope you'll
> start using the word *liberated* territories. A Jew has every
> right to settle these liberated territories of the Jewish land.
> —Begin, May 1977, two days after his election as prime minister

In line with his deeply cherished belief in the importance of Jewish sovereignty over the entire land of Israel, Begin as prime minister
actively encouraged Jewish settlement throughout Judea and Samaria, the historic biblical lands conquered from Jordan during the
1967 Six-Day War. He was in no way deterred from this policy by
the million Arabs living on the West Bank. Begin's pro-settlement
policy was supported by Jews on Israel's political right, and bitterly
opposed by Israelis left of center, on the grounds that these settlements permanently would preclude the possibility of resolving
peacefully the Israeli/Palestinian conflict.

When American President Jimmy Carter urged Begin to halt the
creation of new settlements on the West Bank, the prime minister
presented him with a list of a large number of American cities with
biblical names (e.g., Hebron, Bethlehem, Salem, Jerusalem) and
asked: "What would you say if the governors of those states said
no Jews could live in those towns?" (cited in Eric Silver, *Begin: The
Haunted Prophet*, page 168).

Begin's hopes notwithstanding, no political leaders of any society
has referred to Judea and Samaria as "liberated territories."

*　　*　　*

> A week ago, the Knesset adopted the Golan law, and again
> you declare that you are "punishing" Israel. What kind of
> talk is that, "punishing" Israel? Are we a vassal state? A
> banana republic? Are we fourteen-year-old boys, that if
> they don't behave they have their knuckles smacked? I will
> tell you of whom this government is composed. It is com-
> posed of men who fought, risked their lives and suffered.
> You cannot and will not frighten us with punishments and
> threats. . . . The people of Israel have lived for 3,700 years
> without a memorandum of understanding with America

597

and will continue to live without it for another 3,700 years.

—Message transmitted by Prime Minister Begin to American
Ambassador Samuel Lewis to be transmitted to President Reagan
and to Secretary of State George Shultz, (December 1981);
cited in Eric Silver, *Begin: The Haunted Prophet*, pages 245–246

When Israel in effect annexed the Golan Heights (conquered from Syria in the Six-Day War), the Reagan administration announced that implementation of the recently approved U.S.-Israel memorandum of understanding would be put on hold, and certain financial benefits promised Israel would be withheld. This was the third time in six months that America had "punished" Israel (first, in response to the June destruction of the Iraqi nuclear reactor, then in reaction to the bombings that summer directed against terrorist outposts in Beirut).

Begin's fierce response brings to mind a lesson he had learned from his mentor, Valdimir Jabotinsky, that Jews always have to act with *hadar*, pride. He believed strongly that Jews had to counter acts that seemed to lessen Jewish pride. During his years as head of the Irgun, the British sentenced some captured Irgun soldiers to floggings. Begin immediately ordered some British troops in Palestine captured and flogged, and the floggings of Jews stopped.

*   *   *

Goyim kill *goyim* and the Jews are blamed.
—Reaction to the Sabra-Shatilla massacre, September 1982

When pro-Syrian terrorists murdered incoming Lebanese President Bashir Gemayal (who had promised to make a peace treaty with Israel), Gemayal's followers, the Christian Phalangists, invaded the Palestinian refugee camps of Sabra and Shatilla (supposedly to disarm PLO terrorists), and murdered some one thousand people, few of whom were PLO fighters. At the time, Israel, which controlled West Beirut, was bitterly condemned for allowing the Phalangists into the camps.

Begin responded with the above words, questioning why Jews

should be condemned when Christians kill Muslims. Given that Israel controlled West Beirut and permitted the Phalangists into the camps, his statement was a somewhat disingenuous attempt to evade responsibility. Indeed, the Kahan Commission, assigned to investigate the massacre, concluded that "the Jewish public's stand has always been that the responsibility for such deeds falls not only on those who rioted and committed the atrocities, but also on those who were responsible for safety and public order."

*   *   *

Begin rhymes with Fagin.
> —*Time* magazine, May 1977, after Begin's election
> as prime minister

Time rather unsubtly expressed its contempt for Israel's new leader by linking Begin's name to one of the most odious antisemitic stereotypes in literature (Fagin is the Jewish villain of Charles Dickens's *Oliver Twist*). In response to many irate Jews, the newsweekly's editors denied any antisemitism in this characterization; few believed, however, that they would have chosen to explain the pronunciation of Ronald Reagan's name in the same way.

My outraged father, Shlomo Telushkin, commented at the time, "How would they like it if people went around noting that *Time* rhymes with crime? Or slime?"

*   *   *

Mr. Prime Minister, there can either be a compromise, albeit a painful one, between the two peoples in this land, or else perpetual war. There is no third alternative.
> —Israeli novelist and essayist Amos Oz in an open letter to Prime
> Minister Begin, *Yediot Aharonot*, June 21, 1982; see Amos Oz,
> *The Slopes of Lebanon*, page 30

Oz's letter, written early during the Lebanese War, was an appeal to Begin to start thinking in terms of compromise on the West Bank, and with the PLO. Oz titled his open letter, "Hitler's dead, Mr. Prime Minister," a rejoinder to Begin's repeated comparison of

Yasir Arafat and the PLO to Hitler and the Nazis. Thus, in justifying Israeli bombings in Beirut, Begin said: "If Adolf Hitler were hiding out in a building along with twenty innocent civilians, wouldn't you bomb the building?" To which Oz responded, "Adolf Hitler destroyed one-third of the Jewish people, among them your own parents and relatives, and some of my family. There are times when, like many Jews, I feel sorry I didn't kill Hitler with my own hands. I'm sure you feel the same way. There is not, and there never will be, any healing for the open wounds. . . . But, Mr. Begin, Adolf Hitler died thirty-seven years ago. Pity or not, the fact is: Hitler is not hiding in Nabatiyah, in Sidon, or in Beirut. He is dead and buried in ashes."

90

"IT IS GOOD TO DIE FOR OUR COUNTRY"

Other Zionist Leaders and Other Quotes About Israel

It is good to die for our country (in Hebrew, *Tov lamut be'ad artzaynu*).
   —The last recorded words of Joseph Trumpeldor (March 1, 1920). An accomplished one-armed soldier, Trumpeldor was helping defend the northern outpost of Tel-Hai from an Arab attack, when he suffered a fatal shot to the stomach.

*   *   *

Masada shall not fall again.
   —Yitzhak Lamdan, "Masada," 1927

Masada was the final Jewish outpost during the failed Jewish revolt against Rome. When it fell in 73 C.E., three years after Jerusalem was conquered and the Temple destroyed, its 960 defenders committed suicide rather than fall into the Roman army's hands.

To the Hebrew poet Yitzhak Lamdan, Masada became a metaphor for Palestine, which he saw as the final refuge to which Jews had fled from a hostile world. Therefore, it was imperative that "Masada" not be permitted to fall again. As Lamdan wrote, "This is the limit. From here on, there are no boundaries."

To this day, the fortress at Masada remains one of the most popular destinations for Jewish tourists visiting Israel. On occasion, Israeli officers are brought there to swear the oath "Masada shall not fall again."

*   *   *

If that is the "messiah," may he not come in my time.
—Ahad Ha'am, 1922

Ahad Ha'am, the early Zionist thinker and leader of what was known as "Cultural Zionism," was responding to the reported murder of an innocent Arab boy, an act apparently committed by Jews retaliating for previous Arab murders of Jews. For him, it was inconceivable that Jews would return to Zion "and befoul its soul by the shedding of innocent blood" (cited in Anita Shapira, *Land and Power*, page 178); if this was where the messianic dreams of Zionism would lead, he wanted no part of it.

While Arab terrorists have killed far more Jews than Jewish terrorists have killed Arabs (and almost never have been criticized by Arab governments or leaders for doing so), there have been a number of Jewish terrorist acts against Arabs.

Most shocking was the February 25, 1994, murder of twenty-nine Arabs praying at a Hebron mosque by Dr. Baruch Goldstein, a follower of the late Meir Kahane. A small number of extremist Israelis expressed support for Goldstein (who was beaten to death by Arabs immediately after the shooting); he even was extolled in a eulogy by a Rabbi Yaakov Perin, who declared, "One million Arabs are not worth a Jewish fingernail." But the far more representative response, both within Israel and among Jews worldwide, was horror and shame. Israeli Prime Minister Yitzhak Rabin declared before the Israeli Knesset:

> As a Jew, as an Israeli, as a man and as a human being, I am ashamed over the disgrace imposed upon us by a desperate murderer. . . . To him and to those like him, we say: You are not a part of the community of Israel. . . . You

are not partners in the Zionist enterprise. . . . Judaism spits you out. . . . You are a shame on Zionism and an embarrassment to Judaism.

—Excerpt from Rabin's statement, printed in
The New York Times, March 1, 1994, page 14

Many Israelis commented upon the irony that some Jewish terrorists, while claiming to be religious, lived by values more similar to those of Arab terrorists than to those of Judaism. Thus, Rabin referred to the murderer as a "Jewish Hamas member" (Hamas is the most unyielding and antisemitic of the Palestinian terrorist groups), while Israeli novelist and essayist Amos Oz denounced such Jews as "nothing other than Hezbollah in a skullcap."

* * *

Like a rabbi who carries his prayerbook in a velvet bag to the synagogue, so carry I my sacred gun to the temple.
—Avraham Stern (1907–1942)

Stern, a Hebrew poet, founded *Lekhi,* the Freedom Fighters of Israel (popularly known as "the Stern Gang"), an anti-British terrorist organization. His dream was to oust the British from Palestine and immediately establish a Jewish state, which could serve as a haven to Jews fleeing Nazi rule. He thus opposed calling off the fight against the British even after World War II erupted and England was fighting the Nazis (Stern was killed by the British in 1942).

It is revealing to contrast Stern's poetic exultation of the "sacred gun" with the writings of the far more moderate and thoughtful Abraham Isaac Kook, the first Ashkenazic Chief Rabbi of Palestine:

It is not fitting for Jacob [that is, the people of Israel] to engage in political life at a time when statehood requires bloody ruthlessness and demands a talent for evil.
—Rabbi Abraham Isaac Kook, cited in Arthur Hertzberg, ed.,
The Zionist Idea, page 422

*   *   *

Rabbi Kook (known everywhere as Rav Kook), a passionate proponent of the Jewish return to Israel, never understood the widespread opposition of many Orthodox leaders to Zionism:

> "How can one not be a Zionist," he asked on the last Friday night of his life, "seeing that the Lord God has chosen Zion?"
> —Cited in Jacob Agus, *High Priest of Rebirth,* page 126

*   *   *

Israel has no foreign policy, only a defense policy.
> —General Moshe Dayan

Aware of Israel's exceptionally bitter internal debates, American Secretary of State Henry Kissinger later sardonically restated Dayan's words: "Israel has no foreign policy, only a domestic political system."

*   *   *

> A Government that prefers . . . the Land of Israel above peace would cause us grave difficulties of conscience. A Government that prefers settlements across the Green Line [i.e., on the West Bank in Judea and Samaria] to the ending of the historic conflicts . . . would raise questions for us about the justice of our cause.
> —Open letter in Israeli press, March 1978, signed by some 350 Israeli reserve army officers, urging Prime Minister Begin to be open to making territorial compromises in his negotiations with Egyptian President Anwar Sadat. Their letter was the catalyst for the founding of the dovish Israeli peace lobby, Peace Now.

*   *   *

TWO AMERICAN PRESIDENTS AND ISRAEL'S BIRTH

> There are serious doubts in my mind that Israel would
> have come into being if Roosevelt had lived.
>> —David Niles, assistant to President Franklin Delano Roosevelt,
>> Truman's predecessor; this comment is cited and discussed by the
>> eminent historian Howard Sachar (*A History of Israel*, page 255),
>> who concludes that Niles's assessment "was probably correct."

Although widely perceived by Zionists and other Jews as a devoted friend, Roosevelt repeatedly vacillated in his support for a Jewish state. On April 5, 1945, a week before his death, he assured Saudi Arabia's King Ibn Saud, a virulent anti-Zionist, that he would not adopt a stance hostile to the Arabs. He also informed Judge Joseph Proskauer, president of the American Jewish Committee, that "on account of the Arab situation, nothing could be done in Palestine."

* * *

> God put you in your mother's womb so that you could be
> the instrument to bring about the rebirth of Israel after
> two thousand years.
>> —Comment of the Israeli Chief Rabbi upon meeting
>> President Harry Truman in 1949. A year earlier, Truman had
>> strongly supported Israel's establishment, and became the
>> first head of state to recognize her.

Merle Miller reports that when the former president related this story to him some eleven years later, "great tears started rolling down Harry Truman's cheeks" (see Merle Miller, *Plain Speaking*, page 218).

EMBATTLED JERUSALEM

The late W. H. Auden remembered standing in 1970 with Teddy Kollek, the liberal mayor of Jerusalem, on a terrace overlooking the Old City and the pink, bare luminous hills beyond. Palestinian terrorists had just exploded a hand grenade at a busy intersection in downtown Jerusalem, wounding several pedestrians. Orthodox rioters had just clashed with the police in a northern suburb. In an offhand manner, the mayor remarked that Jerusalem would be a beautiful place if it were not for the wars, and the orthodox of all faiths, their squabbles and their riots. He said this, Auden recalled, "as one might say in London that it would be lovely except for the weather."

—Cited in Amos Elon, *Jerusalem: City of Mirrors,* pages 81–82

91

ANTI-ZIONISM AND ANTISEMITISM

Israel to the Arab world is like a cancer to the human body, and the only way of remedy is to uproot it just like a cancer. . . . We Arabs total about fifty million. Why don't we sacrifice ten million of our number and live in pride and self-respect?
—King Saud of Saudi Arabia, quoted by the Associated Press,
January 9, 1954

Several things are striking about King Saud's comment, most obviously, the virulence of his hatred for Israel. His speaking so casually of sacrificing ten million of his *own* people demonstrates the obsessive nature of his hatred. In addition, given that Israel's entire population at the time was a little over one million, Saud's estimate that it would take ten million Arab soldiers to destroy her suggests that he saw the Jews in superhuman physical terms. It also is not clear whether the king was himself willing to be one of the ten million people sacrificed to destroy Israel.

Although for many years Saudi Arabia and other Arab states bribed and pressured many African nations to break off diplomatic relations with Israel and support anti-Israel resolutions in the United Nations, one, the Ivory Coast, refused to be intimidated. Ambassador Arsene Assouan Usher responded to Saudi pressure with the statement: "Saudi Arabia may be used to buying Negroes [a reference to the slave traffic] but it can never buy us" (I. L. Kenen, *Israel's Defense Line,* page 159).

*   *   *

Those [Israelis] who survive will remain in Palestine. I estimate that none of them will survive.
—Ahmed Shukeiry, founder of the Palestine Liberation
Organization (PLO), predicting the future of Israeli Jews
if the Arabs succeeded in defeating Israel; Yasir Arafat
took over control from Shukeiry after the 1967 Six-Day War.

WESTERN ENEMIES OF ISRAEL

On the Day of Judgment, the gravest crime standing to the German Nationalists' account might be, not that they had exterminated a majority of Western Jews, but that they had caused the surviving remnant of Jewry to stumble.
—Arnold Toynbee (1889–1975), *Study of History,*
Vol. VIII, page 290n

Toynbee, author of the multivolume *Study of History,* was probably the most famous historian of the first half of the twentieth century. Unfortunately, he had a vicious hatred for Zionism, as reflected in the above passage, which suggests that the greatest Nazi sin was not carrying out the Holocaust, but moving surviving Jews to become Zionists.

Toynbee had a particular fondness for drawing comparisons between Nazis and Jews: "The Nazi Gentiles' fall from grace was less tragic than the Zionist Jews," he wrote on one occasion; on another, " . . . in the Jewish Zionists I see disciples of the Nazis" (*Reconsiderations,* pages 627–628). Perhaps the most important assessment of Toynbee's writings on Zionism and Jews is Oskar Rabinowicz's book-length treatment, *Arnold Toynbee on Judaism and Zionism.* In a letter to the editor of the *Jewish Frontier* (January 10, 1955) he commented, "The tragedy of recent Jewish history is that, instead of learning through suffering, the Jews should have done to others, the Arabs, what had been done to them by others, the Nazis."

The late Professor Marie Syrkin notes of Toynbee's odious comparison: "I am concerned with the moral perversity which views as equal the systematic murder of six million men, women and children, and the resettlement of 800,000 Arabs" (*The State of the Jews,* page 175).

Toynbee proved to be one of the Arab world's most important Western supporters in its fight against Israel. No figure of comparable stature was willing to go on record equating Zionism and Nazism (a particular irony, given that many Arabs had been supportive of the Nazis during World War II, in large measure because of Nazi antisemitism).

Toynbee's view of Judaism was not much higher than his opinion of Zionism. He regarded it as "a fossil of the Syriac civilization," which had little reason to continue existing after the rise of Christianity. He even claimed that Judaism, with its belief in monotheism, introduced bigotry into the world: "The irony of Jewish history surely is that the Jews have been the chief sufferers from a spirit which they themselves originally kindled" (the same letter of January 10, 1955). On another occasion, he claimed that "Hitler's main idea—the fanatical worship of a jealous tribal god, at the bidding of a prophetic leader—is the original (though not ultimate) *Leitmotif* of the Old Testament" (cited in Rabinowicz, page 321). Toynbee claims that he heard this astonishing idea from a Jewish scholar, though he does not mention the scholar's name.

*   *   *

All persons who seek to view the Middle East problem with honesty and objectivity stand aghast at Israel's onslaught, the most violent, ruthless (and successful) aggression since Hitler's blitzkrieg across Western Europe in the summer of 1940, aiming not at a victory but at annihilation—the very objective proclaimed by Nasser and his allies which had drawn support for Israel.

—Henry P. Van Dusen, former president of Union Theological Seminary, a leading school of liberal Protestantism; letter to the editor, *New York Times,* July 7, 1967

Van Dusen's linking of Israel and Hitler, a standard feature of both Soviet and Arab propaganda, was, as far as I know, a view never previously articulated by any American church leader. However, subsequent to the publication of his widely discussed letter, this odious comparison became an all-too-common feature in religious and radical left-wing writings on Israel.

Van Dusen's comparison of Israel's and Hitler's fighting styles is particularly outrageous given that World War II and the Six-Day War had nothing in common. Israel fought only after surrounding Arab states repeatedly made threats to exterminate her (see pages 593–594), threats that apparently prompted no equal published expressions of outrage by Van Dusen. Moreover, the charge that Israel sought to annihilate her Arab opponents represented a second equation with the Nazis, who *did* annihilate six million Jews. The Israelis defeated the Arab armies but never, in any way, moved to exterminate Arab civilians or, for that matter, Arab soldiers.

Historian Jack Wertheimer rightly has characterized Van Dusen's attack as "the most savage" unleashed against Israel by an American clergyman (*A People Divided,* page 31). Almost as disturbing to many American Jews was the neutral posture so many liberal Christian clergy adopted during the month preceding the Six-Day War, when bloodcurdling anti-Israel and antisemitic threats poured forth daily from Arab heads of states. As Professor Jacob Neusner wrote at the time: "It seems to me that the silence of most, though not all, leaders of American Christianity in the face of what then seemed impending genocide, but what was most certainly intended and well planned genocide, against the people of the State of Israel, cannot be ignored" (*Judaism,* Summer 1967, 16:3; page 363).

IS ANTI-ZIONISM ANTISEMITISM?

The libel of "Zionism equals racism" is the . . . contemporary equivalent of *Christ-killer, traitor, usurer, international conspirator.* All this has stolen into vogue under the sham disclaimer of "I'm not antisemitic, I'm just anti-Zionist"—the equivalent of "I'm not anti-American, I just think the United States shouldn't exist."

—Benjamin Netanyahu, *A Place Among the Nations: Israel and the World,* page 88

DENNIS PRAGER'S FOUR GUIDELINES FOR DISTINGUISHING AN ISRAEL-HATER FROM A CONCERNED CRITIC OF ISRAEL

1. When a person begins talking about the unfairness of Israel's creation, know that you are listening to an Israel-hater. Almost every country on earth was born in bloodshed, yet this person challenges only one's legitimacy—that of the one Jewish state.

Ask the person why he or she doesn't raise questions about Pakistan's birth. While Israel's birth was accompanied by the death of a few thousand Palestinians and Jews, Pakistan's birth resulted in the killing of about a million Muslims and Hindus. Why then does the person question only Israel's right to exist? Jews know the reason—Israel is Jewish.

2. Is the critic of Israel prepared to admit that of all the nations surrounding it, Israel is the only democracy, the only state with an independent judiciary and press, freedom of religion and, most important, its own mechanisms for self-criticism? If not, he is an Israel-hater.

3. Ask the person if he or she is as vocal about the rights of Tibetans occupied by China or blacks killed by the Sudanese government as he is about Palestinian statehood. If not, why? Jews know the reason.

4. If the person is over fifty, ask if he or she was as vocal on behalf of a Palestinian state when the West Bank was occupied by Jordan before June 1967? If not, why all of a sudden, when Palestinians came under Israeli occupation, did the critic begin to be so concerned with Pales-

tinian statehood? Jews know the reason, and it isn't because of the individual's newfound love of Palestinians.

—Dennis Prager, "Why Anti-Zionism Is Antisemitism,"
Ultimate Issues, October–December 1990, page 16

*   *   *

While [Israel] struggles for the right to exist, [its citizens] . . . feel, as Jews have felt all through this century, that to kill a Jew is a political virtue, whereas in the Middle Ages, it was a religious one.

—Alfred Kazin, "The Heart of the World," in Eva Fleischner,
Auschwitz: Beginning of a New Era?, page 65

Kazin's observation on the similarity of medieval antisemitism and modern anti-Zionism is acute. Jew-haters such as the Crusaders were willing to let Jews who accepted Jesus Christ live, while anti-Zionists who support the destruction of Israel are willing to leave anti-Zionist Jews alone. Both, however, see the overwhelming majority of Jews as their enemies.

PART VIII

ON BEING A JEW

Modern Reflections

Judaism, done right, has the power to save your life from being spent entirely on the trivial. . . . But it can do more than that. Its goal is not just to make *your* life more satisfying. Its goal is not the survival of the Jewish people. That is a means to an end, not an end in itself. The ultimate goal is to transform the world into the kind of world God had in mind when He created it.

—Rabbi Harold Kushner, *To Life!*, page 297

*   *   *

It was my Jewish nature alone that I had to thank for two characteristics that proved indispensable to me in my life's difficult course. Because I was a Jew I found myself free from many prejudices that hampered others in the use of their intellects; and as a Jew, I was prepared to take my place on the side of the opposition and renounce being on good terms with the "compact majority."

—Sigmund Freud, in speech to the Society of B'nai B'rith, Vienna, May 6, 1926; Freud's speech is printed in Steve Israel and Seth Forman, eds. *Great Speeches Throughout Jewish History*, pages 81–83.

*   *   *

The pursuit of knowledge for its own sake, an almost fanatical love of justice, and the desire for personal inde-

pendence, these are the features of the Jewish tradition
which make me thank my lucky stars I belong to it.
—Albert Einstein (1879–1955)

Upon Chaim Weizmann's death in 1952, Israeli Prime Minister
David Ben-Gurion invited Einstein, an ardent supporter of Zionism
and other Jewish causes, to become Israel's second president. The
great physicist, who had no particular affinity for diplomatic work,
thanked Ben-Gurion for the honor, but turned down the invitation.

*   *   *

You feel oppressed by your Judaism only as long as you
do not take pride in it.
—Bertha Pappenheim (1859–1936)

I believe that Pappenheim is a great unsung hero of modern Jewish life. An early feminist and an ardent fighter against "white slavery" and other kinds of prostitution (she also is famous in
psychoanalytic history as the patient described by Freud as Anna
O), Pappenheim was a deeply committed Jew, one who criticized
those who abandoned Jewish identification (as evidenced by the
above quote) while goading her rabbinic contemporaries to alleviate
injustices committed in the name of Jewish law.

After World War I, a number of Jewish women in Europe were
left uncertain of the fate of husbands who had disappeared in battle.
Because Jewish law accepts only eyewitness testimony in establishing
an individual's death, these women were forbidden to remarry (in
Hebrew, such women are called *agunot*), since there was a theoretical, if very slight, possibility that their husbands might still be alive.
Confronting German rabbis at a conference, Pappenheim told them:
"Gentlemen, when the capitalist economy developed to a point
where it was no longer possible to observe the Torah's explicit prohibition against lending money for interest, your predecessors managed to find within the *halakha* an acceptable way to circumvent
the law. From your failure to act now, I can only conclude that the
halakha, as you interpret it, places higher value on economic concerns than on the needs and rights of these pathetic and unfortunate

women" (quoted by Ernst Simon in Marvin Fox, ed., *Modern Jewish Ethics,* page 52).

*   *   *

I still hope the day will come when the Jews who are great will become great Jews.
> —Among the final words of Israeli Chief Rabbi Abraham Isaac Kook (1935), addressed to his physician, a Dr. Zondek, whose adherence to Judaism apparently was somewhat tenuous (cited in Jacob Agus, *High Priest of Rebirth,* page 126).

*   *   *

When I was young, I asked my father, "If you don't believe in God, why do you go to synagogue so regularly?" My father answered, "Jews go to synagogue for all kinds of reasons. My friend Garfinkle, who is Orthodox, goes to synagogue to talk to God. I go to talk to Garfinkle."
> —American writer Harry Golden

*   *   *

When it's not terrible to be a Jew, it's wonderful.
> —Helen Telushkin

*   *   *

In order for a caterpillar to become a beautiful butterfly taking its beauty out into the world, it must first spend time in a cocoon. In order for a Jew to become a beautiful Jew taking his or her beauty into the world, he or she too must first spend time in a cocoon. Unfortunately, most non-Orthodox Jews don't believe in the cocoon, and most Orthodox Jews don't believe in flying into the world.
> —Dennis Prager

Prager believes that the small number of Jews living Jewish lives out in the world and actively propagating Judaism's values there is dangerous both to Jews and to the world: "If Jews do not teach the world ethical monotheism, they will be victims of a world they didn't influence."

*　　*　　*

One of the great teachers of twentieth-century Jewry was the late Rabbi Joseph Soloveitchik (1903–1993), a man with an unrivaled knowledge of the Talmud. During the more than forty years in which Rabbi Soloveitchik taught at Yeshiva University, he ordained some two thousand rabbis. In the course of one lecture, Rabbi Soloveitchik described the role played by centuries of Jewish learning in weaving together countless generations of Jews:

> Whenever I start my lesson, the door opens up and another old man comes in and sits down. He is older than I am. He is my grandfather and his name is Reb Hayyim Brisker, without whom I cannot teach Torah. Then the door opens quietly again and another old man comes in. He is older than Reb Hayyim. He lived in the seventeenth century. His name is Shabbetai ben Meir ha-Kohen, the famous "Shakh" who might be present when you study Talmud. And then more visitors show up. Some of the visitors lived in the eleventh century and some lived in the twelfth century, some in the thirteenth century—some even lived in antiquity: Rashi, Rabbenu Tam, Rava, Rashba. More and more come in. Of course, what do I do? I introduce them to my pupils and the dialogue commences. The Rambam says something. Rava disagrees. A boy jumps up, he has an idea. The Rashba smiles gently. I try to analyze what the young boy meant. Another boy intervenes and we call upon Rabbenu Tam to express his opinion, and suddenly a symposium of generations comes into existence.
>
> —Cited in Joel Grushaver, *40 Things You Can Do to Save the Jewish People,* page 223

BIBLIOGRAPHY

A NOTE ON CITATIONS FROM JUDAISM'S CLASSIC TEXTS

When citing statements from the Hebrew Bible, I have generally followed the translation of the Jewish Publication Society (Philadelphia, 1985), an excellent and highly readable rendering of the Bible into contemporary English. On occasion, however, I have translated the verses myself, or utilized other translations which seemed to me preferable for a specific verse.

In quoting from the Talmud, I have often relied on the highly accurate and literal translation of the Soncino Press (London, 1935), the only complete translation of the Talmud into English. Currently, Random House is publishing a translation of large sections of the Talmud into English, following the Hebrew translation of Rabbi Adin Steinsalz. Art Scroll, a large Jewish publisher in Brooklyn, is currently bringing out a translation of the Talmud into English as well, and plans to have the entire Talmud completed within a few years. So far, both of these translations have been excellent, and I have occasionally consulted them both. Nonetheless, many of the talmudic texts cited in this book have been translated by me from the original. Where I have utilized translations that have appeared in other books (e.g. William Braude's translation of *The Book of Legends*), I have acknowledged the source within.

There are several English translations of the Mishna, among them one by Herbert Danby (Oxford: Clarendon Press, 1933), and a recent translation by Jacob Neusner, *The Mishnah,* published by Yale University Press (1988). Yale University Press has likewise published Judah Goldin's translation of *The Fathers According to Rabbi Nathan* (1955), and Dov Zlotnick's translation of *The Tractate Mourning* (1966).

Over a period of several decades, Yale University Press has also published translations of all fourteen volumes of Maimonides's *Mishneh Torah,* under the title *The Code of Maimonides.* Unfortunately, the sixteenth-century standard code of Jewish law, the *Shulkhan Arukh,* has, with the exception of a few small sections, not been systematically translated into English. Rabbi Shlomo Ganzfried's nineteenth-century legal code has been recently retranslated by Eliyahu Touger and published in a two-volume English edition under the title *Kitzur Shulchon Oruch: The Classic Guide to the Everyday Observance of Jewish Law* (Brooklyn, N.Y.: Moznaim, 1991).

The citations of the Midrash Rabbah generally follow the ten-volume Soncino translation (London, 1983), although I have checked all translation against the original, and have generally made some alterations. The *Mekhilta* has been translated and published in three volumes by the Jewish Publication Society (Philadelphia, 1933).

THE TEN MOST IMPORTANT COLLECTIONS OF JEWISH QUOTES AND TEXTS: A PERSONAL SELECTION

Baron, Joseph. *A Treasury of Jewish Quotations.* Northvale, N.J.: Jason Aaronson Inc., 1985. A wide-ranging collection of some 18,000 quotes assembled by the late Rabbi Joseph Baron during his long rabbinic career.

Bialik, Hayim Nahman, and Yehoshua Hana Ravnitzky. *The Book of Legends: Legends from the Talmud and Midrash* (translated from the Hebrew *Sefer Ha-Aggadah* by William Braude). New York: Schocken Books, 1992. This is probably the most extensive selection of ethical and legendary material from the Talmud and Midrash ever assembled, and one of the classic works of Jewish literature. Its recent translation into English fills an important gap.

Bokser, Ben Zion, and Baruch Bokser. *The Talmud: Selected Writings.* New York: Paulist Press, 1989. A particularly beautiful, and morally insightful, compilation of significant passages from the Talmud.

Cohen, A. *Everyman's Talmud*. New York: Dutton, 1968 (originally published in 1932). A wonderful guide and overview to the Talmud's contents.

Glatzer, Nahum. *Hammer on the Rock: A Midrash Reader*. New York: Schocken Books, 1948, 1962. The late Dr. Glatzer was one of Jewish literature's master anthologists. This work, although short, contains many of the Midrash's profoundest gems.

Hertzberg, Arthur. *Judaism: An Anthology of the Key Spiritual Writings of the Jewish Tradition*. New York: Simon and Schuster, 1991. An eminently useful, and provocative, assemblage of key Jewish writings, by an important and widely-read Jewish scholar.

Klagsbrun, Francine. *Voices of Wisdom: Jewish Ideals and Ethics for Everyday Living*. New York: Pantheon, 1980. An extraordinary collection of Judaism's most beautiful and important passages. This book is a classic.

Petuchowski, Jakob J. *Our Masters Taught: Rabbinic Stories and Sayings*. New York: Crossroad, 1982. A short, but powerful, collection of important talmudic anecdotes by one of American Jewry's great (and recently deceased) teachers.

Siegel, Danny. *Where Heaven and Earth Touch: An Anthology of Midrash and Halachah*. Northvale, N.J.: Jason Aronson, Inc., 1989. Danny Siegel is a distinguished Jewish poet, and his extraordinary renderings of numerous talmudic quotes raises the art of translation to a new height.

Weiss, Saul. *Insights: A Talmudic Treasury*. Jerusalem: Feldheim, 1990. Rabbi Saul Weiss has culled 500 important, and many of them overlooked, talmudic quotes, and provided a far-ranging, insightful and very interesting commentary.

BIBLIOGRAPHY OF BOOKS AND ARTICLES CITED

Agus, Jacob. *High Priest of Rebirth: The Life, Times, and Thought of Abraham Isaac Kuk*. New York: Bloch, 1970.

Alcalay, R. in collaboration with Mordekhai Nurock. *Words of the Wise*. Jerusalem: Masada Press, 1970.

Alexander, Philip S., ed. and trans. *Textual Sources for the Study of Judaism*. Manchester, England: Manchester University Press, 1984.

Almog, Shmuel. *Nationalism and Antisemitism in Modern Europe 1815–1945*. Oxford: Pergamon Press, 1990.

————ed. *Antisemitism Through the Ages*. Oxford: Pergamon Press, 1988.

Alter, Robert *After the Tradition: Essays on Modern Jewish Writing*. New York: E. P. Dutton (pbk.), 1971.

Amichai, Yehuda. *Amen*. New York: Harper and Row, 1977.

Aptowitzer, Viktor. "Observations on the Criminal Laws of the Jews," *Jewish Quarterly Review*, Philadelphia, Vol. XV, 1924.

Avidor Hacohen, Shmuel. *Touching Heaven, Touching Earth: Hasidic Humor and Wit*. Tel Aviv: Sadan Publishing, 1976.

Avineri, Shlomo. *The Making of Modern Zionism*. New York: Basic Books, 1981.

Ayalti, Hanan, ed. *Yiddish Proverbs: The Essence of Yiddish Wit and Wisdom, in Yiddish and English on Facing Pages*. New York: Schocken Books, 1949; paperback, 1963.

Baraka, Imamu Amiri (LeRoi Jones). *Black Magic: Collected Poetry 1961–1967*. Indianapolis: Bobbs-Merrill, 1969.

Bellow, Saul. *Seize the Day*. New York: Penguin, 1976.

Ben-Sasson, Haim Hillel. *Trial and Achievement: Currents in Jewish History (from 313)*. Jerusalem: Keter Publishing House, 1974.

Berenbaum, Michael. *The World Must Know: The History of the Holocaust as Told in the United States Holocaust Memorial Museum*. Boston: Little, Brown and Company, 1993.

Berkovits, Eliezer. *Faith After the Holocaust*. New York: Ktav, 1973.

———. *Jewish Women in Time and Torah*. New York: Ktav, 1990.

———. *With God in Hell: Judaism in the Ghetto and Deathcamps*. New York: Sanhedrin Press, 1979.

Biale, Rachel. *Women and Jewish Law: An Exploration of Women's Issues in Halakhic Sources*. New York: Schocken Books, 1984.

Bialik, Hayim Nahman. "After My Death," in S. Y. Penueli and A. Ukhmani, *Anthology of Modern Hebrew Poetry*, Vol. 1. Jerusalem: Institute for the Translation of Hebrew Literature and Israel Universities Press, 1966.

Bleich, J. David. *Contemporary Halakhic Problem*, Vol. II. New York: Ktav and Yeshiva University Press, 1983.

———. *Judaism and Healing: Halakhic Perspectives*. New York: Ktav, 1981.

Blidstein, Gerald. "Capital Punishment: The Classic Jewish Discussion," in Alan Corre, ed. *Understanding the Talmud*. New York: Ktav Publishing, 1975.

Block, Gay, and Malka Drucker. *Rescuers: Portraits of Moral Courage in the Holocaust*, prologue by Cynthia Ozick. New York: Holmes and Meier, 1992.

Blue, Lionel, with Jonathan Magonet. *The Blue Guide to the Here and Hereafter*. London: Collins, 1988.

Bok, Sissela. *Lying: Moral Choice in Public and Private Life*. New York: Pantheon, 1978; New York: Vintage Books (pbk), 1979.

Borowski, Tadeusz. *This Way for the Gas, Ladies and Gentlemen*. New York: Penguin Books, 1959, 1967.

Brandon, S.G.F. *Jesus and the Zealots: A Study of the Political Factor in*

Primitive Christianity. New York: Charles Scribner's Sons, 1967.

Breitman, Richard. *The Architect of Genocide: Himmler and the Final Solution.* New York: Knopf, 1991.

Broun, Heywood, and George Britt. *Christians Only.* New York: Vanguard Press, 1931.

Brown, Steven M. "Parents as Partners with God: Parenting Young Children," in Rela M. Geffen, ed. *Celebration and Renewal: Rites of Passage in Judaism.* Philadelphia: Jewish Publication Society, 1993, pages 32–52.

Buber, Martin. *Meetings,* edited with an introduction by Maurice Friedman. La Salle, Ill.: Open Court Publishing Company, 1973.

———. *Tales of the Hasidim. Book One: The Early Masters, and Book Two: The Later Masters.* New York: Schocken, 1975.

———. *Ten Rungs: Hasidic Sayings.* New York: Schocken, 1962.

Buckley, William F., Jr. *In Search of Anti-Semitism.* New York: Continuum, 1992.

Bunim, Irving. *Ethics from Sinai: An Eclectic, Wide-Ranging Commentary on Pirke Aboth,* 3 vols. New York: Feldheim, 1966.

Cargas, Harry James. *Shadows of Auschwitz: A Christian Response to the Holocaust.* New York: Crossroad, 1992.

Carlebach, Julius. *Karl Marx and the Radical Critique of Judaism.* London: Routledge and Kegan Paul, 1978.

Carmell, Aryeh. *Masterplan: Judaism: Its Program, Meaning, Goals.* Jerusalem: Jerusalem Academy Publications, 1991.

Cohen, Jeremy. "Traditional Prejudice and Religious Reform: The Theological and Historical Foundations of Luther's Anti-Judaism," in Sander Gilman and Steven Katz, eds. *Anti-Semitism in Times of Crisis.* New York: New York University Press, 1991, pages 81–102.

Cohn, Norman. *Warrant for Genocide: The Jewish World Conspiracy and the Protocols of the Elders of Zion.* New York: Harper and Row, 1966, 1967.

Colson, F. H. trans. *Philo,* Vol. 7, Loeb Classical Library, London: William Heinemann, n.d., although the preface is dated January 1937.

Condition of Jewish Belief, The, a symposium compiled by the editors of *Commentary* magazine. New York: Macmillan, 1966; reissued: Northvale, N.J.: Jason Aronson, 1989.

Cowan, Lore, and Maurice Cowan, eds. *The Wit of the Jews.* Nashville, Tenn.: Aurora Publishers, 1970.

Dalin, David G., ed. *American Jews and the Separationist Faith: The New Debate on Religion in Public Life.* Washington, D.C.: Ethics and Public Policy Center, 1993.

Davies, Alan T. "Response to Irving Greenberg," in Eva Fleischner, ed., *Auschwitz: Beginning of a New Era? Reflections on the Holocaust.* New York: published jointly by Ktav Publishing, The Cathedral

Church of St. John the Divine, and the Anti-Defamation League, 1977, pages 57–64.

Davidowicz, Lucy. *A Holocaust Reader*. New York: Behrman House, 1976.

———. *The War Against the Jews*. New York: Holt, Rinehart and Winston, 1975.

Dinnerstein, Leonard. "Antisemitism in Crisis Times in the United States: The 1920s and 1930s," in Sander Gilman and Steven Katz, eds. *Anti-Semitism in Times of Crisis*. New York: New York University Press, 1991, pages 212–226.

———. "A Dreyfus Affair in Georgia," in Leonard Dinnerstein, ed., *Antisemitism in the United States*, pages 87–101.

Eban, Abba. *Personal Witness: Israel Through My Eyes*. New York: Putnam, 1992.

Eliach, Yaffa. *Hasidic Tales of the Holocaust*. New York: Oxford University Press, 1982.

Eliot, T.S. *Collected Poems 1909–1935*. New York: Harcourt Brace, 1936.

Epstein, Joseph. *Pertinent Players: Essays on the Literary Life*. New York: W.W. Norton, 1993.

Evans, Eli N. *The Lonely Days Were Sundays: Reflections of a Jewish Southerner*. Jackson, Miss.: University Press of Mississippi, 1993.

Fackenheim, Emil. "The Holocaust and the State of Israel: Their Relation," in Eva Fleischner, ed., *Auschwitz: Beginning of a New Era? Reflections on the Holocaust*. New York: published jointly by Ktav Publishing, The Cathedral Church of St. John the Divine, and the Anti-Defamation League, 1977, pages 205–215.

———. *The Jewish Return into History: Reflections in the Age of Auschwitz and a New Jerusalem*. New York: Schocken, 1978.

Feldman, David M. *Birth Control in Jewish Law: Marital Relations, Contraception, and Abortion as Set Forth in the Classic Texts of Jewish Law*. New York: New York University Press, 1968.

Flannery, Edward. *The Anguish of the Jews: Twenty-three Centuries of Anti-Semitism*. New York: Macmillan, 1965.

Fleg, Edmond. *Why I Am a Jew,* translated from the French by Louis Waterman Wise. New York: Bloch, 1929.

Fleischner, Eva, ed. *Auschwitz: Beginning of a New Era? Reflections on the Holocaust*. New York: published jointly by Ktav Publishing, The Cathedral Church of St. John the Divine, and the Anti-Defamation League, 1977. This book is a collection of some twenty-five papers given at the International Symposium on the Holocaust held at the Cathedral Church of St. John the Divine in New York City, June 3–6, 1974.

Fox, Marvin, ed. *Modern Jewish Ethics: Theory and Practice*. Columbus, Ohio: Ohio State University Press, 1975.

Frank, Anne. *The Diary of Anne Frank*. Garden City, N.Y.: Doubleday, 1952; New York: Simon and Schuster, Pocket Books (pbk.), 1963, 1974.

Freud, Sigmund. *The Future of an Illusion*. New York: Norton, 1961.

———. *Jokes and Their Relation to the Unconscious*, New York: Norton, 1963.

———. *Moses and Monotheism*, translated from the German by Katherine Jones. New York: Knopf, 1939.

Friedman, Dayle. "The Crown of Glory: Aging in the Jewish Tradition," in Rela M. Geffen, ed., *Celebration and Renewal: Rites of Passage in Judaism*. Philadelphia: Jewish Publication Society, 1993, pages 202–225.

Friedrich, Otto. *The End of the World: A History*. New York: Coward, McCann, 1982.

Fromm, Erich. *The Sane Society*. New York: Rinehart, 1955.

Geffen, Rela M., ed. *Celebration and Renewal: Rites of Passage in Judaism*. Philadelphia: Jewish Publication Society, 1993.

Gellman, Rabbi Marc. In David G. Dalin, ed., *American Jews and the Separationist Faith: The New Debate on Religion in Public Life*. Washington, D.C.: Ethics and Public Policy Center, 1993, pages 53–56.

Gilbert, Martin. *Auschwitz and the Allies*. New York: Holt, Rinehart and Winston, 1981.

———. *The Holocaust: A History of the Jews of Europe During the Second World War*. New York: Henry Holt and Company, 1985.

Gilder, George. *Naked Nomads: Unmarried Men in America*. New York: Quadrangle/The New York Times Book Co., 1974.

Gilman, Sander, and Steven Katz, eds. *Anti-Semitism in Times of Crisis*. New York: New York University Press, 1991.

Ginsberg, Benjamin. *The Fatal Embrace: Jews and the State*. Chicago: University of Chicago Press, 1993.

Ginzberg, Louis. "The Gaon, Rabbi Elijah Wilna," in his *Students, Scholars and Saints*. Philadelphia: Jewish Publication Society, 1928.

Glatzer, Nahum, ed. *A Jewish Reader*. New York: Schocken Books, 1946, 1961.

Glendon, Mary Ann. *Rights Talk: The Impoverishment of Political Discourse*. New York: Free Press, 1991.

Gold, Michael. *Does God Belong in the Bedroom?* Philadelphia: Jewish Publication Society, 1992.

Gould, Allan, collector and editor. *What Did They Think of the Jews?* Northvale, N.J.: Jason Aronson, Inc., 1991.

Green, Arthur. "A Contemporary Approach to Jewish Sexuality," in Michael and Sharon Strassfeld, *The Second Jewish Catalog*. Philadelphia: Jewish Publication Society, 1976, pages 96–99.

Greenberg, Hayim. *The Inner Eye: Selected Essays*, Vol. II, edited by

Shlomo Katz. New York: Jewish Frontier Association, 1964.

Greenberg, Irving. "Cloud of Smoke, Pillar of Fire: Judaism, Christianity and Modernity After the Holocaust," in Eva Fleischner, ed., *Auschwitz: Beginning of a New Era? Reflections on the Holocaust.* New York: published jointly by Ktav Publishing, The Cathedral Church of St. John the Divine, and the Anti-Defamation League, 1977, pages 7–55.

Grishaver, Joel Lurie. *40 Things You Can Do to Save the Jewish People.* Los Angeles: Alef Design Group, 1993.

Ha'am, Ahad. *Selected Essays,* trans. Leon Simon. New York: Meridian Books, 1962.

Halkin, Hillel. *Letters to an American Jewish Friend.* Philadelphia: Jewish Publication Society, 1977.

Heer, Friedrich. *God's First Love.* New York: Weybright and Talley, 1967.

Heinemann, Benno. *The Maggid of Dubno and His Parables.* New York: Feldheim, 1978.

Hentoff, Nat. *Free Speech for Me, but Not for Thee: How the American Left and Right Relentlessly Censor Each Other.* New York: HarperCollins, 1992.

Herberg, Will. *Four Existentialist Theologians: A Reader from the Works of Jacques Maritain, Nicholas Berdyaev, Martin Buber and Paul Tillich.* Garden City, N.Y.: Doubleday, 1958.

———. *Judaism and Modern Man.* New York: Atheneum, 1979.

Herring, Basil. *Jewish Ethics and Halakhah for Our Time: Sources and Commentary.* New York: Ktav and Yeshiva University Press, 1984.

———. *Jewish Ethics and Halakhah for Our Time,* Vol. II. Hoboken, N.J.: Ktav and Yeshiva University Press, 1989.

Hertzberg, Arthur. *The French Enlightenment and the Jews: The Origins of Modern Anti-Semitism.* New York: Schocken Books, 1970.

———. *The Jews in America.* New York: Simon and Schuster, 1989.

———. ed. *The Zionist Idea: A Historical Analysis and Reader* (an anthology drawn from the writings of thirty-seven of the leading thinkers of the Zionist movement). New York: Harper and Row, 1959.

Herzog, Isaac. *Judaism: Law and Ethics.* London: Soncino, 1974.

Heschel, Abraham Joshua. *The Earth Is the Lord's: The Inner World of the Jew in Eastern Europe.* New York: H. Schuman, 1950.

———. *Man's Quest for God: Studies in Prayer and Symbolism.* New York: Scribner, 1954.

———. *A Passion for Truth.* New York: Farrar, Straus and Giroux, 1973.

Himelstein, Shmuel. *A Touch of Wisdom, a Touch of Wit: A Sparkling Treasury of Jewish Anecdotes, Ideas and Advice.* Brooklyn, N.Y.: Mesorah Publications, 1991.

Himmelfarb, Milton, ed. *The Condition of Jewish Belief.* New York: Macmillan, 1969.

———and David Singer, eds. *American Jewish Year Book—*

1986. Philadelphia: American Jewish Committee (New York) and Jewish Publication Society of America, 1986.

Hitler, Adolf. *Mein Kampf,* English edition, trans. R. Manheim. Boston: 1943.

Howe, Irving. *The Critical Point: On Literature and Culture.* New York: Horizon, 1973.

———, and Eliezer Greenberg, eds. *Ashes Out of Hope: Fiction by Soviet Yiddish Writers.* New York: Schocken Books, 1977.

Israel, Steve, and Seth Forman, eds. *Great Speeches Throughout Jewish History.* Northvale, N.J.: Jason Aronson, Inc., 1994.

Jacobs, Louis. *Jewish Law.* New York: Behrman House, 1968.

———. *Principles of the Jewish Faith.* New York: Basic Books, 1964.

———. *Religion and the Individual: A Jewish Perspective.* Cambridge, England: Cambridge University Press, 1992.

———. *What does Judaism Say About . . . ?* New York: Quadrangle, 1973.

Johnson, Paul. *Intellectuals.* New York: Harper and Row, 1988.

Joseph, Morris. *Judaism as Creed and Life.* New York: Bloch, 1925.

Josephus, Flavius. *Against Apion, Antiquities,* and *The Jewish War* are all available in the Loeb Classical Library, 9 vols. Translated by H. St. J. Thackeray, Ralph Marcus, and Louis Feldman, 1926–1965.

Kaplan, Lawrence. "The Hazon Ish: Haredi Critic of Traditional Orthodoxy," in Jack Wertheimer, ed., *The Uses of Tradition: Jewish Continuity in the Modern Era.* New York: Jewish Theological Seminary, 1992, pages 145–173.

Katsh, Abraham, trans. and ed. *The Warsaw Diary of Chaim A. Kaplan.* New York: Macmillan, 1965; Collier (pbk.), 1973.

Katz, Dov. *T'nuat Ha-Mussar (The Mussar Movement),* 5 vols. Tel Aviv, published 1945–1952.

Katz, Jacob. "Was the Holocaust Predictable?" in Yehuda Bauer and Nathan Rotenstreich, eds., *The Holocaust as Historical Experience.* New York: Holmes and Meir, 1981, pages 23–41.

Kaufmann, Walter. *Religions in Four Dimensions: Existential, Aesthetic, Historical, Comparative.* New York: Reader's Digest Press, 1976.

Kellner, Menachem, ed. *Contemporary Jewish Ethics.* New York: Sanhedrin Press, 1978.

Kenen, I. L. *Israel's Defense Line: Her Friends and Foes in Washington.* Buffalo: Prometheus Books, 1981.

Kirschenbaum, Aaron. *Equity in Jewish Law: Halakhic Perspectives in Law: Formalism and Flexibility in Jewish Civil Law.* Hoboken, N.J.: Ktav, 1991.

Kirschner, Robert. *Rabbinic Responsa of the Holocaust Era.* New York: Schocken Books, 1985.

Koch, Edward, with Daniel Paisner. *Citizen Koch: An Autobiography*. New York: St. Martin's Press, 1992.

Kurzman, Dan. *Ben-Gurion: Prophet of Fire*. New York: Simon and Schuster, 1983.

Kurzweil, Arthur. "The Treatment of Beggars According to Jewish Tradition," in Danny Siegel, *Gym Shoes and Irises: Personalized Tzedakah*. Spring Valley, N.Y.: The Town House Press, 1982, pages 103–117.

Kushner, Harold. *To Life! A Celebration of Jewish Being and Thinking*. Boston: Little, Brown and Company, 1993.

———. *When All You've Ever Wanted Isn't Enough*. New York: Summit Books, 1986; Pocket Books (paperback), 1987; the page citations in this book are from the paperback edition.

Lamm, Maurice. *The Jewish Way in Love and Marriage*. New York: Harper and Row, 1980.

Lamm, Norman. "Ecology in Jewish Law and Theology," in his *Faith and Doubt: Studies in Traditional Jewish Thought*. New York: Ktav, 1986, pages 162–185.

Langer, Jiri. *Nine Gates to the Chassidic Mysteries*. trans. Stephen Jolly. Northvale, N.J.: Jason Aronson, Inc., 1993.

Laqueur, Walter. *A History of Zionism*. New York: Holt, Rinehart and Winston, 1972.

———. *The Terrible Secret: Suppression of the Truth About Hitler's "Final Solution.'* Boston: Little, Brown and Company, 1980.

Levi, Primo. *Survival in Auschwitz*. trans. S. Woolf. New York: Collier, 1961.

Levine, Peter. *Ellis Island to Ebbets Field: Sport and the American Jewish Experience*. New York: Oxford University Press, 1992.

Levkov, Ilya. *Bitburg and Beyond: Encounters in American, German and Jewish History*. New York: Shapolsky Publishers, 1987.

Lichtheim, George. *Collected Essays*. New York: Viking Press (pbk.), 1973.

Linzer, Norman, ed. *Understanding Bereavement and Grief*. New York: Ktav and Yeshiva University Press and Jewish Funeral Directors of America, 1977.

Lipstadt, Deborah. *Denying the Holocaust: The Growing Assault on Truth and Memory*. New York: Free Press, 1993.

Lowenthal, Marvin, ed. and trans. *The Diaries of Theodor Herzl*. New York: Dial Press, 1956.

———. trans. *The Memoirs of Gluckel of Hameln*. New York: Schocken Books, 1977.

MacArthur, Brian, ed. *The Penguin Book of Twentieth-Century Speeches*. London and New York: Viking, 1992.

Maccoby, Hyam. *The Day God Laughed: Sayings, Fables and Entertainments of the Jewish Sages*. New York: St. Martin's Press, 1978.

————. *Early Rabbinic Writings*. Cambridge, England: Cambridge University Press, 1988.

————. "Halakha and Sex Ethics," in Walter Jacob and Moshe Zemer, *Dynamic Jewish Law: Progressive Halakha*. Pittsburgh: Rodef Shalom Press, 1991, pages 131–146.

————. *Revolution in Judaea*. New York: Taplinger, 1980.

Maimonides, Moses. *The Guide of the Perplexed*, trans. with introduction by Shlomo Pines. Chicago: University of Chicago Press, 1963.

————. *The Preservation of Youth: Essays on Health*. trans. from the Arabic by Hirsch Gordon. New York: Philosophical Library, 1958.

Marcus, Jacob. *The Jew in the Medieval World*. New York: Union of American Hebrew Congregations, 1938; Harper and Row, Harper Torchbooks (pbk.), 1965.

Maritain, Jacques. *A Christian Looks at the Jewish Question*. New York: Longmans, 1939.

Marrus, Michael, and Robert Paxton. *Vichy France and the Jews*. New York: Basic Books, 1981.

Marx, Karl. "On the Jewish Question," in *Early Writings,* trans. Rodney Livingston and Gregor Benton. New York: Random House, Vintage Books (pbk.), 1975.

Matt, Daniel, trans. *Zohar: Book of Enlightenment*. New York: Paulist Press, 1983.

Meisels, Zvi Hirsch. *Mekadshei Ha-Shem*, Vol. I, published by the author, 1955.

Miller, Avigdor. *Rejoice O Youth*. New York: 1962.

Miller, Judith. *One by One by One: Facing the Holocaust*. New York: Simon and Schuster, 1990.

Miller, Merle. *Plain Speaking: An Oral Biography of Harry S. Truman*. New York: Berkley Publishing, distributed by G. P. Putnam, 1974.

Mosley, Leonard. *Lindbergh: A Biography*. New York: Doubleday, 1976.

Netanyahu, Benjamin. *A Place Among the Nations: Israel and the World*. New York: Bantam Books, 1993.

Newman, Louis, in collaboration with Samuel Spitz. *The Hasidic Anthology: Tales and Teachings of the Hasidim*. New York: Schocken Books, 1963.

O'Brien, Conor Cruise. *The Siege: The Saga of Israel and Zionism*. New York: Simon and Schuster, 1986.

————. "Three Zionists: Weizmann, Ben-Gurion, Katznelson," in his *Passion and Cunning: Essays on Nationalism, Terrorism and Revolution*. New York: Touchstone, 1989.

O'Neill, William L. *A Democracy at War: America's Fight at Home and Abroad in World War II*. New York: Free Press, 1993.

Oppenheim, Carolyn Toll. *Listening to American Jews: An Anthology of Sh'ma*. New York: Adama Books, n.d.

Orlinsky, Harry. "The Biblical Concept of the Land of Israel: Cornerstone of the Covenant Between God and Israel," in Lawrence A. Hoffman, ed., *The Land of Israel: Jewish Perspectives*. Notre Dame, Ind.: University of Notre Dame Press, 1986, pages 27–64.

Oz, Amos. *The Slopes of Lebanon*. San Diego: Harcourt Brace Jovanovich, 1987.

Pasternak, Boris. *Doctor Zhivago*, trans. Max Hayward and Manya Harari. New York: Pantheon, 1958.

Pawel, Ernst. *The Labyrinth of Exile: A Life of Theodor Herzl*. New York: Farrar, Straus and Giroux, 1989.

Pearl, Chaim. *Rashi: Commentaries on the Pentateuch*, selected and translated by Chaim Pearl. New York: Viking Press, 1970.

Peli, Pinchas. *Torah Today: A Renewed Encounter with Scripture*. Washington, D.C.: B'nai B'rith Books, 1987.

Penueli, S. Y. and A. Ukhmani, eds. *Anthology of Modern Hebrew Poetry*. Tel Aviv: Institute for the Translation of Hebrew Literature, 1966.

Philipson, David. *The Reform Movement in Judaism*. New York: Macmillan, 1931; reissued by Ktav, 1967.

Philo, "On the Decalogue," in Colson, F. H., trans. *Philo*, Vol. 7, London: Heinemann, 1949–1962.

Plaut, W. Gunther. *The Rise of Reform Judaism: A Sourcebook of Its European Origins*. New York: World Union for Progressive Judaism, 1963.

Pliskin, Zelig. *Love Your Neighbor: You and Your Fellow Man in the Light of Torah*. Brooklyn, N.Y.: Aish HaTorah Publications, 1977.

Poliakov, Leon. *The History of Anti-Semitism: From Voltaire to Wagner*. New York: Vanguard Press, 1975.

Polner, Murray, ed. *Jewish Profiles: Great Jewish Personalities and Institutions of the Twentieth Century*. Northvale, N.J.: Jason Aronson, Inc., 1991.

Potok, Chaim. *The Chosen*. New York: Simon and Schuster, 1967.

Prager, Dennis. "Is This Life All There Is?," *Ultimate Issues*, Spring 1987.

———. "Judaism, Homosexuality, and Civilization," *Ultimate Issues*, April–June, 1990.

———. "What Bitburg Revealed About the Jews," *Ultimate Issues*, Summer 1985.

———. "Why Anti-Zionism Is Antisemitism," *Ultimate Issues*, October–December 1990.

Prager, Dennis, and Joseph Telushkin. *The Nine Questions People Ask About Judaism*. New York: Simon and Schuster, 1981.

———. *Why the Jews? The Reason for Antisemitism*. New York: Simon and Schuster, 1983.

Rabinowicz, Oskar. *Arnold Toynbee on Judaism and Zionism: A Critique*. London: W. H. Allen, 1974.

Rauschning, Hermann. *Hitler Speaks*. London: T. Butterworth, 1939.

Raz, Simcha. *A Tzaddik in Our Time: The Life of Rabbi Aryeh Levin*, translated from the Hebrew, revised and expanded by Charles Wengrow. Jerusalem and New York: Feldheim Publishers, 1976.

Reich, Mordechai Menachem. *The Crown of Wisdom*. Vol. II, Lakewood, N.J.: distributed by C.I.S. Publishers and Distributors, 1989.

Reichik, Morton. "Chaim Grade," in Murray Polner, ed., *Jewish Profiles: Great Jewish Personalities and Institutions of the Twentieth Century*. Northvale, N.J.: Jason Aronson Inc., 1991, pages 80–92.

Ringelblum, Emanuel. *Notes from the Warsaw Ghetto: The Journal of Emanuel Ringelblum*, ed. and trans. Jacob Sloan. New York: McGraw Hill, 1959.

Robinson, Armin, ed. *The Ten Commandments*, preface by Herman Rauschning. New York: Simon and Schuster, 1944.

Rosenberg, Bernard, ed., and Fred Heuman, co-ed. *Theological and Halakhic Reflections on the Holocaust*. New York: Ktav and Rabbinical Council of America, 1992.

Rosenstock, Morton. "Are There Too Many Jews at Harvard?," in Leonard Dinnerstein, ed., *Antisemitism in the United States*. New York: Holt, Rinehart and Winston, 1971, pages 102–108.

Rosenthal, A. M. "Forgive Them Not for They Knew What They Did," in Albert Friedlander, *Out of the Whirlwind: A Reader of Holocaust Literature*. New York: Schocken Books, 1976, pages 451–457.

Rosner, Fred. "The Jewish Attitude Toward Abortion," in Fred Rosner, M.D., *Modern Medicine and Jewish Law*. New York: Yeshiva University Press, 1972, pages 53–78.

Rossel, Seymour. *When a Jew Seeks Wisdom: The Sayings of the Fathers*. New York: Behrman House, 1975.

Roth, Philip. *The Counterlife*. New York: Farrar, Straus and Giroux, 1986.

———. *Operation Shylock: A Confession*. New York: Simon and Schuster, 1993.

———. *Portnoy's Complaint*. New York: Random House, 1969.

Rubenstein, Richard L. *After Auschwitz: Radical Theology and Contemporary Judaism*. Indianapolis: Bobbs-Merrill Company, 1966.

———. *The Cunning of History: Mass Death and the American Future*. New York: Harper and Row, 1975.

———. *Power Struggle: An Autobiographical Confession*. New York: Charles Scribner's Sons, 1974.

Sachar, Howard M. *A History of Israel: From the Rise of Zionism to Our Time*. New York: Alfred A. Knopf, 1986 (originally published 1976).

Sachs, Nelly. *O the Chimneys*, selected poems translated from German by Michael Hamburger. New York: Farrar, Straus and Giroux, 1967.

Safire, William. *Lend Me Your Ears: Great Speeches in History*, selected and introduced by William Safire. New York: Norton, 1992. The speech cited in this book by Clarence Darrow is found on pages 327–335.

Samuel, Maurice. *The Great Hatred*. New York: Knopf, 1941.

Saperstein, Marc. "The Land of Israel in Pre-Modern Jewish Thought: A History of Two Rabbinic Statements," in Lawrence A. Hoffman, ed., *The Land of Israel: Jewish Perspectives*. Notre Dame, Ind.: University of Notre Dame Press, 1986, pages 188–209.

Sartre, Jean-Paul. *Anti-Semite and Jew*. New York: Schocken Books, 1948; paperback, 1965.

Scholem, Gershom, ed. *Zohar, The Book of Splendor: Basic Readings from the Kabbalah*. New York: Schocken Books, 1949.

Schwartz, Helene. *Justice by the Book: Aspects of Jewish and American Criminal Law*. New York: Women's League for Conservative Judaism, 1976.

Schwartz, Howard. *Gates to the New City: A Treasury of Modern Jewish Tales*. New York: Avon, 1981.

Schwartz, Richard H. *Judaism and Global Survival*. New York: Atara Publishing Company, 1987.

———. *Judaism and Vegetarianism*. Marblehead, Mass.: Micah Publications, 1988.

Segev, Tom. *The Seventh Million: The Israelis and the Holocaust*. New York: Hill and Wang, 1993.

Shabbetai, K. *As Sheep to the Slaughter?* Bet Degan, Israel: Keshev Press, 1962.

Shapira, Anita. *Land and Power: The Zionist Resort to Force 1881–1948*. New York: Oxford University Press, 1992.

Sharansky, Natan. *Fear No Evil*. New York: Random House, 1988.

Shenker, Israel, and Mary Shenker, eds. and compilers. *As Good as Golda: The Warmth and Wisdom of Israel's Prime Minister*. New York: The McCall Publishing Company, 1970.

Shepherd, Naomi. *A Price Below Rubies: Jewish Women as Rebels and Radicals*. Cambridge, Mass.: Harvard University Press, 1993.

Sherwin, Byron, and Seymour Cohen. *How to Be a Jew: Ethical Teachings of Judaism*. Northvale, N.J.: Jason Aronson, Inc., 1992.

Shimoni, Gideon. *Gandhi, Satyagraha and the Jews: A Formative Factor in India's Policy Towards Israel*. Jerusalem: The Hebrew University of Jerusalem: The Leonard Davis Institute for International Relations, 1977.

Sifakis, Carl. *The Encyclopedia of Crime*. New York: Facts on File, 1982.

Silver, Abba Hillel. *Where Judaism Differed*. New York: Macmillan, 1956; paperback, 1972.

———. *The World Crisis and Jewish Survival*. New York: R. R. Smith, 1941.

Silver, Eric. *Begin: The Haunted Prophet.* New York: Random House, 1984.

Singer, David, ed. *American Jewish Year Book—1990.* Philadelphia: American Jewish Committee (New York) and Jewish Publication Society, 1990.

Singer, Isaac Bashevis. *The Slave,* translated from Yiddish by the author and Cecil Hemly. New York: Farrar, Straus and Cudahy, 1962.

Snyder, Louis. *Encyclopedia of the Third Reich.* New York: Paragon House, 1989 (paperback).

Sperling, S. David. "Bloodguilt in the Bible and in Ancient Near Eastern Sources," in Ruth Link-Salinger (Hyman), ed., *Jewish Law in Our Time.* Bloch Publishing Company, 1982, pages 19–25.

Spero, Shubert. *Morality, Halakha and the Jewish Tradition.* New York: Ktav Publishing, 1983.

Stein, David, ed. *A Garden of Choice: 200 Classic Jewish Quotes on Human Beings and the Environment.* Wyncote, Pa.: Shomrei Adamah, 1991.

Steinberg, Milton. *Anatomy of Faith,* ed. Arthur Cohen. New York: Harcourt, Brace and Co., 1960.

Stern, Guy. "The Rhetoric of Anti-Semitism in Postwar American Literature," in Sander Gilman and Steven Katz, eds., *Anti-Semitism in Times of Crisis.* New York: New York University Press, 1991, pages 291–310.

Sykes, Charles J. *A Nation of Victims: The Decay of the American Character.* New York: St. Martin's Press, 1992.

Synnott, Marcia Graham. "Anti-Semitism and American Universities: Did Quotas Follow the Jews?," in David Gerber, ed., *Anti-Semitism in American History.* Urbana and Chicago: University of Illinois Press, 1987, pages 233–271.

Syrkin, Marie. *Blessed Is the Match: The Story of Jewish Resistance.* Philadelphia: Jewish Publication Society, 1976.

———. *The State of the Jews.* Washington D.C.: New Republic Books, 1980.

———, ed. *Hayim Greenberg Anthology.* Detroit: Wayne State University Press, 1968.

Tarr, Herbert. *The Conversion of Chaplain Cohen.* New York: Avon Books, 1966.

Telushkin, Joseph. *Jewish Literacy: The Most Important Things to Know About the Jewish Religion, Its People and Its History.* New York: William Morrow and Company, 1991.

Tucker, Gordon. "Jewish Business Ethics," in Joseph Lowin, ed., *Jewish Ethics: A Study Guide.* New York: Hadassah, 1986, pages 33–34.

Ulmann, Liv. *Changing.* New York: Knopf, 1977.

Vidal-Naquet, Pierre. *Assassin of Memory: Essays on the Denial of the*

Holocaust, translated and with a foreword by Jeffrey Mehlman. New York: Columbia University Press, 1992.

Visotzky, Burton, translator and annotator, *The Midrash on Proverbs.* New Haven: Yale University Press, 1992.

von Treitschke, Heinrich. "A Word About Our Jewry," trans. Robert Chazan and Marc Lee Raphael, eds., *Modern Jewish History: A Source Reader.* New York: Schocken Books, 1974.

Vorspan, Albert, and David Saperstein. *Tough Choices: Jewish Perspectives on Social Justice.* New York: UAHC Press, 1992.

Weiner, Herbert. *9 1/2 Mystics.* New York: Holt, Rinehart and Winston, 1969.

Weiss, James David. *Vintage Wein: The Collected Wit and Wisdom, the Choicest Anecdotes and Vignettes of Rabbi Berel Wein.* Brooklyn, N.Y.: Shaar Press, distributed by Mesorah Publications, 1992.

Weizmann, Chaim. *Trial and Error.* New York: Harper and Bros., 1949.

Wertheimer, Jack. *A People Divided: Judaism in Contemporary America.* New York: Basic Books, 1993.

Wiesel, Elie. "Art and Culture After the Holocaust," in Eva Fleischner, ed., *Auschwitz: Beginning of a New Era? Reflections on the Holocaust.* New York: published jointly by Ktav Publishing, The Cathedral Church of St. John the Divine, and the Anti-Defamation League, 1977, pages 403–415.

———. *Night.* New York: Hill and Wang, 1960.

———. *One Generation After.* New York: Random House, 1970.

———. "A Plea for the Dead," in *Legends of Our Time.* New York: Schocken (paperback), 1982, pages 174–197.

Wiesenthal, Simon, *Justice Not Vengeance.* New York: Grove Weidenfeld, 1989.

———. *The Sunflower.* New York: Schocken Books, 1976.

Wisdom of the Ages. New York: CLAL, the National Jewish Center for Learning and Leadership, 1993.

Wyman, David. *The Abandonment of the Jews: America and the Holocaust 1941–1945.* New York: Pantheon, 1984.

Yacover, Maurice. *In Method of Madness: The Comic Art of Mel Brooks.* New York: St. Martin's Press, 1981.

Yadin, Yigael. *Masada: Herod's Fortress and the Zealots' Last Stand.* New York: Random House, 1966.

Zevin, Shlomo Yosef. *A Treasury of Chassidic Tales on the Torah,* Vol. 1, trans. Uri Kaploun. Jerusalem and New York: Mesorah Publications Ltd. in conjunction with Hillel Press, 1980.

Zimmels, Rabbi Dr. H. J. *The Echo of the Nazi Holocaust in Rabbinic Literature.* published by the author, Republic of Ireland, 1975.

PERMISSIONS

Grateful acknowledgment is made for permission to quote from the following publications:

Crossroad Publishing Company: From *Our Masters Taught: Rabbinic Stories and Sayings* by Jakob J. Petuchowski. Copyright © 1982 by Jakob J. Petuchowski. Reprinted by permission of the Crossroad Publishing Company.

Farrar, Straus and Giroux, Inc.: Excerpt from "Aloft" from *The Counterlife* by Philip Roth. Copyright © 1986 by Philip Roth.
Excerpt from "The Kotzker and Job," from *A Passion for Truth* by Abraham Joshua Heschel. Copyright © 1973 by Sylvia Heschel as executrix of the estate of Abraham Joshua Heschel.

Godine: From *Voices of Wisdom* by Francine Klagsbrun. Original copyright © by Pantheon Books, a division of Random House, Inc. Currently published by Godine; reprinted by permission of the author.

HarperCollins Publishers: "My Father's Memorial Day," fourteen lines from *Amen* by Yehuda Amichai. Copyright © 1977 by Yehuda Amichai. Reprinted by permission of HarperCollins Publishers, Inc.

Jason Aronson, Inc.: From *Where Heaven and Earth Touch* by Danny Siegel. Copyright © 1989. Reprinted by permission of the publisher, Jason Aronson, Inc., Northvale, N.J.

Jerusalem Academy Publications: From *Masterplan: Judaism: Its Program, Meanings, Goals*. Copyright © 1991 by Jerusalem Academy Publications, distributed by Feldheim, 1991; reprinted by permission of the author.

Jewish Publication Society: Extract by Rabbi Arthur Green from *The Second Jewish Catalog* by Michael and Sharon Strassfeld. Copyright © 1976; and from *Halakhic Man* by Rabbi Dr. Joseph Soloveitchik, translated from the Hebrew by Lawrence Kaplan. Copyright © 1983 by the Jewish Publication Society of America. Reprinted by permission of the publisher.

Oxford University Press: From *Hasidic Tales of the Holocaust* by Yaffa Eliach. Copyright © 1982 by Yaffa Eliach. Reprinted by permission of the author and Oxford University Press.

Paramount Publishing: From *Operation Shylock* by Philip Roth. Copyright © 1993 by Simon and Schuster, a division of Paramount Publishing. Reprinted by permission of the author and Simon and Schuster, a division of Paramount Publishing.

Paulist Press: Reprinted from *The Talmud: Selected Writings,* translated by Ben Zion Bokser. Copyright © 1989 by Baruch M. Bokser. Used by permission of Paulist Press.

Penguin USA: "This Way for the Gas, Ladies and Gentlemen," from *This Way for the Gas, Ladies and Gentlemen* by Tadeusz Borowski, translated by Barbara Vedder. Translation copyright © 1967 by Penguin Books Ltd. Original text copyright © 1959 by Maria Borowski. Used by permission of Viking Penguin, a division of Penguin Books USA Inc.

Random House: From *The Book of Legends* by Bialik and Ravnitzky, translated by William Braude. Copyright © 1992 by Random House, Inc. Reprinted by permission of Schocken Books, published by Pantheon Books, a division of Random House, Inc.

From *A Jewish Reader,* edited by Nahum Glatzer. Copyright © 1961 by Schocken Books. Reprinted by permission of Schocken

Books, published by Pantheon Books, a division of Random House, Inc.

From *The Sunflower* by Simon Wiesenthal. Copyright © 1976 by Opera Mundi SA. Reprinted by permission of Schocken Books, published by Pantheon Books, a division of Random House, Inc.

From *Tales of the Hasidim* by Martin Buber. Copyright © 1948 by Schocken Books. Reprinted by permission of Schocken Books, published by Pantheon Books, a division of Random House, Inc.

Reich, Mordechai Menachem: From *The Crown of Wisdom, Volume Two,* by Mordechai Menachem Reich. Copyright © 1989. Distributed by C.I.S. Publishers and Distributors, Lakewood, N.J. Reprinted by permission of the author.

UAHC Press: From *Tough Choices* by David Saperstein and Albert Vorspan. Copyright © 1992. Reprinted by permission of UAHC (Union of American Hebrew Congregations) Press.

Women's League for Conservative Judaism: From *Justice by the Book* by Helene E. Schwartz. Copyright © 1976 by Helene E. Schwartz, and published by the Women's League for Conservative Judaism. Reprinted by permission of the author.

INDEX

Aaron, 60–61, 104, 264
Abandonment of the Jews: America and the Holocaust, 1941–1945 (Wyman), 35
Abba Tahnah the Pious, 183–184
Abba the surgeon, 434–435
Abbaye, Rabbi, 47–48, 146, 209–210, 435
Abel, 45, 409, 469
Abortion, 161–167
"Abortion in Halakhic Literature" (Bleich), 165
Abraham, 24, 25, 59, 90, 100, 104–105, 201, 214, 263, 304, 320, 336, 375, 567
Abraham Lincoln: The War Years (Sandburg), 124
Abram, Morris B., 553
Abramowitz, Jacob, 255
Abridged Code of Jewish Law (Ganzfried), 23
Absalom, 149
Adam, 24, 88–89, 135, 143, 188, 264
Adams, John, 498
Addictions, 243–244
Adenauer, Konrad, 546, 547
Ad meah v'esrim shana, 251
Adoption, 146, 376–377
Adultery, 43, 80, 136, 138, 139–140, 208, 214, 348
Advice, 28, 72
Afikomen, 385
After Auschwitz (Rubenstein), 311–312, 315
Afterlife, 257, 276–279, 333
"After My Death" (Bialik), 269–270
After the Tradition (Alter), 239, 240–241
Agag, 194, 551
Agca, Ali, 193–194
Age, aging, 248–254

admiration and, 182
agonies of, 251–253
expectations and, 253–254
longevity, 250–251
of parents, 150–153, 340
sense of justice and, 404–405
Torah study and, 153, 340
wisdom and, 182, 249–250, 404
Agnon, Shmuel Yosef, 27–28
Agnosticism, 284
Agrippa, 227
Aqunot, 170, 614–615
Agus, Jacob, 604, 615
Ahab, 43, 545
Ahad Ha'am, 382, 420–421, 472, 602
Ahai, Rabbi, 154
Ahasuerus, 36, 93, 345–346, 459
Ahavah, Adda bar, 250–251
Ahavat Chesed 16, 25
Ahaz, 101
Ahlwardt, Rector, 499
Ah-reivin, 91
AIDS, 29–30, 493–494
Ain kei'loheinu, 357
Aishet khayyil, 128
Akiva, Rabbi, xxiii, 6, 21, 29, 84–85, 106–108, 129, 156, 169–170, 174, 223, 251, 272, 286, 320–321, 337–340, 358–359, 412–413, 429–430
Albo, Joseph, 450
Aleichem, Sholem, 202, 430
Alexander of Macedon, 405–406
Alexandri, Rabbi, 191–192
Alienation, 239–242, 510–511
Aliyah, 298
Allen, Woody, 283, 426
Almog, Shmuel, 501
Alnakawa, Israel ben Joseph, 150, 153

Alston, Walter, 509
Altalena, 596
Alter, Robert, 239, 240–241
Alterman, Natan, 582
Altizer, Thomas, 312
Altneuland (Herzl), xx, 572–573
Amalric, Arnaud, 316–317
Amen (Amichai), 270
America First Committee, 488–490
American Freedom and the Social Sciences
  (Deese), 246
American Jewish Year Book, 1986
  (Himmelfarb and Singer), 493
American Jewish Year Book, 1990 (Singer),
  493–494
American Jews and the Separationist Faith
  (Dalin), 166–167, 292
Amichai, Yehuda, 270
Amidah 359–360
Amin, Idi, 462
Amir, Michael, 549
Ammi, Rabbi, 30
Amon, 144
Amos, 8
Amos, Book of, 298–299, 568
Amram the Pious, 132
Amush, 251
Anarchy, 393–397
Anatomy of Faith (Steinberg), 283
Anger, 155–156, 214, 344
  with God, 303–306
Anguish of the Jews. The (Flannery), 560
Anielewicz, Mordechai, 534
Animals, xxiv, 442, 444–453
Anthology of Modern Hebrew Poetry, 269
Anti-Defamation League of B'nai B'rith,
  483, 494
Antiochus, 85, 320
Anti-Semite and Jew (Sartre), 459–460
Antisemitism, 95, 197–198, 457–495
  and the American-Jewish experience,
    480–495
  in American universities, 483–486
  antizionism and, 607–612
  Black Death and, 322–323
  blood libel and, 471–472, 487, 497
  as catalyst for repentance, 346
  as cause for assimilation, 503–504
  and chosenness, 298–299, 301–302, 466
  Christian, 465–471, 496–497, 499–500,
    558, 560, 609–610
  as double standard, 464
  during economic downturns, 395
  Eichmann trial and, 543
  from the far right and left, 490–495
  Ford and, 67, 486–488, 490
  Frank case and, 482–483
  Freud on, 213
  Grand Union Affair and, 481–482
  Lindbergh and, 462, 488–490

Marx and, 95, 472–473
  reasons for, 459–462
  twentieth-century literary, 457–479
  as unappeasable hatred, 462–463
  during U.S. Civil War, 480–481
  Voltaire and, 197–198, 471–472, 498
"Anti-Semitism and American Universities"
  (Synnott), 485
Antisemitism Through the Ages (Almog),
  501
Antiwar statements, 418–420
Aptowitzer, Viktor, 163
Arad, Yitzchak, 526–527
Arafat, Yassir, 600, 608
*Architect of Genocide, The: Himmler and
  the Final Solution* (Breitman), 521
"Are There Too Many Jews at Harvard"
  (Rosenstock), 484
Arguing, 70–75, 284–287
  "from design," 284–285
  with God, 286–287, 365
Arif, Abdel Rahman, 594
Arnold Toynbee on Judaism and Zionism
  (Rabinowicz), 608
Aronsfeld, C.C., 519
Arouet, Francois-Marie (Voltaire), 197–198,
  292, 471–472, 498
Arrogance, 227–229
Arukh ha-Shulkhan(Y. Epstein), 272
Asceticism, 230–238
Asch, Sholem, 158
Ashes Out of Hope (Howe and Greenberg),
  511
Ashtoreth, 334, 506
Assai, Rabbi, 30
*Assassins of Memory: Essays on the Denial
  of the Holocaust* (Vidal Naquet), 556
*As Sheep to the Slaughter? The Myth of
  Cowardice* (Shabbetai), 533–534
Assimilation, 503–505
Atheism, 277, 290–293, 312–313, 475, 501
Auden, W. H., 479, 502, 605–606
Augustine, Saint, 272, 349
Auschwitz, 35, 82, 212, 234, 277, 304–305,
  311–315, 327, 489, 502, 504–505,
  524–525, 542, 558
Auschwitz: Beginning of a New Era?
  (Fleischner), 293, 310, 515, 559–560,
  612
Auschwitz and the Allies (Gilbert), 35
Autobiography. An (Roosevelt), 499
Av, fifteenth day of, 388
Avidor Ha-Cohen, Shmuel, 64, 201
Avineri, Shlomo, 589–591
Avtalion, Rabbi, 341
Ayalti, Hanan, 127
Azariah, 222

Baal Shem Tov, Israel, 132, 174–175, 355,
  363

Babylonia, 273, 394–395, 568–569
Babylonian Talmud, *see* Talmud,
    Babylonian
Baeck, Leo, 307, 537
Bacr, Dov, 232
Bahya ibn Pakuda, 271–272, 284–285
Balfour, Arthur James, 499, 580
Balfour Declaration, 457, 499, 577, 579–
    583, 589
Bal tashkhit, 438–441
Baltimore Sun, 478
"Bankrupt" (Greenburg), 530–531
Barabbas, 465–468
Barach, Ann Louise, 114
Baraita, 258–259
Baraka, Amiri, 478–479
Bar-Kochba, Simeon, 321
Bartenura, Obadiah of, 134, 367
Baruch, Bernard, 555
Barukh dayan emet, 287
Barzillai, 252
Bashert, 119
Bashfulness, 343–344
Bathsheba, 43, 214, 256
Beggars, 14, 15–16, 18–20, 22, 23
Begin, Menachem, 202, 545–549, 569, 584,
    591, 596–600, 604
Begin: The Haunted Prophet (Silver), 597–
    598
Beinoni, 367
Beirut, 598, 599–600
Belloc, Hilaire, 467
Bellow, Saul, 194
*Belzec Sobibor, Treblinka: The Operation
    Reinhard Death Camps* (Arad), 526–
    527
Ben-Gurion, David, 42–43, 543, 545–549,
    551, 588–592, 596, 614
Ben-Gurion, Paula, 591
Ben-Gurion: Prophet of Fire (Kurzman),
    590
*Ben-Gurion: The Burning Ground, 1886–
    1948* (Teveth), 588
Benjamin, 91–92
    tribe of, 396
Ben Kalba Sabua, 106–107
Ben-Sasson, H. H., 323
Bentham, Jeremy, 452
Ben Zoma, 187–188
Berdyaev, Nikolai, 25, 469
Berenbaum, Michael, 520, 529
Bergelson, David, 510
Bergen-Belsen concentration camp, 553
Bergmann, Shmuel Hugo, 551
Berkovits, Eliezer, 105, 113–114, 312, 327,
    529, 533, 542, 557
Bermant, Chaim, 14
Beroka of Hoza, 184–185
Beruriah, 265–266, 349
Bettelheim, Bruno, 247

Biale, Rachel, 131
Bialik, Hayim Naham, 47, 52, 156, 192,
    210, 269–270, 287, 430, 581
"Biblical Concept of the Land of Israel,
    The" (Orlinsky), 567
"Biblical Diet as an Ethical System, The"
    (Milgrom), 451
Bichri, Sheba ben, 81
Billings, Josh, 355
Birth, 4, 108–109, 119, 135, 256
Birth Control in Jewish Law, 164–165
Bitburg, 544, 552–553
Bitburg and Beyond (Levkov), 544, 552
Black Death, 322–323
Black Magic: Collected Poetry 1961–1967
    (Baraka), 478
Bleich, J. David, 50, 64, 165, 292, 411,
    420
"Blessed Is the Match" (Senesh), 540–541
Blessed Is the Match (Syrkin), 541
Blidstein, Gerald, 151, 413
Block, Gay, 515
Blood, consumption of, 450–451
Blood avenger, 548–549
Blood libel, 471–472, 487, 497
"Bloodguilt in the Bible and in Ancient
    Near East Sources" (Sperling), 548–
    549
Bloom, Allan, 496
Blue, Lionel, 15, 432
Blue Guide to the Here and Hereafter The
    (Blue), 15
Boaz, 211–212
Boerne, Ludwig, 458
Bokser, Ben Zion, 93, 405–406
*Book of Directions to the Duties of the
    Heart, The* (Hyamson and Mansoor),
    284–285
Book of Legends. The (Bialik and
    Ravnitzky), 47, 52, 192, 210, 430
Book of the Dead, The, 276
Book of the Pious (Sefer Hasidim) (Judah
    the Pious), 23, 123, 225, 362, 436,
    447
Bork, Robert, 408
Borowski, Tadeusz, 524–525
Brandeis, Louis, 202, 245
Brandon, S.G.F., 466
Braude, William, 47, 52, 192, 210, 430
Braun, Eva, 194–195
Breitman, Richard, 521
Brett, George, 477
Bribery, 7, 8, 82–83
Brickner, Balfour, 165–166
Broder, Henry M., 544
Brodkey, Harold, 159
Brothers Karamazov, The (Dostoevsky),
    290
Broun, Heywood, 477
Brown, Steven, 150

Buber, Martin, 41, 90, 176, 180–181, 221,
  240, 311, 354, 422–423, 551
Buchanan, Patrick, 490–492, 494
Buchenwald, 247, 527, 5331
Buckley, William F., Jr., 189–190, 491–492
Bundism, 309
Bunim, Irving, 20
"Burbank with a Baedeker, Bleistein with a
  Cigar" (Eliot), 476
Burial, 24–25, 40, 271, 372, 440
Burns, Arthur, 544
Business, xxiii, 3, 12, 40, 46–48, 50–51,
  250, 371, 417–418, 441–442
Bystanders, 33–38

Caesar, 75
Cain, 45, 409, 469
Camus, Albert, 320, 425
Cantos (Pound), 476
Capek, Karel, 497
"Capital Punishment in the Noachide
  Code" (Bleich), 411
"Capital Punishment—The Classic Jewish
  Discussion" (Blidstein), 413
Carelbach, Julius, 473
Cargas, Harry James, 554, 557
Carmell, Aryeh, 36–37, 192–193
Carter, Jimmy, 136, 305, 597
Cathars, 316–317
"Chaim Grade" (Reichik), 510–511
Chaim of Sanz, 19, 389
Chalutzim, 224
Changing (Ullman), 109
Charity, 10, 11–25, 196
  acceptance of, 13–14
  anonymous, 14–15
  to beggars, 15–16, 18–20, 22, 23
  and changes in fortune, 22–23
  charlatans and, 18–20
  determining amount of, 18, 19–20
  and dignity, 21–23
  fasting and, 17–18
  gemilut chesed vs., 24–25
  and God's will, 20–21
  highest form of, 11, 24–25
  idolatry and, 16
  knowing a person by, 214
  lowest form of, 15
  as a *mitzvah*, 22
  by the poor, 14
  pragmatic reasons for, 23–24
  to protect travelers, 332
  repentance and, 353
  steady, 17–18
  from stolen money, 331
  subtlety in, 23
  see also Needy, neediness
Charlatans, 18–20, 132
Charles, Prince of Wales, 212
Charmed Circle (Mellow), 241

Chelbana 367
Chesed shel emet 25
Children, 3, 4, 119, 121, 147–160
  adoption of, 146, 376–377
  adult, 159
  of an adulterous relationship, 140
  conversion of, 163–164, 376–377
  death of, 149, 256, 263–266
  determining sex of, 135, 368
  and disagreements with parents, 149–150,
    351
  as duty, 135–136, 143–146
  environment and, 245–246
  favoritism among, 157, 336
  and financial hardship, 145
  as Holocaust victims, 522–523
  and human inclination toward evil, 207–
    208
  of immoral marriages, 122–123
  of intermarriages, 506–507
  justice of the Sanhedrin and, 253, 404–
    405
  Kaddish recited by, 116–117
  lying and, 58, 154–155
  male vs. female, 108–109, 116–117, 135
  number of, 145
  obligation of, to parents, 147–149
  parental blessing of, 360, 382
  parents' obligation to, 153–154, 340,
    344, 359
  Passover and, 385
  punishment of, 155–156
  religious identity of, 115
  see also Parents
Chesterton, G. K., 272
Chmelnitzki massacre, 286
Chomsky, Noam, 492, 554–555
Choni, 181, 258, 259–260
Chosen, The (Potok), 298
Christian Looks at the Jewish Question, A
  (Maritain), 463
Christianity and Anti-Semitism (Berdyaev),
  469
Christian Phalangists, 598–599
Christians, Christianity:
  antisemitism among, 322–324, 379, 465–
    471, 496–497, 499–500, 558, 560,
    609–610
  belief in afterlife and, 277
  belief in Jesus Christ and, 6, 74–75, 174
  converts to, 6, 95, 322–324, 379
  Holocaust and, 557–560
  idealization of poverty in, 18
  loss of Jewish identity and, 506–507
  missionizing, 299–300
  principles of Torah in, 6, 174, 358
  proof of God's existence and, 284–285
  salvation as viewed by, 375
Christian Science Monitor, 487
Christian Scientists, 433–434

Christians Only (Broun and Brett), 477
Chronicles, First Book of, 418–419
Churchill, Winston, 500–501
circumcision, 4, 24, 141, 153, 375
Citizen Koch: An Autobiography (Koch and
    Paisner), 262
City College of New York, 485
Civil War, U.S., 30, 480–481
Claudius, emperor of Rome, 130
Clemens, Samuel L. (Mark Twain), 498
"Cloud of Smoke, Pillar of
    Fire"(Greenberg), 310, 315, 559
Code of Jewish Law, The (Shulkhan Arukh)
    (Karo), xxiv, 13, 17, 36, 44, 57, 63,
    89, 140, 260, 261, 268, 343, 413
Cohen, A., 109, 133
Cohen, Hermann, 26–27
Cohen, Jeremy, 470
Cohn, Haim, 465–466
Cohn, Norman, 555
Cokely, Steve, 493–494
Collected Essays (Lichtheim), 473–474
Collier's 486
Columbia University, 485
Commentary, 491–492, 504
Communism, 501, 510–511, 590–591
Community, 91–98, 182–183, 366–367,
    506–507
Companionship, 180–181
Compassion, 182–186, 192, 193, 253, 272,
    444–447, 451
Complete Essays of Mark Twain, The
    (Neider), 498
Compromise, 41–43, 398
Conception, 244
Condition of Jewish Belief, The (Rackman),
    283–284, 301
Confession, prayers of, 356, 359–360
Congressional Black Caucus, 493, 494
Conley, Jim, 483
"Contemporary Approach to Jewish
    Sexuality, A" (Green), 137
Contemporary Halakhic Problems (Bleich),
    420
Contemporary Jewish Ethics (Kellner), 166
Contempt, 241–242
Conversion, 299, 319, 374–381, 503, 538
    advantages and disadvantages of, 376–
      378
    in ancient Rome, 374–376, 379
    to Christianity, 6, 95, 322–324, 379
    God's love of, 378–379
    of minors, 163–164, 376–377
    secularism and, 379–380
    special place of, 378–379
Conversion of Chaplain Cohen, The (Tarr),
    148
Corinthians, Book of First, 136
Cornell University, 485
Counterlife, The (Roth), 464

Courtesy, 27, 187–190
Covetousness, 43, 208
Cowan, Lore, 250
Cowan, Maurice, 250
Cowardice, 417–418
Crescas, Hasdai ibn, 157
*Critical Point, The: On Literature and
    Culture* (Howe), 478–479
Criticism, 76–79, 200, 351
*Crown of Glory The: Aging in the Jewish
    Tradition* (Friedman), 254
Crown of Wisdom, The (Reich), 149
Crucifixion, 414, 468
Cruelty, 194, 264, 291, 404–405, 414–415,
    447, 449, 450, 452
Cunning of History The (Rubenstein), 312
Czerniakow, Adam, 539

Dachau, 247, 536
Dafni, Reuven, 540
Dalin, David, 167, 292
Dama, 152
Dangerfield, Rodney, 127
Daniel, Book of, 62
Danzig, Abraham, 63
Darkei shalom, 40
Darrow, Clarence, 246
David (Maimonides's brother), 267–268
David, king of Israel, 7, 43, 81, 100, 103,
    137, 149, 178–179, 210–211, 214,
    251, 256, 261, 299, 379, 418, 506
Davidowicz, Lucy, 488, 518
Davies, Alan, 559
*Day God Laughed, The: Sayings, Fables
    and Entertainment of the Jewish
    Sages* (Maccoby), 74, 346
Dayan, Moshe, 604
Days of Ziklag, The (Yizhar), 240–241
Dearborn Independent, 486–488
Death, 23–25, 63–64, 255–270
    afterlife and, 257, 276–279, 333
    as a blessing, 257–260
    burial and, 24–25, 40, 271, 372, 440
    of a child, 149, 256, 263–266
    foreknowledge of, 255, 347
    of God, 290–293, 311–312
    inevitability and irreversibility of, 256–
      257
    of a parent, 116–117, 149, 256
    remarriage and, 123–124, 614–615
    Sabbath and, 261
    of a spouse, 256
    and submission to God, 287
Death penalty, 407–416
    circumstantial evidence and, 410–411
    confessions and, 410, 411, 416
    as deterrent, 408, 413
    in Eichmann trial, 550–551
    Maimonides on, 410, 411, 414
    pregnant women and, 162–163

Death penalty *(continued)*
  restrictions on, 409–416
  under Roman rule, 412–413
  Sanhedrin and, 412–413
  in times of emergency, 413–414
"Decalogue, The" (Jacob), 383
Decter, Midge, 492
Deese, James, 246
Delilah, 361, 505
Democracy at War, A (O'Neill), 489
Denying the Holocaust (Lipstadt), 464, 555
Deprivation, symbolic acts of, 234
Derekh eretz, 228
Detroit *Jewish Chronicle,* 508–509
Deuteronomy, Book of, xxiii, 11, 21, 24,
  26, 30, 38, 41, 43, 44, 54, 61–62,
  69, 73, 122, 140, 147, 168, 181,
  228, 249, 250, 251, 286, 317, 333,
  334, 338, 357–358, 384, 386, 393,
  396, 408–409, 415, 417–418, 422,
  429, 438, 439, 444–445, 451, 505
"Dialogue Between Heaven and Earth"
  (Buber), 311
Diana, Princess of Wales, 212
Diaries (Kafka), 239
Diaries of Theodor Herzl, The (Lowenthal),
  572–578
Diary of a Young Girl, The (Frank), 48, 186
Diet, 199, 231–232, 329–330, 385, 448–
  453
Dignity, 21–23, 133
Dinnerstein, Leonard, 482
Din Torah 305
Disputation of Paris (1240), 74
Disputes, 41–43, 60–61, 70–75, 149–150,
  228, 259, 433
Divorce *(get),* xxiii, 104, 108, 114–115,
  116, 119, 126, 127, 134, 140, 168–
  173, 569–570
D'mai, 409
Doctor's Guide (Israeli), 436–437
Doctor Zhivago (Pasternak), 504
Does God Belong in the Bedroom? (Gold),
  137, 140
Domestic workers, 31–32, 54–56, 249
Donin, Hayim, 356
Dordai, Eleazar ben, 346–347
Dostoevsky, Feodor, 290
Dred Scott v. *Sandford* 30–31, 317
Dreyfus, Alfred, 474, 497–498, 576
"Dreyfus Affair in Georgia, A"
  (Dinnerstein), 482
Drinking, 214, 231, 385
Drucker, Malka, 515
Drysdale, Don, 509
Dubno Maggid, 216–218
Duke, David, 395
"Dust of slander," 208–209
Duties of the Heart (Bahya ibn Pakuda),
  271–272, 284–285

Earth Is the Lord's, The (Heschel), 300
Eban, Abba, 582, 593
Ecclesiastes, Book of, 181, 183–184, 199,
  215, 218–219, 231, 238, 255, 256,
  345, 348, 429, 438
Ecclesiasticus (Ben Sira), 69, 156
Ecology, 438–443
Edels, Samuel Eliezer (Maharsha), 17–18
Education, 153, 207, 359, 429, 483–486,
  614
Egypt, xxi, 26, 91–92, 94, 104–105, 141,
  157, 211, 276, 311, 334–335, 336,
  367, 385, 446, 491, 577, 582, 593–
  595, 604
Ehrman, Avi, 249
Ehrman, Zvi, 227
Eichmann, Adolf, 408, 416, 534, 543, 550–
  551
Einsatzgruppen, 293
Einstein, Albert, 203, 449, 457–458, 614
Eisenhower, Dwight, 554
Ekhad, 321
El-Am Talmud, 227, 249
Elazar, 274–275
Elazar, Rabbi, 6, 62, 168, 171–172, 230,
  356
Elazar ben Arakh, 264–265, 266
Elazar ben Azarya, 77, 412
Elazar ben Simeon, 93
Eleazar ben Harsom, 341, 342
Eleazar ben Pedat, 19, 258–259, 374–375
Eliach, Yaffa, 305–306, 324–326, 427–428
Eliezer, 336–337
Eliezer, Rabbi, 6, 73–74, 108–113, 116,
  138, 264, 347–348
Eliezer ben Hyrcanus, 105, 110
Elijah, 4, 29, 74, 184–185, 210–211, 235,
  545
Elijah, Rabbi, 236–237
Elimelekh of Lyzhansk, 62–63
Eliot, T. S., 475–476
Elisha, 210–211
Elitism, 95, 227–229
Ellis Island to Ebbets Field (Levine), 509
Elon, Amos, 606
Emile (Rousseau), 496
Empathy, 102, 175
Employees, 38–39, 54–57
Employers, 54–57
Encyclopedia Judaica, 129, 433
Encyclopedia of American Crime, The
  (Sifakis), 404
Encyclopedia of the Third Reich (Snyder),
  536–537
Endangerment of life, 80–87
  abortion and, 161–162, 164
  emotional blackmail and, 133–134
  passive complicity in, 81–85
  pregnancy and childbirth as, 143–144
  ritual observance and, 85–87, 134, 261

and saving one's own life, 80–82
  see also Murder
End of the World, The (Friedrich), 316–317
Enemies, 191–195
Entebbe, raid on, 487
Envy, 202, 210–211
Ephraim, 360
Ephron the Hittite, 201
Epistles (Seneca), 257
Epstein, Joseph, 478
Epstein, Yechiel, 272
Equity, 5, 38–39, 40
Equity In Jewish Law (Kirschenbaum), 401–402
Erasmus, Desiderius, 496
Esau, 104, 200, 419
Eshkol, Levi, 66, 593
Esterhazy, Colonel, 497
Esther, 36, 93, 105
Esther, Book of, 36, 93, 129, 346, 459, 543
Eternal Light, 353
"Eternity of Israel, The" (Greenberg), 505
Ethics from Sinai (Bunim), 20
Ethics of the Fathers (Pirkei Avot), xxiii, 4,
  6, 9, 46, 52, 72, 93, 97, 175, 187,
  189, 198, 199, 200, 201, 220, 225,
  229, 232, 235, 251, 263, 279, 330,
  331, 337, 342–344, 354, 393–394,
  403, 425
Ethiopia, 98, 313
Eulogies, 263, 269–270
Euthanasia, 257
Evans, Eli, 241
Eve, 135, 143
Everyman's Talmud (Cohen), 109, 133
Evil, 8
  caused by religion, 290
  within a congregation, 367
  in God's name, 316–319
  from good ideology, 296–297
  harnessing of, 213–215
  hatred of, 408–409
  human inclination toward, 207–210,
    393–394, 449
  propensity for, 212–213
Evil eye, 198
Excommunication, 95, 110–111, 261
Exodus, Book of, xxiii, 16, 18, 26, 31, 58,
  59, 74, 99, 105, 115, 136, 139, 147,
  158, 161, 165, 191, 250, 256, 285–
  286, 316, 317, 367, 382, 386, 399,
  407, 421, 422, 429, 433, 439, 444,
  446, 459, 568, 570
Exodus, Operation, 98
Extended Circle, The (Wynne-Tyson), 452
"Eye for an eye," 402–403
Ezra, 338

"Face of God, The: Thoughts on the
  Holocaust" (Lamm), 310

Fackenheim, Emil, 312–314, 524
Faith, 212, 276, 283–284, 311–315, 363–
  364
Faith After the Holocaust (Berkovits), 312,
  327, 529, 533, 557
"Faith and the Holocaust" (Wyschogrod),
  314
Falk, Marcia, 431
False humility, 226
False testimony, 43, 399–401, 408
Falwell, Jerry, 166
Fame, 211–212, 213–214
"Family of Eight" (Reisin), 431
Farrakhan, Louis, 299, 493–495
Fasting, 17–18, 56, 86, 95, 237, 305, 306–
  307, 388–389, 530
Fatal Embrace, The (Ginsberg), 494–495
Fathers According to Rabbi Nathan, The,
  60–61, 100, 175, 263–265, 340,
  425
Faunce, William, 483–484
Faurisson, Robert, 492, 554–555
Favoritism, 157
Fear No Evil (Sharansky), 327–328
Feldman, David, 164–165
Feldman, Louis, 376, 383
Fichte, Johann, 472
First Love and Other Sorrows (Brodkey),
  159
Fischer, Louis, 423
Flannery, Edward, 560
Fleg, Edmund, 287
Fleischner, Eva, 293, 310, 515, 559–560,
  612
Ford, Edsel, 487
Ford, Henry, 67, 486–488, 490
Forgiveness, 259, 350–353, 389, 545–546,
  562–563
"Forgive Them Not, For They Know What
  They Did" (Rosenthal), 543
Forman, Seth, 614
*40 Things You Can Do to Save the Jewish
  People* (Grushaver), 616–617
Forward, 494
Four Existentialist Theologians (Herberg),
  311
Fox, Marvin, 614–615
Frank, Anne, 48, 186, 475
Frank, Hans, 521
Frank, Leo, 482–483
Frankfurter, Felix, 30–31, 529
Frankl, Viktor, 247, 542
Free-Loan Societies, 12
Free Speech for Me but Not for Thee
  (Hentoff), 493
Free will, 243–247, 434
Freiburg, Dov, 526–527
French Enlightenment and the Jews, the
  (Herzberg), 471–472
Freud, Ernst, 213

Freud, Sigmund, 22, 213, 288–289, 292, 461, 613–614
Friedlander, Albert, 364
Friedman, Dayle, 254
Friedman, Milton, 202
Friedrich, Otto, 316–317
Friendship, 178–181, 257–260, 553
Frimer, Norman, 57
Fromm, Erich, 290
Frum, David, 189–190
Fuglsand-Damgaard, H., 537
Funerals, 261–263
Future of an Illusion, The (Freud), 292

Gaffney, Frank, 491
Galut 505, 585
Gambling, 243–244
Gamliel, Rabbi, 261–262
Gandhi, Mohandas K., 422–424
Gandhi Satyagraha and the Jews (Shimoni), 422
Ganzfried, Solomon, 23
"Gaon, Rabbi Elijah Wilna, The" (Ginzberg), 236–237
Garden of Choice Fruit, A: 200 Classic Jewish Quotes on Human Beings and the Environment (Stein), 443
Garraty, John, 31
Gates of Repentance, The (Gerondi), 353
Gates to the New City: A Treasury of Modern Jewish Tales (Schwartz), 102
Gellman, Marc, 166–167
Gemayal, Bashir, 598
Gemilut chesed 9, 10, 24–25, 86
Generosity, 12, 17, 18, 207, 359
Genesis, Book of, xxi, 24, 56, 59, 77, 91–92, 104, 116, 118, 119, 122, 135, 143, 145, 157, 172, 199, 200, 201, 207, 211, 213, 218, 245, 252, 255, 263, 264, 267, 304, 336, 343, 375, 401, 407, 409, 419, 448–450, 567, 570
Gerondi, Jonah, 353
Gershom, Rabbi, 170
Get, see Divorce
Gibbons, Edward, 130
Gide, Andre, 474
Gienanth, Kurt Freiherr von, 521
Gifts, 199
Gilbert, Martin, 35, 525–526, 537, 539–540
Gilder, George, 118–119
Ginsberg, Benjamin, 494–495
Ginzberg, Louis, 236–237
Glatzer, Nahum, 362, 364–365
Glendon, Mary Ann, 34–35
Gluckel of Hameln, 269
God:
  absence of, in Song of Songs, 129
  adultery as sin against, 139
  anger with, 303–306
  arguing with, 286–287, 365
  converts loved by, 378–379
  creation of the world by, xxi, 89, 90, 99, 120, 216, 438, 570–571
  David tested by, 214
  day of death concealed by, 255
  "death of," 290–293, 311–312
  deepest hope of, 177
  desecrating name of, 316–319, 368, 397
  as exemplar of *gemilut chesed*, 24–25
  expecting an immediate answer from, 208–209
  faith in, 212, 277, 283–284, 311–315, 363–364
  fear of, 248–249, 289
  first questions of, 3–4, 46
  free will and, 244–245, 434
  Holocaust and, 212, 277, 303–315, 363–364
  illness and, 434
  independence from, 73–75
  individual experience of, 285–286
  Israel promised by, 567–571, 604
  in Jewish history, 287–289, 300, 311–312
  love of, 147, 176, 286, 303, 358–359
  mankind created by, 88–89, 407
  as marriage broker, 120
  meat forbidden by, 449–450
  murder as punished by, 415–416
  as a necessity for morality, 290–293
  old age as blessing from, 250–251
  as one, xxi, 10, 300, 357, 388
  "pity" for, 304
  and the poor, 20–21, 430
  praise of, 356, 357–359
  prayer of, 369
  preparation for praying to, 356–357
  proof of the existence of, 284–285
  questioning of, xxii, 100
  responsibility of, 304–306
  and reward for *mitzvot*, 332
  sacrifice to, 144, 182, 233
  sanctifying name of, 316–328, 523–524, 538
  seeking of, 285–286
  speaking truth to, 61–63
  submission to, 287
  suffering and, 223, 276, 286–287
  Torah given by, 74, 116, 377, 385–386, 447
  worshipping of, 9, 61–63, 213
God's First Love (Heer), 471
God's Presence in History (Fackenheim), 314
Goebbels, Joseph, 519–520
Goethe, 213
Gold, Michael, 137, 140
Golden, Harry, 615
Goldstein, Baruch, 602–603

Goldstein, Isaac, 50
Goldwyn, Samuel, 257, 436
Goliath, 103
Gomorrah, 100
Gonnif, 594
Goodness, xxi, 202
    hard life of, 220–221
    harnessing evil for, 213–215
    intellect vs., 227–229
    reward for, 220
    and treatment of animals, 446–447
Gordon, Martin, 230–231
Goring, Hermann, 489
Gossip, 8, 67–68, 228
Gottfarstein, Yosef, 523–524
Gould, Allan, 476, 499, 502
Grade, Chaim, 510
Grand Union Hotel, 481–482
Grant, Ulysses, 480–481
Gratitude, 187–190, 378–379
Great Assembly, 61–62
Great Hatred, The (Samuel), 461
Great Revolt, 233, 273–274
Great Speeches Throughout Jewish History
    (Israel and Forman), 613–614
Greece, 163, 383
Green, Arthur, 137–138
Greenberg, Eliezer, 511
Greenberg, Hank, 508–509
Greenberg, Hayim, 55, 269, 505, 530–531
Greenberg, Irving, 4, 225–226, 293, 310,
    315, 369, 386–387, 426, 509–510,
    559
Groth, Paul, 526–527
Grudges, 176–177
Gruenbaum, Yitzchak, 296–297
Grushaver, Joel, 616–617
Guest, Edgar, 508–509
Guests, 187–190
Guide to the Perplexed (Maimonides), 333,
    445
Guns, 50–51, 533
Gurley, John Addison, 480

Habakkuk, 8–9, 303
Habakkuk, Book of, 303, 394
Hadar, 13, 538–539, 598, 614
Hadassah, 116
"Ha-Derashah" (Hazaz), 240
Hadrian, 153–154, 222, 463–464
Haffetz Hayyim, *see* Kagan, Israel Meir Ha-
    Kohen
Haganah, 540
Haig, Alexander, 491
Ha-karat ha-tov, 188
Ha-Ketav ve-Ha-Kabbalah, 118
"Halakha and Sex Ethics" (Maccoby), 133–
    134
Halakhic Man (Soloveitchik), 371–372
Halevai, 376

Halevi, Yehuda, 571
Halkin, Hillel, 380
Halpern, Ben, 240
Haman, 36, 93, 105, 345–346, 459, 543
Hamas, 603
Hananiah, 222
Hanina, Rabbi, 19, 222, 329
Hanina ben Gamliel, 155
Hanina ben Teradion, 321–322
Hannah, 105, 320, 361–362
Hannuka, 389
Hanokh of Aleksandrov, 219–220
Happiness, 219–220
Harijan, 422
Harlow, Jules, 359, 387–388
Harper's, 352–353
Harvard University, 483–485
Hasidei Ashkenaz, 237–238
Hasidic Anthology, The (Newman), 232
Hasidic Tales After the Holocaust (Eliach),
    305–306, 324–326, 427–428
"Hatikvah" ("The Hope") (Imber), 574
Hatred, 196–198
    of evil, 408–409
Hattushilis, 548
Hatzolah, 86
Hausner, Gideon, 550–551
Havdalah 265
Hayim Greenberg Anthology (Syrkin), 471,
    505, 530–531
Hayyim of Brisk, 151
Hazaz, Haim, 240
"Hazon Ish, The: Haredi Critic of
    Traditional Orthodoxy" (Kaplan), 42
"Heart of the World, The" (Kazin), 612
Heer, Friedrich, 471
Heine, Heinrich, 449, 520
Heinemann, Benno, 216–218
Henrietta Szold: Life and Letters
    (Lowenthal), 116–117
Hentoff, Nat, 493
Herald, George, 352–353
Herberg, Will, 291, 311
Herring, Basil, 63, 423
Hertzberg, Arthur, 87, 471–472, 571, 585,
    603
Herzl, Theodor, xx, 103, 460, 541, 569,
    572–579
Herzog, Isaac, 436
Heschel, Abraham Joshua, 182, 289, 300,
    320, 350–352
Hesped, 263, 269–270
Heuman, Fred, 310
Hevra Kadisha 63–64
Hezekiah, 101, 144
High Priest of Rebirth (Agus), 604, 615
Hillel:
    on divorce, 169
    on essence of Judaism, xix-xx, 5–6, 202
    on holiness, 236

Hillel *(continued)*
  on the human condition, 216
  on isolation, 97
  long life of, 251
  on number of children, 145
  poverty of, 341, 342, 429–430
  School of Hillel, 70–71
  on sexual needs of women, 134
  Torah study reestablished by, 339
  on white lies, 59–60
Hilton, Conrad, 481
Hilton, Henry, 481–482
Himelstein, Shmuel, 13, 226, 270, 389
Himmelfarb, Milton, 493, 507
Himmler, Heinrich, 520–521
Hinckley, John, 50
Hirsch, Samson Raphael, 230–231
Hisda, Rabbi, 96, 157, 401–402, 414, 430
*History of Anti-Semitism: From Voltaire to
  Wagner, The* (Poliakov), 197–198,
  471
History of Israel, A (Sachar), 577, 605
*History of the Decline and Fall of the
  Roman Empire* (Gibbon), 130
History of the Jews in America, A (Sachar),
  482, 484, 485, 486, 487, 490
History of Zionism, A (Laqueur), 574
Hitler, Adolf, 67, 144, 194–195, 290, 301,
  307, 312–315, 422, 423, 457, 462,
  471, 472, 475, 478, 487–488, 494,
  517–518, 537, 554, 558, 576, 586,
  588, 599–600, 609–610
Hiyya (son of Rav), 154
Hiyya, Rabbi, 22, 338–339, 381
Hiyya bar Abba, 222
Hokhmat he-Adam (Danzig), 63
Holiness, 40–41, 137, 236, 382, 442
Holocaust, 303–315, 515–563
  Allied indifference to, 35, 84, 529
  American isolationism and, 462, 488–
    490
  American Jewry and, 530–531
  anger from, 303–306, 542–544
  Auschwitz as symbol of, 504–505
  "bargaining" in, 82–84
  book burning in, 519–520
  children as victims of, 522–523
  Christians and, 557–560
  commemoration of, 234, 312
  cowardice in, 524–526, 532–535
  denial of, 554–556
  Eichmann trial and, 408, 416, 534, 543,
    550–551
  faith in God and, 212, 277, 311–315,
    363–364
  FDR and, 529
  forgiveness for, 350–352, 545–546, 562–
    563
  Gandhi's response to, 422–424
  German acknowledgment of, 543–544
  German-Jewish business boycott and,
    306–307
  God's role during, 306–310
  Great Revolt compared to, 233
  guilt of survivors of, 84–85
  Hitler's "prophecy" and, 517–518
  hunger in, 427–428
  intellectuals in, 292–293
  Jabotinsky and, 585–587
  martyrs of, 324–327
  Nazis on, 517–521
  prayer from, 363–364, 365, 368–369
  as punishment, 306–310, 311
  Reagan's visit to Bitburg and, 544, 552–
    553
  refugees from, 457, 528–529, 581, 603
  religious responses to, 536–538, 557–560
  reparations for, 545–549, 569
  resistance to, 532–535, 537, 540
  shame and, 532–535
  Wagner-Rogers bill and, 528–529
  weakness of the Jews and, 225–226
  Western reactions to, 528–531
  Zionist Executive Committee debate on,
    296–297
  as Zionist hoax, 492
Holocaust, The (Gilbert), 525–526, 537,
  539–540
*Holocaust and the State of Israel, The:
  Their Relation* (Fackenheim), 524
Homosexuality, 129–130, 141–142
Honesty, 7–8, 18, 46–53
  animals and, 447–448
  in business, 3, 46–48, 50–51, 250, 371
  in a dishonest world, 51–52
  employees and, 56–57
  full, 52–53
  of rabbis, 371
  see also Lies, lying; Stealing; Truth
*Honor Thy Father and Mother: Filial
  Responsibility in Jewish Law and
  Ethics* (Blidstein), 151
"Hope, The" (*"Hatikvah"*) (Imber), 574
Hosea, Book of, 182, 568
Howe, Irving, 457, 478–479, 511
How to Get Up When Life Gets You Down
  (Blue and Magonet), 432
Human condition, 216–221
Humanism, 290–293
Human nature, 207–215
  and the desire for fame, 211–212, 213–
    214
  envy and, 210–211
  and harnessing evil, 213–215
  and the inclination toward evil, 207–210,
    393–394, 449
  and neighbor's pain, 212
  and the propensity for evil, 212–213
  testing oneself and, 214–215
Humiliation, 77

Humility, 70, 225–229
Huna, Rabbi, 158
Hunger, 232, 427–428, 446
Hunting, xxiv, 250, 448–449
Hussein, Saddam, 463, 491–492
Husseini, Hajj Amin al-, 589
Hyamson, M., 284–285

Ibn Ezra, Moshe, 197
Ibn Gabirol, Solomon, 68, 279
Ibn Verga, Solomon, 363
Idleness, 126, 441
Idolatry, 10, 16, 80, 196, 245, 294–297, 334, 397, 506
Iggeret ha-Kodesh, 141
Illustrated Sunday Herald, 500
Imber, Naphtali Hertz, 574
Im eshka-kheikh yerushalayim 569
Im tirzu, ein zoh aqgadah, xx, 573
Incest, 80, 138, 165
Individuality:
    and community responsibility, 91–98
    and experience of God, 285–286
    infinite value of, 88–90, 409
    nature vs., 442–443
    and the world's fate, 92–93, 425
Infanticide, 109, 163
Infertility, 172–173, 361–362
Informed Heart, The (Bettelheim), 247
Ingratitude, 187–190
Injustice, xxii, 405–406, 420–421
Inner Eye, The (Greenberg), 55, 269
Innocent III, pope, 317, 467
Innocent IV, pope, 467
In Search of Anti-Semitism (Buckley), 189-190, 491–492
Insights: A Talmudic Treasury (Weiss), 72–73, 95, 346
Intellectuals (Johnson), 473
Interest, 7, 12, 615
Intervention, 33–38, 76
International Jew, The, 67, 486–488
Interpretation, 451
"In the City of Slaughter" (Bialik), 287
Iran, 462
Iraq, 463, 490–492, 594, 598
Irgun, 596, 598
Isaac, 25, 104, 252, 320, 336–337, 567
Isaac, Jules, 562
Isaac, Rabbi, 122, 159–160, 333
Isaiah, 101, 144
Isaiah, Book of, xxi, 8, 171, 299–300, 346–347, 419, 449–450, 532
"Isaiah Wall," xxi, 419
Ishmael, Rabbi, xxiii, 303
Isolation, 93–95, 97–98, 366–367
Israel, ancient:
    anarchy in, 396
    children born in, 119
    exile from, 374, 568–569

Philistine rule over, 360–361
    as promised land, 567–571, 604
    refuge in, 457
    Roman rule over, *see* Rome
    waning of Torah study in, 338–339
Israel, modern, 565–612
    American relations with, 490–493, 597–598, 605
    defense of, 424, 581–582, 604
    and direction faced during prayer, 366
    establishment of, xx, xxii, 499, 575, 580–583, 587, 603, 611
    German reparations to, 545–549, 569
    God's purpose and, 300
    Herzl buried in, 578
    immigration to, 97–98, 581, 586, 588–590
    Nazi trials in, 408–409, 416, 534, 543, 550–551
    opposition to existence of, 479
    partition of, 584–585
    Persian Gulf War and, 490–492
    return of territories by, 87, 594, 597–600, 611–612
    Senesh buried in, 541
    Western enemies of, 608–610
    women drafted in, 42–43
    see also Six-Day War; Zionism
Israel, Steve, 614
Israeli, Isaac, 436–437
Israel of Rizhyn, 238
Israel of Vishnitz, 78–79
Israel's Defense Line (Kenen), 103, 607–608
Isserles, Moses, 260
Issi, Rabbi, 56
"Is This Life All There Is?" (Prager), 277
Jabesh Gilead, 396
Jabotinsky, Eri, 587
Jabotinsky, Vladimir, 584–587, 591, 598
"J'accuse" (Zola), 497
Jacob, 91–92, 104, 122, 157, 200, 267, 336, 419, 567
Jacob, Aha ben, 112
Jacob, Benno, 383
Jacob, Rabbi, 323
Jacobs, Louis, 237–238, 245–246, 300, 318, 394, 406
Janowska Road Camp, 324–326, 427–428
Japhet ben Eliyahu of Acco, 268
JAP jokes, 135
Jehovah's Witnesses, 422, 434
Jelenski, Konstantyn, 460
Jeremiah, 288, 427
Jeremiah, Book of, 5, 6, 62, 154, 395
Jeremiah, Rabbi, 73–74
Jeroboam, 245
Jerusalem: City of Mirrors (Elon), 606
Jesse, 137
Jesus and the Zealots (Brandon), 466

Jesus Christ, 6, 74–75, 85, 136, 174, 193, 241, 358, 413, 419, 420–423, 464–468, 515, 558, 612
  see also Christians, Christianity
Jesus et Israel (Isaac), 562
Jethro, 99, 446
"Jew, Disease Incarnate, The" (Pound), 476
Jew and Gentile in the Ancient World (Feldman), 376, 383
Jew in the Medieval World, The (Marcus), 470
"Jewish and Gay" (Marder), 142
"Jewish Attitude Toward Abortion, The," 165
"Jewish Business Ethics" (Tucker), 47
Jewish Ethics and Halakhah for Our Time (Herring), 63, 423
Jewish Frontier. 608
Jewish Law (Jacobs), 318, 406
Jewish Literacy (Telushkin), xx, 309
"Jewish Peril, The," 487
Jewish Profiles (Polner), 510–511
Jewish Quarterly Review, 383
Jewish Quest for Religious Meaning, A (Frimer), 57
Jewish Reader, A (Glatzer), 362, 364–365
Jewish Return into History, The (Fackenheim), 312–314
Jewish Social Ethics (Novak), 416
Jewish State, The (Herzl), 572
Jewish Theology, A (Jacobs), 300
Jewish Way in Love and Marriage, The (Lamm), 138, 386–387
Jewish Week 451
Jewish Women in Time and Torah (Berkovits), 105
Jews, Judaism:
  alienation among, 239–242
  capitalist ethic and, 38
  as chosen people, 298–302, 466
  conversion to, *see* Conversion
  denominations of, 509–510
  eponymous father of, 92
  essence of, xix-xx, 3–10, 202, 297
  goal of, 613
  God's role in history of, 287–289
  hierarchy of values in, 442–443
  Holocaust and faith of, 311–312
  modern reflections on, 613–617
  nonbelievers and, 311–315
  race and, 298–299, 301, 501–502
  as reaction to antisemitism, 459–460
  renunciation of, 377
  U.S. law vs. laws of, 34–35, 51, 317
Jezebel, 43
Job, 263, 264
Job, Book of, xxi-xxii, 51, 56, 266, 303
Joel, Book of, 419–420
Johanan, Rabbi, 81–82
John, Book of, 85

John XXIII, pope, 469, 559
John Paul II, pope, 193–194
Johnson, Paul, 473
Jokes and Their Relationship to the Unconscious (Freud), 22
Jones, LeRoi, 478–479
Jonathan, 178–179
Jordan, 594, 597
Joseph, 91–92, 122, 139, 157, 211, 267, 336, 342, 360, 401
Joseph, Morris, 299
Joseph, Rabbi, 47
Josephus, Flavius, 274–275, 375–376
Joshua, Rabbi, 6, 73, 198, 233–234, 264, 430
Joshua ben Hananiah, 22, 71–72
Joshua ben Korcha, 144–145, 218, 285–286
Joshua ben Levi, 16–17, 29–30
Joshua ben Perakhia, 100
Jotham, 101
Journal of Jewish Thought, 230–231
Judah, 91–92
Judah, Rav, 38
Judah ben Asher, 353–354
Judah ben Rabbi Nahmani, 158–159
Judah ben Tabbai, 100
Judah the Pious, 23
Judah the Prince, Rabbi, xxiii, 112, 121–122, 144–145, 153, 157, 214, 234–235, 257–258, 273, 322, 347, 348, 404–405, 447
Judaism, 308–309, 314, 610
Judaism (Hertzberg), 87
Judaism: Law and Ethics (Herzog), 436
Judaism and Global Survival (Schwartz), 26–27
Judaism and Healing (Bleich), 64
Judaism and Modern Man (Herberg), 291
Judaism and Vegetarianism (Schwartz), 450, 452, 453
Judaism as Creed and Life (Joseph), 299
"Judaism, Homosexuality, and Civilization" (Prager), 130, 142
Judea, 394, 465–468, 597
Judges, Book of, 136, 224, 360–361, 396, 505
Justice, xxi, 5, 8, 41–43, 49–50, 398–406, 614
  and animal slaughter, 450
  burden of proof in, 401–402
  delayed, 403
  for enemies, 193
  "an eye for an eye" in, 402–403
  falsehood avoided in, 399–401
  from God, 100, 245, 304
  guiding principles of, 398–403
  Maimonides on, 398
  mercy and, 398, 399
  subtlety in, 403–404
Justice by the Book (Schwartz), 411–412

Justice Not Vengeance (Wiesenthal), 562
Juvenal, 376

Kabdai-hu ve-hashdai-hu, 500
Kaddish 116–117, 256, 268–269, 366
Kaddishl 116
Kafka, Franz, 239, 453
Kagan, Israel Meir Ha-Kohen, 16, 25, 68–69, 284
Kahan Commission, 599
Kahane, Meir, 602
Kamenev, Lev Borisovich, 501
Kametko, Archbishop, 557–558
Kaplan, Chaim, 539
Kaplan, Lawrence, 42, 371–372
Kaplan, Louis, 97
Kaplan, Mordechai, 220, 301–302
Kapos 82–83, 561
Karelitz, Avraham Yeshayahu, 42–43
Karl Marx and the Radical Critique of Judaism (Carlebach), 473
Karo, Joseph, xxiv, 13
Kashrut, 3, 230, 330, 335, 386, 448–453
Kaskel, Cesar, 480
Katz, Dov, 261, 331–332
Katz, Jacob, 586
Katz, Samuel, 173
Katznelson, Berl, 587
Katznelson, Yitzchak, 522–523, 542
Katzya, 405–406
Kazin, Alfred, 612
Kean College, 494
Keating, Edward, 469
Kellner, Menachem, 165–166
Kelman, Wolfe, 123, 350–352
Kenen, I. L., 103, 607–608
Kennedy, Jacqueline, 263
Kennedy, John F., 103, 263, 319
Kerensky, Alexander, 194
Ketuba, 126, 169, 170–171, 569–570
Khalid Abdul Mohammad, 494
Khomeini, Ayatollah Ruhollah, 462
Kiddush, 382
Kiddush ha-Shem, 316–328, 523–524, 538
Kilpatrick, James Jackson, 491
Kimelman, Reuven, 125
Kimhi, David, 273
Kindness, 5, 6, 70, 182–186
  loving-, 9, 10, 24–25, 86
Kings, First Book of, 43, 210, 245, 252, 334–335, 388, 506, 545
Kings, Second Book of, 210, 295
Kirschenbaum, Aaron, 401–402
Kirschner, Robert, 29–30, 306
Kisei eliyahu, 4
Kishinev pogrom, 287
Kissinger, Henry, 491, 604
Kitzur Shulkhan Arukh, 149–150
Klagsbrun, Francine, 62–63, 150, 152, 202, 219–220, 322

Koch, Ed, 262
Kohl, Helmut, 552–553
Kolitz, Zvi, 363–364
Kollek, Teddy, 605–606
Kol Nidre, 95
Kook, Abraham Isaac, 179–180, 197, 224, 440, 603–604, 615
Kook, Nahum, 125–126
Korakh, 386
Korban Ha-Eida, 171–172
Kortner, Fritz, 250
Kosher, 3, 230, 330, 335, 386, 448–453
Kotler, Aharon, 23
Koufax, Sandy, 509
Kovner, Abba, 532–533
Kranz, Yaakov, 216–218
Krauthammer, Charles, 491
Kreiser, Aaron, 196–197
Kristallnacht, 528, 537
Kristol, Irving, 292
Ktavim (Jabotinsky), 584
Ku Klux Klan, 483
Kula, Irwin, 4, 88–89, 285
Kultura, 460
Kurzman, Dan, 590
Kurzweil, Arthur, 15
Kushner, Harold, 68, 220, 299, 332, 337, 372–373, 415–416, 442, 468, 579, 613
Kuwait, 490–492

Labyrinth of Exile, The: A Life of Theodor Herzl (Pawel), 578
Ladies' Home Journal, 400
La Guardia, Fiorello, 399
Lahai Roi (Levin), 439–440
Lailah, 244
Laing, R. D., 102, 213
Lamdan, Yitzhak, 601–602
Lamentations, Book of, 273, 427, 463
Lamm, Maurice, 138
Lamm, Norman, 310, 442
Land and Power (Shapira), 602
Landau, Ezekiel, xxiv, 448
Langer, Jiri, 97
Language of Faith, The (Glatzer), 365
Lanzmann, Claude, 534
Laqueur, Walter, 529, 543, 574
Lashon hara, 65–66, 359–360
Law:
  Jewish vs. U.S., 34–35, 51, 317
  letter of, 38–39, 40, 50, 334–335
  precedence of, 80
  of the state, 395
Lazare, Bernard, 574
Lazeit y'dei shamayim 50
Lazerov, Judah Leib, 289
Leadership, 99–103
Leah, 122, 360
Lebanon, 462–463

Lebrou, Henri, 471
Leibowitz, Samuel, 403–404
Lekhi, 603
Lend Me Your Ears: Great Speeches In History (Safire), 246
Lenin, Vladimir Ilich, 194, 501, 510
Leprosy, 29–30, 356
Lerman, Miles, 305
Letter in Defense of the Jews (Innocent IV), 467
Letters of Sigmund Freud and Arnold Zweig, The (Freud), 213
Letters to an American Jewish Friend: A Zionist's Polemic (Halkin), 380
Levi, Primo, 368–369
Levi, Rabbi, 256, 285
Levin, Aryeh, 125–126, 179–180, 224, 439–440
Levin, Hannah, 125–126
Levin, Yitzchak Itshe Meir, 176, 296–297
Levine, Peter, 509
Leviticus, Book of, xxiii, 6, 12, 14, 22, 28, 33, 40, 41, 47, 52, 58, 65, 76, 80, 84, 95, 115, 124–125, 137, 139, 141, 147, 149, 153–154, 174, 176, 211, 228, 236, 248–249, 333, 340, 386, 387, 388, 398, 403, 445
Levi Yitzkhak of Berditchev, 176, 286–287, 364–365
Levkov, Ilya, 544, 552
Lewis Samuel, 598
Libya, 463
Lichteim, George, 473–474
Lichtenstein, Aaron, 441
Liebknecht, Karl, 242
Lies, lying, 58–64, 154–155, 318, 353, 354
Life:
  endangerment of, *see* Endangerment of life; Murder
  final stages of, 260–261
  infinite value of, 88–90, 409
  longevity in, 250–251
  in pain and nothing more, 257–260
  see also Age, aging
Lifnim me-shurat ha-din, 39
Lincoln, Abraham, 124, 480
Lindbergh: A Biography (Mosley), 489, 490
Lindbergh, Anne Morrow, 489
Lindbergh, Charles, 462, 488–490
Linzer, Norman, 256
Lippmann, Walter, 126, 477
Lipstadt, Deborah, 464, 555
Listening to American Jews (Oppenheim), 50
Lloyd George, David, 500
Loans, 7, 12, 23
Loneliness, 118–119, 180–181, 241, 257–260
Lonely Days Were Sundays, The: Reflection of a Jewish Southerner (Evans), 241

Lookstein, Joseph, 203
Lorincz, Shlomo, 202
Lot, 344
Love:
  acknowledging of, 199
  of God, 147, 176, 286, 303, 358–359
  hatred vs., 197
  between parents and children, 147
  romantic, 128–130, 380–381
Love Your Neighbor (Pliskin), 31–32, 44
"Love your neighbor as yourself," xx, xxi, 5–6, 33, 36, 124–126, 147, 174–178
Lowell, A. Lawrence, 484
Lowenthal, Marvin, 116–117, 269, 578
Luce, Claire Boothe, 515
Lueger, Karl, 576
Luke, Book of, 466
Lulav, 331
Luria, Solomon, 379
Luther, Martin, 469–471
Luxembourg, Rosa, 241–242

Maccabees, First Book of, 85
MacArthur, Brian, 540
Maccoby, Hyam, xxii, 74, 133–134, 346, 466, 468
McLaughlin Group, 490
Madness, 101–102, 126, 133, 134
Maggid of Dubno and His Parables, The (Heinemann), 216–218
Magic Carpet, Operation, 98
Magnes, Judah, 588
Magonet, Jonathan, 15, 432
Maharsha (Samuel Eliezer Edels), 17–18
Mah nishtana ha-lie-lah ha-zeh meekol ha-leilot, 385
Mahzor for Rosh Hashana and Yom Kippur (Harlow), 387–388
Maimonides (Moses ben Maimon), xxiv, 10, 138
  on charity, 11, 15, 20
  on confessions of murder, 410, 411
  on criticism, 77
  on death penalty, 410, 411, 414
  on destruction of the environment, 439, 442
  on divorce, 114–115, 170
  epitaph of, 269
  on extravagant speech, 201
  on free will, 244–246
  as healer, 433, 442
  on injuries, 44
  on intervening on behalf of a neighbor, 36
  on isolation, 93–94
  on justice, 398
  on killing to save one's own life, 82
  on marriage, 113–115
  on mentally disordered parents, 151
  mourning of, 267–268

on murder ransoms, 407–408, 548–549
on old age, 253
on overrighteousness, 231
on physicians, 434
on rationale for *mitzvot*, 333
on rejoicing, 384
on repentance, 348–349, 387
on self-defense, 82, 423
on selling weapons, 50
on sounding of the shofar, 387
on stealing, 50
on the suffering of animals, 445
on teaching, 344
on violating the Sabbath, 85–86
on waste, 440
on who should study Torah, 339–340
on widows and orphans, 27
on women, 113–115
Making of Modern Zionism, The (Avineri),
   589–591
Malachi, Book of, 183
Mamzer, 140
Manasseh, 144, 295
Mann, Alonzo, 483
Mansoor, Menahem, 284–285
Man's Quest for God (Heschel), 289
Man's Search for Meaning (Frankl), 247
Mar, 360
Marcus, Jacob, 470
Marder, Janet, 142
Mari ben Isak, 401–402
Maritain, Jacques, 461, 463
Marriage, xxiii, 4, 80, 118–127, 136, 153
  arranged, 121
  benefits of, 118–119
  after the death of a spouse, 123–124,
    614–615
  discontented, 126–127
  early, 131
  God as broker of, 120
  infertile, 172–173
  inter-, 313, 505–507
  ketuba for, 126, 169, 170–171, 569–
    570
  Maimonides on, 113–115
  military service and, 417–418
  for money, 122–123
  polygamous, 121–122, 139, 170
  proposals of, on fifteenth of Av, 388
  rape within, 140–141
  respect in, 124–126
  two sides in, 400
Marrus, Michael, 558
Marshall, George, 554
Marshall, Louis, 485, 487
Martyrdom, 85, 247, 320–328, 358–359,
  413
Marx, Groucho, 458
Marx, Karl, 95, 472–473
Masada, 274–275, 601–602

Masada (Yadin), 274–275
"Masada" (Lamdan), 601–602
Masaryk, Thomas, 421, 497
Masmid, 342
Masterplan: Judaism:Its Program Meanings,
  Goals (Carmell), 36–37, 192–193
Matt, Daniel Chanan, 99
Mattathias, 85
Matthew, Book of, 136, 174, 193, 334,
  376, 420, 421, 465–468, 558
Mauthausen, 533
Mazal, 430, 440
Medicine, 64, 433–437, 485
Meetings (Buber), 180
Mein Kampf (Hitler), 518, 554
"Mein Yingele" ("My Little Son")
  (Rosenfeld), 431–432
Meir, Golda, 593–595
Meir, Rabbi, 20–21, 53, 219, 265–266,
  267, 323, 349
Meir of Rothenburg, 95
Meisels, Zvi Hirsch, 82–84
Mekadshe Ha-Shem (Those Who Sanctified
  God's Name) (Meisels), 82–84
Mekhilta, xxiii, 46, 94, 220, 330
Meklenburg, Jacob Zvi, 118
Melamed, Eliezer, 525–526
Mellow, James, 241
Memoirs of Gluckel of Hameln, The
  (Lowenthal), 269
Menahem Mendel of Kotzk, 90, 344
Menashe, 360
Mencken, H. L., 477–478
Mendele Mokher Seforim, 255
Menorat ha-Maor (Alnakawa), 150, 153
Mensch, 33–45
  compassion and, 182
  compromise and, 41–43
  covetousness and, 43
  equity and, 38–39, 40
  holiness of, 40–41
  intervention by, 33–38
  and the letter of the law, 38–39, 40
  property and, 38, 40, 44
Menstruation, 138, 185
Merab, 146
Mercy, 9, 10, 86, 194–196, 356, 398, 399,
  446–447
Meshech Hokhmah (Simkha), 143
"Message to the First Zionist Congress"
  (Mohilever), 571
Messiah, 425, 449–450, 557, 571, 602
Mezuzah, 358–359
Micah, xxi, 5, 6, 8
Michal, 146
Middah k'negged middah, 409
"Midnight Rescue, The" (Carmell), 36–37
Midrash:
  Proverbs, 266
  Psalms, 145

Midrash: (continued)
   Rabbah, xxiii, 14, 18, 22, 47, 52, 56, 77,
      95, 99, 116, 137, 153–154, 158,
      159, 172, 183–184, 199, 211, 213,
      215, 218, 219, 220, 222, 228, 236,
      256, 273, 285–286, 343, 348, 367,
      379, 419, 429, 438, 439, 446, 463
   Tanhuma, 9, 56, 152, 192, 335, 336,
      375, 378
Midrash on Proverbs, The (Visotzky), 265–
      266
Mikveh, 138
Milcom, 334, 506
Milgrom, Jacob, 451
Military service, 42–43, 417–424
Milk, Harvey, 244
Miller, Avigdor, 309–310, 311
Miller, Judith, 563
Miller, Merle, 605
Milton, John, 118
Minyan, 366
Miracles, 74–75, 434
Miriam, 104, 356
Misalliance (Shaw), 437
Mishael, 222
Mishna, xxiii, 9, 46–47, 49, 51, 88–89,
      108, 110, 126, 129, 134, 135, 145,
      162, 169, 277, 287, 294, 342, 353,
      367, 385, 386, 389, 409, 412, 414,
      435, 441, 569–570
Mishnato shel David Ben-Gurion (Ben
      Gurion), 589–591
Mishneh Torah, see Maimonides
Mitzvot, 22, 32, 78–79, 93, 137, 188, 196,
      254, 260, 329–335
Moab, 179
Mobs, 210
Modena, Leon da, 68
Modern Jewish Ethics (Fox), 614–615
Modesty, xxi, 5, 9, 447–448
Mohammed, 358
Mohilever, Samuel, 571
Mommsen, Theodore, 464
Montaigne, Michel de, 257
Mordechai, 36, 93, 105, 346, 543
Moredet, 114–115
Moscone, George, 244
Moses, 7, 14, 24, 61–62, 90, 94, 99, 104–
      105, 116, 245, 249, 251, 285–286,
      356, 367, 385–386, 422, 446, 577,
      595
Moses, Operation, 98
Moses and Monotheism (Freud), 288–289,
      461
Moses ben Maimon, see Maimonides
Moshe of Coucy, 319
Moshe of Kobryn, 220–221
Moshe of Leib of Sassov, 176
Moshe Yitzchak of Ponovezh, 270
Mosley, Leonard, 489, 490

Mourning, 24–25, 111, 133, 156, 255–270
   community and, 366–367
   consolation and, 263–270
   eulogies and, 263, 269–270
   excessive, 233–234, 267, 268
   funerals and, 261–263
   Kaddish in, 116–117, 256, 268–269, 366
   lamenting and, 268
   silence in, 263, 267
   for suicides, 271–272
   time limits for, 267, 268
   weeping and, 262–263, 268
Movshovitz, Daniel, 523–524
Muravchik, Joshua, 491–492
Murder, 33–34, 43, 80–87, 109
   death penalty and, 407–416
   and destruction of the first Temple, 196
   forgiveness for, 352–353, 562–563
   free will and, 244, 246–247
   God's punishment of, 415–416
   by Jewish terrorists, 602–603
   multiple, 88, 408–409
   in Noahide law, 397
   passive complicity in, 81–85
   premeditated, 407
   ransom for, 407–408, 548–549
   repentance for, 352–353
   to save one's own life, 80–82
   of a slave, 317
   suicide as, 156, 272
   witnesses to, 409–416
   see also Endangerment of life
Mussar, 201
Mussar Movement, The (T'nuat HaMussar)
      (Katz), 261, 331–332
Mussolini, Benito, 422
"My Father's Memorial Day" (Amichai), 270
"My Favorite Assassin" (Herald), 352–353
"My Little Son" ("Mein Yingele")
      (Rosenfeld), 431–432
"My Negro Problem and Ours"
      (Podhoretz), 504
My Religion (Tolstoy), 468

Nachamson, Jennie, 241
Nachmanides, Moses, 141
Nachman of Bratslav, 101–102, 200, 213,
      231–232, 436
Nadler, Allan, 308–309
Naftali of Rotchitz, 64
Nahman, Rabbi, 159–160
Naked Nomads (Gilder), 118–119
Navasky, Victor, 492
Naomi, 178–179, 374
Napoleon I, emperor of France, 367–368
Nasser, Gamal Abdel, 594–595, 609
Nathan, Rabbi, 74
Nation, 491–492
National Review, 492
Nation of Victims, A (Sykes), 243–244, 246

Navot, 43
Nazis, Nazi Germany:
  atheism of, 290, 312–313, 475
  German-Jewish businesses boycotted by, 306–307, 538
  on the Holocaust, 517–521
  intellectuals in, 292–293
  Jewish rage at, 542–544
  kapos, 82–83, 561
  Lindbergh and, 462, 488–490
  racial superiority and, 298–299
  reparations from, 545–549, 569
  Skokie march of, 562
  Toynbee's view of, 608–609
  trials of, 408–409, 416, 521, 550–551
  see also Holocaust
Nebuchadnezzer, 222, 288
Needy, neediness, 26–32
  advice to, 28
  poverty vs., 27–28
  rabbis as advocates for, 371–372
  ritual observance and, 31–32
  taking advantage of, 28
  waste and, 440–441
  see also Charity
Neider, Charles, 498
Neighbors, neighborliness, 6, 7, 9, 43, 200, 212, 401
  see also "Love your neighbor as yourself"
Netanyahu, Benjamin, 586, 610–611
Neusner, Jacob, 610
Newman, Louis, 232, 484
New Testament, 135–136, 193, 207, 334, 420–423
New York Daily News, 493
New York Review of Books, 492, 555–556
New York Times, 458, 491, 543, 553, 602–603, 609
New York Times Book Review, 592
New York World, 486
"Next year in Jerusalem," 327–328
Niemoller, Martin, 536–537
Nietzsche, Friedrich, 290, 292
Night (Wiesel), 527
Niles, David, 605
9½ Mystics (Weiner), 360
Nine Gates of the Chasidic Mysteries (Langer), 97
Nine Questions People Ask About Judaism, The (Prager and Telushkin), 212, 284, 288
Nissenbaum, Yitzchak, 538
Noah, 99–100, 376, 450
Noahide laws, 397
Non-Jews:
  aged, 248
  antisemitism's effects on, 462–463
  conversion of, *see* Conversion
  darkei shalom and, 40
  Jewish actions perceived by, 318–319

  Marx as viewed by, 473
  righteous, 375
  stealing from, 48
Nonviolence, 420–423, 468
Non-Violence in Peace and War (Gandhi), 422
Nordau, Max, 460–461, 573–574
Notes from the Warsaw Ghetto: The Journal of Emanuel Ringelbaum (Ringelbaum), 543
Novak, David, 416
Numbers, Book of, xxiii, 153, 220, 356, 378–379, 386, 407, 457, 548–549
Nuremberg, 408–409, 521

O'Brien, Conor Cruise, 576, 587
Obscenity, 141
"Old, The" (Zevin), 253
One by One by One (Miller), 563
One Generation After (Wiesel), 561–562
O'Neill, J. J., 486
O'Neill, William, 489
On Equal Terms: Jews in America, 1881–1981 (Davidowicz), 488
On Orthodoxy (Chesterton), 272
On Patience (Augustine), 272
"On Resistance" (Chomsky), 492
On the Decalogue (Philo), 152
"On the Jewish Question" (Marx), 472, 473
On the Jews and Their Lies (Luther), 470
Operation Shylock (Roth), 65–66
Oppenheim, Carolyn, 50
Oppenheimer, Suss, 324
Order No. 11, 480–481
Orhot Zaddikim (The Ways of the Righteous), 17, 225
Original sin, 207
Orlinsky, Harry, 567
Orphans, 26, 27, 384
Orwell, George, 477
Oswald, Lee Harvey, 319
O the Chimneys (Sachs), 516
"Our Balance Sheet with the English" (Ben-Gurion), 589–590
Our Masters Taught (Petuchowski), 172, 340–342
Out of the Whirlwind: A Reader of Holocaust Literature (Friedlander), 364
Oz, Amos, 599–600, 603
Ozick, Cynthia, 515, 562–563

Paisner, Daniel, 262
Palestinian Liberation Organization (PLO), 462, 598–600, 608
Palestinian Talmud, *see* Talmud, Palestinian

Palgi, Yoel, 532
Papa, Hanina bar, 244

Papa, Rabbi, 262, 429
Pappenheim, Bertha, 109, 614–615
Pappus ben Judah, 337–338
Parents, 147–160
  adult children and, 159
  aged, 150–153
  bad-tempered, 155, 156
  blessing of children by, 360, 382
  children's obligations to, 147–149
  commonsense guidelines for, 154–157
  death of, 116–117, 149, 256
  and disagreements with children, 149–
    150, 351
  honoring of, 9, 108, 115, 147–148, 150–
    153, 250, 360, 568
  influence of, 158, 344
  marriages arranged by, 121
  mentally disordered, 151–152
  obligations of, to children, 153–154, 340,
    344, 359
  see also Children "Parents as Partners
    with God"(Brown), 150
Parker, Dorothy, 257
Partisan Review, 240
Pascal, Blaise, 286
Passion for Truth, A (Heschel), 304
Passover, 27–28, 94–95, 384–387, 465,
  487, 497
"Passover Celebrants, The" (Agnon), 27–28
Pasternak, Boris, 504
"Patrick J. Buchanan and the
  Jews"(Muravchik), 491–492
Patton, George, 554
Paul (Saul of Tarsus), 136
Pawel, Ernst, 578
Paxton, Robert, 558
Peace, 39–40, 76–77, 86, 87, 353, 419
Peace Now, 604
Pearl, Chaim, 571
Pearls of Wisdom (Ibn Gabirol), 68, 279
Peel Commission, 580–581, 584, 585
Peixotto, Benjamin Franklin, 481
Peled, Yossi, 582
People Divided, A (Wertheimer), 610
Perle, Richard, 491
Persian Gulf War, 490–492
Peli, Pinchas, 72, 451
*Penguin Book of Twentieth-Century
  Speeches* (MacArthur), 540
Penueli, S. Y., 270
Peres, Shimon, 553
Peretz, Haym, 116–117
Perin, Yaakov, 602
Personal Witness (Eban), 582, 593
Pertinent Players (Epstein), 478
Pesikta d'Rav Kahana, 16–17, 120, 285,
  300
Petition, prayers of, 356, 360, 368
Petuchowski, Jakob, 172, 340–342, 561
Petura, Ben, 84

Phagan, Mary, 482
Pharaoh (Ramses II), 94, 104, 255, 311,
  367, 458–459, 467, 577
Philipson, David, 383
Philistines, 360–361
Philo, 152
Philosemitism, 496–503
Physically disadvantaged, 28, 163, 164,
  243–244, 246, 248–249, 251–252
Physicians, 64, 433–437, 485
"Piety and Politics: The Case of the Satmar
  Rebbe" (Nadler), 308–309
Pikuakh nefesh, see Endangerment of life;
  Murder
Pilate, Pontius, 465–468, 482
Pinsker, Sanford, 189–190
Pirkei Avot, see Ethics of the Fathers
Pirkei d'Rabbi Eliezer, 116
Pius X, pope, 576
*Place Among the Nations, A: Israel and the
  World* (Netanyahu), 586, 610–611
Plain Speaking (Miller), 605
Plato, 129–130
Playboy, 136
"Plea for the Dead, A" (Wiesel), 535
Pliskin, Zelig, 31–32, 44
PLO (Palestine Liberation Organization),
  462, 598–600, 608
Podhoretz, Norman, 492, 504
Poland, 304, 309, 323–324, 586–587, 589
Poliakov, Leon, 197–198, 471
Polner, Murray, 510–511
Polygamy, 121–122, 139, 170
poor, poverty, 13–14, 40, 427–432
  as demeaning, 429–430
  favoring of, 399
  God's will and, 20–21, 430
  idealization of, 18
  neediness vs., 27–28
  physicians and, 434–435
  Torah study and, 341, 342
Portnoy's Complaint (Roth), 159
Possession, legal aspects of, 401
Potiphar, 139
Potocki, Valentine, 323–324
Potok, Chaim, 298
Pound, Ezra, 296, 476–477
Power Struggle (Rubinstein), 311
Prager, Dennis, 130, 142, 175–176, 195,
  212, 277, 284, 288, 335, 461–462,
  463, 510, 560, 611–612, 615–16
Praise, 67–68, 179
  prayers of, 356, 357–359
Prayer, 356–370
  action vs., 367–368
  to alter the past, 368
  community and, 95–96, 366–367
  of confession and introspection, 356,
    359–360
  expecting immediate answer to, 208–209

facing Israel during, 366
God's, 369
to have children, 105
from the Holocaust, 363–364, 365, 368–369
inappropriate, 367–369
petitionary, 356, 360, 368
of praise, 356, 357–359
for punishment of enemies, 349
by the simple, 363–363
of thanksgiving, 356
unusual, 360–365
see also specific prayers
Preface to Morals, A (Lippmann), 126
Pregnancy, 143–144, 368
Premarital sex, 137–138
Preservation of Youth, The: Essays of Health (Maimonides), 442
President Masaryk Tells His Story (Capek), 497
Price Below Rubies, A: Jewish Women as Rebels and Radicals (Shepherd), 109, 242
Pride, 13, 538–539, 598, 614
Principles of the Jewish Faith (Jacobs), 245–246
Procrastination, 330
Property, 27, 31, 38, 40, 44, 46, 200, 243, 408, 443
Proskauer, Joseph, 605
Protocols of the Elders of Zion, 486, 490, 555
Proudhon, Pierre Joseph, 473–474
Proust, Marcel, 498
Proverbs, Book of, 23, 38, 39, 55, 106, 115, 128, 156, 193, 237
Psalms, Book of, xxi, xxii, 7, 145, 230, 251, 274, 294, 303, 356, 439, 446, 447, 532, 568–569
Puah, 104
Publicity, 211–212
Purim, 231, 389
Pushke, 17, 357

Qaddafi, Muammar al-, 463
Quarrels That Have Shaped the Constitution (Garraty), 31

Rab, 189
Rabbah bar Nahmani, 430, 435, 441
Rabbinic Responsa of the Holocaust Era (Kirschner), 306
Rabbis, 371–373, 562
Rabin, Yitzhak, 66, 602–603
Rabinowicz, Oskar, 608
Rachel (wife of Jacob), 122, 360
Rachel (wife of Rabbi Akiva), 106–108
"Racial Motif in Renan's Attitude to Jews and Judaism, The" (Almog), 501
Rackman, Emanuel, 283–284

Radak, 273
Radical Theology and the Death of God (Altizer), 312
Rakover, Yossel, 363–364
Ramses II, *see* Pharaoh
Ransom, 407–408, 548–549
Rape, 80, 137, 140–141, 164, 165, 344
Rappleye, William, 485
Rasha, see Evil
Rashi, 112–113, 398–399, 448, 570–571
Rashi: Commentaries on the Pentateuch (Pearl), 570–571
Rathenau, Mathilde, 352–353
Rathenau, Walter, 352–353, 449
Rauschning, Hermann, 475
Rav, 154–155, 214, 369
Rava, 51, 80–81, 259, 430
Rav Ashi, 295
Ravina, 360
Ravnitzky, Y. H., 47, 52, 192, 210, 430
Raz, Simcha, 125–126, 179–180, 224
Reagan, Ronald, 50, 552–553, 598–599
Rebecca, 104, 337, 360
Reconsiderations (Toynbee), 608
Reconstructionism, 301–302
Rector of Justin, The (Auchincloss), 330
Redemption of the world, 3, 4, 52–53, 87, 269
Reform Movement in Judaism, The (Philipson), 383
Reich, Mordechai Menachem, 149
Reichik, Morton, 510–511
Reisin, Abraham, 431
Rejoice, O Youth (Miller), 309
Reliqion and the Individual (Jacobs), 394
Religion in Life 301
Renan, Ernest, 501, 549
repentance, 345–355
Maimonides on, 348–349, 387
on Rosh Hashana and Yom Kippur, 387, 389
for stealing, 354–355
three guides to, 353–354
true, 348–349
unequaled power of, 348
useless, 350–353
Rescuers: Portraits of Moral Courage in the Holocaust (Block and Drucker), 575
Resh Lakish, 258–259, 378
Responsa Mistip'tei Uziel (Uziel), 166–167
Responsa *Nodeh B'Yehuda*, 449
Responsibility, 216–218, 223, 243–247, 276, 304–306, 599
Reuben, 211
Reuven, Rabbi, 291
Revenge, 176–177, 548
Revolution in Judaea: Jesus and the Jewish Resistance (Maccoby), 466, 468
Rezza v. United States Department of Justice et al., 243–244

"Rhetoric of Anti-Semitism in Postwar American Literature" (Stern), 479
Rich, John, 228
Rieger, Pastor, 324
Riemer, Jack, 101–102, 141, 352–353
Righteousness, 7, 8, 24, 41, 94, 106, 116, 200, 220, 245, 276, 348, 367, 375, 393
Rights Talk (Glendon), 34–35
Rimalt, Elimelekh, 546
Ringelbaum, Emanuel, 543
Riskin, Shlomo, 451
Robinson, Armin, 475
Rogers, Edith Nourse, 528
Rokeakh, Shalom, 184
Romania, 481
Rome, 16–17, 20–21, 163, 196, 235, 273–275, 294, 303, 320–322, 337–338, 374–376, 379, 383, 412–413, 465–468, 601
Roosevelt, Eleanor, 529
Roosevelt, Franklin Delano, 489, 529, 605
Roosevelt, Theodore, 499
Rosenberg, Bernard, 310
Rosensaft, Menachem, 553
Rosenstock, Morton, 484
Rosenthal, A. M., 491, 543
Rosenzweig, Itzik, 327
Rosh Hashana, 387–389, 509
Rosner, Dr. Fred, 165
Roth, Philip, 65–66, 159, 464
Rothschild, Baron, 473
Rothschild, Lionel, 580
Rousseau, Jean-Jacques, 496
Rubenstein, Richard, 311–312, 315
Rumkowski, Chaim, 539–540
Russell, Bertrand, 290–291
Ruth, 178–179, 211–212, 299, 374, 379
Ruth, Book of, 178, 374, 379

Sabbath, xxi, 382–383
    death and, 261
    endangerment of life and, 85–87, 261
    holiness as ultimate goal of, 382
    love poem recited before, 128
    observing of, xxi, 3, 13, 31–32, 331, 386, 420
    parental blessing on, 360, 382
    Torah reading on, 382
    treatment of animals on, 444
    violations of, and the Holocaust, 306–307, 309
Sabbath Prayer Book (Kaplan), 301–302
Sabra-Shatilla massacre, 598–599
Sachar, Howard Morley, 482, 484, 485, 486, 487, 490, 577, 592, 605
Sachs, Nelly, 516
Sacrifice, 144, 182, 233, 367
Sadat, Anwar, 604
Safire, William, 246

Safra, Rabbi, 7–8
Sahlins, Marshall, 555–556
St. Louis, S.S., 529–530
Salanter, Israel, 13, 25, 31–32, 67, 72–73, 86, 201, 226, 261, 331–332, 342, 371
Samaria, 597
Samson, 360–361, 505
Samuel, 105, 194, 213, 361, 414, 551
Samuel, Books of, xxii, 43, 81, 100, 105, 146, 159, 178–179, 194, 252, 256, 273, 360, 419, 550
Samuel, Maurice, 461
Samuel, Rabbi, 157, 318
Sandburg, Carl, 124
Sane Society, The (Fromm), 290
Sanhedrin (Jewish high court), 83, 253, 327, 412–413
Santayana, George, 257
Saperstein, David, 29
Sapiro, Aaron, 487
Sarah, 59, 104, 201, 263, 360
Sartre, Jean-Paul, 459–460
Saud, King of Saudi Arabia, 605, 607–608
Saudi Arabia, 114, 491, 605, 607–608
Saul, King of Israel, 100, 146, 179, 194, 273, 274
Saul of Tarsus (Paul), 136
Sawyer, Eugene, 493–494
Scherman, Nosson, 208
Schneeweiss, 324–326
Scholem, Gershom, 278
Schwartz, Helene, 411–412
Schwartz, Howard, 102
Schwartz, Richard, 26–27, 450, 452, 453
Schweitzer, Albert, 221
Sefer ha-Hinnukh, 76
Sefer Ha-Ikkarim (Albo), 450
Sefer Hasidim (Book of the Pious) (Judah the Pious), 23, 123, 225, 362, 436, 447
Sefer Minhagim of Worms, 323
Segev, Tom, 296, 546–549, 569, 582, 588
Seize the Day (Bellow),
Self-defense, 420–424
Self-denial, 230–238
Self-improvement, 200
Selfishness, 96–97, 207–208
Seligman, Joseph, 481–482
Semag (Moshe of Coucy), 319
Seneca, 257, 376, 383
Senesh, Hannah, 532, 540–541
"Sermon, The" (Hazaz), 240
Service Book (Rabin), 66
Seventh Million, The (Segev), 296, 546–549, 569, 582, 588
Sex, 108, 114–115, 131–142
    desirability of, 135–136
    and destruction of the first Temple, 196
    and emotional blackmail, 133–134

female drive for, 131, 134–135
forbidden, 139–141, 397
frequency of, 134–135
homosexuality, 129–130, 141–142
Jewish vs. New Testament views of, 135–136
male drive for, 131–134
other commandments vs., 137
premarital, 137–138
refraining from, on Yom Kippur, 388
thoughts of, 131–133, 208–209
value in, 138
Shabbetai, K., 533–534
Shadows of Auschwitz (Cargas), 554, 557
Shaliakh mitzvah gelt, 332
Shame, 60, 132, 210, 212, 532–535
Shamir, Yitzhak, 584
Shammai, School of Shammai, xix, 5, 59, 60, 70–71, 108, 134, 145, 169, 187, 216
Shammas, 27–28
Shapira, Anita, 602
Shapira, Hayyim Elazar, 306–307, 310
Shapiro, David, 326–327
Sharansky, Anatoly (Natan), 327–328
Sharansky, Avital, 328
Shatz, David, 425
Shavuot, 384, 385–386
Shaw, George Bernard, 301, 437
Sheftel, Ariel, 546–547
She'iltot (Ahai), 154
Shekhina, 276
Shepherd, Naomi, 109, 242
Sheshet, Rabbi, 441
Shifra, 104
Shimoni, Gideon, 422
Shirat Yisrael (ibn Ezra), 197
Shiva, 266, 366
Shlilat ha-golah, 240
Shlomo of Karlin, 97
Sh'ma, 7–8, 268, 321, 324, 357–359, 362
Shmaya, Rabbi, 341
Shmelke of Nikolsberg, 15
Shmuel (displaced boy), 365
Shnorrer, 22
Shoah, 534
Shochet, 448
Shofar, sounding of, 387
"Should a Jew Sell Guns?" (Bleich), 50
Shragai, S. Z., 304
Shukeiry, Ahmed, 608
Shulkhan Arukh (The Code of Jewish Law) (Karo), xxiv, 13, 17, 36, 44, 57, 63, 89, 140, 260, 261, 268, 343, 413
Shultz, George, 598
Sickness, 24, 29–30, 40, 63–64, 222, 251–252, 256, 433–437
Siddur Sim Shalom (Harlow), 359
Siege, The (O'Brien), 576
Siegel, Bugsy, 403

Siegel, Danny, 263–265, 340, 344
Sifakis, Carl, 404
Sifra, xxiii, 12, 28, 141, 333
Sifre, xxiii, 181
Silence, 78–79, 224, 263, 267, 400, 536
Silver, Abba Hillel, 288
Silver, Eliezer, 15
Silver, Eric, 597–598
Silver Platter, The (Alterman)
Simeon, Rabbi, 6, 264
Simeon ben Gamliel, 126, 230, 412–413
Simeon ben Lakish, 30, 81–82
Simeon ben Shetach, 415
Simha Bunam of Pzysha, 354
Simkha, Meir, 143
Simlai, Rabbi, 7
Simon, Ernst, 240, 614–615
Singer, David, 493–494
Singer, Isaac Bashevis, 189–190, 286, 450, 453, 502
Six-Day War, 66, 87, 590, 591, 593–595, 597–598, 608, 609–610
"614th commandment," 312–315
Slander, *see* Gossip; Speech, negative
Slaton, John, 482–483
Slave, The (Singer), 286
Slavery, 30–31, 92, 111–113, 311, 317, 334, 408, 493
Slopes of Lebanon, The (Oz), 599
Smith, Gerald L. K., 488
Snyder, Louis, 536–537
Sobibor concentration camp, 526–527
Sobran, Joseph, 492
"Socialism and the Jews" (Lichtheim), 473–474
Socrates, 257
Sodom, 100, 344, 441
Solomon, 210, 221, 334–335, 505–506
Solomon, Operation, 98
Soloveitchik, Hayyim, 86, 350–352, 371–372
Soloveitchik, Joseph, 87, 262–263, 371–372, 616–617
Some Turns of Thought in Modern Philosophy (Santayana), 257
Song of My Slaughtered People (Katznelson), 522–523
Song of Songs, 129–130, 172, 222, 343
Soviet Union, 95, 98, 194, 290, 313, 393, 464, 501, 510–511, 591
Specter, Yitzchak Elchanan, 20
Speech, 27, 51
extravagant, 201
gossip, 8, 67–68, 359–360
Maimonides on, 201
misappropriating of, 52–53
negative, 65–69, 180, 208–209, 359–360
while in pain, 223
to parents, 150, 351
of praise, 67–68, 179

Speech *(continued)*
  in public, 203
  silence and, 78–79
  truthful, to God, 61–63
Sperling, David, 548–549
Spinoza, Baruch, 241
Spira, Israel, 324–326, 427–428
Sports, 508–509
Sprinzak, Yosef, 297
Stalin, Josef, 501, 571
Stangl, Franz, 559
State of the Jews, The (Syrkin), 609
"Status of the Embryo in Jewish Criminal
  Law" (Aptowitzer), 163
Stealing, 40, 43, 47–53, 153, 210, 331,
  354–355, 397
Stein, David, 443
Stein, Gertrude, 241
Stein, Leopold, 383
Steinberg, Milton, 283
Steinsalz, Adin, 16
Steinschneider, Moritz, 467
Stern, Avraham, 603
Stern, Guy, 479
Stockhammer, Shimshon, 326–327
Strangers, 26–27, 147, 38
Study of History (Toynbee), 608
Success, 175, 198, 220
Suffering, 222–224, 276, 363–364, 366,
  445–446, 452
Suicide, 244, 271–275, 320, 423
  justified, 273–275
  as murder, 156, 272
Sukkot, 384, 386–387
Sunflower, The (Wiesenthal), 350–352, 563
Supreme Court, U.S., 30–31, 317, 483
Sureties, 91–92
Survival in Auschwitz (Levi), 368–369
"Sweeney Among the Nightingales" (Eliot),
  475
Sykes, Charles, 243–244, 246
Symposium (Plato), 129–130
Synnott, Marcia Graham, 485
Syria, 594
Syrkin, Marie, 471, 505, 530–531, 541, 609
Szold, Henrietta, 116–117
Szonyi, David, 343

Tacitus, 163, 383
Taft, William Howard, 487
Tales of the Hasidim—Later Masters
  (Buber), 176, 220–221, 354
Talmud, xxiv
  on the death penalty, 409–416
Talmud, The: Selected Writings (Bokser),
  93, 405–406
Talmud,Babylonian, xxii–xxiii
  Arakhin, 77
  Avodah Zara. 230, 295, 321–322, 346–
    347, 394

Bava Bathra, 13, 14, 20, 21, 67, 108,
  157, 208, 223, 233, 234, 356, 441
Bava Kamma, 96–97, 122, 225, 243,
  253, 395, 401, 402, 433, 434, 441
Bava Mezia, 38–39, 54, 74, 110, 124,
  149, 200, 258–259, 318, 338, 401–
  402, 405–406, 429, 447
Berakhot,. 17, 48, 58, 90, 96, 105, 111,
  123, 144, 158, 187–188, 222, 223,
  227, 249, 276, 287, 289, 321, 337–
  338, 348, 349, 357, 360, 361–362,
  446
Betzah,. 182
Eruvin,. 70, 71–72, 126, 214, 216, 326,
  448
Gittin, 14, 17, 40, 48, 119, 155, 168,
  273–274, 303, 354–355, 386
Hagigah, 343
Hullin, 53, 231–232, 366, 451
Ketubot, 16, 18, 19, 44, 59, 106–107,
  122, 131, 135, 141, 157, 169, 170,
  222, 258, 376, 402, 441, 570
Kiddushin, 93, 108, 112–113, 121, 122,
  131–133, 146, 147–148, 151, 153,
  210, 248, 329, 332, 339
Kritot, 367
Makkot, 8, 413
Megillah, 10, 116, 231, 297, 345, 366
Menahot, 100, 112, 381
Mo'ed Kattan, 253, 267, 430
Nedarim, 29
Niddah, 116, 135, 244
Pesachim, 24, 53, 80–81, 101, 141, 330,
  332, 374, 434
Rosh Hashana, 389
Sanhedrin, 18, 29, 33–34, 35–36, 42, 51,
  64, 75, 81, 121, 123, 128, 133, 146,
  148, 210, 214, 227, 295, 334, 397,
  398, 402, 403–404, 410–416, 420,
  503
Semakhot, 156, 227, 271–272
Shabbat, 3, 5, 13, 22, 61, 77, 85, 92,
  107, 156, 157, 199, 224, 235–236,
  250, 252, 261, 331, 336, 347–348,
  385
Shevuot, 91, 399–400
Sotah, 25, 110, 119, 147, 418
Sukkah, 58,131,132,155,158,209
Sukkot, 24, 331, 338–339, 386
Ta'anit, 94, 145, 159–160, 181, 184–185,
  212, 250–251, 259–260, 388, 434–
  435
Yevamot, 9, 41, 58, 78, 124, 135–136,
  138, 143, 154, 164, 377, 379
Yoma, 62, 80, 105, 177, 196, 208, 318,
  340–342, 348, 358–359
Talmud, Palestinian, xxii–xxiii, 56, 66, 81,
  87, 107, 110, 171–172, 174, 189,
  230, 231, 318
Tamid, 342

Tanchum, Rabbi, 75
Taney, Roger, 30
Tanna d'Bai Eliyahu, 177
Tarfon, Rabbi, 4, 77, 339, 412–413, 425
Targum Jonathan, 69
Tarr, Herbert, 148
Teaching, 101–102, 189, 344, 359, 400, 485
"Tearing Off the Veil" (Barach), 114
Techow, Ernst Werner, 352–353
Tefillin, 286, 358–359
Teitelbaum, Yoel, 307–310
Telushkin, Dvorah, 450
Telushkin, Helen, 111, 615
Telushkin, Joseph, 212, 284, 288, 463
Telushkin, Nissen, 15, 226, 342–343
Telushkin, Shlomo, 342–343, 599
Temple, 144, 367
Temple, first, 334, 394, 506
  destruction of, 123, 196–197, 273, 305, 394, 539
Temple, second, destruction of, 123, 196–197, 233, 305, 539, 601
Ten Rungs: Hasidic Sayings (Buber), 41, 90
Teresa, Mother, 38
Terrible Secret, The (Laqueur), 529, 543
Tetrachordon (Milton), 118
Teveth, Shabtai, 588
Tevye the Dairyman (Aleichem), 430
Text of the Holocaust, The (Aronsfeld), 519
Thanksgiving, prayers of, 356
That Jesus Christ Was Born a Jew (Luther), 470
Theological and Halakhic Reflections on the Holocaust (Rosenberg and Heuman), 310
Theresienstadt, 537
This Way for the Gas, Ladies and Gentlemen (Borowski), 524–525
Thompson, Dorothy, 528
Those Who Sanctified God's Name (Mekadshe Ha-Shem) (Meisels), 82–84
"Three Zionists: Weizmann, Ben-Gurion, Katznelson" (O'Brien), 587
Tikkun, 386
Tikkun olam, 3, 4, 52–53, 87, 269
Time, 599
Tisha Be'Av, 305, 539, 586
Tisso, Joseph, 558
T'nuat Ha-Mussar (The Mussar Movement) (Katz), 261, 331–332
To Life (Kushner), 299, 337, 442, 468, 579, 613
Tolstoy, Leo, 421, 468
To Pray as a Jew (Donin), 356
Torah, xx, xxi
  afterlife not mentioned in, 276
  blessing of, 298
  as divine fiat vs. reasoned law, 333–335

essence of, 5–6, 46, 84–85
eternal words of, 322
giving of, 74, 116, 377, 385–386, 447
influence of, 336–337
Sabbath reading of, 382,
613 laws of, 7–8, 76, 377
strict application of, 40
study of, *see* Torah study trial of, 74
Torah study, 336–344, 413
  acts vs., 317–318, 339
  asceticism and, 232, 235–237
  and destruction of the Second Temple, 196
  and elitism, 226–229
  and essence of Judaism, 5–6, 9–10
  excuses for avoidance of, 340–342
  and God's first questions, 3, 4
  as lifeblood of the Jewish people, 337–339
  old age and, 249–250, 253
  parents' obligations and, 153, 340, 344, 359
  preeminence of, 339
  techniques for, 342–344
  waning of, 338–339
  women and, 105–107, 110–111, 113
Torah Today, 451
Torture, 197–198, 222–223, 410
Tosefta, xxiii, 48, 82, 277, 291
Touching Heaven, Touching Earth (Avidor Ha-Cohen), 64, 201, 226
Touch of Wisdom, a Touch of Wit, A (Himelstein), 270, 389
Tough Choices: Jewish Perspectives on Social Justice (Vorspan and Saperstein), 29
Toynbee, Arnold, 608–609
"Traditional Prejudice and Religious Reform: The Theological and Historical Foundations of Luther's Anti-Judaism" (Cohen), 470
Treasury of Chassidic Tales on the Torah, A (Zevin), 78–79
Treatise on the Gods (Mencken), 477
Treblinka, 559
Treif, 448
Trial and Achievement (Ben-Sasson), 323
Trial and Death of Jesus, The (Cohn), 465–466
Trial and Error (Weizmann), 580
Trotsky, Leon, 55, 501
Truman, Harry, 605
Trumpeldor, Joseph, 601
Truth, 58–64
  to the dying, 63–64
  ethical argumentation and, 70–71
  to God, 61–63
  half-, 58–61, 64
  recognizing of, 403–404
  see also Honesty; Lies, lying

T. S. Eliot: Collected Poems, 1909–1935 (Eliot), 475–476
Tucker, Gordon, 47
Turner, Nat, 110
Twain, Mark (Samuel L. Clemens), 498
Tweed, Boss, 481
Twersky, Abraham, 61
Twersky, Rebecca, 262–263
Tzaddik in Our Time, A (Raz), 125–126, 179–180, 224
Tzibbur 367
Tziporah, 105
Tzitzit, 184, 185, 380–381

Uganda, 462, 487, 569, 575–576
Ukhmani, A., 270
Ullman, Liv, 109
Ultimate Issues, 277, 462, 611–612
U'mipnei chata-einu galeenu meartzainu, 306
"Unbeliever and Christians, The"(Camus), 425
Understanding Bereavement and Grief (Linzer), 256
U-ne-taneh Tokef, 387–388
United Jewish Appeal, 97–98
United Nations, xxi, 419, 462, 607
Uriah, 43
Usher, Arsene Assouan, 607–608
Ussishkin, Menachem, 577
Utopianism, 425–426
Uziel, Ben Zion, 166–167
Uzziah, 101

Van Dusen, Henry P., 609–610
Vatican II, 1965 declaration of, 469
Va'Yoel Moshe (Teitelbaum), 308–309
Vegetarianism, 449–453
Vichy and the Jews (Marrus and Paxton), 558
Vidal, Gore, 492
Vidal-Naquet, Pierre, 556
Vintage Wein (Weiss), 526
Visotzky, Burton, 265–266
Vivekananda, 232
Voices of Wisdom (Klagsbrun), 62–63, 150, 152, 202, 219–220, 322
Voltaire (Francois-Marie Arouet), 197–198, 292, 471–472, 498
Von Jan, J., 537
Von Treitschke, Heinrich, 474
Vorspan, Albert, 29

Wages, 54–57
Wagner, Robert Ferdinand, 528
Wagner-Rogers bill, 528–529
War, 417–424, 438, 450
  see also Six-Day War
War Against the Jews, The (Davidowicz), 518

Warrant for Genocide (Cohn), 555
Warsaw Diary of Chaim Kaplan, The (Kaplan)
Warsaw Ghetto, 324, 326–327, 363–364, 534–535, 538, 539, 543
Waste, 440–441
"Was the Holocaust Predictable?" (Katz), 586
Ways of the Righteous, The (*Orhat Zaddikim*), 17
Wealth, 5, 14, 18, 22, 27, 107, 218–219, 279, 340–342, 399
Weeping, 262–263, 268
Wein, Berel, 526
Weiner, Herbert, 360
Weinstein, Jacob J., 269
Weiss, James David, 526
Weiss, Saul, 72–73, 95, 346
Weissmandl, Dov Baer, 557–558
Weizmann, Chaim, 457, 576, 577, 579–583, 614
Weltsch, Robert, 538–539
Welt von Gestern, Die (Zweig), 578
Wertheimer, Jack, 610
"What Bitburg Revealed About the Jews" (Prager), 461–462
What Did They Think of the Jews? (Gould), 476, 497, 502
What Does Judaism Say About . . . ? (Jacobs), 237–238
When All You've Ever Wanted Isn't Enough (Kushner), 68, 220, 372–373
Where Heaven and Earth Touch (Siegel), 263–265, 340, 344
White, Dan, 244
White lies, 58–61
White Paper, 581, 588–589
Who Is Man? (Heschel), 320
"Why Anti-Zionism Is Antisemitism"(Prager), 611–612
Why I Am a Jew (Fleg), 287
Why the Jews? The Reason for Antisemitism (Prager and Telushkin), 463
Widows, 26, 27–28, 32, 79, 384
Wiesel, Elie, 84–85, 98, 303, 515, 527, 535, 557, 559–562
Wiesenthal, Simon, 350–352, 562, 563
Will, George, 491
Wilson, Woodrow, 487
Wisdom, 5, 202, 249–250, 279, 404
Wisdom of the Ages (Kula), 285, 369
With God in Hell (Berkovits), 542
Wit of the Jews, The (Cowan and Cowan), 250
Wolf, Simon, 481
Women, 104–117
  abortion and, 161–167
  in biblical law vs. narrative, 104–105
  Kaddish recited by, 116–117

as "light-headed," 108
Maimonides on, 113–115
marriage proposals by, 388
menstruation and, 138, 185
military service of, 42–43, 418
moral influence of, 116–117
and obligation to have children, 143–144
positive views of, 115–116
pregnancy and, 143–144, 368
Rabbi Eliezer on, 109–112, 113
Rashi on, 112–113
remarriage by, 614–615
sex drive of, 131, 134–135
as slaves, 111–113
Talmud's negative view of, 105–109, 349, 614–615
and Torah study, 105–107, 110–111, 113
valorous, 128
Women and Jewish Law (Biale), 131
"Word About Our Jewry, A" (von Treitschke), 474
Words of Wisdom, Words of Wit (Himelstein), 13
World Crisis and Jewish Survival (Silver), 288
World Must Know, The (Berenbaum), 520, 529
World of the High Holy Days, The (Riemer), 352–353
Worry, 201
Wurm, Mathilde, 241
Württemberg, Duke of, 324
Wyman, David, 35
Wynne-Tyson, Jon, 452
Wyschogrod, Michael, 314

Yadin, Yigael, 274–275
Yahrzeit, 256
Yalkut Shimoni, 255
Yalta, 231–232
Yannai, Rabbi, 227–228
Yehiel, Rabbi, 201
Yehudi, 92
Yemen, 98
Yevtushenko, Yevgeny, 419
Yiddish proverbs, 64, 90, 127, 150, 202, 220, 275, 279, 302, 369–370, 430
Yiddish Proverbs (Ayalti), 127
Yitgadal ve-Yitkadash Shmei Rabbah, 268
Yizhar, S., 240–241
Yochanan ben Zakkai, 6, 30, 56, 158, 187, 222, 229, 248, 251, 258–259, 264–265, 266, 289, 369, 425

Yohai, Shimon bar, 152, 172–173, 235–236, 300
Yom Kippur, 86–87, 95, 324–326, 356, 363, 387–389, 508–509, 537
Yosef, Ovadia, 87
"Yossel Rakover's Appeal to God"(Kolitz), 363–364
Yossi, Rabbi, 51, 171–172, 264, 369
Yossi ben Halaphta, 120
Yossi ben Judah, 144–145
Yossi ben Kisma, 252
Youth, 182, 249–250, 252, 253, 326–327

Zangwill, Israel, 457, 510, 574
Zedekiah, 273
Zeira, Rabbi, 212, 250–251
Zemba, Menahem, 326–327
Zevin, Shlomo Yosef, 78–79, 253
Zimmels, H. J., 84
Zinoviev, Grigory Yevseyevich, 501
Zionism, xx, 224, 240, 479, 565–612
anti-, 607–612
and the coming of the Messiah, 571
communism vs., 501, 590–591
as elevated to idolatry, 296–297
First Congress of, 571, 574–575
Herzl's Uganda plan and, 569, 575–576
Holocaust as hoax of, 492
Holocaust as punishment for, 307–310
Jabotinsky and, 584–587
Kishiner pogrom and, 575–576
medical anticipation of, 571
Sixth Congress of, 569, 575–576
slogan of, xx, 573
Weizmann and, 457, 576, 577, 579–583
"Zionism Versus Bolshevism: A Struggle for the Soul of the Jewish People" (Churchill), 500
Zionist Idea, The (Hertzberg), 571, 585, 603
Zmirot, 31
Zohar, 165, 277–278
Zohar, The Book of Splendor (Scholem), 277–278
Zohar: The Book of Enlightenment (Matt), 99
Zola, Emile, 497
Zonah, 138
Zuckerman, Yitzchak, 534
Zutra, Rabbi, 369
Zweig, Stefan, 578
Zygelboim, Shmuel, 324